CUBA'S REVOLUTIONARY WORLD

CUBA'S REVOLUTIONARY WORLD

Jonathan C. Brown

 Harvard University Press

Cambridge, Massachusetts
London, England
2017

First Printing

Library of Congress Cataloging-in-Publication Data

Names: Brown, Jonathan C. (Jonathan Charles), 1942– author.
Title: Cuba's revolutionary world / Jonathan C. Brown.
Description: Cambridge, Massachusetts : Harvard University Press, 2017. |
    Includes bibliographical references and index.
Identifiers: LCCN 2016046018 | ISBN 9780674971981 (cloth)
Subjects: LCSH: Revolutions—Latin America—History. |
    Military government—Latin America—History—20th century. |
    Dictatorship—Latin America—History—20th century. | Cuba—Politics
    and government—1933–1959. | Cuba—Politics and government—
    1959–1990. | Latin America—Politics and government—1948–1980. |
    United States—Foreign relations—Latin America.
Classification: LCC JC491 .B79 2017 | DDC 303.6/409809045—dc23
    LC record available at https://lccn.loc.gov/2016046018

To Lynore Brown, my partner in life, research, and editing

Contents

CUBA'S REVOLUTIONARY WORLD

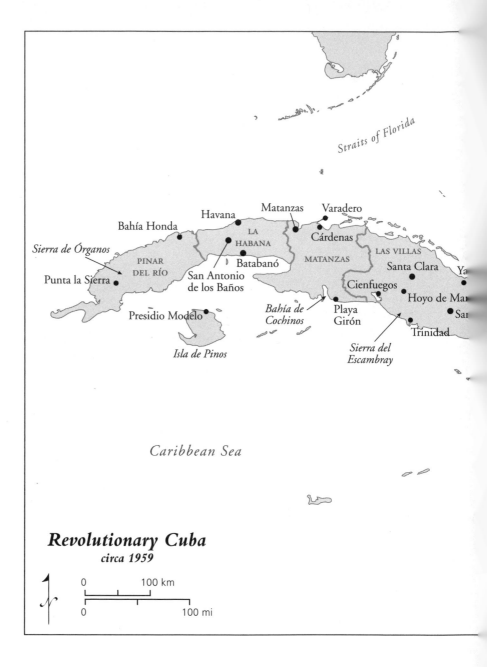

Straits of Florida

Matanzas   Varadero
Havana   Cárdenas
Bahía Honda   LA
                    HABANA
Sierra de Órganos   MATANZAS   LAS VILLAS
         PINAR   Santa Clara   Ya
         DEL RÍO   Batabanó   Hoyo de Ma
Punta la Sierra   San Antonio   Cienfuegos
              de los Baños   Bahía de   Playa   Sa
                              Cochinos   Girón
Presidio Modelo   Trinidad

         Isla de Pinos   Sierra del
                              Escambray

Caribbean Sea

Revolutionary Cuba
circa 1959

0   100 km

0   100 mi

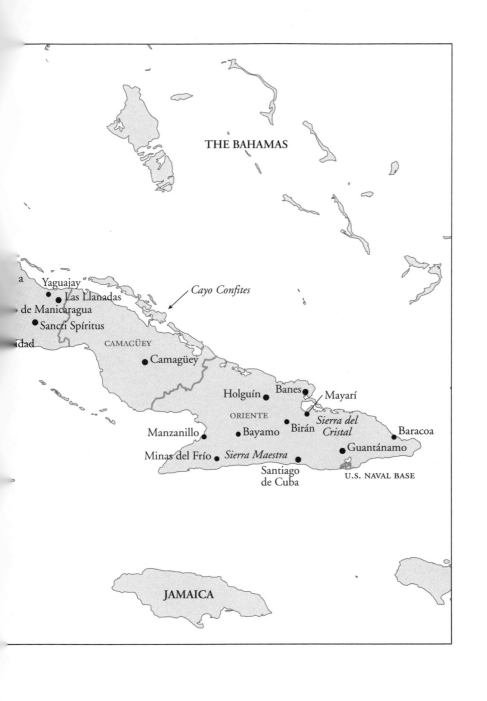

THE BAHAMAS

a
Yaguajay
Las Llanadas
de Manicaragua
Sancti Spíritus
idad

Cayo Confites

CAMAGÜEY

Camagüey

Holguín   Banes
Mayarí
ORIENTE   Birán   *Sierra del Cristal*
Manzanillo   Bayamo   Baracoa
Minas del Frío   *Sierra Maestra*   Guantánamo
Santiago de Cuba   U.S. NAVAL BASE

JAMAICA

Introduction

AT DAWN ON New Year's Day, 1959, euphoria broke out among the residents of Havana as news spread that the rebellion against Fulgencio Batista had triumphed. The dictator had resigned the previous night. Batista had secretly informed his cabinet and military leaders during a midnight coffee reception at his mansion in Havana's military base at Camp Columbia. He was leaving the armed forces in the hands of Major General Eulogio Cantillo. The dictator conferred with Cantillo momentarily before boarding a Cuban Air Force plane, then leaned out from the door of the plane and shouted "salud, salud" (health, health) to a small group of supporters. At 2:00 A.M., the plane took off for the Dominican Republic with family members and close associates aboard. Commanding some twenty thousand soldiers at Camp Columbia, General Cantillo resolved to form a military junta, as the US embassy had been suggesting for more than a month. He ordered the army commander in Santiago de Cuba to arrange a truce with the guerrilla leader, Comandante Fidel Castro.

Batista's army numbered some forty thousand officers and men in late 1958, while Castro's guerrillas and other fighting groups may have amounted to little more than three thousand combatants. The contrast in esprit de corps made up for the difference in force levels. Batista's army was beset with corrupt, ineffectual leaders and poorly trained soldiers. Their indiscipline led to exceptional brutality. The guerrillas, on the other hand, earned the admiration of the Cuban people for their audacity and pluck.[1] In addition, the rebels had hundreds of sympathizers variously organized in groups of poorly armed urban activists. Thousands more, especially in the middle class, just wanted Fidel to win. New Year's Day suddenly ended the seven-year nightmare of dictatorship.

Batista's flight caught Comandante Castro by surprise, though hardly unprepared. On New Year's morning, he and his own column of two hundred guerrillas were five hundred miles away, closing in on Cuba's second most populous city, Santiago de Cuba. Not three days beforehand, he had conferred face-to-face with General Cantillo outside this city. After five years of civil war and nearly three thousand deaths, these enemy commanders had agreed on ending the turmoil. They were to combine rebel and regular troops on two conditions—that Batista and other "war criminals" not be allowed to get away and that no military junta should seize political power. Cantillo had now broken that agreement.

Fidel was eating breakfast on that first morning of 1959 when an aide brought him the news of events in Havana. "It's a cowardly betrayal!" he exclaimed. "They're trying to steal the triumph that belongs to the revolution."[2] Fidel Castro immediately went on Radio Rebelde to address the nation. "I am ordering a rebel advance on Santiago and on Havana, and I am now proclaiming a general strike," he said. "We will never accept any solution other than a civilian government. This long and arduous battle will not brook any outcome other than the triumph of the Revolution. Let no one be deceived. We will not accept a military junta."[3] He claimed that General Cantillo was trying to prevent the guerrillas from entering Santiago de Cuba. He asked all *santiagueros* to resist this order. Castro compared his guerrillas to the *mambises,* the peasant fighters who were decommissioned by American military intervention in the Independence War against Spain. "The history of 1895 will not be repeated," Fidel proclaimed. "Today the *mambises* will enter Santiago de Cuba."[4]

Castro immediately ordered two other columns of his guerrilla forces in the province of Las Villas, located midway between Havana and Santiago, to take charge of the military and police facilities in the capital. They were to force General Cantillo's junta to step down and allow the government-in-exile to take power. Comandantes Ernesto "Che" Guevara and Camilo Cienfuegos directed their separate commands, each numbering a few hundred men, to set off for Havana in separate caravans. Before they arrived, Havana's urban militias, made up of clean-shaven youths of the urban resistance, had taken over patrolling the streets. They maintained a joyful order, preventing most looting and revenge killings.[5] Meanwhile, on New Year's Day, *batistiano* officials, police captains, and military officers—even American Mafia bosses—were leaving on yachts and small planes. Other Batista loyalists fled to the sanctuary of foreign embassies in Havana. On this holiday, none of them could get to their bank deposit boxes.

Castro had thought ahead about giving a revolutionary task to urban workers, who had arrived late to the anti-Batista struggle. "Workers," he proclaimed, "this is the moment for you to assure the victory of the Revolution. This time nothing and no one can impede the triumph of the Revolution."[6] His labor command sent out the order. "The Cuban workers, directed by the Workers' Sections of the Revolutionary Movement of the 26th of July, must today take over all syndicates dominated by [Batista labor boss Eusebio] Mujal and his henchmen, and organize themselves in the factories and labor centers so that the total paralysis of the country will begin at dawn tomorrow."[7] Laborers helped make General Cantillo's rule untenable, and army discipline buckled.

Castro then turned his attention to securing control of Santiago with several columns of guerrillas of the Movimiento 26 de Julio (M26), which had grown rapidly toward the end of the revolutionary war. The guerrillas of M26 distinguished themselves by wearing olive-drab *(verde olivo)* battle dress and sporting scraggly, unruly beards. Soldiers of Batista's army feared and the people revered these *barbudos,* or bearded ones. Castro's younger brother, Raúl, could not grow impressive facial hair. He compensated with a ponytail beneath his beret and with resolute leadership of the guerrillas' Second Front, operating in the Crystal Mountains of the brothers' boyhood home in Birán. Fidel Castro spent New Year's Day accepting the surrender of army forces in Guantánamo City and Santiago de Cuba. On January 2, Castro dictated a bulletin detailing the Batista regime's crimes. "General Cantillo betrayed us," he said. "The most criminal act of the Camp Columbia coup was allowing Batista . . . and other master crooks to escape. They let them escape with their millions of pesos, three or four hundred million that they had stolen, and it's going to prove very expensive for us because now they'll be making propaganda against the Revolution from Santo Domingo and other countries." Others who had thought ahead already had fat bank accounts abroad as well.

The people of Santiago de Cuba and Oriente Province had always favored the rebels. Since 1956, the *santiagueros* had supported Fidel's small band in the nearby Sierra Maestra with arms, money, and recruits. The *guajiros* (peasants) of the mountains finally joined as guerrilla volunteers in late 1957 and 1958, once the M26 forces were able to protect them from Batista's incompetent army. Fidel and Raúl had grown up among them, spoke their language, and mastered their culture. In fact, support for the guerrillas was so great among the well-off and the rural workers that Batista's armed forces had to conduct themselves in Oriente Province like an army of occupation. On his first visit to Santiago de Cuba, following the assassination of M26 urban leader Frank País in July 1957, US ambassador Earl E. T. Smith was confronted by a picket line of middle-class white women with signs reading "Stop killing our sons"—this in a city inhabited by an Afro-Cuban majority. Widespread funding for Fidel from the upper classes, including Santiago's business community, convinced the Central Intelligence Agency and the US State Department that the rebels could not be communists.[8] Most M26 leaders had come from the upper middle class of the province.

For a guerrilla fighter, Fidel Castro proved himself a great orator. His previous university law training and political work had prepared him well for this moment of triumph. As president of the law student association at the University of Havana in 1948, Castro attended a student conclave with nationalist overtones in Colombia's capital of Bogotá. Students from all over Latin America gathered conterminously with a meeting of the Organization of American States. In the midst of both conferences, an assassin killed the popular presidential candidate Jorge Eliécer Gaitán, provoking a week of urban riots known as the *Bogotazo*. Castro spent three days in the rioting until he was able to get out of Colombia. Back in Cuba, he joined the new Orthodox Party of Eduardo Chibás. Chibás was gaining popularity for his oratory and for his exposés of the rampant corruption of ruling Authentic Party presidents at a time when most students at the University of Havana aligned themselves with the Partido Auténtico of their fathers. When, unexpectedly, the popular Chibás committed suicide during his radio show in

1951, Castro figured among the Orthodox Party leaders who spoke at his funeral.

As a young lawyer, Castro ran for the House of Deputies on the Orthodox Party ballot in the 1952 election campaign, which the ex-general and ex-president Fulgencio Batista terminated with an army coup d'état. When student protests against the *golpe de estado* reached a stalemate, Fidel used his party leadership to recruit some 150 young men to make an attack on Moncada Barracks in Santiago de Cuba. The date of the attack, July 26, 1953, lent its name to his subsequent revolutionary movement. The Moncada attack failed. In his trial for treason, Castro said famously, "Condemn me, it doesn't matter. History will absolve me." Fidel, his brother Raúl, and twenty other survivors spent two years in jail until they were amnestied in 1955. He left for the United States, offering his military skills to political leaders of the Authentic and Orthodox Parties exiled by Batista's coup.

Castro collected donations from the émigré community in the United States, then formed and trained a Cuban expeditionary force in Mexico City. There he met the young Argentine doctor Ernesto Guevara de la Serna and recruited him to serve as a military doctor with the expedition. They traveled together to Cuba on the yacht *Granma* in late November 1956. Some twenty of eighty-two of them survived an army ambush to reach the Sierra Maestra. Thereafter, President Batista mistakenly ignored the guerrillas until their force had grown sufficiently to hold territory in the mountains and recruit local students and peasants. Why? Batista believed that his greatest enemies were his own generals and not the few ragtag guerrillas living in the wilderness. In two years of guerrilla warfare in the sierras of eastern Cuba, Guevara became the most successful of Castro's lieutenants. At the end of December 1958, Comandante Che Guevara's column of some three hundred combatants seized the central city of Santa Clara from some eight thousand soldiers in Batista's garrison there.[9] That battle precipitated the dictator's departure.

At 1:00 A.M. on January 2, 1959, Fidel Castro addressed his people, the *santiagueros,* about what the triumph of the revolution would mean for Cuba. "The Revolution will be a very difficult undertaking, full of danger," he told the celebrants gathered before him in Santiago's central plaza. "This time, luckily for Cuba, the Revolution will truly come into power. It will not be like 1895, when the North Americans came and made themselves

"We will have no thievery, no treason, no intervention. This time it is truly the Revolution." Fidel Castro, Santiago de Cuba, January 2, 1959.

masters of our country. . . . It will not be like 1933, when [President Gerardo] Machado was ousted and the people began to believe that a revolution was taking place; but then Batista took over the reins and instituted a dictatorship lasting eleven years. It will not be like 1944, when the multitudes were fired with the idea that at last the people had come to power, but those who had really come to power were the thieves." Then the rebel comandante paused to allow the excited crowd to settle down. "We will have no thievery, no treason, no intervention," Castro shouted. "This time it is truly the Revolution."[10]

Thus did the Cuban Revolution launch a powerful wave of political change that the capitalist West could not escape and the Eastern Bloc could not ignore. A violent phase of the Cold War was descending on Latin America.

EXPORTING REVOLUTION AND COUNTERREVOLUTION

This book deals with changes in transnational relations provoked by social revolution on the biggest island in the Caribbean Sea. It focuses on the first decade of revolution in Cuba, from 1959 to 1968. The study also chronicles the consequences of the Cuban Revolution for the countries of the Caribbean Basin and South America, where domestic politics were already embroiled in conflict and unrest in the 1960s. Of necessity, this book explains essential events of the 1950s and 1970s in order to round out the historical context of the tumultuous sixties.

Historical actors in this drama include members of Fidel's revolutionary inner circle as well as occupants of the White House, the Kremlin, and Beijing's Communist Party compound. Latin American presidents and generals also appear. However, they did not occupy center stage all alone. Leaders had to react to and accommodate countless individuals who joined radical groups, whether on the left or on the right. Numerous of these mainly youthful agents took up arms to resist authority. Some fought against Cuba's revolutionary state, and others joined the militias to defend it. Still others volunteered to carry out invasions from Cuba against dictatorships in the Caribbean Basin or from Miami and other locations against Cuba. Moreover, the 1960s and early 1970s formed the preeminent period of guerrilla warfare in Latin America. Thousands of young men and hundreds of women participated in rural and urban paramilitaries that, weapons in hand, challenged both authoritarian regimes and democratic ones. Popular movements developed among peasants and rural workers to claim the haciendas and *fazendas* owned by members of the oligarchy.

All revolutions disrupt, but some have greater historical impact. France in 1789 falls into the latter category. The French Revolution began a national transformation that involved all of Europe in prolonged warfare, which French revolutionary armies carried to Central Europe, Egypt, Russia, and the Iberian Peninsula. The slave revolt of Saint-Domingue (Haiti) followed in 1791. It destroyed the sugar plantations of France's Caribbean colony and contributed to Cuba's first sugar boom as a substitute world supplier. Needing money, Emperor Napoléon Bonaparte in 1803 sold the vast Louisiana territory to the United States. France's invasion of Iberia sent the Portuguese royal family fleeing to its colony of Brazil. It also resulted in the incarceration of the Spanish king. French occupation of Spain gave rise to the unconventional warfare we know today by the Spanish word *guerrilla* and sparked colonial insurrections for independence in Spanish colonies from Buenos Aires to Mexico. So powerfully did the French Revolution influence the next half century of Western history that historians know this period as the Age of Revolution.[11]

Social revolutions by their very nature contain disruptive power. They establish alternative forms of domestic government and distribution of wealth. Social revolutions also disrupt neighboring states governed by older political and economic institutions. France substituted a republic and then an empire for the Bourbon monarchy, with the result that the remaining hereditary rulers in Europe united to contain the spread of revolutionary ideas to their own realms. New ideas of citizenship practiced in revolutionary France also threatened the wealth and privilege of aristocracies throughout Europe. Neighboring principalities reacted by harboring refugees of France's Old Regime and encouraging French counterrevolutionaries. In response, the revolutionary state in Paris sought security and legitimacy through military expansion. It mobilized the people for war. It promoted rebel movements abroad to weaken or overthrow monarchical enemies.[12] Fidel Castro, as a law student in the late 1940s and as a political prisoner in 1954, read extensively in French history.

Of the four social revolutions in Latin America during the twentieth century, Castro's of 1959 had the greatest impact on international affairs. It far surpassed the disruptiveness of the revolutions in Mexico in 1910, Bolivia in 1952, or Nicaragua in 1979. Actually, one might say the Nicaraguan Revolution resulted from the Cuban Revolution. Scholars have classified social revolutions according to five distinctive characteristics: violent uprisings against the established political order; destruction of the military establishment defending the old order; mobilization of the popular classes by one or more revolutionary factions; downward redistribution of both income and property; and strengthening of state institutions that intervene in economic and social affairs.[13] The revolutions of Mexico, Bolivia, and Nicaragua shared with Cuba all these internal changes. Cuba's revolution greatly altered the international landscape beyond even the Western Hemisphere. Therefore, one could easily add a sixth hallmark of social revolution: disruption of nation-state arrangements on a regional and international scale.

The revolutionary reforms in Cuba broke radically with the status quo in neighboring countries. First, the revolutionaries destroyed Cuba's military establishment, which certainly would have resisted economic and social change. Then, Fidel utilized members of the domestic communist party and formed alliances with the Soviet Bloc. He socialized rural and urban properties and confiscated all foreign and domestic businesses, many owned by US capitalists. The revolutionary regime provided universal and free programs in public education and health care. In 1961, Castro and his worker and peasant militias defeated a counterrevolutionary invasion engineered by the Central Intelligence Agency (CIA). The Cuban Revolution delighted students, dissidents, nationalists, workers, and peasants in neighboring countries. It struck fear into the landowning elites, the propertied middle class, business interests, and military officers everywhere in Latin America.

This revolution caught the imagination of Latin America's youth. Many who flocked to Havana to celebrate Cuba's victories stayed on to train in guerrilla warfare. They were already dissatisfied with the economic lethargy of their homelands and with the resistance to basic social change by powerful landowners and foreign interests. The powerlessness of electoral governments to effect change alienated many secondary and university students. They resented dictatorships even more and blamed the United States for supporting tyrants in the interest of "political stability." Latin American *jóvenes* who made their way to Cuba for military training returned home to start their own revolutions.[14] Cuban-trained fighters operated in Guatemala, Nicaragua, Venezuela, Colombia, Peru, Bolivia, and Argentina. Moreover, Panamanian and Brazilian politicians adjusted to the popular ferment that a successful Cuban challenge of US hegemony had generated.

The Cuban Revolution came to fruition at a moment when dictatorship in Latin America was in decline. Once Batista fled from Havana, only four old-fashioned dictators remained in power in the smaller countries—Haiti, Dominican Republic, Nicaragua, and Paraguay. Fidel Castro permitted armed assaults to be launched from Cuba against three of these dictators.

Failing to overturn them, Havana undertook to spread the revolution systematically to other countries through guerrilla insurgencies. Latin American youth disdained the feckless elected presidents who never seemed able to deal with national weaknesses. The generals also disrespected civilian politicians and took advantage of rising Cold War tensions to bring down elected governments. Within two decades of Castro's victory speech in Santiago de Cuba, the vast majority of Latin American citizens lived under dictatorship. Military rule became institutional in nature, administered by faceless juntas that ruled repressively over the long term. The last generals in power did not leave until 1990, in Chile.

Could events in Cuba, a nation of a mere six million people, really determine that 140 million out of 180 million Latin Americans had to suffer government by dictators?[15] Yes—but only because of Cuba's geopolitical location and the ideological intensity of the age in which Castro came to power. First of all, each revolution creates its own counterrevolution made up of people and interests injured by social reforms. The American Revolution had the Tories; the Bolsheviks engendered the White Russians; and the Cuban Revolution produced *bandidos* and *gusanos*. The counterrevolutionaries were not in fact "outlaws" or "worms" at all. The revolutionaries merely branded them with these demeaning names in order to discredit the resistance. Those who opposed Fidel Castro's turn toward socialism viewed themselves as patriots, loyal Cubans, good Catholics, and men and women who risked their lives for the country they loved.

The so-called bandit uprisings that began in 1959 had their origins in the resistance of some peasants to Cuban agrarian reform. Many small property owners with coffee trees or tobacco plants or a few head of cattle feared the redistribution of private lands. Many landless rural laborers also joined the fight against the "communists" who administered agrarian reforms, a fact that the revolutionary government could not admit publicly. Castro's followers maintained that the "real peasants" supported the revolution. Indeed, rural residents who benefited from land reform did fill out the militia units that fought rebels in the Escambray Mountains and elsewhere on the island. The Cuban counterrevolution, in this regard, compares to the Vendée in France, the Cristero Revolt in Mexico, kulaks in the Soviet Union, and the Contra movement of Nicaragua. By 1966, however, the *bandidos* were vanquished.

Fidel's consolidation of power and his alliance with the Cuban communists also led, in the first half of the 1960s, to the mass emigration of approximately 260,000 mainly middle-class opponents. More refugees left in the second half of the decade. Castro called them *gusanos,* or worms. Ironically, many of these Cuban urban professionals had backed Fidel in the struggle against Batista and had cause to accuse him of betraying the revolution by dealing with the communist party. Former collaborators against Batista—and more than a few from within M26—broke with the revolution over the prominence of communists among Fidel's state administrators. Castro and his mass following labeled as "counterrevolutionary" anyone who mentioned that party members really did not do much fighting against the dictatorship. *Al paredón*—"to the execution wall"—became a common refrain in mass assemblies where Fidel denounced the counterrevolutionaries. Most opponents fled from Cuba; others spent time in jail for treason; a minority suffered execution. Secondary and university students felt betrayed because they had collaborated with Castro in the overthrow of the dictator Batista. The pro-Castro university student federation expelled these protesters, many of whom fled to Miami from 1959 through 1962. Some joined anti-Castro armed groups. The CIA recruited and trained members of this urban middle-class counterrevolution for the Bay of Pigs invasion. Still others formed semi-independent commando groups in Miami in order to mount armed attacks against Cuba.

It is no exaggeration to say that the Castro regime exported both its revolution *and* its counterrevolution. These two exports account for a portion of the outsized international influence of revolutionary events on the Caribbean island.[16] The Cold War was likewise a precondition for Cuba's explosive international impact. The post–World War II era featured an international order dominated by two powerful ideological foes. Washington in alliance with Western Europe represented capitalism. Moscow directed the socialist pact of Eastern European states and communist China. Castro's revolution upset the equilibrium between them when Havana denounced the United States as an imperialist power and joined the Eastern Bloc. The Gulf of Mexico and Caribbean Sea had once been "America's lakes," key to US hegemony, which reached through the Panama Canal to the west coast of South America. Cuba, as the first socialist republic in the Western Hemisphere, proved so disruptive to international order that, in October 1962, its military ties to the Kremlin nearly led to thermonuclear war. Cold War currents interpenetrating with the hot waters of Castro's revolution created a stormy mixture. Jean-Paul Sartre called it the "Cuban hurricane."

THE IDEOLOGICAL STRUGGLE

Three of Latin America's social revolutions occurred in the backyard of the United States. That fact raises many questions about smaller, less developed countries maturing in the shadow of a culturally different hegemon. This book will not delve into these issues directly. The point I wish to make is that timing and international context mattered. Mexico's revolutionaries in the second decade of the twentieth century could find no foreign sponsor to substitute economically for the United States. They queried an imperial Germany otherwise engaged in World War I and came up empty handed. The *sandinistas* of Nicaragua sought Moscow's military and economic assistance only to discover that the Soviets were preoccupied with subsidizing Cuba and invading Afghanistan. The lack of an alternative international patron meant that the revolutionaries sooner or later had to find accommodation with the United States.

In contrast, Castro's timing turned out to be impeccable. It is difficult to imagine a more propitious moment to seek Soviet assistance than 1959. Cuba's revolutionaries confronted a wholly new orientation of Soviet policy that might not have existed had Premier Joseph Stalin not died in 1953. Stalin had maintained a strict postwar policy of Socialism in One Country, meaning to strengthen the economic and military security of the Soviet Union, surrounded by socialist republics to the west and east. His successor, Nikita Khrushchev, began to involve the USSR in the affairs of the Third World, lending support to Gamal Abdel Nasser and his nationalization of the Suez Canal.[17]

The Soviet Union also had recovered from the devastation of the Second World War. It was industrialized, militarily equipped, and secure from Western hostility behind a buffer of East European client states. Khrushchev, its brash new premier, had consolidated power and had plans to be a worthy successor to if not the equal of Joseph Stalin himself. He had the atom bomb and missiles to deliver it. He presided over the space program that bested the West in sending a man-made object, Sputnik, into the outer atmosphere and then a human being, cosmonaut Yuri Gagarin. Both fell back to earth and survived, which attested to the superiority of socialism over capitalism. At least, this is how the Cuban revolutionaries in 1959 interpreted current events.

Moreover, Khrushchev was beset with challenges that made him willing to take risks. The communist regime of China disputed Moscow's claim as the uncontested leader of the Socialist Bloc. Beijing believed that Mao Zedong, as the greatest living revolutionary, should assume Stalin's mantle. To the Chinese, Khrushchev was a mere apparatchik, a child of revolution rather than one of its creators. In this climate, Moscow looked for something bold to accomplish to reestablish its leadership. Then, in April 1959, Army General Raúl Castro contacted the Kremlin, requesting military instructors for the Cuban rebel armed forces. Cautious at first, Khrushchev warmed to the idea of supporting a socialist republic in the backyard of the United States. Little did he contemplate that Cuba would be his undoing.

The Cuban Revolution also changed Washington, capital of the richest and most powerful nation on earth. Prior to Castro, the US government had been so convinced of the benefits that American investment bestowed on Latin America that presidents had routinely ignored the region. True, President Dwight D. Eisenhower had commissioned the CIA to undermine a democratically elected government of Guatemala in 1954. What had this small nation done? The country's president had displayed great "immaturity" in giving government jobs to a few communists as an anticorruption measure and in proposing to redistribute to peasants property that belonged to a US banana company. The CIA created an invasion force in Honduras led by an exiled military opponent. Psychological operations broadcasts spread fears of an armed invasion, and bombing raids in the capital seemed to prove it. The Guatemalan army intervened and overthrew the president.

Washington's concerns about Latin America receded to complacency yet again. It was short lived. In quick succession in 1959 and 1960, the Cuban revolutionaries executed officers of the previous regime, brought communists into the government, instituted land reform, provoked the defection of moderate politicians, and expropriated American businesses. These actions amounted to far more than the Guatemalans had accomplished. Castro's overtures to the Soviet Union became a decisive issue in the 1960 American election. In the first presidential debates, Senator John F. Kennedy famously skewered Eisenhower's vice president, Richard M. Nixon, for allowing communists to seize a nation just ninety miles off the Florida coast. Suddenly, the Cuban Revolution became a major issue in American politics.

At no time in American history—before or since—did Washington spend so much effort and treasure on Latin America than it did between 1959 and 1968. In this brief period, President Kennedy produced the Alliance for Progress, the Bay of Pigs invasion, the Peace Corps, and the military doctrine of counterinsurgency. Kennedy and his successor, Lyndon Baines Johnson, dealt with Soviet missiles in Cuba, Castro's export of revolution, the Panamanian flag riots, the Dominican civil war, and numerous guerrilla uprisings and military coups d'état. The Cuban Revolution had introduced the Cold War to the Western Hemisphere.

The decade of the Cuban Revolution was not kind to electoral governments. Historians blame either the radical foreign policy of Cuba or, more often, the reactionary one of the United States. An alternative explanation suggested in this book places Latin Americans themselves at the center of the crisis of the 1960s.[18] After all, it was for them to choose whether to steer their nations to the left, or to the right, or straight on to democratic transition. To ascribe less prominence to them would be to diminish their agency and to consider Latin Americans as lacking influence over their own fate.

The only thing that Americans and Cubans did together was to involve other countries in the Cold War. After 1959, every nation tended to internalize the world's ideological struggle. The left in Central and South America embraced Havana; the right sided with Washington. Electoral parties mostly gave up the field to those willing to commit violence in settling the ideological disputes. In most countries, the revolutionaries lost and the reactionaries won. Beginning in 1962, civilian regimes toppled one after another until, by 1973, a majority of Latin Americans lived under military rule.

US military forces seldom engaged the "Communist threat" in Latin America directly—with the notable exceptions of the 1962 Missile Crisis and the 1965 invasion of the Dominican Republic. Even the CIA-planned assault in the Bay of Pigs was fought by Cuban émigrés without American combat support. These dramatic conflicts form the subject of many excellent books. In contrast, this study focuses on the lesser-known covert struggles in which both Havana and Washington utilized surrogates in a strategy known as "secret war." It included paramilitary incursions, sabotage, hit-and-run attacks, and subversion. Cubans and Americans trained their Latin American allies in guerrilla warfare and counterinsurgency tactics. They worked through third parties, a process that eventually brought the left- and right-wing extremists of many other nations into the struggle. American and Cuban leaders did not always direct these operations. Often, they were planned and carried out by subalterns—hundreds of workers, peasants, and students who had no official portfolios but nonetheless acted on their own agency. Political conflicts between leftist radicals and reactionaries heated up in Guatemala, Nicaragua, Panama, and nearly every country of South America. Thus did secret war spread throughout the Western Hemisphere in the first decade of the Cuban Revolution.

This book also seeks to explain several paradoxes of international relations in the 1960s. First, Cuba's promotion of guerrilla warfare throughout the hemisphere complicated its relationship to the two greatest socialist powers of the Cold War. Mao Zedong approved of Castro's revolutionary expansionism. Soviet premiers Nikita Khrushchev and Leonid Brezhnev did not. The Kremlin belittled guerrilla warfare as dangerous "adventurism." It promoted "peaceful coexistence" and détente. Even though he depended on Soviet aid, Castro would not renounce the export of revolution. Khrushchev and Brezhnev embraced him despite these differences. Therefore, Mao denounced Castro as a "revisionist," in spite of their ideological affinities.

Second, try as it might to defeat the Cuban Revolution, Washington could not have been more instrumental in assuring its longevity. Everything American policymakers did to combat communism reinforced Fidel Castro's rule and undermined his domestic enemies. One might speculate that Fidel succeeded because Washington opposed him.

Third, democratic politicians in Latin America hesitated to denounce Fidel Castro because pro-American policies did not win elections. Kennedy had temporarily won them over with the promise of funding development through the Alliance for Progress. But political parties in the region grew increasingly cynical when Alliance funding fell far short of expectations. On the other hand, military men did not have to appeal to voters. They could support anticommunism with impunity. Although American diplomats would have preferred electoral democracy, military regimes easily bought them off by pursuing anti-Castro policies.

Fourth, although Presidents Eisenhower, Kennedy, and Johnson promoted progressive reforms at home, they pursued reactionary policies abroad. In order to deflect accusations from conservatives about "creeping socialism," American presidents felt compelled to find a compensation for tackling problems of poverty and civil rights at home. A "tough" foreign policy proved politically popular with Congress and with voters. Therefore, US policy-makers treated foreign politicians who sought remedies for poverty and discrimination in their own countries as subject to communist subversion. For the United States, the decade of the 1960s was a time of reactionary liberalism.

Finally, the strategies and tactics utilized by American presidents to undermine the Cuban Revolution changed in the 1960s. They never really considered the use of US military forces. The anti-Castro strategy began with draining Cuban society of its professional middle classes and terminated with an open-ended humanitarian rescue that, to this day, is reserved for no other nation's refugees. It went from CIA sponsorship of anti-Castro commando raids to reliance on Latin American militaries to prevent revolutions in their own countries. The year 1965 formed the watershed between Washington's aggressive anti-Castro crusade and acquiescence to rule by the generals. The reason was simple. Aggressive policies proved counterproductive, and acquiescent ones produced tolerable results, albeit not for democracy.

Castro's consolidation of the Cuban Revolution exposed these paradoxes of the Cold War in Latin America. It is how Cuba began to change the world, for good or for ill. As Fidel promised, "This time it is truly the Revolution."

PART ONE

REVOLUTION AND COUNTERREVOLUTION IN CUBA

CHAPTER ONE

How to Consolidate a Revolution

ALL OF CASTRO'S political maneuvers to consolidate power might have come to naught if Fulgencio Batista's army had survived the dictator's downfall. It did not. Batista had thoroughly destroyed the institutional integrity of the officer corps with his promotions of incompetent cronies and vicious enforcers. Police brutality provoked even more resistance from university students and alienated their middle-class families. He permitted Los Tigres of the gangster Rolando Masferrer to conduct political rallies and collaborate with American Mafiosi who built casinos and paid off the president's political supporters.[1]

Batista had pretended to be the magnanimous political manipulator, rigging elections with one hand and granting amnesty to political prisoners with the other. He publicly depreciated the capabilities of the Revolutionary Directorate in Havana and of Fidel Castro's 26th of July Movement in Santiago de Cuba. He doted on the children of his second wife and partied with friends and cronies in the Presidential Palace and at his rural estate, the Finca Kuquine. When Fidel got into the Sierra Maestra with some two dozen fighters in January 1957, the dictator refused to believe Castro was even alive.

In June 1958, it was already too late when the dictator finally woke up to the danger. He sent in twelve thousand poorly trained raw recruits to chase the guerrillas, now numbering three hundred, out of the Sierra Maestra, while his best units remained in their garrisons close to the big cities.[2] Unable to defeat Castro's rebels, the army abandoned its arms and left the Sierra Maestra. Neither could it rout one thousand guerrillas of two armed movements operating independently of Castro in the Escambray Mountains, the Revolutionary Directorate and the Second Front. When the M26 guerrilla columns of Ernesto "Che" Guevara and Camilo Cienfuegos marched from the east toward the center of the island, few army units dared to oppose them. Only the air force sent out warplanes and bombers, which the guerrilla columns easily avoided by traveling at night. The surrender of more than six thousand soldiers, policemen, and Masferrer's Tigres at Santa Clara to several hundred guerrillas under Che Guevara's combined command— along with the simultaneous fall of a second garrison to Comandante Camilo Cienfuegos—sealed the doom of the military establishment.

By January 1, 1959, the collapse of the old-regime army had been complete. The dispirited troops, some of whom had not been paid for months, welcomed the guerrillas as "brothers." Castro's guerrilla commanders took control of every major military installation and police station on the island, and his tribunals began to execute some six hundred "war criminals." Batista's supporters had killed up to three thousand victims, but not the twenty thousand claimed by the revolution's propagandists.[3] The old army no longer existed when the various revolutionary factions began to jostle for power.

¿ARMAS PARA QUÉ?

The kernel of counterrevolution germinated within the revolution itself, not among the *batistianos* who had just lost power. This fact accounts for Fidel Castro's political actions following the departure of the dictator. In that first week of 1959, Castro had no intention of rushing to Cuba's capital city. He did not need to behave like every other petty politician seeking immediate advantage. To do so would have been a sign of weakness. Exiled party politicians were catching the first Cubana and Pan Am flights to Havana's Rancho

Boyeros Airport. They had hopes of getting appointments in the interim government. Inside Cuba, army and naval officers who had been imprisoned by Batista hurried to Havana from the Isle of Pines. Guerrilla bands not affiliated to Fidel's M26 arrived in Havana on January 2.

Not Fidel. He knew he was the man of the hour, the master of the situation. Castro's urban militias, made up principally of young men of middle-class origins, had quickly established order in the cities. These members of the urban underground were not *barbudos* and did not wear *verde olivo* (olive-green) battle dress. The youthful militiamen announced their affiliation and authority in the streets with black-and-red M26 armbands. These urban militias prevented violence, except on January 1, when crowds in Havana looted homes of notorious *batistianos* and the casinos of American mobsters.[4] Thereafter, calm and celebration prevailed.

Under Fidel's orders, guerrilla columns of M26 *barbudos* took over police stations and army barracks in towns and cities all over the island. Comandante Camilo Cienfuegos and one hundred men took charge of the sprawling Camp Columbia, on the outskirts of Havana, early on the morning of January 3. He promised the ten thousand Batista troops still there that he harbored no rancor toward them, only toward their corrupt former officers.[5] Che Guevara's column quietly entered the capital after dark and established his headquarters at the eighteenth-century La Cabaña Fortress on the east side of the Bay of Havana. Both comandantes arrived fresh from their victories in Las Villas in caravans of commandeered army jeeps and trucks. Castro could have become a military dictator if he had wished, ruling the country like the Somozas of Nicaragua or Trujillo of the Dominican Republic. American investors, members of Congress, and even the White House would have acquiesced. But he wanted something more than ending up like another Fulgencio Batista.

The public had heard Fidel speak ever since his men had set up Radio Rebelde, a shortwave transmitter that had broadcast more trustworthy news than the government media. Since the summer of 1958, Cuban shops could not stock enough shortwave radio receivers for the public to pick up Rebel Radio.[6] Fidel frequently spoke to the nation, as he did when he ordered the general strike against the junta of General Eulogio Cantillo of Batista's army, but his followers wanted to see the brave *barbudos* in person. Fidel's victory caravan took its time traveling toward Havana so that he could meet his people, speak to them, and celebrate with them now that the ordeal of Batista's repression had ended. He wanted them on his side, come what may.

The Caravan of Liberation, as they called it, traveled the Central Highway from Santiago to Bayamo, then to Holguín, where correspondent Jules Dubois of the *Chicago Tribune* caught up to Castro. Fidel once again disavowed any relationship with the communists. He also said that he sought amicable relations with the Americans, "as long as the United States is friendly to us."[7] Castro made long speeches, usually late at night, in major cities like Santa Clara. The Mexican journalist Carlos Castañeda rode in Castro's car for part of the trip. They listened together as the car radio announced the names of the ministers who were to serve in President Manuel Urrutia's interim cabinet. Castro said he did not know many of them. That may have been true literally, but Urrutia's ministers in exile had been collaborating with M26 for two years.[8] Everyone in the émigré community had no other choice but to associate with the men of the Sierra Maestra.

Fidel had been saying in his speeches that he would not serve in the interim government; he desired only to reestablish the honor of the new Cuban armed forces. Passing through the port city of Cienfuegos, Fidel had dinner with Comandante William Morgan of the allied rebel group the Second Front. Morgan was one of the few Americans to gain a leadership position in the fight against Batista. He and his colleagues fought in the Escambray Mountains and occupied the port of Cienfuegos on the day Batista fled from Cuba. They wanted prominent positions in the new military.[9] Ed Sullivan and his television crew were waiting for Fidel's entourage in Matanzas to record the first American TV interview with the victorious Castro. Fidel told Sullivan that Batista would be the last dictator of Cuba. "Now we are going to improve our democratic institutions," Castro said. "This is a fine young man," Sullivan announced during his Sunday night variety show. "With the help of God and our prayers and the help of the American government, he will be able to come up with the sort of democracy down there" that the United States enjoys.[10] Castro also visited the parents of the deceased anti-Batista resistance leader José Antonio Echeverría, who died in an attack on the Presidential Palace in 1957. Castro also went to Echeverría's gravesite in the town of Cárdenas. In victory, Castro acknowledged the martyrdom of someone who, had he lived, might have been a postrevolutionary rival. But animosities remained between M26 and Echeverría's Revolutionary Directorate (Directorio Revolucionario or DR).

In January 1959, the rural guerrillas of the DR, who had joined Che Guevara in the battle of Santa Clara, were spoiling for high-level participation in the new government. For this reason, surviving DR operatives occupied the Presidential Palace. They turned over the palace to interim president Manuel Urrutia a few days later, but not without some tense negotiations with Comandante Camilo Cienfuegos.[11] In the meanwhile, DR fighters broke into the armory of the military base at San Antonio de los Baños, south of the capital. There they seized hundreds of rifles and machine guns.

Revolutionary Directorate militants stored these weapons at the University of Havana, where many had been students protesting the Batista regime before they took up arms with Echeverría. The cache served to reinforce their demands for political influence. The only American guerrilla in the ranks of Fidel's M26, Neill Macaulay, had stopped by the university during the DR occupation. "The rebels at the University were quite different from the peasant and working-class *barbudos*," he later wrote. Macaulay observed more than three hundred students at the university who identified deeply with the veterans of the Presidential Palace attack. "They were intense, animated young men with ideas and strong convictions," he said.[12]

Finally, shortly after noon on January 8, 1959, Fidel's caravan entered Havana. A crowd numbering in the tens of thousands had been waiting along the Malecón. Not a single other revolutionary chieftain or returning politician received such a reception. "I must see him!" a woman said to an American news reporter. "He has saved us! He has liberated us from a monster and from gangsters and assassins!"[13] Fidel Castro greeted the multitudes in a slow procession along this famous seaside boulevard that terminated at the Presidential Palace. Interim president Urrutia greeted him at the ornate doorway. Fidel invited the crowd to his speech that night at Camp Columbia.

Before anything else, Fidel would have to deal with the Directorio Revolucionario. For that purpose, he resolved to utilize his popularity and oratorical skills in his major address of January 8, 1959, before the new Revolutionary Army. As Castro, not yet thirty-three years of age, began to address his troops and the thousands of others gathered at Camp Columbia, someone released three white doves. Two landed on the speaker's rostrum, and one alighted on the shoulder of the fatigue-clad Fidel Castro. The doves stayed there during part of the speech. The idea that God himself was anointing this young guerrilla leader crossed the minds of the awed onlookers.

"¿Armas para qué?" (Weapons for what?) he asked during the speech, referring to the Revolutionary Directorate. "To fight against whom? . . . Today there is no torture, assassination or dictatorship. Today there is only happiness."

"Weapons! What for?" Castro asked again. "So that we can watch gangsterism and daily skirmishes flourish? Weapons for what? Well, I say to you that two days ago, members of a certain organization entered the San Antonio barracks . . . and took 500 machine guns and other weapons. . . . If they were seeking provocations, what they lacked was not guns but only men of the people to support them."[14] The commandant of Camp Columbia, Camilo Cienfuegos, stood behind Fidel on the platform. Fidel turned to him in the middle of his address and asked, "¿Cómo voy, Camilo?" (How am I doing, Camilo?) "Vas bien, Fidel," said Cienfuegos— "You're doing fine."[15]

Castro's speech swayed Cuban public opinion, and the Directorio Revolucionario capitulated. It abandoned its occupation of the University of Havana, gave up the weapons, and joined the rebel army in subordination to its *comandante en jefe* Fidel Castro. Leaders of the Revolutionary Directorate and also those of the splinter rebel group, the Second National Front of the Escambray, accepted positions in the rebel armed forces. They retained their ranks as comandantes as well as the facial hair. These included Fauré Chomón and Rolando Cubela of the DR and Eloy Gutiérrez Menoyo and the American William Morgan of the Second Front. Not all future challenges would be so easy to resolve, however, as some revolutionaries realized. "This Revolution [will be] more difficult than the war of liberation that ended on the 31st of December," Comandante Camilo Cienfuegos said. "The difficulties, the real sacrifices, and the most intense work began on the first day of January of the year 1959."[16]

THE ART OF ELIMINATING RIVALS

It was as if Fidel Castro had learned all the dirty tricks of the early modern doges of Venice. This author has found no conclusive evidence that Castro had read *The Prince* by Machiavelli. Nevertheless, he did become a master politician and an international figure of major stature. Quite possibly, he learned merely by participating since his university days in the byzantine world of Cuban politics. As a law student, Castro had even engaged in the *grupos de acción,* action groups of enforcers. He ran for office in university politics, becoming president of the association of law students at the University of Havana while failing in his quest for the student federation presidency. His book education came after he earned his law degree. Two years as a political prisoner on the Isle of Pines for the Moncada attack of 1953 provided ample opportunity for him to immerse himself in reading. He had a photographic memory and devoured books.[17]

Fidel read extensively on the Latin American revolutions for independence of Simón Bolívar and on the nineteenth-century Cuban revolutionaries José Martí and Antonio Maceo. He sampled the work of other authors including Victor Hugo, Karl Marx, and Sigmund Freud. Fidel became a student of the French Revolution—and Napoléon Bonaparte. Friends sent books and letters to his hospital cellblock, where political prisoners were held at Modelo Prison on the Isle of Pines. Fidel made it a point not to claim extra liberties just because his brother-in-law, Rafael Díaz-Balart, was serving as Batista's deputy minister of the interior. "These past days, many books have gone through my hands," he wrote to a friend. "I've rolled up my sleeves and have undertaken the study of world history and political doctrines."[18] Fidel Castro was no uneducated dilettante. He acted shrewdly and understood human nature.

Throughout 1959 and 1960, Fidel and his closest advisers from the Sierra Maestra consolidated control over the new revolutionary military and the government. They were bound to encounter opposition from former collaborators—from those ex–government officials who lost their jobs and went into exile with Batista's 1952 coup and from party politicians of the late 1940s. Fidel handled these politicos rather easily. Greater danger derived from men with guns, particularly from within his own revolutionary group, the M26. Eventually, opponents relocated to Miami and, with the assistance of the US government, would continue the counterrevolution from abroad. The measure of Fidel's political genius was in how he baited them with the Cuban communist party and maintained his rivals in a state of disunity. Each of them claimed revolutionary status for having advanced the cause against Batista, and each of them suffered a lonely exit. Moreover, Castro demonstrated remarkable restraint with political rivals because they could become useful and not particularly dangerous. With armed opponents, on the other hand, Fidel utilized *la mano dura,* the iron fist.

In exile during the 1950s, the Auténticos participated in the resistance from a distance. This political party's leader, ex-president Carlos Prío Socarrás, financed and armed several groups, all of them disconnected from Castro's M26. The first was the Revolutionary Directorate of José Antonio Echeverría. The other was the Second Front of Eloy Gutiérrez Menoyo. The third, a seaborne expedition, ended in Batista's army executing some two dozen armed men from the yacht *Corinthia* in May 1957. The Auténticos also dominated the first attempt at forming a government-in-exile in December 1957 with the Pact of Miami. Castro subverted that effort with a long accusatory letter demanding the input of his 26th of July Revolutionary Movement. Later in July 1958, the exiles were anticipating victory and finally settled with M26 on the outlines of a future government in the Pact of Caracas.[19] Fidel forced the Cubans abroad to accept Manuel Urrutia, a judge, as president of the government-in-exile. Having no party followers and few political skills, Urrutia satisfied everyone who hoped eventually to displace him.

The Auténticos in Miami felt that they had contributed invaluably to the overthrow of Batista. They had sent money, had smuggled arms, and had bad-mouthed Fulgencio Batista to the American press. Most of all, they had portrayed the revolution in electoral terms. The émigrés had said that the young fighters in Cuba were not communists but proponents of fair elections. If anything, Prío Socarrás had told reporters, the communist party supported Batista. Thus the exile community succeeded in reversing a US policy that had supported the Batista dictatorship. President Eisenhower had smiled and shaken hands with Batista at an international conference in Panama. Vice President Richard M. Nixon had visited Havana; there had been more smiling and glad handing for the cameras. The US military mission in Cuba had delivered weapons and even tanks to Batista's army, all in the name of "Hemispheric Defense" against a Russian invasion. Both the émigré leaders and the rebels had complained incessantly about Batista's airmen using US warplanes to bomb and strafe peasant villages. Finally, news stories about police atrocities in Cuba changed public opinion in the United States. In March of 1958, Washington imposed an arms embargo on Batista; in July, it ended the delivery of ammunition to the Cuban Air Force.[20] The rebel victory came five months later.

Former president Carlos Prío Socarrás returned to Cuba in January 1959, even though he had no formal government position. Rumor had it that he had come to reclaim some of the real estate holdings that he had acquired as a politician in the 1940s. He expressed support for the revolution. Prío Socarrás even endorsed the May 1959 land reform decree "in principle" and urged Cubans to unite behind Fidel's slogan *patria o muerte,* "fatherland or death." As late as October 1960, at the height of the confiscation of foreign companies, he praised the revolutionary program for its dedication "to the defense of the humble, the peasants and the workers."[21] Chagrined American diplomats speculated that former president Prío Socarrás was getting back at the United States for his brief incarceration and legal problems in Miami stemming from illegal arms trafficking in the late 1950s.

Older politicians who had returned to Cuba after Batista's ouster encountered familiar difficulties and perils in going back to exile. They escaped by boat or took refuge in foreign embassies in Havana. Prío Socarrás had some luck in this regard. He eventually went to Brazil on a "lecture tour" that provided a safe exit from Cuba.[22] Later, back in Miami, Prío Socarrás played little role in the proliferating anti-Castro movements. He retired comfortably and permitted a younger generation of political refugees to collaborate in anti-Castro activities.

Castro set out to entrap these competitors for power, allowing them to take the bait, then springing the trap. The communist party, known in Cuba as the Popular Socialist Party (PSP), became the bait. Known communists suddenly appeared in military training academies and in important government ministries. There were no press announcements at all, and party politicians in the interim cabinet were becoming nervous. The PSP hardly contributed to the struggle against the tyrant until the very end, they complained.

Fidel's courtship with the communists posed risks, as it had the potential of provoking a confrontation with the United States.[23] Castro's closest advisers knew that they could not have their revolution without an eventual conflict with their northern neighbor, but they wished to have it later rather than sooner. Therefore, until he flushed out most of his domestic opponents, Fidel Castro could not announce his alliance with the PSP. To have done so would have united his rivals against him. And Washington too. It greatly helped that Castro, unlike Guatemalan president Jacobo Arbenz in 1954, had no autonomous military establishment to block his policies. Fidel could count on the rebel army to afford him maximum political maneuverability.

DECLINE OF THE INTERIM GOVERNMENT

Another exile leader, José Miró Cardona, eventually had much more expo-sure than most of the old party stalwarts in both the interim government and the Cuban counterrevolution in Miami. In neither of these positions did he have much authority. In fact, the lack of authority seemed to be Miró Cardona's lot in life, and also his political allure. He had just enough pres-tige to merit political appointments, but not enough followers to threaten rivals. Miró Cardona obtained the prime ministry in January 1959 because of his former job as head of the Cuban Bar Association. From there, he gained his anti-Batista credentials as defense counsel of army officers implicated in the conspiracy in 1956.[24] After his defendants lost their case in court, Miró Cardona fled the country. His work in exile organizing the Caracas Pact gained the notice of another nonthreatening political personality, Manuel Urrutia, Fidel's choice for the interim presidency. Urrutia rewarded Miró Cardona with an appointment as prime minister of the first revolutionary government.

During his six weeks as chief cabinet minister, Miró Cardona participated in the major events only sparingly. The disarmament of the Revolutionary Directorate, the trials and executions of *batistianos*, reorganization of the po-lice and military, demands for US extradition of the tyranny's "war crimi-nals," and the expulsion of the US military mission—Fidel and his military chiefs performed these tasks, not the prime minister. Did not American mili-tary advisers instruct Batista's army how to lose? Castro asked by way of explaining the eviction of US military personnel. "If they are going to teach us that, it would be better [that] they teach us nothing."[25]

Prime Minister Miró Cardona attempted one reform during his brief tenure. He proposed ending the scourge of gambling on the island that had attracted the American Mafiosi during the Batista tyranny. His cabinet voted in favor of the proposal. But gambling had attracted tourists and filled hotel rooms as well, and hotel workers went to Fidel Castro with complaints about losing jobs and family income. Commander of the rebel army Castro sum-moned the ministers to his suite at the Hilton Hotel and told them to re-scind the decree.[26] Miró Cardona did the only thing a powerless official could: he offered to resign. Castro convinced the prime minister to stay on, but still no one listened to a figurehead, so Miró Cardona quit a second time in mid-February. "I resigned," he told one newspaper. "Cuba did not protest; it accepted, it applauded."[27]

Miró Cardona arrived back in Miami in 1960 in time to receive the offer of another powerless position, that of leading the Cuban Revolutionary Council (CRC). This umbrella coalition served ostensibly as the political arm of the Bay of Pigs invasion, over which the agents of the CIA allowed the CRC absolutely no control. The ex–prime minister soon became angry at the CIA for botching the invasion. His son was a member of the landing force and spent twenty months as a prisoner in Castro's jails. Miró Cardona remained on the Council's payroll until he resigned in 1963.

Back in Cuba, Fidel took the initiative in defining who was revolutionary and who was not. He introduced the terms "reactionaries and counterrevolutionaries" as early as March 1959 to denounce defense attorneys who so ably defended Batista's air force officers that a court acquitted the pilots of criminally bombing and strafing peasant villages during the uprising. Castro also applied these terms to newspaper editors who questioned the prominence of communists in the government despite having been notably absent in the rebellion.[28] His speeches began to refer to opponents as *gusanos,* or worms.

The first M26 *gusano* was Major Pedro Luis Díaz Lanz. Before the revolution, he had been an airline pilot. In March 1958, the future comandante Huber Matos contracted the services of Díaz Lanz to fly a shipment of arms from Costa Rica to the Sierra Maestra. Just before the critical guerrilla defense against Batista's summer offensive of June 1958, Díaz Lanz made a second flight—illegally—from Florida into the Sierra Maestra with more arms and ammunition. Díaz Lanz evaded both the state police in Florida and Batista's warplanes over Cuban airspace. His passenger, M26 operative Carlos Franqui, praised his flying skill as he negotiated the high peaks. "Díaz Lanz's risky landing was successful," he wrote. "It was more a plowed meadow than a landing field."[29] In June 1958, General Cantillo assembled a force of twelve thousand troops below the Sierra Maestra. Yet the much-ballyhooed Fin de Fidel (End of Fidel) campaign stalled, and, within two months, government forces lost arms and momentum to the rebels. One infantry company even joined up with the guerrillas.

President Urrutia had known of his arms deliveries and appointed Díaz Lanz as head of the rebel air force in the first week of 1959. He subsequently served on the second tribunal that convicted Batista-era pilots for bombarding peasant villages. But the sudden presence of communists in the military academies bothered the air force chief. In June 1959, he spoke to reporters about "indoctrination classes" that Raúl Castro's instructors from the Soviet Union were teaching to military personnel. Fidel heard about his remarks and asked for his resignation. Díaz Lanz returned home, bundled his family into a small boat, and crossed the Straits of Florida to Miami. Within weeks, he appeared as a witness before a Senate investigative committee in Washington, DC. There, Díaz Lanz accused Fidel Castro of being a communist. His defection and testimony in Washington placed his friends back home in an awkward situation. President Manuel Urrutia and other moderate ministers felt obliged to denounce Díaz Lanz for treason and opportunism.[30] They also realized that the competition had begun.

Some *batistianos* had been flying light aircraft from Florida over Cuban airspace for months. Pedro Díaz Lanz himself piloted several flights in the fall of 1959. Fidel used these occasions to rush to the TV station and deliver full-throated denunciations of counterrevolutionaries and their CIA sponsors. Castro easily associated Díaz Lanz with the discredited *batistianos*, several of whom had also testified before the United States Congress. Thereafter, Fidel identified every defector as a Díaz Lanz–like traitor.[31]

President Manuel Urrutia also had impressive revolutionary credentials. Six years before he became the interim leader, he had served as a judge in Santiago de Cuba. Like others, he had been surprised when the little-known politician Fidel Castro and one hundred others attacked the second-largest army base on the island, Moncada Barracks. Batista's soldiers repulsed the assault and later rounded up several hundreds of suspects implicated in the attack. Judge Urrutia oversaw some of the legal proceedings.

Later, he presided over the trial of captured M26 veterans of the *Granma* expedition who had become separated from Fidel's small group of survivors due to an army ambush in December 1956. Judge Urrutia gained instantaneous renown among Batista's enemies by setting these prisoners free. In rising up in arms against the government, he ruled, "the defendants had been acting within their constitutional rights." Among those absolved that day were the twenty-three-year-old leader of the Santiago uprising and head of the National Directorate of the M26, Frank País. Because Fidel Castro completely depended on País and his network of supplies and recruits, the guerrillas of the Sierra Maestra demonstrated their gratitude by advocating Manuel Urrutia as leader of the government-in-exile. Moreover, Urrutia had neither a political entourage nor a party apparatus behind him like the prestigious exile leader Felipe Pazos.[32]

The Pact of Caracas promoted Judge Urrutia to the presidency-in-exile of Cuba. Urrutia arranged to fly into Santiago de Cuba on January 1 in order to stand behind Fidel Castro during his first speech following the resignation of the dictator. He managed to confer with the guerrilla chieftain about the cabinet assignments before flying west to Havana but arrived to find the Presidential Palace occupied by the Revolutionary Directorate. Following the DR's capitulation, he met with Prime Minister Miró Cardona and his cabinet frequently. But when Fidel took over the prime ministry in February, he called fewer meetings and often failed to invite President Urrutia. The latter's main duty was to sign the government's laws, such as the agrarian reform decree in May 1959. Apparently, he began to delay signing statutes with which he did not agree. His stalling set the plot for his ouster in motion. During a television interview, someone asked what he thought about the communists. President Urrutia vented his frustrations. "I saw no Communist sacrifices of blood and life in the Cuban Revolution," Urrutia recounted in a memoir written in exile four years later.[33] *Hoy,* the newspaper of the communist PSP, criticized the president's remarks as unfitting for a revolutionary.

Apparently, President Urrutia did not realize that he had taken the bait. In his memoir he wrote: "In the early morning of July 17, I received the surprising news that Fidel Castro had resigned as Prime Minister and was nowhere to be found. At once I went down to the second floor of the Presidential Palace, where I found almost all the Ministers in Council Hall. None of them knew what was happening nor [*sic*] where Castro was, but I detected a distinct reserve on the part of those who were Castro's Ministers."[34]

The day passed without any explanation. The government stopped working, and labor leaders called for walkouts. Fidel had disappeared from view. The leading television station announced that the prime minister would address the nation at 11:00 A.M. Then a new time was set for noon. Still no Fidel. In a long afternoon of uncertainty, a large crowd gathered at the Presidential Palace. The multitude began to chant a plea to the absent prime minister: "Do not quit. Do not quit." Urrutia went to the balcony of his office and tried to placate the people below. "What you should do is ask Doctor Fidel Castro that he not renounce, because he's the only one who can withdraw his resignation, in view of the fact that it is he who directed Cuba's liberation and he alone is responsible for the success of the Revolution."

Finally, Fidel himself appeared on television before a table of news reporters. "I have resigned," Castro said, "because it is impossible for me to continue exercising my duties in view of the difficulties issuing from the presidency of the Republic."[35] The prime minister complained that President Urrutia was holding up the revolution by delaying the signing of revolutionary laws, especially those that dealt with the imposition of the death penalty for counterrevolutionary crimes. Castro charged that Urrutia had given himself the same "exorbitant" salary as Batista and was beginning to buy expensive real estate. Castro's television interview continued for another three hours, at the end of which a news bulletin announcing Urrutia's own resignation brought the show to an end. The prime minister resumed his duties immediately, and the cabinet approved the appointment of a new president, Osvaldo Dorticós, the University of Havana–trained lawyer who had been serving as the minister of revolutionary laws.[36]

The Urrutias took refuge in the Venezuelan embassy for nearly a year until the Cuban government allowed their safe passage out of the country. The former president spent the rest of his days in Queens, New York, teaching Spanish.

ELIMINATING THE MODERATES

Felipe Pazos, the economist, earned the respect of both Cubans and American diplomats as a principled and able public servant. Until the 1952 coup, he served in the cabinet of President Prío Socarrás as president of the Cuban National Bank. Subsequently, during the struggle against Batista, Pazos exercised the most effective leadership of the large number of Auténticos. He convinced reporter Herbert Matthews to visit Castro in the Sierra Maestra early in 1957. The resulting stories in the *New York Times* painted the rebellion in romantic hues as a fight against tyranny.[37] The smaller M26 became more famous abroad than the powerful Revolutionary Directorate. Along with Orthodox Party leader Raúl Chibás, Pazos also visited Fidel's guerrilla headquarters and cowrote the Sierra Manifesto, which expressed the objectives of the revolution in noncommunist terms. "Do the Sierra Maestra rebels not want free elections, a democratic regime, [and] a constitutional government?" asked the manifesto. "We are here because we want them more than anyone else."[38] At the time, Pazos had a ten-year-old son, also named Felipe, who would become famous acting next to Spencer Tracy in the movie version of Ernest Hemingway's *The Old Man and the Sea*. His elder son, Javier, accompanied his father to Castro's hideout. Javier Pazos stayed on with the M26 guerrillas for several months while his father was serving as an eloquent spokesman for the anti-Batista forces in the United States. Javier suffered bullet wounds in a firefight against Batista's troops in November 1957 but survived and eventually fled to the United States.

His peers abroad practically anointed Pazos as the next Cuban president in the Miami Pact of October 1957. However, the men of the sierra proved powerful enough to subvert that agreement. In June 1958, M26 forced the exile community to accept the Caracas Pact instead, which designated a public figure of lesser stature, Judge Urrutia, as the president-in-exile.

In January 1959, Pazos obtained appointment to the job he had previously performed—president of the National Bank. This portfolio ostensibly made him one of the chief ministers for economic planning in the interim cabinet. However, his cabinet position of 1959 gave him none of his old authority, because Che Guevara's secret planning committee was laying the foundations for a more socialized economy. Castro's trip to Washington in April accorded Felipe Pazos his moment in the revolutionary sun. He accompanied his new prime minister on the trip, which led the State Department to hope that the liberals had influence in the revolutionary government. The presence of Pazos and other moderates comforted American diplomats who feared that Castro was in danger of falling in with communism.[39] That Fidel requested no American aid for the new revolutionary government dumbfounded both moderates like Pazos and the State Department. The prime minister knew—and his moderate ministers did not—that his brother Raúl Castro was initiating contact with the Kremlin at that very moment.

Perhaps Castro realized that the fall of so many anticommunists might precipitate unwelcome and hostile reaction from the US embassy. As long as his moderate cabinet ministers dropped in to the American embassy to assure Ambassador Philip Bonsal that they could reason with the prime minister, Fidel could count on a few more months of US indecision. But the purges took a toll on Pazos, and he disagreed with Fidel's decisions. Castro gave Pazos the benefit of the doubt. Pazos resigned his National Bank presidency in October 1959 without denouncing communism or criticizing Prime

Minister Castro. He retired without recrimination, and Che Guevara replaced him at the National Bank.

At the beginning of 1960, Felipe Pazos received diplomatic appointment as Cuba's ambassador-at-large for economic affairs with Europe. It might have provided his ticket for a graceful exile. However, in August, when Castro was engaging in the confiscation of the assets of foreign businesses and industries in the country, Pazos received word that the government had dismissed him from this diplomatic post. As he resigned, he reportedly said that the government was taking the revolution in a different direction than what had been its original objective. "There is less liberty in Cuba today than any period in the past," he said.[40] Felipe Pazos found a way to leave the country in safety. President Kennedy ultimately appointed Pazos as director of the economic planning committee for the Alliance for Progress.

Minister of Agriculture Humberto Sorí Marín, an attorney and a longtime Auténtico, joined Fidel Castro in the Sierra Maestra. There he drafted the Law of Revolutionary Justice, which introduced the death penalty for treason and murder. It formed the legal basis for numerous executions in the Sierra Maestra during the guerrilla war and for the executions of *batistiano* war criminals in January through March of 1959. Sorí Marín also had written the Sierra Maestra agrarian reform decree based on the Constitution of 1940. It allotted peasants private property rights to lands confiscated from Batista supporters in M26 territory. For these services, he was promoted to the rank of comandante in the Sierra Maestra. Then he became minister of agriculture in the interim revolutionary government of President Urrutia. He served on the tribunal that sentenced the *batistiano* Captain Jesús Sosa Blanco to death for torture and murder.[41]

Sorí Marín had another side to him. He was also a Catholic nationalist and organized many Catholic students into the Rural Commandos. This group provided educational outreach to prepare peasants in the Sierra Maestra for the future exercise of their property rights under the forthcoming national agrarian reform. Like Lieutenant Manuel Artime, Catholic students who had supported the revolution worked directly under Sorí Marín's ministry. The *comandos rurales* provided literacy instruction for children by day and adult education in basic literacy and agricultural technology by night. Nevertheless, Che Guevara and Antonio Núñez Jiménez excluded Sorí Marín while drafting the May 1959 land reform decree.[42] The minister of agriculture ultimately objected to the new communist-dominated National Institute of

Agrarian Reform, or INRA. Humberto Sorí Marín resigned from the interim government in June and left the island later that autumn.

During 1960, as its economy underwent socialization, Sorí Marín prepared to return to Cuba. He started organizing among other émigrés involved in Catholic nationalist groups. The CIA trained Sorí Marín to lead the anti-Castro uprising that was to accompany the Bay of Pigs invasion. Landing with a boatload of saboteurs equipped with arms and explosives, he infiltrated back into Cuba in March 1961. Castro's spies had penetrated the network of anticommunist groups in Miami and Havana. State Security captured most of the members of the Sorí Marín expedition at the same time that Castro's military forces defeated the invasion of twelve hundred anti-Castro Cubans at the Bay of Pigs.[43] A firing squad executed the former M26 comandante and minister of agriculture shortly thereafter. Ironically, Sorí Marín fell afoul of the successor of the death-for-treason law he had first drafted three years beforehand in the Sierra Maestra. He was one of the few former cabinet ministers who resorted to guns against Castro.

Minister of Public Works Manuel Ray Rivera had received his degree in engineering at the University of Utah and became the project manager for the construction of the Havana Hilton Hotel (in which Fidel resided in 1959). During the late 1950s, Manuel Ray had become the Havana director of Civic Resistance, another group opposing the Batista regime. As leader of the urban underground, Ray urged consumers to buy only essentials, thus depriving the dictatorship of tax revenues on luxury items. "Don't go to places of amusement," he advised. "Cuba is in mourning."[44] Ray's Civic Resistance also collected funds for the rebels in the Sierra Maestra.[45] He cooperated with the National Directorate of the M26 in the April 1958 general strike that ended in defeat and repression at the hands of the Batista police. Manuel Ray had been fortunate to escape arrest through December 1958. In January 1959, he accepted President Urrutia's appointment as minister of public works with the interim government. Known as a revolutionary but anticommunist and pro-American, he maintained cordial relations with the US embassy.

Manuel Ray continued in his ministry into the fall of 1959, even as President Urrutia and many others were leaving government service and going into exile. The defining event of the autumn proved to be the Huber Matos affair (discussed in greater detail in the following section). Comandante Huber Matos resigned from his command of the military district of

Camagüey in October. His letter of resignation expressed abhorrence at the undue influence of the communists in serving a revolution they had little role in bringing about. Fidel ordered the arrest of Matos.[46] Manuel Ray joined Felipe Pazos and two other cabinet ministers in opposing plans to try Matos for treason, but they lost the debate as well as Fidel's confidence. Manuel Ray Rivero resigned his ministerial post in November 1959 and retired to private life.[47]

Opposition among the professional middle class was growing. Many doctors, lawyers, and engineers purchased passage on the planes leaving the country, and a few began clandestine operations against the regime. In October 1960, Manuel Ray was organizing an anti-Castro group called the People's Revolutionary Movement (MRP). The US embassy viewed Ray as one of the influential leaders who might unite the various resistance factions. The diplomats interpreted the MRP's program as the restoration of the 1940 Constitution, respect for civil liberties and the rule of law, and economic and social reforms without communism. They likened Ray's ideology to "Fidelismo without Fidel."[48] Manuel Ray Rivero slipped out of Cuba in November 1960 on a boat to Tampa, Florida—most likely with the assistance of the CIA.

The Eisenhower administration immediately tapped Manuel Ray for the board of directors of the Cuban Revolutionary Council. The CIA formed the CRC as a cover organization that pretended to supervise the CIA-devised invasion for which Cuban exiles were training in the Panama Canal Zone and Guatemala. In this new task, Ray became reunited with his former cabinet boss, the ex–prime minister and now director of the CRC, Miró Cardona. White House advisers in the new Kennedy administration grew to admire Manuel Ray's anticommunist reformism. Presidential adviser Arthur Schlesinger Jr. wrote eloquently about visiting Ray in the headquarters of the CRC. Schlesinger saw the other leaders such as Miró Cardona and Antonio "Tony" Varona as indecisive and out of touch—but not Manuel Ray. He was youthful and energetic by comparison. "I had a long talk with Manuel Ray, who seemed more reasonable and realistic than the others," Schlesinger wrote.[49] The CIA did not share the White House's enthusiasm for Ray. The Agency disliked his liberal politics and preferred counterrevolutionary leaders with more conservative outlooks. Anyway, the defeat at the Bay of Pigs undermined the CRC in the counterrevolution, centered now in

Miami, yet the ex-minister Manuel Ray Rivera would still find a role to play in the anti-Castro crusade.

MEN WITH GUNS

Fidel and his revolutionary officers had a tolerant approach toward civilian rivals. They kept them on long enough to mollify American policymakers, preventing Washington from breaking diplomatic relations until it suited the revolutionaries. Prime Minister Castro dismissed his cabinet members from their duties when he needed their jobs or when the men left in disgust over their powerlessness. Fidel also allowed the civilian politicians to escape from Cuba rather than line them up at the *paredón,* the "execution wall." Abroad in Miami, the former government officials might continue to serve the revolution's interest as discredited and reviled enemies, whose return the Cuban people would have to suffer if Castro fell from power. Only those civilians who resorted to arms, like the ex-agriculture minister Sorí Marín, faced the firing squads. This hard-line policy also applied to dissident officers of the Revolutionary Armed Forces. If these defectors with guns did not evade capture, they went to prison for a long term or to the wall. Four case histories suffice to sustain this point.

The resignation of Comandante Huber Matos caused the greatest political crisis of 1959. Matos had joined the M26 as a young schoolteacher and manager of his father's rice farm in Manzanillo, Oriente Province. Early in 1957, Matos had wanted to go into the Sierra Maestra to join up with the small guerrilla force. But Fidel himself sent a note. "Here you will be one more man," wrote the guerrilla chief. "We lack arms and bullets. If you come with a rifle, we will accept you."[50] Forced into exile for his anti-Batista views, the schoolteacher and rice farmer fled to Costa Rica, where he met Venezuelan and Nicaraguan refugees as well as Cubans. His father sent money, and with the assistance of the Costa Rican ex-president José "Pepe" Figueres, he purchased military armament and a C-46, a World War II transport plane.

In March 1958, Díaz Lanz piloted this cargo plane with Matos, the arms, and six members of M26. Matos came to the Sierra Maestra with enough weapons for many men. Eventually, Castro promoted Matos to the command of his own guerrilla column. His troops were participating in the siege of Santiago when Batista fled the island.[51] On January 8, 1959, Matos rode into Havana on the same military truck with Fidel and Camilo in the grand parade up the Malecón.

Matos took over army command in the province of Camagüey, a cattle- and sugar-producing region. He became alarmed at how the communists were becoming prominent in military affairs. In May, Captain Antonio Núñez Jiménez, who joined Che's forces just before the assault on Santa Clara, became director of the National Institute of Agrarian Reform. The INRA became the most powerful new government bureaucracy created by Fidel's land reform decree. INRA's overzealous land-reform activities in his command area of Camagüey disquieted Comandante Matos. Military orders arrived at his headquarters instructing Matos to use army troops to seize cattle farms of landowners who resisted the orders of the local INRA office. Matos believed that these interventionist measures went beyond the intent of the more moderate agrarian reform law of May 1959.

Fidel refused to talk to Matos about his complaints. Instead, Prime Minister Castro laid a trap that nearly cost Matos his life. A minor member of the M26 went on television in October 1959 to accuse Comandante Huber Matos of several treacherous acts. It was the final insult. Matos resigned from the Revolutionary Armed Forces and sent a scathing letter to Fidel Castro, who promptly publicized its contents. "Now, Fidel, you are destroying your own work," it said. "You are burying the revolution."[52]

Fidel ordered Camilo Cienfuegos to go to Camagüey and place Huber Matos under arrest for treason. As Cienfuegos and his armed *escolta* (escort) approached the gates of the army post, Matos ordered his guards not to shoot. Cienfuegos entered the command post alone and sat down with Matos over *café cubano*. Matos agreed to submit peaceably to his arrest for he wanted no bloodshed. "Be careful, Camilo," Matos said, according to his memoirs. "Your popularity is a cause of worry for Fidel and even more for Raúl."[53] Sixteen of Matos's staff officers, most of them *barbudos* like their chief, dropped their pistol belts and volunteered to accompany their comandante under arrest.

In the meantime, Fidel Castro himself showed up at the Camagüey headquarters of the National Institute of Agrarian Reform, where he raised a mob of three thousand men. They headed for the military camp to make sure that Matos had given himself up. Raúl Castro's security chief, Ramiro Valdés, took custody of the prisoners from Camilo Cienfuegos and transported them to Havana to await trial.[54] It did little to help Matos, but just as the crisis of this high-level military resignation made the news, his old colleague from the arms-smuggling days in the Sierra Maestra, Pedro Díaz Lanz, appeared in the sky over Havana once again. He dropped more anti-communist leaflets. The flyover angered Castro all the more because of CIA collusion with a possible military rebellion. Fidel and Raúl subsequently testified for the prosecution at Huber Matos's trial for treason. The three-man military tribunal pronounced him guilty and sentenced him to death by firing squad. Fidel commuted the death sentence to twenty years in prison.[55]

Additional consolidation of power occurred in the rebel armed forces. Just two weeks after Cienfuegos arrested Huber Matos, the former's small plane supposedly plunged into the sea during a severe thunderstorm. Raúl Castro interrupted a cabinet meeting to notify his brother the prime minister that Camilo's plane had gone missing. Right there in the cabinet room they laid out the military maps and traced possible flight routes. Fidel ordered Raúl to investigate the matter.[56] Ultimately, searchers found no signs of the wreckage. No bodies were ever recovered. Fidel's detractors do not believe the government's version of Camilo's death. Years later, Huber Matos remembered Camilo once confiding in him that "Fidel praises me in public but in private he underestimates me, and sometimes he treats me like shit."[57] Others who fled Cuba for exile entertain the story of a fighter plane that took off from the same airport that Camilo's aircraft had departed.

The US embassy staff had numerous conversations with disgruntled, mainly middle-class applicants for visas to the United States. American diplomats knew that Cubans held Camilo in greater esteem than his boss, the defense minister Raúl Castro. In fact, people filled the streets in joyous celebration when rumors spread through the capital that Camilo had been found alive. Fidel went on television stating definitively that Camilo had died, and he then devoted the rest of his remarks to criticizing US authorities for allowing rogue aircraft to take off from Florida in order to drop firebombs on Cuban sugar mills. Moreover, the government refused to accept assistance from US Navy ships and planes from the Guantánamo Naval Base to help find the wreckage of Camilo's downed aircraft.[58]

The embassy also noted that, unlike Fidel and Raúl, Camilo seldom denounced the United States in his public speeches. Hatred of plantation owners and dictators and praise for the revolution's social programs—especially agrarian reform—occupied most of Camilo's public remarks. He loathed counterrevolutionaries and, just days prior to his death, he spoke of Huber Matos as a traitor of the likes of Díaz Lanz and Urrutia.[59]

Some sources suggest that the lightheartedness of Camilo Cienfuegos often offended Fidel and other committed revolutionaries. Several days before he disappeared, Camilo had burst unannounced into a meeting—which was his habit—between Fidel Castro and Carlos Franqui. Castro was complaining that Franqui's newspaper, *Revolución,* was publishing articles about the recent revolutionary war that were inaccurate. Franqui responded that his stories reflected the recollections of several different witnesses, the more the better to arrive at the truth. Suddenly, Cienfuegos added some levity to the discussion. "One has to write history, Fidel, because one day you will be old and old men say many lies, and Camilo will not be here to tell you: 'Vas mal, Fidel,' [you're doing badly]." Fidel did not appear amused and ended the meeting. "You don't change, Camilo," he said.[60]

Until Cuban documents become available, historians have to grapple with the unanswered questions about Camilo's death. Was he a popular obstacle eliminated for the good of the revolution? No one doubted his bravery. In coordination with Che, he led seventy-two men into the center of the island to Yaguajay, an important garrison town north of Santa Clara, Cuba's third-largest city. But as Guevara directed the attack from the south on Santa Clara, Camilo became bogged down in a protracted siege of the Yaguajay garrison. He wasted days converting a bulldozer into a battle tank for two inconclusive assaults on the garrison. Che finished the conquest of Santa Clara in December 1958 without Camilo, then sent his former protégé the weapons to finish the siege—a bazooka and a mortar.[61] And just in time to carry out Fidel's order to occupy Camp Columbia in Havana.

Camilo Cienfuegos spent the early months of the revolution reorganizing the army with a high degree of conciliation. For the first seven days, he was the public face of M26 in Havana. Che kept a low profile in La Cabaña Fortress, where he directed the roundup of *batistiano* policemen and soldiers accused of human rights abuses. Fidel took his time coming to the capital. President Urrutia admired Cienfuegos and, in the meantime, appointed him commander of the armed forces for Havana Province.[62] Camilo's vision was of a small military force, lean and competently led, and he had little regard for having to eventually protect the revolution from North American hostility. In an address to the first graduating class of the new officers' school, Cienfuegos proclaimed: "We are going to have a small Army of selected

Comandante Camilo Cienfuegos of M26 (in the cowboy hat) reviewing troops of the new Revolutionary Army that he commanded until his death in October 1959. Costa Rican ex-president José "Pepe" Figueres marches on his right.

men." Thirty-five thousand men in the army, Camilo said, were unduly draining the Cuban economy.[63] When Raúl Castro took over as minister of defense, he changed course. Raúl directed a huge military buildup complete with peasant, worker, and student militias.

There was another disagreement between the Castros and Cienfuegos. Issues of the communist newspaper *Hoy* turned up in April for free distribution to army troops at Camp Columbia, Camilo's headquarters. Raúl Chibás once walked into Camilo's office and found him reading a copy of *Hoy*. Camilo threw it to the floor and said, "What shits these communists are!" It was also true that his brother and aide-de-camp, Osmany Cienfuegos, held membership in the communist party, the PSP. Nonetheless, army chief Camilo Cienfuegos banned the distribution of *Hoy* in his headquarters at Camp Columbia. The armed forces chief Raúl Castro rebuked him. Only the

return of Fidel from his trip to Washington and South America finally resolved the dispute—in Raúl's favor.[64]

Camilo Cienfuegos never developed into a workaholic revolutionary. Not
much evidence exists that he became involved in the long-range planning
accomplished in dusk-to-dawn discussion sessions among Che Guevara's
brain trust. Camilo enjoyed women, dancing, and the nightlife. The *habaneros* absolutely adored Camilo, the only M26 comandante born in the capital city. Fidel, Che, and Raúl shunned the nightlife and preferred working
into the early morning hours rather than going to the clubs.[65]

His premature death preserved Camilo's reputation on both sides of
the Straits of Florida. Cubans in Miami revere his memory as a victim of
the treachery of the Castro brothers. Cubans in Havana remember Camilo
as a native son who died serving the revolution. In this, Camilo resembles
José Antonio Echeverría, shot dead during the attack on the Presidential
Palace, and Frank País, killed in an ambush by Batista's police in Santiago.
All three "revolutionary heroes" died before they had to choose between
Fidel and his opponents. Only Camilo Cienfuegos, however, might have
become that one formidable counterrevolutionary able to unite the opposi-
tion like no other defector.

Two other men with guns managed to take their anti-Castro struggle
abroad. Lieutenant Manuel Artime, a medical doctor trained at the University of Havana, joined the M26 in his home province of Oriente during the
last months of the struggle against Batista. When the dictator fled, Artime
stayed on with the new revolutionary armed forces. In May 1959, Castro as
prime minister decreed the first land reform law and established the National
Institute of Agrarian Reform under military control. Captain Núñez Jiménez
became the first director of INRA and assigned Lieutenant Artime to ad-
minister the agrarian reform in the district of Mansanillo in Oriente Province.
He continued working with the so-called Rural Commandos established
earlier by the Ministry of Agriculture.[66] Artime claimed that he began to be
bothered by the increasingly anti-American and anti-Catholic rhetoric of
the revolution's leadership. The Huber Matos affair also jolted him.

Artime was to say that Fidel himself precipitated his defection. The
breaking point arrived in October when Prime Minister Castro and new National Bank president Che Guevara addressed officials of INRA. They both
indicated that the revolution would continue its turn toward socialism, as
Artime subsequently indicated in his letter of resignation. "To keep people

calm, we may hand out a few deeds," Artime quoted Fidel as saying to IN-RA's top administrators, "but this will be an exception. Land will become state property."[67] Artime sent a copy to be published by one of the few newspapers not yet taken over by the government. Its appearance caused a sensation. The government accused Artime of being a reactionary under the orders of US imperialism. His superiors at INRA claimed that he had embezzled public money, a common accusation against defecting officials.[68]

Artime vacated his post and entered into the protection of an underground organization run by the Catholic Church. In a Havana safe house, he met with other dissidents and formed the MRR, the Movement for Revolutionary Recovery. He then proposed to go abroad to seek US support, while his associates remained in Cuba. Priests ultimately directed him to CIA agents, who smuggled Artime out of Cuba on a Honduran freighter. Other CIA men awaited his arrival in Miami. (They gave him a lie detector test, which greatly impressed the defector.) There, the Cuban publication of his renunciation had given Manuel Artime great credibility and profile. CIA agent Howard Hunt says that Artime "exuded the intangible charisma of leadership."[69] He joined the Cuban Revolutionary Council governing board, and when the CIA recognized his leadership potential, they sent him to train with Brigade 2506, the émigré combat force. In Guatemala, Artime was instrumental in mediating a mutiny of anti-Batista trainees against officers who had served in Batista's army. In April 1961, Castro's militias captured Manuel Artime together with a thousand others. He spent twenty months in Cuban prisons, returning to Miami in December 1962. Together with Gutiérrez Menoyo and Manuel Ray, Artime would continue the struggle as a commando in the CIA's secret war against the Cuban Revolution.

True to their bargain with Fidel in the first days after Batista fled, Comandantes Eloy Gutiérrez Menoyo and William Morgan of the Second Front joined the new rebel army. They had fought since February 1958 in the Escambray Mountains, where ex-president Prío Socarrás had set up several Auténtico armed men as rivals to the M26 guerrillas. Many of them had survived the assault on the Presidential Palace that claimed José Antonio Echeverría's life in March 1957. However, in the Escambray, an internal dispute split the Revolutionary Directorate into two factions. Gutiérrez Menoyo, whose elder brother had died in the palace attack, formed the Segundo Frente Nacional del Escambray, better known as the Second Front. Others fought on separately as heirs to Echeverría's original DR.[70] In October 1958,

Che Guevara came to the Escambray with his M26 column of fighters, adding extra tensions among the guerrillas. The Second Front refused to take orders from the Argentinean comandante, but, in the last days of the dictatorship, the Second Front did accomplish its share of military operations in tandem with Che's battle at Santa Clara.[71]

Gutiérrez Menoyo, Morgan, and other Second Front officers continued service in Las Villas Province for the revolutionary armed forces. There they played an important role in defeating one of the few armed incursions by counterrevolutionary partisans of Batista. The incident occurred in August 1959, a time by which communist influence in the new armed forces was rising. Gutiérrez Menoyo and Morgan had made moderate statements in the Cuban press. Dominican dictator Rafael Trujillo knew that many members of the opposition had fled to Cuba and were in military training there. Trujillo believed he could enlist the leaders of the Second Front into a conspiracy. Batista's ex-officers in the Dominican Republic made contact with Comandantes Gutiérrez Menoyo and Morgan in order to involve them in the conspiracy. They were planning to coordinate an internal insurrection against Castro with the landing of a planeload of exiled *batistianos* from the Dominican Republic. However, Gutiérrez Menoyo and Morgan helped the rebel army capture the men on the plane and arrest five hundred other soldiers of the old army.[72] Fidel appeared on television and praised the loyalty of Comandantes Gutiérrez Menoyo and Morgan.

The Second Front began to lose influence within the revolution after its leaders challenged Che Guevara. In one TV interview, a union leader criticized Guevara for having a known Batista collaborator on his staff. Photos and documents were furnished. Che responded by smearing the unions for "doing nothing for the revolution." The labor leader countered by pointing to the presence in the TV studio of Majors William Morgan and Eloy Gutiérrez Menoyo as testimony to his outstanding service in the overthrow of Batista.[73] A month later, Gutiérrez Menoyo yielded to pressure. He disbanded the Second Front and its affiliated political arm, the Organización Auténtica. Gutiérrez Menoyo said he now desired to bring together all revolutionary elements into "a single movement under a common program based on the ideals of Martí and the radical essence of our liberating action."[74]

Gutiérrez Menoyo and his men did not embrace communist participation in the government. Whenever he gave interviews, Gutiérrez Menoyo voiced opposition to the threats posed by exiled *batistianos* and their Dominican sponsor, Rafael Trujillo. But Gutiérrez Menoyo made no denouncements of US "imperialists" for harboring pro-Batista "war criminals." He did not criticize American sponsorship of the counterrevolution, even though this accusation had already become a staple of Fidel's speeches. On TV, a reporter once asked the comandante what opinion he had of the communists. "Well, about the communists I don't have an opinion," Gutiérrez Menoyo replied, "because in the Escambray Mountains I didn't see any."[75]

Ultimately, Gutiérrez Menoyo took refuge back in the Escambray, where many of his former associates were rising up against the communists running the National Institute of Agrarian Reform. His colleague William Morgan was captured in Havana, tried for arming domestic counterrevolutionaries, and executed in October 1960.[76] In January 1961, Gutiérrez Menoyo and twenty armed men of the Second National Front of the Escambray fled Cuba by boat. CIA agents greeted them in Miami and, unsure of their loyalties, shipped them out to a refugee camp on the Rio Grande in Texas.[77] They arrived too late to enlist with Brigade 2506 for the Bay of Pigs landing. Still, their counterrevolutionary days did not come to an end. Gutiérrez Menoyo eventually collaborated with the CIA in order to establish a Florida-based commando unit to fight Castro from abroad.

In his memoirs, the last American ambassador in Havana, Philip Bonsal, sounded a recurrent theme. He said that Fidel Castro's domestic enemies relied on the United States to rid them of the revolutionary leader rather than uniting to do the job themselves. The opposition could not believe that the Americans would allow communists to take over the island.[78] Certainly, the moderates remained disunited, but Bonsal's view underestimates the political genius of Fidel Castro. With his audacity, Castro survived and influenced world history like no other leader of a nation of just six million people.[79]

Fidel proved his mastery with a multifaceted strategy of political consolidation. He did not execute many of his civilian enemies. Castro simply eliminated the moderates one by one by forcing them into lonely, compromising situations. Individually, they found ways to get out of Cuba to go to Miami. There they continued to serve Fidel's longevity in power through vain efforts to undermine him from abroad. Nothing served this revolutionary more than to have enemies close at hand, threatening to take the benefits of social reform from Castro's supporters.

Moreover, Fidel Castro used charm, promises, and occasional back-tracking to prevent the opposition from forming a united front against him. He mobilized the masses with revolutionary theater, property redistribution, and warnings of the danger of counterrevolution. Meanwhile, without announcement or proclamation, he allowed the members of the old Popular Socialist Party to infiltrate the army and bureaucracy. The communists knew how to follow orders, and, unlike the moderates, they would not defect to the United States. PSP members also linked the regime to the Sino-Soviet bloc, a more revolution-tolerant foreign alternative to the United States. In this process of consolidating the Cuban Revolution under the nostrils of the North American behemoth, timing was everything.

Fidel Castro also kept Washington perplexed as to his true intentions. Thereby, his revolutionary government avoided direct confrontation with the world's foremost military power. He molested neither the three thousand Americans still living in Cuba, nor US embassy personnel, nor the servicemen at the Guantánamo Naval Base. He merely criticized the Americans for harboring war criminals like Esteban Ventura and Rolando Masferrer and counterrevolutionaries like his former brother-in-law, Rafael Díaz-Balart, and his former air force chief José Luis Díaz Lanz. These denunciations provided good propaganda at home. Washington dithered while Castro eliminated his former revolutionary collaborators. At the same time, Fidel, Che, and Raúl were secretly arranging for the visit of the first Soviet dignitary—this in January 1960. The point is this: in consolidating his power, Fidel Castro forced his former collaborators into the counterrevolution, which they took abroad into exile.

As Fidel used to say, "Within the Revolution, everything. Outside the Revolution, nothing."

CHAPTER TWO

The Caribbean War of 1959

IN APRIL 1959, a yacht from Cuba carrying nearly ninety armed men landed on the Atlantic coast of Panama. It seemed like a mirror image of Fidel Castro's own voyage from Mexico to Cuba with eighty-one Cuban armed men and one Argentinean on the *Granma* less than three years beforehand. The *Granma* expedition touched off the final phase of Fidel's successful fight against the Batista dictatorship. Now that Fidel had gained power, he promised repeatedly to help Latin American political refugees in Cuba return to their homelands and win revolutions against the remaining dictatorships in the Caribbean Basin. However, the Panama landing did not conform to Fidel's pronouncements. The Republic of Panama was not a dictatorship. Moreover, only six members of the armed invasion were Panamanians. All the rest were Cubans dressed in olive-green battle uniforms and some with full beards.

The timing and location of the Panama expedition arouse curiosity. The expeditionaries landed close to the Atlantic entrance to the Panama Canal Zone—a fifty-mile-wide swath of land dividing North and South America that served as the chief symbol of US imperialism in Latin America. At the time, April 1959, Prime Minister Fidel Castro and an entourage of Cuban officials were visiting Washington, DC. Fidel had left military details to Che Guevara, Camilo Cienfuegos, and Raúl Castro. Since these men were his closest advisers, it is inconceivable that Castro did not know the specifics of the Panama expedition.

As prime minister, however, Fidel had plausible deniability. He could pretend that he was preoccupied with domestic affairs and with the activities of a cabinet composed of a few members of his own 26th of July Revolutionary Movement and moderate politicians. Some speculated that the radicals within the rebel army resented Fidel's impending trip to the United States. After all, according to US diplomats, it had been the "responsible group of Cuban financial technicians" (cabinet members Rufo López-Fresquet and Felipe Pazos) who had arranged the trip for the purpose of obtaining American financial assistance for the new government. However, neither the Americans nor the moderate Cubans knew the full story. In Havana, Raúl Castro was preparing to make the first direct contact with the Kremlin. This remained a state secret within the revolutionary armed forces. Therefore, Raúl and Che "were concerned" that Castro's trip and his "friendly attitude" toward the United States were giving the Soviets a mixed message. Raúl actually phoned Fidel at his hotel to warn that supporters at home feared that he was selling out to the Yankees.[1] Fidel reacted angrily to his brother as his moderate ministers stood by.

In any case, the Eisenhower administration was not keen to have Castro in Washington. He traveled to the US capital at the invitation of the association of newspaper editors. He neither requested nor received an invitation for a state visit to the White House. Fidel forbad his aides to ask for a loan. The American secretary of state, Christian Herter, had already expressed reservations about "the apparent resurgence of the communists in Cuba." President Eisenhower himself did not want to be in Washington during Castro's visit. He departed for a golfing trip to Augusta, Georgia.[2] Fidel did meet with Vice President Richard Nixon, who later wrote famously that Castro was "either incredibly naïve about Communism or was under Communist discipline." The Cuban revolutionary expressed his outrage about Nixon's patronizing attitude.[3]

When the news from Panama broke, Fidel Castro expressed embarrassment about the role of Cuban fighters. He disassociated his government from those who carried out the adventure, but he also mocked Panama's president

As Fidel Castro met Vice President Nixon in Washington, the Cuban invasion of
Panama was unfolding. "Whatever we may think of him," Nixon reported, "[Castro]
is going to be a great factor in the development of Cuba and very possibly in Latin
American affairs generally."

Ernesto de la Guardia for calling in the Organization of American States (OAS).[4] Nevertheless, Castro's visit to the United States appeared to be a triumph, even though he had been forced to disavow communism repeatedly. But the Eisenhower administration did not trust him. "It would be a serious mistake to underestimate this man," concluded one after-action report. "Castro remains an enigma and we should await his decisions on specific matters before assuming a more optimistic view."[5] Eventually, the Cuban invaders were repatriated after the Cuban government assured President de la Guardia that no other force would be allowed to attack Panama. Castro's army arrested the returnees for a possible court-martial. However, within a month, all of them were set free.[6] The radicals in the Cuban revolutionary family appeared to be winning Fidel Castro from the moderates.

The Cubans offered mea culpas. Fidel called the Panama invasion "embarrassing, inopportune, [and] unjustified." Cuba at all costs must safeguard the principle of nonintervention, he said. Raúl hinted that the CIA had staged the faux expedition in order to undermine the Cuban Revolution, and Che said that Cuba exported revolutionary ideas but not revolution itself.[7] The Americans remained suspicious. "It is likely that certain Cuban officials knew and approved of the expedition," US intelligence analysts speculated. They believed that Che Guevara had engineered the whole business. Panama made perfect sense, Costa Rica's ex-president José Figueres told them, for the Cubans might have wanted to provoke a US military intervention that would alienate all Latin Americans. At this juncture, CIA director Allen Dulles briefed a meeting of President Eisenhower's National Security Council about how a contagion of "Castro-itis" was afflicting Central America.[8]

Only four dictatorships remained in Latin America in 1959, and already in January Havana was attracting their political opponents and youthful dissidents. Fidel Castro and his closest advisers decided to take advantage of the hope and popularity that the revolution had generated in the region. As undisputed military commander, Fidel proposed to liberate the Americas of the remaining Caribbean dictatorships in Nicaragua, the Dominican Republic, and Haiti. The Paraguayan dictatorship lay beyond reach for the moment. But numerous refugees from the three neighboring countries had already come to Cuba seeking Fidel's assistance. He imagined a region free of dictators—a laudable goal that his ministers and Washington could not dispute though they might object to the means. If the Nicaraguans should take to the mountains and fight for their freedom, Fidel declared, they could count on the complete support of the Cuban people. Thus began Cuba's foreign policy project of "exporting its revolution." It would soon gain another name throughout the Western Hemisphere: "Communist subversion."

This first stage in the export of revolution featured rebel military leaders in the full flush of victory encouraging the establishment of guerrilla movements in Caribbean countries ruled by dictators. Of course, Caribbean tyrants such as Luis Somoza, François Duvalier, and Rafael Trujillo were already fighting a regional wave of democratization and feared a Cuban-style revolution even more. In fact, Trujillo was providing a haven and assistance to former military officers in Batista's defunct army who conspired to return to political power. But the addition of Panama to the revolutionary hit list indicates that Cuba's military radicals had something much more complex in mind—a war against imperialism and its collaborators in Latin America.[9]

Moreover, Cuba's support for revolutions abroad played out in a specific domestic context in which the military radicals were maneuvering to displace the moderates within the revolutionary government. In this process of political consolidation, the aggressive domestic agenda begat a radical foreign policy and vice versa. Foreign enemies became useful in rousing the peasants and workers to make revolution at home in the face of opposition from domestic counterrevolutionaries. Nothing united domestic support for the revolution quite like having powerful enemies abroad. As for Panama, the Cuban military radicals desired to demonstrate simultaneously their anti-American fervor to Moscow and the youth of the Americas. Fidel Castro demonstrated his audacity by threatening the symbol of US imperialism at the same time that he toured the United States.

In addition, the military radicals had another audience. They utilized an aggressive foreign policy as a means to mobilize the Cuban population to complete the revolution at home. Fidel placed agrarian reform as the number one transformation on his agenda.

A CONTAGION OF CASTRO-ITIS

Fidel's speeches served notice to the remaining Caribbean tyrants that they might soon suffer the same fate as Fulgencio Batista. Trujillo, Duvalier, and

Luis Somoza were preparing their defenses. Trujillo had permitted Fulgencio Batista to take refuge in the Dominican Republic, although eventually the Cuban would leave for permanent exile in Portugal. Several of his former supporters and army officers remained in the Dominican Republic plotting a return to Cuba. General José Pedraza, for example, was training an exile force to overthrow Castro. Trujillo offered Pedraza the facilities of the Dominican army for his preparations. However, Castro denied any intention to intervene with Cuban military forces against the remaining dictators. He only promised to help train and guide political exiles from these countries. Castro even signed on to the proposal of Rómulo Betancourt, Venezuela's president-elect, that the dictatorships be expelled from the OAS.

From the beginning, Cuba's intentions aroused suspicions. For their part, US diplomats brokered an agreement that settled the differences between Honduras and Nicaragua to better control the movements of exile combatants from one country to the next. The United States also bolstered dictatorial regimes in the Caribbean with economic and military aid. "Although Haitian President Francois [sic] Duvalier's position has been strengthened by the recent granting of US financial and economic aid," reported the State Department in 1959, "he is still faced with a serious economic situation and widespread opposition both within the country and abroad."[10] Duvalier promised that he would "lop off heads" and "burn Port-au-Prince" before he gave up Haiti to an exile invasion. Trujillo of the Dominican Republic announced that he would consider an attack on Haiti as an attack on his country too. With Duvalier's approval, Trujillo placed Dominican troops at the border and sent his patrol boats into Haiti's coastal waters.[11]

Neither did Castro's efforts gain the confidence of the democratic movements of the Caribbean. Instead, it alienated them. Betancourt and the former Costa Rican president José Figueres declined to back Cuba's favored exile factions from Nicaragua and the Dominican Republic because of their procommunist tendencies. Figueres decided to talk to his Cuban friends and pay them a visit. Castro held a rally at the end of March 1959 and allowed the former Costa Rican president to address Cuban workers. But the visiting statesman had his own agenda. He refused to criticize Washington's policies, advocated negotiation with foreign companies, and suggested that Cuba join the western democracies against communism. The leader of the Cuban Labor Confederation, David Salvador, seized the microphone from ex-president Figueres and forcefully rejected his views. Fidel then launched into a two-hour

harangue on why the revolutionary government should refute the suggestions of Costa Rica's former president, who had to sit and listen. The entire
program was broadcast nationwide.[12]

José Figueres took the insult personally because, just one year previously,
he had been instrumental in facilitating shipments of arms from Costa Rica
to Castro's guerrillas in the Sierra Maestra. In the meantime, President
Betancourt spoke of the dangers of a Caribbean war. These maneuverings
alerted the dictators and the United States to the sites of possible invasions,
which explains why the very first invasion from Cuba came as a great surprise. A group of rebels landed on the coast of Panama!

President de la Guardia's Panama did not qualify as a dictatorship so
much as an aristocratic polity of endlessly conspiring elites. "We recognized
perfectly well that no iron dictatorship existed in Panama," said one Cuban
invader, "but we knew that four or six families exchanged the presidency
among themselves through rigged elections."[13] A young man from a prominent Panamanian family, Rubén Miró, came to Havana to approach the
famous American comandante William Morgan and asked him to help
organize a group of five hundred men to invade Panama and overthrow the
president. Morgan declined. De la Guardia was experiencing a political crisis,
punctuated by a February riot and general strike in the capital. He uncovered
a sergeants' plot in March and ordered the arrest of thirty-three noncommissioned officers of the Panamanian Guardia Nacional. Two opponents,
both cousins of de la Guardia, conspired to seek the aid of Cuba's revolutionaries. They were Rubén Miró and Roberto Arias, the latter a wealthy
former ambassador to England.

The plot had ripened with Roberto Arias's arrival in Havana at the end
of January accompanied by his famous wife, Dame Margot Fonteyn. Then
a thirty-nine-year-old prima ballerina renowned for her partnerships in dance
with Rudolf Nureyev, Fonteyn played on Castro's vanity, begging his assistance for husband Roberto's plot against de la Guardia.[14] With the prime
minister's help, Miró acquired two Cuban fishing yachts in order to coordinate amphibious assaults on Panama's Atlantic coast, which were to coincide
with cousin Roberto's attacks on the Panamanian police force, the Guardia
Nacional.

However, a separate revolutionary group within Panama set out to establish a Castro-like guerrilla insurrection even before the Miró expedition
could depart from Cuba. In the first week of April 1959, a group of fifteen

armed young men arriving at night in three cars held up the small town of San Francisco in the highlands of Veraguas Province in Panama. They took food supplies from a store in exchange for a chit promising to pay in full "when the revolution triumphs." The poorly armed youths announced that they represented the Movement of Revolutionary Action (MAR), whose armbands they sported on the sleeves of their blue uniforms. They tarried in San Francisco for a time, waiting for other associates to join them. Several of their fellow members, including their leader, a youthful poet and former student leader at the University of Panama, Polidoro Pinzón, never showed up. The fifteen eventually set off on foot to establish a guerrilla base at Cerro Tute, the highest peak in western Panama.

The MAR proclaimed three principal objectives: to terminate US control of the Canal Zone, to reform and expand the nation's educational system, and to overturn Panama's corrupt oligarchy.[15] Therefore, these youthful guerrillas of middling socioeconomic background actually were struggling against the political interests of Roberto Arias's aristocratic family and those of President de la Guardia as well.

Once word of the Veraguas insurrection got back to the president, he turned to the commandant of his police force, the Guardia Nacional. General Bolívar Vallarino agreed that the government should avoid making the mistake of Cuba's Fulgencio Batista, who ignored Fidel Castro's uprising in the Sierra Maestra until it was too late. General Vallarino acted immediately. He appointed one of his young officers, Captain Omar Torrijos, as commander of a special task force of 125 men to pursue the small band of MAR guerrillas. Torrijos, a native of Veraguas Province, knew the terrain. Within two days, he transported his policemen to two bases in the province. Soon, a peasant showed up at his headquarters and informed him of the probable location of the fledgling guerrillas. Immediately, Captain Torrijos assembled twenty-five men and led them on the trail of the armed insurrectionaries.

The Panamanian rebels may have been inspired by Fidel's example, but they did not measure up in terms of organizational skills and leadership. The combatants of the Movement of Revolutionary Action—the youngest being fifteen and the eldest twenty-four years old—did have relatives in Veraguas who helped them get into the mountains. Family connections also helped most of them escape alive after two brief firefights with the Guardia Nacional. But their academic preparation at the National Preparatory School, the nation's premier high school, and at the University of Panama did not prepare them for guerrilla warfare. Physically and mentally, the youthful guerrillas proved to be ill equipped for operating in the wilderness. Long marches, hunger, and sleep deprivation took a toll on their esprit.

Within a few days, Captain Torrijos's column caught up to the fifteen would-be guerrillas climbing slowly up the Cerro Tute. The two left behind as the rearguard ambushed the National Guard column. "I told them to surrender," Captain Torrijos wrote in his report. "They responded with rifle fire that struck my cap but miraculously did not kill me."[16] Torrijos took grazing bullets to the hand, arm, and shoulder on his right side. Still he directed his men to flank the two guerrillas on the right and left, killing them after a brief gun battle. Two coups de grâce made sure the guerrillas were dead.

The main body of thirteen others heard the battle from above but decided that they, armed with pistols and .22-caliber hunting rifles, were powerless to help their colleagues. They anxiously assessed the situation and concluded that their revolution was collapsing. These friends from high school and college broke up into groups of two and three and fled from the mountainside. Several fell into the hands of the Guardia, while most made their way back to Panama City and took refuge in the Chilean and Brazilian embassies.

Their ostensible leader, Polidoro Pinzón, who never caught up to the main group at Cerro Tute, also decided to flee Veraguas Province. He and two others tried to get out on foot and walked into an ambush set up by a squad of National Guardsmen. His two friends died and he got away. He too fled to the Chilean embassy, thence to Chile, then to Cuba. Back in Panama City two years later, under a government amnesty, Pinzón died in an explosion at his apartment.[17] Fidel Castro's revolution may have inspired the guerrillas of the Movement of Revolutionary Action, but their insurrection actually ended just days before the Cuban-sponsored expedition landed two hundred miles away, near Nombre de Díos on the Atlantic coast.

Meanwhile, on April 14, Roberto Arias and the ballerina Margot Fonteyn departed Havana for Panama City. There they coordinated the dropping of weapons along the Pacific coast for an attack on the National Guard garrison at Chorrera, ten miles west of the capital. Arias and Fonteyn sailed their yacht out from Panama City on the Pacific side to meet up with a shrimp boat that contained weapons for their fellow conspirators. Fonteyn returned to the capital on her yacht, while Arias joined the small crew in the shrimper. The boat ran aground, and a water leak damaged some of the weapons. Once freed from the rocks, the crew headed out to sea to test the weapons again and dumped overboard about a third that did not fire. By then, the Guardia Nacional had gone on alert, and Arias decided to put in at a nearby casino and resort. He buried the weapons in the sand and attempted to escape. One of his coconspirators, an Afro-Panamanian student radical named Floyd Britton, engaged in a firefight with a squad of policemen in order to cover Roberto Arias's escape.

Several of their confederates were captured, but Britton and Arias managed to flee. Britton suffered a gunshot wound and found treatment among friends in Panama City. He finally took refuge in the Guatemalan embassy. On foot and under cover of night, Roberto Arias reached one of his family's ranches and then caught a ride back to the capital. In the meantime, his ballerina wife had returned with the yacht to Panama City, where the police detained and interrogated her for twenty hours at the women's prison. The police confiscated address books that had the names of Hollywood movie stars like Errol Flynn and John Wayne, neither of whom had any part in this drama. However, John Wayne had been a business partner with Roberto Arias in the shrimping business.[18] To avoid a diplomatic incident with the British government, President de la Guardia put the English ballerina Margot Fonteyn on a plane to London. Her conspiratorial husband, Roberto Arias, found asylum in the Brazilian embassy. The couple rejoined each other in Rio de Janeiro two months later. Despite Arias's planning, the uprising had ended before his confederates from Cuba even landed on the opposite coastline.

Miró's expedition departed by boat on April 19 from the Cuban port of Batabanó. The armed men cast off in broad daylight, sailing out of port past a Cuban patrol boat. "We were waved goodbye enthusiastically by the crew," one Cuban remembered.[19] The expeditionaries landed on Panama's coast at a spot fifty miles southeast of Colón, the Atlantic terminus of the Panama Canal. Remarkably, the Panamanians on board the fishing boat were outnumbered—eighty Cubans and one Puerto Rican to only six Panamanians. A few of the Cubans had participated in Fidel's guerrilla forces during the revolution, and the conspiracy's expedited timetable left them little time for training. The Panamanian commander, Enrique Morales Brid, drowned during the landing, but the expedition managed to take over the colonial port town of Nombre de Díos on April 27.[20] The conspiracy's second-in-command, Rubén Miró, stayed behind in Cuba to launch additional men in a second boat.

President de la Guardia immediately appealed to the Organization of American States, which condemned the invasion of one member country from another. The US Caribbean Command in the Canal Zone sent out ships and planes to patrol the Panamanian coastline for the expected second boat. Guatemalan arms and planes arrived on April 29, and Colombia and Ecuador promised to lend assistance. De la Guardia also requested additional US aid. He reminded the Americans that Panama's Guardia Nacional was but an urban police organization and that the invasion might spark a coup d'état of his government from any number of divergent groups that "possess arms and could take advantage of the guard's preoccupation with the invasion."[21]

OAS and Cuban mediators soon arrived in Panama. "The bulk of the invasion force, assured that their lives would be spared, surrendered to the Panamanian National Guard on May 1," reported the American embassy in Panama City. Five of the invaders took to the hills but soon fell into the hands of National Guardsmen. Miró had stayed behind in Cuba to launch a second fishing boat of armed men. They turned back upon learning of the conspiracy's failure. Officials in Havana, who feigned embarrassment at the revelations of Cuban complicity in the Panama incident, arrested the expeditionaries.[22] They were released within a few weeks. Although not technically a dictatorship, the Republic of Panama had become the first target of Cuba's campaign to eliminate the last dictators in Latin America.

NO BLOODSHED!

Shortly thereafter, the Somoza regime of Nicaragua came under threat of revolution from abroad. Apparently, many inside Nicaragua were anticipating some sort of intervention from Cuba because they had been closely monitoring the speeches of Fidel Castro and Nicaraguan refugees in Cuba predicting the demise of tyranny. The anti-*somocista* Nicaraguans were a fine example of the political divisions that afflicted most opposition groups in the Caribbean Basin at the time. Mexico City had been the center of Nicaraguan exile groups, and many there quickly made their way to Havana once Batista fled.

Che Guevara may already have met some of these leaders in 1955 and 1956 while training in Mexico City. In Havana, he designated the more radical

Rafael Somarriba, a naturalized American citizen of Nicaraguan birth, as military leader. Somarriba got Che's nod as commander because he had been an officer in Somoza's police force.[23] Afterward, Che himself acted to bring together three other groups under the Somarriba umbrella. All of these factions signed a joint declaration in February that adopted a "progressive socio-economic program around which all Nicaraguans could rally." Members called themselves the MRN (Movimiento Revolucionario Nicaragüense) and named a political moderate as president-in-exile. State Department analysts subsequently were able to name dozens of the members of these multiple factions as well as list their political affiliations.[24]

As the hasty training of Nicaraguans went forward in Cuban military camps, Che held late-night discussions with Somarriba and with future Sandinistas Carlos Fonseca and Tomás Borge. Only one "unaffiliated Nicaraguan revolutionary" in Cuba, Chester Lacayo, a conservative activist, did not meet Che's approval. Guevara stopped two of Lacayo's unauthorized expeditions and arrested all sixty of his men. American newspaper correspondent Ruby Hart Phillips saw these Nicaraguans under guard at the Camp Columbia army base on the outskirts of Havana. They were released the following day.[25]

Additional anti-*somocista* exiles had taken refuge in Costa Rica. These represented conservative business and oligarchic families that had been shoved aside, beginning in the 1930s, with the rise of General Anastasio Somoza. His two sons, Luis and Anastasio Jr., now ruled as president and National Guard commander, respectively. These conservative students had a chaplain among them, a Catholic priest who had been their instructor at the Colegio Centro-América in Granada, Nicaragua, where many of the rebels had gone to secondary school. The rebels in Costa Rica derived entirely from the upper and middle strata, because few opponents could afford to pay for their own exile. In contrast, the political refugees in Cuba received financial support from the Cuban revolutionary armed forces. These conservative youths admired what the Cuban Revolution had accomplished against Batista. After arriving in Costa Rica in late 1958, these "Nicos" had learned about the M26 in the Sierra Maestra from none other than their resident patron, José Figueres. This ex-president had supported Fidel's rebellion. Nevertheless, his conservative young men in Costa Rica remained leery of the more radical MRN operating out of Havana.[26]

Having populist origins in the Guardia Nacional, the Somozas had humbled the old political power (though not the wealth) of the aristocratic politicians and landed families of Nicaragua. The patriarch of the Somozas, Anastasio, trained as a young man with US Marine instructors who established the country's Guardia Nacional during the American occupation. Augusto César Sandino, on the other hand, fought a legendary guerrilla insurrection against US occupation. Somoza ultimately became commander of the national police forces before the Marines departed in 1933. General Somoza utilized the National Guard first to eliminate his rival Augusto César Sandino through assassination, then to shut out the elite families who had provided most presidents of Nicaragua.

General Somoza dominated the nation for twenty-three years and finally made himself head of state. The elder Somoza prepared his sons, Luis and Anastasio Jr., well. They both studied at universities in the United States, Luis at Louisiana State University and Anastasio at the US Military Academy. After graduating, both joined their father's National Guard. The elder son, Luis, succeeded his father to the presidency when the latter fell mortally wounded by an assassin's bullet in 1956. Anastasio took command of the Guardia.[27] By the late 1950s, the earlier populist appeals of the Somozas to the middle class and labor unions had given way to corruption, scandal, and repression. The family and their cronies acquired land and wealth and socialized with North American businessmen and diplomats. Both the old right and the new left inspired by Cuba's revolution opposed the Somozas. The conservatives exiled in Costa Rica made the first move.

On June 1, two planes from Costa Rica flew in more than one hundred armed youths of the anti-*somocista* Conservative Party and landed them in a field near the mountain town of Santo Tomás, east of the capital city of Managua. Several fellow conspirators greeted the invaders with packhorses and supplies. As the invaders headed out, a warplane of Somoza's National Guard spotted the landing site. The invaders wore battle dress of *verde olivo,* the same as Castro's M26. News reporters from Managua actually arrived at the invasion area before the National Guard, reminding the combatants of how reporter Herbert Matthews of the *New York Times* went into the Sierra Maestra in 1957 to make Fidel Castro a celebrity.[28] A platoon of guerrillas remained behind at the landing zone to lay an ambush for the first infantry unit to appear. They succeeded in blunting the National Guard

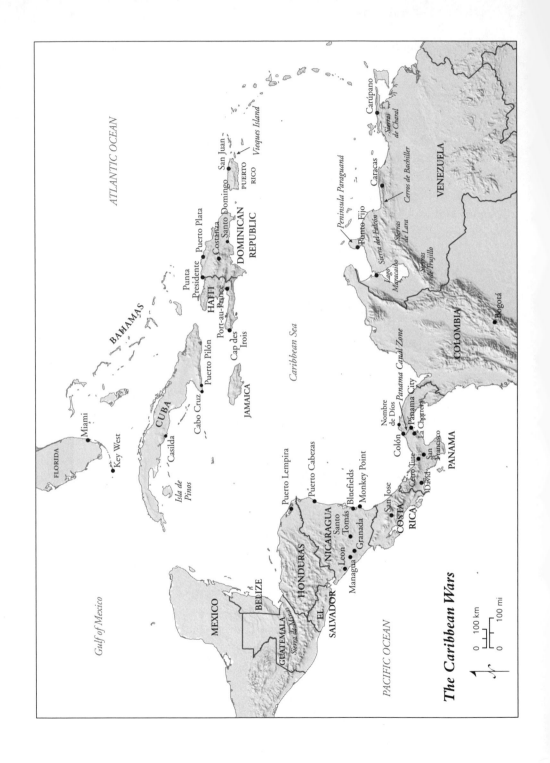

The Caribbean Wars

advance on the retreating conservative rebels, but now three wounded companions hampered their foot speed. Meanwhile, shopkeepers in Managua and other cities shut down businesses in sympathy for the youthful invaders of the Conservative Party.

However, the peasants found it difficult to identify with the educated, urban youth. "Our radio went dead," one thirty-year-old guerrilla commander said. "We were always short of food and the peasants in these mountains do not have enough to spare."[29] Units of the Guardia Nacional ultimately surrounded the ill-trained rebels. Exhausted, many just wanted to give themselves up. "Surrender?" shouted Comandante Luis Cardenal, imitating Fidel Castro's famous speech. "On our knees, for what?" The guardsmen too invoked the Cuban Revolution. "GIVE UP, BARBUDOS," they shouted back. These conservative rebels quickly ended their rebellion and surrendered to Somoza's forces. Somoza's commander in the field congratulated his officers and men, all of whose families enjoyed fewer privileges than their rebel prisoners. He also referred to the Cuban example when he said threateningly: "The life of one [National] Guard private is worth more than all of these Fidel Castros together."[30]

"No bloodshed," President Luis Somoza ordered his younger brother, Anastasio, the commander-in-chief of the Guardia Nacional. The Somoza regime showed forbearance toward these right-wing youths, and the Conservative Party challenge to the Somoza regime ended without further incident. In the meantime, the Nicaraguans in Cuba were completing their final preparations for their own invasion.

Three weeks later, Che Guevara's champion Rafael Somarriba landed with sixty armed revolutionaries on the Caribbean coast of Honduras, just north of the Nicaragua border. Cubans and Guatemalans accompanied the Nicaraguans, a mixture of nationalities that would become a trademark of Guevara.[31] Somarriba encamped his force in one isolated location for two weeks as he made preparations to cross the border into his homeland. Discipline deteriorated with the inactivity, and sentries failed to go out at night to protect the camp. In the meantime, units of the National Guard rushed to the border to repulse the leftist interlopers from Cuba. However, the government of Honduras had already dispatched its own armed forces to intercept the Nicaraguan band. Honduran soldiers surrounded the rebels one night and, at first light, commenced firing at close range into the tents. Six would-be guerrillas died, fifteen suffered wounds, and the rest surrendered. "It wasn't

Soldiers of Anastasio Somoza's National Guard processing rebel prisoners of the Liberal Party youth in June 1959. Cuba provided haven and military training to many Nicaraguans in the anti-Somoza opposition for the next two decades.

a battle, it was the most terrible of massacres," said the wounded Carlos Fonseca. "Rafael [Somarriba] is an honorable man, but that is not enough to be a leader in times like ours."[32] Somarriba, the ex–National Guard officer and aspiring guerrilla leader, eventually left Honduras for the United States and retired from the Nicaraguan resistance.

Members of the Nicaraguan student federation at the Universidad de León denounced the Honduran regime for killing and capturing rebels who were only attempting to bring "democracy" to Nicaragua. The students had heard—incorrectly as it turned out—that one of their former colleagues, the future Sandinista Carlos Fonseca, had died in the firefight. They mounted a protest march in July. Somoza's National Guard troops opened fire on the procession, wounded many, and killed four students. In the capital, Managua, American diplomats wrote a dispatch to Washington identifying the university protest as "Communist inspired."[33] This label already explained many complex phenomena in US embassy reports from Latin America.

Several members of this band of revolutionaries eventually returned to Cuba for a lengthy exile. A seriously wounded Fonseca was among them. He had taken a bullet through the lung and recovered in a Havana hospital. Che Guevara continued to take a personal interest in training the Nicaraguan contingent. Future Sandinistas like Carlos Fonseca and Tomás Borge underwent military training, regrouped with other Nicaraguan exiles, and planned for future incursions. Che gave them money for their expenses.[34] Cuba's efforts eventually bore fruit two decades later. By force of arms, the Sandinistas led an alliance of opposition groups to triumph in 1979, although without the participation of one of its architects, Carlos Fonseca, who had died in battle three years before.

In the meantime, officials in Washington found much assurance in Luis Somoza's steadfast anticommunism. His father had been a useful ally in the 1954 CIA-backed military rebellion in Guatemala. The Somozas still refused to negotiate with the "responsible opposition," meaning the Conservative Party. After the leftist invasion of 1959, Washington became concerned. The Eisenhower administration ordered the US Navy's "air and surface units" to patrol the coast of Nicaragua.[35] Luis and Anastasio Somoza subsequently provided the launching site in Nicaragua for the CIA's Bay of Pigs assault as well as smaller commando raids against Cuba. Better a family dictatorship than a communist one, American policymakers reasoned. But the White House's attitudes toward another dictator, the Dominican general Rafael Trujillo, remained much more reserved.

PALE FACES, TREMBLING HANDS

Fidel Castro already had a history of anti-Trujillo activities. As a young law student at the University of Havana, Castro took time off in 1947 to join an invasion force organized by Cuban president Grau San Martín. At the time, Grau was participating with Costa Rican president José Figueres and the Venezuelan exile Rómulo Betancourt in a democratic crusade against dictatorship called the Caribbean Legion. The combat leaders established a base on Cayo Confites, a barren island off the northeastern coast of Cuba. Castro joined the force training there. Among his fellow trainees was Rolando Masferrer, a Spanish Civil War veteran who went on to fame as the leader of the pro-Batista thugs known as Los Tigres and who would go into exile in Miami. Trujillo learned of Cayo Confites and complained to President Harry S. Truman. The United States put pressure on President Grau, who lost interest. Eventually, the expedition fell victim to political feuding and gang violence. Fidel Castro had to escape by diving off the ship transporting him and others into custody and swimming ashore through shark-infested waters.[36]

Once in power, Castro again made Rafael Trujillo a prime target. "Cuban officials have shown some tendency to look favorably on communist-influenced Dominican and Nicaraguan groups," State Department analysts concluded in May 1959. Trujillo's fall seemed a logical goal for the revolution because the Dominican dictator offered haven to many *batistianos*. Trujillo had organized an "Anticommunist Foreign Legion" to defend his regime and staffed it with Cuban refugees. Papa Doc Duvalier of Haiti cooperated by forming his own "anti-Communist" foreign legion, equipped by Trujillo and led by retired Dominican generals.

Comandante Camilo Cienfuegos was working with the Dominican Patriotic Union (UPD), whose five-man executive committee consisted of leftist radicals. They wrote up a revolutionary program featuring land reform, a literacy program, and social services. Captain Enrique Jiménez Moya acted as the UPD's military leader and had been training Dominican fighters in the Escambray Mountains, where he had served under Che Guevara at the end of the revolutionary war. Jiménez Moya participated in the battle of Santa Clara. His Dominicans prepared the invasion at a military camp in the Sierra Maestra. Most of them had been in exile for years and had limited communication with supporters back in the Dominican Republic.[37] Eighteen Cuban advisers, most of them veterans of the revolutionary war, volunteered to accompany the Dominican fighters in the invasion. Captain Delio Gómez Ochoa from the army staff of Camilo Cienfuegos commanded the Cuban advisory group.[38]

The Dominican Republic presented the Eisenhower administration with a dilemma. Trujillo had ruled even more brutally than his temporary guest exile, Fulgencio Batista. Eisenhower's advisers speculated that such a dictator could provoke a Castro-like rebellion from within that might lead to another radical regime. When Venezuelan president Rómulo Betancourt criticized the Dominican dictator, Trujillo responded by attempting to have him assassinated. The White House desired that Trujillo resign, an option dictators always resist. President Eisenhower and his advisers settled on OAS sanctions against the dictator, even though Eisenhower lamented that "he knew of no alliance in which indecisiveness is so great" as that of the Organization of American States.[39] In fact, Washington was attempting to defuse the Caribbean crisis by restricting the sales of military equipment to both revolutionary Cuba and the Dominican dictatorship, the two major sources of the tension in the Caribbean.[40] Between Trujillo and Castro, it had been a matter of who would strike whom first.

The band of leftists from the Dominican Republic had precipitously advanced the date of their air and sea assault, against the advice of their handler, Comandante Camilo Cienfuegos. The plan called for simultaneous air and amphibious assaults, so the plane would leave three days following the departure of the boats.[41] Both Camilo Cienfuegos and Delio Gómez Ochoa saw off the 150 expeditionaries on the three boats. But the voyage across the straits met with delays, while the air assault went on as planned. In addition, the dictator Trujillo may have had spies among the group.

On June 14, 1959, a combined force of sixty Dominicans and Cubans prepared the plane for takeoff at the airstrip in Oriente Province. Immediately, curious peasants surrounded the plane. Painters changed the C-46's coloring to match that of the Dominican Air Force. One of the Cuban advisers later explained that he had no doubts about the "adventure loving" nature of the pilot, a Venezuelan. He did entertain suspicions about the Dominican copilot, who complained of an upset stomach just before takeoff. But Captain Manuel Rojo del Río of Camilo's staff also believed the Dominicans were inexperienced and undisciplined. He watched as they boarded the C-46 "with their pale faces and trembling hands." Camilo Cienfuegos arrived at Santa Lucía late, ten minutes after the plane had departed. He then drove to Manzanillo to report to Raúl Castro.[42]

On his return, the Venezuelan pilot said that the C-46 had landed successfully at Constanza Airport in the interior of the Dominican Republic, taking the Dominican garrison there by surprise. During eight tense minutes on the runway, the pilot reported, all of the invaders quickly exited the C-46. Shots rang out, and several bullets fired by Dominican army troops struck the C-46 as it took off. When the plane returned to Cuba, Comandante Camilo Cienfuegos showed up again at the landing field. He ordered Cuban soldiers to "arrest" the pilots in order to provide plausible denial of Cuban involvement. Then Cienfuegos and his aide Captain del Río flew in a second plane to report to Fidel Castro in Havana about the successful landing at Constanza. They met with Castro at about 3:00 in the morning. Clad in his pajamas, Fidel "could not contain his feelings of contentment." He turned to del Río and suggested that he get trained as a C-46 pilot so that he might carry out such operations in the future.[43] The memory of that suggestion chilled del Río, who defected six months later.

Meanwhile, the Dominican incursion was not going according to plan. After the plane full of Dominican and Cuban invaders had landed at Constanza, two of the rebels were captured. Probably under torture, they alerted Trujillo's soldiers to the imminent arrival of additional rebels, who were to land on the northern coast. The guerrillas who got to the mountains held out for two weeks as their supplies dwindled. Peasants in the region did not help them with food or shelter, and army patrols kept the rebels on the run. Trujillo's soldiers took few prisoners and executed most of the rebels who fell into their hands.

The marine landing ended in disaster for the rebels. One of the three boat pilots had deliberately gone off course, causing the two Cuban PT boats escorting the flotilla to waste several days in reassembling it. Seasickness, vomiting, and dehydration afflicted members of the assault team. The landing's postponement allowed Dominican army forces to redeploy to await the sea landing. The Cuban escorts advised the Dominicans to return to Cuba, but they refused. The Cubans suspected their trainees of having a death wish. Cuban boat pilots quoted one Dominican as saying, "We're all going to die, so it's all the same to me."[44]

Behind schedule, three boats loaded with 150 armed revolutionaries came ashore near Puerto Plata. "They arrived on the coastline after navigating six days on fragile boats, suffering from cold and hunger," said one Cuban report. "They debarked exhausted, for which they were in no condition to maintain the struggle."[45] Trujillo's soldiers were waiting, and his air force strafed and dropped napalm on the invaders. Trujillo's spokesmen broke silence on June 23 and announced that "the force that sought to instigate an armed rebellion in national territory has been completely exterminated, all of its participants having died."[46]

An estimated two hundred combatants participated in the combined air and sea assault, inflicting "substantial" losses to the Dominican army, mainly in the mountains. The invasion apparently met with little popular support or domestic preparation, and Trujillo's army troops easily defeated the rebel invaders. Only a few invaders survived. Trujillo spared the life of the Cuban

comandante Delio Gómez Ochoa, who returned to his homeland after Trujillo was assassinated in 1961. But the generalissimo ordered his soldiers to
torture the other prisoners before execution, be they of Puerto Rican, Venezuelan, or Cuban nationality.[47] Several Dominican army officers who
plotted Trujillo's assassination two years later suggested that this butchery
had turned them against the long-term dictator.

Trujillo promised to retaliate militarily against the country sponsoring
these raids. He threatened to unleash the *batistiano* general José Pedraza
against Cuba but yielded to US diplomatic cautions—for two months, at
least. In the meantime, Santo Domingo's police looked the other way while
Cuban refugees sacked the Cuban embassy and beat up the ambassador's
driver. Castro responded with criticism of Trujillo for violating both diplomatic immunity and the human rights of prisoners of war.[48] One thing that
Generalissimo Trujillo did not do was to appeal to the Organization of
American States. President Betancourt promised that he would block the
OAS from assisting Trujillo as it had Panama and Nicaragua. Indeed, most
OAS members were reluctant to come to the aid of the brutal dictatorship,
then in its twenty-ninth year.

Two final engagements in the Caribbean War of 1959 remained. Both
took place in August. Haiti became the final republic to be assaulted by
armed revolutionaries leaving from Cuba—at about the same moment that
the *batistianos* from the Dominican Republic were assaulting the Cuban city
of Trinidad. Thirty Cubans participated in this Haitian venture too, accom-
panying the few anti-Duvalier Haitians who were not deterred by news of
the Dominican debacle. Che Guevara had given them a three-month training
course at a base outside of Havana. They launched the invasion on boats from
Baracoa on the easternmost coast of Cuba. The expeditionaries landed at
Cap des Irois at night on August 12, while the group's exiled political leaders,
being older, remained in Cuba. The army of dictator François "Papa Doc"
Duvalier sprang into action. In two firefights followed by pursuit, Papa
Doc's armed forces killed nearly all the invaders. Four Cuban youths were
captured, interrogated, and sent home. They were mere teenaged boys, unable
yet to grow beards.[49]

Nearly simultaneously in August, Cuban security police discovered the
revenge plot hatched by Trujillo and General Pedraza. The Second Front of
Escambray, now subordinate to M26 commanders in the new Revolutionary
Army, had been conspiring with *batistianos* operating out of the Dominican

Republic. But Comandantes Eloy Gutiérrez Menoyo and William Morgan actually were acting under Castro's instructions. The ostensible plan consisted of an air assault of armed *batistianos* landing at the airport of Trinidad in central Cuba in coordination with an uprising of a group of former Batista soldiers. Several priests in Trinidad also participated. Before the expedition landed, however, Cuban forces rounded up one thousand men in the armed forces who were suspected of participating in the conspiracy. Gutiérrez Menoyo and Morgan then signaled for the plane to land while Fidel's troops waited in ambush. They killed and captured all the armed invaders on board as the plane landed on the runway in Trinidad.[50] Trujillo's counterthrust against Castro ended even more quickly than the latter's authorized invasion of the Dominican Republic.

Where Fidel failed to dislodge Rafael Trujillo, the United States eventually succeeded. Dominican army dissidents, armed with US weapons provided by the CIA, gunned down Generalissimo Rafael Trujillo in 1961. The elimination of Trujillo after three decades of dictatorial rule permitted the election of Juan Bosch as president. A veteran of the Caribbean Legion, Bosch had been one of the Dominican exiles who trained with Fidel Castro at Cayo Confites in 1947.

AGRARIAN REFORM OR DEATH

Cuba's revolutionary leaders used the Caribbean War in order to radicalize the domestic revolution. For this reason, Fidel Castro accomplished these foreign operations without informing the moderate ministers still in the interim government. Cuba's flurry of conspiracies against the dictatorships coincided with its boldest revolutionary action at home, the first agrarian reform. The land law of 1959 initially met tepidly favorable responses among the powerful Cuban Association of Cane Growers *(colonos)* as well as from the high clergy. They favored the expansion of private ownership of the land by reducing the size of plantations and guaranteeing each peasant household a parcel of sixty-six acres.

The land reform decree stated that every peasant had a right to own land, as stipulated by none other than the 1940 Cuban Constitution. Those most disadvantaged by the decree would be the largest plantation owners such as the Cuban and American corporations that owned and operated the great sugar refineries. The US State Department affirmed Cuba's right to readjust its land tenure system but not without immediate compensation to American investors. Revolutionary leaders took umbrage at criticism coming from the United States. They pointed out that these same foreigners who now opposed the land reform were the very ones who protected Caribbean dictators and *batistiano* "war criminals."

Perhaps, more importantly, the manner in which the authorities carried out the agrarian decree indicated that political considerations trumped its moderate intent. Land reform roused the peasant population to the side of the revolutionaries and alienated the bourgeoisie. The decree also established a new state bureaucracy in the National Institute of Land Reform. Army Captain Antonio Núñez Jiménez assumed the directorship of INRA; he had participated in the final battle of Santa Clara. American diplomats in Havana described him as "a member of the PSP," Cuba's old communist party.[51] Moreover, the rebel armed forces became involved in carrying out land reforms that went way beyond the decree's moderate stipulations.

In the midst of the armed incursions in the neighboring dictatorships, revolutionary soldiers in the summer of 1959 seized cattle farms in Camagüey Province. They accused the owners of resisting land reform and holding cattle off the market in an attempt to drive up meat prices. Then revolutionary leaders held rallies of small growers and agricultural workers throughout the country. Raúl Castro's speech to *campesinos* in Pinar del Río revived the anti-American diatribes that had lain dormant since Fidel Castro's trip to Washington. Fidel himself came up with a new slogan: *Reforma agraria o muerte*, "agrarian reform or death." In that very same week, the revolutionary government broke relations with the Trujillo regime for its harboring of Cuban counterrevolutionaries and for "mass extermination of war prisoners."[52]

The first land reform decree widened the breach between the moderates who had supported the fight against Batista and the M26 leaders who had fought to bring about his downfall. In the thirty days following the promulgation of the land reform decree, these critical internal events occurred:

Sugar mill owners protested to the US embassy.

The influential association of *colonos* went on record against land reform.

The conservative newspaper *Diario de la Marina* opposed and the communist *Hoy* supported the agrarian reform.

Rebel air force commander Pedro Luis Díaz Lanz fled to Florida and denounced the communists in Cuba.

Rebel armed forces commander Raúl Castro replaced white stars with red stars at all military installations.

Sabotage, bombings, and shootings began against police and the revolutionary government.

US diplomats and American newspaper editors criticized the Cuban land reform.

Eighty thousand peasants and workers rallied in Santa Clara in favor of agrarian reform.

The cabinet of the interim government was reshuffled and the minister of agriculture Humberto Sorí Marín resigned.

Catholic prelates criticized the communist leanings of the agrarian reform institute, INRA.

President Manuel Urrutia denounced the communists and took refuge in the Venezuelan embassy.

Anti-Castro guerrilla activity commenced in Los Órganos Mountains of Pinar del Río, indicating that not all peasants approved of agrarian reform.

The above events of the four-week period following the land tenure decree defined the Cuban Revolution for the next fifty years. The redistribution of rural property coincided with four Cuban foreign policy initiatives, the armed assaults on Panama, Nicaragua, the Dominican Republic, and Haiti. The aggressive foreign policy reflected the radical tendencies of the consolidation of power. Subsequently, the domestic revolutionary process involved nationalizing the foreign industries, educating the illiterate, mobilizing the militias, and defeating an invasion of Cuban émigrés. Under such conditions, the policy of supporting guerrilla movements abroad also expanded.

The military radicals designed both the agrarian reform of 1959 and the military excursions into four neighboring countries in the Caribbean Basin. The timing could not have been accidental at all. The Panama invasion coincided with Prime Minister Castro's trip to Washington and Raúl Castro's first direct communication with the Kremlin. The incursions against Somoza and Trujillo took place in June just as Fidel Castro unveiled the centerpiece of his domestic policy, the agrarian reform. Castro had delegated the planning and training of exile groups and invasion plans to Raúl, Che, and Camilo. All three preferred giving aid to procommunist militants, while liberal and conservative exiles chose to find havens in Venezuela and Costa Rica.

One might conclude from the case studies of these invasions that their architects displayed great haste and lack of planning and coordination. These deficiencies undoubtedly led to the defeat of the expeditions and the needless loss of lives of both Cubans and foreign nationals. No matter. Neither Fidel Castro nor his radical advisers seemed perturbed. It appeared more important to their supporters at home that the revolution demonstrated influence beyond the Cuban shoreline and that Cuban revolutionary aspirations approximated those of other peoples for liberation from the imperialism of the United States and its Latin American client rulers. Success in establishing revolutionary movements in Panama, Nicaragua, the Dominican Republic, and Haiti would have been beneficial to Cuba, but success was not necessary. The effort of exporting the revolution sufficed to rally the popular classes to the task of making the revolution at home.

The military radicals of the Cuban Revolution in 1959 pursued a multifaceted process of consolidation that included outflanking moderate politicians, mollifying US diplomats, rousing the masses, making contact with the Soviet Union, and beginning internal social reforms. Spreading revolution to Caribbean neighbors ruled by dictators formed an integral part of the process. The watershed domestic policy of the revolution in 1959 consisted of the redistribution of property in the guise of agrarian reform. Obviously, the dispatch of revolutionary expeditions abroad at the very same moment that interest groups debated the consequences of the revision of landholding at home cannot have been accidental. After all, the same revolutionary faction that fashioned the agrarian reform also designed the revolutionary excursions. Furthermore, neither of these actions had been triggered by American sanctions against the Cuban government.[53]

In the end, Cuba's emphasis on the export of its revolution may have mobilized the reactionaries of Latin America as much as the radicals. Trujillo and the Somozas subsequently turned aside US suggestions to negotiate with their moderate domestic opponents; instead, they seized the banner of saving Latin America from communism. As one CIA report concluded, "Moderates and conservatives with no love for authoritarian rule in their countries, but fearful of the implications of drastic social and economic upheaval on the Cuban model, have rallied to support the status quo."[54] The export of revolution from Cuba provoked an equal but more powerful reaction in one country after another in Latin America. By 1976, a majority of Latin American citizens lived under military rule, as opposed to 1958, when only a small minority did. The hemisphere was heading toward unity, all right. But it was the counterrevolution that would eventually win out—not the guerrilla movements nurtured by the Cubans. However, failure did not deter the revolutionaries, which suggests that the export of revolution served other objectives than toppling a few dictators.

A French historian once observed how such an aggressive foreign policy affected his country's revolution of 1789. "La guerre révolutionna la Révolution," Marcel Reinhard wrote. "War revolutionized the Revolution."[55]

CHAPTER THREE

Cuba and the Sino-Soviet Dispute

"WE FLEW INTO Havana at twilight," remembered a member of the Soviet delegation. "What a contrast compared with 1960!"[1] Arriving in Cuba for his second visit, Soviet deputy minister Anastas Mikoyan did not expect a warm welcome. Mikoyan was coming in November 1962 directly from Washington, where he had finalized arrangements ending the October missile crisis. He knew that Cuban leaders could not contain their fury against the Soviets for having resolved the missile crisis behind their backs. He was right. Outwardly, the revolutionary government treated the number two man in the Kremlin's political hierarchy with respect. Fidel Castro, Ernesto "Che" Guevara, and Soviet embassy officials met Mikoyan at the airport. A smiling Castro held a bouquet of flowers. During his month-long visit, the official newspaper *Revolución* quoted Soviet and Cuban officials expressing solidarity with each other. However, in private meetings, expressions of disappointment and disagreement abounded.

Months earlier, the Cubans had accepted the Soviet offer of placing medium-range nuclear weapons on their island "for the good of international socialism," as Fidel had put it. Premier Nikita Khrushchev had convinced

Castro that Soviet rockets in Cuba would protect socialist republics everywhere from US aggression. Faced with an American naval blockade of Soviet ships entering the Caribbean, Khrushchev lost his nerve. He negotiated the withdrawal of the rockets with President John F. Kennedy without consulting Castro. The Cubans felt betrayed when the Soviets concluded an agreement in exchange only for President Kennedy's verbal pledge not to invade Cuba with US armed forces. Now Mikoyan had to convince Castro that the Khrushchev-Kennedy accord had saved the Cuban Revolution.

"We will not give our consent for [US] inspection," Castro informed Mikoyan. "Come what may. We have a right to defend our dignity." But Mikoyan had already promised the Americans that they could monitor the withdrawal of missiles from Cuba. "I don't understand such a sharp reaction to my proposal [for inspections aboard Soviet vessels in Cuban ports]," he told his hosts.[2] As if to illustrate Cuba's lack of security from US hostilities, *Revolución* featured multipage coverage of the capture of "the Principal Chief of the CIA in Cuba," an infiltrator who intended to sabotage a mining operation and an electrical plant.[3]

The Cuban leadership gave Mikoyan a severe reprimand at their meetings in Havana. Fidel told the Soviet vice premier that the Cuban people had been prepared to fight the imperialists, "and suddenly—concessions!" Moreover, Moscow did not consult at all with Havana. Everything happened rapidly, Mikoyan responded, and "the threat of aggression was so critical that there was no time for consultations."[4] The Cubans then boycotted further talks with Mikoyan. With no warning whatsoever, they left him waiting in the Soviet embassy for ten days. Mikoyan could not even return to Moscow for his wife's funeral.

Fidel disagreed with the removal of the missiles and the bombers and stated that Kennedy's verbal promises could not be trusted. US flyovers were "bad for the morale of our people and [made] them resentful." Che Guevara objected to the fact that the American-imposed economic boycott against Cuba would continue despite the USSR's removal of missiles and bombers.[5]

A month later, in Moscow, Khrushchev himself tried to convince dubious Cuban envoys that the Soviet withdrawal had guaranteed the survival of the Cuban Revolution. "We spent millions of rubles to save Cuba and you attack us in your press like the Albanians and the Chinese," the Soviet premier complained. "Mikoyan scarcely left Cuba alive." Longtime Cuban communist Carlos Rafael Rodríguez explained to the Soviet premier that "for Fidel the acceptance of the missiles was not meant to satisfy the needs of Cuba . . . but was to be for the benefit of the [entire] socialist camp."[6] The Cubans claimed that the outcome of the crisis did not at all protect them from violations of Cuban airspace by US warplanes. The Americans could continue the economic blockade and mount armed attacks on Cuba by émigré commandos. Moreover, United States Marines still occupied the Guantánamo Naval Station.

It seemed positively paradoxical. Cuba, an island nation of six million citizens, was demanding to be treated as an equal by the two greatest military powers of the Cold War. Cuban representatives considered that they had a right to question the decisions of their mighty ally, the Union of Soviet Socialist Republics, on whom they depended for political and economic survival. The Revolution of 1959 had converted Cuba into an international actor of considerable leverage. No one could have imagined any great power bringing the world to the brink of nuclear conflagration over a small Caribbean republic like Nikita Khrushchev did in 1962.

This dangerous episode resulted from the intersection of social revolution and the Cold War. Most remarkably, the leaders of the Cuban revolutionary government had chosen to place themselves in this pivotal position. They had gone out of their way to seek alliance with Moscow and with Beijing, too, knowing that the Goliath of the Western Hemisphere, then locked in ideological conflict with world communism, would object. What logic of social revolution in the age of Cold War impelled the Cubans to choose such a controversial and dangerous foreign policy?

Revolutionary Cuba determined its own fate. Its revolutionaries in the 1960s enticed both the Soviet and the Chinese communist regimes to compete for Cuba's favor during a time of internal conflict known as the Sino-Soviet dispute. The rancor between the Russians and the Chinese within the Socialist Bloc presented the Cubans with some roadblocks—including the missile crisis. But the rift between the two socialist giants also provided commodities and arms with which the Cubans successfully defended their revolution from United States aggression. In a way, Khrushchev had been right: members of the Socialist Bloc did help secure the Cuban Revolution. The rivalry between the USSR and the People's Republic of China (PRC) offered remarkable opportunities to the revolutionaries of the Caribbean.

CUBA'S SEARCH FOR ALLIES

At the height of the Cold War in the 1960s, the Soviet Union, the People's Republic of China, and revolutionary Cuba would seem to have been steadfast allies in the struggle against imperialism. All three regimes considered the United States to be their primary enemy. However, though they all had revolutionary origins, these countries did not share an international communist solidarity. The PRC and the USSR developed a long-simmering rivalry that split the socialist countries into two hostile encampments in the 1960s. They argued over economic and foreign strategies and disputed the leadership of the international communist movement. Isolated geographically from its socialist allies, Cuba attempted to chart its own independent path.

In the first instance, the timing of the three revolutions had placed the Soviet Union and China on different trajectories by the time that Cuba became socialist in the 1960s. Since only ten years separated the revolutionary triumphs of China in 1949 and of Cuba in 1959, these two regimes found much in common. Both China and Cuba believed in confronting imperialism with armed struggle. They shared the belief that spreading revolution to other countries would provide for the survival and longevity of young revolutions encircled by enemies.

In contrast, the USSR had reached the age of maturity in the 1960s. It concerned itself less with achieving radical ideological purity and more with modernizing economically. Soviet leaders promoted détente and mutual trade with the capitalist nations as a strategy to preserve the USSR and international socialism. The Soviets wished to avoid entering into World War III with the West. In the nuclear age, they believed both sides would annihilate each other. Of the three revolutionary regimes, only the USSR had an industrial economy, possessed nuclear weapons, developed rocket science, and had just bested the United States in thrusting the first satellite (the Sputnik) into space. It had also developed security after World War II by creating a buffer zone of satellite states between Russia and Western Europe.

The Soviets and Chinese were maintaining a tenuous but fitful unity in the international socialist movement just as the Cuban Revolution burst onto the scene. At the time of the 21st Congress of the Communist Party of the Soviet Union, in February 1959, the ideological trajectory of the month-old Cuban Revolution had yet to coalesce. Nevertheless, Castro had already legalized the seventeen-thousand-member Cuban communist party, the Partido Socialista Popular (PSP). Some PSP leaders attended the 21st Congress. Soviet leaders warned them that the new Cuban regime might "go to the right." They stressed trade union organization and publicity campaigns against US bases and missions. This strategy amounted to the official Soviet doctrine for revolution in Latin America, whose capitalist structures were considered too immature to be conducive to revolution. The Latin American communists in attendance reportedly respected and submitted to Moscow's leadership. Yet they complained privately about "Soviet aloofness."

Several Latin American communists traveled to Peking (today Beijing) following the congress. Mao Zedong and Liu Shaoqi, chairmen of the party and of the state, respectively, received them cordially. Chinese leaders explained their own anti-imperialist policies as distracting and dispersing imperialist forces and forcing them "to spread themselves thin over a vast area." The PRC sought to "strike blows against the United States without engaging directly in military actions." Mao and Liu said that the Cuban Revolution had demonstrated that "the battle could be carried to the imperialist rear."[7] Mao also advocated the union of Latin American countries into one national entity, in order to strengthen the fight against imperialism. The Chinese promised to set up training programs for Latin American communist leaders.[8]

In the immediate aftermath of its Great Leap Forward industrialization project, which the CIA counted as a failure of "mismanagement" and which historians credit with having caused famine and starvation, the PRC seemed poised to challenge Soviet leadership in the world.[9] The challenge to Moscow coincided with the temporary demotion of Mao's leadership within the Chinese government. Beijing moderated its domestic economic policies against Mao's wishes and simultaneously engaged with the world according to Mao's own hard line.[10]

Fidel Castro's revolutionary faction sought out relations with the socialist republics in an attempt to cultivate allies against US interests. Raúl Castro, himself a former member of the PSP's youth wing, first initiated contact with the Soviets for reasons of military defense. He dispatched longtime communist labor leader Lázaro Peña to Moscow. This trip occurred in April 1959 while Fidel Castro was on tour in the United States. It resulted in the arrival of veterans of the Spanish Civil War to instruct Cuban soldiers in Marxism-Leninism.[11] Neither Fidel nor the Soviets, in their secret communications, wanted to provoke the United States. The Cubans at first sought only trade ties with Communist Bloc countries. "No weapons," Fidel told one KGB officer in Havana. "We do not ask for any." While Castro's speeches addressed none of these things, brother Raúl and Che Guevara were speaking privately about "the construction of socialism."[12]

In June 1959, Guevara toured North Africa and Southeast Asia in search of diplomatic and trade alternatives to dealing with the United States. CIA agents had knowledge of Guevara's meeting with President Gamal Abdel Nasser of Egypt. Guevara spoke bitterly against the Americans. If one deals with US imperialists, Nasser reportedly told him, one loses 5 percent of one's resources. But if one negotiates with the communists, one loses all assets. The Argentinean revolutionary also gained a poor opinion of India's prime minister Jawaharlal Nehru, who preferred to talk to him about food rather than international politics.[13] However, US intelligence apparently did not know that Che secretly made visits to the Soviet embassies in these countries.

The Soviet security agency known as the KGB served as a direct linkage between Havana and Moscow. Nikolai Leonov, as a young secret agent, had obtained an assignment in 1953 to travel to Mexico to learn Spanish. By chance, he shared a ride with Raúl Castro on a freighter returning the latter to Havana after attending a communist youth meeting in Vienna. They became friends during the trip. In July 1959, Leonov escorted Raúl Castro on his first visit to Moscow, where he was to meet Khrushchev at the Kremlin's invitation. Not until October did another KGB officer, Aleksandr Alekseyev, take up residence in Havana to provide liaison between the Cubans and Leonov in Moscow. The KGB link to the Cuban revolutionary left wing was solid.[14] The Soviet and Cuban foreign ministers took a back seat. Prime Minister Castro discussed none of these matters with his moderate cabinet ministers.

The first Cuban travelers to the People's Republic of China produced mixed results. Comandante William Gálvez made a goodwill tour of socialist countries early in 1959. He had two audiences with Chairman Mao Zedong and told him that the Cubans desired to intensify their "intimate relationship" with the Chinese people in opposition to the "imperialists of the US."[15] Another revolutionary comandante, Faure Chomón of the Revolutionary Directorate, visited Beijing in October 1959. He praised the Chinese Revolution but claimed that communism would not work in Cuba. "If anyone tried

Che Guevara, conferring here with Aleksandr Alekseyev, KGB officer and Soviet ambassador to Cuba. Fidel and Raúl Castro actively sought the aid of the People's Republic of China and the Soviet Union.

to take the country down the path of Communism," Chomón said, "he would fail because the people would not support him."[16] Obviously, neither Gálvez nor Chomón belonged to Castro's inner circle.

As it turned out, both the Soviet and the Chinese leaders responded quickly if cautiously to Cuban requests for assistance. While Fidel's public denunciations of the United States certainly piqued their interest, it was the growing breach between the Soviets and the Chinese that explains the attentions that both powers lavished on the Cubans. Each communist superpower was looking to enlist allies against the other. The Soviets moved first.

Vice Premier Anastas Mikoyan arrived in Havana with a Soviet trade fair in January 1960. The Cubans welcomed Mikoyan with lavish attention even though Fidel "belittled everything [he] saw at the [Soviet] exhibit."[17] Mikoyan and the Cuban revolutionaries agreed to future purchases of Cuban sugar amounting to one million tons per year over a five-year period, plus the advancement of a one-hundred-million-dollar commercial loan at 2.5 percent interest.[18] The Soviets also cooperated in providing petroleum to Cuba so that Fidel could end the country's dependence on US-controlled oil supplies from Venezuela. Shell and Standard Oil's refusal to process Soviet crude in their Cuban refineries provided Castro the excuse in June 1960 to nationalize the industry.

The Cubans actively sought Soviet Bloc weapons after the March 1960 explosion of *La Coubre,* a French vessel bearing Belgian arms, in Havana Harbor. Fidel accused CIA agents of sabotage in the incident. Throughout the rest of the year, he kept up his charges that the United States was preparing an invasion of Cuba. Khrushchev still hesitated to conclude a formal Soviet arms deal, and the Cubans continued buying small arms from Western European countries.[19] Eisenhower had had enough. He approved a CIA plan to organize an invasion of Cuba with anti-Castro Cuban émigrés. The CIA advised the White House not to worry about a response from Moscow. "The USSR would not hesitate to write off the Castro regime before involving itself in a direct military confrontation with the U.S.," the CIA predicted, incorrectly, as it turned out.[20]

But the Soviet premier liked Fidel's anti-American diatribes. In July, Khrushchev pleased the Cuban revolutionaries with a statement indicating his willingness to use Soviet military forces in protecting the revolution. "Soviet artillerymen can support the Cuban people with their rocket fire should the aggressive forces in the Pentagon dare to start [an] intervention against

Cuba," Khrushchev announced.[21] Armed Forces Minister Raúl Castro traveled secretly to Moscow within a few days of this announcement. Just before meeting the Soviet premier, he had received a briefing on the "incorrect views" of the Chinese leadership. Raúl learned that the Kremlin would send rifles and a few older tanks to Cuba free of charge—not from the Soviets but from the Czechs. "We don't want war and you don't either," Khrushchev explained to Raúl Castro.[22] Subsequently, Khrushchev seized a high-profile opportunity at a United Nations meeting to demonstrate his support of the Cuban Revolution. The Soviet premier went to meet the Cuban leader at the latter's hotel in Harlem.[23] Never had even the most obsequious East European ruler received such an honor from a Soviet leader. The photo of Khrushchev giving Castro a bear hug appeared in newspapers around the world.

China too demonstrated an interest in supporting the Cuban Revolution. In January 1960, Beijing increased China's handouts of money and arms to Africa and Latin America.[24] Longtime Cuban communist Blas Roca traveled to Beijing and received a warm welcome. The government officials invited him to address the nation via television, the first foreign dignitary to do so. He informed the Chinese of Cuba's land reform, formation of the people's militias, and confiscations of American properties. By June 1960, the US government had learned of the presence of Chinese technicians at military training centers and at the Cuban Institute of Agrarian Reform. Chinese dance troupes, youth groups, and labor and trade delegations arrived in Havana.[25] "China supports Cuba because it is a revolution against imperialism and it is an example of how to struggle against the USA," the foreign ministry in Beijing announced. The "Chinese support [Cuba] with all possible means, despite Cuba maintaining ties with Taiwan."[26] Havana soon broke diplomatic and trade relations with Taiwan.

President Eisenhower and his National Security Council monitored the rising influence of Moscow and Beijing in Cuban affairs, as the CIA and US military had begun training for the Bay of Pigs invasion. Events moved rapidly. Following the expropriation of American- and British-owned oil refineries, Cuba responded to the US reduction of sugar imports by nationalizing all remaining American businesses and sugar mills. Both the Soviets and the Chinese established embassies in Havana, and the first shipments of Czech arms arrived.[27] US intelligence learned of the September arms shipment, which included ten tanks, one hundred antiaircraft guns, and a large number of machine guns. Moreover, Cuban soldiers had begun training with advanced Soviet weaponry in Czechoslovakia.[28] Thereafter, every Cuban officer attended military schools behind the Iron Curtain.

Che Guevara emerged as the earliest ideological collaborator of the Soviets and Chinese. As the chief planner for the socialization of the Cuban economy, he led a delegation to the USSR and PRC in the last months of 1960 and the first month of 1961. Che had moderate success selling sugar to and obtaining loans from the USSR on his first stop in Moscow.[29] The Kremlin courted him as a distinguished visitor. He stood with members of the Soviet Presidium atop Lenin's Tomb during the parade in Red Square commemorating the October 1917 Revolution. Che seemingly ignored Sino-Soviet differences emerging in Moscow during an international communist conference. As CIA director Allen Dulles described it in a briefing for President Eisenhower: "The chief Chinese Communist delegate . . . made a four hour speech attacking Khrushchev personally. Khrushchev was alleged to have lost his temper twice."[30] This competition within world communism proved beneficial to Che as each socialist superpower sought to draw Cuba to its side in the dispute.

On traveling subsequently to Beijing, Che Guevara again uncritically accepted the red carpet treatment. His audience at the Sino-American Friendship Association greeted him with a standing ovation. Che's speech did not express a preference for the Soviets or the Chinese but assumed an international communist unity that scarcely existed. He praised Khrushchev and acknowledged Soviet leadership. "China, in conjunction with the other socialist countries headed by the Soviet Union," Guevara said, "has opened a new historical era in extending generous aid."[31]

He had several meetings with Chairman Mao and Zhou Enlai, who charmed Che by praising his writings on guerrilla warfare. "[You] could be regarded as an intellectual," Zhou gushed. Mao appeared well briefed for the meeting and asked many questions about Latin America. He also drew parallels between the Chinese and Cuban Revolutions, though Che did acknowledge Cuba's easy path. The imperialists "didn't concentrate their forces," he said. Mao also imparted much advice on how to deal with the United States. "Be firm to the end," he advised Guevara, "and imperialism will find itself in greater difficulty." Later Guevara came away with a sixty-million-dollar loan that Foreign Minister Zhou Enlai assured him "was not disinterested." The Chinese considered Cuba to be at the forefront of the anti-imperialist struggle. Therefore, if Cuba could not repay the loan, Zhou reportedly told Che, "[it was] not at all important." Che subsequently signed an agreement to sell the PRC one million tons of Cuban sugar and to have Cubans receive technical instruction from the Chinese. Concluded Che, "Truly, China is one of those countries where you realize that the Cuban revolution is not a unique event."[32]

In Beijing, Guevara announced that Cuba was urging other Latin American countries to follow its example of armed uprising. He especially backed the Chinese position on the need for armed struggle by communist parties in the developing countries. He said at one reception that the Chinese Revolution had "revealed a new road for the Americas." Cuba watchers in Washington concluded that Guevara was "apparently siding with the Chinese on several key points in the Sino-Soviet dispute."[33] Although he toured collective farms, Che saw no evidence of how Mao's ambitious industrialization program, the Great Leap Forward, had brought a devastating famine to the countryside.[34] He proposed industrialization for Cuba as well.

Soviet leaders apparently did not want to be outdone by China's generosity. On his way back to Cuba through Moscow, Che received increased offers of loans above and beyond the Chinese. Guevara sought sugar sales and technical assistance in order to underwrite his elaborate plans to convert the island nation into an industrial power. The socialist countries did not disappoint him. Guevara acquired Soviet and East European agreements for the Cuban acquisition of factories, petroleum, textiles, foodstuffs, chemicals, paper, and technicians to run the new factories.[35] The Kremlin committed capital at 2.5 percent interest and no payments for ten years as well as technology to build a steel plant in Cuba. The Chinese also provided credit but did not require any interest at all. "Find me a capitalist country that would do the same!" Che exclaimed.[36] Eventually, he wanted to phase out Cuba's dependency on sugar exports and devote most resources to industrialization.

Guevara came away from his trip to the Soviet Union and China with an inflated view of their economic prowess. "[China's] articles of export are of the highest quality," he told one journalist. "They have a maxim that says that the Chinese worker can make whatever any other worker in the world can make."[37] His view of Cuba's position in the Cold War was more accurate. On Havana radio, Che Guevara gave a report about his trip to the PRC and the USSR. "We are not spectators in the struggle between [the United

States and the Socialist Bloc]," he said. "We are an important part of this struggle."[38]

Che Guevara based his economic programs on moral incentives, tight state controls, and voluntary labor. But when the Cuban economy responded with deteriorating production, he began to turn against Soviet economic policies. The missile crisis served as the turning point. Thereafter, he did not accuse Khrushchev of being too orthodox in his Marxist economics but of not being orthodox enough. Che opposed Moscow's limited introduction of prices and profits. "The moment you introduce profits into the socialist economy," he said, "you subvert socialism to capitalist revisionism." But the stalwart communists of the old Popular Socialist Party, notably Carlos Rafael Rodríguez, criticized Che's rigid state controls and upheld Khrushchev's model of economic incentives. Said Rodríguez: "The economy must run on profit, must earn," or else the national economy cannot "grow, develop, or advance."[39] This debate went on during Che's entire term as president of the National Bank and minister of industry.

In fact, Moscow did not approve of Che's plans for industrialization any more than it had liked China's Great Leap Forward. "Guevara was impossible," said Anatoly Dobrynin, the Soviet ambassador to Washington. "He wanted a little steel mill, [and] an automobile factory. We told him Cuba wasn't big enough to support an industrial economy. They needed hard currency, and the only way to earn it was to do what they did best—grow sugar."[40] Ultimately, Che's plans did not succeed, despite the assistance of his socialist economic partners. The factory machinery they sent him was outmoded and inefficient. Moreover, the revolutionary government's economic miscalculations contributed to a decline in agricultural production. "Another point that adds to Guevara's bitterness against the Russians," CIA analysts observed, "is that they have refused the help that he considered necessary for the immediate development of the industry of Cuba and insisted that the country concentrate on agricultural development."[41]

There remained another aspect in which Che Guevara posed a problem for Sino-Soviet relations. He was an unrepentant revolutionist. Che often quoted one of Fidel's early dictums, "The duty of the revolutionary is to make the revolution." His classic primer *Guerrilla Warfare* stated that "the guerrilla fighter is above all an agrarian revolutionary."[42] In this policy, the Cubans remained true to Chinese ideological tenets. US intelligence in 1963 concluded that the Cuban revolutionaries wanted "all the benefits of Soviet economic and military aid but insist[ed] upon a unique position in the Bloc without submitting to the discipline and control imposed on Soviet Satellites."[43] Thus did rising disagreements within the socialist world complicate Cuba's foreign and domestic policies.

THE SINO-SOVIET RIFT

The rupture between the Soviets and the Chinese grew wider at the 1961 Communist Party conference in Moscow. Beijing had always considered that Khrushchev's campaign against the cult of Joseph Stalin intended to tarnish Mao Zedong's revolutionary reputation as well. Zhou Enlai therefore pointedly laid a wreath at Stalin's grave. It was inscribed to "the great Marxist-Leninist." In a carefully worded speech, Zhou did not attack Nikita Khrushchev directly. But he seemed to imply that Soviet policy was insufficiently militant in its support of revolutionary struggles in the Third World. Zhou and the Chinese delegation walked out of the conference on October 23, the very day that the Communist Party Congress voted to remove Stalin's body from the Kremlin's mausoleum. Meanwhile, the Soviets halted deliveries of Russian oil to Beijing and resolved not to share nuclear technology with the Chinese. Thereafter, the Communist Parties of China and the Soviet Union continued to attend the same international meetings to level thinly veiled criticisms at each other.[44] Most—but not all—communists in Latin America sided with the Soviets.

Khrushchev grasped the importance of Cuba in this struggle. He sought to enhance his prestige at home and abroad by championing the Cuban revolutionaries while looking the other way as Fidel tightly controlled Cuba's communist party. Within Fidel's revolutionary family, many of his former guerrilla leaders still harbored animosity toward the pro-Moscow PSP for its inactivity during the fight against Batista. Domestically, the Castro brothers and Che Guevara never allowed the communist old-timers much influence over policy but utilized them as compliant bureaucrats. The most ambitious of them, Aníbal Escalante, faced dismissal and humiliation in 1962 and again in 1967. Fidel chose again to demonstrate independence from the USSR. In 1965, he handpicked the membership of the new Cuban

Communist Party.[45] The relationship between Havana and Moscow ebbed and flowed according to domestic and international events. The invasion at the Bay of Pigs in 1961 tightened that revolutionary kinship.

Eastern Bloc arms certainly arrived in time to contribute to Cuba's defense. At the military parade celebrating the first anniversary of the Revolution on January 2, 1960, Cuba already had one hundred thousand soldiers armed with mainly Batista-era and Belgian weapons. A year later and just three months before the Bay of Pigs invasion, foreign news reporters had tangible evidence of the rumored arrival of Soviet arms and equipment. They counted fifty battle tanks with 55- and 105-millimeter cannons and numerous truck-mounted rocket launchers.[46]

In the spring of 1960, the CIA received the directive of President Eisenhower to prepare an invasion force of Cuban exile combatants in order to overthrow Fidel Castro. This operation had to appear to be a Cuban affair. "Our hand should not show in anything that is done," Eisenhower said.[47] CIA operatives subsequently recruited young men of the Cuban exile community in Miami and sent them to Guatemala to be trained by US Army personnel. Miami's Cuban community buzzed with chatter about their youths going off for training, and Castro's spies among them got word back to Castro's G-2. Cuba's allies in the Socialist Bloc also knew of the military training. An East German diplomat in China wired his government that "preparation for direct intervention in Cuba is taking place in Nicaragua and Guatemala. So far intervention attempts have not been dangerous since conspirators do not find support in the Cuban army."[48]

President-elect John F. Kennedy learned of the planned invasion shortly before his inauguration and could hardly refuse the CIA plan. After all, in his presidential debates with Vice President Richard Nixon, Kennedy had criticized the Eisenhower-Nixon administration for tolerating a "communist" regime just ninety miles from Key West, Florida. Moreover, CIA directors assured Kennedy that three-quarters of the Cuban population did not support Castro. The mere landing of an invasion force would spark a massive uprising against the "communist" regime. True to his predecessor's admonition that the "hand of the US must not be shown," the newly inaugurated president Kennedy also wanted to send a similar message. "First I want to say that there will not be, under any conditions, an intervention in Cuba by the United States Armed Forces," he announced at a press conference.[49]

The exile force, called Brigade 2506, numbering more than twelve hundred men, landed at Playa Girón in the Bahía de Cochinos on April 17, 1961. The exile air force's B-26 bombers had raided Cuban airfields two days before, destroying many of Castro's fighter aircraft. Mindful of international public opinion, President Kennedy called off a second strike. The few surviving Cuban fighter planes quickly established air superiority over the battlefield. Then they chased the B-26s from the skies and sank the ships carrying the invaders' supplies. The men of Brigade 2506 found themselves stranded, and no popular uprising materialized.

Indeed, the poorly armed revolutionary militias took heavy casualties but prevented the invaders from getting off the beachhead until Fidel himself arrived with regular army units.[50] They deployed some of those newly arrived Czech weapons such as antiaircraft and artillery batteries and T-34 tanks. Twelve hundred members of Brigade 2506 surrendered and spent the next twenty months in Cuban prisons.[51] Raúl Castro admitted that Soviet Bloc military equipment had arrived just in time. "There were tankers and artillerymen who learned how to maneuver with their weapons on their way from Havana to Playa Girón," said Raúl. We won, "but we suffered heavy losses."[52] It bears mentioning that Nicaragua and Guatemala, both fearing the spread of Cuba's revolutionary example, had cooperated with the CIA's invasion preparations.

Soviet support had helped the Cubans defend their revolution. "Without this help [of the socialist countries]," one Cuban diplomat told the East Germans, "the defeat of the invasion would have been impossible. Cuba's Revolutionary Army was supplied with Czechoslovak, Soviet and Chinese weapons." Thereafter, Havana's embassies behind the Iron Curtain were informing their hosts that "Cuba is following the socialist path."[53]

Khrushchev seized upon Kennedy's failure at the Bay of Pigs to embarrass the American president when they met a few months later in Vienna. The Soviet premier jabbed his finger in the president's face and spoke nearly nonstop for half an hour while Kennedy responded with feeble platitudes. "The President's decision to launch a landing in Cuba only strengthened the revolutionary forces and Castro's own position," said Khrushchev, "because the people of Cuba were afraid that they would get another Bastista [sic] and lose the achievements of the revolution." He added, "Castro is not a Communist but US policy can make him one." Khrushchev asked, "Can six million

[Cubans] really be a threat to the mighty US?"[54] The Soviet premier scolded the American president for supporting the "most reactionary" regimes.

Thereafter, Khrushchev looked for additional victories over a weak American president, the better to solidify his leadership over Mao in the world communist movement. He permitted his clients in East Berlin to prevent the German brain drain to the West by erecting the Berlin Wall. The move surprised the Americans who had saved West Berlin from Joseph Stalin with the Berlin Air Lift of 1948. "It's not a very nice solution," President Kennedy said, "but a wall is a hell of a lot better than a war."[55] Khrushchev's next gambit in the Cold War held the possibility of greater stature over the Chinese. Instead, it was Mao who reaped a measure of revenge in the late fall of 1962.

THE MISSILES OF OCTOBER

The plan to place medium-range missiles in Cuba originated in the Kremlin. It resulted from Khrushchev's linking the Cuban Revolution to superpower conflict over Berlin and Turkey and to his sluggish economy at home.[56] He needed another victory abroad. The longtime Soviet ambassador to Washington, Anatoly Dobrynin, explained. "Was Khrushchev's decision prompted only by his desire—and it was a sincere one—to defend Cuba? I doubt it," he wrote. "The move was part of a broader geopolitical strategy to achieve greater parity with the United States that would be useful not only in the dispute over Berlin but in negotiations on other issues." The Soviets only had three hundred long-range missiles. The United States had five thousand. Khrushchev wanted his medium-range missiles in Cuba to counterbalance the Americans' advantages in long-range capabilities.[57]

Fidel knew that the Kremlin had been cautious about direct weapons deliveries between the two countries and asked why the missiles were needed. The Soviets exaggerated the threat of an imminent attack on Cuba by American armed forces, and Havana dutifully sent Raúl and Che to Moscow to finalize the plans.[58] The Kennedy administration's continued threats against Cuba had given no hope to anyone in Moscow and Havana that US antagonism toward the Cuban Revolution would abate. Reports of a Soviet military buildup had prompted the White House to order spy planes into the sky over Cuba. They discovered missile sites and feverish military activities on Cuban soil. After several days and nights of secret, high-level meetings,

Kennedy and his security advisers decided to impose a naval blockade to prevent Soviet shipping from getting through with nuclear warheads. US intelligence surmised that the missiles had not yet been armed.

The government of the People's Republic of China initially supported the Soviets in placing defensive missiles on Cuban soil. The Chinese government issued a statement praising Moscow's resolve not to withdraw the missiles and supporting "this just stand of the Soviet government." It urged the Cubans to fight. "US imperialism is, after all, a paper tiger," said the lead editorial of the *Ta Kung Pao* newspaper. "Its desperate struggles will intimidate no people fighting for national independence, democracy, and socialism. To deal with US imperialism, the most important thing is to wage a resolute and blow-for-blow struggle against it." But the article also reminded readers of Mao's 1958 qualification about US imperialism: "This tiger can still bite."[59]

When Kennedy ordered the naval blockade, the Kremlin backed down. Beijing's support for the Soviets dissolved when Premier Khrushchev made an agreement to withdraw the missiles in exchange for President Kennedy's promise not to invade Cuba with US troops. The accord ordered Soviet ships to return to port and the missiles to be dismantled. The Chinese press expressed incredulity: Khrushchev's capitulation in the missile crisis was a "victory for US diplomacy." In a public rally in Beijing, Peng Zhen of the Politburo compared Cuba's to the Chinese Revolution; both were "armed revolutions" of the type that Khrushchev was now reluctant to advocate. Peng said that it was an "unshirkable international obligation of the people of the socialist camp" to support "the Cuban people's struggle against US war provocation." During Mikoyan's mission to Havana, Beijing supported the resentments of Fidel Castro and the Cuban revolutionaries. The PRC hailed the "Five Conditions" that Fidel defiantly appended to the Soviet-US agreement.[60]

Castro's five demands were that the United States must end the economic blockade, launch no other forms of harassment, stop Cuban exile hostilities against the island, end the U-2 flights, and abandon the Guantánamo Naval Station. In addition, Fidel said that he would not allow US inspections of Soviet missile sites—which Khrushchev had condoned.

Indeed, Fidel's disappointment with Soviet leaders ran deep. He had permitted the armed militias to parade through the Havana streets chanting, "Nikita, mariquita; lo que se da, no se quita" (Nikita, you little sissy: what you give, do not take back). Vice Premier Mikoyan suspected that the Chinese diplomats in Havana were influencing Fidel in this defiant attitude. During the contentious talks of November 1962, Fidel wanted Mikoyan to admit that placement of the rockets and bombers in Cuba had been a mistake on the part of the Soviets. Mikoyan replied that the Soviet Union had "reasons of its own" for placing these weapons in Cuba.

It was at this point that an angry Fidel Castro broke off discussions with Mikoyan, leaving the Soviet deputy premier waiting in the Soviet embassy for ten days. Finally, Fidel returned and told Mikoyan that he wished to remain a friend of the USSR but reserved the right to find "new friends, who might be more devoted to Cuba." The Soviet envoy took this to mean the Chinese. Mikoyan concluded that Castro was "almost like a mule in his obstinacy."[61] Instead of Kennedy's verbal promise not to invade, Fidel wondered why Khrushchev had not swapped the missiles at least for the American base at Guantánamo.

CASTRO CHOOSES MOSCOW

After the missile crisis, Cubans were saying that "Fidel's head is with Moscow but his heart is with Beijing."[62] Ideologically, the island's revolutionary leadership had more in common with the Chinese than with the Soviets. Cuba continued its subversive activities in Venezuela and sent a small cadre of guerrillas to Argentina.[63] The CIA calculated in 1963 that three thousand Latin Americans had received guerrilla training from the Cubans. Che Guevara planned for armed uprisings elsewhere, designed to strengthen the Cuban Revolution in its struggle with the United States. This activity in the "export of revolution" increased the friction between the Cubans and the Soviets. Moscow viewed Havana's aggressive revolutionary stance as a threat to the pro-Soviet communist parties. Schisms broke out in every country in Latin America between the cautious communist old guard and the youthful guerrillas. Cuban speeches on the need to sponsor revolution abroad received very positive responses in the People's Republic of China. Both Fidel's and Che's remarks on the subject always made the front pages of government newspapers in China. On the other hand, Soviet media hardly mentioned Cuba's promotion of guerrilla warfare in Latin America.[64]

Still, the Cubans did not spare their criticism of Chinese policies either. Castro faulted the PRC for not intervening more forcefully in the October missile crisis and always asked them for more arms, loans, and trade.[65] Moreover, the Cubans sought to act as a disinterested broker between the PRC and the USSR and to draw together the two sides at international conferences. The only problem with this short-lived effort: China had little to offer Cuba. To secure the revolution, Fidel had to choose between a generous industrial benefactor with different ideas and a parsimonious ideological fellow traveler.

Following the missile crisis, Moscow pressed the Cubans to sign an economic assistance pact that would bind them to the USSR and save this Caribbean island as a symbol of Soviet leadership in international socialism. Khrushchev wanted to preserve communism ninety miles off the shores of his capitalist rival, the United States. For this purpose, he invited Castro to come to the USSR in May 1963. Soviet leaders patiently listened as Fidel talked about his commitment to "national-liberation" movements.[66]

Fidel learned accidentally about one of the real reasons that Moscow had sent missiles to Cuba—that they might serve as a bargaining chip in more important disputes elsewhere. Mikoyan had not briefed him on that part of the Moscow-Washington agreement. As Fidel reported later, in one of their discussions during his visit to Moscow, Khrushchev himself was reading documents out loud. The Spanish translator recited them to Fidel, and the Soviet premier inadvertently read one about the US removal of missiles from Turkey. "How's that?" Castro asked. "Repeat that part." That was when "Nikita realized he had read the paragraph by mistake."[67] In addition to not invading Cuba with American troops, Kennedy had also promised to dismantle Jupiter missiles in Turkey. The Soviets intended to keep this part of the agreement secret—even from Castro. Nevertheless, Khrushchev gained positive publicity standing next to Fidel at state functions, because the socialist world acclaimed Fidel Castro for his defiance of the United States. His 1963 trip to the Soviet Union lasted five weeks.[68] The Chinese could not have been happy as Fidel addressed a mass rally in Red Square. "Without the existence of the Soviet Union, Cuba's socialist revolution would have been impossible," he pronounced. "The might of the Soviet Union and of the whole socialist camp stopped imperialist aggression against our country."[69] The media in Beijing printed few reports of Castro's presence in Moscow.

Despite his triumphant visit to Moscow in May 1963, Fidel worried that Moscow might still make a deal with Washington at Cuba's expense. Soviet minutes of his meetings with Khrushchev indicate that Castro always turned the conversation to the subject of military cooperation. He wanted the Soviet brigade to stay on in Cuba. "It is our opinion that Soviet military personnel located in Cuba are like the celebrated missiles," Fidel said. "So long as they are there, American military circles are convinced that an attack on Cuba would inevitably lead to war with the Soviet Union, which is something that they don't want and fear." Nikita replied that "Soviet forces cannot stay forever, especially since there is evidence of a strong guarantee given confidentially by Kennedy not to invade." Likewise, Khrushchev deflected Castro's request for the newest Soviet tanks. "The defense of Cuba will not come only with building up Cuban military power," the Soviet premier advised, "but in effective intelligence activity abroad."[70]

For their part, Cuban revolutionary leaders did not wish to break with the PRC and took care to communicate with Chinese embassy officials in Havana. "For us, the Sino-Soviet dispute is one of the saddest events," Che Guevara said. "We are trying to mediate."[71] Nonetheless, the Cubans wanted Soviet weapons. Defense Minister Raúl Castro may have exaggerated a bit in Moscow when he suggested that the United States was creating a joint Latin American military strike force to invade Cuba.[72] Havana could not depend only on verbal promises. Its insecurity heightened following the assassination in November 1963 of the American president, who had made that verbal promise not to invade. No one in Havana could be certain the new American president would honor an informal, unsigned agreement.

Castro's second trip to the USSR in January 1964 met the expectations of both Nikita and Fidel. The premier reportedly informed the Cubans that the Soviet Union was not in a position, due to the dispute with the Chinese, to engage in direct military action to protect the revolution in the Caribbean. Soviet troops actually were engaged in reinforcing positions along its border with China. But Khrushchev said he would continue his generous military and economic aid to Cuba.[73] American intelligence surmised that Castro's visits to Moscow served three major purposes. First, the Soviets tried to persuade Castro to use caution in fomenting revolution elsewhere in Latin America. Then they gave Fidel a contract for the delivery of sugar at high fixed prices for the long term. Third, they brought Cuba over to Moscow's side in its dispute with Beijing.[74]

Following these sojourns in Moscow, Castro momentarily stopped attacking North American imperialism. He actually signaled for the improvement of United States–Cuba relations. But he reiterated that the

Americans would have to accept that Cuba would never abandon Marxism-Leninism in order to improve relations. "There is no way back," he said. "Cuba will always be with the Soviet Union and the Socialist Camp." In 1964, Cuba was sending five million tons of sugar per year to Eastern Europe and another one million to China.[75] The military aid proved timely. Exile commando groups backed by the CIA were still attacking coastal ports and military installations, and Cuban militiamen, freshly armed after their service at the Bay of Pigs, were flushing out the remaining counterrevolutionary bands from the island's mountains.

However, the rapprochement between Havana and Moscow did not save Khrushchev. The presidium removed him from power in the autumn of 1964. "You insisted that we deploy our missiles on Cuba," read the brief against Khrushchev. "This provoked the deepest crisis, carried the world to the brink of nuclear war, and even frightened terribly the organizer of this very danger [Khrushchev himself]. . . . This incident damaged the international prestige of our government, our party, [and] our armed forces, while at the same time helping to raise the authority of the United States."[76] Plainly, Khrushchev had overextended himself in the Sino-Soviet dispute and in Cuba.

The tight relationship between Havana and Moscow greatly displeased Beijing. Cuba and China still shared identical attitudes about revolutionary action. Yet the Chinese delegates attending the 1964 Havana Conference of Latin American Communist Parties attacked the hosts for not breaking relations with the Soviets. As the CIA reported, "The pro-Chinese elements also wanted the Cubans to condemn pro-Soviet elements in Latin American communist parties because they refused to advocate armed revolution."[77] Beijing had not yet given up on Latin America or its own emphasis on armed resistance.

Che skipped the November 1964 meeting of the Latin American communist parties. He had resigned his economic posts and was visiting the new premier, Leonid Brezhnev, in Moscow. Then in December he left for the United Nations meeting in New York and thereafter took a long trip to northern and central Africa. He finished up with the February 1965 speech in Algiers.[78] Everywhere he went, Che Guevara chided the Soviets and advocated aggressive assistance to national liberation movements.

The Western Hemisphere had become a Sino-Soviet battleground, even though China's presence was comparatively small. Beijing's call for revolutionary struggle appealed to dissident activists eager to wrest power from the Moscow-oriented old guard that dominated the communist parties in every country of Latin America. These dissidents looked both to Havana and to Beijing in their arguments against party leaders. The Chinese had increased their financial backing and training of militant revolutionists. China had only one embassy in Latin America, in Havana, and its trade with Cuba amounted to two hundred million dollars, mainly rice in exchange for sugar. Some brave Chinese factory workers and peasants were openly wondering, "Why export to Cuba when we don't have enough to eat?" Moreover, 150 Chinese advisers were working in Cuba. But Cuba's dependence on Soviet trade and arms had cooled its relations with the PRC. The Chinese began referring to the Cuban leaders as "revisionists."[79]

TENSIONS WITHIN THE COMMUNIST BLOC

Cuba could not rely solely on ideological kinship with the Chinese; trade and military assistance drew Castro into the Soviet camp. Thus it was that Chinese leaders began to distance themselves from Cuba following the Havana meeting of Latin American communist parties in November 1964. When the next delegation of Latin American communists traveled to Beijing, they met with an icy reception. Mao Zedong was particularly furious with the "revisionist" resolutions of the Havana conference, according to CIA informants. "He reminded his listeners that 650 million Chinese are behind the Chinese Communist Party," the report said. "In reply to a remark by the Uruguayan delegate, Mao demanded to know how many people the Uruguayan communist party represented." (The CIA estimate was six thousand members.) Cuba's pro-Moscow communist leader Carlos Rafael Rodríguez attempted a feeble retort, but Mao interrupted. There were three demons in the world, said the Chinese party chairman: imperialism, the atomic bomb, and revisionism. "Fidel Castro was still afraid of the first two," said Mao. Rodríguez responded that Cuba did not fear imperialism or the bomb and "was absolutely independent of everybody and uninvolved in any disputes."[80]

Che Guevara's own thinking began to sour on both the Soviet and the Chinese camps. He relinquished his economic oversight and resigned as minister of industries. By that time, rationing of basic commodities had become a quotidian fact of life. Even so, Fidel continued to utilize moral incentives and strict state controls under the economic leadership of Orlando Borrego, Che's protégé. However, Castro terminated the industrialization drive and returned to sugar production, as Moscow had advised, though without adopting the Soviet policies on material incentives and decentralization.

Guevara thereafter resolved to devote himself to constructing revolutionary solidarity with the postcolonial nations of the Third World. He departed from Cuba on December 18, 1964, for an extended trip through Africa and Asia. As he traveled, his speeches drew parallels between African guerrilla movements and that of Castro in the Sierra Maestra. Che also linked the "progressive revolutionary" states of Africa with the Cuban Revolution. All the struggles of Africans were against "neocolonialism," he said, and Cuba should be their natural ally rather than the USSR or the PRC. Che Guevara offered Cuban military and medical training to the African liberation movements.[81]

However, Che Guevara still wished to repair the Sino-Soviet rift because these two powers could bankroll and arm the anti-imperialist movement. He returned to China in February 1965, but Party Chairman Mao Zedong refused to meet with him. Instead, Che faced the ire of the government's chairman. Liu Shaoqi scolded Guevara for Cuba's entry into the camp of the Soviet revisionists. Liu claimed that the People's Republic of China had been generous in helping Cubans. "However, we now realize," said Liu, "that the Cubans are and have been actually led by the Soviets and are in fact in the revisionist camp." Che shot back with criticism of the Chinese for the stubborn positions they had taken at the Havana conference. "The fourth interview ended with a violent exchange between Liu and Che, who announced that there was nothing to be gained by continuing the conversations," the CIA reported. Guevara departed from China earlier than expected. Later, he would admit to Fidel Castro that the Chinese were "useless to Cuba."[82]

Guevara never broke openly with the Castro brothers despite his disillusionment with both Moscow and Beijing. Armed forces chief Raúl Castro meanwhile had become the leading proponent of a Soviet alliance. He visited the Soviet Union on numerous occasions, conferring with the Soviet defense minister on arms deals and the training of Cuban military and intelligence personnel.[83] Observed Carlos Franqui, editor of the newspaper *Revolución,* "Che and Raúl were good friends in the early days of the [revolutionary] war, but they drifted apart during the times of heavy Party politics, when Che began to criticize the Soviet system and the Czechs, who had sold us the junk they couldn't use."[84] Guevara's last public speech in Algiers in February 1965 proved inflammatory. He accused the Socialist Bloc of behaving like imperialists in its trade deals with Latin America and Africa and also in its diplomatic relations with the United States at the time of the Vietnam War. No one could mistake Che's inference when he said, "The socialist countries have the moral duty to put an end to their tacit complicity with the exploiting countries of the West."[85] To many observers, Che was leveling his criticism toward the Soviet Union.

Che's forthright expressions of distaste for Soviet party bosses exasperated Fidel, who, after all, had a nation to govern. On Guevara's return from Algiers, Castro met him at the airport, immediately whisking his Argentine *compañero* into a private office. They had a long, occasionally heated, discussion. Cuba could not fight both the United States and the Soviet Union, Fidel implied.[86] At that moment, Raúl Castro was attending a communist party meeting in Moscow that the Chinese delegation was boycotting. His presence there signaled that the Cubans were aligning with the Soviets. Defense Minister Raúl Castro also worried that Guevara's bitter denunciation of Moscow's foreign policies might disrupt Soviet-Cuban military cooperation. Che's views expressed in Algiers were "extreme and out-of-place," Raúl told East European leaders. Guevara was "marked by obstinacy, a cause for serious discussions within the Cuban leadership."[87] Nonetheless, the Castro brothers agreed that Che would pursue his activist agenda in Africa, while Fidel and Raúl fulfilled their duties to preserve the Cuban Revolution.

One of the most photographed and newsworthy personalities of the era, Che Guevara dropped out of sight in March 1965. No one knew where he was or whether he was alive or dead. The FBI advised the administration of President Lyndon Baines Johnson that "perhaps" Fidel had shot Che in the midst of a heated argument. CIA agents suggested that Guevara might be resting in a Soviet psychological hospital after suffering a mental breakdown.[88] Of course, Fidel knew of yet never revealed Che's whereabouts. In fact, in the last two and one-half years of his life, Guevara was engaging in revolutionary struggles of the type that the Chinese would have approved of and the Soviets would have criticized as "adventurous."

With the blessing of Castro, the Argentinean revolutionary organized, trained, and led a team of Cuban advisers into the eastern Congo in support of Laurent Kabila's rebel forces. Both China and the USSR had stock-piled weapons with the leftist governments of Tanzania, Ghana, Egypt, and Algeria. Che's group availed itself of several tons of these stocks. In a way, Chinese generosity toward Africa had spurred the Soviets to respond with comparable supplies.[89] "Boats keep arriving with plenty of high quality weapons," Che wrote about the Congo. "It was pitiful to see how [the rebels] squandered the resources of friendly countries." However, socialist arms could not prevent CIA-supported mercenaries from routing Kabila's forces. Guevara had to go into hiding at the Cuban embassy in Tanzania in order to write a lengthy report to Fidel about the African debacle. "This is the history of a failure," his analysis began.[90]

Despite leaning toward the Soviets, Castro did not give up on Che's projects in support of the revolution abroad. In January 1966, Fidel invited to Havana more than five hundred delegates from more than eighty countries of Latin America, Africa, and Asia. They came for the Tricontinental Conference. Revolutionary unity suffused the air among an assortment of communists, socialists, Trotskyists, and Gramskyists that the Tricontinental sought to coalesce for the goal of defeating imperialism worldwide. Cubans touted the Tricontinental Conference of Asian, African, and Latin American revolutionaries as an antidote to US aggression. They informed the foreign delegations about US counterinsurgency training, the effective suppression of liberation movements, and the rise of military dictatorships. The message reiterated that revolutionaries worldwide needed to defend themselves.[91]

Fidel Castro put up all the conferees at the Havana Hilton, renamed the Hotel Habana Libre. The delegates lacked for little in terms of food and beverages. Lázaro Cárdenas, Salvador Allende, Carlos Marighela, Luis Augusto Tucios, and Régis Debray circulated through the crowds, as did Robin Blackburn, the British intellectual representing Bertrand Russell's Council of World Peace.[92] However, the world's foremost guerrilla leader, Che Guevara, did not show up. Fidel informed the delegates that Che was working elsewhere for world revolution. Guevara's defeat in the Congo had not yet become known.

Despite the show of unity, the Tricontinental Conference let loose another series of squabbles stemming from the Sino-Soviet dispute. The Chinese delegates accused Moscow of being soft on imperialism, for allowing the United States to transfer troops from West Germany for service in

Vietnam. In turn, the Soviets suffered a blow when the delegates did not endorse the policy of "peaceful coexistence" and expressed strong support for the "anti-imperialist" struggle in Vietnam.[93] The Cubans too were drawn into the disputes. Fidel reacted strongly to China's sudden reduction in the delivery of rice supplies. He cited the gesture as proof of China's having joined the US economic blockade. "We do not blame the Chinese government exclusively for the reduction of this ration," Fidel said. Cubans should also blame themselves "for having believed in the international spirit of the Chinese government."[94] Also there arose a question about China's dissemination of anti-Soviet propaganda among Cuban officials and military officers. Mao's propagandists lumped Fidel Castro together with the Soviet "revisionists." The Sino-Soviet rift threatened the main business of the conference: the establishment of a solidarity organization uniting the anti-imperialist forces of Asia, Africa, and Latin America.

Shortly after the Tricontinental Conference, internal upheaval occasioned China's withdrawal from international socialism once again. The Great Proletarian Cultural Revolution that began in 1966 served as the catalyst when internal party struggles between the left and right mobilized the Red Guards movement, discredited the communist bureaucracy, involved the People's Liberation Army in political disputes, and retarded China's economic recovery. Liu Shaoqi and Peng Zhen died, as did the commander of the armed forces, Lin Biao. The future chairman, Deng Xiaoping, underwent years of internal exile, and Zhou Enlai was one of the few moderates to survive. Mao strengthened his domestic rule and then turned on the so-called Gang of Four, including his wife, Jiang Qing, who had aided him in reestablishing his authority. He finally used the army to suppress the Red Guards. As the CIA concluded, the Cultural Revolution "contributed to China's growing isolation in the world."[95] Certainly, China's export of arms, foreign trade, and funding of foreign revolutionary movements dried up.

Back in Cuba, in the summer of 1966, Che Guevara began organizing yet another foreign venture. With the assistance of Castro's intelligence agencies, Che began to train a small band of Cubans and Bolivians for an armed uprising in Bolivia. "The cordillera of the Andes will be the Sierra Maestra of Latin America," he quoted Fidel as saying.[96] Che and his men arrived in Bolivia in November 1966. A 1967 issue of the *Tricontinental* journal published his last article. In the piece, Che praised the North Vietnamese struggle against US imperialism and urged his comrades to create "two, three, many

Vietnams" in order to stretch thin American military power. This was a Maoist strategy Che believed he could carry out in Bolivia. But the Moscow-aligned Bolivian Communist Party refused to cooperate.

Soviet premier Leonid Brezhnev voiced annoyance that Che and Cuban guerrillas were operating in Bolivia and that Moscow had not been consulted beforehand. It violated the understanding between the communist parties of Latin America, Brezhnev said, and it provoked the United States government. The Soviet premier also implied that the USSR might *not* come to Cuba's aid if the United States attacked.[97] At this tense moment in Soviet-Cuban relations, Alexei Kosygin traveled to the United States in order to confer with President Johnson in June 1967. The president brought up the subject of Cuba. Although Johnson did not mention Che Guevara's presence in Bolivia, he did tell Kosygin that the United States had evidence of "Cuba's encouragement of guerrilla operations in seven Latin American countries," and these were dangerous to peace. Johnson later confided to former president Eisenhower that Kosygin acted "like he was a little upset with Castro."[98]

Kosygin stopped in Havana on his return to Moscow and reiterated Soviet objections to the presence of Che Guevara and Cuban guerrillas in Bolivia. Castro defended Che. In fact, "Fidel expressed strong criticism of the Soviet Union for going too far in making concessions to imperialism in its efforts to foster détente," admitted one Soviet diplomat in Havana.[99] Castro refused to apologize for Cuba's attempts to foster revolution abroad.

Premier Brezhnev had had enough. The Kremlin decided to get tough with Fidel, particularly now that the Chinese were shutting out the world during the Cultural Revolution and could not intervene. The Soviet Union reduced the supplies of low-priced oil along with other aid that it delivered to Havana, and the Cuban economy began to sputter. Castro responded that Cuba should be able to chart its own course free from outside interference.[100]

At this juncture, the career of the Cuban Revolution's most celebrated comandante was rapidly coming to an end. In April 1967, Bolivian forces had captured one of Che Guevara's accomplices, the radical French journalist Régis Debray. He revealed for the first time in more than two years that Che was indeed alive. This exposure led to several important developments that sealed the doom of Che's guerrillas. First, Bolivian politicians used the specter of a "foreign invasion" in order to foster a nationalist reaction in the zone of combat. Not a single Bolivian peasant joined Che's revolution. Second, the United States sent in military equipment and trainers. Special Forces instructors arrived to help create an elite battalion of Bolivian rangers, one unit of which finally captured Che Guevara in October 1967.[101] He was executed shortly thereafter.

Why was the fate of this Argentinean revolutionary important to the relationship between the Soviet Union, China, and Cuba? The rigid ideologue of the Cuban revolution, Ernesto "Che" Guevara, had to give way to the pragmatic revolutionary, Fidel Castro. Thereafter, Castro was free to make the inevitable decision to preserve the Cuban Revolution by confirming its military and economic alliance with the Soviet Union rather than the People's Republic of China.[102]

Nevertheless, the Sino-Soviet dispute had offered a timely opportunity to America's first socialist republic. The dispute broke into the public view during Cuba's revolutionary infancy, when international condemnation and internal opposition presented the revolutionaries with the greatest danger of being overthrown. They needed allies with deep pockets and a willingness to spend. The timing could not have been better for young revolutionaries located so far from the centers of international communism. In 1959, China was just emerging from the internal turmoil of the Great Leap Forward and preparing itself to reengage with the outer world. Mao's return to the international stage motivated Moscow to embrace the Cuban Revolution. Thus, Raúl Castro in 1960 could negotiate to get Czech arms, which arrived just before the Bay of Pigs invasion. Thus, Che Guevara could fly from Moscow to Beijing and back again to Moscow early in 1961 in order to pry generous economic concessions from both communist rivals. Castro obtained additional economic and military aid in two visits to Moscow, in 1963 and again in 1964. It is doubtful that Nikita Khrushchev would have been so forthcoming in the absence of Mao Zedong's challenge to his international communist leadership. Thus, the Kremlin tolerated Cuba's Mao-like export of revolution—up to a certain point.

By 1966, when the Cuban Revolution had become firmly established, the Chinese rulers reentered another period of internal turmoil, the Cultural Revolution, during which Beijing ended its efforts to make friends through trade and diplomacy. By this time, the Cubans no longer needed Russian artillerymen. This Caribbean island's revolutionary army and militia forces were trained, indoctrinated, and armed. The Cuban people mobilized to defend the revolution, and Soviet subsidies were undergirding Cuba's redistributive economy. Moreover, the island nation's primary aggressor, the United States, was moving the site of its anticommunist crusade from the Caribbean Basin to Southeast Asia. The Cuban Revolution had established a modicum of security.

In August 1968, therefore, Cubans expected that Fidel would revert to his independent tendencies by condemning the Soviet invasion of Czechoslovakia during the Prague Spring movement. But Castro turned the tables. Czech leaders had blundered in their reform measures, he reasoned, and failed "to maintain contact with the masses." Furthermore, the Czechs were negotiating loans with the imperialist powers and getting involved with the CIA. "We were convinced that the Czechoslovak regime was heading toward capitalism and was inexorably heading toward imperialism."[103] Fidel Castro sided with the USSR all right, but with a logic that would have pleased Che Guevara himself.

The Soviets restored full economic trade after Castro's pronouncements on Czechoslovakia. This is not to say that the bargain was ever easy, for the Soviets paid dearly for their sponsorship of the only socialist republic in the Western Hemisphere. They sold petroleum cheaply and bought sugar dearly as well as subsidizing arms and technology for Cuba. Moscow grew accustomed to tolerating Cuba's more aggressive foreign policies in Latin America and Africa, as an indulgent parent might ignore the occasional poor behavior of a beloved but willful child.

"You mustn't think of Castro as [a] little man with a beard from Cuba—a wild demagogue. He is not in the least primitive or unstable," a Soviet diplomat was heard saying. "He is a very able man; he can be a very dangerous opponent, and is quite clever and subtle enough to be able successfully to play Moscow off against Beijing, and vice versa. It is vital for us [Soviets] that Cuba doesn't slide gradually into the Chinese camp. We have to hold on to Castro tight, and we can only do it with economic aid. This the Chinese cannot give."[104]

CHAPTER FOUR

The *Gusano* Counterrevolution

FIDEL CASTRO CALLED them *gusanos,* Spanish for worms.[1] To supporters of the revolution, the term refers to those brought up in upper-middle-class comfort. This meant homes with live-in servants, education in Catholic primary and secondary schools, and entrance to the universities—even education abroad. Young men born to these circumstances then entered the professions as lawyers, engineers, and doctors and eventually obtained prestigious positions in the government. They married within their class and destined their children for the same advantages. Many of these youths had favored the struggle against the Batista dictatorship, but not the move to the left with Castro's consolidation of power. According to the revolutionary lexicon, Antonio "Tony" Zamora qualified as a *gusano.* He kept going straight when the revolution veered left.

Even though Tony was too young to join the revolution against the Batista regime, he and his schoolmates felt that they were contributing. Zamora enrolled in Havana's Catholic secondary school of La Salle. His senior class of one hundred students walked out of classes, observing the call for the April 1958 general strike against Fulgencio Batista, notwithstanding that the dictator's two sons also attended La Salle. In repressing the strike, Batista's police killed an older friend of Zamora's.

Tony Zamora took inspiration from the resistance activities of an older brother. Juan Clemente Zamora knew people involved in the Havana underground, although he was not hard core. Also Tony himself had had a run-in with Batista's police. As an avid skin diver, he and some friends planned a fishing trip to the waters off Varadero Beach in Matanzas Province. He arrived first and had forgotten the spearguns, known as *rifles* in Spanish. From the hotel, he phoned his friends back in Havana to bring the "rifles." A black Oldsmobile sedan, the preferred vehicle of the ruthless military secret police called the SIM (Military Security and Intelligence), soon pulled up, and out jumped an officer notorious for his brutality. Someone had listened in on Tony's phone conversation and informed the military police. The seventeen-year-old Tony Zamora spent several harrowing moments until he remembered the name of a family friend, a senator in Batista's government, who vouched for him by phone.

Tony graduated from La Salle and, the University of Havana being closed, enrolled at the University of Miami in the fall of 1958. Thus he missed the final months of the revolutionary war. He returned to Havana four days after Batista fled the country, at about the moment that a mob captured and strung up a Matanzas police officer by the neck. He waited for classes to resume at the University of Havana, where he wished to follow his brother's path of getting a degree in law. Time passed, and when classes resumed in 1960, the revolution had come to the universities. Purges had begun and communists replaced moderates on the faculty.

In the meantime, the attorney Juan Clemente Zamora found work in several ministries of the interim revolutionary government with some of his friends in Havana's M26 underground. He mingled with the likes of Raúl Roa in foreign affairs, Armando Hart in education, and even Fidel Castro himself. Nevertheless, Juan Clemente became concerned about members of the PSP turning up in important government positions. So did Tony. He obtained work in the Ministry of Foreign Affairs for a year along with two friends, one of whom was the son of the former minister and important Auténtico Party figure Aureliano Sánchez Arango. "We started very supportive of the Revolution," Tony writes, "but in early 1960 we saw the growing influence of the Soviet Union and Cuban Communists and turned against the government."[2] One of his spearfishing friends had worked in the M26 underground and received a commission as officer in the new rebel army. On the other hand, Tony was becoming disaffected and decided to act. He would use his skills as a skin diver against communist influences.

When a Chinese freighter berthed in Havana Harbor, he and a few skin-diving friends laid plans to sink the ship. They contacted the American embassy to acquire limpet mines for the operation. CIA agents dissuaded them from the idea and recruited the young men for a "special operation" abroad. Through the CIA, Tony obtained a visa and an airline ticket. He arrived in Miami in October 1960, a bit chagrined to find "so many Batistianos in the United States."[3] However, his two workmates in the Ministry of Foreign Affairs had run afoul of Castro's security agents. They were captured in December 1960 and imprisoned for betraying the revolution. In February 1961, Tony flew from Miami's Opa Locka Airport to Guatemala, there to train with the émigré Brigade 2506. Neither Zamora nor his friends viewed themselves as counterrevolutionary scum. They were the true Cuban patriots Fidel Castro had betrayed.

Tony Zamora's story brings up an important question. The revolutionary leadership knew that the US embassy had contacts with the dissidents and was spiriting them out of the country. Fidel's own security agents identified American intelligence officers and their Cuban collaborators by name. The Interior Ministry kept tabs on political moderates, suspected turncoats, and outspoken opponents of the regime. G-2 intelligence had moles in several underground organizations. Castro also knew about the Cuban exiles training in Guatemala and had been warning his countrymen for many months about the coming invasion. Yet he did not order the shutdown of the US embassy. Why not? American diplomats had been complaining about revolutionary policies since the executions of "war criminals" began in February 1959. They objected to land reform in the summer of 1959. US officials also criticized the presence of communists and the seizures of US businesses in 1960. Still the revolutionary government tolerated them. One can only conclude that the close proximity of the enemy and their *gusano* allies served a purpose for the revolution. It gave Fidel Castro another excuse to rally and organize his supporters. The Bay of Pigs invasion, in which Tony Zamora participated, offered Fidel that final provocation. Castro used it to get rid of his internal enemies.

Cuba's counterrevolution consisted of two branches. One originated among the urban middle class, and the other in the traditional sectors of rural society. Resistance in the cities commenced mainly among educated youngsters whose older siblings and families had supported the uprising against Fulgencio Batista. The trials and executions of *batistiano* war criminals did not bother them in the least, for the butchery and corruption of the "tyranny" had appalled them. After all, Batista's victims had come predominantly from the middle class too. Many of these youngsters did not object to the agrarian reform. Rather, the presence of communists in the revolutionary government provided the basic motivation for many young men and women and their families to turn against Fidel Castro.

There was another reason that drove the professional classes. Fidel appeared to be provoking them with his revolutionary actions. May and June 1959 marked the turning point. Not only were members of the communist party (the PSP) staffing army training centers, but many also began to fill positions in the government ministries. The rise of the communists triggered opposition in the Catholic Church as well. Its middle-class followers had not forgotten that the PSP had played a very small role in the revolutionary war, a last-minute one at that. Therefore, the idea took hold that Fidel Castro was deviating from the democratic nationalist revolution that the professional classes had embraced.

The Central Intelligence Agency developed contacts with anti-Castro activists, especially students whose faculty were being purged by the pro-communist student federation. These young counterrevolutionaries chanted anticommunist slogans, engaged in shoving matches with urban militiamen, and disrupted mass rallies with small bombs. With CIA help, the opposition youth groups even started to arm themselves. They never actually mounted a serious uprising because Castro's intelligence agents kept them off guard. Therefore, many anti-Castro activists began to leave Cuba, joining their families in the massive exodus of the island's bourgeoisie. These opponents in the cities had resources to escape abroad relatively quickly, and the US embassy and consulates facilitated their departure. In just two years and several months, the *gusano* counterrevolution had moved entirely offshore to Miami. In contrast, the other counterrevolution, the one in the countryside, persisted three years longer, until 1965.

How did Castro's opposition relocate to Miami so quickly and so thoroughly? The answer has to do with the United States's policies enabling the migration of Castro's opponents. Urban activists such as Tony Zamora had greater access to the avenues of escape. Fidel Castro did little to block the exits because the departure of his opponents strengthened the revolutionary state and hastened the restructuring of Cuban society. US intelligence surmised that Castro's internal enemies were not succeeding, and sought to expedite their escape abroad. American agents and politicians believed that they could make the counterrevolution more powerful from Florida than from Havana. In the process, US policymakers unleashed an unexpectedly massive exodus. There were no refugee camps to spawn generations of embittered youth. Instead, entire families, generously subsidized, settled in and began to Latin Americanize South Florida. In the end, the counter-revolution in Miami proved to be just as ineffective as it had been in Havana. The size of the immigrant flow from Cuba to Florida actually enervated the anti-Castro movement because it incentivized anti-Castro dissidents to remain disunited, competing among themselves for economic resources rather than fighting Fidel.

MIDDLE-CLASS YOUTH

In the private secondary schools, most of which were operated by the Catholic Church, students came of age in the late 1950s visualizing themselves as part of the revolution against Batista. Their elder siblings at the public universities had started the protests against the "tyrant." They routinely planted homemade bombs—not to kill people but to disrupt city life. They revered the memory of José Antonio Echeverría, the university student leader who died in the 1957 attack on Batista's Presidential Palace. Then the dictator shut down the public universities. The middle-class youth who attended them, whether rebel or neutral, forewent classes and graduation. Older brothers of university age opposed Batista by performing acts of defiance against Batista's police forces and the SIM. SIM officers under Batista usually patrolled the cities dressed in street clothes but fully armed and driving in unmarked black Oldsmobiles.[4] Middle-class kids in Havana grew up cautious of black Olds.

The secondary schools of Belén and La Salle competed for the top students in Havana. Their teachers were Jesuit and Christian Brothers priests principally of Spanish birth and politically conservative. Fidel, who once studied under them at Belén, later called these clerical teachers "Falangists," right-wing followers of Generalissimo Francisco Franco. Yet not all priests, nor many of the families whose children they educated, particularly supported the Batista dictatorship. The Catholic secondary students walked out of classes during the April 1958 general strike called by the National Directorate of the 26th of July Movement.[5] These students felt themselves to be part of the revolution.

Armed activism belonged to middle-class youth—not to their parents. In times of national stress, Cuban parents had always reacted in ways that protected their families, usually not risking income and children. Unmarried students of university age, on the other hand, were free to react. Thus it had been in 1895 against Spanish rule and in 1933 against the prolonged presidency of Gerardo Machado. As the university generation of 1952 protested against Batista's coup, so too did the students of 1959 come to reject Castro's rule. These latter youths were ten to twelve years younger than Fidel, Raúl, and Che. They were enrolled in Catholic primary schools when Fidel attacked Moncada Barracks in 1953. They started taking classes at Belén and La Salle when Echeverría of the Revolutionary Directorate died in the assault on the Presidential Palace in 1957. Some were about to enroll in the universities in Havana, Santa Clara, and Santiago de Cuba when Batista closed down those roiling campuses. However, the Catholic University of Villanueva remained open. Its rector, Father John J. Kelly, had refused to allow political expression on campus, despite the fact that several Catholic youth organizations had endorsed the rebel movement.[6]

Once the revolution had triumphed, the new government under Prime Minister Fidel Castro began to make piecemeal decisions that alienated the younger generation of students. "Fidel seems to have forgotten completely that the students once supported his movement to the hilt. . . . Don't forget that plenty of us were killed by Batista's police," said one Villanueva student. Castro "only won because thousands of boys and girls risked their lives day and night in order to dynamite barracks and public buildings, collect information and generally undermine the morale of Batista's troops."[7] Even church officials, while officially seeking clemency in many cases, did not denounce the trials of "war criminals." They acknowledged the heinous killing and torturing of several thousand Cubans by the Batista regime. In January 1959, Archbishop Enrique Pérez Serantes said that the measures of the new revolutionary government "were not more numerous, not more harsh, than those applied in other places in similar circumstances by exceptionally responsible men."[8] But as the trials continued for several more months, church leaders became uneasy. It was the same with land reform.

The revolutionary state sought to transform the traditional autonomy and political activism of the universities—to eliminate white middle-class privilege from higher education. Castro betrayed his own origins. He picked on the Catholic students first, suspending classes at Villanueva University, because they had continued their studies in the last months of the fighting. Castro's education ministry refused to accept credits earned at Villanueva while the public universities had been shut down. Some high school and college graduations were invalidated. The revolutionaries heaped scorn on Father Kelly and his fifteen fellow North American Augustinians, who ran Villanueva University during the last years of the Batista dictatorship. Archbishop Pérez Serantes protested that the Castro government was denying the right of parents who wanted freedom of choice for religious education. He also requested that the state provide religious instruction in the public schools. He reminded his parishioners that Fidel himself had obtained his education at religious institutions, at Dolores in Santiago and at Belén in Havana.[9] Castro rejected the archbishop's requests.

When Father Kelly criticized these decisions, the government likened the Villanueva students to *batistianos* and *vendepatrias,* "sellers of the homeland" and collaborators with foreign capitalists. The Catholic Church again reacted defensively. Villanueva "is not, as it was affirmed the other day, a Yankee-land University," the bishops responded in an open letter to Fidel. It is a Catholic and national university, "a work of the Church whose faculty is formed almost entirely by Cubans."[10] The American-born Father Kelly resigned. In June 1959, the authorities permitted instruction at Villanueva University to begin under the administration of the Cuban-born Father Eduardo Boza Masvidal.[11] Some disenchanted youths found a natural ally in the Catholic Church.

University autonomy, the right of the faculty and students to run the public universities, did not survive the revolution's encroachment. Before classes resumed, the interim government held elections for the influential Federation of University Students (FEU), the student government of the nation's three autonomous public universities.[12] With his considerable prestige, Fidel Castro endorsed the candidacy of Comandante Rolando Cubela, veteran fighter of the Revolutionary Directorate. Cubela had subordinated himself to the M26 military leadership of Che Guevara at the battle of Santa Clara and turned over the DR's weapons following Fidel's "Arms for what?" speech. He won the student federation election handily.

Student activists had always shunned the communists in Cuba. In the struggle against Batista, the first protesters from the University of Havana in 1952 and 1953 scrupulously sought to exclude members of the Popular Socialist Party from their anti-coup rallies.[13] Echeverría's Revolutionary Directorate had no communist participants in its assault on the Presidential Palace in 1957. However, when classes resumed after the revolutionaries had triumphed, the communist party, the PSP, had become more emboldened and could no longer be excluded. Cubela's FEU began to purge faculty members and replace them with communists such as the very competent Carlos Rafael Rodríguez. Organization of a student militia force followed, staffed with one hundred youths who tolerated its Marxist-Leninist indoctrination. Commander-in-Chief Fidel Castro himself led the students and veteran M26 fighters on training marches through the Sierra Maestra.[14] Noncommunist students noticed that moderate politicos in the government were capitulating one by one and slipping into exile.

FEU president Rolando Cubela formed tribunals to dismiss students and faculty suspected of being insufficiently loyal to the revolution. In April 1960, he announced that the rebel armed forces would sponsor scholarships for the sons and daughters of the workers and peasants. Fistfights broke out on campus between opposing groups when the communist Carlos Rafael Rodríguez showed up to teach Marxist economics. FEU president Cubela denounced this "small group of playboys" for causing disturbances at the University of Havana. "As they are frankly involved in the counterrevolution," he went on, "they should be in the military prisons with the criminals of war, in order that they be judged before the Revolutionary Tribunals. We are not going to let them continue to come to the University to perturb our Revolution."[15] A student group affiliated with the Auténtico Party openly opposed the FEU for purposely subverting university autonomy. By the end of 1960, Cubela and the FEU had completely transformed the university's student body and faculty. More than one hundred former rectors and professors of the Universities of Havana, Santa Clara, and Santiago had fled to Miami.[16] Former university students followed—others preceded—their families into exile.

THE CATHOLIC OPPOSITION

As the revolution entered its second year, a group of Catholic activists decided to take action. Youth at Villanueva University had formed the Student Revolutionary Directorate, the DRE. It had its origins among the anti-Batista and now anti-Castro Catholic youth movement of the late 1950s. Its founders had been in Havana's Catholic *colegios* and Villanueva University in the final year of the Batista regime, and their opposition led them to revere the martyrdom of José Antonio Echeverría.[17] They named their action organization after Echeverría's Revolutionary Directorate. To them, Echeverría represented the pro-Catholic, anticommunist viewpoints to which they subscribed. They also resented the government's confrontation with the administrators of their Catholic university.

While the public universities were still closed early in 1959, some of these young men decided to act out their revolutionary commitment with Agriculture Minister Humberto Sorí Marín and M26 lieutenant Manuel Artime. Members of the DRE joined the Rural Commandos. Several journeyed to the foothills of the Sierra Maestra to prepare landless peasants for the expected redistribution of plantation lands into small farms. After all, this provision appeared in none other than the 1940 Constitution. They taught literacy classes and basic agronomy to landless rural workers.[18] However, Castro's land reform decree purposely transferred authority over agrarian reform from the Ministry of Agriculture to the National Agrarian Reform Institute, or INRA. The latter came to be dominated by communist bureaucrats and their Chinese advisers.[19] The bishops supported the idea of giving property titles to a new class of smallholders. But when INRA began collectivizing plantations, the clergy joined the critics. Church leaders accused Castro's revolutionaries of having "drunk from the same fountain" as the "moscovitas."[20]

Cuba's first land reform decree of May and June 1959 orphaned these youthful reformers of the DRE. Their benefactor, Minister of Agriculture Sorí Marín, resigned. But his Catholic acolytes enjoyed a brief reprieve when Lieutenant Manuel Artime of the M26 received an appointment at INRA to head up the land reform in Manzanillo. Though out of step with INRA's communist leadership, Artime and the Catholic youth leaders continued with their Rural Commando activities. Not long after the Comandante Huber Matos affair later that year, his superiors at INRA accused Lieutenant Artime of "misappropriating" state funds, a standard denouncement for corruption. They forced him to resign and go into hiding. The Catholic Church and the CIA helped Artime escape from Cuba.

Rural Commando participants Alberto Müller, Juan Manuel Salvat, and Luis Fernández Rocha returned to Havana and regrouped. They reconnected with friends of the Catholic University of Villanueva and immediately fell into the maelstrom of events surrounding the revolution's takeover of education. The US embassy was in touch with anticommunist student leaders such as Salvat and Müller, who edited the Catholic student publication *Trinchera,* which they distributed at Villanueva and the University of Havana.

Their opportunity to mount a noticeable protest came during the February 1960 visit of Anastas Mikoyan. The vice premier of the Soviet Union placed a flowered wreath, adorned with the hammer-and-sickle emblem, before the statue of José Martí. This monument to Cuba's *padre político* graces Havana's Central Park, located on the busy boulevard opposite the Capitolio, a governmental building resembling the US Congress. About an hour later, Müller, Salvat, and one hundred young men of the Catholic youth filed into Central Park and attempted to remove the wreath. They chanted, "¡Cuba, sí. Rusia, no!" Pro-government supporters who had witnessed Mikoyan's visit immediately reappeared carrying *Viva Fidel* signs. Policemen with pistols drawn surrounded the anticommunist protesters. There was scuffling. Alberto Müller and others subsequently served several days in "protective custody."[21] The incident figured among the first public protests against the revolutionary regime.

At about the same moment in March 1960 that President Eisenhower ordered the CIA to arrange for Castro's downfall, his intended victim was devising another institution for the revolution's survival. The French ammunition ship *La Coubre* had just exploded in Havana Harbor. It had been filled with arms and ordnance the revolutionary government had purchased in Europe. Fidel accused the CIA of sabotage. By that, he meant Cuban *gusanos* employed, armed, and directed by the American intelligence agency. A few months later, on his return from the United Nations, Fidel announced the formation of the Committees for the Defense of the Revolution, the CDRs, from the balcony of the Presidential Palace. "We're going to set up a system of revolutionary collective vigilance. And then we shall see how the lackeys of imperialism manage to operate in our midst," Castro said. "When the masses are organized there isn't a single imperialist, or a lackey of the imperialists, or anybody who has sold out to the imperialists, who can

Catholic youth marching to Havana's Central Park in the first public protest against communist party participation in the government. "Revolution, yes; Communism, no," one sign reads. "Castro saved Cuba," another proclaims. "Mikoyan wants to crush it."

operate." As he was speaking, two petards exploded nearby. "¡Al paredón!" the audience shouted, "to the execution wall."[22] The very next day, thousands began organizing at neighborhood levels, pressuring others less enthusiastic about the revolution. The CDRs served as neighborhood watch groups. They turned in the names of suspected counterrevolutionaries to the security police. Eventually, they gained the privilege of redistributing properties belonging to families going into exile. The CDRs also organized people in their neighborhoods for voluntary work in the countryside.[23] But the full implication of the organization of the committees did not become evident until the Bay of Pigs invasion.

During this process, the American embassy gathered intelligence on the internal resistance. Its analysis of revolutionary events tended to reflect the thinking of those middle-class dissidents the diplomats debriefed. The embassy's chargé d'affaires wrote a lengthy report on the domestic opposition in December 1960. He prefaced this document by estimating that the revolution's supporters amounted to less than one-quarter of the population. "At present it is within this largely uneducated, unthinking, highly emotional mass that Castro draws his main support."[24] Opposition among the professional middle class was growing, the diplomat said. Many doctors, lawyers, and engineers booked passage on the planes leaving the country, and a few remained to begin clandestine operations against the regime. When its upper-crust contacts disparaged Fidel's popularity with the masses as a form of demagoguery, so did US intelligence.

Cuban security agents posing as dissidents had contacts with CIA agents from the embassy. They assembled the names of these American operatives. Louis C. Hervert directed CIA intelligence in Havana between 1959 and January 1961. Robert E. Van Horn held the title of head of public affairs, a cover for his real job with the CIA. Agents John Z. Williams (code-named Frank) and political officer David Morales (a.k.a. Carlos Domínguez) held CIA staff positions. Cuban double agents were able to identify various coordinators of Manuel Artime's new counterrevolutionary movement, the Movement for Revolutionary Recovery, MRR. The CIA brought in arms for this fledgling group. One MRR leader in Las Villas, Cuban G-men reported, came from a wealthy family, studied at the Colegio de Belén, and belonged to the same university Catholic action group as Artime.[25] Government espionage networks may have lacked sophistication in the early days of the revolution, but they effectively monitored the dissidents. Cuban agents had already penetrated many of these *gusano* groups.

Cuba's G-2 also monitored the activities of CIA agent Austin Young. Young was posing as a tourist when, in March 1960, he succeeded in getting out the San Román brothers, José Alfredo and Roberto Pérez, both lieutenants in Batista's army. The San Románs were destined for command positions at the Bay of Pigs. Castro's police apprehended Young but later let him go. He left the country, then returned with another American, Peter Lambton. G-2 accused Lambton of recruiting about thirty rebels in order to commence a combat operation in the mountains of Pinar del Río Province. Authorities arrested Young once again and sentenced him to prison. Released in April 1963, Austin Young left definitively for the United States.[26]

Needless to say, the Agency was to depend on its linkages to the anti-Castro underground as its principal source of intelligence on the Cuban Revolution. It had no access inside Cuba to peasants and workers. US intelligence agents relied on Cuba's professional classes for their wishful interpretation of what was happening inside the country as the *brigadistas* (members of Brigade 2506) prepared for the invasion at the Bay of Pigs. They knew that

A CIA agent on trial for fomenting rebellion against the revolutionary government in 1960. Cuban State Security monitored such activity and succeeded in breaking up urban resistance groups.

Castro was announcing that the US invasion was coming. Yet they wrote off his warnings. "These moves by Fidel have caused the people to begin to laugh at him," CIA reports indicated, "which is the first indication of the downfall of Latin dictators."[27] CIA intelligence reported on the unpopularity of Castro: large groups were preparing to go into the hills as guerrillas; police quashed 350 electricians on strike; a thousand workers marched in protest.[28] One informant's brother-in-law inside Cuba reported that only 30 percent of the island supported Fidel. "In the 30 percent are included the negroes, who have always followed the strong man in Cuba, but will not fight," the informant said. "During the Batista regime, all negroes followed Batista's government."[29]

The titles of the CIA reports belied their misinformation. "Increasing Opposition to Castro" and "Indications in Camaguey of Increasing Dissatisfaction with CASTRO Government" lent credence to CIA planners of the Bay of Pigs. Many were predicting that the landing of Brigade 2506 would incite widespread uprisings throughout the island. Another trend in the reports coming into CIA headquarters at Langley confirmed a second assumption of the Bay of Pigs planners—that the growing numbers of militia units would not fight. "The militiamen left for the [Escambray] zone of fighting [against the rural counterrevolution] with little enthusiasm and only because they had no alternative," said one report. "It is generally believed," another source reported, "that approximately 75 to 80 per cent of the militia units will defect when it becomes evident that the real fight against CASTRO has begun."[30] Finally, just two days before the air strike that failed to take out all of Castro's fighter planes, the CIA issued its final intelligence analysis before the Bay of Pigs attack. "The pace of anti-Castro activity both inside Cuba and among Cuban exiles is mounting, and sabotage efforts against Cuban industrial and commercial installations are being stepped up," it stated. "Insurgent bands are actively engaging Castro's forces in several Cuban provinces."[31]

CIA agents at the US embassy monitored the situation, offering assistance to domestic opposition groups. Like the original DR, the DRE passed from unarmed protests to armed resistance. Isidro Borja of the Student Revolutionary Directorate returned to Cuba from several years in Canada studying for an engineering degree. He and his acquaintances in the DRE planned a raid on a weapons depot at the Mariel Naval Base. Approximately a dozen young men whose families had already abandoned Cuba agreed to join the operation. A police informer betrayed the conspiracy. Borja and others fled to the Costa Rican embassy, which arranged their travel to San José and Miami under diplomatic immunity.

At the end of 1960, a nucleus of DRE members gathered in Florida. They continued their anti-Castro activities with the assistance of the CIA station located on the south campus of the University of Miami. Some took training classes in light weapons and plastic explosives. Others learned radio communications at Viéques Island, Puerto Rico, and in the Panama Canal Zone. An English-only CIA agent named "Roger" prepared them to sneak back into Cuba in order to lead the anticommunist uprising that was to accompany the invasion of Brigade 2506. Borja spoke English fluently. He would meet the American agent for coffee, and "Roger" would hand over brown paper bags filled with thousands of dollars.[32]

CIA speedboats infiltrated Müller, Salvat, and others back to Havana, where they hid in safe houses of the underground. The closing of the US embassy in January 1961 deprived them of an easy exit and CIA support inside Cuba. On arriving in Havana, Müller penned a long letter to the newly inaugurated president Kennedy. He explained that his generation of students was fighting against communist control of government. Müller promised to

struggle for the restoration of private property rights in Cuba. He also promised to fight for the reinstatement of the noncommunist university faculty and
for freedom "of the pastoral activities of the Catholic bishops."[33] Müller's
uncle was the bishop of Holguín Province.

On a flight from Mexico City, the DRE's Isidro Borja returned to Havana
carrying a briefcase with one hundred thousand pesos in the false bottom.
Not only did he speak English, the result of three years' studying abroad,
but he had also been born while his Cuban parents were living in Mexico.
Borja's Mexican passport sped his way through customs. The DRE was
supposed to stockpile arms for the uprising, but the Cuban boat pilots arranged by the CIA failed to deliver. Feeling vulnerable in Havana, Müller
and several others decided to find refuge outside the capital. They returned
to the exact spot in the Sierra Maestra near Manzanillo where they had
worked two years before as Rural Commandos.

The creator of the Rural Commandos, former minister Humberto Sorí
Marín himself had stayed in Miami long enough to confer with his ex–prime
minister, José Miró Cardona, the head of the CIA's new Cuban Revolutionary Council. He received a briefing on the invasion plans for Brigade
2506. Sorí Marín resolved to return clandestinely to Havana to help prepare his friends in the underground. He chose a symbolic date to land by
boat east of Havana. It was March 13, 1961, the fourth anniversary of Echeverría's assault on Batista's office. However, Cuba's G-2 had already penetrated the Havana dissidents, and Castro's agents confiscated two tons of
weapons Sorí Marín had brought with him. Within three days, troops of
State Security surrounded the home in which the ex-minister was meeting
with underground leaders. They shot and wounded Sorí Marín as he tried
to escape. Several leaders of the pro-Catholic MRR were also captured with
him.[34] Fidel's former M26 lawyer from the Sierra Maestra was recovering
in jail when the brigade of exiles commenced its invasion.

THE BAY OF PIGS

Dawn on April 15, 1961, saw the quick unraveling of the urban resistance
inside Cuba. "I first learned about the Bay of Pigs invasion on Cuban radio,"
Cuban exile infiltrator Félix Rodríguez writes. "Outside I could see hundreds
of military trucks moving in the streets, and soldiers, armed."[35] The five-day

event known as the Bay of Pigs assault commenced on that date with an air strike. Fidel had prepared his supporters for the long-awaited invasion. The militias formed up, and the neighborhood watch organizations, the CDRs, collaborated in apprehending one thousand potential domestic enemies of the revolution. The government had thought that several small landings would occur all over the island. No one suspected the Bay of Pigs, surrounded by a swamp and distant from the Escambray Mountains, where the rural counterrevolution was already under way.

Government militiamen, G-2 agents, and CDR leaders mobilized even before the public learned of the invasion. "These forces, armed with machine-guns, systematically arrested anti-CASTRO Cubans and searched their homes," the CIA reported in the aftermath of the invasion. "The mass arrests, although involving many people who were innocent, succeeded in eliminating the Cuban underground." Those arrested and detained filled the movie theaters, the Havana Sports Palace, El Príncipe Prison, El Morro Castle, and the fortresses of La Cabaña and La Punta. Pro-government forces detained up to one hundred thousand suspected dissidents throughout the island.[36] One hundred thousand!

Other infiltrators in the anti-Castro urban underground scrambled to escape. José Manuel Salvat and Miguel García Armengol of the Student Revolutionary Directorate could not avoid capture. But a rapid and sloppy processing of so many detainees allowed Salvat to sneak out and find refuge in the Vatican's embassy. Others escaped to the Brazilian and Venezuelan embassies.[37] The DRE's Isidro Borja took advantage of his Mexican passport and left on a flight to Mexico City. His Mexican brother-in-law accompanied him and did all the talking at the airport so that Borja's *cubañol* accent would not tip off the guards. Others found refuge in the embassies. More than thirty days passed before the CIA's Félix Rodríguez found refuge. The MRR underground hid him until one of its operatives arranged to drive him to the Venezuelan embassy. Rodríguez bolted past the Cuban guard straight into the embassy's kitchen. He recognized the startled man having breakfast there and said, "Good morning, Mr. President."[38] It was former president Manuel Urrutia, still awaiting permission to leave the country after nearly two years.

The unfortunate went to prison. In Oriente Province, a company of militiamen detained the DRE's leader, Alberto Müller, as he was traveling toward Santiago de Cuba. At his Rural Commando base at a small town at the foot of the Sierra Maestra, they also rounded up some one hundred thirty others, principally peasants. They were waiting in vain for an expected cache of weapons to arrive by plane from the CIA air base in Guatemala. Müller was armed with a mere pistol, for which the judges sentenced him to seventeen years in prison. His crime had been to leave the country, enter into the service of the CIA, and return to Cuba in the *gusano* underground.[39] These acts amounted to treason. Nevertheless, the revolutionary tribunal treated the peasant followers of the *comandos rurales* with leniency.

Former agriculture minister Humberto Sorí Marín, on the other hand, paid the ultimate penalty. He and the MRR leaders were tried and executed as the last members of Brigade 2506 were losing the battle on the beach known as Playa Girón.

Tony Zamora, the spearfisherman who became a *brigadista,* did not hang around to be captured at Playa Girón. He had been a lieutenant with a mortar company of Brigade 2506. As a forward observer, he directed mortar fire on advancing revolutionary militia units. Then the infantry ran out of ammunition and was ordered back to the beach. In the third and last day of battle, his fellow *brigadistas* prepared to surrender. Lieutenant Zamora separated from the disorganized units and found a boat and shoved off into the surf. Days later he found himself floating near a mangrove swamp on the Isle of Pines, today the Isle of Youth. He could see the rooftops of Modelo Prison, which housed so many political prisoners over the years, including Fidel Castro. Soon two motorboats with *milicianos* aboard were coming at him from both sides, firing warning shots. Tony Zamora had no weapon. The militiamen on the two boats started to argue with each other over who was to get credit for the capture. "I spoke up and told them to share the credit," Tony recalls, and the *milicianos* agreed. "It was then I knew I would be a decent lawyer."[40]

CIA predictions about the cowardice of the militias and the certainty of a popular rebellion against Castro—these things did not transpire. The biggest failure of the Bay of Pigs, according to the CIA inspector general, arose "from the operators' failure to secure accurate intelligence."[41] Thus began the rapid decline of the *gusano* counterrevolution. But not without the final denouement of the clergy.

The church also became implicated in the Bay of Pigs invasion. Manuel Artime, founder of the pro-Catholic armed group, the MRR, was third-in-command in Brigade 2506. Three Spanish-born priests also accompanied the *brigadistas* as chaplains. One of them had a proclamation with him when captured. "We have come in the name of God," it stated. "Our struggle is that of those who believe in God against the atheists, the struggle of democracy against communism."[42]

The Catholic Church of Cuba had ministered principally to the urban middle class. In the 1950s, more than two hundred Catholic schools operated on the island, educating a total of sixty-two thousand students. More than half of the 1,872 clergymen and -women on the island taught at these Catholic schools. Less than one-third of the priests and nuns were Cuban by birth, and Spaniards made up the majority of the foreign-born clergy.[43] There were also fifty Protestant schools, one of which in Santiago had educated the future M26 revolutionary Frank País. The Bay of Pigs gave the revolutionary government the excuse it needed to nationalize all the private schools.

The church hierarchy fought back with words—no match for the revolutionary government. Militiamen showed up at religious masses and even looted a few church offices. In September 1961, on the feast day of the Copper Virgin of Charity (Virgen de la Caridad del Cobre), four thousand parishioners attended mass in Havana. Whipped up by the anti-government homily of Monseigneur Eduardo Boza Masvidal, the faithful marched on the Presidential Palace. A melee broke out. There was some gunfire, killing a bystander. Soon thereafter, the revolutionary government expelled 130 priests and religious leaders, sending them to Spain on the steamer *Covadonga*.[44]

The bishop of Holguín missed the ship. Earlier in the year, when his nephew, the DRE founder Alberto Müller, fell into the hands of the militias, the bishop sought refuge in the Argentinean embassy. He remained there until the following year, when Argentina's government broke diplomatic relations with Cuba and closed the embassy. According to the recollection of Fidel Castro himself, Müller's uncle retired peacefully to a Cuban "rest home" arranged by the Vatican's representative.[45]

Closely identified with the counterrevolutionary resistance, the church as an institution met its final demise during the invasion. The militias, made up of men of the popular classes not traditionally served by the Catholic Church in Cuba, surrounded the places of worship. Cardinal Arteaga sought asylum at the Argentine embassy; eight bishops on the island found themselves under house arrest. Many foreign-born priests who asked to leave voluntarily found refuge, while the government took over the religious schools where these priests had taught the sons of the Cuban bourgeoisie. "I know of no plans by Church authorities to take countermeasures against Castro," said one foreign-born priest when he landed in Miami.[46] Yet religious belief proved far more difficult to stamp out. An estimated eighty thousand people turned out for the Easter procession at La Parroquía de la Caridad in Havana. People on balconies and on the street waved white handkerchiefs as the new archbishop Boza Masvidal led the procession. Parishioners filled the churches on the island.[47] Still, the Bay of Pigs invasion marked the end of church influence in domestic affairs on the island.

Fidel's opponents certainly did not see themselves as "worms" or even as counterrevolutionaries. They did not deviate from the original goals of the revolution—namely an end to the police state and to rigged elections. It was Castro and his lieutenants who made the revolution something else altogether. Therefore, to criticize the communists amounted to patriotism, not treason. To oppose restrictions on educational and religious choice epitomized liberty. Refusing to join the militias and the Committees for the Defense of the Revolution proved no less one's love for country and way of life. Castro's critics did not view themselves as "selling out the fatherland." Those who delivered the *patria* to the Russians deserved that epithet, Castro's opponents reasoned.

THE EXODUS

Like the revolution itself, the Cuban immigration crisis seems to have come as a surprise to the Eisenhower administration. The White House had been preoccupied with US interests being damaged by the land reform decree, the oil refinery crisis, communist infiltration, Soviet sugar purchases, US reduction of Cuban sugar quotas, and the resultant nationalization of American-owned businesses. The president could be forgiven for being startled by the exodus to Miami of Cuba's formidable middle class. Nothing like this had ever occurred before. Out-of-favor Cuban politicians had resided in Florida always temporarily, ever since the nineteenth century. What astonished Floridians and Washingtonians alike was the exodus of such a large portion of Cuba's middle class.

Even before the watershed moment of the first land reform, there were signs. In March 1959, urban landlords could not mistake the import of Premier Castro's edict reducing rents by 50 percent. It chagrined property owners and pleased the popular classes.[48] Many cane farmers, *colonos,* were middle-class urban residents who made their living in the professions or politics. They owned farms and hired laborers and contracted tenants to manage them. From the beginning, the communist party bureaucrats appointed to the INRA had favored cooperative farms over private property units. Government bureaucrats were conducting the land reform in ways not at all stipulated by the May agrarian reform decree.

Then came the indignity to many *habaneros* living in middle-class neighborhoods—they had to open up their homes to peasants in July 1959. Fidel had invited his country supporters to Havana by the thousands to celebrate the first 26th of July anniversary, which was the revolution's most sacred holiday. That was when professionals, students, and Catholic nationalists began leaving for Florida to join—uneasily—the Díaz-Balarts, Rolando Masferrer, Esteban Ventura (the White Angel of Death), and other *batistianos* who fled in the first days of January 1959. Batista's supporters already had had a good five months to consolidate their positions in Miami. Beginning in May, many in the Cuban middle class began to grow weary of the politics of revolutionary consolidation and started to leave the island. They lined up by the hundreds at the US embassy and consulates in order to apply for visas. When Washington broke diplomatic relations with Havana in January 1961, reported CIA director Allen Dulles, "50,000 applicants for US visas in Cuba were very distressed."[49] Thus did the Cuban counterrevolution move abroad to roost in Miami.

The massive inflow from the island nation overwhelmed Florida. Authorities in Dade County wrote President Eisenhower that Miami's welfare system could not absorb the thousands of new Cubans arriving there on tourist visas. They needed state and federal assistance.[50] Orders went out from the Oval Office to investigate the enormity of the problem. Respondents reported that the migratory flow from Cuba had gained strength as the revolutionaries took over private property and equated opposition to communism with treason. "The middle and upper classes are clearly being systematically destroyed," American travelers reported. "The majority of these elements, including most of Castro's original supporters in the middle and upper groups, appear . . . to be jittery, demoralized and disillusioned."[51]

As for political refugees, Cubans had always made Miami the preferred destination in the twentieth century. The number of political exiles living in Miami had risen nearly sevenfold during the repressive years following Batista's coup d'état in 1952, reaching some fifteen thousand émigrés in 1956.[52] The total included one former president, Carlos Prío Socarrás, and an entourage of ex-officials of his government. Fidel passed through, collecting money from them, while his men trained in Mexico. Then in the first month of 1959, as the Auténtico and Ortodoxo party members traveled in the other direction to Havana, several thousand *batistianos* arrived as exiles in Miami. Many Batista collaborators had had the good sense beforehand to deposit in Florida banks the cash they had acquired in government service.

However, the new immigration to Miami that began in 1961 differed from the bags-of-money sort that the *batistianos* had typified. Those applying to leave the country, beginning in 1961, lost their jobs as they waited for their departure passes. Castro's revolutionaries did not allow money transfers or property sales. When members of the middle class fled from revolutionary Cuba, the government allowed them only a few dollars in cash before they boarded the Pan American and Cubana flights. Militiawomen at the airport zealously strip-searched society women and confiscated gold earrings and diamond rings.[53] The government took over the urban and rural properties of those who left. These new arrivals doubled and tripled up on housing in downtown Miami. They sent their children to public schools, paying the fifty dollars per year in noncitizen's tuition for an education that cost the city three hundred fifty dollars per pupil. Local school districts exempted some immigrant families who could not pay the fee. Cuban kids got free lunches at school. The budget of the Miami School Board grew by hundreds of thousands of dollars in 1960 merely to accommodate Cuban youngsters.

The Southern Democratic establishment of Florida had to raise taxes to support the growing Cuban community. But because the immigrant scale had grown beyond anyone's expectation—thirty-two thousand Cubans inhabited South Florida in 1960—the state appealed to the federal government.[54] Presidents Eisenhower, Kennedy, and Johnson alike responded generously. So did the Catholic charities and individual and corporate donors. The new immigrants were refugees from international communism, after all.

While the US government searched for long-term solutions, charities and donations provided some immediate relief. The Catholic Church established

Two young girls wait at the Cuban Refugee Center in Miami while their parents undergo processing.

the Catholic Hispanic Center in Miami. It placed Cuban immigrants in jobs, provided money for needy families, dispensed medical care, collected canned and dried foods, gave free classes on traffic rules, and collected thousands of dollars from the Palm Beach Women's Society. The Texaco Oil Company pledged a donation of one hundred thousand dollars. Cardinal Spellman of New York sent out a call for monetary offerings in the nation's Catholic parishes. The Rockefeller Foundation also responded with aid. Florida's governor, LeRoy Collins, set up a job registry to record the skill set of each Cuban looking for work. State employees discovered that more than three hundred physicians had arrived in the immigrant flow. However, neither the Florida state government nor the charities could match the enormity of the problem. In some weeks, one thousand Cubans arrived. President Eisenhower pledged to spend one million dollars from the federal budget on Cuban relocation. The federal government also sent tax dollars to help state employment agencies handle twenty thousand unemployed Cubans.[55]

Finally, the outgoing Eisenhower administration established the United States Committee for Cuban Refugees under the direction of Tracy S. Voorhees. He was the logical choice for the job. Voorhees had performed the same function for thirty-two thousand refugees from communism when Russian troops crushed the 1956 Hungarian Rebellion.[56] The much larger Cuban program owed much to America's prior experience with the Hungarian exodus. Voorhees immediately began a survey of the Cuban immigration problem. "No Cuban refugee . . . is now without an immediate source of assistance if he seeks it," Voorhees told Congress in January 1961. "None for the time being need go without food, clothing, housing, emergency medical care, or assistance in finding employment."

Voorhees found that fifty thousand Cubans then were living in the United States, thirty-six thousand in South Florida alone. An additional four thousand congregated in Newark, New Jersey, and still others in the New York area. Sixty-five hundred Cuban children, described as "generally a very high type of student from ambitious, education-minded families," were going to Miami public and parochial schools. "There are a lot of very fine people coming into our schools," one Miami principal told Voorhees. "They can be fine ambassadors for us, if they return to Cuba; or fine potential citizens of the United States, if we handle things right." In addition, the University of Miami provided twenty college scholarships to Cuban young men and women. The Federal Refugee Center registered 112 accountants, 125 lawyers, 140 physicians, 142 professors and teachers, 81 engineers, and 166 business managers.[57] This immigrant group had solid middle-class origins. There were surplus food programs, care for unaccompanied children, English courses for doctors and lawyers, and scholarships of one thousand dollars per year for Cuban students at American universities. Special loan programs for Cubans helped finance university education even before federal Pell grants were available for US citizens. Government insiders in 1963 were saying that six of every ten immigrants drew "money from the Cuban refugee relief program."[58]

United States taxpayers paid the bill for an extensive airlift of Cuban refugees. The flights allowed Castro's supporters to express their resentments of the privileged middle class. "At the airport, the *milicianos* made us disrobe and they checked all of our personal belongings," said one woman. "They were so arrogant, those *milicianos*. But we didn't say anything because if we did, they wouldn't let us leave."[59] Castro nationalized the private schools after the Bay of Pigs, alarming parents. Even before they themselves could get visas, mothers and fathers sent their children out of the country in the Peter Pan program. "I did not get to finish my third year in high school," one refugee remembers. "Also, there were rumors that the government intended to take all children away from their parents for indoctrination. Panic had set in."[60] The *disgustados* (those unhappy with the revolution) resisted the coerced recruitment of their children into the Young Pioneers, a communist youth group. Said one father, "I do not want the boys to be ruled by anyone but me."[61] The religious orders and the US government cooperated in assisting middle-class families with exit documentation.

Unaccompanied by mothers or fathers, ten-to-eighteen-year-old kids in the Peter Pan program also suffered humiliation as they exited the country. "I was ten years old, but I had just learned how to tie my own shoelaces," writes Carlos Eire. "I had never cut my own steak or buttered my own toast. I'd never lifted a finger to do anything around the house. No chores. No responsibilities."[62] Housework at the home of young Carlos had been the responsibility of Afro-Cuban housemaids. Most of the Peter Pan children were white. Fidel called them the "pampered children." Carlos Eire described his own flight from Cuba as "sheer torture." Those working-class youths who joined the militias and supported the revolution resented the privileged upbringing of the Peter Pan kids. Stern-faced, uniformed airport personnel separated ten-year-old Carlos from his mother and placed him for three hours in a glassed-off waiting room he called the "fish bowl." He could not talk to his loved ones or caress them prior to takeoff. He subsequently lived in Chicago and other locations with foster parents arranged by Catholic charities. He waited for three years for his mother to gain permission to leave Cuba.[63]

More than fourteen thousand children arrived in Florida during the first two years of the Peter Pan program. Relatives took in about half of the newcomers, and religious charities in Florida, Nebraska, New Mexico, Colorado, and Louisiana cared for the others until the families could be reunited. The US government was paying $5.50 per day for an unaccompanied child in a private home and $6.50 per day in group settings.[64] Miami residents of the Protestant and Jewish faiths opened their homes to the Peter Pan kids who arrived in Florida without their parents. When the adults finally arrived, American taxpayers kicked in for the cost of reuniting parents and Peter Pan kids.

Cuban immigration also overwhelmed the African American community of Miami. The chapter of the National Association for the Advancement of Colored People in South Florida complained of the jobs that black employees lost to the newcomers. "There are many . . . categories of employment . . . that Negroes no longer enjoy as a direct result of the Cuban influx," wrote one black leader. He said that his organization supported refugees from communist dictatorship. "We feel, however, that the Federal Government must exercise its responsibilities toward the economically oppressed . . . as well as toward the political oppressed."[65] Florida's government acknowledged the social disruptions that the Cuban refugees had caused. "Their presence has created tremendous economic problems especially among our Negro citizens who were filling positions with service establishments such as hotels, restaurants and other non-skilled areas of employment," the governor informed the White House.[66] Florida officials conferred in Washington, DC, with the secretary of the Department of Health, Education, and Welfare. The federal government was paying to resettle thousands of Cuban professionals outside of Florida.[67]

The US airlift ended with the October 1962 Missile Crisis. Immigration did not. The economic boycott imposed on Cuba by the US government closed off all direct air traffic between the two countries. In 1963 and 1964, more Cubans of the white middle class had to flee through a variety of indirect means. They flew to Mexico City and crossed the Rio Grande. They hijacked a ferryboat and sailed it into the Guantánamo Naval Base. They abandoned their fishing boats on the Yucatán in Mexico and headed north. Cubans got themselves to Madrid, Jamaica, and the Bahamas and applied for US visas. Ships heading toward the Panama Canal picked up Cuban refugees in foundering boats and dropped them off in the Canal Zone. The United States proved reluctant to turn these people away.[68] By 1966, the Cuban population of the United States had grown to 260,000. The

White House announced in 1965 that the cost of the Cuban Refugee Program amounted to thirty-two million dollars per year.[69]

The Cuban Revolution had succeeded in changing Florida and the United States. Refugees also benefited from funding from the US government—very generous subsidies indeed when compared to those destined for Puerto Ricans and Dominicans. Cuban refugees became the most successful Hispanic immigrant population in America—and a politically conservative group as well. The Mexicans, whose ancestors once claimed all of the US Southwest, fared poorly by contrast. The fact that Cubans were refugees from communism made all the difference. Mexicans, Puerto Ricans, and Dominicans came predominantly for jobs.

One other characteristic distinguished these first Cuban immigrants. Few of them applied for citizenship. All intended to return to Cuba as soon as someone drove Castro from power.

THE COUNTERREVOLUTION ABROAD

Following the Bay of Pigs debacle of April 1961 and the missile crisis of October 1962, the White House lost all illusions about a quick return of the refugees to Cuba. In fact, the situation worsened. "While Miami has performed remarkably thus far, local facilities are being taxed and tensions are rising," the National Security Council informed President Lyndon Johnson. "The general feeling of the government officials on the spot is that there must be a further outflow of refugees from the Miami Area."[70] One hundred and forty thousand Cubans lived in Miami, and their numbers were growing with the arrival of nearly one thousand more every week. One White House adviser said it was time to "free up the [the federal government's] resettlement capability. By now, many in Miami ought to realize they are not returning to Cuba soon and might be willing to resettle out of Florida." Other states and locals could "get a deal" with the influx of professional Cubans, the presidential aide speculated.[71]

The enormity of the émigré flow provoked an effort to relocate the Cubans (at government expense) to areas of the country in need of professional services. Leaders of the Cuban community especially resisted resettlement because they feared that, once removed from South Florida, say, to Abilene, Texas, repatriation to Cuba itself might fade from the agenda. "Once the exile colony is gone from Miami and scattered across the United States," said one immigrant politician, "the Cuban issue is dead. That's what happened with the Hungarian Refugees."[72]

An additional form of cash infusion to the exile community consisted of CIA payments to the families of the *brigadistas*. The CIA considered members of Brigade 2605 as employees. From April 1961 to January 1962, the CIA disbursed a total of $311,500 monthly to dependents of the prisoners. Each member's family received between $175 and $350 per month, depending on the number of dependents. CIA director John A. McCone opined that the Agency should continue to make payments to family members as long as the brigade members remained imprisoned in Cuba. "To cut off payments might subject the American government to charges of bad faith and of placing a dollar value on human beings," McCone said. "Further, we might be subjected to possible legal action."[73]

Now, in 1963, the United States government braced itself for another embarrassment. Many Cubans in Miami began turning against the host government and its CIA handlers. The Agency's counterrevolutionary allies were blaming their failures on Washington. "Public opinion [among the resistance] is unfavorable to the United States," one agent reported, "which is considered to have been the cause of defeat." The CIA-appointed Cuban Revolutionary Council and its director, José Miró Cardona (whose *brigadista* son was then languishing in a Cuban prison), were held in low regard. Others said that the captured *brigadistas* talked too much in Cuban-televised interrogations.[74] The anti-American feeling spread particularly among the majority of the Bay of Pigs prisoners housed in El Príncipe Prison in Havana and at Modelo Prison on the Isle of Pines. Their commander, José San Román, had lost prestige among the men, and individual *brigadistas* faced ostracism for admitting to being trained by the CIA. But San Román's executive officer, Erneido Oliva, helped reestablish morale with military discipline. Family members in Cuba who visited prisoners were reporting that "the majority of the Brigade has a marked anti-U.S. feeling."[75] Miami émigrés speculated that returning brigade members might criticize the United States government.

Thereafter, the CIA refurbished its intelligence conduit for arriving refugees. In March 1962, the Agency set up the Caribbean Admission Center at the former Marine air base at Opa Locka. The Immigration and Naturalization Service had established reception services there as well. The CIA interviewed males between sixteen and sixty years of age. They solicited information on the respondents' past addresses, service in the military, biographical data, and membership in revolutionary and anti-Castro organizations. In 1962, the interrogators also inquired about "Sino-Soviet Bloc personnel, and activities in Cuba and names of members of the Cuban internal security forces." US intelligence agents generated 5,500 reports and 75,000 documents. They were also making assessments about those Cuban young men who would be "candidates for anti-Castro clandestine activity or actively engage in such activity."

The payoff came in early June 1962. Refugees were reporting "suspicious Soviet activities and rumors that offensive military weapons, especially long-range missiles, were to be introduced into Cuba."[76] Based on these reports, the US government sent reconnaissance flights of U-2 spy planes over Cuba and discovered the Soviet missile buildup. The subsequent Cuban Missile Crisis may have been a triumph for Kennedy, but America's victory over the Soviet Union did not make it possible for the Miami émigrés to reclaim their properties and political positions in Cuba. The refugees on whom the US government had lavished much financial support now blamed their benefactor.

The return to Miami of the freed fighters of Brigade 2506 presented the Kennedy administration with another kind of resettlement problem. The American government could not abandon more than a thousand Bay of Pigs veterans who had just spent eighteen months in Cuban prisons. The administration decided to drop the "unduly rigid adherence to current high induction standards" in order to conduct US Army basic training courses for the returnees. Those who chose this training could serve as members of the Army Reserves. US armed forces would provide English language training. Attorney General Robert Kennedy suggested that the Cubans might serve in Special Forces teams in Latin America. "Their firsthand experience with Communism," he speculated, "could be used to great advantage in Latin American countries in explaining the threat of Communism." Other Cuban refugees could become intelligence agents, and still others could travel in Latin America as scholars, lecturers, and student leaders.[77] US officials did not want the embittered Brigade 2506 veterans to "turn hostile."

When the *brigadistas* did return in January 1963, the CIA also paid the former prisoners a bonus of $250 on landing at Homestead Air Force Base. Then the agency released the men to federal welfare rolls, which entitled them "to the benefits and assistance afforded to normal Cuban political refugees." The federal Department of Housing, Education, and Welfare paid each arrival an additional $100 ($60 for emergency expenses and $40 for clothing). All payments to the dependents were made through the Cuban Revolutionary Council. In fact, the CIA continued to pay the *brigadistas* their monthly paychecks through April 1963.[78]

Finally, the Kennedy administration pondered the creation of a special Cuban brigade in the United States Army. All veterans of the "Armed Forces of Liberation" (denoting those who trained for and / or fought at the Bay of Pigs) received an invitation to undergo basic training in the army. Officers of Brigade 2506 automatically entered officers' training courses. Noncommissioned officers and soldiers qualified for the basic training program for enlisted personnel. Antonio "Tony" Zamora, who wanted to sink a Chinese ship with an underwater limpet mine, qualified for officer training in the Navy Reserves.[79] Many Cuban young men who did not serve in Brigade 2506 also enlisted in the training courses.

Two years after the assault on Playa Girón, more than twenty-three hundred Cuban young men were participating in military training programs at Fort Jackson, South Carolina. The first company of 207 men had already completed basic training, with another two hundred finishing every week thereafter until twelve companies of Cuban soldiers had completed basic training. Most returned to civilian life and served in Army Reserve units. Others signed up for a two-year tour of active duty in the US Army. An estimated twenty-seven hundred Cubans were taking American military training. Not all were former *brigadistas*.

In this cauldron, the Kennedy administration prepared the next stew for Fidel Castro. The *Miami Herald* broke the news that Bobby Kennedy was heading up the anti-Castro project. He had already interviewed several leaders of Brigade 2506 in the attorney general's office in Washington, DC. Photos of this meeting appeared in the nation's newspapers showing broad smiles on the face of the attorney general and on those of Manuel Artime, Erneido Olivo, Enrique Ruiz Williams, and José and Roberto San Román. The Cubans at Fort Bragg came to be known as "Bobby's Boys." Manuel Artime, who was traveling in Central America at CIA expense, arranged a special visit to the officer trainees at Fort Bragg. Speculation in Miami had it that Bobby's Boys would soon be engaging in hit-and-run raids on Cuba.[80]

While its founder, Alberto Müller, languished in a Cuban prison, the DRE regrouped in Miami under the leadership of Juan Manuel Salvat. Isidro Borja's and Salvat's harrowing escapes after the Bay of Pigs fiasco boosted the group's prestige. Hundreds of youths in Miami enrolled in the DRE. Corresponding members included Cuban students pursuing their studies in other countries of Latin America. Miami leaders of the DRE took extensive trips to Bolivia, Peru, Brazil, and Chile. They appeared at anticommunist student rallies informing like-minded Latin American youth about the communist takeover of the Cuban Revolution and about Müller and other students still held in Castro's prisons. They gained press coverage in Latin America for their work. DRE representatives concentrated on the private, Catholic institutions of higher education rather than the public universities that formed the cradle of pro-Castro agitation in the 1960s. Representatives of the DRE lobbied delegates at meetings of the Organization of American States in Washington and Latin America.

Salvat and his colleagues engaged in armed struggle on just one occasion. No one at the White House or at Miami's CIA station had authorized the attack. The DRE obtained two fast boats and a small arsenal of machine guns and cannons. In late August 1962, twenty-two young men overcame the jitters and maneuvered their boats alongside the oceanfront Hotel Icar in the fashionable Havana suburb of Miramar. The hotel was known as a hangout for Soviet and East European advisers, who were holding a reception there on the evening of the attack. The DRE operatives opened a fusillade of gunfire. No one was killed in the lightning raid. The attackers purposely aimed high so as to avoid casualties. After just seven minutes, the attackers turned their boats northward and sped off before Cuban naval craft could respond.

Time magazine featured a photo of Juan Manuel Salvat and three accomplices posing on one of the boats. Later, Salvat told the press that the raid "was all Cuban—planned and executed by Cubans without any foreign organism having anything to do with it." Isidro Borja mentioned that DRE contacts in Havana informed them about a massive Russian military buildup that would lead to the October missile crisis. "We were told to launch the action on a Friday night," Borja said, "because that was the time Russian and Czech 'technicians' gathered [at the Hotel Icar]."[81] Following the hotel assault, Salvat and others launched a speaking tour of the United States, collecting cash donations along the way.

In a letter to President Kennedy, DRE leaders compared their colleagues in the Cuban diaspora to the Hungarians of 1956 who had stood up to Soviet tanks. Their letter extolled the imprisoned *brigadistas* who fought against Russian tanks at the Bay of Pigs and Müller's Rural Commandos of the Sierra Maestra who opposed the Red Tyranny while "the nations of the Free World limited their aid to reticent moral support." The DRE did not shy away from a more active but unspecified role by the United States in overthrowing Fidel. But when the American government sought to ransom the imprisoned *brigadistas,* the DRE said no. Giving aid to Castro would weaken the anticommunist underground inside Cuba, spokesmen said.[82] The DRE's opposition to paying for the release of imprisoned Brigade 2506 prisoners alienated other Cubans in Miami who wanted their relatives returned.

The Hotel Icar assault concluded the armed resistance of the Student Revolutionary Directorate, and thereafter they returned to traveling abroad in support of US anti-Castro policies in Latin America. Several DRE members joined conservative Ecuadorians in the capital of Quito in celebrating their government's break of diplomatic relations with Cuba. Ecuador's Catholic cardinal addressed the "tens of thousands" of his countrymen who had gathered to denounce godless communism. Several DRE members shared the stage and arranged to present the cardinal with a Cuban flag. One intelligence agent stationed in Quito described the Student Revolutionary Directorate as "run by the [CIA's] Miami station and in some countries the local representatives are run directly by station officers." Later, this same agent, Philip Agee, encountered the DRE in Uruguay. "More anti-Cuban propaganda," Agee observed from the CIA station at Montevideo. "Representatives of the Revolutionary Student Directorate in Exile . . . an organization financed and controlled by the Miami station, arrived today. They're on a tour of South America hammering away at the Cuban economic disaster."[83]

The subsequent history of the DRE illustrates well the limitations of the counterrevolution abroad. It became an anti-Castro propaganda machine, funded generously by the CIA. Moreover, it served Castro well. The DRE and many other groups of this kind in Miami did not threaten the regime at all. To the contrary, their existence and visibility served Castro's own propaganda machine that sustained popular mobilization at home and reminded his supporters abroad of US threats. Premier Fidel Castro wanted the world to know that he condemned "the recent Havana raid by counter-revolutionary mercenaries of US imperialism. We hold the US Government responsible for this new and cowardly attack upon our country," Castro stated. "Before world opinion we condemn the aggressive plans which imperialism is preparing against Cuba." For the domestic audience, the pro-government newspaper *Revolución* ran photographs of the damage at the Hotel Icar.[84] The revolutionary government found it very advantageous to portray itself at home and abroad as a victim of a powerful neighbor and its *gusano* surrogates.

Members of the DRE continued to travel, to give interviews, to spread warnings of communist subversion, and to plead with their handlers to give them more military assets. Regular reports about DRE activities and plans went out to the CIA. But DRE leaders took it upon themselves to organize an armed resistance group capable of invading Cuba. With the assistance of conservative politicians and military generals, they set up a training camp at a remote coastal military zone in the Dominican Republic and commenced, with pistols and hunting rifles, to engage in military training in the hot sun. It all came to naught in April 1965, when a constitutionalist army revolt in Santo Domingo prompted President Johnson to send US troops into the Dominican Republic. He wanted to avoid the dreaded "second Cuba" in the old-fashioned way—not by the CIA and not by Cold War surrogates like the DRE. Instead, Johnson intervened in the internal affairs of a Latin American country with US armed forces for the first time since President Franklin Delano Roosevelt had proclaimed the Good Neighbor Policy in 1933.

The exodus helped Fidel Castro stay in power over the long term in two ways. It first helped flush out internal opposition at no cost to the revolutionary state. In fact, the United States paid the expenses for the relocation of whole families—indeed, for a substantial portion of Cuba's middle class. Fortunately for Fidel and his followers, theirs was an island revolution. The defecting dissidents could not take up positions just across a land border, as the so-called Contras did later against the *sandinista* revolutionaries of Nicaragua. The regime merely had to be vigilant but did not have to build the equivalent of a Berlin Wall or an Iron Curtain. The émigrés in Miami lived close enough for propaganda purposes yet were separated from Havana by the Straits of Florida.

Second, the out-migration gave Fidel's government a permanent enemy with which to rally those who remained behind. Men and women of pre-revolutionary privilege who turned their backs on "the people" served the revolutionary state very well. Moreover, to have these dissidents removed to the United States, the historical threat to Cuba's full sovereignty, allowed revolutionaries to utilize the powerful tool of nationalism. "Patria o muerte," intoned Fidel at the end of every speech. Also, revolutions by their very newness require a clear and present "danger" to mobilize the citizenry. "To develop himself, the revolutionary needs his antithesis," the editors of *Revolución* wrote in February 1959, "which is the counterrevolutionary."[85] For the next half century, Fidel Castro's revolution survived by reminding citizens that they stood to lose schools, medical clinics, housing, and basic subsistence if the Miami Cubans returned to reclaim their properties. The argument, often repeated in Castro's speeches, sufficed to elicit demonstrations of public support. Everyone could hate the formerly privileged *gusanos.*

The anti-Castro activities of the counterrevolution abroad actually helped Fidel perfect the revolution at home. He did not attempt to censor news about armed attacks. Unlike Batista, he did not ignore his opponents. To the contrary, Fidel frequently cited such activities in his speeches and *Hoy, Revolución,* and the photo weekly *Bohemia* publicized the armed attacks and the verbal assaults of the DRE and other anticommunist groups. The message: these Cubans of privileged birth want their property back. And so do their imperialist American backers.

All during the counterrevolutionary struggle, Castro's government blamed the CIA for sponsoring, financing, and directing the Cuban counterrevolution. His many denunciations of US meddling served the purpose of highlighting international opposition to the Cuban Revolution. He mobilized his domestic and international supporters to resist both the United States and the counterrevolution. Fidel Castro was not completely wrong. Politics in Washington could not accommodate the Cuban Revolution, which explains why the White House directed the CIA to assist counterrevolutionary movements inside and outside of Cuba. Yet the counterrevolution proved so divided and factionalized that no amount of US financing and assistance could mold it into a coherent mass. In fact, the presence of CIA money favored some Cuban organizations—the Cuban Revolutionary Council and the Student Revolutionary Directorate—and alienated others until factionalism ruined any chance for unity among anticommunist Cubans in Miami. Thanks to US generosity, the *gusano* counterrevolution had entirely relocated to Miami by the end of 1961. There it waited, nourished on CIA largesse, until the United States did something to get rid of Fidel.[86] Meanwhile, the anticommunist dissidents abandoned the battlefield inside Cuba to the counterrevolutionaries in the countryside.

For a brief while, even the automobiles driving up and down the Havana waterfront on the Malecón engaged in ideological battle. Many cars carried a sticker saying, "We are Catholics, in case of accident please call a priest." Others had messages stating, "We are Communists, in case of accident please call a doctor."[87]

CHAPTER FIVE

The *Bandido* Counterrevolution

THE REVOLUTIONARY STATE disparaged them as *bandidos,* "outlaws, criminals." Yet several leaders of the rural counterrevolution had fought in or sympathized with the local resistance to Fulgencio Batista. They saw themselves passed over for jobs and rewards by communist bureaucrats. Communism was changing Cuba and their way of life for the worse, and they were willing to die or serve long prison terms for their resistance. No, in their own minds, they were not mere brigands. These rebels were *alzados,* those who rise up in rebellion for the sake of justice and patriotism. The term *alzados* originally referred to runaway slaves who escaped into several of the island's mountain ranges. It also applied to the followers of José Martí and Antonio Maceo in the 1895 rebellion for independence from Spain.[1] Now, in late 1959, the *alzados* again took up arms, and, for a while, Osvaldo Ramírez was their champion.

Like other counterrevolutionaries, Ramírez too had fought against Batista. When he joined the Second National Front of the Escambray in 1958, Ramírez had been driving a truck, hauling sugarcane during the harvest and timber from the Escambray Mountains during the "dead season." He served as a lieutenant under Comandantes Eloy Gutiérrez Menoyo and William Morgan. Osvaldo Ramírez distinguished himself in the revolution. His reward after the victory consisted of a position in the new National Revolutionary Police Force.[2] In May 1959, when Prime Minister Fidel Castro decreed the land reform law, former members of the Second Front began meeting in conspiratorial groups. They smuggled arms and supplies to their old hideouts.

In October 1959, Osvaldo Ramírez rose in revolt *(alzarse)* in opposition to the presence of communists in the Castro regime. Early in the uprising, a government militia force came upon Ramírez's rebels. His eighteen men engaged these first militiamen in a firefight and forced them into retreat. Months later, Osvaldo was leading a force of thirty-eight men. Another militia unit trapped them at the edge of a cliff. "We can die here fighting," Ramírez told his men as night approached, "or we can jump."[3] They jumped into the ravine below and escaped in the darkness.

Thousands of revolutionary militiamen pursued several small bands of outlaws throughout 1960, yet the number of *bandidos* rose. Osvaldo's group dispersed and escaped encirclement on several occasions, only to regroup later on. Ramírez himself was captured and escaped miraculously by throwing himself over another, higher cliff.

Osvaldo Ramírez became a well-known figure when he single-handedly created another martyr for the revolution. The National Agrarian Reform Institute (INRA) in 1961 engaged literacy teachers to prepare the peasants for their revolutionary roles. Volunteer mentors went into the hills between the cities of Cienfuegos and Trinidad at the same time that the counterrevolutionary bands began to multiply. One of these volunteers was an Afro-Cuban young man named Conrado Benítez. Osvaldo's band captured the teacher together with the head of the peasant family with whom Benítez was living. According to government sources, the rebel leader became enraged when the literacy teacher would not renounce the Castro revolution. "The stoning and knife stabs did not cease until the moment that Osvaldo decided to string him up by the neck," an *alzado* later confessed. "The body was suspended and lowered on various occasions as if it were a doll until [Conrado Benítez's] life expired, at which time we just left him hanging."[4] Fidel Castro himself eulogized the literacy teacher in his next speech. "He was poor, he was a Negro, and he was a teacher," Fidel said of Benítez. "There you have three reasons why the agents of imperialism assassinated him."[5]

Castro's accusation contained an element of truth. Urban allies belonging to the Auténtico Party network in Havana had been using connections to the CIA at the American embassy to direct airdrops into the Escambray for Osvaldo's *alzados*. President Eisenhower closed the embassy in January 1961, which complicated the delivery of arms. Thereafter, Auténtico operatives in Havana had to make arrangements by radio with Miami. Nonetheless, government forces recovered most airdrops, and some of the equipment landed by boat as well.

In the meantime, rumors of Osvaldo Ramírez's escapades had attracted more rebel volunteers. He now was leading more than two hundred men. His group successfully ambushed a militia patrol, killing seventeen and seizing their weapons.[6] Osvaldo's other victims included local INRA officials and peasant leaders of the new cooperative farms. The *alzados* also ambushed buses and army trucks. Ramírez and his men were assembling an impressive arsenal seized in firefights or acquired from sources in Miami. A militia attack on one of the group's hideouts uncovered four shoulder-mounted cannons, sixty Springfield rifles, hand grenades, radios and batteries, and five knapsacks of medicines.[7] The military equipment bore US identification.

Finally in April 1961, news of the Bay of Pigs invasion gave the *alzados* a welcome respite, as Castro's militia units left the Escambray to converge on Playa Girón. Many volunteers in Osvaldo Ramírez's band believed that final victory against Castro's communist regime was close at hand.

The following tells the story of the rural rebels who resisted the revolutionary state. The rural rebellion attracted disaffected residents all over the island nation, not just in the hotbed of the Escambray. Whereas the *gusano* counterrevolution reflected urban middle-class resistance, the *bandido* affair concerned smallholders and their rural allies. Cuba's rural counterrevolution from 1959 to 1965 had even deeper roots in the peasantry than did Fidel's M26. Therefore, in order to discount the farmer origins of the anti-Castro movement, the very same revolutionary leaders who exaggerated the peasants' contributions to the struggle against Batista had to explain away the greater role they played in the anti-Castro rebellion. Revolutionaries now decried the isolation, ignorance, and misguided fanaticism of Cuba's rural residents as relics of the prerevolutionary era. Thus they dug up the word *bandido,* the term by which the Spaniards defamed the rebels of the independence war and that Batista had used to describe Castro's guerrillas.

Remarkably, the rural *bandido* counterrevolution outlasted the *gusano* counterrevolution. The Bay of Pigs invasion of April 1961 spelled the end of the urban middle-class opposition in Havana and other cities. Yet Castro's regime did not extinguish resistance in the countryside until mid-1965. Faced with the revolutionary state's overwhelming repression, how did the *bandido* counterrevolution endure so long?

The answer had to do with the origins of the *alzados.* The rural rebellion arose not from traditional capitalist exploitation on plantations but from the rapid transformation of social relationships that the revolution had set in motion. True, the regime's land reform decree ended the unjust plantation system in Cuba. But it also created an institution, the INRA, that intervened in the daily lives of an independent peasantry that had existed at the margins of the sugar industry. The National Agrarian Reform Institute became the instrument by which the revolutionaries mobilized rural residents to socialize the economy. Such rapid change was bound to meet resistance, which in turn propelled the government to invest greater resources in pacifying the countryside. Guerrilla warfare resumed in Cuba because of agrarian reform. In the time of Osvaldo Ramírez, armed resistance sprouted like the thorny *marabú* bushes in some of the remotest parts of the countryside.

However, these rural guerrillas of the 1960s differed greatly from Castro's fighters of the late 1950s. The *alzados* mainly fought in small groups without an effective centralizing leadership. The size of Osvaldo Ramírez's outlaw gang in 1961 did not at all fit the norm. Therefore, the government's defeat of one band of resisters merely led to new uprisings elsewhere until exhaustion set in after six whole years of rural unrest. The linkage to political rivalries of the 1950s contained some relevance in the beginning. Rural rebels also had support from Cuban political exiles abroad, which, in the 1960s, remotely connected the rebels to the CIA. However, following the Bay of Pigs debacle, Washington recognized the futility of trying to back the *alzados* and drew down its active assistance.

Nevertheless, the rural rebels continued the struggle. In the process, one of history's legendary guerrilla leaders, Fidel Castro, also became the master of counterinsurgency. Once the cycle of resistance continued year upon year, it became plain that unrest in the countryside had its root causes in the land reform process itself. Membership of the guerrillas and the profile of their victims indicate that the rebellion targeted personnel connected to the INRA's restructuring of rural society. The *alzados* also targeted other revolutionary organizations, the pro-Castro small farmers, the provincial Committees for the Defense of the Revolution (CDRs), and Castro's first ruling party called the Integrated Revolutionary Organizations or ORI.[8] In the final reckoning, when the last "outlaw" gave up, the National Agrarian Reform Institute and other revolutionary organizations reigned supreme throughout the hinterlands. Moreover, the revolutionary state's security apparatus penetrated deeply into every village and hamlet.

CLEANSING THE ESCAMBRAY

The first *bandido* uprisings occurred relatively simultaneously in the late summer of 1959 within two to three months following Fidel's land reform decree. Rebels escaped to the Órganos Mountains of Pinar del Río on the western end of the island republic. They gathered up arms in the hills of Matanzas overlooking the lowland sugar plantations dating from the eighteenth century. Resistance cropped up also in the highlands of Las Villas and Camagüey in the center of the island. Even in Oriente Province, where loyalties to Fidel Castro remained strong, some mountain people found cause to *alzarse,* "to rise in revolt," in the recent M26 strongholds of the Sierra Maestra and the Sierra del Cristal.

Traditional sugar plantations did not characterize these locations. Rather, one found smallholders, tenant farmers, and *guajiro* squatters. Some residents of these highland zones went down to the plantations to cut cane during the *zafra*. However, few of these mountain men belonged to powerful pre-revolutionary organizations such as the Union of Sugar Mill Workers and the Association of Landowners *(colonos)*. After the revolution triumphed, rural resistance sprang up in the most remote areas of the countryside. But the heartland of rebellion spread in all directions from the highest elevation, Topes de Collantes, in the mountains of the Escambray. This location constituted the area of operations of Osvaldo Ramírez and his successors.

In the Escambray, the first counterrevolutionary outbreak lived up to its name. An ex-sergeant of Batista's secret police, the SIM, led seven others into resistance to the revolution. The group, representing elements of the discredited regime, did not make much of an impact.[9] Then, in late 1959, the national leaders of the anti-Batista guerrilla group the Second National Front of the Escambray began to communicate their reservations about the Castro government to several of their former followers.

Comandante William Morgan of the Second Front had returned to the Escambray and established a farm, raising bullfrogs and producing frogs' legs for export to the United States. His "capitalist" operations did not sit well with Félix Torres, the Las Villas provincial boss at the INRA. Torres proved to be a doctrinaire communist who carried out the first agrarian reform decree with scant regard for the sensibilities of the region's farmers. Former supporters of the Second Front relied on Morgan to protect them from dispossession by the INRA. Morgan obliged. He warned the Castro government that it risked armed resistance from the *guajiros* (rustic rural people) of the Escambray if it did not dismiss Félix Torres. Castro's security forces detained William Morgan. A military tribunal sentenced him to death for treason, and he faced the executioners soon thereafter.[10]

However, Morgan's confederate, Comandante Eloy Gutiérrez Menoyo, and a handful of his top lieutenants succeeded in fleeing into the Escambray Mountains once again.[11] Gutiérrez Menoyo reassembled some of his ex-guerrillas and then left by boat to Miami to secure financing and arms for the uprising. He never returned to the Escambray. Nor did he obtain much patronage or direction from the CIA, which did not trust him for having helped Castro put down the right-wing invasion from the Dominican Republic in August 1959. Nonetheless, rural resistance within Cuba took on a life of its own.

Following the land reform decree of May 1959, the intrusion of the revolutionary state into the social life of the countryside proceeded rapidly. The INRA acted as the vanguard. In less than two months, its Las Villas director, Félix Torres, confiscated two hundred plantations with more than 2.7 million acres of land and established dozens of people's granaries and cooperatives.[12] He was one revolutionary who pushed the agrarian reform beyond its original intent, which aimed to convert plantations into small properties for landless farmers. Director Torres had powerful patrons. He had been one of the few members of the communist party (the PSP) to raise arms against Batista. His small band of fighters had joined the M26 column of Camilo Cienfuegos in the last battles of December 1958. Che Guevara commended his service in the pages of the military journal *Verde Olivo*.[13] Also, Torres distinguished himself among the *barbudos* by sporting a long, wispy Ho Chi Minh beard.

The struggle itself justified the increasing intrusion into the countryside by agents of the revolutionary state. Conferences took place. Instructions went out. Political and military authorities scrutinized the rural population like never before. One "order of the day" for the Escambray in September 1961 instructed local authorities to take the pulse of the people to see "if the *guajiros* are understanding the Revolution better; if they are liberating themselves from the influence of the old bosses; if they are disposed to joining up with the local militias; if they can still be attracted by the *alzados;* or if they assist in collaborating with them and helping them."[14]

Shortly after the Bay of Pigs, the revolutionary state began to encroach on the smallholders. It created the National Association of Agricultural Producers, ANAP. This new bureaucracy took charge of closing the free market for agricultural products, forcing peasants to sell to the government at low prices, and confiscating produce for distribution as rationed foodstuffs. ANAP's intrusion led to producer resistance in all provinces except the Oriente, where the small farmers still supported the revolution. Modest landholders suspected that "full socialization" was coming soon. The state was already creating cooperatives out of the old cane plantations. Private owners still held more than half of the land used in food as well as coffee and tobacco production.[15] The state controlled the rest.

THE REBELS

The resistance existed as decentralized, dispersed, and short-lived groups. They differed greatly from the anti-Batista rebel bands of the late 1950s that had grown exponentially over a period of two years. Fidel's own M26 in Oriente Province had developed into a rural fighting force of three thousand armed men with a central command structure. In the Escambray Mountains, the Second Front of Comandantes Gutiérrez Menoyo and Morgan claimed to number two thousand men. In contrast, the resistance bands of the early 1960s averaged fewer than twenty men. Few *alzados* remained in the field for more than several months; only a handful stayed in the fight beyond one year. The difference depended on the response of the government.

Batista's army did not press the rebels, and Castro's military forces gave them no quarter.

Moreover, few outsiders commanded these *alzados*. The leaders and followers had local roots. They moved around in areas where they had grown up and had kinfolk and friends for support. They rested out of sight during the day and moved only after dark. *Bandidos* attacked targets away from their hideouts and then returned to their home territory for rest and supplies. They maintained networks of informants in the local population that provided intelligence about targets and the location of government militia units. The rebel bands planned attacks and laid ambushes in the late afternoon or early evening. After a brief firefight, the attackers dispersed individually or in pairs and used the cover of darkness to evacuate back to their home bases. New recruits had to break contact with their families, could not leave the group without permission, and worked on chores around the encampments until the guerrillas trusted them. Attempted desertion or collaboration with the government could result in the group leader ordering the offender's immediate execution. "As for supplies of arms and ammunition," stated one state security study, "these [counterrevolutionary groups] utilize those captured in assaults and robberies, infiltrations from abroad by air or sea, and from some ex-members of the militia or Armed Forces who ran away."[16] Therefore, the small *alzado* groups carried out operations that differed little from Castro's own tactics early in 1957 when he had had just two dozen men.

The *bandido* counterrevolution represented all social types found in the countryside with only a few nearby urban residents as possible connections to the *gusano* counterrevolution. Young men between the ages of twenty and forty-five predominated. Government agents interrogated captured rebels and recorded their names, origins, and jobs. They identified several who had been soldiers in the army and police of Batista and those who had served in the anti-Batista guerrilla bands in the late 1950s. The list even mentions an ex-captain of the Revolutionary Army. Men of the Second Front figured prominently as leaders in the first years.[17] Others on the list included mechanics, manual laborers, a fisherman, a student, an English teacher, a priest, and a medical doctor.

Leaders and collaborators of the small groups derived from the middle strata of rural society. "Luis Molina, petty bourgeois, owner of two pharmacies and who is disgusted by the revolutionary laws, joined up with the MRR movement," as one report characterized the chief of one small band.

Authorities described another leader as a "medium peasant belonging to the rural bourgeoisie, who in his civil life had the reputation of being an agitator of the masses."[18] The story of Ciro Vera Catalá seems quite mundane. When captured in Havana in 1963, he was thirty-six years old. Catalá was a small property owner when he joined the rebels in the Escambray. He served with several different chieftains for a period of seventeen months. Finally, Catalá fled to Havana but could not escape capture by State Security. He went before a tribunal and received a sentence of thirty years in prison.[19] This *alzado* seemed to have no other motive than fear of revolutionary change.

Although the government claimed the allegiance of the peasantry, many *campesinos* (farmers) and rural workers figured among those detained by government forces. "All these bands consist of peasants and workers of our province," one militia officer reported, "who for their ignorance and for their political outlook cooperate with the outlaws in one form or another."[20] Only a few on the lists faced the firing squad—one a Revolutionary Army deserter and another a government employee who had assassinated one of Castro's security agents. "Regarding the social composition of the bandits," said one veteran militiaman, "the great majority were peasants, workers, employees, and ex-soldiers of the dictatorship."[21] Professionals and doctors collaborated but seldom ran away into the mountains. Only a few Afro-Cubans appeared to have joined the *bandidos*. "Look how a black man joined the fight against the Revolution," an Escambray resident once exclaimed, "when this is the only Government that has done anything for blacks."[22] Afro-Cubans tended to support the government and trained for the militias in significant numbers.

Indeed, Las Villas Province contained a higher percentage of whites among the people of the countryside than Castro's revolutionary Oriente Province. Land ownership had become a mark not only of independence and self-worth but also of white masculinity. Consequently, the loss of land suggested descent into the loss of manhood and of one's wife to prostitution. Rumors equated the communal aspects of INRA cooperatives with Director Félix Torres's sexual license with unchaperoned young girls.[23] The revolution seemed to mobilize the landless Afro-Cubans into the militias and the cooperatives. The slogan "Neither Black nor Red" became the call for opposition to state institutions in cities as well as the countryside.[24]

Militiamen in training to suppress resistance to the agrarian reforms in the countryside. White Cubans predominated among the rebels, while Afro-Cubans rendered service to government militias.

The Castro government considered the clergy to be active supporters of the counterrevolution. Military commanders reported that many Catholic priests and lay activists in Trinidad had become involved as supporters, collaborators, and volunteers for the *bandido* gangs. Some Catholic priests helped the *alzados* find supplies and food, others gave religious services for the rebels, and a few went into the mountains. Many clergymen resided together in the House of Priests in Trinidad. Militiamen had orders not to molest them. But they did keep an eye on the group and took note when visitors came to see them during the night. One prisoner testified that two priests in Trinidad were providing sanctuary and food to *alzados*.[25] Such clerical collaboration ended definitively when the priests sailed into exile at the end of 1961.

The rebels mainly engaged in the destruction of property and in this way avoided confrontations with armed troops. They committed sabotage, set fire to tobacco drying sheds, and descended to the plains to burn fields of maturing sugarcane. In the eight months following November 1961, authorities reported nearly fourteen hundred cases of cane fires throughout the country.[26] Setting cane fields ablaze did not begin in the struggle against the revolutionary regime but had a long history in Cuba. Rebels in the struggle for independence in the 1890s also destroyed Cuba's cash crop, and so did anti-Batista plantation workers during the struggle against the tyranny in the late 1950s.[27]

Assaults took several different forms, but the common victim was an agent or a collaborator with the revolutionary government. In the countryside, human targets of the *alzados* worked either in public health and educational institutions or in various levels of the National Agrarian Reform Institute. The counterrevolutionaries laid ambushes for officers and men of the militias, attacked young teachers in the literacy campaign of 1961, and shot at officers and workers in agricultural cooperatives set up by the INRA. They also mounted armed assaults on "people's farms," "people's stores," and primary schools.[28] Granted, evidence and statistics on this "terrorism" comes from sources of the revolutionary government. Three former members of State Security authored the principal books on the *bandido* counterrevolution published in Cuba. Historians have to be cautious about the revolutionary state's use of the terms "terrorism" and "outlaws." But racism certainly had been a factor in the murder of the Afro-Cuban Benítez. Evelio Duque, second-in-command to Osvaldo Ramírez, explained the motives behind the brutal treatment of the literacy teacher. "Conrado Benítez," he told his men, "has died for being a communist, for being a thief, for being a rapist, and for coming to the Escambray to abuse our *campesinos!*"[29] Duque's explanation deployed many of the coded prejudices that whites entertained about Afro-Cubans.

THE MILITIAS

Several guerrilla veterans in the rebel army in August 1960 received orders from the commander-in-chief, Fidel Castro, to organize units of bandit hunters. They set up training camps for the fifty thousand militiamen recruited from among young males of Havana and Pinar del Río. By 1961, the revolutionary government had placed these recruits into eighty battalions on the whole island: five battalions in Matanzas; ten each in Pinar del Río, Camagüey, and Oriente; twenty in La Habana; and twenty-five in Las Villas. Some of the earliest militiamen to fight against the bandits in the fall of 1959 also became instructors of the new Militia Training Academy at La Campana near Hoyo de Manicaragua. Instruction commenced in September 1960.[30]

"As the counterrevolutionary bands initially rose up, I joined the recently created peasant militias," an ex-militiaman remembers. His first unit going into action was "composed of peasants from all over the Escambray." Five hundred men in his battalion had no time to complete the training course at La Campana. They entered the war zone in September 1960 under the command of officers from the Revolutionary Army. Many militia units suffered a number of casualties, particularly in ambushes.[31] All in all, fifty thousand *milicianos* participated in the first cleansing of the Escambray. Most of them came from Havana and Pinar del Río, and only a few knew the mountains of southern Las Villas Province. By comparison, President Batista sent only twelve thousand poorly trained army troops against Fidel's three hundred guerrillas in the summer of 1958—and lost.[32]

Fidel tasked the new militias with carrying out La Limpia del Escambray, the cleansing of the *alzados* from the mountains. Their training developed the military tactic of encircling and combing *(cerco y peine)*, consisting of surrounding the suspected location of a group of rebels with a superior force of militiamen. Then the officers sent a column or two of troops to comb the area within the encirclement in order to flush out the hidden *alzados*.[33] In fact, Commander-in-Chief Fidel Castro himself showed up and participated with the militiamen in *cerco y peine* operations from time to time. (Batista had never joined troops on the front lines fighting Castro's rebellion.) These first bandit-hunting units tracked down the rebel chieftain Sinesio Walsh and captured his group.[34] The militiamen succeeded because the *bandidos* were poorly armed, hungry, and constantly on the run. "Do not fire. I am Sinesio Walsh. We don't have ammunition to fight, not even for two minutes. I don't care if I die, but I don't want my men slaughtered."[35]

The campaign against the bandits created martyrs for the revolution. The teacher Conrado Benítez was not the first. The army's commander in the Escambray, Manuel "Piti" Fajardo, died in battle in the last days of November 1960, actually two months before Benítez. Elements of the revolutionary army and the intelligence services of the Ministry of the Interior responded to a report of arms stolen from a government installation below Topes de Collantes. As Comandante Piti was setting up a circle-and-comb maneuver, his men came under intense rifle fire from the *alzados*. The commander retreated to his vehicle with gunshot wounds and collapsed. He died while his men were transporting him to the hospital at Trinidad.[36]

In contrast to Batista, Fidel Castro as commander-in-chief frequently visited the sites of the rebel uprising. He involved himself in all phases of the combat, from training, to planning, to leading columns of militiamen, to talking with peasants, and to debriefing *alzados*. The government had purchased FAL assault rifles made in Belgium for NATO troops. "Your little kisses burn," said one *miliciano* of his FAL.[37] Toward the end of 1960, the first deliveries of Czech weapons, especially the M-52 assault rifle, bolstered the firepower of the militias. Now the militiamen had better weapons than the World War II–era American weapons used by most *bandidos*. "From Trinidad we followed the direct instructions that Commander in Chief (Castro) sent to us," recalls one former militia commander, "not only with his spoken words and personal orders, but also with his constant presence in the area where the combat actions were carried out."[38]

The cleansing of the Escambray continued up to the Bay of Pigs invasion, by which time the bandits had not been eliminated. Casualties mounted in the government forces, and hospitals and morgues in Sancti Spíritus and Trinidad became strained. Nevertheless, the militias rose to the occasion at the Bay of Pigs, while these counterrevolutionaries were unable to lend support to the exile forces of Brigade 2506 some distance away at Playa Girón.

The standard measure of sufficient forces to contain a guerrilla outbreak at the time was a ten-to-one ratio of soldiers to rebels. The cleansing of the Escambray met this standard many times over. In one operation, the government sent in fifteen hundred men to hunt down a leader named Ojeda and his seven men. Agents of the Department of State Security (DSE) located the group. The *milicianos* converged on the area, and still Ojeda and his men broke through the encirclement. One government official explained the reason for the mission's failure. "The personnel who found themselves in the operation at that moment," he wrote, "were farm workers with little experience in that type of combat." The outlaws took advantage of the opportunity to succeed in escaping.[39] In a separate incident, two militia units operating along the border between the provinces of Las Villas and Camagüey commenced firing at each other "without any order" to do so, frightening nearby peasants. The writer of the report suggested the remedy for such incompetence. "Only when each one of the [*milicianos*] in the companies pass[es] through the [training] schools . . . will we achieve right away a total reduction of shooting without cause."[40]

All in all, Castro's counterinsurgency program was controlling but not defeating the "outlaws." The government was achieving an important objective nonetheless. The *bandido* uprising served as a training ground for Castro's supporters to become actively involved in defending the revolution. The government called in more militia units from Havana, Camagüey, and Oriente. Each spent a couple of months tracking bandits. But the *milicianos* were not terribly effective. As soon as men got to know the territory, they left to go back home.[41] Nevertheless, the very struggle itself paid dividends in terms of revolutionary mobilization. By 1961, three hundred thousand young men throughout the island had joined the militia forces.[42] Only a small portion of these men and women ever had any participation in fighting against Batista.

THE UNITED STATES

The revolution's leadership interpreted the *bandido* counterrevolution as a rebellion propagated by the CIA. The propagandists implied that there would have been no local resistance to the revolution without US intervention. One commander of the government's anti-bandit campaign suggested that the US imperialists had the power to change strategies that the *bandidos* used. According to Comandante Raúl Menéndez Tomassevich, the CIA ordered the outlaws "to intimidate the revolutionary peasantry through bloody acts" such as assassinating state agents, burning schools, and assaulting the people's stores.[43] Fidel Castro often said that same thing. The CIA did many things to undermine the Cuban Revolution. In its formative years, the counterrevolution in the cities and in the countryside preoccupied the CIA. That much is true. However, the more intriguing question would be about the effectiveness of CIA agents and their Cuban collaborators in manipulating anti-Castro impulses.

American intelligence agents operated out of the US embassy in Havana during the first two years of the Cuban Revolution. Apparently, the revolutionaries believed that the CIA's presence close at hand helped more than hindered the process of consolidation. Fidel did not expel embassy personnel even in January 1961. They left of their own accord because the Eisenhower White House knew the men of Brigade 2506 were preparing to invade Cuba.

However, the CIA took care to leave several Cuban collaborators behind with shortwave radio transmitters. One of them, ironically, had adopted the code name of Comandante Augusto Sandino, after the Nicaraguan rebel who fought against the US Marines in the 1930s. That anti-Castro resistance director was José Ramón Ruiz Sánchez, a nephew of Tony Varona, the Auténtico activist in Miami. Comandante Augusto and the shortwave radio in his Havana home had already been linking *bandido* groups to the Havana underground and their CIA patrons at the embassy. He tried to coordinate CIA airdrops to *alzados* in the Escambray.[44] At least, that was the theory. Many rebel chieftains did not have radios.

Cuban exile pilots flying C-47 transport planes for Brigade 2506 out of Guatemala made airdrops in order to supply arms and equipment to the anti-Castro guerrillas. They came in at a low altitude at night and dropped pallets filled with weapons, ammunition, explosives, communications equipment, battle dress, foodstuffs, and medicines. The CIA made the first airdrop in October 1959. However, the logistics and communications proved impossible to coordinate. Sometimes, the planes did not come. At other times, they missed the designated drop zones. Moreover, the winds often wafted the parachutes away from targets that *bandidos* lit up at night. The émigré airmen turned out to be inexperienced and timid, dropping the pallets far from the prearranged zones.[45] One night in February 1961, CIA planes parachuted thirty pallets at Cabaiguán in the Escambray. Government forces captured nearly all of them. In the meantime, the Revolutionary Army set up antiaircraft batteries to fire at C-47 cargo planes flown by émigré pilots, forcing one to make an emergency landing in Jamaica.[46]

In all, the CIA's Cuban pilots made sixty-eight airdrops. Only seven arrived to the *alzados,* while militia forces recovered the rest.[47] The Castro government transferred the captured American weapons to military bases where foreigners were training for the export of revolution. By the end of 1961, the CIA abandoned air supplies altogether.

While the CIA was planning for the Bay of Pigs invasion, its agents collected intelligence on the rural rebellion against Castro. The Agency's initial plans called for armed Cuban exiles to join with the rebels in the Escambray. Brigade 2506 would have landed near Trinidad on the south coast of Las Villas Province, then pushed into the mountains. Indeed, intelligence agents assigned to the US embassy in Havana sent information about the counterrevolution back to CIA headquarters at Langley. Director Allen Dulles passed on the latest intelligence to President Eisenhower and his National Security Council. Dulles reported on the growing unrest in the countryside, informing the president that "there are about 1000 guerrillas in the Escambray Mountains." Americans still working in Cuba told agents at the embassy that travel on the roads in southern Las Villas Province had become hazardous. Gunfire sometimes continued throughout the night. "However, the guerrilla groups in this area are not cooperating [together] effectively," reported CIA director Dulles.[48]

Infiltration and exfiltration of agents and supplies continued, but military patrolling of the coastline minimized the secure landing of supplies. Many a Cuban émigré boat pilot lost his nerve when approaching the shoreline and found excuses (engine trouble, high waves) to head back to Miami. Getting into the mountains and meeting up with bandit gangs also complicated outside deliveries.[49] Infiltrators had a higher chance of crossing paths with militia patrols than with the *bandidos*. Descending to the coastlines to pick up supplies increased rebels' vulnerability. Yet, at the time of the Bay of Pigs, seven hundred to eight hundred *alzados* were roaming the mountains seeking to disrupt the revolution. But none of the radio operators in the anti-Castro underground knew when or where the actual invasion was to take place.[50] They were unable to coordinate the rebel uprising in the cities and countryside with the landing of Brigade 2506. Anyway, Allen Dulles said later that the "popular uprising" had never been part of the plan. Bay of Pigs planners did not believe that the domestic insurgency could defeat the revolutionary government. Thus, the CIA changed plans for Brigade 2506 to head into the mountains for a prolonged anti-Castro insurgency.[51] The Bay of Pigs invasion instead was meant for quick victory.

Others also worked in the underground ostensibly under the supervision of the CIA. John Meples Spíritto had served with Gutiérrez Menoyo and Morgan's Second Front against Batista. From his home in Havana, he regularly distributed rifles and machine guns to representatives of bandit gangs. He even lunched with them at the Riviera Hotel. "Our agents," wrote one of Miami's CIA directors, "belonged largely to the Cuban middle class."[52] Spíritto had also helped direct sabotage attacks on electrical units and oil refineries in Havana. Cuban intelligence had had him under surveillance for months. When it appeared that Spíritto was leaving the country in December 1962, Cuban G-2 intelligence agents arrested him.[53]

After the Bay of Pigs, American intelligence agents either lost interest in the *bandido* counterrevolution or received little information on it. The extensive CIA reports on Cuba contain little on the *alzados*. Even the Miami Cubans forgot about them. For all the money that the CIA was pouring into Miami's anti-Castro groups, they did not have much communication with the *bandido* resistance.

Yet Cuban military intelligence continued to connect the bandit gangs to the offshore counterrevolutionary groups. In a report dating from June 1962, Cuban army officers counted the small bands and grouped them according to the anti-Castro organizations. They suggested that 223 separate rebel groups belonged to the Democratic Revolutionary Front (FDR), connected to the Auténtico Party and led by Tony Varona from Miami. Two hundred four additional armed groups allegedly had ties to the Movement for Revolutionary Recovery (MRR) of Manuel Artime.[54] The sources did not at all indicate how they made these determinations.

The FDR and MRR at the time were receiving CIA funding in Miami. How much of this money was actually reaching the *alzados,* the documentation does not speculate. In any case, the purported ties to the Miami resistance and the CIA did not make the rebels particularly well armed. By 1961, the militias were using Czech assault weapons. The rebels, on the other hand, carried weapons reminiscent of Castro's M26 guerrillas: Garands, Springfields, M1s, M3s, submachine guns, Browning 30-06s, and Thompsons. Other reports mentioned various kinds of revolvers, Remingtons, Winchesters, shotguns, .22-caliber rifles, and a Brazilian rifle.[55] In comparison to the militias, the *bandidos* found themselves poorly armed. Still, the *bandido* counterrevolution lingered on until mid-1965. CIA responsibility for rebellion in the countryside seems exaggerated.

OSVALDO'S STORY CONCLUDED

In the early days of the *bandido* counterrevolution, José Ramón Ruiz Sánchez, a cooking oil merchant and Tony Varona's nephew, attempted to coordinate operations from his home in Havana. He lived in a "luxurious home" in the Siboney section of the capital. Ruiz Sánchez had a radio transmitter with which he could communicate with his uncle in Miami, the US embassy in Havana, and the rebels in the Escambray. He assumed national command of the counterrevolution under the code name of Comandante Augusto Sandino. His communication hub theoretically supported groups numbering nearly six hundred men dispersed throughout the nation and the Escambray.[56] Like many other dissidents, he also maintained contact with CIA agents in the US embassy until it closed down in January 1961.

At least one anti-Castro chieftain in the Escambray attempted to go around Ruiz Sánchez. Evelio Duque, another ex-fighter with the Second Front, briefly held a post with INRA until he rebelled. The government claimed that he had used his position to take bribes. From his camp in the Escambray, Duque sent a radio message intended for the CIA station in the embassy. In it, Duque complained about the underground leader code-named "Comandante Augusto." Ruiz Sánchez's radio receiver in Havana picked up the message, and he promptly declared Evelio Duque a traitor. He dismissed Duque from his command in the "anticommunist army" and promoted Osvaldo Ramírez in his place. The underground leader in Havana signed the order as Comandante Augusto.[57] Evelio Duque ultimately fled to Miami. The veteran fighter announced that he intended to return to the Escambray. "We have the men," Duque said, "give us the arms!"[58] Like so many others, Duque never did return.

Neither did Comandante Augusto. When he left Cuba, Ruiz Sánchez claimed that the chieftains in the Escambray had asked him to represent them in Miami. The man who took Sandino's name as his nom de guerre then sent a message to Osvaldo Ramírez. He suggested that the rebel chieftain find a way to exfiltrate to the United States, where the CIA would give him training. Ramírez refused.[59]

In July 1961, Osvaldo Ramírez gathered together several other bandit chieftains and proclaimed himself commander-in-chief of the National Liberation Army. By then, he had become famous for having killed the Afro-Cuban literacy teacher Conrado Benítez as well as other representatives of the revolutionary state. Ramírez appointed six captains to head up guerrilla activities in separate combat zones throughout Las Villas and Camagüey Provinces. Despite the image of centralized control, the separate groups within his unified command continued to operate on their own. Other resistance leaders in the region did not acknowledge Osvaldo's authority. Moreover, the constant militia patrols kept them all in survival mode rather than on the offensive.

In July 1962, the revolutionary government had organized a second offensive, the struggle against the bandits, or LCB, to systematically suppress the many *alzados* on a nationwide scale. Raúl Menéndez Tomassevich, himself a former guerrilla fighter in Raúl Castro's Second Front, took command of eight militia battalions of the Highlands Division (División Serrana).[60] This civil war became a struggle between insurgents and former insurgents, and the latter began to gain the upper hand against the National Liberation Army of Osvaldo Ramírez.

At one point in his rebellion, Ramírez proclaimed the death sentence on some two dozen of his local enemies—whom he described as *comunistas y chivatos,* "communists and informers." The decree issued from his hideout in the Escambray applied even to the sons and wives of the principals. Osvaldo signed the document above his signature block as "Comandante en Jefe" of the Democratic National Front, the Auténtico action group in Miami.[61] Evidence gathered by the government points to the fact that the bandits committed acts of terror. Castro's government wanted the Cuban people to understand the nature of counterrevolution. The newspaper *Revolución* often featured articles and photos of *bandido* atrocities. The destruction of property and killing of peasants and occasionally of teenagers cast the *alzados* as terrorists.[62] The bandits of the Escambray had no code of conduct and no tribunals. They had no lawyers such as Humberto Sorí Marín, who had lent legal legitimacy to Castro's M26 in the Sierra Maestra.

A case in point was the assault on Las Llanadas. The date of March 13 approximated an Auténtico day of commemoration. On that date in 1957, José Antonio Echeverría died leading the attack on the dictator Batista at the Presidential Palace. Twenty armed men in 1962 chose March 13 to seize the peasant village of Las Llanadas. They lined up the villagers so that they could witness the burning of the *pueblo*'s cooperative store, called the Center for Social Welfare. As the *alzados* left, they kidnapped the administrator of the public granary and a local representative of the ruling party, the ORI. The *alzados* executed these two men just outside of town.[63] This assault amounted to the most spectacular operation of the *bandido* counterrevolution, though this group acted without the authorization of Osvaldo Ramírez.

Unity in the struggle against Castro eluded these rebels. From abroad, Miami's political leaders arranged the infiltration back into Cuba of the representatives of five different anti-Castro political factions then attempting to support *bandidos*. They sought to unite all rebels throughout the country. Osvaldo's subordinates met with several of these delegates in March 1962 and agreed on arrangements "to supply him with money, ammunition and arms." In other words, only with the provision of arms and supplies would the disparate groups cooperate with offshore politicians. Ramírez's men told the visitors of their commander-in-chief's plan to seize Osvaldo's hometown of Sancti Spíritus, cutting communications between east and west. "We responded that although it sounded to us a bit hair-brained and that no one had enough resources to carry it out successfully," one of the dissidents later told Castro's G-men, "if Osvaldo was disposed to put the plan into action, we would be disposed to assist it nationally."[64] No one could complete the bargain. Cuban security agents captured many of these infiltrators before they could return to Miami, and Ramírez's liberation army could not leave the Escambray without running into revolutionary troops.

Meanwhile, government security officers regularly kept an eye out for suspicious people at hotels and railway and bus stations in areas of *alzado* activity. Once, they apprehended the mother of Osvaldo's second-in-command because she was headed toward the mountains with oversized luggage filled with medicines and preserved food.[65] Such vigilance paid dividends for revolutionary forces.

The intelligence branch of Tomassevich's command closed in on the supply network of Osvaldo Ramírez's National Liberation Army. *Alzados* did have collaborators in the cities who helped supply them and facilitate their activities. Authorities uncovered one such associate in Trinidad. This person held the position of paymaster for state cooperatives, a job that gave him an excuse to go into the hills. The paymaster, whose code name was Pancho el Grande, played a critical role in Ramírez's supply system. Residents of one safe house would transport recruits and couriers to the next safe house, a couple of miles down the road. Government intelligence agents detained Pancho el Grande after he returned home from taking food to a band of Osvaldo's men. The Escambray commander, Raúl Menéndez Tomassevich, came to lecture Pancho el Grande that land reform did indeed benefit the *campesinos*. Whoever said differently was a liar, said Tomassevich. Pancho el Grande accepted the offer of cooperating with the LCB commander in order to expose the *alzados* and their collaborators. Cooperate or be executed—those were the options. It was Pancho el Grande who finally led government forces to Osvaldo Ramírez.[66]

Osvaldo's death came in April 1962. Guided by Pancho el Grande's information, the militias again cornered the liberation army's commander and about forty of his men. The *bandido* who had become known for his remarkable ability to escape encirclement and ambushes again sought to flee through the thick vegetation of a ravine. A militiaman fired at Osvaldo from the hill above and mortally wounded him. His second-in-command, Tomás San Gil, took over the dwindling group, now numbering only a dozen *alzados*. San Gil had raised cattle in the shadow of the Escambray. He took up arms after a heated discussion with an INRA official over whether his pastures belonged to the "people" or to San Gil, who had paid for them. "I'm going into the monte," San Gil told him. "Come and find me. I'll be waiting for you." San Gil and his dwindling band perished in battle eleven months later.[67] In the year that Osvaldo Ramírez and Tomás San Gil died, the revolutionary forces captured six hundred *bandidos*. Yet hundreds of *alzados* remained in the field against the revolutionary government in every one of Cuba's six provinces.

THE STRUGGLE AGAINST THE BANDITS

Other bands held out in the Escambray. The rebellion that began here in November 1959 ended with the capture of the last *alzado* in July 1965. "The struggle in the Escambray was very complex, as it covered a very great area, some parts unpopulated, and others with numerous peasants, who for their low level of political consciousness helped the bandits," said one militia commander who fought the *alzados*. "But to be correct, one can say also that a large portion of the peasantry was our ally in this battle."[68]

In July 1962, the government reorganized the national counterinsurgency campaign and called it La Lucha Contra los Bandidos, or the struggle against the bandits. The campaign became better known by its Spanish acronym, LCB. The armed forces divided up the country into five theaters of operations. The Escambray Mountains, the largest area of contention in the civil war, formed Zone A. The government now recruited, trained, and deployed militiamen exclusively from within the same zones in which they lived.

Henceforth, they fought against their rebel neighbors, lending militiamen the same knowledge of the terrain and local customs as the enemy. "When they created the structure of the Struggle Against the Bandits, many of these men were mobilized in a permanent fashion," remembers one former army officer. "[The government] solicited recruits at their work centers, listed them in the military enrollment, and paid them from Army funds. From that moment on, they formed part of the permanent mobilization."[69] Comandante Raúl Menéndez Tomassevich, the man who had hunted down the bandit king Ramírez, assumed overall direction of the LCB.

Fighting units trained for several different types of "combing," or armed forays through territories marked off by encircling troops. The *cercar y peinar* strategy would flush out suspected bandit encampments identified by intelligence agents. The systematic LCB training secured one victory after another for government forces between 1962 and the end of the campaign in 1965. Toward the end, the militiamen had perfected the tactic of forming up two or three *cercos*. "If the guerrillas broke through the first ring, they would find themselves caught between the first and the second ring," says a surviving *alzado*. "If they broke through the second ring, they faced a third."[70]

Still, no single victory proved decisive. For every three bands of *alzados* rounded up, two others popped up elsewhere. The capture and killing of no single leader ended the uprising until the dissidents became exhausted and accepted the presence of state institutions in the countryside. The INRA organized and managed the collective farms fashioned out of the big plantations. The ANAP brought the private farmers under state control.

Training and overwhelming force were the orders of the day. Tomassevich had a term for it. "Let's dress the zone of combat in olive green." Everyone involved in the LCB turned out in full *verde olivo* battle dress with the Che Guevara–style black beret. Training and discipline among government forces emphasized the humane treatment of captives, a strategy having antecedents among the M26 guerrillas in the Sierra Maestra. "Our troops never abused a single prisoner," said one militia commander. "We never mistreated a single one, even though those prisoners had committed a great many murders, and we hated them."[71] Troop morale was rising just at the right patriotic moment. In October 1962, Fidel Castro, the commander-in-chief, called the militiamen away from hunting outlaws in order to fend off a possible invasion by US armed forces during the missile crisis.[72]

A unit of militiamen captures two rebels during a circle-and-comb operation in the Escambray Mountains.

Perhaps the LCB's most significant result for the revolutionary state turned out to be its contribution to the professionalization of the security services. The counterrevolution gave the state an excuse to develop G-2 intelligence into an institution capable of reaching into the hinterlands. Prime minister and commander-in-chief Fidel Castro, the Defense Ministry under the command of his brother Raúl, and the Ministry of Interior constructed the security apparatus from scratch. Most of these men of the intelligence services had been born in the 1930s, a few in the 1920s. They came principally from the provinces. Most State Security agents had had a rudimentary education and joined local resistance groups affiliated loosely with Castro's M26. Only a few had served in the Sierra Maestra or in the columns of Raúl, Che, and Camilo Cienfuegos. Others entered the intelligence services because of their affiliation with the old communist party—though none of these had actually been combatants against "the tyranny." Some entered the military and received advanced training, while others had gone through police training provided by the Interior Ministry. Individuals who demonstrated commitment to the Revolution by joining the militias of workers and peasants also came to the notice of the Interior Ministry recruiters. All recruits underwent intensive training in Cuba. Some undertook six months of higher-level training with the KGB in the Soviet Union. Selected personnel received ideological training in six-month courses at the School of Revolutionary Instruction "Carlos Marx" in Havana.[73]

Many G-2 recruits in the early 1960s served in the struggle against the bandits. Seventy-seven of them died in action from January 1960 to June 1965. They lost their lives confronting counterrevolutionaries attempting a boat landing or a seaborne arms drop; others, in the act of apprehending suspected collaborators. Intelligence agents also died in firefights with *alzados* or in attempts to prevent the illegal emigration of armed opponents.

A few of the G-men volunteered or were selected for the most dangerous work—joining the *bandidos* as spies. Among the first was José Martí Medina González, who joined the Department of Intelligence of the Revolutionary Army. In 1959, he insinuated himself into the entourage of the Second Front of the Escambray, the source of many *alzado* chieftains in the mountains of Las Villas Province. His work assisted in uncovering the plot orchestrated by Comandante William Morgan in 1960, whom Medina González exposed as a traitor. Another spy, Antonio Santiago García, had served in the Escambray during the dictatorship with the Directorio Revolucionario guerrillas. Thus he was a natural to undertake espionage among outlaw groups whose members knew of his prior service. However, one bandit leader discovered his cover and had him executed. Other G-2 spies suffered similar fates.[74]

LCB forces actually captured one undercover agent code-named El Águila among the *alzados* he had penetrated. El Águila did not reveal his intelligence affiliation and spent time in jail. There he continued to provide information to his G-2 handlers. "I went through everything others did in prison," he said later. "There they were not using torture, but definitely it was not a good life either."[75] Even El Águila's family thought he was a counterrevolutionary. Dedication to the revolution and professionalism rather than cronyism seemed to motivate Castro's security personnel. He expected them to behave the same way abroad as at home.

The revolutionary justice system penetrated the countryside as another institution meant to build loyalty and productivity. The revolutionary criminal justice system dealt firmly but not arbitrarily with *bandidos* and their collaborators. Military tribunals condemned to death a few leaders who had blood on their hands. Most of the followers received prison sentences of up to twenty years. On the other hand, for the collaborators there was internal exile and rehabilitation. "Complete families of peasants accused of harboring and helping anti-Castro guerrillas are being rounded up and broken up," reported one British diplomat in Cuba. "Heads of families are sent to penal battalions for forced labor on the land. Mothers and children are taken to Havana—the mothers to special compounds under detention and the children to crèches or child institutions."[76]

Soviet advisers in 1961 introduced the Cubans to Agrarian Methods, a policy they had developed in fighting Russian counterrevolutionaries in the 1920s. It amounted to a system of reinserting resisters back into society—yet away from their home province. Peasants who supported the *bandidos* were relocated to Ciudad Sandino (also named for the Nicaraguan rebel) in the westernmost province of Pinar del Río. When Stanford University's Richard Fagen visited Ciudad Sandino in the mid-1960s, he found that two-thirds of the town's population hailed from the Escambray. Fagen described several hundred homes, day care centers, and schools that taught the construction trades as well as standard academic courses. The residents worked on two people's farms. Granja Sandino specialized in the cultivation of blond tobacco for cigarettes, and Granja Simón Bolívar, in citrus and other fruits. The farms had commons-style food halls and barracks for visiting workers from the city. It was a time of "voluntary labor," the plan originated by Minister of Industry Che Guevara. Bureaucrats from the Ministry of Foreign Affairs came regularly for the harvests. Fagen noted that the diplomats worked faster in the fields than did the clerical workers, drivers, and mechanics from Havana.[77]

Fidel Castro took great pride in the performance of his revolutionary justice system during the struggle against the bandits. "It is necessary to say that not one single [outlaw] went unpunished. It is necessary to say that none of those doers of evil deeds who had killed [literacy] brigade members, teachers, workers and peasants, managed to escape. It is necessary to say that law and justice fell on the guilty ones."[78]

Finally, it was over. In Matanzas, the last band of rebels, numbering only three, fell to government forces in January 1965.[79] At the eastern end of the island, where the government charged that some *alzados* escaped with the assistance of the US Navy at Guantánamo, the last band gave up in May 1965.

In Pinar del Río, on the western end of Cuba, the rebellion had actually begun in January 1959. It came to an end with the capture of the brothers Camargo Piloto in August 1965.[80] In the Escambray, the last rebels came in from the cold on July 24, just two days before Fidel Castro celebrated the twelfth anniversary of the attack on Moncada Barracks. He chose to do it at Santa Clara, several dozen miles north of the hotbed of the *bandido* counterrevolution.

EPITAPH FOR REVOLUTIONARY VIOLENCE

Nationwide, the *bandidos* fielded nearly three hundred separate bands of anti-Castro rebels. In the Escambray itself, 177 outlaw gangs operated, most on a short-term basis, between September 1959 and July 1965. Two thousand combatants took up arms, and at least six thousand collaborators participated in the anti-Castro uprising. The people of the Escambray bore about one-half of the burden in the fight against the revolution.

The headquarters of the LCB drew up the statistics for the entire nation. They set the total number of anti-government fighters at four thousand and their collaborators at ten thousand. The government counted 549 deaths among all revolutionary forces. More than two hundred additional soldiers, militiamen, and security officers suffered incapacitating injuries. Three hundred victims of *bandido* violence died as well. The number of *alzados* killed or captured in the entire campaign totaled thirty-five hundred in the six years of fighting. An additional twenty-five thousand rural residents may have been relocated away from the Escambray.[81] Cuba at that moment had a population of some seven million inhabitants.

Practically every book published in Cuba on the internal counterrevolution quotes a number of conclusions derived from Castro's speeches. One of them concerns the role of the United States and the CIA. Cubans on the island with little variation treated the *bandido* uprisings as if the US government had orchestrated them directly from Washington, DC. "Agents of imperialism"—Castro used that term frequently. Revolutionary leaders explained the fact that thousands of peasants went into the mountains to join the bandit gangs by claiming that their isolation and ignorance made them easy prey for imperialist spies. "These are actions of tiny groups of stupid and misguided men," Che Guevara told the *milicianos* in 1960. "No real threat."[82] Nevertheless, the Castro government took the threat seriously and responded with massive force.

Evidence taken from Cuban sources suggests an alternative narrative. It indicates that the counterrevolution in the countryside had powerful organic origins. The appeal of *bandidismo* stemmed from the discomfort some rural producers felt toward rapid social change. Mass mobilizations disrupted the normal rhythms of rural life. The invasion of the countryside by the National Agrarian Reform Institute altered the structures of producing, buying, and selling agricultural products. Those who benefited by the new order—and they appeared to have been in the majority—remained loyal to the revolution. Those who calculated that they might lose out acted on their resentments.

True, the CIA did encourage Cuba's rural rebellion. The *bandidos* could have been collaborators, a fifth column that might provide American policymakers with allies in overthrowing the first socialist republic in the Western Hemisphere. But the obstacles to American interference in Cuba's rural affairs remained powerful. CIA incompetence in delivering arms to the *alzados* figures as the greatest drawback. The dedication of the militiamen is another. Lack of communication is a third. Historians should not automatically accept the government's explanations emphasizing "ignorance." To do so would rob the rural people of their agency. The evidence demonstrates much independent initiative being exercised by those who chose to flee into the mountains, for resistance did not turn out to be an easy existence. The outlaws won few victories in six years of fighting, and still newcomers ran away to take up arms.

The analyst also has to come back to the political instincts of Fidel Castro. His masterful consolidation of revolutionary power enabled him to coordinate all the state agencies in quelling the internal rebellion. The ministries and the mass organizations snapped to his orders. Teachers, security agencies, police, militiamen, officers and soldiers, agrarian officials, neighborhood committees, communist administrators, peasant leaders—all marched to his commands. Moreover, he used the strength of both the *gusano* and *bandido* counterrevolutions to heighten the dedication of his followers. CIA meddling merely raised their enthusiasm for the revolution.

One more question demands explanation. If Washington did not control and direct the *bandido* insurrection, why did it end at the precise moment in 1965 that President Johnson transferred the anticommunist campaign from Cuba to Vietnam? After all, the White House shut down Manuel Artime's commandos and the Miami CIA station simultaneously in that year.

Actually, evidence from Cuba does not point to an abrupt end to the rebellion in 1965. That year instead marked the last whimper, the final gasp. The rebellion of the outlaws actually started its decline with the death of Osvaldo Ramírez in 1962. The declining intensity of the antirevolutionary struggle could be measured in the number of *alzados* that revolutionary forces captured in the Escambray. Those figures tapered off every year from a height of 235 captured in 1961 to just fourteen in 1965.[83] When President Johnson finally pulled funds and personnel from the anti-Castro campaign, the outlaw rebellion had already reached extinction. The rebels had not gone into the hills because of the CIA. Nor did the *bandidos* abandon the struggle when Washington lost interest.

Be that as it may, there is good reason for the historian to lump together the violence of the revolution against Batista with that of the counterrevolution. Castro's attack on Moncada Barracks in 1953 commenced twelve years of nearly continuous guerrilla warfare in Cuba. The violence ended with the last *alzados* surrendering in the summer of 1965. When the fighting concluded, the total number of deaths in the *bandido* counterrevolution equaled that of the guerrilla war against Batista. The final, combined death toll amounted to five thousand men and women. Thereafter, little internal or external armed aggression threatened the Cuban Revolution.

As usual, the victors had the last word. "Guerrilla warfare is a formidable weapon when fighting against exploitation, against colonialism, against imperialism," Fidel Castro announced on the twelfth anniversary of the Moncada attack. "But guerrilla warfare will never be an adequate or useful instrument for counterrevolution—for the imperialists to fight against the exploited, to fight against the people."[84]

CHAPTER SIX

Commandos of the Caribbean

FORMER M26 OFFICER and Bay of Pigs leader Manuel Artime brought his anti-Castro MRR resistance group from Havana to Miami. Attorney General Robert F. Kennedy had given a new lease to Artime's Movement for Revolutionary Recovery after the Brigade 2506 prisoners returned to the Miami Orange Bowl. The Kennedy administration utilized the CIA to support Artime's organization with money, arms, and contacts with the Somoza regime in Nicaragua. The MRR mission was to operate independently of the US government while attacking Cuban military targets in order to stimulate a rebellion from within. President Lyndon Baines Johnson inherited the MRR together with the entire Kennedy foreign policy toward Cuba. That is where matters stood in September 1964, as Johnson looked forward to the election that would confirm his continued residence at the White House.

There followed an event that threw the exiles' anti-Castro campaign into question, particularly the White House's support for it. In the early morning darkness of September 15, the MRR mother ship delivered fast boats to the Caribbean waters east of Oriente Province. One of the armed fast boats came upon a sixteen-hundred-ton freighter steaming toward Cuba. The boat circled the freighter, which was displaying its full complement of running lights, then sped off. Three boats returned shortly thereafter and commenced firing on the ship's bridge with rocket launchers and .50-caliber machine guns. "Attacking boats presented appearance of pleasure craft," rescue crews cabled from the US Naval Station at Guantánamo. The seaborne assault left the ship a "burning hulk," dead in the water. A Dutch freighter responded to SOS transmissions and rescued nine survivors out of a crew of twenty, taking them to the Bahamas. A US Navy helicopter from Guantánamo picked up eight wounded crew members and the bodies of three killed in action. The latter consisted of the captain and two officers of the deck.[1]

Later that day, exile sources claimed that anti-Castro commandos linked to Manuel Artime had attacked a Cuban ship carrying sugar. However, Artime's personal spokesperson denied attacking any vessel on the previous evening. He had good reason for denial. The raiders believed they had attacked the *Sierra Maestra,* the largest cargo vessel of the Cuban merchant marine. In point of fact, the *Sierra Maestra* was en route to China with a cargo of sugar.[2] The MRR had actually attacked the *Sierra Aranzazu,* a Spanish vessel carrying general cargo.

The government of General Francisco Franco, as well as those of Great Britain and France, had not broken off diplomatic and commercial relations with Castro's Cuba. Flights still proceeded between Havana and Madrid, making Spain the principal center of Cuban refugees in Europe. Under pressure from the United States, Spanish officials had agreed to end shipping to Cuba during the next year. However, the *Sierra Aranzazu* incident incensed the Spanish government so much that it contemplated canceling the agreement. The foreign ministry issued an accusatory news release: "Such acts would never have taken place were it not for the piracy and banditry against Cuba which has been carried out by the US government using bases situated in North American territory and in other Caribbean and Central American countries." Spain's foreign ministry went on to state that the "US Government knows perfectly well who carried out this attack since the authors were mercenary elements equipped, paid and directed by the Central Intelligence Agency."[3] The *Aranzazu* affair came in the midst of the final stages of the 1964 presidential campaign. It also exposed the thin red line between freedom fighters and terrorists.

Here we will analyze those paramilitary groups that continued the counter-revolution outside of Cuba. Evidence of North American complicity with these surrogates of the secret war had abounded despite efforts of the White House and the CIA to maintain a "plausible deniability" in their operations. "Beginning in 1961," as one government document admitted, "the CIA developed a major capability for paramilitary operations against Cuba. A substantial number of Cubans have been selected and intensively trained in all aspects of paramilitary work, including commando tactics and sabotage. . . . Only a small percentage of the trained personnel has been employed."[4]

The Kennedy administration approved the funding of a handful of these groups and encouraged them to operate offshore in the less-than-democratic countries of Nicaragua and the Dominican Republic. However, the exile paramilitaries seldom conformed to the wishes of their handlers of the CIA station in Miami. They trumpeted their ties to the US government, launched illegal attacks from the Florida Keys, held news conferences, and sought to manipulate their handlers. This aspect of the secret war turned out to be not so secret. Finally, the Johnson administration realized the futility of the project and ended it, giving the émigré commando groups the opportunity to blame their failures on the US government.

Few members of these paramilitary groups considered themselves counterrevolutionaries and often incorporated the term "revolution" into the titles of their organizations. Above all, they claimed to be anticommunist and patriotic Cubans. The CIA favored two of the three most prominent groups, led by men who had participated in the overthrow of Fulgencio Batista and who had served for a time in the revolutionary government of Fidel Castro. They were Manuel Artime and the former minister of public works Manuel Ray. Of the three most important leaders of covert operations, one was a Catholic conservative and the other two favored liberal reforms. Of the three, only Eloy Gutiérrez Menoyo did not receive monthly checks from the CIA. All three commando leaders claimed that they had not betrayed the revolution. Fidel had.[5]

Two questions merit consideration. Why did the US government covertly support the offshore counterrevolution, and how did this policy become self-defeating and counterproductive? American officials tolerated and in some instances paid for exiled counterrevolutionaries because, following the failure of the Bay of Pigs invasion in April 1961, American political leaders had devised no other viable policy to bring down Castro's communist regime. Into this policy vacuum stepped the Cuban exiles. In their covert operations, émigré combatants sought publicity for their exploits, broke US laws, threatened the Cold War allies of the United States, and committed piracy and terrorism. American security officials, hoping to achieve deniability, relinquished control over the Cuban counterrevolutionaries. Their desperate tactics yielded the moral high ground to their enemy, Fidel Castro. Ultimately, the covert activities of the anticommunist commandos accomplished more to confirm Castro's power than to undermine it.

COUNTERREVOLUTION IN MIAMI

The *batistiano* exiles were the first to organize armed resistance groups in the United States, but they received no assistance whatsoever from Washington. Batista's former deputy minister of interior Rafael Díaz-Balart started the White Rose. He and supporters of the ex-dictator in New York City attempted to take advantage of the first press criticism of the revolution toward the end of January 1959 for Castro's execution of former army and police officers. Díaz-Balart engaged mainly in publicity. In July 1960, he sent a telegram to the White House requesting "nothing else but guns in order to take out of Cuba the imperialist hands of Russia and Red China."[6] Cuba is a small place. Rafael Díaz-Balart's sister, Mirta, had married Fidel Castro in 1948 and divorced him in 1955. Therefore, Batista's deputy interior minister was a brother-in-law of Castro and uncle to Fidelito.[7] Most American officials wanted nothing to do with the *batistianos*. Foreign policy experts blamed the violence and corruption of Batista's followers for fomenting Castro's revolution.

American security agents placed their trust in those Cubans who had helped overturn the dictatorship. Despite the failure of the Bay of Pigs, the CIA continued training small teams of infiltrators and wireless communications operators. The CIA established a complex of offices in South Miami on property of the University of Miami—the CIA's Miami station. It had a budget of fifty million dollars per year and four hundred employees. Probably fifteen thousand Cubans earned income working on projects sponsored by the Miami station.[8] Agents in Miami worked on these plans with most exile groups, seven of which showed "promise as instruments for establishing internal assets (inside Cuba)." Their mission: "possible sabotage." These agents saw José Miró Cardona and the Cuban Revolutionary Council as a problem. The agency was subsidizing this organization at the rate of $137,000 per

Table 6.1   Monthly CIA Financial Payments to Cuban Exile Groups, 1963

Name of Organization	Amount of Payment
Cuban Workers Confederation in Exile (CTC)	$ 1,500
Cuban Women's Crusade (CFC)	$ 5,000
Movement for Revolutionary Recovery (MRR)[a]	$ 7,000
Revolutionary Unity (UR)	$ 9,000
Labor Revolutionary Democratic Front of Cuba (FORDC)	$ 10,000
Revolutionary Teachers Directorate (DMR)	$ 30,000
Student Revolutionary Directorate (DRE)	$ 51,000
Cuban Revolutionary Council (CRC)[b]	$137,000

Source: Desmond Fitzgerald, "Financial Payments Made by the Central Intelligence Agency to Cuban Exile Organizations," Apr 1963, National Security Files, box 48, John F. Kennedy Presidential Library.

[a.] The Artime group received millions of dollars from other CIA accounts.

[b.] Includes payments made to former Brigade 2506 members.

month. "Miro has used the funds to support individuals of his choosing and has not devoted attention to strengthening internal Cuban opposition," one agent concluded.[9] Anti-Castro leadership had become a profitable career option for some émigrés.

Miami's Cuban community propagated many transient groups possessing a few fishing boats and some guns that pretended to organize attacks on Soviet shipping and Cuban military targets. Others landed "infiltrators," as the CIA called them ("saboteurs" was Castro's definition), onshore near Havana or close to the island's several mountain ranges. Coast Guard commanders, the FBI, the CIA, and Florida and Miami authorities had knowledge of these activities because young men of the émigré community talked incessantly about them. Not having the financial resources to set up bases in third countries, many groups broke US neutrality laws. They launched armed forays directly from Florida and Puerto Rico.

Publicity rather than secrecy seemed to be the tactic of many groups—especially those with few prospects. If US agents had learned the details of these counterrevolutionary plots, Castro's espionage network knew them as well. Agents of State Security planted spies among refugees fleeing from Cuba, and, from time to time, CIA agents were able to expose Castro's spies operating in the United States. Indeed, Fidel acknowledged publicly that he knew everything the counterrevolutionaries were up to.[10]

The Cuban government informed its own people and the international community about what the Miami-based commandos were doing. Ernesto "Che" Guevara used his address to the General Assembly of the United Nations in December 1964 to expose the aggression. "Finally, distinguished delegates, it must be made clear that in the area of the Caribbean, maneuvers and preparations for aggression against Cuba are taking place, on the coasts of Nicaragua above all, in Costa Rica as well, in the Panama Canal Zone, on Vieques Island in Puerto Rico, in Florida, and possibly in other parts of United States territory and perhaps also in Honduras," Che said. "In these places Cuban mercenaries are training, as well as mercenaries of other nationalities, with a purpose that cannot be the most peaceful one."[11]

Endless requests for financial support sparked skepticism and ambivalence among many American policymakers, which explains why so few anti-Castro groups received funding. "Basically, I do not think that the Cuban exiles have much to offer the US by way of significantly helping us to solve our Cuban problem," wrote one White House aide. National Security adviser McGeorge "Mac" Bundy cautioned that support for the counterrevolution made the United States appear hypocritical, especially while seeking OAS votes condemning Cuba for its sponsorship of guerrilla fighters in Latin America. On the other hand, he observed, "We will still be living with Castro some time from now, and . . . we might just as well get used to the idea. At the same time, we should probably continue our present nasty course; among other things, it makes life a little tougher for Castro and raises slightly the poor odds that he will come apart and be overthrown."[12] Said another White House aide, "As things stand, he seems convinced that we are tied into the raids—as indeed we are."[13] Notwithstanding the skepticism, support for the counterrevolutionaries continued into the mid-1960s. Following the failure of the Bay of Pigs invasion and Operation Mongoose (which ended in 1962), two prior CIA projects against the revolution, no other policy remained to eliminate Fidel Castro.[14] The public policy was to isolate revolutionary Cuba; the secret one was to bring about the overthrow of the Castro government by the Cubans themselves.

Due to the reservations of many Johnson administration officials, the CIA chose to fund only a few of these many groups sufficiently to operate offshore in the greater Caribbean theater. The leaders of these favored commando units did not suffer the taint of having served under Batista's dictatorship. Instead, each had collaborated with Castro in the revolution and in the provisional government. In US security lexicon, they were "liberals." Washington selected Manuel Ray and especially Manuel Artime as champions of the counterrevolution.[15] Eloy Gutiérrez Menoyo operated mostly on funding from exile donors. Their stories reveal large expenditures, collaboration with autocratic regimes in Central America, the weakness of the counterrevolution abroad, and the strength of the Cuban revolutionary regime. These anti-Castro forces produced no devastating blows against the revolution and frequently embarrassed United States policymakers.

The White House operated under the policy that came to be known as the Kennedy Doctrine. "We in this hemisphere must . . . use every resource at our command to prevent the establishment of another Cuba," President Kennedy told the audience of the Inter American Press Association at his last public speech in Miami on November 18, 1963.[16] He delivered this speech just days before he arrived in Dallas, Texas.

FIDELISMO SIN FIDEL

Manuel Ray Rivera was the highest-ranking defector to receive financial support from the CIA. He was also the least competent combatant. Castro's former public works minister left Cuba on November 7, 1960, and arrived in the United States in time to have the White House appoint him to the Cuban Revolutionary Council, the political front for the Bay of Pigs invasion. Most émigré leaders distrusted Ray for his leftist ideas and his ten months in the revolutionary government. They said he favored "Fidelismo sin Fidel." When the Bay of Pigs operation failed, Ray broke with the CRC in order to form the Cuban Revolutionary Junta (JURE).

Walt Rostow of the Kennedy team had been among the first to suggest CIA support for Cuban paramilitary units. Rostow and his fellow New Frontiersman Arthur M. Schlesinger Jr. favored Manuel Ray because they believed he still had an "underground" in Havana capable of sabotage and resistance against Castro.[17] As Ray explained to the CIA, he would run his organization "as independently as possible of any official US connection." Even though CIA agents considered Ray "difficult to handle," they offered him financial support. He had even promised not to break US neutrality laws, since his activities would be carried out "solely within Cuba." He established operations in Puerto Rico, where he had a government job and built houses for a living.[18]

JURE got into action following the release from jail of the Bay of Pigs prisoners at the end of 1962. Paramilitary groups were being formed in South Florida, many of which sought scarce donations from the Cuban community and from the US government. For publicity and profile, Ray and his associate picketed in Washington, DC, when the Organization of American States was considering sanctions against Cuba. He supported Venezuela's charge that Castro had intervened in that country's internal affairs by supporting a guerrilla uprising. JURE members also manned a picket of protesters at the Brazilian consulate in Miami during the presidency of João Goulart, who maintained diplomatic relations with the Castro regime. Ray let it be known that he kept all public actions perfectly legal so that JURE would not jeopardize its good standing with the US government.[19] Like many others, Manolo Ray wanted American officials to know that he was worthy of financial support.

Subsequently, word went out that Manolo Ray and his associates in JURE would be fighting in Cuba on Independence Day, May 20, 1964. The day was important because Fidel had ended public celebrations of the date in 1902 on which the American occupation had transferred the government to Cuban politicians. Ray advertised the date with the objective of bolstering JURE's reputation in the Miami community as well as to encourage resistance in Cuba to coincide with JURE's landing. "Wasn't this Martí's mistake? And Castro's?" asked one intelligence analyst.[20] The rebel armed forces were on alert but not yet mobilized. Meanwhile, JURE was training its recruits in the mountains of Puerto Rico. One of those men, later captured inside Cuba, told Castro's G-2 that "we underwent guerrilla training at the JURE headquarters of Fernández Junco: Assembling and dismantling of US-made weapons, explosives, and wireless equipment. We also learned to orient ourselves and to follow maps."[21]

Ray's plan called for a boat landing at a place near Havana, where thirteen men in disguise and with false identification papers would infiltrate and head for a prearranged safe house. His vessel, the *Venus,* was to leave from Puerto Rico on May 19 at full throttle.[22] Informants mentioned that friction developed within JURE when some newly integrated members discovered they would not be involved in the operation. Ray told them that their continued training would lead to a balanced, long-term struggle. At the last moment, plans changed. The departure was to be made not from Puerto Rico but from a base in Costa Rica.[23]

On the appointed day, May 20, 1964, Manolo Ray was neither in Cuba nor in Costa Rica. He was on board a boat in the Florida Keys. His third plan now called for a boat trip to the mangrove islands off the north coast of Matanzas Province, where collaborators would meet him. He had acquired communications equipment from the United States so that he could demonstrate to his contacts in Cuba that he had US support. Ray's intention now was to infiltrate and begin a campaign of sabotage and propaganda in Havana. JURE's spokesperson asked Washington for more money. What had Ray done with all the money he had collected from his "several fund-raising campaigns"? It was spent on preparations, the spokesman answered.[24]

In the meantime, JURE's publicity campaign began with great fanfare. The *New York Times* published articles based on interviews with Manuel Ray. The articles created the impression in the exile community that Ray had CIA backing, as Cubans in Miami considered the *Times* to be "the official US policy organ." Rival paramilitary groups resented the preferential coverage given to Manolo Ray; it was akin to Herbert Matthews's having been kingmaker to Fidel Castro.[25]

Therefore, it was with great anticipation that JURE partisans awaited Manolo Ray's radio broadcast from inside Cuba. Saturday, May 23, was to be the appointed moment. But no radio contact was made. "JURE reps believe that no news is good news," concluded the CIA's informants, "and the only reason for this is that Ray has not yet had an opportunity to communicate with them."[26] Within a few days, a spokesperson for Ray reported that he had not yet arrived in Cuba because "vigilance by the United States authorities over the activities of JURE [representatives] in Florida is making the support of Ray's effort extremely difficult."[27] Cuba was waiting for Manuel Ray's return as well. News articles about a May 20 landing had been appearing for weeks. The government declared that militiamen and army personnel continued to work in the cane harvest but were prepared to react to any invasion. As late as May 29, Castro announced that he had yet to learn of any counterrevolutionary "desembarque."[28]

Finally, on June 3 came word from British authorities: they had spotted a boat adrift in Bahamian waters. The HMS *Decoy* headed to the site, where its crew discovered arms, ammunition, and explosives aboard and apprehended the pilot and seven passengers. It was Manuel Ray. He was accompanied by two American newsmen, one a writer and the other a photographer. The State Department called Ray a "laughing stock" for having been caught in the Bahamas ten days after he was supposed to have landed in Cuba.[29] Nonetheless, the CIA gave him extra money beyond his monthly stipend to enable Ray to recover from this "humiliating and noisy" fiasco.

Back in Miami, Manuel Ray continued with a whirlwind of alternative plots meant to throw off Castro's agents or the CIA's—or both. Ray planned a new action. In July 1964, the Coast Guard intercepted two boats of the JURE, warning the passengers that if they continued on to Cuba, "they might be met with hostile action." Manuel Ray turned the boats around and headed back to Key West. He went out again a few days later, but high waves swamped his boat. Subsequently, Ray informed State Department officials that his plan was to infiltrate and begin an urban insurrection. "Ray considered that [the] vital element in getting [the] campaign started would be his own presence in Cuba in order to raise resistance morale." The officials reminded him that Washington disapproved of armed raids launched from US territory. Ray promised to "do everything possible to carry out [JURE's] plans without coming into conflict with [US government] policy." The agents advised him that he would be wise to operate from somewhere else than Florida.[30] Manuel Ray took the advice.

Not until six months later did the CIA report that Ray and his followers were in Puerto Rico again. They were preparing to depart for JURE's base in the Dominican Republic. There they were to take on small arms and .50-caliber machine guns, but repairs to the radar system of the *Venus,* his mother ship, caused delays. JURE also had thirteen men (all listed by name in the CIA cable, including Huber Matos Araluce, son of the former M26 comandante who was then languishing in Castro's prisons). From the Dominican base, the *Venus* was to head for the coast of Oriente Province to mount armed raids against targets along the coastline.[31]

However, ship repairs resulted in more delays in Puerto Rico, and his men became disillusioned. "They are all anxious to see action but Ray has been giving them nothing but promises and plans," the CIA reported. The skipper of the *Venus,* José Rabel Núñez, was said to be plotting a mutiny. Intrigue continued among the group into February 1965 as members left the organization.[32]

The *Venus* ultimately arrived at a naval base in the Dominican Republic, where it remained through April 1965, when the constitutionalist military rebellion broke out. The rebels attempted to confiscate the ship and its arms but were thwarted by pro-government forces. Subsequently, Captain Rabel Núñez of the *Venus* returned to Miami, then sailed his own boat into Cuba "to pick up [his] family." There Castro's forces captured him.[33] Manuel Ray retired from his undistinguished career in paramilitary warfare. He returned to Puerto Rico to do what his university training had prepared him for—the construction of buildings. Said one intelligence operative from the Miami station: "Working with Ray seemed to be a marginal venture at best."[34]

AN EXPERIENCED GUERRILLA FIGHTER

Eloy Gutiérrez Menoyo, the former anti-Batista guerrilla chieftain and comandante in the rebel armed forces, escaped from Cuba just as he was resolving to fight against Fidel Castro. He had been preparing to reenter the Escambray Mountains, where many of his associates were battling the government militias. In January 1961, Menoyo fled by boat with several close colleagues and began four months of interrogation and CIA training in Texas. Andrés Nazario Sargen arrived on the boat with Gutiérrez Menoyo, Lazaro Ascencio, and Armando Fleites. "Four comandantes arriving together produced a stir in the growing exile community," Nazario Sargen recalls. They formed Alpha 66 in October 1962. "It was a revolutionary movement made up for the most part of veterans of the II Front of Escambray."[35]

Menoyo and his lieutenants arrived too late to join Brigade 2506 at the Bay of Pigs. In Miami, they formed Alpha 66, which operated under his leadership together with his old anti-Batista group, the Second Front. These groups would specialize in infiltration and sabotage.[36] Menoyo went into action following the Cuban Missile Crisis and the return of the Bay of Pigs prisoners. His first anti-Castro forays excited the émigré community and embarrassed the White House and the State Department.

Alpha 66 held news conferences in Miami and Washington, DC, to publicize Menoyo's initial fast-boat raid on the Cuban port of Sagua el

Grande. He claimed to have inflicted casualties to a dozen Soviet sailors and troops, some of whom had been dressed in Cuban militia uniforms. "Cuba has been taken over militarily," Alpha 66 spokesmen claimed. They informed reporters that the anti-Castro militants had launched the raid from a base "somewhere in the Caribbean not from the US or from the British Bahamas." Funding for the groups' operations came from sympathetic Central American countries and American citizens. The commandos did not work for and were not beholden to any agency of the US government. Reporters asked the spokesmen why they made this raid. "It is the duty of every Cuban," they answered, "to combat intensively against Soviet-Chinese occupation of the fatherland." Moreover, they asserted that such raids would foment internal rebellion against the Castro regime.[37]

Gutiérrez Menoyo's second raid in March 1963 provoked a rebuke from the Soviet Union because two Russian freighters had come under attack. US intelligence determined that the commandos shot up one ship, the *L'Gov*, and also attacked the freighter *Baku*. They breached the hull of the second ship with a "floating bomb," and it ran aground in the harbor of Caibarien. Also, US intelligence established that the attack boats had departed from Miami—not a foreign port somewhere else in the Caribbean. On learning of the attack on the Russian merchant ships, Foreign Minister Andrei Gromyko summoned the US ambassador to the Kremlin. The Soviet official said that he could not accept Secretary Rusk's statement disavowing any responsibility for the incident. "How can [the United States] make such statements and at the same time act in direct contradiction to them?" Gromyko demanded to know. "Can [the US government] really hope to find serious people who can believe that it is not involved, when this exile scum was sitting under [the] US wing?" Ambassador Foy D. Kohler responded that the USSR shares the blame for getting involved in a dispute between Cubans— an ironic accusation for an American diplomat. Kohler also faulted the Soviets for violating the missile crisis agreement, because US inspectors were not allowed into Cuba.[38] In point of fact, Fidel Castro and not the Soviets prevented US inspectors from entering Cuba.

President Kennedy himself felt obliged to rebuke Menoyo's fighters. "We don't think a rather hastily organized raid which maybe shoots up a merchant ship or kills some crewman, comes back, holds a press conference represents a serious blow to Castro," he said during a televised press conference, "and, in fact, [it] may assist him in maintaining his control." He contrasted the irresponsible commandos to five hundred veterans of the Bay of Pigs who were undergoing basic training with the US Armed Forces. "The commander of the brigade, [Erneido Oliva], who is a Cuban, a Negro, got all of his marks at 100 in joining the service," Kennedy said. "So I think there are a good many . . . persistent Cubans who are determined that their island should be free, and we wish to assist them."[39] The US Coast Guard and the FBI had to step up their interdiction of raids launched from the United States so as to avoid acts of piracy and violations of the Neutrality Act.

The Menoyo incident provoked a debate between John McCone of the CIA and Secretary of State Dean Rusk. McCone admitted that the raiders could not be controlled "because they are brave men fighting for [the] freedom of their country." Moreover, the émigré attacks caused trouble for Castro inside Cuba and discredited him abroad. Rusk countered that hit-and-run raids that could not be controlled would yield no benefits. "If anyone is shooting Russians we ought to be doing it," Rusk argued. The president sided with his secretary of state, and McCone followed instructions to inform the commando groups not to attack merchant vessels.[40] President Kennedy's embarrassment may have provided the reason to withhold funding from Gutiérrez Menoyo. Donations in Miami and New York, while not as generous as government subsidies, did suffice for him to continue.

Divisions among the Cubans manifested themselves in President Kennedy's visit to Miami just days before his assassination in Dallas. The more conservative groups were planning opposition rallies yet settled for delivering letters to the president's aides. They faulted Kennedy's speech for not suggesting stronger measures against the Castro regime. On the other hand, the factions of Eloy Gutiérrez Menoyo and Manuel Ray found satisfaction in the president's support of the "anti-Communist progressive and revolutionary elements."[41]

It was President Kennedy himself who signed the executive order that unleashed the émigré commandos. There had been unanimity among his foreign affairs advisers that the CIA should encourage Cuban émigrés to infiltrate the island for purposes of sabotage. The CIA informed the advisers that it would not do this because such infiltrators would certainly be caught. Lyndon B. Johnson inherited this paramilitary project when he took over the Oval Office. However, the new president hesitated when the CIA informed him about the training of a small commando group that would attack the Matanzas power plant. President Johnson canceled the raid. He did not want to provoke Soviet retaliation on the U-2s providing inspection flyovers of the Cuban missile sites. At the time, Soviet crews still controlled the surface-to-air missiles but had condoned American aerial reconnaissance following the 1962 missile crisis.[42]

Perhaps to restore his funding under President Johnson, Menoyo approached the CIA with Plan Omega, in which his organizations would send armed infiltrators back into the Escambray Mountains. Menoyo himself was to lead the first of three groups. He also pointed out for the benefit of his CIA handlers that he was seeking training bases in the Yucatán Peninsula, Panama, and the Dominican Republic (now that Menoyo's nemesis, the dictator Rafael Trujillo, had died in an assassination plot). Additional financial support would come from ex-president Carlos Prío Socarrás, he announced.[43] Menoyo claimed that the Second Front also had assets in Venezuela, where President Rómulo Betancourt, himself challenged by leftist guerrillas, supported anti-Castro activities. A member of the Second Front met with Herbert Matthews of the *New York Times* in hopes of gaining publicity for its activities.[44]

Plan Omega in action lacked the coherence promised on paper. The State Department reported that several of Menoyo's associates felt marginalized, and that there remained those in Miami wary of the Second Front. Factionalism abounded in the exile community. However, Gutiérrez Menoyo did build up credibility by organizing a boycott of English products in protest against Great Britain's sale of busses to the Castro government.[45]

Frequent press conferences created the image of activity and commitment, two qualities that attracted donors. "The Communists . . . stole our revolution," Menoyo's people told reporters. "The Castro regime is demoralized. The resistance of the Cuban people, when added to the industrial decay of the Communist regime, makes it possible to carry the war to Cuba and to pursue it to final victory on Cuban soil."[46] Some officials of the US government expressed approval of his "resolute" personality. At the State Department, he was known as a "Spaniard who only became a Cuban citizen in 1959 [and who] keeps his own counsel and is secretive to a degree almost unknown among Cubans."[47] Subsequent events would chip away at this image of resolve and secrecy.

In May 1964, Eloy Gutiérrez Menoyo disappeared from view, setting the émigré community abuzz with anticipation. Menoyo's wife came to the door of their home to inform reporters that her husband had left and would be gone "for a while." A report from the Dominican Republic suggested that fast boats of the Second Front had just departed for Cuba. An associate attempted to mislead the public by indicating that Menoyo had gone to New York. Rumors persisted nevertheless that he was in Pinar del Río Province with some seventy armed combatants who had trained in Venezuela and the Dominican Republic.[48] Agents learned of Cuban troop mobilizations and the movement of tanks and heavy weaponry in the far western part of the island. Government forces there reported having killed a number of counterrevolutionary guerrillas in the Órganos Mountains. Some speculated also that Menoyo's men were planning an air attack on a British merchant ship.[49] The CIA station in Miami did not appear to know where Menoyo was operating. The rumors died down, and six months passed without a sighting.

Evidently, Menoyo really lacked supporters willing to return to Cuba as a sizeable guerrilla unit. His strategy changed back to an incremental infiltration of small armed groups. Dominican military authorities had given Menoyo permission to utilize Punta Presidente, Santo Domingo, for equipping and arming thirty infiltrators who were to enter Cuba, one group at a time. Menoyo himself would lead the first small group. They would hide in the mountains for a month in order to establish friendly relations with the peasant population. Then, additional small units would reinforce this vanguard.[50] Menoyo chose a landing site at the base of the Sierra del Cristal near Baracoa, at the extreme northeastern end of Cuba. He and three men finally landed back in Cuba shortly after Christmas Day 1964.

Nothing transpired according to plan. Workers' militias from the nearby town of Guatánamo answered the alert and pursued the small group of counterrevolutionaries until they surrendered. Prensa Latina in Havana announced that Menoyo and his three accomplices had been captured. Fidel Castro himself flew to Baracoa.[51] American naval officers at Guantánamo Bay reported heavy concentrations of militia units in the area. "[Government] troops were observed in [Guantánamo] city. Troops were in soiled field uniforms and were rejoicing because they had captured [four] armed bandits in Baracoa."[52]

Just a few weeks later Eloy Gutiérrez Menoyo, the revolutionary turned counterrevolutionary, appeared on television with his three compatriots. Viewers watched as he answered the questions of a team of interrogators. Menoyo admitted to having defected from Cuba early in 1961. On arriving in the United States, he said, he was held at a detention center in Texas for four months. There he eventually accepted an offer of military training with the United States Army. Subsequently, Menoyo joined the CIA for instruction on handling explosives and machine guns. His Cuban interrogators asked to what purpose Menoyo applied these new skills. He replied that he organized a group of counterrevolutionary combatants, raised fifty thousand dollars in the Miami area, purchased arms and watercraft, and directed six or seven armed attacks on Cuban targets. Menoyo claimed to be the leader of several allied organizations: the Second National Front of the Escambray, Alpha 66, and the Revolutionary Movement of the People.

The interrogators inquired as to how Menoyo and his three associates had been able to obtain sophisticated weaponry and to set up bases offshore in the Bahamas, Puerto Rico, and the Dominican Republic. They replied that American authorities protected these assets, as did the Dominican armed forces. What do you think of the counterrevolutionary organizations abroad, interrogators asked. "Very bad," Menoyo answered. "They have pretty low moral standards." He confessed that his men had mounted attacks on Cuba in order to raise more money and that, yes, "it is within the realm of possibility" that innocent people might have been killed in these attacks.

The interviewers also asked Menoyo about the workers and peasants of Cuba. "I had to go to many houses—the houses of peasants," Menoyo said of his armed incursion. "I found that they were hostile to us and that as soon as we left, they reported to the armed forces that we were in the area. . . . We were surrounded and captured on 23 January, at which time I could see that hundreds of production workers had left their work and had taken up weapons and gone out to pursue us."[53] The TV broadcast seemed to confirm two important arguments that Fidel Castro had been making after taking power in 1959: first, that "traitors" like Menoyo were working for the CIA and, second, that the masses supported the revolution.

Meanwhile, White House aides scrambled for a policy statement, even as they denied any complicity with Menoyo's group. Nor would Washington intercede on Menoyo's behalf. Any admission that he was a CIA asset in Cuba would "make things worse for him." Our connections to Gutiérrez Menoyo "will be a blow to anti-Castro morale in Cuba," wrote one adviser in President Johnson's National Security Council. "Also, it shows how efficient the Cuban Government is; Menoyo is an old experienced guerrilla fighter who, in the past, has impressed [us] with his intelligence, security, and carefulness."[54]

Therefore, the US government did nothing as Cuban interrogators interviewed the four captives on television. The story appeared in US newspapers, which quoted Menoyo as saying, "I worked for a while with the CIA."[55] The subsequent military trial in Cuba condemned Eloy Gutiérrez Menoyo. Shortly thereafter, Castro interrupted a talk he was delivering at the University of Havana and asked if Menoyo should be executed or ransomed. The students voted by acclamation for ransom.[56] In a rare show of unity, the "liberal" organizations of the Cuban community in Miami signed petitions for clemency. Such pleas also came from Spanish cellist Pablo Casals and Mexico's ex-president Lázaro Cárdenas, a frequent guest of the Cuban revolutionary government.[57] Ultimately, Menoyo did gain a reprieve—though no ransom—and spent twenty-two years in Cuban prisons.

GOLDEN BOY OF THE CIA

No counterrevolutionary émigré received as much support from the US government as did Manuel Artime. He arrived in Miami in January 1960 with a high profile as an anticommunist. He had been a lieutenant in the Sierra Maestra with Castro's M26. Artime supported moderate land reform and resigned from his job in Castro's National Institute of Agrarian Reform when its communist leaders introduced collectivization of the land. The Catholic underground gave Artime shelter as he formed a few friends into a domestic resistance group, the MRR. He then proposed to go abroad to seek American support, while his associates remained in Cuba. Priests ultimately directed him to CIA agents, who smuggled him out of Cuba on a Honduran freighter. Other CIA men awaited his arrival in Miami. They impressed him greatly with their polygraph tests.[58] These guys know how to operate, he thought.

Artime wasted no time in forming a branch of the Movement for Revolutionary Recovery. In June 1960, three colleagues joined him in issuing the obligatory proclamation about "why we fight." The document mentions betrayal of the revolution by Fidel Castro, Artime's former guerrilla commander. "The MRR has been organized," Artime and colleagues wrote, "because Castro is decided to sacrifice Cuba to the expediency of Soviet International Policy."[59]

Once President Dwight D. Eisenhower had approved the operation that became the Bay of Pigs invasion, CIA handlers decided that Artime's reputation made him a candidate for leadership. They helped him write and publish a book denouncing Cuban communism and sent him on a Latin American lecture tour. Back in Miami, he helped recruit the military leadership of Brigade 2506 of the Bay of Pigs invasion. The CIA then sent him to the Panama Canal Zone for training in jungle warfare and military communications.

In November 1960, when liberal-minded exile trainees mutinied against their *batistiano* commanders, José San Román and Erneido Oliva, the CIA sent Artime. As a conservative Catholic but also a junior officer in M26, Artime had gained the trust of liberals and *batistianos* for the way he had broken so publicly with the revolution. He spoke to an assembly of officers and men about the need for unity against Castro. He said that everyone's life depended on the military training of the officers who had served Batista, yes, but honorably and without blemish.[60]

He stayed on as the unit's political officer and liaison to the Cuban Revolutionary Council. Once launched from bases in Nicaragua, the invaders made an amphibious landing at Playa Girón. Brigade 2506 suffered a crushing defeat. When militia and rebel army troops captured most of the surviving *brigadistas,* Artime attempted to flee to the Escambray but wandered aimlessly in the swamps until apprehended by Castro's forces. He spent more than a year and a half in prison. According to his own testimony, Fidel Castro came to see the imprisoned *brigadistas* one night. He had come to inform them that the revolutionary courts had handed down prison sentences, up to thirty years for Artime, rather than execution. Before Fidel left, he turned to Manuel Artime and said, "It's a pity you're not a Communist," to which Artime replied, "It's a pity you're not a democrat."[61]

Artime gained release with the other *brigadistas* just two months after the Cuban Missile Crisis of 1962. During the welcoming ceremony at the Miami Orange Bowl, he and the commanders presented President Kennedy with the flag of Brigade 2506, as First Lady Jacqueline Kennedy stood at his side. "I can assure you that this flag will be returned to this Brigade in a free Havana," the president said. The First Lady added that it was an honor for her "to be today with a group of the bravest men in the world."[62] Artime accompanied the delegation of Brigade leaders who visited Robert F. Kennedy.

President John F. Kennedy and First Lady Jacqueline Kennedy greet officers of
Brigade 2506 at the Orange Bowl in January 1963. The officers appearing in khaki
shirts include *(left to right)* José San Román and Manuel Artime.

The attorney general conferred with them in his offices and at his home in
Hickory Hill. "The whole [commando] operation was set up as a result of
Artime's discussion with the Kennedys," said one CIA officer.[63] Bobby
Kennedy and his brother the president were looking for the next proxies to
carry on their anti-Castro crusade now that Operation Mongoose's plans
for assassination and sabotage had proven unproductive.

Castro's prisons did not diminish Artime's enthusiasm for overturning
the revolution. The veteran foreign correspondent Jules Dubois, whom Castro
had expelled from Cuba for his championing of press freedoms, printed a
quote from Artime's first speech after returning to Miami. "We owe it to
the mothers of the 300 men who died in the liberation-attempt on the
beaches of the Bay of Pigs," Artime told a crowd of four thousand, "to maintain the unity of Brigade 2506 and prepare to fight to rescue our fatherland
from international communism!"[64] Asked by another journalist if he thought
that President Kennedy's economic blockade would cause the collapse of Castro's regime, Artime answered, "It is like trying to cure cancer with a ban-

dage. Many types of cancer require radical surgery. Communism is one of these; it can only be cured by the knife."[65]

In Miami, Manuel Artime served as a unifying figure as few others could. Former president Prío Socarrás called to tell Artime that he wished to be identified with his Movement for Revolutionary Recovery.[66] The Cuban Revolutionary Council disintegrated when José Miró Cardona resigned in mid-1963. Miró bitterly criticized his formerly generous patrons at the CIA Miami station for the CRC failures. At that time, Robert F. Kennedy promised to sponsor a unity organization. Artime's MRR pledged unity as did many others—even the *batistianos*.[67]

Former Nicaraguan president Luis Somoza came to Miami in July 1963. He also attempted to unify various Cuban microfactions by vowing to work "with a single leader." He favored Manuel Artime. Other factions reacted tepidly.[68] For years, their obsequious attitude toward United States policies had ingratiated the Somozas with Washington policymakers. They were courting the Kennedy administration just as much as Manuel Artime.[69] The upshot was that Somoza would provide base facilities at Puerto Cabezas to Artime's commando organization in order to launch hit-and-run seaborne raids on Cuba. One of the groups to sign on was the L-66, run by former officers in Batista's navy.[70] Miami Cubans regarded the naval officers as heroes because they had mounted the greatest military resistance to Batista's rule with a massive uprising in 1955 in the port of Cienfuegos.

The CIA found Artime a logical choice for financial support. A famous dissident, a Catholic nationalist with advanced military training, and a Bay of Pigs hero—even former president Carlos Prío Socarrás admired him. Prío used his prestige and his connections to assist Artime's MRR. He negotiated with Dominican army officers for logistical support and with Luis Somoza to facilitate the journey of recruits to join the MRR at its Nicaraguan base. Prío also knew—as did other exiles—that the CIA supported the MRR. Artime was very ambitious, Prío once said, and he had "the backing of the Jesuits."[71]

However, it was the CIA's backing that made Artime's outfit the best equipped and most effective paramilitary force in the Caribbean. Unlike most other resistance leaders, such as Gutiérrez Menoyo, he did not have to spend time dunning people for a few bucks here and there at fundraising dinners. Artime denied that he took money from the CIA. The Cuban community in Miami and New York knew differently, that he was the CIA's biggest beneficiary. Cuban exiles admired—and envied—him for that. Artime's staff also received training directly from CIA operatives—especially in advanced communications. Moreover, Manuel Artime did not have to operate in violation of US neutrality laws because his MRR possessed the wherewithal to mount armed raids against Cuba from several bases outside of American territory. He assembled about three hundred men and two hundred tons of arms, costing the CIA approximately six million dollars. "We're going to overthrow Castro," he told his recruits. "This time we're really going to do it."[72]

Every group seemed to have its detractors within the leadership of the Cuban community. Manuel Ray and JURE voiced their disgust that Artime had agreed to work out of a Nicaraguan base supported by the Somozas. They called it an "incredible pact between one exile sector and a tyrannical Somoza dynasty." Ray's JURE described itself, in contrast, as a "true revolution which advocates economic development and social justice within the framework of democratic freedoms."[73] Eventually, the Americans' lack of control over anti-Castro commando groups, even the best of them, would bring down the whole project.

TERMINATION

Artime's reputation and CIA support provided numerous advantages in recruiting the best men available. Once accepted for MRR training, young volunteers in Miami received $150 to $250 per month. In the last week of December 1963, upward of 150 Cubans were already training in Costa Rica. One of Artime's men who had prior US Army training took the job of preparing the Costa Rican training camp. "I never worked so hard in my life," one MRR recruit says. "With explosives and a bulldozer, we cleared a twenty-three mile trail through the bush," in order to complete six training camps for the infiltration teams.[74]

Artime had made friends with the brother of the Costa Rican president and with the vice president of the legislative assembly. MRR fighters were training on the ranch of Ludwig Starke, leader of an anticommunist paramilitary organization called the Free Costa Rica Movement. Government officials, with the assistance of Nicaragua's Somoza brothers, helped Artime acquire arms.[75] MRR leaders realized that these patrons were profiting from the rental of facilities, the importation of arms, and the purchase of supplies for the Cuban fighters.

Information about the relationship between the politicians and the anti-Castro Cubans soon reached the Costa Rican public. Left-wing commentators publicized the fact that Cuban émigrés were undergoing military training in Costa Rica. Communist leader Manuel Mora Valverde went on radio and denounced the émigrés for preparing "an invasion of Cuba." Valverde accused the government of President Francisco Orlich of arming not only the Cubans but also the Costa Rican right-wing paramilitaries. "Word will soon get out," lamented one American diplomat after the Valverde broadcast.[76] Indeed, the Communist party leader sent reports to communists and Castro in Havana.

Personnel at the embassy in San José did not have to wait long. *La Prensa Libre* in San José sent its reporters to the training areas. They found no Cubans but did discover evidence of target practice in discarded cartridges and empty ammo boxes. Nevertheless, training proceeded. Fifty members of the right-wing Costa Rican paramilitary and the seventy Cubans prepared for joint military maneuvers while news stories linked President Orlich's brother to the training sites.[77] Therefore, the Costa Rican president was in a glum mood when he made a state visit to Washington, DC. He inquired as to the attitude of the Johnson administration toward the Cuban counterrevolutionaries. Thomas Mann of the State Department answered for President Johnson. He merely stated that Manuel Artime and others "were trying to help Cuba return to freedom and we sympathized with their objective."[78]

Expectation concerning Artime's plans for 1964 was building in the Cuban exile communities throughout the Caribbean. MRR members spread the word that one hundred men were training in Nicaragua, Costa Rica, Honduras, and the Dominican Republic (though the number was actually larger). MRR spokespersons claimed that they were getting "full material support" from the US government. A leading Cuban exile in Venezuela referred to Artime as the "golden boy of the CIA."[79]

However, its exposure in Costa Rica prompted the MRR to lose some momentum as it moved men and materiel next door to Nicaragua. With the backing of the Somozas, Manuel Artime did not have to confront embarrassing left-wing criticism. He found in Anastasio Somoza, commander of the Nicaraguan National Guard, a companion-in-arms in the fight against communism—and a spokesman for his conservative cause. "Whoever is backing Artime on the American side should not send him people with whom he cannot work," Somoza told a CIA informant, "but let Artime run the show and forget about replacing him with someone else—if, in fact, any serious thought is being given to this idea." Somoza said he did not care if MRR raiders fell into Castro's hands and revealed that Nicaragua was aiding the organization. "In light of proved acts of terrorism through infiltration of revolutionaries, some of whom are in Nicaraguan jails, Nicaragua is taking all steps necessary to retaliate" against Castro.[80]

General Anastasio Somoza fully supported MRR operations, enabling Artime to concentrate on military training. The Nicaraguan consul in Miami, himself a lieutenant of the Guardia Nacional, expedited the MRR's communications and travel. His government waived the usual customs requirements for freighters supplying the MRR.[81] A newly constructed airstrip facilitated air support. Evidence suggests that the Somoza regime even backed the MRR in security and disciplinary matters. In one instance in Puerto Cabezas, three Cubans in handcuffs were turned over to the Guardia Nacional and transported to Managua. Informants believed these men might have been spies for Fidel Castro.[82]

Even in Nicaragua, the presence of counterrevolutionaries could not be kept secret. Newsmen and radio commentators in Managua talked openly about Cuban activities at Puerto Cabezas. They reported that the émigrés would soon launch an invasion "with [the] help of U.S. armed forces." American embassy personnel in Managua scrambled to deny rumors of American military involvement, even though they did not know for certain what was transpiring on Nicaragua's Caribbean coast.[83] Nor did Artime's financier, the CIA station in Miami.

Intelligence reports coming to Washington, DC, indicated that the MRR was assembling an impressive paramilitary apparatus. The MRR naval station at Monkey Point was located within a military security zone on Nicaragua's Caribbean coast. Government security measures undercut land usage in the area, and property values began to plummet. The Somozas thereupon commenced buying up the cheap lands, enhancing the isolation of the Cuban trainees. MRR crews in fast boats traveled back and forth between Bluefields and Monkey Point. Landing craft were spotted in training along the coastline. Cuban personnel often took time off in the bars of Puerto Cabezas and Bluefields. When all of them headed back to their camps in mid-May 1964, informants believed that some sort of raid was imminent.[84] They were correct.

The MRR attacked the Cuban sugar refinery at Puerto Pilón on May 13 and claimed a great victory. Information circulated that the raiders had destroyed the mill, the fuel storage depot, and a radio tower. Despite the refinery being fully manned by work crews, a member of the seaborne attack team said that only two women were slightly injured. "At a distance of 25 to 30 miles at sea, flames from the burning target were still clearly visible," reported the MRR fighter.[85] But the CIA had its doubts, stating that the raid had only burned two sugar warehouses and several thousand bags of sugar. Secretary of State Dean Rusk himself verified the truth of the attack but pointed out that this anti-Castro raid did not originate from US territory.[86]

National Security advisers in the White House continued to monitor the activities of the MRR. "Artime is expected to strike again sometime during the week," one aide speculated in June 1964. "There appears to be little to do except to hold onto your hat along with the rest of us."[87] Eventually, in August, the MRR carried out another armed raid, this one an assault on a radar station at Cabo Cruz on the southern coast of Oriente Province. In a press conference in Panama, Artime said that his commandos "destroyed" a radar station from which 150 Cubans and three Russian advisers supposedly were tracking boats carrying refugees fleeing Cuba.[88] Such claims always appeared exaggerated to observers at the CIA in Miami and Langley too.

It was at this moment that Artime's fast boats attacked the Spanish merchant ship *Sierra Aranzazu*. The White House was now convinced that it had to temper the monster it had created with CIA funding. It was one thing to encourage émigré groups to infiltrate into Cuba and commit acts of subversion but quite another to allow these groups to select their own hit-and-run targets. The latter sort of operation posed less risk to the commandos but greater international condemnation for the United States. It was for Cuba's threat to the security of Venezuela that the United States pressed the Organization of American States to isolate Castro's regime. Now American policies seemed duplicitous as well. The Franco government in Madrid demanded explanations from the US government.

Spanish protests were temporarily mollified when American officials promised to investigate. CIA agents knew full well that the MRR had mounted the attack on the *Sierra Aranzazu*. But for security reasons, they convinced the White House that it must deny prior knowledge of the attack and reject the notion that any group funded by the United States had attacked the Spanish freighter.[89] Staff members of President Johnson's

National Security Council worked on "talking points" to give the Spaniards "the minimum [information] necessary to keep them from thinking that we are trying to deceive them."[90]

White House aides also gave instructions to the president's press secretary. He was to say that the US investigation had established that the attack on the *Sierra Aranzazu* was not launched from American territory and thus broke no American neutrality laws. If asked, the press secretary was to say, "The allegation that Artime works directly under the CIA is false."[91] Technically, this statement was accurate. The US government only provided financial support to the MRR—not the sort of operational direction with which it had managed Brigade 2506.

After the *Sierra Aranzazu* incident, Manuel Artime's status with the CIA began to decline. But General Anastasio Somoza refused to pass on a warning to Artime. Somoza said he would talk to his friend but not threaten him in any way with a withdrawal of US aid. In fact, Somoza said that he was hoping that Castro might pinpoint Artime's Nicaraguan base and try to bomb it. "Somoza looks upon this as an opportunity," one CIA official reported, "for the entrapment of Castro in an aggressive action which could justify additional measures against him."[92]

Over the next few weeks, US security officials requested that Artime cancel further attacks until after the presidential election in early November 1964. President Johnson was on the ballot. In the meanwhile, the CIA undertook a reassessment of its relations with the MRR, still "the strongest of the active Cuban exile groups." Artime defended himself, pointing out all of the allies whom he was cultivating inside Castro's regime. He named Efigenio Ameijeiras, an M26 comandante and government vice minister; deputy minister Juan Almeida, a Moncada and *Granma* survivor; comandante Faustino Pérez, a *Granma* veteran and critic of Cuba's old-line communists; and Majors Rolando Cubela and Juan Nuiry Sánchez of the old Revolutionary Directorate. Artime led the CIA to believe that they were planning "a coup against Castro." Therefore, Langley recommended not cutting ties to Artime just yet.[93]

In fact, CIA agents had been working with Cubela for several years. Rolando Cubela was a survivor of the 1957 attack on the Presidential Palace, veteran of the Escambray, and the past president of the student federation that had purged the University of Havana of anticommunist professors and students in 1960. "He has never given [us] bad information," one White

House adviser wrote. The CIA sent Artime to Paris to talk to Cubela about a plan that involved rebel army commanders joining MRR infiltrators in order to stage a coup against Fidel Castro, after which Artime would gain Washington's recognition for a junta he would lead. Cubela received money and a promise of a weapon and silencer with which to assassinate Fidel Castro.[94] Apparently, Cuba's G-2 had been monitoring Cubela's activities. The secret police arrested him in Havana.[95] Quite likely, Rolando Cubela had been a double agent working a sting on the CIA for Fidel Castro. Meanwhile, US agents reminded Artime of their ban on new armed raids.

Artime and his MRR nevertheless managed to mount one final raid on a Cuban target. In February 1965, his fast boats attacked a fuel depot at Casilda on the south coast of Las Villas Province. Little damage resulted. The boats never approached the target but preferred to exchange fire with Cuban army units from afar. American officials doubted Artime's claim that the fight lasted nearly two hours. Cuban accounts corroborate these doubts. *Bohemia* reported that militia forces repelled the attackers and that "the aggressors were obliged to precipitously abandon the area."[96] "State [Department] has just about had it with the Artime group and seems to be leaning in favor of an immediate cut-off of ties with Artime," a staffer informed presidential adviser McGeorge Bundy.[97] Foggy Bottom also warned that Artime's intrigues with Castro's military commanders were "almost certain to fail" and "may even be a trap."[98] The paramilitary phase of the secret war between the United States and the Cuban Revolution had come to an end. Other struggles lay ahead.

The question remains: Why did the American policymakers support the counterrevolution in the Caribbean and risk exposing the United States' meddling in Latin American affairs—confirming for the whole world the most simplistic notions about US imperialism? Part of the answer has to be that foreign policy advisers believed that the final objective of ridding themselves of Fidel Castro through subversion outweighed the cost of these covert tactics, which amounted to five million dollars per year.[99] The CIA financially sponsored commandos operating offshore while none of its agents actually directed operations or selected targets. Technically, American policymakers could, with straight faces, say that the Cuban paramilitaries did not operate "under the control" of the US security agencies. One might say that these "autonomous" émigré groups gave cover to the politicians. "They're freedom fighters," government spokespersons were able to say with sufficient room for interpretation.

Moreover, these commando-type operations did not blatantly "show our hand in it," as President Eisenhower once said. Of course, he was referring to what became the Bay of Pigs invasion, which ultimately violated the kind of deniability that the president was seeking.[100] But the offshore counterrevolutionaries like Artime, Ray, and Gutiérrez Menoyo did offer greater cover to American political leaders. The MRR, JURE, and Alpha 66 secured their own bases abroad, cultivated leaders of countries targeted by Cuban-trained revolutionists, and chose their own targets and the means to engage them. Most of all, armed raids and infiltration of saboteurs required no action on the part of US military forces. As one CIA assessment concluded, "Externally mounted raids against Cuban targets have helped sustain hope among the many Cubans disillusioned with [Castro's] regime."[101] Yet that hope never resulted in an island-wide uprising against the communists. Apparently, most "disillusioned" Cubans no longer lived on the island.

American policymakers did fret over their hypocritical stand in the OAS against Cuban sponsorship of terrorism, but they knew it did not matter much. The overt policy of isolating Cuba within the concert of American republics (except for Mexico and Canada) was successful, so much so that President Johnson received OAS backing for his 1965 military intervention to prevent a communist takeover in the Dominican Republic. Moreover, American policymakers also recognized that highbrow diplomacy would not bring Castro down. Therefore, they secretly funded exiled counterrevolutionaries who might be able to spark an internal rebellion in Cuba or, with rare luck, assassinate Fidel.

If inexpensive covert action offered potentially rich returns, however unlikely, why did the White House discontinue the CIA program aiding the Cuban counterrevolution in the Caribbean? Because it had become counterproductive! Menoyo's revelations on Cuban television embarrassed the world's most powerful nation. Artime's faux pas proved more devastating. The interdiction of neutral shipping in the Caribbean Sea threatened the alliance that preserved the uneasy Cold War truce in America's most strategic region—Western Europe. That the counterrevolutionaries would attack British or Spanish merchant vessels in international waters horrified the Americans. Even if these countries did not join the economic boycott against

Cuba, the United States still needed their assistance in the more important task of holding back the Soviet juggernaut in Europe.

Finally, American policymakers realized they were actually enabling Fidel to strengthen his personal power. The counterrevolutionaries were giving him an excuse to arrest potential enemies and to eliminate contenders for power. They gave Fidel the motivation—even the necessity—to organize the militias, confiscate the properties, fill the prisons, militarize the island, organize neighborhood surveillance, and mobilize the people. Every exposure of conspiracy generated arrests and purges. One CIA report concluded that Castro considered American tolerance of counterrevolutionary raids as "a propaganda gift," for it reminded the Cubans of US hostility.[102] In the end, policymakers had to admit that commando forays may have reinforced the longevity of the communist regime. "The Cuban exiles in general refuse to believe that liberation is not around the corner," the CIA's Richard Helms observed in 1964.[103]

Frustrated by his lack of policy options toward Cuba, President Johnson once asked Thomas Mann of the State Department how he could rid himself of Fidel Castro. "As long as that army is loyal to him," Mann replied, "he's going to be there until he dies."[104]

CHAPTER SEVEN

The Export of Revolution

CUBA'S DEFEAT OF the CIA-directed invasion at the Bay of Pigs in April 1961 electrified university students throughout the hemisphere. Julio García of Argentina was one of them. He began engaging in debates over radical ideas while attending the University of Buenos Aires.[1] In this atmosphere of anti-imperialism, various leftist factions collaborated in a recruitment drive. One militant asked Julio if he would be interested in taking courses in Cuba on "guerrilla warfare." He consented and left Buenos Aires on July 1, 1962. Julio traveled through Montevideo to Santiago de Chile. There the Cuban embassy issued him travel money and a visa to visit Havana. Julio took flights to Brazil and to Trinidad, finally landing in Havana on July 5. His decision to take guerrilla training far from home might seem impulsive. If so, Julio typified many recruits who flirted with revolution without considering the consequences.

Hundreds of Latin American youths were arriving for the July 26 anniversary celebration of Castro's attack on Moncada Barracks. "We are not only Cubans but also Latin Americans," they heard him say. "We are not only Latin Americans, but also . . . socialists; we are Marxist-Leninists."[2]

Thousands gather in Santiago de Cuba to commemorate the eleventh anniversary
of the Moncada Attack, which took place there on July 26, 1953. These and other
revolutionary celebrations attracted hundreds of foreign visitors, many of whom
stayed on for guerrilla training.

Those gathering at the military camps afterward were divided into groups
based on nationality, and other Argentineans joined Julio. At the end of July,
two Cuban instructors led them on their first of many foot marches through
the Órganos Mountains of Pinar del Río Province. During rest periods, the
Argentinean trainees naturally fell into political discussions. The socialists
and communists among them engaged in disputes with the leftist Peronists,
followers of former president of Argentina Juan Domingo Perón. Julio
was still undergoing instruction in October 1962 when the missile crisis
intervened. His training class "volunteered" to join up with the militia forces
poised to defend the revolution from an expected US military invasion.

Julio's military education resumed in November with classes on Marxist
"political economy." Then the trainees went into the field again to practice
firing infantry weapons. They learned to handle Mausers and M1 Garand

rifles, Browning carbines, Thompson submachine guns, mortars, and anti-tank bazookas. The recruits also received instructions in explosives and communications. Then they moved to another area in the mountains for instruction in "guerrilla tactics," which included digging trenches, sleeping in hammocks, setting up wire entanglements, and practicing small-unit ambushes. Julio studied the texts of Ernesto "Che" Guevara and Mao Zedong.

The Argentineans grew tired as the training extended into December 1962. Some of Julio's fellow trainees refused to take another long march in the rain, and the Cuban trainers punished them by withholding food rations. Some young men, including Julio, lost their motivation and left the camp. Of the forty-five Argentineans who had begun the training course with Julio, less than half completed the instruction.[3] In pairs or threesomes, they shipped out of Cuba by way of Czechoslovakia. There, Julio slipped away from his colleagues, crossed the border into Austria, and told his story to Western European security officials.

Thousands of young Latin Americans, mainly men, made their way to Cuba in the early 1960s to celebrate the revolution, many as guests of the Cuban government. Fewer than half of them, like Julio, took military training. Even fewer actually completed the full training courses, and still fewer became guerrilla fighters. Nonetheless, they set off a wave of rebellion that impacted the hemisphere, most often in unintended ways. It is undeniable that Cuban leaders devoted valuable resources to promote the spread of their revolutionary example.

Prime Minister Fidel Castro had assigned Comandantes Che Guevara and Camilo Cienfuegos to sponsor filibustering expeditions throughout the Caribbean Basin in 1959. When these off-the-shelf, hastily organized efforts ended in failure, the revolutionaries reassessed and added rigor to the project. They established guerrilla training camps. They actively recruited leftists from targeted countries. The Cubans indoctrinated a generation of activists in Marxism-Leninism that destined many an idealistic youth to an early grave. Not only did Fidel Castro target the dictators, but he also denounced the democrats who appeared too close to the United States. In the absence of success in its Caribbean ventures of 1959, why did Cuba continue to export its revolution to the rest of Latin America, even at the risk of impoverishing the homeland?

The best source for this study would be the documentation of the state security agencies. But the Cuban government has not made available documents concerning its export of revolution to Latin America.[4] What historians do have, declassified US documents, suggest that the motivation for spreading revolution abroad resided in Havana's continuing struggle against the internal and external counterrevolution and against the intransigent, unyielding hostility of the United States. Guerrilla warfare elsewhere in Latin America was intended to stretch thin the forces of imperialism. Successful revolutions would create momentum in the struggle with the United States and force it to accept socialism in the Western Hemisphere. Ultimately, the revolutionaries believed, capitalism might collapse before the anti-imperialist onslaught. Moreover, an additional purpose for the export of revolution had to do with Cuba's own domestic revolutionary processes—the efforts to fully socialize the economy and the continuing drive for property and income redistribution.

Above all, the export of revolution was not a game—not a diversion or an avocation. It amounted to a religious calling. A mission.[5] The revolutionaries of Cuba had become true believers, convinced that they held insights into human redemption that the Soviets had lost. As if he were the messiah, Fidel Castro sought to project his revolutionary message far and wide throughout the developing world of Asia, Africa, and Latin America. Che Guevara committed himself to a crusade for which its apostles could expect martyrdom. Everyone else's deaths amounted to little. The revolution was everything.

ESPIONAGE AND COUNTERESPIONAGE

The leadership in Havana took a hiatus from foreign adventures in the second and third year of the revolution. They devoted themselves to promoting the Soviet alliance and defending Cuba from US hostility. In 1961, Fidel launched the literacy campaign that mobilized thousands of youthful teachers to live and work among illiterate peasants. There was the counterrevolution to contend with, followed by the October missile crisis. But the export of revolution continued to preoccupy Che Guevara and Fidel Castro. They did not abandon the project so much as prepare a firmer base for its launching. Stage two of Cuba's export of revolution became bureaucratized. The Americas section of the General Directorate of Intelligence (DGI) assumed responsibility for administering Cuban support of revolutionary groups abroad. US agents called the DGI "Cuba's highly professional espionage and subversion agency."[6] It functioned as the foreign operations branch of the Ministry of Interior and had at least five Soviet intelligence advisers throughout the 1960s. The first group of Cuban agents arrived in Moscow for training with the Soviet state security in 1963, just as Prime Minister Castro started his first visit to the Kremlin.[7]

Ramiro Valdés, a Moncada veteran and comandante in Che's M26 column, which had besieged Santa Clara, headed up the Ministry of Interior. His subordinate, the brilliant leader of the DGI Manuel Piñeiro, had served under Raúl Castro's command in the M26's Second Front during the revolutionary war. After the fall of Batista, Piñeiro briefly commanded the rebel army in Santiago before Raúl brought him to Havana. His prominent red beard gave this *barbudo* the nickname of Barba Roja. Fidel did not assign any members of the Popular Socialist Party (PSP) to the leadership of either the Ministry of Interior or the DGI. Perhaps, the older communists lacked the "true calling," as evidenced by their ambivalence during the fight against Fulgencio Batista. Trusted members of Castro's M26 ran the state security agencies. Valdés and Piñeiro reported directly to Fidel and professed no other loyalty, as did the PSP to the Kremlin.

The General Directorate of Intelligence had a separate line item in its overall budget specifically dedicated to funding revolutions offshore. This agency distributed funding only when revolutionary groups submitted "acceptable plans for armed struggle," said one CIA report. The Agency surmised that Venezuelan guerrillas received more than $1 million between 1960 and 1964: $250,000 had gone to Guatemala, $50,000 to El Salvador, $30,000 to Panama, and $15,000 to Nicaraguan operatives.

In addition, the DGI oversaw the training centers for "national liberation" movements from abroad. Its budget also provided food, clothing, and pocket money for foreign trainees in Cuba. "The DGI's methods of selecting, training, and assigning espionage agents and guerrilla warfare specialists reveals a high degree of professionalism," according to the CIA. "Moreover, the DGI has developed complex travel arrangements designed to hide the fact that Latin Americans coming to Cuba to receive training have actually been in Cuba." Guerrilla trainees numbered upward of twenty-five hundred and learned from the Cubans how to train still others in their home countries. Therefore, concluded the CIA, these trainees were "capable of exploiting local resentments and stimulating activities which could develop into diffi-cult internal security problems in several Latin American countries."[8]

According to Mexican intelligence agencies, the DGI consisted of eight departments. Three of them engaged in "foreign operations including the collection of information and promotion of revolutionary subversive activi-ties." One of its external offices was located in Prague, which Mexican in-telligence described as "the connection point between Cuba, the Soviet Bloc and Western Europe," as well as the easternmost terminal of Cubana Air-lines.[9] East German diplomats, sensitive about Chinese influence on Cuba's revolutionaries, had concluded that "those following the Chinese position are to be found in the Cuban intelligence services."[10]

Apparently, the Cuban embassies also played a subordinate role to the General Directorate of Intelligence in foreign policy. Proof of diplomatic spy craft came in 1960 when Cuban exiles broke into the Cuban embassy in Lima. They found incriminating documents, according to the *Chicago Tri-bune*'s correspondent Jules Dubois, who himself had been expelled by Fidel Castro after several years as foreign correspondent in Cuba. Dubois reported that the Cubans had spent twenty thousand dollars per month "to suborn political leaders, legislators, leaders of the youth movement, and news-papermen" in Peru. A defecting Cuban diplomat subsequently provided corroboration of the subversionary mission of Castro's embassies when he delivered secret documents to the press in Buenos Aires.[11] The Cuban Min-istry of Foreign Relations charged that the purported Cuban documents published by anti-Castro Cubans had been forged. One Cuban defector from the embassy in Paris testified that "virtually the entire staff—except the ambassador and the counselor—were Intelligence personnel. I was an official of D.G.I.; at the same time I held the post of third secretary and was the embassy's protocol officer."[12] The embassy in France handled travel be-tween Cuba, Prague, and Latin America. As the KGB dominated Soviet embassies abroad, so did the DGI preside over the Cuban diplomatic corps.

US intelligence suspected that "several hundred" DGI agents operated throughout the Western Hemisphere. The recruits selected to operate abroad came mainly from the Communist Youth Organization and were approved by the ministers of foreign relations and the interior. They received extensive training prior to postings. Some worked with revolutionary groups and others in collecting intelligence. The DGI even trained foreigners to be spies in their native countries. Foreign and domestic trainees often spent time on the job with Cuban army units operating against *bandido* counter-revolutionaries in the Escambray Mountains.[13] "We were told that our recruitment lessons were based on the experiences of Soviet Intelligence," says one former DGI agent. "Most emphasis was placed on recruitment based on ideological sympathies."[14]

The DGI conducted spy operations among the Cubans living abroad, especially in Miami. From the very beginning, this organization had trained and planted informers among Cuban exile groups to monitor conspiracies and terrorist operations against Fidel Castro.[15] No doubt the DGI had operatives spreading disinformation and collecting intelligence among those active in the commando groups. Castro's agents also planted themselves amid the Cuban émigré communities in Caracas, Santo Domingo, Madrid, Mexico City, and New York. According to one DGI staffer who defected in 1987, these agents promoted divisions and infighting among the exile groups. One DGI agent obtained work in Miami with small boats and reported back to Havana on infiltrators and saboteurs. The defector even claimed that the CIA had recruited several Cuban double agents to do its intelligence work from the mid-1960s onward. Max Lesnik of the old Second National Front of the Escambray says that "all [commando groups in Miami] were always penetrated" by Castro's spies.[16]

Cuba's expansion of espionage abroad provoked the United States to mount countermeasures. In 1963, the CIA managed more than one hundred anti-Castro Cubans as agents and subagents on the island. However, over the decade, the DGI planted double agents among these spies. These counteragents disseminated misinformation and exposed and captured Cubans working for the CIA.[17] Therefore, the CIA headquarters at Langley employed about two hundred Cuba watchers. Its station in Miami, called Quarters Eye, took care to verify intelligence gathered in Cuba and Miami. In the early days of the 1960s, while the young comandantes and older communists were still disputing the ideology of the revolution, the CIA gained access to informants at the highest echelons. One agent in June 1963 was able to report information obtained from "a high-ranking Cuban Official . . . who has access to significant political and economic information by virtue of his reputation and expertise and his close personal connections with top-level Cuban government personalities."[18] Another report derived from information provided by a Peruvian trained in Cuba. Defectors also provided valuable intelligence. The CIA debriefed a former pilot of Cubana Airlines whose flights had taken him to Mexico City and also to Moscow. He provided American agents with data on the travel of "subversives" to Cuba.

Other sources within Cuba did not have government portfolios, only personal contacts with officialdom. One CIA report on Cuban guerrilla training cited the informant as "a retired Cuban lawyer with occasional access to military information through friends in the Army."[19] This source was not accorded the highest endorsement for veracity. "An increasing amount of intelligence was flowing from Cuba as new agents were recruited in Miami and infiltrated back into Cuba," wrote the ex–CIA agent David Atlee Phillips. "There the neophyte spies contacted friends and relatives to work with them. Usually their reports were useful, but often these enthusiastic agents would report the wildest of rumors. In Quarters Eye there were regular morning meetings where . . . officers would review the messages . . . to decide which reports were valid."[20]

By the mid-1960s, the CIA had marshaled some thirty agents working in Washington at the Cuban branch. For the rest of Latin America, the Agency trained and employed one hundred officers in and around Langley headquarters and an additional two hundred agents in the stations, operating on a budget of thirty-seven million dollars.[21]

The CIA also counted on collaborators throughout Latin America. US intelligence agents had regular contact with politicians, labor leaders, business-people, police officers, military officers, intelligence personnel, and students. All of these informants received payment for their cooperation. It is clear from reports that the CIA maintained lines of communication to members of the communist parties throughout Latin America. US agents paid cash to these party members, who generally provided the CIA with information.[22] "We know a great deal about . . . travel from our penetrations of the Communist parties," one secret document concluded, "and from [deleted] travel control authorities in Latin American countries." In addition, operatives in the field obtained additional information "in confessions of captured guerrillas who had been in Cuba." Some information about Brazilian operations came into the hands of agents from a cache of documents belonging to a Cuban agent who died in the crash of an airliner. In Peru, the Agency had been able to assemble a list of two hundred thirty-five individuals who had visited Cuba for extended periods of time.[23]

American military and security agencies shared information, where they deemed it necessary. One former Kennedy staffer mentions how military intelligence officers would send reports on Latin American subversives to the headquarters of the United States Southern Command in the Panama Canal Zone. From there, the information arrived at the US military groups of American embassies and then on to the militaries of the host countries.[24]

Collecting reliable information turned out to be a messy business. The CIA rapidly expanded its presence in Miami and Latin America in the early 1960s. Few of their newly recruited agents had any Spanish capability. They relied on informants who spoke little English.[25] Because of the Cuban Revolution, the United States government moved to treble and quadruple the number of intelligence agents in American embassies throughout the region. Recruits came from the graduating classes of several Ivy League universities, where they had taken European studies and French language courses. They received some six months of training in intelligence work and then found themselves shipped off to embassies in countries about which they knew little. Most did not know Spanish or Portuguese. The eyes and ears of the secret war against the Cuban Revolution functioned but imperfectly.

THEORIES, *FOCO* AND OTHERWISE

In addition to providing the organizational basis for spreading the benefits of revolution, the Cuban leadership sought to create the theoretical foundation as well. Che Guevara assumed this task. After all, he had been the diarist of M26 and had maintained a log of the major events in the revolutionary war. Photos of Che in the Sierra Maestra caught him holding a diary book in hand or in the pocket of his tunic. His classic primer came out in 1960 as *Guerra de Guerrillas,* dedicated to the memory of Comandante Camilo Cienfuegos. Instantaneously, it gained a wide audience and was translated into many languages, printed and reprinted multiple times. Che devoted the bulk of the book to tactics and practical lessons. With characteristic directness, he explained the model he devised from his experience fighting in the Sierra Maestra and the Sierra del Escambray.

The Cuban revolutionary war taught us three lessons about the possibility of success of similar movements in other countries of Latin America, wrote Che on the very first page of his text.

(1) Popular forces can win a war against the army.

(2) It is not necessary to wait until all conditions for making revolution exist; the insurrection can create them.

(3) In underdeveloped America, the countryside is the basic area for armed fighting.[26]

Immediately, the world's leftists took note that Che Guevara was revising Moscow's doctrine of social revolution, to which communist parties in the Third World subscribed. Latin America did not have to wait for industrialization and capital accumulation to reach a breaking point sufficient to produce the conditions for wholesale change. A guerrilla force rather than the party apparatus would lead the revolution, he said, and this vanguard could successfully operate among peasants in agrarian societies. These concepts contradicted the Kremlin's revolutionary doctrine. The Soviets gave primacy to prior capitalist development, to the party vanguard, and to urban and industrial workers. On the other hand, Chinese communists could identify with Che's notions. They had come to power in 1949 in a rural environment with peasant rather than worker armies—though not without party leadership.

One of the major theoretical caveats of Guevara's first text concerned the nature of the regime to be overthrown. A revolutionary movement like that of Fidel Castro's M26 could succeed against the army of a dictatorship, Che explained, but not necessarily against an electoral regime. "Where the government has come into power through some form of popular vote . . . and maintains at least an appearance of constitutional legality, the guerrilla outbreak cannot be promoted, since the possibilities of peaceful struggle have not yet been exhausted."[27] In the first three years of the revolution, Fidel and Che too were violating this principle. The struggle in Venezuela between pro-Cuban rebels and the elected government encouraged the revolutionary leaders to focus their efforts against civilian presidents hostile to the Cuban regime.

Therefore, Che had to revise his ideas when Fidel turned bellicose again in 1963. Castro's speech commemorating the tenth anniversary of the attack on Moncada Barracks returned to the rhetoric of "inevitable revolutions." He declared that Latin American conditions were ripe for revolution. "The duty . . . of Latin American revolutionaries is not to wait for the change in the correlation of forces to produce the miracle of social revolution," he stated, but "to make revolution in each nation."[28] However, Castro denied that Cuba "exported" revolution. It sent no weapons or military to fight in other countries, Fidel said. Rather, he viewed Cuba as a source of guidance and inspiration for revolutionaries elsewhere. Three hundred Latin Americans had traveled to Cuba to attend the July 26 festivities. The CIA expected that many would remain there for several weeks of "ideological indoctrination and training in the practical arts of subversion."[29]

Within weeks, Che Guevara revisited and updated his ideas on guerrilla warfare in order to give structure to Cuba's renewal of the project. In September 1963, he unveiled several new concepts that reflected rather than redirected current Cuban foreign policy. The most important concerned revolution and elected governments. In the first edition of *Guerrilla Warfare,* published in 1960, he had posited that revolutionary movements would be unlikely to succeed against even pseudodemocratic governments. However, several elected leaders were working with Washington against the revolution. Indeed, Presidents Manuel Prado of Peru and Rómulo Betancourt of Venezuela had collaborated with American policy of isolating Cuba within the Organization of American States so effectively that, by 1963, only a handful of elected governments still had diplomatic relations with the island republic. For this reason, Fidel and Che sought to undermine these "democratic" enemies. They wished especially to reinforce the active resistance movement against Betancourt's elected government in oil-rich Venezuela. As the theoretician of the revolution, consequently, Che came up with the justification for policies already in place.

Guevara arrived at an idea. Those democratic leaders who acted with hostility toward Cuba were merely following the dictates of the reactionary military in their countries. In other words, they were no better than the generals themselves. Betancourt kowtowed to the Venezuelan army; President Arturo Frondizi had served the interests of the Argentine officer corps; the generals in Colombia and Guatemala manipulated their elected presidents. Only the Chileans, Bolivians, Brazilians, Uruguayans, and Mexicans did not merit such denunciations because they still hosted Cuban embassies. The first four would eventually drop from this list as the 1960s proceeded. Therefore, the 1963 version of Che's theory of guerrilla warfare dispensed with any mention of "peaceful means" needing to be utilized against civilian governments.[30] His 1963 manifesto declared that the guerrilla uprising could produce the conditions for revolution equally in elected as in dictatorial regimes.

In *Cuba Socialista,* Che Guevara explained yet again that "it is not always necessary to wait for all the conditions for revolution to exist; the insurrectionary focal point can create the necessary conditions." Che advanced a new idea that justified encouragement of guerrilla warfare in hostile countries governed by constitutional "bourgeois governments." The guerrilla insurrection would force them to "unmask themselves" and resort to violence and suppression, because the true nature of these electoral regimes approximated the "brutal dictatorships led by reactionaries." Exploitation everywhere in Latin America made conditions ripe for revolution. He mocked the so-called democratic governments as an "apologetic form for representing the dictatorship of the exploitative classes." Elections in Latin America amounted to fictions, "with the delivery of power to another gentleman of mellifluous voice and angelic face," who merely stood in for the military. The generals, in turn, represented "mere instruments of domination for the reactionary classes and the imperialist monopolies. . . . They aspire only to maintain their prerogatives."[31] He implied that the repressive responses of the civilian government would reveal its true reactionary nature to the aggrieved masses.

Che's other new idea proposed that the revolutionary guerrilla uprising against the electoral regime would provoke the military to seize power from the civilians. This kind of *golpe de estado* would advance the revolution by focusing the hatred of the masses on the generals. Democratic governments posed a greater menace than outright dictatorships since it was harder for rebels to arouse the populace against them. Therefore, he urged the Venezuelan left to destroy the democratic framework of the state and compel the military to take power. The military coup and subsequent repression would serve as a transitional stage toward revolution.[32] Of course, Che's ideas on revolution still ran contrary to the views of Latin American communist parties. Under Soviet influence, they sought not to destroy the "national bourgeoisie" but to work with it against foreign interests.

The *foco,* defined as the focus or center, was not a concept that Che Guevara himself devised. Rather, the *foco* theory, or *foquismo,* derived from Che's writings as interpreted by the radical French journalist Régis Debray. Guevara went underground in 1965 at about the time that Debray arrived in Cuba to write a book on the revolution. Debray interviewed Fidel Castro

and other revolutionaries and read Che's writings on the subject of revolution. Che had published a series of chronological vignettes on the struggle
in the Sierra Maestra taken from his diaries. They appeared in various issues of the military journal *Verde Olivo* for the instruction of soldiers of the
revolutionary armed forces.[33] Debray studied all these.

In his 1963 reformulation on the theme of guerrilla warfare, Guevara did
say that "there are three conditions for survival of a guerrilla group . . . constant mobility, constant vigilance, constant distrust."[34] From this, Debray
defined the *foco* as "the center of guerrilla operations rather than a military
base." That is, to avoid destruction by a force of more numerous and better-
armed soldiers of the regime, the guerrilla *foco* had to be incessantly on the
move. Fixed encampments only invited coordinated assaults on and an-
nihilation of the rebel fighters. As an example, Debray cites Che's own
establishment of a fixed base at Hombrito in the Sierra Maestra. In October 1957, a unit of Batista's troops overran the hospital, mess hall, electrical plant, and the printing and boot repair shops and sent Che's column
of sixty men retreating back into the mountains.[35] The *foco* had to retreat
to survive.

Another concept on which Debray elaborated from the Cuban revolutionary war pertains to the area of guerrilla operations—the countryside
rather than the city. He quoted Fidel as saying that the city was the "cemetery of revolutionaries." The French journalist identified the rural area as
critical to the revolution because of the support that the peasants would give
guerrillas. Country people would provide supplies and recruits for the
struggle. He cited Fidel's 1958 order to M26 operatives in the cities: "All
arms to the Sierra!" Throughout that final year of the insurrection, Debray
observed, Castro's main guerrilla *foco,* composed of peasant volunteers, reproduced one column after another commanded by subordinates like Che
Guevara, Raúl Castro, Camilo Cienfuegos, and Juan Almeida. Debray suggested that "urban terrorism" merely complemented the authentic rural
base of guerrilla action by distracting thousands of troops in order to guard
the urban infrastructure against sabotage.[36] Thus was born the theory of the
rural *foco* or *foquismo.*

The intended targets of Guevara's and Debray's revolutionary ideas took
notice immediately. The United States Army and other armed forces in the
Western Hemisphere already had incorporated *Guerrilla Warfare* (1960) into
the curricula of their war colleges. They added Che's 1963 article and Régis

Debray's 1966 edition.[37] The CIA maintained a log of Fidel's speeches and monitored those of Che Guevara as well. Few military officers in Latin America remained unaware that destruction of their cherished professions would be the first casualty of social revolution. Both Fidel and Che constantly reminded them. Commenting on the 1963 military *golpe de estado* against the elected government of the nationalist Juan Bosch in the Dominican Republic, Fidel again pointed out the revolutionary truth in Latin America. The military class must first be destroyed, he said, and "their principal leaders executed."[38] Che had been saying this since his 1954 stay in Guatemala. Remarks such as these, uttered frequently by Cuban revolutionaries in interviews and speeches, did not go unnoticed in army barracks throughout the Americas.

The export of revolution did not meet the favor of Cuba's chief benefactor, the Soviet Union. The Kremlin objected to Che's writings on guerrilla warfare on the grounds that they violated Marxism-Leninism. Soviet leaders criticized his essays as "ultrarevolutionary bordering on adventurism." The Soviet ambassador to Cuba, Aleksandr Alekseyev, who was also a KGB officer, came under criticism from the Kremlin. His superiors suggested that Alekseyev had "gone native" for not having restrained the revolutionary adventurism of the Cubans.[39] On the other hand, the Chinese hailed Havana's commitment to revolutionary warfare. Che's negation of the prospects for Soviet-style collaboration with "bourgeois regimes" coincided nicely with the more confrontational doctrine of Chairman Mao. Chinese periodicals in 1963 widely reprinted Che's "Guerrilla Warfare: A Method," that appeared in *Cuba Socialista* in 1963.[40] These were not ideas that pleased the Kremlin.

Shortly after the October missile crisis, a conversation between Guevara and Vice Premier Anastas Mikoyan teased out the differences between Cuba and the Soviet Union on the subject of the export of revolution.

E. Guevara: It seems that the further development of the revolutions in Latin America must follow the line of simultaneous explosions in all countries. Only this way can they succeed.

A. I. Mikoyan: This is incorrect. The countries of Latin America have their own national characteristics, which cannot be ignored. Because of these features, the revolution cannot occur simultaneously in all countries. These revolutions can happen shortly one after another, but an overall explosion is unlikely.

E. Guevara: Unless there is a simultaneous explosion, the revolutions in individual countries will be suppressed by the reactionary forces in alliance with imperialism. This is confirmed, in particular, by the events in Venezuela and several other countries.

A. I. Mikoyan: Speaking specifically about this case does not really prove the point. . . . As for the theory of a simultaneous explosion, I would like to say that during the first years after the October Revolution [in Russia], we were also waiting for socialist revolutions in other countries. Many people thought that if such revolutions do not take place, we would not make it. And in fact a socialist revolution broke out in Hungary and Bavaria. However, these revolutions were soon crushed by the reactionary forces. Some time passed, and we saw that the time for revolutionary crises in capitalist countries had passed, and then we made an important decision and announced that capitalism had entered a period of partial stabilization, and we need to build socialism on our own.[41]

American experts on guerrilla warfare who had been working with the MIT economist Walt W. Rostow analyzed the implications of Che's ideas. President Kennedy had assigned Rostow to a planning group at the State Department that conducted a wide-ranging study of communist guerrillas operating in South Vietnam, Laos, Malaysia, and Latin America. "[President Kennedy] instructed me to . . . get him some materials to read about guerrilla warfare in general," Rostow wrote. "He soon had the works of Mao and Guevara around the Mansion."[42] Rostow and this group also studied how Castro's own small band of guerrillas had succeeded in destroying Batista's army. The task force subjected Che's views to a stage model similar to Rostow's classic text on economic modernization, *The Stages of Growth.* Here is how the group interpreted the stages involved in Che's concepts on armed struggle:

1. Forming the guerrilla force in a remote rural area;
2. Developing forces and winning the support of the *campesinos;*
3. Initiating hit-and-run operations against government forces;
4. Harassing urban and rural communications and supply lines;
5. Moving guerrillas toward urban areas as disarray of army permits;
6. Linking up with urban forces to overthrow government; and
7. Appealing for Socialist Bloc aid after victory is achieved.[43]

The Achilles' heel of the entire sequence of Che's ideas concerns step 2. Recruiting and converting peasants into revolutionary fighters presupposes a Batista-like nonresponse to the guerrilla uprising. In January 1957, Castro's handful of rebels had been able to establish a degree of security in the Sierra Maestra because the overconfident dictator in Havana depreciated the rebels at the opposite end of the island. His corrupt generals did not take seriously the poorly armed, isolated, hungry, and ragged fighters. Moreover, Batista had cashiered those officers who had developed their professionalism in military science rather than in obsequious politics.

Army incompetence had allowed Castro's M26 to establish a safe haven, *territorio liberado,* where the authority of Che and Raúl over the peasants went unchallenged. They educated the peasant recruits, gave them land and hospitals, and protected them from poorly disciplined army patrols. Fidel slowly armed *guajiro* fighters too. The honor student of Colonel Alberto Bayo's school in Mexico, Che Guevara, set up his own military training school for peasant recruits in the Sierra Maestra. Even so, it was not until November 1957, nearly a year after Castro entered the Sierra Maestra, that peasants began joining the rebels.

Successful completion of step 2 accounted for the success of the Cuban revolutionaries. Eventually, the revolutionaries multiplied, broke out, and followed steps 3 through 7 more or less as Rostow's study group interpreted Che's ideas. After New Year's Day, 1959, when the destruction of Batista's army became dramatically manifest, no military establishment in the Americas would again adopt Batista's cavalier attitude toward armed rebels. Indeed, they resolved to apply maximum firepower against the rural *foco* at the first moment it appeared. Suffice it to say that Che's entire revitalized theory of spreading the revolution abroad suffered from another, even greater leap of logic.

Che and Fidel proceeded as if they believed that the Cuban Revolution had legitimized communism as an alternative model of governance. These true believers imagined that the popular classes in other countries would anticipate the promises of socialism in the same fashion that the Cuban masses had rallied to them after 1959. Therefore, Cuban guerrilla training emphasized Marxist-Leninist ideology. Che and Raúl had been indoctrinating the guerrilla fighters in their commands during the revolutionary war. But all the other M26 comandantes, including Fidel, had not. M26 operatives had had many ideological tendencies—nationalism and electoral democracy based on the 1940 Cuban Constitution comprising the most salient of them.

In other words, Castro's guerrilla forces had achieved victory with an amorphous, non-Marxist political ideology. Revolutionary leaders quoted José Martí and believed in the verses he had composed for Cuba's national anthem that "to die for the *patria* is to live." On the connections between M26 and the communist PSP during the struggle against Batista, State Department analysts concluded in 1958 that "little evidence . . . exists to prove a strong tie between the two groups."[44] Even Che Guevara had to admit to the noncommunist ideology of his guerrilla chieftain. "Fidel isn't a communist," Che told Argentinean reporter Jorge Ricardo Masetti in the Sierra Maestra. "Politically you can define Fidel and his movement as 'revolutionary nationalist.' Of course he is anti-American, in the sense that the Americans are anti-revolutionaries."[45]

Fidel occasionally admitted afterward that Cuba's communists had been slow to support the guerrilla struggle. The veteran Cuban communist Blas Roca had dismissed Castro's 1953 "putschist" attack on Moncada Barracks as a "bourgeois revolution." Therefore, Castro quipped on rare occasions that the communists were "hiding under the bed" during the Cuban revolutionary war.[46] More recently, Castro claimed that, had he espoused Marxist-Leninist doctrines in 1957 and 1958, the Cuban middle class (the backbone of his movement's supporters) and the peasants and workers, too, would have rejected him. He reasoned that the elite-owned media and Catholic Church had long "deceived" the masses and bourgeoisie about the "benefits" of communism.[47] Only Raúl Castro had been a party militant and Che a confirmed anti-imperialist. Fidel subsequently adopted communism in order to gain the support of the socialist world, item 7 in the stages of armed struggle. The implications of this contradiction proved quite devastating to the revolutionary project abroad.

Fidel's governing as a Marxist-Leninist in Havana tended to unmask the very guerrillas whose insurrections he was encouraging in the rest of Latin America. They were doomed in the 1960s to make the insurrections in their own countries as Marxist-Leninists—not as the democratic nationalists Fidel's guerrillas had been in the late 1950s. After 1959, every guerrilla in Latin America was considered to believe in some form of Marxism, whether Stalinist, Trotskyist, Maoist, Castroist, or socialist—all lumped together as *comunista.* And so was every student protester, every peasant land invader, every striking laborer, and every reformist politician! That they were not exporting the same revolutionary model that had brought them to power did not seem to matter to Fidel and Che. They conducted themselves as if they were prophets of revolution.

THE TRAINEE'S LIFE

The first thing each potential guerrilla had to do was get to Cuba. When the Argentinean Julio García traveled to Cuba in 1962, he could not board a flight from Buenos Aires directly to Havana. He had to take a roundabout route. Air travel to and from Cuba became even more constricted as the 1960s progressed. In 1958, eleven foreign carriers served Cuba on flights originating in the United States, Spain, Argentina, and five nations of the Caribbean Basin. Several countries suspended air service beginning in 1960. Still other airlines terminated their connections following the missile crisis of October 1962. Thereafter, only Iberian Airlines of Spain made one flight per week, and Cubana Airlines flew back and forth to Mexico City thrice weekly.

The only new airlines scheduling weekly flights to Havana were Czechoslovak Airlines from Prague and Aeroflot from Moscow. Cubana's flights to Prague passed through the Canadian airport at Gander, Nova Scotia, where the local authorities refused to spy on passengers for the CIA.[48] Aeroflot flew the largest plane to Cuba, the Tu-114, with a normal capacity of 170 passengers. But the Soviets greatly subsidized its service. It had to modify the cabin to accommodate additional fuel tanks for the 7,000-mile flight, thus reducing passenger capacity to sixty. In 1963, Cubana began to run occasional charter flights to Brazil, under a special agreement with the government of President João Goulart, and to the Grand Caymans too.[49]

All in all, the travel restrictions imposed by many countries deprived Cuba of the means for unobtrusively transporting visitors to Havana. On leaving Cuba, many travelers flew to Prague in order to catch return flights from Vienna or Paris back to Latin America. Cuban intelligence agencies arranged complicated travel itineraries with a view to shrouding the identification of trainees. High-profile radicals required extra care. Guatemalan rebel leaders Augusto Turcios Lima and Rolando Morán received cosmetic makeovers from Cuba's Ministry of the Interior. Together with false passports, Turcios and Morán made their way home by way of Prague.[50] The ministry's success was only partial. The reduction of countries having air service to Cuba also enhanced the CIA's ability to monitor the passenger lists of flights heading to and from Havana with the assistance of Mexican security services.[51]

US intelligence sources indicated that the travel restrictions also were reducing the number of visitors to Havana. No doubt the cost of so many foreign guests burdened the socialized economy of Cuba. The total number of travelers declined from approximately five thousand in 1962 to twenty-five hundred in 1963. The CIA furnished Latin American governments with intelligence information about subversive travel, which contributed to efforts to "keep returning trainees under surveillance."[52] Latin Americans traveling from Cuba placed themselves in personal danger. Mexican intelligence agents had been observing the activities of various individuals seen visiting the Soviet embassy. They identified one "Honduran Communist" who subsequently was arrested on his return home. "He was shot when he tried to escape from police headquarters, but he was not seriously wounded," the CIA reported. The man spent an indeterminate amount of time in jail.[53] Guilt by association complicated the lives of many idealists who visited Havana.

The CIA estimated that the "great majority" of trainees flew into Cuba from Mexico City, and calculated the number to exceed forty-nine hundred passengers in 1962. American security personnel pressed hard on the Mexicans to scrutinize and, if possible, to restrict these entries.[54] Mexico's political stability in the 1950s and 1960s enabled the one-party state dominated by the Party of the Institutional Revolution to tolerate a large community of leftist political exiles. Fidel Castro formed the 26th of July Revolutionary Movement in Mexico City. The Argentinean physician Ernesto Guevara took refuge there in 1954 fleeing from the CIA-engineered coup against the Guatemalan revolution. Exiles from dictatorships in Latin America passed through Mexico with great frequency, forming linkages across nationality. The Mexican government maintained surveillance of these groups, mainly to contain the spread of revolutionary ideas to the Mexican left wing, led by ex-president Lázaro Cárdenas.[55]

The CIA estimated that the Cuban military camps processed between one thousand and fifteen hundred Latin Americans in 1962 alone.[56] The Cubans often referred to these trainees as the International Brigade, an allusion to the foreigners who fought for the Republicans in the Spanish Civil War. Units were formed along the lines of nationality so that the trainees might return home as a "packaged cadre" ready to lead the "Liberation Army." Many Africans also showed up in the training camps toward the end of the 1960s. Afro-Cuban veterans of the Cuban revolutionary war served as instructors of prospective guerrillas from the Congo, Guinea-Bissau, and Cabo Verde.[57] Leftists were training in Cuba at the following locations:

El Caney de las Mercedes near Manzanillo in Oriente Province;
Bahía Honda in Pinar del Río Province for small arms familiarization;
Punta la Sierra in Pinar del Río for jungle survival and field maneuvers;
Minas del Frío in Oriente Province for guerrilla tactics, sabotage, hand-to-hand combat, forced marches, and physical training;
various locations in Havana for security procedures, counter-intelligence, codes and communication, political indoctrination, and weapons practice; and
the School of National Liberation on the Isla de Pinos.

While in Havana, the trainees stayed at the hotels Presidente and Riviera in the Vedado neighborhood.[58]

According to a US Air Force intelligence report, the full guerrilla training course consisted of several stages. Stage 1 lasted five weeks and was devoted to small arms familiarization such as assembly, disassembly, maintenance, and firing. Students shot up to one hundred rounds each on American, Belgian, and Czech weapons and practiced on .50-caliber machine guns, mortars, rifle grenades, and antitank bazookas. In stage 2, the trainees spent five to seven weeks on preparing and handling homemade explosive devices. These included Molotov cocktails and antitank and antipersonnel explosives.

Stage 3 consisted of up to six weeks of jungle survival and guerrilla operations. Each trainee in this phase received a blue militiaman's uniform, combat boots, a knapsack, a US-made M1 rifle, sixty rounds of ammunition, and a hammock. They practiced bivouacking without tents, preparing ambushes, and laying booby traps. The US Air Force report mentioned that many men dropped out of the program during and after this rigorous stage.

The next stage, number 4, emphasized political indoctrination and the military, economic, political, and psychological aspects of guerrilla warfare.

It lasted for one month. Trainees studied encirclement operations, map reading, treatment of peasants, and methods of attacking towns and army posts. Here students read and discussed literature on guerrilla strategy and texts on socialism, including the communist newspaper *Hoy*. Stage 5 acted as a fitting two- to four-week conclusion. It dealt with clandestine communications, counterintelligence, and security procedures. Advanced trainees used radio equipment seized from émigré forces captured at the Bay of Pigs. Contingents of trainees capped this final stage with a week's tour of duty in the Escambray Mountains, where they mounted patrols against anti-Castro bandit groups.[59]

Che Guevara staffed the guerrilla training schools with politically reliable combat veterans of the Cuban revolutionary war. Most came from M26 units and a few others from the Revolutionary Directorate that fought in the Escambray Mountains. The training manuals emphasized Marxist concepts and anti-imperialist ideas. Colonel Alberto Bayo authored a primer for trainees called *140 Questions on Guerrilla Warfare*. The Cuban-born Bayo fought in the Spanish Civil War. In 1956, he trained more than one hundred of Castro's associates in Mexico during the formative stage of the M26. Bayo's mimeographed pamphlet used drawings and charts to demonstrate demolition techniques and methods of making Molotov cocktails and other incendiary devices from local materials.[60] As the director of the School of Revolutionary Training, Colonel Bayo worked directly under the orders of his best guerrilla student, El Che.[61] Military trainers provided extra instruction to selected men who would teach their countrymen back home. Moreover, Cuba combat veterans also traveled to meet up with guerrilla forces in Argentina, Colombia, and Venezuela as advisers in the field of battle.

The manuals of Che Guevara and Mao Zedong taught apprentices that they were to obtain their weapons close to home. Meanwhile, Fidel denied that Cuba was providing arms to the revolutionaries. We "are experts on ideas," he declared, sharing them openly with revolutionaries all over the world.[62] Che Guevara, Cuba's minister of industry, reiterated to a hall full of economists that Cuba did not engage in international arms smuggling. "We cannot leave off exporting the example, as the United States wants, because the example is something spiritual that crosses borders," Che announced to the OAS economic ministers in August 1961. "That which we do give is our guarantee that not one rifle will be moved from Cuba, that not a single arm will leave Cuba, to go to fight in another country of America."[63] The Cuban leadership did not always keep its pledge.

There were many other sources of arms in the Western Hemisphere. One Peruvian recently returned from Cuba revealed that revolutionaries were to live off the land and arm themselves by seizing the weapons of the police and soldiers.[64] Therefore, most of the training in the Cuban camps featured American weapons that the trainees were likely to come across in their own countries. They received training in the use and maintenance of M1 Garand and M3 rifles and Browning and Hotchkiss machine guns. US military advisory programs distributed such World War II and Korean War weapons to military forces throughout Latin America. Cubans told leaders of militant groups from Venezuela, Brazil, and Peru that they could count on funding, training, and technical assistance but no weapons. Up to the end of 1963, no one had uncovered evidence that guns of Cuban origin had reached local guerrilla forces. "This is *not* to say," one CIA document cautioned, "that we are positive weapons have *not* been sent from Cuba."[65]

The Cubans stockpiled older American military equipment, which they used in their training camps. The rebel armed forces pulled maintenance on Batista's Korean War arms and on more up-to-date military hardware captured at the Bay of Pigs and in the CIA airdrops in the Escambray. M1 Garand infantry rifles, incendiary bombs, and battery-operated communications equipment found their way to Latin America in support of guerrilla activities in Venezuela and Argentina. "The thing was equitable," one Argentinean trainee wrote. "The Yankees promoted the counterrevolution and the Cubans, revolution."[66] Despite their denials, the Cubans did provide limited amounts of arms and money to foreign guerrilla fighters.

Neither the CIA nor the State Department could substantiate the supply of arms from Cuba to Latin American revolutionary groups before December 1963, when a cache of arms traced to Cuba turned up on the coast of Venezuela. There were plenty of rumors, particularly of Czech weapons entering Latin America. But State Department analysts concluded in 1962, "So far there has been little to indicate Soviet bloc or Cuban complicity in arms traffic." The American agents noted the difficulties of Cuba's using airdrops and fishing trawlers for such arms delivery.[67] Plenty of other sources existed. Central American insurgents purchased illegal arms shipped from the United States. In just two years, American officials had seized twenty-one illegal shipments heading south containing 20 mm cannon, rifles, machine guns, bazookas, automatic firearms, pistols, grenades, and grenade launchers.[68] Many other shipments had slipped through undetected.

For those guerrilla fighters who survived, the 1960s had been a decade of hope, privation, adventure, and defeat. One Peruvian trainee reflected on his youth, "The fact is that we spent the sixties in military training camps under truly tough conditions that tested the firmness of our resolve. Traveling with false passports in Europe and Latin America, hidden in safe houses in Bolivia, crossing the Bolivian jungle on foot or by other means, making secret contact and fooling the police. . . . And, finally, fighting in the sierra of Peru."[69] It cannot be claimed that all young men who trained in Cuba actually entered into combat on returning to their countries. Most enlisted from within their social milieus without having visited Cuba beforehand, although nearly all the guerrilla leaders in Latin America—whether *foquistas* or urban fighters—had some connection to that revolutionary isle just ninety miles from Key West, Florida.

UNIFIED AND SIMULTANEOUS REVOLUTIONS

Even the limited export of arms and cash became increasingly costly to the socializing economy of Cuba. Revolutionary propaganda proved to be far less expensive. American security agents monitored Cuban radio broadcasts to the United States and to other Latin American countries. Radio Habana Cuba broadcast two hundred hours of propaganda per week in Spanish, Haitian Creole, Portuguese, French, English, and Arabic. Entertainment and music shows interspersed with news programming pitched messages to justify the policies of the Cuban government. Other programs served the national liberation movements in Latin America. The guerrilla organizations of Peru, Guatemala, and the Dominican Republic each had fifteen minutes of programming twice weekly. Brazilian and Haitian leftists made up seven hours each.

What did these broadcasts do to subvert governments in Latin America? Principally, they denounced both the constitutional and dictatorial governments for favoring the oligarchy and foreign interests. The programming also exhorted the masses to fight to overturn these regimes. They conflated democracies and dictatorships, just as Che had instructed. Here are some examples of the incendiary content:

21 March 1962: "The Trujillista Council of State [which governed after Trujillo's assassination] is not competent to resolve the serious national problems. . . . That is why it must be overthrown and replaced by a government of the people whose hand will not tremble in liberating the country from feudal extortion and Yankee imperialist domination."

22 March 1962: "Cuba has said . . . that it is not necessary to export revolution, because each of the oligarchical, tyrannical, and despotic governments under which America suffers is itself preparing the conditions necessary for the people to rise up against it."

4 April 1962: "The present [Guatemalan] government of Ydígoras Fuentes must be forced to abandon office, and the Congress, composed mainly of deputies who held office as a result of fraud and imposition, must be dissolved."

1 May 1962, a speech by Che Guevara: "The working class, helped and strengthened by the peasant class, must never seek the most bloody battle, because it will cost thousands . . . of lives of their sons. But the seizure of power by the working class is a historic necessity, and no one can oppose history."

24 November 1962: "Venezuela is the weakest trench in the imperialist front in the Americas. It is not to be forgotten that the traitorous regime [of President Rómulo Betancourt], despite all appearances, is under fire from a great popular offensive."

7 January 1963: "The military government junta may rest completely assured that there will be revolution in Peru and the people will take over. . . . We wonder if among the members of the armed forces there is not a group of truly honorable and patriotic men who love the people of Peru and are ready to place their weapons at the service of the people."[70]

Che and Fidel also reserved a role for the Latin American news service Prensa Latina. The Cuban revolutionary leadership organized Prensa Latina to counteract the dominant "capitalist" news services, the Associated Press and the United Press International. Both outlets wired news stories across the so-called Free World, including Latin America. Che originated the idea of an alternative distributor of news favorable to revolution and critical of the United States's activities in Latin America. In fact, Guevara had worked in Mexico in 1955 as a photographer and stringer for Juan Perón's South American news service, Agencia Latina. The army's coup d'état against Perón in September 1955 terminated the operations of Agencia Latina, ending young Ernesto's source of income.[71] Prensa Latina commenced operations in June 1959.

Che Guevara left his mark on the news service by staffing its headquarters with Argentinean expatriates like its first managing director, the journalist Jorge Ricardo Masetti. Masetti had reported on the Cuban revolutionary war from the Sierra Maestra. He wrote articles and eventually a book on his experiences with Fidel and Che. As a journalist, he even gained a scoop by using Radio Rebelde, the transmitter station set up in the Sierra Maestra. Masetti sent out live reports on the revolution that reached Cuban short-wave listeners as well as radio audiences in Mexico and Venezuela.[72]

Prensa Latina under Masetti also employed Che's ex-wife, the Peruvian Hilda Gadea, who helped assemble a weekly economic review on Latin America. Within a year of its founding, Prensa Latina had branch offices in the larger cities of Latin America as well as in Rome, Paris, London, Moscow, and Prague. Among his reporters and editors in the home office in Havana, one found non-Cuban writers such as the Argentinean Rodolfo Walsh and the Colombian Gabriel García Márquez. The former became a rebel in his own country, and the latter a Nobel laureate in literature. Masetti himself had toured Latin America spreading good news about the Cuban Revolution, once giving a lecture at the University of Buenos Aires. "In America a profound revolution can be made," he told students in March 1960. "The Cuban Revolution is the major proof that a total revolution is possible."[73]

However, once the Cuban Revolution took a hard turn to the left and the Prensa Latina began distributing what many editors regarded as propaganda, one host country after another closed down its branch offices. By 1964, only Mexico, Chile, Uruguay, Bolivia, and Brazil still tolerated Prensa Latina's presence. Its correspondents went underground in the other countries but still maintained communications between the Cuban government and its former trainees in the leftist groups of Central and South America. According to the Mexican intelligence services, Prensa Latina inexorably became involved in Cuba's bureaucratic squabbles between the M26 veterans (including Guevara) and members of the old communist party, the PSP.[74] Masetti eventually had to resign in 1961. His resignation freed him to lead Che's first guerrilla band in Argentina.

The difficulties of the struggle throughout the hemisphere did not dissuade Fidel Castro from his mission. Beginning in 1964, he commenced a series of three international conferences intended to unify revolutionary forces worldwide. One change in the overall strategy of revolution in Latin

America came to light in the November 1964 meeting in Havana of the Latin American Communist Party leaders. In the communiqué that concluded this conference, Cuba promised to support only those guerrilla groups endorsed by the country's orthodox communist party. It was an easy compromise. The pro-Cuba Goulart government in Brazil had succumbed to the military coup of April 1964, and an Argentinean *foco* sponsored by Che had collapsed as well. For their part, the orthodox communists promised to "intensify solidarity in the anti-imperialist struggle" and promote "solidarity with Cuba." The Colombian Communist Party, which heretofore had ignored the guerrillas in favor of gaining power through peaceful means, now switched sides. It endorsed the Cuban-supported guerrilla groups.[75] The show of unity did not have much effect one way or another. The old-line communists, many of whose leaders had grown cautious after decades of semilegality, still refused to take up arms. Neither Fidel nor Che expected much from the pro-Soviet parties.

At the beginning of 1965, Havana still concentrated on three guerrilla movements that Castro said "cannot be crushed"—Colombia, Venezuela, and Guatemala. Che also singled out these three countries in his address to the United Nations in New York City. He admitted that Cuba had helped the "freedom fighters" of Venezuela to "acquire military knowledge." Che reiterated that "bullets not ballots" would bring revolution to Latin America.[76] In only his second meeting with an official of the US government, Che Guevara told Senator Eugene McCarthy that Cuba's support of armed revolution was the only hope of progress in Latin America. Certainly, the Alliance for Progress was doomed to failure, he told McCarthy, because it underwrote the vested interests and the status quo. Venezuela and Central America needed revolutions, Che said.[77]

But events in the Dominican Republic in 1965 came as another setback for Cuba. The CIA speculated that Cuba had trained fifty Dominicans who participated in the 1965 Constitutionalist uprising. Most belonged to the 14th of June Group (APCJ). But during the crisis of April, Cuban news of the events in Santo Domingo played down Castro's linkages to rebel leaders. It refrained from labeling them "pro-Castro" and "Communist" in a vain effort *not* to provoke the intervention of the US Armed Forces. The CIA triumphantly speculated that the US intervention in the Dominican Republic "served to convince Castro that his 'inevitable' revolution is not imminent."[78] Fidel and Che persevered anyway.

A guerrilla band in the Sierra de Minas of Guatemala, 1966. Third from the left is the Mexican photographer Rodrigo Moya; next to him are César Montes and a woman known only as "la guerrillera Rosa María."

International conferences for national liberationists began the new, presumably more economical phase. At the Tricontinental Conference in January 1966, Castro had urged greater commitments to armed revolution in Latin America, Africa, and Asia. More than five hundred conferees representing eighty countries attended. Lázaro Cárdenas of Mexico, Salvador Allende of Chile, and guerrilla Luis Turcios of Guatemala represented their countries at the Tricontinental. From Bolivia, the "conservative" communist party chief Mario Monje succeeded in capturing control of the delegation from the rival Trotskyists and Maoists. Everyone voted on seventy-three resolutions, including on the right "to resort to all forms of struggle . . . including armed struggle" to win political independence.[79] Fidel gave the final address.

In 1967, the Cubans hosted the foundational meeting of the Latin American Solidarity Organization (OLAS). Stokely Carmichael, the Black Power leader from the United States, was visiting Cuba too, and Castro introduced him to the conferees. He suggested that black America could be the vehicle for expanding the revolution into the "bastion of world imperialism."[80] The OLAS meeting could not remedy the very problem for which it had been convened—namely to resolve the disunity on the left in Latin America. One hundred sixty-four delegates and more than one hundred observers and guests attended the weeklong event. The delegates voted on a resolution stating that "it is a right and duty of the peoples of Latin America to carry out the Revolution."[81]

Rodney Arismendi, leader of the Uruguay communists and also a traveling companion to Fidel Castro in his first trip to the Soviet Union, attempted to work out a compromise. At the OLAS meeting, he attempted to bridge the differences between the ultraleft revolutionaries and the pro-Moscow parties. Arismendi's proposal acknowledged that the armed struggle constituted one of the higher forms of revolutionary activity, but popular front activities of the mainline parties contributed to revolution as well. Even his pro-Soviet colleagues from other countries did not agree with him, and the Uruguayan's proposal met rejection.[82] If disunity did not mar the meeting, the breakdown of security did. A functionary at the Cuban embassy defected with the list of Latin American leftists who traveled back and forth to Havana under Cuba's diplomatic auspices. The defector turned the list over to American security agents.[83] It served as his ticket to a comfortable exile in Miami.

Soviet Bloc countries also monitored the continued confrontational style of the Cubans at the OLAS conference. The East Germans took Castro's comments personally. "The struggle with the leadership of the Communist Party of Venezuela was actually addressed to all the parties that did not share the Cuban position of armed struggle as the only revolutionary way forward in Latin America," reported the diplomats of the German Democratic Republic (DDR). "Castro's strong critique of the parties as out-of-date and out-of-touch . . . was probably also aimed at the 'revisionist' parties in Europe." The East Germans surmised that the OLAS conference deepened the breach between the communists and the "revolutionary petite bourgeois [guerrilla] groups." The diplomats deemed the latter groups "vulnerable to state repression." Do not underestimate the Cubans, advised the East Germans. "Most likely Cuba will dedicate even more energy towards the realization of its political goals and activities in the guerrilla movement."

The East Germans also predicted that Castro would "focus all resources on Venezuela in order to create a Latin American Viet Nam."[84]

Cuba's export of revolution was not a secretive project. Both Fidel and Che had talked openly and often with reporters and public officials abroad and with mass audiences at home. They spoke as prophets spreading the gospel about how to bring about redemption to the poor and oppressed of the world. "There is no solution but armed struggle—for the people to take power out of the hands of the Yankee imperialists and the small group of the bourgeoisie that work with them," Che told a reporter for England's *Daily Worker*. "Cuba has shown that small guerrilla groups . . . can be converted into an army which eventually can destroy the armed forces of the class enemy. We say that this can be done in a large number of Latin American countries."[85]

Che Guevara further clarified his own evolving ideas in a speech to a delegation of Central Americans attending the fourth anniversary celebration of the Cuban Revolution. Clearly, he was thinking in hemispheric terms when he told them that they must prepare "for united and simultaneous revolutions" in all their republics. Any idea that they could gain power by other methods was a myth, he said. "No Communist Party had ever achieved power thru [*sic*] the vote," the CIA quoted him as saying. Che left the Central Americans with confident predictions. Within the next year, he speculated that Chile would be communist because the party there had a large following among the peasants. Venezuela was the linchpin of continental revolutionary strategy. Che said that communist guerrillas in this oil-rich nation would begin attacking foreign companies that invest in Venezuela, causing them to pull out. In the resultant economic chaos, he predicted, Latin America will fall to the communists. Che chided the Nicaraguans for their recent failures, because they were "completely out of touch with the masses inside Nicaragua." Then he warned that "the revolution would not be easy." He said that counterinsurgency military groups knew his book on guerrilla warfare and were "capable of crushing any uprising in Latin America."[86]

As Che called on the radical left to overthrow the reactionaries, the latter prepared themselves to annihilate the revolutionaries. The right wing had the arms and the motivation to act on their apprehensions. For this, Latin America's generals needed no American advisers to warn them of the consequences of inaction. They only had to contemplate the results of Batista's strategy of ignoring the guerrillas until it became too late.

In 1968, United States intelligence suggested that American officials could rest easy. The danger of revolution had passed. "We judge that the factors impeding revolutions are appreciably stronger than the factors conducive to them," the CIA reported. By the same token, the Agency noticed no "improvement in the basic economic conditions of many Latin American countries, and a gradual worsening in social conditions." Therefore, intelligence agents did not rule out that some circumstance of "intolerable conditions" might provoke a future revolution.[87] This latter observation proved a prescient caveat that Nicaragua would corroborate in 1979.

However, despite the *sandinistas*, the eventual triumph accrued to the military dictators. The export of revolution from Cuba provoked an unequal and more powerful reaction in one country after another. Che Guevara's prognostications did not come to pass. He viewed revolution as an international phenomenon sweeping up all Latin America in its wake. Guevara had a Bolivarian vision of the peoples of Mesoamerica and South America uniting in revolutionary anti-imperialism. Instead, the generals won out. By 1976, a majority of Latin American citizens lived under their rule, as opposed to in 1959, when only a small minority did.

"The establishments which now control the larger Latin American Countries are much stronger than any proponents of revolutionary violence." This CIA report concluded that the three remaining active insurgencies—Guatemala, Colombia, and Venezuela—had no chance of success. Cuban-inspired uprisings in the last three countries lasted longer and developed greater military capabilities. Other insurgencies, such as the one in Ecuador, ended rather abruptly. In any case, they never amounted to the "unified and simultaneous revolutions" that Che Guevara had sought. However, guerrilla uprisings profoundly affected inter-American relations and the domestic political climate of every republic in the region. The hemisphere was heading toward unity all right. But it was the counterrevolution that would eventually win out—not Che's cherished guerrilla movements. The great counterrevolution initiated by the secret war between Washington and Havana did not diminish despite Cuba's eventual cancellation of its revolutionary export project. As if physics were behaving illogically, the reaction became much more powerful and more vicious than the original action.

The spread of revolution threatened too many entrenched interests in Latin America, of which the military was the most salient. "If the Communists came to power," one Ecuadorian general told an American political scientist, "they would replace the army with a militia!"[88]

PART TWO

THE SECRET WAR
FOR SOUTH AMERICA

CHAPTER EIGHT

Revolutionary Diplomacy and Democracy

THE WELCOME BEFITTED a hero. Fifty thousand Venezuelans awaited the arrival of Fidel Castro at Maiquetía Airport on January 23, 1959. Not yet a member of Cuba's new government, the thirty-three-year-old leader of the 26th of July Revolutionary Movement (M26) had assumed only the title of commander-in-chief of the Revolutionary Armed Forces. The revolution had not yet entered its second month, but Castro had found time to accept an invitation of the student government of the Central University of Venezuela. He came to help the nation celebrate the first anniversary of the fall of the dictatorship of General Marco Andrés Pérez Jiménez. Admiral Wolfgang Larrazábal, former head of the junta that replaced the dictator, and student federation leaders waited at the airport to welcome the visiting revolutionary. Castro expressed his gratitude to Larrazábal for his government's delivery of arms to M26 during its revolution against Batista.

Admiral Larrazábal's interim government had proved to be remarkably sympathetic to the exiled coalition of parties and personalities that supported Castro's M26 fighting against the dictator Batista. No one thought of them as communists. The Cuban government in exile, formed by the so-called

Pact of Caracas, found a haven in Venezuela during Larrazábal's government. The interim Venezuelan president even permitted the Cuban émigrés to collect money and arms and fly them out by plane to Castro in the Sierra Maestra. Cuba's president, Manuel Urrutia, sojourned as an exile in Caracas.[1]

The visit turned into a spectacle. From Maiquetía Airport, Castro traveled up the highway to the city of Caracas in the bed of a truck together with fifty bearded companions, his personal guards. They waved at the bystanders along the way. Olive-green fatigues and bearded faces contrasted greatly with the formal style of the politicians and students of Caracas. The guerrilla chieftain addressed Venezuela's new congress on the very next day. He spoke extemporaneously for two hours, interrupted often by applause. "People have lost faith in the Organization of American States," he said. "It serves no purpose at all." Four dictators still remained in Latin America. They were just like Pérez Jiménez, whom Venezuelans had defeated a year before, and Batista, whose dictatorship Castro had ended twenty-four days earlier.

Castro expressed hope that the remaining dictatorships, of the Dominican Republic, Haiti, Nicaragua, and Paraguay, would soon fall as well. He also expressed disdain for the officers of Latin America's armed forces. Later, Fidel Castro went to the Central University of Venezuela to greet thousands of students who awaited him there. His caravan had difficulty negotiating traffic because of the throngs of people who gathered along the streets.[2] American diplomats in Caracas could not help but contrast Castro's reception to that accorded to Vice President Richard M. Nixon seven months beforehand. Nixon had been stoned. Castro was cheered.

Fidel Castro conveyed the real purpose of his trip to no one else but president-elect Rómulo Betancourt, in a private conversation lasting three hours. Betancourt joked that if the elections had been held during Fidel's visit, the Cuban would have defeated any Venezuelan candidate running on the ballot. "Between us," Castro said to the president-elect, "we'll play a masterful game with the *gringos*." He deliberately used the Mexican term for North Americans rather than the Cuban equivalent, *yanquis*. Would Betancourt lend him three hundred million dollars or provide Cuba the equivalent in crude petroleum? Betancourt had to refuse. The Venezuelan president-elect explained that the oil companies would deduct such country-to-country oil deliveries from their royalty payments to the Venezuelan people. Besides, he too had a large agenda of social reforms to finance.[3]

Betancourt did not know it, but his negative response to Castro foreclosed future collaboration between them.

Though discouraged, Castro stayed one day longer than scheduled so that he could greet a long line of Venezuelans at the Cuban embassy. Among the guests Fidel met and embraced was the future Nobel laureate poet of Chile, Pablo Neruda, who happened to be in town at Betancourt's invitation. The Cubans knew that Neruda was Che Guevara's favorite literary figure. Then, early on the morning of January 27, Comandante Francisco Cabrera, chief of the commander's bodyguards, boarded the plane with Fidel's entourage for the trip back to Havana. He suddenly remembered leaving a gun in another aircraft. Comandante Cabrera descended from the plane and, in the morning darkness, walked into the whirling propeller, dying instantaneously. "To think that after having faced all the dangers of war he should have died like this," Castro said.[4] Thereafter, Fidel Castro would become the prime minister of Cuba. Betancourt would be inaugurated as the first popularly elected president of Venezuela following nearly a century and a half of dictatorial rule. Even though they both had helped defeat a dictatorship in each of their countries, their relationship deteriorated rapidly following their only face-to-face meeting. They became enemies and struggled to unseat each other. Betancourt resorted to the Organization of American States, and Castro, to leftist guerrillas.

Cuba's revolutionary diplomacy presented an enormous challenge to the fragile hegemony of democracy. Among the Spanish- and Portuguese-speaking countries of South America, only Paraguay remained the old-fashioned, personalist dictatorship of an army general, Alfredo Stroessner. All other nations in 1960 had elected governments and civilian presidents. But their tenure depended on these democracies' ability to manage the expectations of an electorate besieged by economic stagnation and the reality of poverty for the many and money and property for the few. Not only did the Cuban Revolution stand out as a new model to solve social inequities, but the brash new leaders of Cuba also actively sought to spread their example and preach the gospel of armed rebellion.

What did the world's paragon of economic dynamism and democracy, the United States of America, accomplish in the 1960s to preserve the electoral experiment in which civilian politicians to the south were engaged?

It offered financial aid that it could not deliver and diplomatic assistance to those who rejected revolutionary Cuba. Unfortunately for democracy, Washington's best allies in the struggle against Castro-communism were the established military officer corps and the most reactionary sectors of privilege and wealth. The secret war for South America boded ill for democracy, because the Cuban revolutionaries scorned most civilian presidents, and US policymakers could not count on them to stem the communist threat.

FIDEL IN BUENOS AIRES

Fidel's trip to Argentina demonstrated that he would not play by the normal rules of inter-American cooperation. Following his visit to the United States, Cuba's new prime minister flew to Buenos Aires on May Day of 1959. Argentineans did not hail Fidel Castro's arrival with the same level of fanfare as had either the Venezuelans in January or even the Americans in April. Union workers and student organizations on both the left and the right took little note of the Cuban leader's visit. The upper-crust ladies of Barrio Norte, on the other hand, mobbed Fidel's limousine as it drove under the elaborate portico of the Alvear Hotel. The "ladies and maidens" of the fashionable neighborhood of Barrio Norte received the *verde olivo*–clad Cuban entourage with particular fervor. The better-off *porteñas* (women of Buenos Aires) mistakenly equated Castro's victory over General Fulgencio Batista with the 1955 Revolución Libertadora, the military's overthrow of President Juan Perón.[5] After all, to the elite, both Batista and Perón were "populist dictators" supported by labor unions.

Castro came to the Casa Rosada for a photo opportunity with the recently elected president, Arturo Frondizi. Then he attended a dinner party hosted by the Guevara and La Serna families of Che Guevara. Argentina's foreign minister spent many hours entertaining the Cuban delegation. Fidel enjoyed grilled beef at the *parrillada* restaurants along the coastal drive of the Río de la Plata and grew to admire the expanse and majesty of Buenos Aires. "One has to take note that we can make these kinds of cities in America," he remarked.[6] Few newspaper reporters asked him about communism. Therefore, Fidel did not have to give elusive denunciations of "foreign ideologies," as he had in Washington just a week earlier.

"The self-appointed Prime Minister of Cuba," as the English-language weekly belittled Fidel, had come to Buenos Aires to attend the Conference of Twenty-One American Republics. The meeting focused on economic development. President Frondizi delivered the inaugural address. He spoke about inter-American economic cooperation and the importance of foreign investment. "[Development] should be based on national labour and savings," said Argentina's head of state, "and upon the contribution of foreign capital, whose aid is indispensable to compensate for the low levels of capitalization" in Latin America.[7] When his turn came to speak, Castro expressed skepticism. He said that underdeveloped countries had "little to share except their poverty." He did not welcome private foreign capital to Latin America but suggested instead that the United States donate thirty billion dollars in outright grants.[8] Latin America's need to fight poverty was just so immense.

Thomas C. Mann represented the administration of President Dwight D. Eisenhower at the Buenos Aires meeting of the Organization of American States (OAS). Due to President Nixon's hostile reception in his 1958 goodwill tour and the Cuban Revolution, the White House was already devising a more proactive policy toward Latin America. The former ambassador to Mexico, who was now working at the State Department, Mann announced his government's new loan policies for Latin America. He said that the Inter-American Development Bank, the World Bank, and the International Monetary Fund would be offering new loan packages for Latin America totaling about nine million dollars.[9]

The delegates could not help but notice the lack of agreement between Castro's proposal (thirty billion) and Tom Mann's frugality. Eventually, the Eisenhower administration would increase the promised loans to fifty million and then to five hundred million dollars. American policymakers also offered interest-bearing loans that had to be repaid—not the outright grants that Fidel Castro had in mind. President Eisenhower had acquiesced to increased foreign aid, but nothing resembling the Marshall Plan for Latin America that so many of the OAS conferees desired.[10] Already, the young revolutionary dressed in olive-green battle dress was disrupting international relations. In truth, Argentina had a long history of internal conflict, which still was working itself out inconclusively when the Cuban Revolution burst onto the scene. This internal conflict would become evident with the arrival of Che Guevara.

THE ALLIANCE WILL FAIL

Fidel Castro's visit to South America in May 1959 had generated moderate excitement. But Che Guevara's trip two years later created great anticipation. What had occurred in the interim—the Bays of Pigs—made all the difference. The Cubans had become David to the North American Goliath. The economic ministers' meeting of the OAS drew Guevara to Uruguay. As minister of industry, Che represented Cuba at the OAS meeting at a moment in which the Kennedy administration had doubled down on its project to isolate revolutionary Cuba. President Rómulo Betancourt had already complained to the OAS about Cuba's support for Venezuela's guerrilla uprising. Several Central American regimes and Peru too had already broken diplomatic relations with Cuba.

President Kennedy sought the means to convince other countries to do the same. The Alliance for Progress served the purpose, for the United States proposed to provide twenty billion dollars in development loans over the next decade to all governments of Latin America if they would sign up for free-enterprise development projects. Actually, the Kennedy administration had not arrived at a total aid package prior to the conference; Treasury Secretary Douglas Dillon had made up the number just to demonstrate US commitment toward Latin America after decades of neglect.[11] Most governments were inclined to accept the financial assistance despite the fact that Latin American public opinion had decisively sided with the Cubans.

Two unavoidable situations complicated White House plans for the OAS economic ministers' conference. First of all, the site of the meeting could not have been more unfavorable for the Americans. The Cuban embassy in Montevideo had already concluded that "the great majority of the Uruguayan people are in solidarity with our Revolution."[12] The Cubans had surveyed the attitudes of various student and union groups, public officials, and civic organizations. Few other nations favored Cuba so much as the Uruguayan people. Supporters had just concluded their Second Congress in Support of the Cuban Revolution, which had been held at the University of the Republic. Only the church and the military disparaged the revolutionary government.[13]

Second, Castro's victory at the Bay of Pigs had given many South Americans a boost of confidence and pride. Therefore, Che's arrival at the international airport in Montevideo commenced a frenzy of excitement. Hundreds of supporters gathered to welcome the Cuban delegation. Uruguayans lined the highways to cheer Guevara and the Cubans, and as the motorcade drove by, they shouted "¡Viva Fidel!"[14] Foreign and domestic reporters followed Che Guevara as he walked from his hotel to the gambling casino where OAS delegates were conferring. They yelled out questions as he and his economic advisers passed by. "Comandante Guevara. What do Latin Americans need to make a revolution like Cuba's in their own countries?" one asked. "Huevos," he shouted back, "balls."[15] Several Uruguayan pro-Cuba support groups came to Punta del Este to greet the head of Cuba's OAS delegation. Local residents regarded the US delegation's arrival with wintery indifference.

Che's press conference attracted an overflow crowd of five hundred newspaper correspondents and photographers. As always, he dressed in olive-green battle dress with a red star on his black beret. Most reporters asked friendly questions, although American correspondents interrogated him about political prisoners and Soviet subsidies. Someone brought up the presence of four anti-Castro activists from Miami.[16] The press even covered Guevara's reunion with family members who crossed the Río de la Plata from Buenos Aires. Che's picnic luncheon hosted by the Uruguayan president brought out the press once again. Che sipped maté from a gourd and chatted with Uruguayan president Eduardo Haedo as an audience of Latin American public officials gathered around.[17] Brazil's Leonel Brizola was present. Everyone seemed to want to see and listen to the comandante who defeated Batista's army at the battle of Santa Clara. The previous day's picnic for the American delegation, led by the American secretary of the treasury, a successful businessman of patrician birth, had passed nearly without notice. The local press took to characterizing Douglas Dillon as "el adinerado," the wealthy one.

Che's opening and closing speeches garnered the greatest attention of the entire proceedings, and the Cuban minister of industry did not disappoint, though Secretary Dillon was caught by photographers smirking and rolling his eyes. Unlike the other heads of delegation, Guevara spoke without reading from a prepared text. He began by attacking Secretary Dillon's misuse of quotations from José Enrique Rodó and José Martí, natives of Uruguay and Cuba and two literary harbingers of Hispanic American nationalism. Che quoted Martí at length. "The people who buy rule; the people who sell serve," he paraphrased. "One needs to balance commerce in order to assure liberty. People who want to die, sell to only one buyer, and the people who want to

Che Guevara expounds his ideas to President Eduardo Haedo of Uruguay and other guests at a picnic reception during the Punta del Este meeting of April 1961. The Cuban delegation opposed the OAS Charter of the Alliance for Progress.

save themselves sell to more than one buyer."[18] The "buyer" obviously referred to the United States.

Che then derided the US offer of only twenty billion dollars, when Fidel Castro himself had insisted that the underdeveloped economies of the region required thirty billion. Guevara also reminded his fellow delegates of the stinginess of the US Congress. "The experience of all the honorable delegates is that the many promises they make here are not ratified there."[19] Furthermore, he said, delegates should take note that the United States would control the project selection process by which the money would be spent. Heading that US-controlled process, Che reminded OAS delegates, would be none other than Felipe Pazos, the very defector and exile whom Che had replaced as president of Cuba's National Bank.[20]

However, Che's policy commitments of the moment led him to miscalculate one particular matter. His overwhelming receptions in Moscow and Beijing in January 1961 had led him to overestimate socialism's economic achievements. "Since the Revolution arrived, that nation has not stopped growing," he told one escort who asked about China. "The economy is in full expansion."[21] To the delegates, he enthused over the possibilities of obtaining huge investments from the socialist countries. He mentioned the millions of dollars that the Socialist Bloc countries were lending to Cuba at low interest rates or none at all—not for primary exports but for industrialization, Latin America's key to prosperity.[22] Actually, before too long, he would be blaming Soviet and Chinese selfishness for Cuba's own economic failures. Yet in 1961 his confidence in the social republics brimmed over.

At the end of the conference, the Cuba delegation refused to sign the OAS resolution sponsored by the United States, which, Che claimed, was designed in the first place to exclude revolutionary Cuba from Western Hemispheric economic affairs. "We have denounced the Alliance for Progress as a vehicle destined to separate the Cuban people from other peoples of America, to sterilize the example of the Cuban Revolution, and afterwards to domesticate other peoples in accordance to the dictates of imperialism."[23] Moreover, the US proposal would increase the strength of the "monopolios imperialistas," further distorting economic development and exacerbating poverty in Latin America. "If the Alliance for Progress fails," Che Guevara warned, "no one will be able to stop the wave of popular movements."[24]

As soon as Che finished his two-hour oration, an anti-Castro protester sent to Uruguay by the CIA broke through security and unfurled a Cuban flag in front of Guevara. "He is an assassin," the protester yelled. "Down with Communism!" He shouted anticommunist slogans and denunciations of Fidel Castro. Che sat stoically until conference security officers ended the disruption. Earlier in the week, the protester, identified as Max Azicri Levi of the Democratic Revolutionary Front, the FRD, had participated with three other Cuban exiles in an anti-Castro meeting organized by the

Uruguayan right wing.[25] The Uruguayan authorities ultimately expelled members of the Cuban exile group.

Despite Che's popularity in South America and the public's goodwill toward the Cuban Revolution, OAS delegates voted for their wallets rather than their hearts. Che cast the only vote against the Alliance for Progress resolution. In his closing statement, Guevara predicted that the project ultimately would fail. "This Alliance for Progress is an effort to seek a solution within the framework of economic imperialism. We consider that the Alliance for Progress, under these conditions, will be a failure."[26]

Che Guevara still was not done. The Cuban embassy had already determined that the students of Montevideo overwhelmingly supported the revolution and objected to US machinations against it. Its study did acknowledge some student organizations that criticized Fidel Castro. "Both tendencies find themselves at constant conflict," Cuban diplomats concluded, "and they even have produced fights between them."[27] Che accepted an invitation to speak at the Universidad de la República in Montevideo.

Supporters mobbed Minister of Industry Guevara when he arrived, and the overflow crowd filled the plaza outside the assembly hall. Several future Tupamaro rebels attended the event. Another leftist popular among students, Senator Salvador Allende of Chile, stood at Che's side during his speech. Guevara repeated many of his main arguments from the OAS conference in Punta del Este. He spoke grandiloquently about the economic future of Cuba's industrialization with Soviet and Chinese assistance. "By the year 1965," he predicted, "Cuba will be fabricating its own ships of at least six thousand tons, perhaps ten thousand tons. That is to say, ships of great tonnage made in Cuba by Cuban laborers with Cuban technologies will begin to sail all the seas of the world at the end of the first Four-Year Plan of Development." The students responded with enthusiastic applause.[28]

However, when Che's motorcade departed from the university, shots rang out and a bystander suffered a mortal wound. He was Professor Arbelio Ramírez, a thirty-year-old historian there to witness history in the making. Days later, his funeral produced an outpouring of support for the Cuban Revolution.[29] Subsequently, the police of Montevideo admitted that they could not identify the history professor's assailants and blamed the crime on Che Guevara himself.

Although Secretary Dillon studiously avoided meeting face-to-face with the famous guerrilla leader, Che had made it known to many delegates that Cuba desired reconciliation with the United States. Brazilian and Argentinean delegates took Che Guevara to an unscheduled meeting with Richard Goodwin, the White House adviser and director of the Alliance for Progress. The diplomats left the two for a private conversation. Goodwin knew no Spanish at all, and Che spoke English haltingly. According to Goodwin's memo, the only document historians have of the encounter, Che opened the conversation with a note of gratitude for the Bay of Pigs. "The Revolution is even more ensconced in power than ever because of the U.S. invasion," Guevara said. He also informed the White House aide that Cuba would welcome a meeting of the minds. We require only that you recognize that the socialist turn of the revolution is irreversible, he said, and that you respect Cuba's national security, meaning an end to CIA support for armed exiles. The United States should also terminate the economic embargo. Guevara also offered to pay American investors for the properties that the revolutionaries confiscated in Cuba. We Cubans would be willing to discuss our support of revolution in other countries, he said.[30]

Goodwin's memorandum to President Kennedy reflects the intransigent attitude of the White House in those post–Bay of Pigs months. The revolutionaries are losing their grip, Goodwin told the president, and we are in a great position to apply even greater pressures. Mindful that the revolutionary government was still holding more than one thousand Bay of Pigs prisoners, Goodwin only recommended provocative actions once the *brigadistas* were released. Guevara's first discussion with an American official produced not understanding but disparagement.

CHE IN BUENOS AIRES

Following the conference in Uruguay, Argentina's president Frondizi risked his tenuous standing with his country's generals by secretly hosting Che Guevara at a private luncheon at the president's residence in Buenos Aires. He wished to broker a peace settlement between Castro and Kennedy. For electoral reasons, Frondizi wanted both development monies from the Alliance for Progress and cordial relations with revolutionary Cuba. Economic stagnation would win no elite- and middle-class votes in coming elections. Breaking with Castro would win no nationalist votes.

Guevara's last visit to Argentina, his homeland, remains a curious episode. In his luncheon with Frondizi, Che said that the Cubans had resolved to construct socialism. However, he emphasized that the Cubans did not desire a regime subservient to the Soviet Union. For this reason, the leaders of the revolution sought economic and trade relationships with all countries of the Western Hemisphere. The Cubans also were open to an equitable arrangement with the United States.[31] About Che's visit, Frondizi said later that "the public position of the Argentinean Government in relation to the problem of Cuba was that of facilitating negotiations between the United States and Cuba in order to avoid that this case would be converted into an aggravating factor in the Cold War." Che's own version of the presidential interview was not so positive. Guevara reported afterward on Havana TV that "the doors had closed" between him and President Frondizi, because the latter had asked Cuba to temper its close relationship with the Warsaw Pact, the military alliance of Eastern Europe. Che responded that Cubans reserved "the absolute right to have friendships that please us."[32]

The military had never trusted Arturo Frondizi and suspected him and his closest advisers of being closet communists. Some officers believed that the president had had an "alleged Marxist education." They cited his early career as an attorney representing "leftist groups" and his influential book of the 1950s entitled *Petróleo y política,* which denounced foreign capital in Argentina's oil industry. His political deal with Perón suggested to his detractors that Frondizi intended ultimately to set up a "popular front" type of regime with the cooperation of the Peronists and the Communist Party. Also, Frondizi's brother Silvio, a professor and lawyer, admitted to Trotskyist leanings.[33] This background of distrust explains why the generals reacted viscerally when they learned of Che's visit.

A dozen military chiefs confronted Frondizi at the presidential residence on the evening following the Guevara luncheon. They told him that he had lost their confidence, but Frondizi refused to resign. Then the president made a speech to the nation on live radio. "A serious and responsible nation cannot practice the policy of the ostrich," he told his listeners, "which consists of explaining away problems by pretending to ignore them." If a Cuban government official was willing to discuss a problem with the Argentinean head of state, Frondizi continued, "we would have failed in our duties as public administrators and as Americans if we had rejected dialogue."[34] Apparently, he believed that his relationship with President Kennedy would save him from the wolves.

Fallout from the Cuban Revolution continued to influence the Argentinean political atmosphere. In September 1961, exiled Cuban leader Tony

Varona of the Democratic Revolutionary Front (FRD) publicized documents exposing Castro's diplomats' attempts to intervene in Argentina's internal affairs. A defecting embassy employee had taken with him the "incriminating" papers from the Cuban embassy in Buenos Aires. They amounted to instructions from Havana for information about Argentinean groups supporting the revolution and an assessment of the esprit de corps of Argentina's military. Right-wing newspapers headlined the documents as showing a "Cuban red plot to subvert [the] Argentine government."[35]

Although Frondizi praised the Alliance for Progress and spoke often of his friendship toward President Kennedy, the White House did not sympathize with the political problems of Argentina's president. The differences became evident when the two elected heads of state exchanged views face-to-face. Two meetings in 1961 following the Bay of Pigs came at the lowest ebb of Kennedy's tenure. At the United Nations, Frondizi told Kennedy of his enthusiasm for receiving Alliance funding. However, Kennedy had to deflate his counterpart's high expectations, stating that Congress had just cut the foreign aid budget from five billion to less than four billion dollars. Turning to the subject of Cuba, President Frondizi informed Kennedy of the reasons why he could not join the US-led coalition against Castro at the OAS. Sanctions against the Cuban Revolution would not win votes in Argentinean elections, Frondizi said. "The problem was to distinguish clearly whether Argentina was a friend or a satellite of the United States," he later observed.[36]

The two presidents met again in December at Kennedy's vacation home in West Palm Beach. There the exchanges became even more discordant. Frondizi hinted that the delay of Alliance for Progress funds hindered his administration from solving Argentina's fiscal problems. The sluggish economy might force Argentina to find new export markets in the People's Republic of China, he said. The suggestion summoned a rebuke from Kennedy. "Red China constitutes such a great and unpredictable threat to all of us in the Western World," he said, "that it would be very unfortunate if anything were done to help the . . . Beijing Government."[37]

Frondizi again requested that Washington not divide the OAS by forcing member nations to isolate Fidel Castro. He expressed concern about pressure from his own country's armed forces for stronger action against Cuba, which Frondizi suspected was "accentuated by stimulation [from] U.S. intelligence sources." Forcing him to join the boycott of Castro would disadvantage his government in the March elections if voters got "stirred up with publicity about . . . sanctions against Cuba." Certainly, the United States could cajole the small Central American and Caribbean nations to vote for the censure of Cuba, Frondizi said, but the elected governments of Mexico, Bolivia, Brazil, Chile, and Argentina wished to abstain from voting on such a proposal. These countries represented a majority of Latin America's population, Frondizi reminded Kennedy.[38] The two presidents parted without agreement, as Kennedy indicated that he would not give up on expelling Cuba from the OAS.

Indeed, during the subsequent, January 1962 foreign ministers' meeting, also held in Punta del Este, the United States clung to its policy of isolating Castro. Members of the Argentinean delegation told Secretary of State Dean Rusk that the smaller countries, many of them dictatorships, should not "force" the larger South American democracies to accept sanctions against Cuba. The delegation representing the government of Brazil too resented US pressure and voted with the bigger South American countries against the proposal. Haiti held out for a multimillion-dollar loan before giving the United States the last of the minimum two-thirds of votes.[39] "Frequently, our patience has been sorely tried," Kennedy later complained to his aides, "by the opposition of some of the larger South American countries to measures we felt to be in our common interest and worthy of their support."[40] The statement betrayed his growing disenchantment with the constitutional leaders with whom he was dealing.

Meanwhile, Frondizi was attempting to save his government. The stalled negotiations over a one-hundred-fifty-million-dollar credit from the United States did not help.[41] For all his expressions of "partnership" with President Kennedy, Frondizi obtained little assistance in maintaining control over his own military leaders. The latter expressed disapproval for Argentina's vote at the OAS meeting. Following several stormy meetings between the president and his generals, Frondizi finally capitulated. His foreign minister complained that the military, "with a pistol [pointed] at the head," had forced Frondizi finally to break relations with Cuba. "This," the minister told the US ambassador, "might at least have been left until after elections."[42] In those elections of March 1962, the Radical Party president Arturo Frondizi allowed Peronist candidates on the ballots. That very fact also annoyed military leaders, who resented the exiled former president Juan Perón for directing the political activities of more than one-third of the Argentinean electorate.

Peronist candidates won nine gubernatorial elections in fourteen provinces. Argentina's second most important elected post, the governorship of Buenos Aires Province, went to a Peronist.[43] This balloting marked Frondizi's final undoing.

The anti-Peronist generals mounted a *golpe de estado,* deposed Frondizi, canceled the election results, and installed a caretaker government. US ambassador Robert McClintock had spoken to several general officers in an attempt to prevent the coup on Frondizi. "He's the only friend President Kennedy has in Latin America," McClintock told them. Replied one admiral: "I am sorry President Kennedy has such bad friends."[44] Following a few expressions of lament, the Kennedy administration recognized the military-imposed government. After all, the Argentinean generals did support American diplomatic objectives against Cuba, and they did promise new elections. In the process, Arturo Frondizi became the second democratic victim of the diplomatic struggle between Cuba and the United States. The first victim had already fallen, as we shall see in the next section.

A MEDAL FOR CHE

Che Guevara's trip to Punta del Este during the previous year's OAS meeting roiled the political waters of Brazil as well as those of Argentina. The problem for Brazil's right wing (not to mention for Washington) lay in President Jânio Quadros's infatuation with the Cuban Revolution. As a presidential candidate, Quadros in April 1960 took a preelection trip not to Washington, as had been customary, but to Havana. Cuban leaders such as Fidel Castro, Che Guevara, and President Osvaldo Dórticos received him as an important state visitor. Back home, his entourage spoke of the Cuban journey as the hallmark of a new Brazilian foreign policy more independent of US influence. Thereafter, Quadros never spoke ill of the Cuban Revolution. "The reforms undertaken by Prime Minister Fidel Castro," he told reporters, "are contributing to the construction of a New World that is awakening now in America. Our duty is to protect the Cuban Government and people."[45] As far as elections went, his Cuban gambit did not harm his campaign. Quadros took 45 percent of the national vote, while two other candidates split the remaining votes.

Officials in Washington and conservatives back home questioned the wisdom of Quadros's Cuban visit. In view of the fact that the new president's

fight against Kubitschek-era inflation would depend heavily on US financial resources, they asked, why would he go to capital-deficient Cuba instead of the United States?[46] One Cuban report predicted that "the armed
forces would not accept an electoral triumph by Jânio Quadros."[47] Nonetheless, the army held back as he delivered his inaugural address and set up
his government.

Such was the situation in May 1961 when President Quadros's financial
minister made a call on the White House. Washington had just pledged
three hundred million dollars for restructuring Brazil's three-billion-dollar
foreign debt. Finance Minister Clemente Mariani was about to institute a
far-reaching monetary stabilization plan advised by the International Monetary Fund (IMF). But Mariani's host in the Oval Office did not even ask
him about it. President Kennedy fixated on Quadros's fascination with the
Cuban Revolution and his refusal to enroll in the American boycott.

Still smarting from the Bay of Pigs disaster and anticipating a difficult
summit with Premier Khrushchev in Vienna, President Kennedy signaled
the new punitive policy toward Cuban-inspired radicalism. He lectured Brazil's finance minister about the dangers of communism. Kennedy said he
knew that President Jânio Quadros had domestic political problems, but "so
have I." He handed Minister Mariani several American newspaper clippings
criticizing Kennedy for approving the loan to Brazil after President Quadros
had espoused neutrality vis-à-vis Cuba. Latin American leaders must recognize, Kennedy continued, that Cuba served as a "weapon used by international communism in its efforts to take over additional Latin American
countries by internal subversion." Therefore, the nations of this hemisphere
must agree to isolate Cuba. Kennedy complained that the Cuban embargo
was not effective "when the leader of the largest nation in Latin America"
did not cooperate. The Brazilian finance minister explained that President
Quadros had "to deal with considerable communist and leftist strength
within Brazil." Nevertheless, Mariani said, President Quadros would move
away from "his pre-electoral position in favor of Castro."[48]

But it was not Castro that Quadros backed away from. It was Mariani's
stabilization plan. No sooner did his minister increase interest rates and stop
printing money than Quadros called a halt to austerity. He received too many
complaints from labor leaders about how the IMF's deflationary measures
were reducing the purchasing power of Brazilian families. Brazil's president

even sought to renew diplomatic and trade relations with the Soviet Union in order to expand foreign trade.[49]

For his part, President Kennedy focused attention on Brazil. Unlike any previous American president, John Kennedy opened the White House to visiting dignitaries from Latin America. In July 1961, preceding his Vienna meeting with Khrushchev, the president hosted a discussion with Brazil's most prominent economist and government planner, Celso Furtado. Both shared ideas about government initiatives to foster economic development. Kennedy touted his Alliance for Progress, while Furtado explained his plan for economic development for the impoverished Brazilian Northeast. At the time, Celso Furtado served as head of the Superintendency for the Development of the Northeast (SUDENE), a regional development agency on the order of the New Deal's Tennessee Valley Authority. SUDENE sought to stimulate more efficient cane production and encourage mass migration into the Amazonian frontier of one million unemployed rural workers. Furtado said the government would provide irrigation projects to landowners in exchange for plots they would donate to peasants to grow food crops.

President Kennedy expressed support for such a development program. US assistance would, of course, be conditioned "by what is available here." However, Congress resisted increasing foreign aid, Kennedy said. There was no discussion of communism, but the president did inquire about peasant organizations advocating land reform. Furtado dismissed their influence.[50] In his memoirs, Furtado later reflected on US policy in Brazil during this period. "The Cuba syndrome prevented the North Americans from seeing reality," he wrote. "They wanted a program of short duration, a façade for public opinion, a thing like fountains for the Alliance for Progress, etc."[51] Furtado suggested that Brazil's problems stemmed from long-term social inequalities rather than from communism.

Truth be told, many Brazilians had become enamored of the Cuban Revolution. The reforms in land tenure, education, and health care appealed to many left-of-center politicians. Nationalists found much to admire in Cuba's confiscation of foreign-owned businesses. Most of all, the Castro victory at the Bay of Pigs filled Latin Americans with admiration. Many exultant Brazilian youths flocked to Havana to help Fidel celebrate the eighth anniversary of the 1953 attack on Moncada Barracks. "Right now there are in my hotel more than a hundred Brazilians who have come to celebrate the

26 of July," wrote the Argentinean John William Cooke in 1961. "There are deputies of all parties, news reporters, representatives of the most important labor unions and peasant leagues, which is to say, the immense majority of the nation is represented."[52]

Defense of Cuba from the threats of the United States motivated students on university campuses across the country. The visit of Che Guevara's mother, Celia de la Serna, to the University of Pernambuco caused a riot in the city of Recife. Local authorities canceled her talk on campus. Students took their protests downtown, battling police and military troops amid clouds of tear gas. Celia de la Serna had to speak to students off campus at a union hall lit with candles. Tensions increased when peasant groups joined the student strike, raising the specter of a rebellion among the impoverished masses. Army troops patrolled the streets, and President Quadros sent investigators to assess the situation.[53]

One incident demonstrates how divisive the Cuban Revolution was becoming in Brazil. It had to do with the OAS meeting of August 1961 that Che Guevara had attended. Finance Minister Clemente Mariani led the Brazilian delegation. One of his delegates, Governor Leonel Brizola of Rio Grande do Sul, became disillusioned when it appeared that Mariani was not going to support Cuba. Brizola had attended the outdoor reception for Che Guevara, who dominated the discussion with his biting criticisms of US imperialism. Brizola agreed with Che. But, like other delegations, the Brazilian group had hopes that the Alliance for Progress would lead to as much economic growth in the Americas as the Marshall Plan had accomplished for Europe. Only Governor Brizola shared Che's view that the Alliance's program for land reform, including the prompt payment for confiscated land, amounted to "a vision alienated from Latin American reality."[54] Brizola left the Punta del Este meeting early and complained to reporters in Brazil that the Quadros government was caving in to US domination.

With Brizola gone, several Brazilian delegates conspired to arrange a meeting between Che Guevara and an unsuspecting White House adviser named Richard Goodwin. Nothing came of the meeting. In any case, President Quadros apparently wished to blunt Brizola's criticism by demonstrating Brazilian independence.[55] He sent Che Guevara an invitation to stop by Brasília on his way from Buenos Aires and Montevideo to Havana so that Quadros himself could present him a high honor. But Guevara was not just any foreign dignitary. He suggested that youthful rebels should destroy their country's military in order to build socialism—at the OAS economics meeting, no less. He had also predicted the demise of Latin America's oligarchy. Nonetheless, Quadros wished to present Che Guevara with the highest award conferred on foreign dignitaries, the Order of the Southern Cross.

Che's visit to Brasília began poorly. Weather delayed his trip from Uruguay by twelve hours, and a late afternoon award ceremony had to be postponed. When members of the presidential guard learned who would pass in review the next morning, they nearly mutinied. The award ceremony began before 8:00 A.M. because President Quadros had another engagement out of town. Che arrived in his rumpled olive-green battle dress, and he and Quadros only had ten minutes afterward to chat. The president quickly requested that the Cuban government provide a safe conduct for all the political defectors crowded into the Brazilian embassy in Havana. Quadros also asked for clemency toward the many Catholic priests accused of treason in Cuba.[56] Such actions would make it easier domestically for President Quadros to remain Cuba's friend.

A firestorm of criticism ensued, and more than just the generals objected. A conservative political rival, Guanabara governor Carlos Lacerda, promised "to take to the streets in defense of Brazil from Communism." He also decided to present the keys of the city of Rio de Janeiro to Tony Varona, the Cuban exile leader from Miami. As a member of the Cuban Revolutionary Council, Varona received a salary from the CIA. Varona had also attended the OAS meeting as an anti-Castro protester. That evening, Varona blasted Castro-communism on Brazilian television. Just days after Che's departure, the opposition in Congress defeated Quadros's agrarian reform bill, and Jânio Quadros suddenly resigned from the presidency. Some suggested that the generals had forced him to quit.[57] The Cuban embassy acknowledged the military's opposition but also mentioned another explanation that was making the rounds. "The current and generally accepted version," diplomats reported to Havana, "is that Quadros was preparing a plan to resign then return to government invested with greater powers as the only man capable of saving the nation from chaos."[58]

Vice President João Goulart had just completed a visit to the People's Republic of China at the moment of the president's resignation. Quadros had sent him there on a diplomatic and trade mission. Mao Zedong graciously received the Brazilian vice president for a private interview. Zhou Enlai hosted a banquet in Goulart's honor in the Great Hall of the People. Chinese trade officials spoke of purchasing more Brazilian coffee beans so that the United States could not manipulate world prices to Brazil's disadvantage. En route home through Singapore, Vice President Goulart learned that the Brazilian generals were refusing to allow him to return to take over the presidency.[59]

The generals had always claimed they were the guardians of the constitution. They remembered that Goulart had been labor minister for President Getúlio Vargas, whom the military had helped remove from office in 1954. Vargas committed suicide and became a martyr for Brazil's poor people.[60] One should bear in mind that the involvement of the armed forces in political transition never involved a military junta—at least not in the first six decades of the twentieth century. Rather, the armed forces permitted a civilian caretaker government to preside over the 1954 presidential election that brought to power Juscelino Kubitschek, the man who built highways and the new capital city of Brasília. He also ran up the country's foreign debt. In 1961, however, the armed forces did not forget João Goulart's connection to Vargas.

Leonel Brizola, the governor of Rio Grande do Sul, rose to defend Vice President João Goulart's constitutional right to succeed to the presidency. It so happened that Brizola was Goulart's brother-in-law. Both were *gaúchos,* natives of the state of Rio Grande do Sul, just like Getúlio Vargas himself. Brizola organized the nationwide Movement for Legality. He forged an alliance with unions, peasant organizations, student radicals, and leftist parties, which only confirmed the suspicions of his enemies. Brizola's campaign forced the generals to save the constitution by amending it. With the military's pressure, the Brazilian Congress voted to establish a parliamentary system with one of its members as prime minister, thereby reducing Goulart to a figurehead president.[61] The generals and the Congress took it upon themselves to reduce presidential power if it meant rule by a pro-left regime.

The CIA reported that Goulart was utilizing the communists in the labor movement and bureaucracy in order "to increase his political strength" within the new parliamentary system. The new president promoted the few officers in the army and police forces who favored the political Left.[62] Already, American intelligence officers were interpreting Brazilian political events according to what their right-wing Brazilian informants were telling them. The White House and the Department of State also adopted the attitudes of Brazil's reactionaries, because they coincided with the anticommunist Cold War rhetoric that dominated American politics. It would not be long before these complementary tendencies would result in a definitive victory for the Brazilian right wing.

EL GRAN ASADO

Meanwhile, El Che was laying plans for his own homeland. Argentina's military had installed a civilian interim government that was preparing for new presidential elections in 1963—with Washington's belated blessings. Guevara, on the other hand, prepared for warfare. On May 25, 1962, he hosted a gaucho-style *asado,* or "barbeque," for some 380 of his *paisanos* then living in or visiting Cuba. The date denotes Argentina's most important national holiday, which commemorates the beginning of the revolution for independence in 1810. The factional squabbling that the Argentineans displayed in the guerrilla training camps had irritated Che. The Peronists debated the socialists, and the communists criticized the Trotskyists. He wanted all leftist factions to unite, for revolution demanded no less. The barbeque was to be Guevara's opportunity to unite his bickering countrymen and -women into a solid leftist coalition.

Che Guevara took advantage of his status as Latin America's greatest guerrilla commander (taking nothing away from Fidel) and deployed his passionate eloquence. "That call to arms of May 25, 1810 was neither the first nor the only battle cry," he said. "Nevertheless, it had the special virtue of guaranteeing and consolidating it; the call to arms had the virtue of triumph in those moments. And the Cuban Revolution today is the same," Che said. "The Argentinean armies crossed the Andes Mountains in order to assist in the liberation of other peoples. When these feats are remembered, our pride always . . . is that of having obtained the liberty in our territory . . . and of having cooperated in the liberation of Chile and Peru with our revolutionary forces." We must unify in alliance, Che said, "notwithstanding that sometimes we divide our own forces with internal quarrels, notwithstanding that sometimes in sterile discussions we fail to form the necessary union in order to fight against imperialism."[63]

Guevara also referred to the imperative of defeating Argentina's military establishment and replacing it with a people's army, as Cuba had demonstrated to the world. Che also left his *paisanos* with his vision of what the continental revolution would approximate. "In this moment of colonialism and imperialism, total change means the advance that we have made," he told his fellow Argentineans, "the advance toward the declaration of the socialist revolution and the establishment of a power that is dedicated to the construction of socialism."[64] Even today, one of the surviving attendees of the famed barbeque, Manuel Gaggero, reminds his Argentinean compatriots "that we were provincial. El Che always strove to create a continental vision."[65]

Not all the Argentineans who visited Cuba and attended training sessions agreed with the strategies that Che derived from his Cuban experiences. Several argued for armed action in the cities rather than the countryside. One older veteran of the Argentine resistance, Vasco Ángel Bengoechea, belonged to the Socialist Party and had a long discussion over the necessity of the *vía armada* (armed struggle) one evening with Guevara. Bengoechea and others, too, had doubts about the wisdom of depending on peasant recruiting.[66]

Bengoechea argued that revolutionary struggle in the cities of Argentina would have a better chance of succeeding. With mature industries, seven million workers, grand urban areas, and a history of mass mobilization in the Peronist movement, he told Guevara, "one has to think that the scene of the struggles has to be Buenos Aires, Rosario, the banks of the [Río] Paraná, Córdoba, Tucumán—the large cities." Che responded with his well-known ideas about the necessity of organizing in the sanctuary of the wilderness, gathering revolutionary forces with the aid of the peasants in mountainous areas such as those of Tucumán and Salta. Alicia Eguren and others on the Peronist left added that "not obtaining the backing of Juan Perón would abort any revolutionary venture in Argentina."[67] Che still was not convinced of Perón's commitment to the revolution. "Before a sharpening of the conflicts," he told another visitor, "imperialism and the reactionary sectors [in Argentina] would orchestrate Perón and Peronism as a brake on the revolutionary advance."[68] He already had a plan to avoid that possibility.

Early in 1962, Che Guevara was planning his own rural uprising in Argentina, and he was careful not to inform his guests at the Gran Asado. Guevara intended to take advantage of Argentina's political turmoil by establishing a group of rural insurrectionaries in a remote area of Salta Province in western Argentina. Guevara picked Argentinean journalist Jorge Ricardo Masetti to lead the group under the name Comandante Segundo.

The title roughly promised that eventually Che himself would join the guerrilla insurrection in southern Salta as Comandante Primero. This nom de guerre also alluded to the heroic gaucho literature of the late nineteenth century and to the novel *Don Segundo Sombra* by Ricardo Güiraldes. Every secondary student in Argentina had read this classic.

Masetti came into prominence as the journalist who introduced the Cuban Revolution to Argentina's reading public through his stories filed from the Sierra Maestra. He also broadcast reports from the Sierra Maestra on Radio El Mundo in Buenos Aires as early as October 1958. Despite his earlier right-wing proclivities, he became fast friends with Che Guevara and published a chronicle of the guerrilla war, *Los que luchan y los que lloran* (Those who fight and those who cry).[69] He stayed on in Havana and founded Prensa Latina at the behest of El Che.

Masetti resigned this job shortly after the Bay of Pigs, as he said, in order "to better serve the Cuban Revolution and to be ready to dedicate myself actively to its works."[70] Actually, Masetti had fallen victim to the sectarian struggle inside the revolution between the older communists and the M26 veterans. Indeed, he went on to train as a guerrilla fighter in Cuba and then in Algiers as an associate of Che's allies, Ahmed Ben Bella and the Algerian independence movement.[71] Masetti took a course in urban guerrilla tactics from the Algerians, who had mastered that craft in fighting against the French colonial regime.

The members of this guerrilla cadre had begun their training shortly after the Gran Asado. Che selected five trainees from non-Peronist leftist groups. He had a strong preference for dissidents of Argentina's Communist Party who embraced armed revolution. From time to time, Che came to visit them at the training sites. He laid out the revolutionary task in blunt terms, the communist Ciro Bustos remembers. As guerrillas, you should count yourselves among the dead, Guevara once told them. "Perhaps some of you will survive but consider that from now on you are living on borrowed time."[72]

Supervised by Che's Cuban handlers, the five Argentinean recruits prepared themselves mentally and physically. They lived in isolation and trained intensively for months. In the interim, they fired, disassembled, cleaned, and reassembled every military firearm used in the Americas at the time. Finally, they practiced on "the best weapon in the world," the Russian AK-47, also known as the Kalashnikov.[73] Once the missile crisis erupted, Che decided they must get out of Cuba quickly through Prague and Bolivia.[74] But the trip actually took six months via a detour from Prague through Rome to Algiers. Complications in post–missile crisis relations within the socialist world slowed travel arrangements. In 1963, the Cubans and Soviets had some issues to settle, including the Kremlin's opposition to Che's revolutionary "adventures."[75]

Frustrated at the travel delays, Masetti sought the assistance of Ben Bella and his friends in Algeria, to whom he once had personally delivered Cuban arms as the Algerians completed their struggle against French colonial forces.[76] However, inactivity in Algeria produced even more strains within the group, and Comandante Segundo and the guerrilla code-named Miguel became estranged. Miguel announced that he was returning to Cuba; Comandante Segundo then subjected Miguel to a guerrilla trial, and his comrades gave Miguel the penalty of death for abandoning the group. They turned him over to the Algerians for execution. Ben Bella declined to carry out the order and returned Miguel to Cuba.[77]

Finally, in May 1963, the Algerians succeeded in getting the guerrilla trainees out of Europe on flights from Rome to São Paulo and La Paz. There the Bolivian Moscow-line communists led by Mario Monje complied with the Cuban request to help the guerrilla band get into Salta Province. However, when they learned of the expedition from Monje, the Argentinean party militants took umbrage that they had not been consulted beforehand.[78]

Che and Manuel Piñeiro, the Barba Roja of Cuban security, had a point man in Bolivia to facilitate revolutionary activities for the Andean region. The Cuban agent in Bolivia was "Papi," the Sierra Maestra veteran José María Martínez Tamayo, who later died with Che in the Bolivian uprising. Papi organized safe houses and travel services for the Cuban-trained Peruvian guerrillas in the Ejército de Liberación Nacional (ELN).[79] Papi acquired a farmhouse on the Bolivian-Salta border. Masetti's group would use this property as a base for supplies and refuge in support of Guevara's incursion into Argentina. The Argentinean side of this logistical planning fell to the artist and communist Ciro Bustos.[80]

At the time, Guevara was coordinating the ambitious plan known as Operación Andina. Cubans from the Americas office were sending out several guerrilla groups to Peru at about the same time. None of these combatants knew about the others, because the Cubans utilized compartmentalization and secrecy to the utmost. Bolivia served as the principal conduit for fighters infiltrating into Peru and Argentina.[81] Masetti's guerrilla band did succeed in getting under way from Bolivia, though under inauspicious circumstances, as we will see in Chapter 13.

It seems evident that Castro and the Cuban revolutionaries held a disparaging view of South American political parties long before Che Guevara formalized these ideas in his 1963 article in *Cuba Socialista*. They had tried working with Presidents Frondizi and Quadros as well as other elected heads of state who did not break diplomatic relations with Havana and who did not vote for US-sponsored proposals to tighten the economic boycott of Cuba. Panama, Venezuela, Peru, and Argentina had become fair game to Cuban interference because their civilian presidents had "followed [the] orders" of the generals to suspend diplomatic ties with Cuba. These regimes could expect no less than Cuba unleashing against them the wrath of their own revolutionary youth.

In the beginning, there were no ambiguities. The secret war antagonists, Cuba and the United States, had clearly drawn the battle lines. The Cubans collaborated with those elected officials who resisted American calls for isolating their revolution from the community of pan-American republics. However, that number dwindled steadily so that by 1964, only Bolivia, Brazil, Chile, Mexico, and Canada counted among those nations still maintaining diplomatic embassies in Havana. Fidel and Che declared war on the elected presidents who voted for US sanctions and actively promoted guerrilla warfare in almost all the other countries. President Johnson followed his predecessor John Kennedy in pressuring the remaining holdouts in South America to join the boycott of the first socialist republic in the Western Hemisphere. To do so, Johnson's ambassadors joined forces with the Latin American right-wing. Washington's allies, the anti-Castro groups in Miami, were already engaged in the hemisphere-wide US project. The secret war was well underway in 1964, and its tragic consequences would soon unfold with unexpected fury.

CHAPTER NINE

Venezuela's Guerrilla War

THE CUBAN REVOLUTION burst onto the South American scene at a critical juncture. As if countries like Venezuela were not already navigating the difficult passage from dictatorship to democracy, the Cuban revolutionaries introduced Cold War ideological struggle. Fidel Castro and Ernesto "Che" Guevara had energized Venezuelan youth who felt left out of the political settlements made by Rómulo Betancourt's older generation. Already university students had vented their frustrations at Washington by attacking Vice President Nixon's motorcade. They felt that the Americans supported dictators in Latin America and ignored the poverty and unequal development produced by US ownership of the Venezuelan oil industry. If Castro could take land from the rich and if he could seize his country's sugar industry from foreigners, why could not this generation of Venezuelans take over the oil fields and redistribute the wealth? The Cuban example found fertile ground among Venezuelan youth. It also inspired a decade-long guerrilla movement bent on unseating not a dictatorship but the moderate democratic transition.

The prospects of a guerrilla victory in such a situation confronted enormous obstacles. Betancourt and the older generation of exiled democratic politicians relied on the revenues generated by the insatiable North American market for petroleum. They embraced the United States as a partner in development. Betancourt and his democratic coalition used oil resources to woo the peasantry and the workers. The democratic government also sought to depoliticize and professionalize rather than to destroy the military that had ruled the country for 150 years. As for foreign policy, the elected governments in Caracas opposed right-wing dictators as well as the Cuban Revolution. Venezuelan politicians also utilized the OAS, that inter-American organization that Castro derided as "useless" and Eisenhower as "indecisive."

One might suppose that, under these conditions, a leftist uprising would sputter and stall. However, Venezuela's guerrillas stayed in the field for ten long years, surviving two national elections and constant police and military harassment. How did these radicals endure for so long? Part of the answer lies in the enduring support that Fidel Castro gave to these anti-imperialist warriors: the training, the weapons, the Cuban instructors, the money, and the encouragement that the Cubans extended to few other foreign guerrilla movements. In the end, however, the Venezuelan leftists could not surmount their own factionalism as well as the defeats suffered by rural guerrilla movements elsewhere in Latin America.

DEMOCRACY'S COALITION

The Venezuelans were overthrowing their last dictator just as Castro's guerrillas were ridding Cuba of its tyranny. The Venezuelan rebellion against General Marco Andrés Pérez Jiménez had not been easy. Students in the secondary schools and universities had begun demonstrations against the regime in 1956, clashing with police, while Cuba's Fidel Castro was still in Mexico. Thereafter, Venezuela's university students reacted violently to the fraudulent Pérez Jiménez plebiscite of December 1958. The church hierarchy too took a public position against dictatorship, and several priests spent time in prison for their efforts. The revolt began in earnest in January 1958 and involved several days of street fighting led by students of the Central Venezuelan University in Caracas. Ultimately, the Venezuelan Navy and Admiral Wolfgang Larrazábal came over to the uprising. Several air force officers also rebelled and flew warplanes over Caracas. Finally, a twenty-nine-year-old journalist named Fabricio Ojeda and his Patriotic Junta issued a call for a general strike.

The Communist Party too was very much involved in the Patriotic Junta.[1] The Communists also joined Ojeda's resistance group along with youth groups of three different political parties. The general strike in Caracas and other cities forced the hand of the generals, who stepped in and engineered the resignation of Pérez Jiménez. The dictator fled on January 23, 1958. "These anonymous deaths, fallen in the streets in an unequal and heroic struggle," wrote Gabriel García Márquez, "have given to Venezuela an indelible date."[2] Still the military did not wish to turn power over to the civilians.

At this delicate juncture, with the transition very much in flux, Vice President Nixon arrived on his goodwill tour. The students turned out en masse and took advantage as the forces of order reached a nadir of indecision. Richard and Pat Nixon suffered the resentments of many Venezuelan civilians toward an officer corps that did not want to relinquish power and prerogative. A hostile crowd greeted them at Maiquetía Airport with gobs of spittle. Young men along the highway to Caracas stopped the vice presidential caravan and assaulted Nixon's car with clubs and stones. His driver finally maneuvered through the mob and delivered the vice president and his wife to the safety of the American embassy. "Caracas was a much-needed shock treatment which jolted us out of dangerous complacency," Richard Nixon said of his narrow escape.[3] By that statement, the vice president was not referring to the Eisenhower administration's previous awarding of the Legion of Honor medal to the dictator Pérez Jiménez. In his previous stops in Argentina and Peru, angry students had confronted him as well. But he was not referring to Washington's intolerance of land reform in Guatemala and tolerance of dictators like Batista elsewhere either. Nixon ascribed these passions to the influence of communism on Latin America's youth. When the vice president returned to New York, he was hailed as the freedom fighter who had defied the communist masses.

Finally, enormous protests by hundreds of thousands of Venezuelans in July 1958 forced the removal of the right-wing generals, permitting the interim government to hold the presidential elections that Betancourt of the Democratic Action Party won in alliance with two other parties—the Christian Democratic COPEI and the Democratic Republican Union or URD.[4] Party leaders, all of whom had spent years in exile, decided to come to an agreement about the limits of competition. At a Caribbean beach resort called Punto Fijo, the three largest parties signed a protocol in October 1958. They agreed to collaborate on a coalition government. Furthermore, they decided to exclude the Communist Party from the Pact of Punto Fijo.[5]

The Communist Party emerged from the 1958 victory over dictatorship in a strong though not dominant position. A White House report admitted that "Communists actively participated with other groups in organizing the general strike which resulted in the overthrow of General Pérez Jiménez; exiled leaders have returned and the Party's opportunities are greatly enhanced."[6] Venezuela's Communist Party had 30,000 members, operated in the open, and commanded more than 180,000 votes in national elections. A few Communist Party members won seats in the Senate and House of Deputies.[7] A number of hacienda invasions by landless peasants during the politically uncertain year of 1958 encouraged the Communists even though Betancourt's Democratic Action (AD) already had affiliations with the peasant leagues. Coalition leaders resolved to deal with the land problem, if only to outflank the Communists.[8]

Locked out of bureaucratic appointments by the multiparty coalition led by Betancourt's AD, the Communists appealed to the anti-American students. Then the *adecos,* as Acción Democrático leaders were called, expelled its own left-wing youths from the party because of their admiration for Fidel. The left wings of the three coalition parties consequently formed the Movement of the Revolutionary Left (MIR). Venezuela's left wing had a vocal minority in Congress with one senator and fifteen congressmen claiming MIR affiliation.[9] The seven deputies and two senators on the left found themselves outnumbered by 166 congressmen and senators who had signed on to the Punto Fijo agreement.

In the meantime, President Rómulo Betancourt could not have been a more stalwart ally in the anti-Castro campaign of the United States. He himself had been a radical revolutionary in the 1928 student insurrection against longtime dictator General Juan Vicente Gómez. Betancourt and his companions became known as the Generation of '28.[10] They had spent many of their formative years in exile as generals succeeded one another until 1945. Betancourt then participated in a joint civilian and military junta. The Trienio government obtained its name from its three years of reformist rule that ended in 1948. In this period, Betancourt's Democratic Action Party helped form the powerful oil workers' union as well as peasant organizations.[11] General Pérez Jiménez overthrew the Trienio in 1948 and ruled Venezuela for the next decade.

Betancourt and his associates lived in exile during the Pérez Jiménez dictatorship. There he collaborated with Víctor Raúl Haya de la Torre of Peru, Juan Bosch of the Dominican Republic, and José Figueres of Costa Rica. They were charter members of the anti-dictator pressure group called the Caribbean Legion. In exile, Betancourt made common cause with other party politicians such as Cuba's ex-president Carlos Prío Socarrás who were plotting in exile against the Batista dictatorship. In 1953, Betancourt even lunched with the young traveler Dr. Ernesto Guevara during the latter's brief stay in Costa Rica. The future El Che preferred Juan Bosch to Betancourt, whom he characterized as being "steadfastly in favor of the United States" and dedicated "to speaking maliciously about the communists."[12] Guevara subsequently journeyed to Guatemala to witness the CIA-engineered coup against the elected government of President Jacobo Árbenz.

The history of his own country left a strong mark on Rómulo Betancourt as well as on his generation of the Venezuelan middle class, now grown more formidable after forty years of oil development. As president, he continued his fight against the Latin American dictators. He withdrew his ambassadors from nations governed by autocrats. Betancourt had a special animus toward Rafael Trujillo, joining the Eisenhower administration to try to oust him. President Dwight Eisenhower had come to equate Trujillo with Batista. This sort of brutal dictator might provoke a second leftist revolution in the Caribbean, something no American politician wished to contemplate. Eisenhower and Betancourt asked the Organization of American States to expel Trujillo. For this, Trujillo sent a conspirator to kill Betancourt with a car bomb that exploded as the presidential motorcade passed by. Betancourt's military aide and chauffeur were killed on June 24, 1960.[13] Eleven months later, the Dominican dictator himself died in an ambush by army conspirators, permitting the eventual election of the Caribbean legionnaire Juan Bosch.

For his part, the fifty-year-old Rómulo Betancourt had good reason to stick with the United States, despite his youthful criticisms of American influence. In exile, he once wrote an influential book criticizing Standard Oil and other US producers in Venezuela.[14] That was all behind Betancourt now. Thanks to the 50–50 agreement of 1948, the government already shared half the oil profits with the foreign corporations. The Saudis quickly followed suit. In fact, Venezuela and Betancourt's elected government in the 1960s pioneered with the Saudis in the foundation of OPEC (the Organization of Petroleum Exporting Countries).[15] Oil exports had expanded exponentially until Venezuela became one of the world's star exporters.

Rising revenues earned from petroleum now underwrote Betancourt's ambitious social programs known as *sembrar el petróleo,* "planting the petroleum," into educational and agrarian reforms and other populist projects. The redistribution of land began during the struggle against the dictatorship of Pérez Jiménez, when peasants had invaded private haciendas on their own or encouraged by communists. The new democratic regime had to respond. Between 1959 and 1963, Betancourt's government distributed more than one and one-half million hectares of land, more than half of which had been expropriated from big landowners.[16] Venezuelan reformers avoided conflict by paying immediate reimbursements to landowners for the confiscated properties. This program conformed perfectly to the prescriptions of President John F. Kennedy's Alliance for Progress.

Oil exports to the United States made it all possible. The petroleum industry that had once kept the military dictators in power now sustained a reformist democratic regime. In 1958, crude oil production amounted nearly to 140 million metric tons and rose steadily in the next few years until total production had risen to 194 million metric tons in 1970. Venezuela had long since become the number one producer in Latin America, outdistancing Mexico in the number two spot by a factor of 9 to 1.[17] That Standard Oil and Royal Dutch Shell dominated the producers of this commodity meant that direct foreign investment in Venezuela topped even that of Brazil, which had a population eight times larger than its northern neighbor's. US foreign investments in Venezuela surpassed $2.7 billion at the end of the 1960s.[18]

Betancourt had another reason to reject Castro's face-to-face request of January 1959. Venezuela's military establishment remained a powerful factor in domestic politics and still smoldered with ambitions and intrigues. Electoral democracy the generals and colonels could accept. But none of them embraced the *barbudos* who had just destroyed the military high command in Cuba—this amounted to an unhealthy precedent. The military men of Venezuela had also taken careful note as Castro dispatched boatloads of armed men throughout the Caribbean in 1959. In 1960, they began reading Che Guevara's texts on revolution. Nor were the generals encouraged when

Cuban envoys turned up in East Berlin, Prague, Moscow, and Beijing. In order to deal with the ever-present conspiracies in his own army, President Betancourt had to remain steadfastly anticommunist. He outflanked Venezuelan communists in the trade unions and peasant organizations. Betancourt also excluded them from bureaucratic sinecures despite communist participation in the resistance against the military dictatorship of Pérez Jiménez. The Communist Party felt betrayed. In Venezuela, therefore, the Marxists found common cause with the university students who supported pro-Castro, anti-*yanqui* alternatives.

Moreover, Fidel's victory in 1959 and his tilt toward the Cuban communist party and the Socialist Bloc reassured members of Venezuela's Communist Party, the PCV. Its leaders voted to embrace armed rebellion, the only established pro-Moscow party in Latin America to do so. Castro's encouragement and Betancourt's enmity encouraged the Venezuelan left to dedicate itself to duplicating Cuba's revolutionary triumph. However, unlike the original Castro guerrilla movement, the rebels did so under the guise of communism, not democratic nationalism. Also unlike the Cuban *barbudos,* the Venezuelan leftists sought to make a revolution in an electoral regime rather than a dictatorship.

Fidel Castro had come to see Venezuela and its giant oil industry as fruit well worth the plucking. The refineries he confiscated from the foreign oil companies in the second year of the revolution had been refining crude petroleum of Venezuela, after all. He would dearly have loved to have such a wealthy, socialist ally in the Caribbean.

OPERATION RAPID VICTORY

In 1960, Cuba again inspired the restless youth of Venezuela. Castro's nationalization of US businesses and his anti-American rhetoric moved thousands of Venezuelan youth to stage demonstrations. Leftist leaders then drafted an insurgency plan for "rapid victory" and resorted again—as in 1958—to urban violence, shootings, and bombings. Other militants took to the hills in M26 fashion as rural guerrillas. Their objective was to create disorder, inducing the military takeover of the government before the presidential elections of December 1963.[19] They took Che's advice that the demise of democracy would mobilize the masses against their real oppressors, the pro-American generals. "We saw that while our leaders had been talking about revolution for thirty years, the Cuba Revolution triumphed in two years of fighting," said one MIR militant. "While Rómulo Betancourt had been talking about agrarian reform for thirty years . . . in Cuba a far-reaching agrarian reform was taking place."[20]

Insurgency began in Caracas in October with a series of urban riots that responded to a futile call by students for a general strike against the Betancourt government. The Communist Party itself had some two hundred militants under arms. Together the insurrectionists killed fifty police officers in this first year of bombings, shootings, and kidnappings. The police themselves rounded up rebels by the hundreds.[21]

For their part, Fidel Castro and Che Guevara favored the communists in their early projects in the export of revolution. The party had cadres in every country that could have been useful in spreading revolution and anti-imperialism. Younger noncommunist radicals who formed the MIR proved to be pro-Castro too. Together these two political organizations in Venezuela, the PCV and the MIR, sponsored a paramilitary organization called the Armed Forces of National Liberation, the FALN. Douglas Bravo became military commander of the FALN. It established an office in Havana, proof to one newspaper editor that the Castro-communist conspiracy was seeking to penetrate Latin America. "Communist Terrorism will only succeed in strengthening the Venezuelan reaction," said the editor of La República. He concluded that the democratic system was the best defense against extremism.[22]

As a tribute to these Venezuelan communist revolutionaries, Fidel pronounced his famous motto for the export of revolution. "The imperialists were given evidence of what revolutionary solidarity is," he said in January 1963, "the active solidarity of revolutionaries who do not sit in their doorways to wait for the corpse of their enemy to pass by, of revolutionaries who understand that the duty of all revolutionaries is to create the revolution."[23] Venezuelan rebels received more outside funds than most other Latin American guerrillas. Castro's monetary contributions to the Venezuelan rebels, aside from the cost of housing and training foreign combatants in Cuba, were quite modest. Customs agents at the Caracas airport once discovered an undetermined amount of US dollars in the false-bottomed suitcases of leftist politician Fabricio Ojeda. He had been the Patriotic Junta leader so instrumental in bringing down the dictatorship. They released him,

An FALN guerrilla unit known as the *internacionalistas* operating in the Falcón Mountains of western Venezuela. They are carrying Belgian FAL assault rifles.

but Ojeda later faced prosecution and served a prison term for being an insurrectionary.[24]

The rebels began Operation Rapid Victory with two goals in mind. They wanted to prevent the state visit of President Kennedy to Caracas and to thwart President Betancourt's subsequent trip to Washington. The left also resented American officials coming to pay homage to Betancourt. US ambassador to the United Nations Adlai Stevenson, Secretary of the Treasury Douglas Dillon, and freshman senator Edward Kennedy came to express support.[25] American diplomats used their visits to Caracas to talk up President Kennedy's Alliance for Progress. On meeting the Venezuelan president, Chester Bowles of the State Department touted Betancourt's commitment to the goals of the Alliance. "Basic changes are necessary in Latin America," Bowles told reporters in Caracas. "An example . . . is the case of taxes. I am happy . . . to see that the government of this country is taking the necessary steps to carry out a tax reform. I hope that other countries of Latin America will follow this example and will move down the road of a just distribution of wealth and obligations."[26] For all of Bowles's enthusiasm, it should be pointed out that progressive taxation never took hold anywhere in Latin America. Not Venezuela, not Brazil, not anywhere. This fact made Venezuela's oil reserves even more important to its survival in the Cold War.

When the left began its insurrection, the military became agitated about the limitations of democratic responses. Continued bombings and attacks on US businesses put military units on the alert. Army convoys rumbled through the streets of Caracas after rebels set fire to a Sears, Roebuck warehouse there, and renegade officers took command of provincial army bases. The capital seethed with rumors of conspiracies in the armed forces.[27] However, junior officers with leftist ideas rebelled rather than the more conservative general officers. In May 1962, one navy captain and 450 marines rose in rebellion at the Carúpano Naval Base east of Caracas. They called for full employment, a raise in workers' wages, an economy free of foreign influence, and a "genuine" agrarian reform. The army quelled this revolt without bloodshed. Then in June, another rebellion broke out at a naval base in Puerto Cabello, resulting in two days of bloody fighting. Government forces suffered two hundred casualties and the rebels even more.[28]

Several junior officers also abandoned their military posts to join the leftist rebels, who welcomed them and praised the armed forces for their patriotism. The guerrillas, meanwhile, borrowed a page from Fidel's tactical manual. They stated that the guerrilla war was not directed against the patriotic military but against the pro-imperialist government. Guerrilla leaders were saying they did not want to fire on soldiers. Instead, rebels trained their weapons on the hated political police officers of Digepol, that "totalitarian creation hated by [the] people."[29] However, the generals remained loyal to the elected government of Betancourt as an alternative to social revolution.[30] This internal dissension in the armed services gave Betancourt another reason to castigate Cuban interventions publicly, to sponsor anti-Castro sanctions in the OAS, and to move closer to the United States—Venezuela's biggest market for petroleum products.

President Betancourt proved adept at stroking the egos of the senior officers. He invited them often to the Presidential Palace for strategy meetings and offered potential troublemakers a "golden exile" to foreign diplomatic posts. Betancourt often visited the barracks. He made sure that oil revenues continued to flow into the military budget. The CIA concluded that "the military is anxious to avoid an arbitrary move against the government which might alienate a large segment of the population."[31] The generals demanded that the president outlaw the Communist Party and dismiss other leftists who enjoyed immunities as elected deputies in Congress. Presidential spokespersons admitted that Betancourt found it difficult "to resist the pressure being applied by rightist military personnel."[32] Now more than ever, said his advisers, Venezuela needed to retain its constitutional democracy.

This situation made Rómulo Betancourt the most reliable democratic ally of the United States in the secret war. Few other constitutional heads of state willingly collaborated in US policies. President Kennedy treated Betancourt deferentially. When Kennedy made his celebrated trip to Caracas in December 1961, Betancourt joined his American counterpart in pressing the other OAS nations to sanction Cuba. But he also told President Kennedy that "any unilateral [American] action against Cuba would destroy the inter-American system."[33] Betancourt warned the United States never to intervene with its armed forces in the internal affairs of any Latin American nation. In the post–Bay of Pigs era, President Kennedy followed this advice, but President Johnson did not.

On his state visit to Washington in February 1963, Betancourt congratulated the president on the successful conclusion of the missile crisis and promised to do more to isolate Castro in the hemisphere. Again, he advised Kennedy not to act unilaterally. If any Cubans died in a US armed invasion, "Latin Americans would not forget," he said. Presidents Betancourt and Kennedy talked of other political hotspots in Latin America. They spoke about arms smuggling through Panama to the Venezuelan rebels and about the two hundred guerrilla trainees Cuba was sending back to Venezuela via Cubana Airlines flights to Mexico City. Betancourt assured the American head of state that "the Communists [would] not be able to overthrow the Government" of Venezuela.[34] In successfully exchanging visits, Betancourt and Kennedy thwarted two objectives of the Venezuelan leftist insurrection.

The slum riots, student violence, and military uprisings certainly challenged the Betancourt presidency. The insurgents concentrated heavy weapons in the core of the capital city, deploying mortars, bazookas, and recoilless rifles. Simultaneously, they launched additional attacks on oil pipelines, communications facilities, and military and police personnel. But rearmament did not suffice to make the revolution. "In January 1962 we were close to victory," said the leftist leader Teodoro Petkoff. "In my opinion, we could have won in 1962 if we had properly combined the armed struggle in the towns with risings by army patriots and revolutionaries."[35]

FALN's military commander, Douglas Bravo, formed a different opinion altogether. His experience in those first days of urban fighting led him to conclude that the slum dwellers could be quite conservative and averse to risk in the struggle against police forces. "The floating population of Caracas," concluded Bravo, "cannot be described as urban, since the 300,000 men who live in ranchos in the city have brought with them typically peasant customs and habits." Bravo said that these unskilled laborers "were neither peasants nor workers."[36] The rebels had failed in achieving any of their objectives in the first three years. Therefore, the combatants of the FALN announced that they would now concentrate on disrupting the December 1963 elections.

This second phase of the insurrection got off to an inauspicious start. One FALN unit shocked public opinion when it attacked a tourist train, killing four national guardsmen and three Venezuelan vacationers. The rebels had intended only to disarm the guardsmen and humiliate them in front of the passengers. Instead, bullets flew. After this disaster, the combatants turned almost exclusively to American targets and inflicted damage on oil companies and multinational corporations. Even here, the rebels made mistakes. Two of them were placing an explosive on an oil pipeline and accidentally set themselves ablaze.

Unfavorable public opinion demonstrated that many Venezuelans feared destruction of the oil industry, the life blood of the country. The rebels halted such attacks. Instead, they invaded the home of an American diplomat attached to the US embassy, spray-painting the walls with slogans and holding his wife and a housekeeper at gunpoint before departing. They firebombed the motor pool of the US military advisory program. In addition, the FALN's spectacular hijacking of the oil tanker *Anzoátegui* in February 1963 and sailing it to Brazil were intended to dissuade President Betancourt from making his trip to Washington. Newspapers published interviews with revolutionary operatives, such as the two leaders of the *Anzoátegui* hijacking.[37] Betancourt turned up at the Oval Office anyway.

The government crackdown in 1963 prior to the presidential election, partly motivated by an assassination attempt on President Betancourt, did yield results. Six congressmen went to jail along with seven hundred other activists connected to the violence. Many of these were turned over to military courts for prosecution.[38] These repressive measures of the democratic government could have played into the plans of the militants to show that Betancourt was no better than—if not a tool of—the military and the imperialists. Yet there is little indication that the public believed this supposition.

Despite the setbacks, the FALN carried on the campaign of terror, desperate to complete its new objective: to provoke the postponement of the December 1, 1963, elections. Election boycotts were not rare phenomena in Latin America. Castro as guerrilla leader in 1958 had urged Cubans not to vote in the sham presidential election of a Batista surrogate during the height of the insurrection. Perhaps, the PCV and the MIR were hoping for similar results. Noise bombs scattered "Don't Vote" leaflets on city streets. FALN militants attempted to set fire to printing plants that were manufacturing the ballots. The government called up three thousand reservists and sent several thousand army troops and police personnel into the streets to secure the voting places.[39] Then the rebels suffered their biggest setback to date.

A fisherman stumbled onto a Cuban arms cache weighing three tons on the beach of Paraguaná Peninsula. The discovery came within a week of President Kennedy's assassination in November 1963 and just three days before national elections. It caused a great stir. The government of Venezuela protested the intervention of Cuba into its internal affairs and called for additional OAS sanctions against Fidel Castro.[40] The weapons proved easy to trace. Their identification numbers corresponded with weapons that Belgian manufacturers had sold to Cuba in 1959. They included "20 bazookas, 5 mortars, 9 recoilless rifles, 31 submachine guns, 81 automatic rifles, 67 high-power demolition charges and a large amount of ammunition," as the *New York Times* noted. Apparently, the weapons had been destined for use in disrupting the elections.[41]

Fidel Castro did not deny dispatching the arms to his colleagues in Venezuela. In his first public speech following the discovery, Castro merely said that these were American weapons that the CIA had delivered to Cuba in order to provoke a counterrevolutionary rebellion. The OAS did not once investigate US arms smuggling into Cuba in the previous four years, Castro declared. But now that the arms showed up on a beach in Venezuela, the OAS proposed to apply a blockade on Cuba for provoking rebellion in another country. "What kind of logic is this?" Castro asked. "What kind of morality is this?"[42]

Nevertheless, the elections came off as scheduled. Raúl Leoni of the Acción Democrática party succeeded Betancourt as president of Venezuela. It marked the second peaceful transfer of power in the history of the republic—the first having occurred with Betancourt's own inauguration in January 1960. Nevertheless, Venezuela's guerrillas and their collaborators in the Communist Party refused to admit defeat.

MILITARY PROFESSIONALIZATION

The insurrection needed readjustments, and the Communist Party of Venezuela did seem ready to make them. Its leaders met in April 1964, at which time the party had lost its political apparatus in the arrests of PCV congressmen during the previous year. Discussions at the meeting glossed over its setback in subverting the elections. Instead party officials congratulated themselves on the amount of disorder they had created in phase one. This kind of environment prepared the masses for the struggle ahead, they boasted. The hard-liners dominated this plenary meeting and rejected a plea from the jailed party general secretary, Pompeyo Márquez. His message requested that the PCV call off the armed struggle. But the leadership reaffirmed its commitment to the Castro-style insurrection and planned for a more protracted, mainly rural guerrilla strategy.[43] The Communists uncritically embraced their role in the FALN paramilitary network, although a few of their number were beginning to have doubts.

Douglas Bravo of the FALN emerged as the chief revolutionary leader and advocate of the rural guerrilla movement. He said that the battle would now shift to the countryside where the rebels had cultivated the support of the peasants, just as Che advised. No more "immediatism." "We did not prepare with the strategic realities in mind," he confessed. "We had only one idea—to overthrow the government immediately."[44] Bravo admitted that the election of Raúl Leoni came as a defeat. Ninety percent of eligible voters turned out on the December 1 election day despite warnings of FALN snipers shooting anyone daring to vote.[45]

Comandante Douglas Bravo had been a *militante del partido* for many years. He belonged to a prominent landowning family in Falcón State and grew up among country folk, much like Fidel Castro did in the Oriente Province of Cuba. The police imprisoned Bravo in 1961, but he escaped and rejoined the rebels operating in the region of his birth. Fabricio Ojeda, hero of the resistance to the dictator Pérez Jiménez, gave Bravo a boost in revolutionary prestige when he joined the FALN in mid-1962. He too fell into the hands of the police, served time, and escaped along with Luben Petkoff.[46] Luben and his brother Teodoro were sons of immigrant parents, the father from Bulgaria and the mother from Poland. Growing up, the boys worked in their father's printing shop, a perfect school for learning radical ideas.[47] Bravo and the Petkoffs now consolidated leadership of the guerrillas.

What elements of society were contributing to the Armed Forces of National Liberation? A journalist in Montevideo put this question to FALN spokesperson Nicolás Sarmiento. He replied that participants included "workers, peasants, employees, students, journalists, professional men in general, and officers, soldiers, and marines." Sarmiento claimed that eight military officers had joined the rebels. Among the important leaders were the student Douglas Bravo, journalist Fabricio Ojeda, and the "peasant" Argimiro Gabaldón. (News accounts later disputed the latter's "peasant" status.) "Women occupy an outstanding position in the various fronts of the armed struggle," Sarmiento said. "They have demonstrated a high degree of combativeness, skill, and personal courage." He mentioned the student Oliva Olivo as an example.[48]

When President Leoni took office, the guerrillas still had the capacity to disrupt. The democratic government had to seek a military solution—to professionalize the army rather than allowing it back into politics. The armed forces responded. As yet, the army lacked the capacity to subdue the rebels, but neither did it wither before the task, as Batista's soldiers had done in the summer 1958 campaign.[49]

At the elected government's invitation, the US military mission in Caracas made an assessment of the thirty-two thousand men in the Venezuelan armed forces and nine thousand National Guard personnel. The 1961 report said the Venezuelan army had "increased its combat capability through the acquisition of vehicles, light arms, artillery, and other armament." However, "the lack of logistic facilities, maintenance, training, and communications" hampered military effectiveness.[50] The Venezuelan armed forces proved incapable of subduing so many small rebel bands in the cities and Andean mountainsides.

The government in Caracas wholeheartedly embraced US military assistance, though without public acknowledgment. American and Venezuelan troops conducted a joint exercise along the Caribbean coastline designed to improve surveillance of infiltrating guerrillas and arms. Green Beret mobile training teams (MTTs) flew in from the Southern Command in the Canal Zone to assist Venezuelans in setting up training facilities. The School of the Americas increased its counterinsurgency training programs for officers and noncommissioned officers from Central and South American countries. Thirty-five enlisted personnel from eight countries received training in medical civic action. The US Air Force stationed in the Canal Zone conducted instruction for Latin American crews in counterinsurgency air operations; the navy there instructed Latin American enlisted personnel in boat maintenance.[51]

However, the Canal Zone training facility that had been in operation since World War II changed very slowly from continental defense to the new counter-guerrilla curriculum. On his 1963 inspection trip to Fort Gulick in the Canal Zone, Attorney General Robert F. Kennedy became upset on discovering that only seventeen of the 435 students were studying the new doctrine. In-country training programs came to be preferred over the School of the Americas. Bringing Latin America military personnel to the Canal Zone cost too much, and Lyndon Johnson in 1966 even entertained proposals to save money by eliminating the School of the Americas altogether. MTTs proved more cost-efficient and culturally satisfying to the host country.[52] The MTTs delivered all instruction in Spanish.

The US military engaged in many training programs designed to professionalize Venezuelan soldiers, who had had a long history of political interference. Declassified US Army records reveal that democratic Venezuela hosted more American counterinsurgency training teams than any other country of South America—thirteen in total from 1962 to 1966. One training visit might easily dissipate its long-term impact, but repeated trips seemed to contribute to the combat effectiveness of the host country's military. The MTTs had the capacity to stimulate improvements in marksmanship, unit movements, the leadership skills of junior officers and NCOs, and the coordination of joint command units. Significantly, such repeat MTTs from the Canal Zone led to the increased proficiency of Venezuelan trainers themselves.

The 8th Special Forces personnel stationed at Fort Gulick did not always conduct the actual training of the Venezuelan soldiers. For one thing, the numbers of American trainers—two or three per MTT—did not suffice to offer training and would reach but one hundred soldiers. Instead, Green Beret instructors trained the local trainers. The latter could train one hundred soldiers several times per year. Second, national sensitivities militated against the American trainers taking direct charge of the instruction. Instead, the Green Berets provided guidance and suggestions to Venezuelan trainers, who had superior linguistic and cultural rapport with the recruits.

One example suffices to explain the consequences of American assistance for Venezuela's campaign against the guerrilla threat. Captain Robert Foote of the 8th Special Forces Group conducted one such MTT in 1963. According to his after-action report, counterinsurgency training in Venezuela was building proficiencies based on incremental progress made by previous mobile training teams. In fourteen weeks of 1963, Captain Foote and one Green Beret sergeant worked with a Venezuelan "instructional group." It numbered four Venezuelan officers and twelve enlisted men. They were engaged in the training of ninety-four national guardsmen in counterinsurgency tactics at three different locations.

American Special Forces personnel advised the Venezuelan instructors in designing the course, writing lesson plans, gathering the instructional materials, preparing the training ranges, and conducting troop exercises. The national guardsmen learned about small arms fire as well as machine gun and mortar operations. They practiced small-unit maneuvers. A combined-arms drill capped the training period. The two-day field exercise consisted of a coordinated attack on a force of twenty guardsmen posing as guerrillas. Venezuelan air force transport and reconnaissance planes collaborated with seventy ground troops in engaging the rebel force in simulated combat.

The Special Forces captain and sergeant concluded that the national guardsmen needed improvements in infantry weaponry. "The Mauser carbines with which many of the National Guard personnel are armed were in very poor condition," reported the Green Berets. "They were inaccurate . . . rusty and dirty."[53] Captain Foote also mentioned that the company officers had failed to demonstrate initiative in directing troop movements. But the report noted that Venezuelan troops demonstrated adequate progress, though "not yet at U.S. standards." The report also made an important suggestion. "If indigenous instructor groups such as this are created in the future," Captain Foote wrote, "there should be an incentive, such as additional pay or promotion considerations to ensure that the best qualified personnel could be selected."

Outmoded equipment posed another problem for the Venezuelan armed forces. The OAS presidential summit meeting at Punta del Este, Uruguay, of April 1967 provided an opportunity for Presidents Leoni and Johnson to address the issue face-to-face. Johnson warmed to the fact that no loans were necessary. Venezuelan petroleum export revenues alone could finance the purchase of some twelve million dollars' worth of military equipment. However, President Leoni suggested that Washington reduce delivery times from eighteen months to just three. President Johnson said that he did not wish to become the arms merchant for Latin America and that Congress limited total military assistance at eighty-five million dollars per year. Vietnam also placed a heavy burden on supplies of military equipment. Let us know what you need, and we will deliver as fast as possible, Johnson told Leoni. "We don't want Venezuela to have to wait one minute to chase the communists."[54]

However, sensitivities abounded in the country concerning American contributions to these advancements. Venezuelan officials and officers did not wish to publicize them in any way. In 1964, the defense minister announced that the Venezuelan armed forces were undertaking two operations against guerrilla groups. One targeted the rebels in the states of Falcón and Lara in western Venezuela, and the other, in the eastern states. At the same time, the defense ministry was carrying out civic action projects among the peasants with medical and educational teams. He added that there had been "no intervention of foreign personnel in these activities."[55] The Venezuelan army did not permit American advisers to accompany either its combat or its civic action operations.

The rebels operated with no such reservations. They relished publicizing the linkage between US and Venezuelan armed forces. American personnel serving in the Military Assistance Program (MAP) became targets of the revolutionaries. Early one morning in November 1963, four armed men kidnapped Colonel James K. Chenault, the deputy chief of the US Army mission in Venezuela. They intercepted him as Chenault was getting into the chauffeur-driven Venezuelan army car that was taking him to work. Later that morning, the embassy received a telephone call advising diplomatic personnel that the kidnapping was "for propaganda purposes only." On the following day, a woman called a newspaper in Caracas, saying that Colonel Chenault had "enjoyed himself last night, as he will tonight and tomorrow night." A week later, members of the FALN released him in a suburb. Chenault hailed a cab and returned home. The colonel reported that he had received good treatment.[56]

In the same neighborhood nearly one year later, Lieutenant Colonel Michael Smolen of the US Air Force mission was seized in front of his home. Kidnappers used machine pistols to force Smolen into a station wagon. The Caracas police set up roadblocks and raided homes of suspected leftists. Within three days, the FALN released Smolen.[57] The police apprehended one youth in connection with Smolen's kidnapping, but the courts soon released him for lack of evidence. The young man then went directly from jail to the Mexican embassy and asked for asylum.[58] Police suppression of the operatives who had kidnapped Smolen threatened the entire urban operations of the guerrillas. Their subversive activity subsequently fell off drastically, and the rebels in the countryside began to complain about the reduction in deliveries of supplies and money.[59] Nevertheless, the FALN successfully publicized the presence of US military advisers. It made little difference. The Venezuelan armed forces were beginning to press the guerrilla bands.

PROLONGED STRUGGLE

Not to be outdone, Cuba stepped up its support for Latin American revolutions. At Havana's First Conference of Latin American Communist Parties in 1964, Fidel Castro touted the Venezuelan guerrilla movement, the only one in Latin America supported by the country's Communist Party. He pledged greater support for the FALN to Alberto Lovera, head of the Venezuelan delegation. Lovera served on the politburo of the PCV. Castro promised delivery of three million dollars from Cuban sugar sales, which were then on the rebound thanks to Cuba's new trade deal with the Soviet Union. The Czechs would provide the guns, he said. In fact, the Cubans had called for another Latin American solidarity meeting as a way to enlist all the communist parties of Latin America to support the Venezuelan guerrilla movement. But Lovera described the attitude of the communist leaders from other countries as "one of grudging tolerance." He also expressed some "surprise" at the optimism of Cuban leaders about the FALN's prospects. Lovera thought that the Cubans exhibited more optimism than the FALN members themselves.[60]

At the November 1964 Havana conference, the Soviets obliged Fidel with support for the Venezuelan armed insurrection. Thereafter, Moscow financed the rebellion in Venezuela through its party apparatus in Italy. Venezuelan intelligence agents had received a tip and met flights from Rome at the Maiquetía Airport of Caracas. They apprehended two Italians, a male whose vest contained one hundred fifty thousand dollars in US currency and a female who had 120 crisp new one-hundred-dollar bills sewn into her corset. They said they intended to buy a business and maybe a racehorse. A check with Interpol identified the couple as Italian communists.[61]

Che Guevara too bragged openly of Cuban support of armed rebellion in Venezuela. During his trip to New York to address the United Nations in December 1964, Guevara told reporters that "Cuba is the free territory of America," meaning that all revolutionaries will find haven, support, and encouragement there. "Our example will bear fruit in the continent as it already has in certain measure in Guatemala, Colombia and Venezuela," Guevara explained. He said that the world would soon see the results of these three guerrilla uprisings. Guevara appeared on CBS television two days later and said that he supported the "armed revolutionary path of socialism."[62] At the United Nations, Che delivered a defiant anti-imperialist attack on United States policies in the Western Hemisphere. "In Venezuela, not only do U.S. forces advise the army and the police, but they also direct acts of genocide carried out from the air against the peasant population in vast insurgent areas," Che told members of the General Assembly. "And the Yankee companies operating there exert pressures of every kind to increase direct interference."[63]

Though Che Guevara did not attend the next two international conferences in Havana, the Tricontinental in 1966 and the Latin American Solidarity Organization (OLAS) in 1967, visiting delegates certainly felt his presence. Fidel Castro renewed his commitment to armed struggle. Despite recent defeats of Cuban-supported guerrilla groups in Argentina and Peru, Castro was redoubling efforts to spread the revolution abroad. Havana's OLAS conference in August 1967 had proposed to establish coordination among various guerrilla groups in the hemisphere. At this meeting, representatives of Colombia's National Liberal Army obtained a promise of enough Cuban arms for five hundred peasants they had organized in eastern Colombia. Talks in Havana between this group and Bravo's FALN had focused on the possibility of joint operations along the Colombian-Venezuelan border. The Leoni government dispatched troops to the border to prevent such an eventuality.[64] Nothing came of the bi-national guerrilla cooperation.

Leaders of the FALN responded to Cuban encouragement by clarifying their new strategies to win the struggle. "The Venezuelan revolutionary movement . . . suffered a tactical defeat in the past Venezuelan elections and the enemy took pleasure in the victory," one communiqué stated in 1965. "National liberation can only be achieved by the creation of an army of the people and through a revolutionary war of an extended nature, which would transform our present relative weakness in the face of a temporarily powerful enemy into a strong movement which will succeed in defeating the mercenary army and the social classes which serve the interests of imperialism." The guerrillas said that they had learned from their setbacks. The objective remained to create the instrument of victory—that is, "the army of the people." The guerrillas said that the FALN had offered to conclude a truce, but the government of President Raúl Leoni responded with even more repression of the "popular forces." Therefore, the vanguard was preparing for a protracted struggle. They concluded their communiqué with the stirring words from prison of communist Pompeyo Márquez: "Struggle is inevitable. Victory is also inevitable."[65]

Nonetheless, the revolution gained little traction. More than fifteen hundred government troops in March 1965 encircled the national liberation force under the command of Douglas Bravo in the western mountains. They blocked the routes of escape to the neighboring state of Trujillo.[66] In June, soldiers of the Urica Anti-Guerrilla Detachment engaged rebel forces in the mountains of Lara State. Official sources reported that they killed sixty-three guerrillas and captured eighty-four others. This unit also confiscated weapons, propaganda, and uniforms. Captured documents indicated that the guerrillas had been receiving outside aid. Interrogators learned of the presence of one Cuban nurse among the three women who accompanied the guerrillas.[67] In June 1965, the army again took the offensive against the guerrillas. They killed and captured rebels in several encounters. Leoni's defense minister told reporters that troops had flushed out all the guerrillas in the mountains of the state of Miranda and were completely in control there. However, he admitted that army units were still dealing with groups of rebels in the mountains of the states of Trujillo, Lara, and Falcón and in the Bachiller Mountains of Miranda State.[68]

The death of one of its talented commanders set back the rebel cause as well. Argimiro Gabaldón had earned the respect of his men and his fellow guerrilla leaders. Gabaldón was not a peasant at all. He was cultured and learned and was also the son of a general hailed for his opposition in the 1930s to Venezuela's brutal dictator, General Juan Vicente Gómez. Initial news of his death, put out by the FALN itself, suggested that Gabaldón had died from an accidental gunshot wound. The defection of another FALN officer revealed a different story. This defector said that Gabaldón had developed cancer and intended to give up and seek medical treatment. However, his fellow rebel commanders decided that Gabaldón's surrender would shatter the morale of the movement. Better that he die a hero. "They decided," said the ex-guerrilla, "that Gabaldon should die for the cause of Venezuelan freedom, to avoid giving a bad example to the people who followed him."[69]

The defector also talked about the toll that the army's offensive was taking on the guerrillas. The encirclement prevented the rebels from replenishing their supplies, said the man whose nom de guerre was Comandante Gavalán. The rebels were running out of food, ammunition, and medicines. He reported that "the guerrillas no longer [had] uniforms and that they are wearing rags and going without shoes." Moreover, members of the MIR and those of the Communist Party began a vicious struggle to succeed Gabaldón. The guerrilla movement in Lara had "fallen into the hands of mere boys," said the defector Gavalán. "There [were] many leaders and few fighters."[70]

The offensive of the Urica Anti-Guerrilla Command continued to create havoc. Army spokesmen reported that the remaining guerrilla zones in the Falcón State had been reduced to two locations. Troops picked up fifteen rebel deserters and found many abandoned encampments in the mountains. Guerrilla leaders from Lara moved out toward the eastern mountains to join up with the group commanded by Fabricio Ojeda, hero of the fight against the last dictator. Meanwhile, other army units in western mountains engaged rebels, killing five and overrunning the campsite. Captured documents indicated that the guerrillas were "suffering from intensive military encirclement and that the men do not have sufficient clothing, food, weapons, and money."[71]

The only signs that rural workers and smallholders may have supported the guerrillas came in the west. There, Douglas Bravo had nurtured good relations with the country people due to his upbringing in rural Falcón. Peasants reported that they had seen Comandante Douglas with a troop of eighty guerrillas.[72] Military sources claimed that a final sweep of the Falcón Mountains resulted in the discovery of sixty guerrilla camps and the seizure of more than five tons of arms, supplies, and medicines.[73] This kind of rebel operation rivaled that of Castro himself in the Sierra Maestra, except that in Falcón the army chased the rebels relentlessly and monitored suspected *campesino* collaborators.[74]

Few peasants in other regions trusted the guerrillas, for a number of reasons. Many of the guerrillas had urban middle-class origins. When officials identified captives and the dead rebels, they discovered that many had been students of the Central University in Caracas—a hotbed of anti-American sentiment.[75] University students comprised the single largest reservoir of recruits and collaborators for the MIR and the FALN. Upward of 40 percent of a student body of eighteen thousand students reportedly supported the guerrillas, urban and rural. Of the eighteen hundred urban and rural activists and supporting personnel, probably 70 percent who had volunteered for duty hailed from the radicalized university environment.[76] The faculty also professed extreme views.

There were other reasons for minimal peasant support for the guerrillas. Unlike M26 in the Sierra Maestra of Cuba, the guerrillas never could sustain themselves in any particular mountaintop because the army sweeps usually kept them on the run. The Venezuelan rebels were seldom able to establish *territorio liberado,* which might encourage peasants to collaborate, even join and undergo training, without being harassed by army patrols.

One other factor played an important role. The government had a functioning agrarian reform program that Presidents Betancourt and Leoni had included in their social program called *sembrar el petróleo.* Raúl Leoni talked about land redistribution as a "Revolution without Communism." Government officials claimed the loyalty of the Peasant Federation of Venezuela, which represented a majority of the country's rural workers. Up to half of Democratic Action Party's vote came from workers and peasants.[77] The government devoted a remarkable 25 percent of the national budget to programs benefiting the poor: land reform, school building, and public housing.[78] Based on the export of crude oil, the economy supporting some 8.7 million citizens was growing by 3 percent per annum. As in other countries, internal migration was proceeding rapidly, so that 71 percent of the entire population lived in cities in 1965, compared to less than 30 percent in 1935.[79] Of course, Venezuela's land redistribution program did not approximate that of the Cuban Revolution, but it sufficed to keep peasants from joining the rebels.

Nevertheless, guerrilla bands continued to pop up everywhere in the country. The army kept moving about from state to state putting down small groups. In the western mountains of Falcón State, four thousand troops and additional airborne units carried out a campaign against the guerrillas. They captured two of its leaders, Hipólito Acosta Blanco and José Marino Colima Leones.[80] Troops in a military convoy foiled the ambush that guerrillas had set up at a bridge. The rebels threw Molotov cocktails at the vehicles, but they failed to ignite.[81] Guerrillas also turned up in the state of Anzoátegui, south of Caracas. Twenty guerrillas in three cars occupied a small town in this state and made off with supplies for their mountain encampment. They identified themselves as members of a detachment headed by the woman known as Comandante Oliva, identified in the Montevideo interview mentioned above as Oliva Olivo. An estimated two hundred guerrillas, in the meantime, were operating in the highlands of a neighboring state.[82] In Sucre State, east of the nation's capital, thirty guerrillas armed with machine guns occupied a small town. "The guerrillas came out of the mountains, stole supplies, held meetings with the townspeople, and painted subversive slogans on buildings." Then they returned to the mountains.[83]

However, the counterinsurgency program of the Leoni government was beginning to pay dividends. In September 1965 alone, Leoni's armed forces captured one hundred guerrillas and soon thereafter apprehended several top leaders. Authorities discovered and occupied a clandestine, underground arms factory that the guerrillas had constructed. In this operation, troops confiscated quantities of rifles, machine guns, grenades, bazookas, and explosives stored there.[84] The standoff awaited a breakthrough for one side or the other.

DIVISIONS IN THE RANKS

The year 1966 became most decisive. Havana's assistance for revolution abroad did not flag but indeed increased when Che Guevara returned from the disastrous Congo venture and secretly organized an expedition to Bolivia. Was this an effort to spread thin the forces of imperialism? To make the continent-wide revolution? It was in 1966 that Luben Petkoff disembarked on a beach in the state of Falcón with forty new trainees from Cuba—this on the July 24 anniversary of Simón Bolívar's birth. Veteran Cuban guerrilla Arnaldo Ochoa, who had fought with Camilo Cienfuegos, accompanied the group as an adviser. Petkoff took his group to join with Douglas Bravo's rebels. There he told a journalist visiting the guerrilla camp that his landing had inflicted a "serious military and political setback for the government, the armed forces and American imperialism." They brought $220,000 in cash as well as extra weapons for guerrilla associates already in the field. Bravo finally acknowledged that the Venezuelan armed forces were the enemies of revolution and had to be destroyed. The junior officers had long ago stopped joining the rebels and were demonstrating more leadership in the campaign by aggressively advancing on guerrilla positions.[85]

Nonetheless, as 1966 began, the CIA reported that "the Venezuelan Communist Movement is undergoing a split of major proportions."[86] The breach severed the alliance between the Communist Party and its military wing, the FALN. The leaders of the Communist Party were becoming disillusioned by the armed rebellion and their part in it. The soft-liners gained strength within the PCV and talked about rebuilding the labor base and drawing down the rural violence. In response, guerrilla leaders such as Douglas Bravo and Luben Petkoff of the FALN complained about the "armchair leadership" of the PCV. They suggested that guerrilla leaders on the front lines of the struggle should take political control as well.[87] In the 1966 meeting, politburo members ordered a suspension of guerrilla activities in order to form a united leftist front for the 1968 elections. Douglas Bravo and Luben Petkoff attempted to seize control of the party's central committee in December. The politburo responded by expelling Bravo from the party.

The Communist leaders joined with the left-of-center Democratic Republican Union, the URD, to appoint Domingo Alberto Rangel, a former MIR member, as the leader of a new campaign coalition called the Party of National Integration. The Kremlin resumed funding for the Venezuelan Communist Party in February 1967, and Pompeyo Márquez walked out of jail to resume his moderating leadership of the party. When guerrillas assassinated the brother of the foreign minister, garnering criticism in the press, the party finally decided to end its support of guerrilla violence. In this, Teodoro Petkoff parted ways with his own brother, Luben Petkoff. Teodoro joined the other members of the Communist Party leadership in admitting errors in their earlier backing of armed revolution. They resolved to oppose further adventurism. "Playing the guerrillaist game has once again confirmed the Leninist truth that the path of the ultraleftist deviations coincides with the positions of the right," PCV leaders concluded. "Unwitting or not . . . , the action of the anarchy-terrorist group today serves the imperialist interest in extending reactionary hegemony and isolating and destroying the revolutionary movement."[88]

Undaunted by the desertion of the Communists, Bravo and Luben Petkoff still led the hard-liners and allied their guerrilla followers with the Cuban Revolution. They found renewed enthusiasm for the revolution with Fidel's material support and encouragement. Castro threw his weight behind the FALN dissidents and changed abruptly from praising the Venezuelan Communists to vilifying them. The party defended itself in detailed communiqués that Cubans buried in the diplomatic archives.[89] But the news from Venezuela bespoke military setbacks and the breakdown of unity among the dissidents.

Douglas Bravo completed the break with the Communist Party and became the commanding officer of the unified command of the FALN. He sent out notifications to the governments of Cuba, the Soviet Union, and the People's Republic of China that the dissidents intended to continue the armed struggle. Luben Petkoff assumed the position of deputy commander. These hard-liners attempted to establish a rival communist party from renegades alienated by the official Moscow faction. Fabricio Ojeda penned a long report accusing the party leaders of denying urban assistance to the men fighting in the mountains. He also informed Fidel. "The morale of our combatants is high," Ojeda wrote. "We shall fight until we overcome."[90] Shortly thereafter, Venezuelan military intelligence agents captured Ojeda for a second time. Several days later, the body of this hero of 1958 was found hanging from the neck in his jail cell.

The CIA reported that "terrorism in Venezuela had to all intents and purposes been suppressed in 1965 when Cuba stepped in with support which renewed it." It maintained that Fidel convinced Douglas Bravo to bolt from the Communist Party. Then, at the OLAS conference in Havana, Fidel called for increased support from conferees for the Venezuelan and other guerrilla uprisings. The vice president of the conference was a former naval officer who had joined the FALN. That group's second-in-command, Luben Petkoff, who had led the 1966 landing at Falcón, publicly thanked the Cubans for their support. "Cuba only has one responsibility," Castro stated in

March 1967, "that of having made a revolution and being disposed to carry it to its ultimate consequences."[91] At his closing address to the OLAS, Fidel denounced the Venezuelan Communist Party for abandoning the revolution and for calling the guerrillas "anarcho-Castroites."[92] Party loyalists back in Caracas denounced the Cubans for intruding in the internal affairs of Venezuela.

The government stepped up its offensive in June 1967. The police caught up with MIR leaders Américo Martín and Leonet Canales and fifteen others. Two weeks later, they arrested Raúl Chirinos and his Chilean girlfriend, whose interrogation led to the capture of fourteen other "Communist terrorists" belonging to Douglas Bravo's FALN. The police also commandeered a cache of weapons and propaganda leaflets.[93]

The factionalization continued. Under pressure, the FALN and MIR broke up into two separate revolutionary factions. Fidel chose to support Luben Petkoff, who left Bravo's men in the Falcón Mountains and moved his MIR faction to the highlands southeast of Caracas. Venezuelan government sources informed the CIA that they believed that eight to ten Cuban advisers were with the MIR. Thirty Venezuelans in the eastern rebel *foco* had received training in Cuba. Caracas reported that 485 men remained in the guerrilla bands, although the MIR and FALN no longer communicated or made any pretense of coordinating with each other.

Castro had to renew his support of the Venezuelan guerrillas or lose all hope for a second guerrilla victory in Latin America. In the second landing on May 8, 1967, the government forces killed the Cuban boat master. Four Cubans and four Venezuelans succeeded in joining the MIR forces in the Bachiller Mountains. Among the most prominent Cubans was Raúl Menéndez Tomassevich, who had commanded the struggle against the *bandidos*. He carried his new weapon, the AK-47 Kalashnikov assault rifle. Conditions among the MIR guerrillas appalled the Cuban newcomers. There was resentment against the FALN, hunger, a lack of esprit, and misuse of good weapons. They reported that Douglas Bravo "lives in the city . . . and he only goes up into the mountains in order to get money when it is sent from Cuba."[94] However, the new MIR *foco* struggled to gain momentum.

Then came the news in October 1967—Che had died in Bolivia. In the January 1968 issue of *World Marxist Review,* shortly before Castro threw his support behind the Soviet tanks in Prague, the party loyalist Teodoro Petkoff penned the epitaph of the Venezuelan guerrilla movement. He admitted that the army had nearly wiped out Bravo's rebel group as well as the MIR. The police performed the same function in repressing and disabling the urban units. "Our big mistake," Teodoro Petkoff said, was organizing 125 peasant villages that were to support the rural guerrillas. "However, when the army mounted an offensive," he concluded, "informers promptly supplied it with lists of our people and their helpers, and nearly 200 people were executed and most of our political organizations were crushed."[95] Few other sources have substantiated Petkoff's claims about government executions, but the guerrillas had reached the end.

Tomassevich and his three other Cuban guerrilla advisers of the MIR now had to scramble to get out of the country. The former commander of the Escambray had fallen gravely ill with amoebic dysentery while in the mountains. He lost weight. His Venezuelan hosts brought him into Caracas for a clandestine rehabilitation. There he obtained a false passport and escaped the country by flying on a commercial airline out of Maiquetía Airport. "If they had discovered me," he said later, "they would have killed me."[96] Raúl Menéndez Tomassevich rendezvoused in Paris with his three other colleagues and finally returned to Cuba.

The election of December 1968 represented the final setback, though anticlimactic. Dissension within the Democratic Action Party permitted Rafael Caldera of COPEI, the Christian Democrats, to win the presidency. Venezuela's new president freed some twenty communists from jail. Caldera brought the Communist Party in from the cold, hoping that the legalization of the PCV might influence the remaining, dwindling cadres of rebels to give up and negotiate with the government.[97] Douglas Bravo moved into the Maoist camp in 1970, criticizing Fidel Castro for abandoning armed insurrections in Latin America while he accepted generous subsidies from the Soviets. Bravo himself accepted a blanket amnesty from the Venezuelan government in 1974.[98] Clearly, the Castro-inspired guerrilla movement was ending with a whimper. Fidel himself pursued other foreign policy objectives, especially in Africa. Yet he continued to offer Cuba as a haven for *sandinistas* and other leftists from Latin America—though Bravo was not one of them.

Venezuela swam against the tide in the 1960s. Most other Latin American countries exercised the military option when confronting internal political crises caused partly, though not entirely, by the Cuban Revolution. The reversion to militarism included the *golpe de estado* and long-term military rule. In the era of secret war, the generals eventually dominated politics in Argentina, Bolivia, Brazil, Chile, Ecuador, Panama, Peru, Uruguay, and most countries of Central America. It seems paradoxical that most of these nations did not confront a decade-long guerrilla insurrection like that experienced by Venezuela—or the even lengthier rebellion in its neighbor Colombia. Yet neither Caracas nor Bogotá took the military option, even though they received among the highest levels of US counterinsurgency training of any of the countries listed above.[99] How does one account for the survival of elected government in Venezuela despite its century and one-half of continuous military rule up to 1958?

First of all, the tradition of militarism in this nation acted as a recent memory of what most politicians did not want—another greedy, arbitrary ruler such as General Marco Andrés Pérez Jiménez. Most citizens seemed to agree that electoral democracy, imperfect though it was, remained the best remedy for guerrilla warfare.

A second factor, economic growth, might have been even more important than the bitter memory of militarism. Most other countries in Latin America in the 1960s encountered economic dislocation at the same moment that they confronted Cuba-inspired insurrections. Not so Venezuela. The vibrant international market for Venezuela's bountiful reserves of crude oil provided enough revenues for reform projects assisting the poor, for middle-class prosperity, and for military armament. The country's leaders did not have to beg for US financial assistance. This fact gave Venezuelans the assurance that they could deal with Washington as an equal rather than as a dependent. Therefore, pro-American sentiments did not hurt Venezuelan politicians at the polls.

Given these two powerful factors favoring electoral forms of governance, we have to return to the question we asked at the outset. How could the guerrillas have lasted so long in such adverse conditions? To answer this, one has to look to the factors influencing the country's youth. Middle-class youngsters and Marxist left-wing politicians had emerged from the struggle against the last military dictatorship in a strong and self-confident position. Their militancy in the streets had brought down General Pérez Jiménez. Yet the older generation of party exiles returned with political programs that did not satisfy the radical changes they had envisioned.

For this very reason, the socialist revolution in Cuba fascinated Venezuela's youth and also the communists. Fidel Castro had the youth and vigor that Rómulo Betancourt did not. Moreover, Fidel lavished the PCV and youthful rebels with attention. He brought them to Cuba for training and ideological indoctrination. Castro helped them to find weapons and funds for the struggle. He sent accomplished guerrilla advisers to fight with them. Fidel gave the Venezuelan guerrillas an honored place in the international anti-imperialist struggle. No other rebellion but Bolivia's received as much Cuban assistance as did the Venezuelan uprising.

In the end, no amount of Cuban assistance sufficed to make the revolution in the birthplace of Simón Bolívar. After 1966, unity on the left fell apart and brought the insurrection to an end. "We all wanted to be Fidel Castro," one *mirista* said. "No one was content to be Che, let alone Raúl."[100]

CHAPTER TEN

Military Counterrevolution in Brazil

FOLLOWING ITS TRIUMPH in the missile crisis, the Kennedy White House began to pursue more aggressive policies against the remaining friends of Cuba. Brazil, the largest country in Latin America, refused to join the boycott. At the meetings of the Organization of American States, Brazilian delegates voted against most proposals sponsored by the United States. Who better to bring Brazil to heel than the director of Operation Mongoose, Attorney General Robert F. Kennedy. In December 1962, Bobby Kennedy flew to Brasília for a chat with President João Goulart at the Palácio do Alvorada. The following summarizes US ambassador Lincoln Gordon's notes about their discussion:

Attorney General Kennedy: President Kennedy is becoming concerned about the "many signs of Communist or extreme left-wing nationalist infiltration" into the Brazilian government, the military, trade unions, and student groups.

President Goulart: Some forces in Brazil are "systematically anti-American." The Communist Party falls into this category, but it is "relatively small."

Brazil "has no animosity against President Kennedy" but in the past "has opposed Republican Party policies." It placed "high hopes on the Kennedy Administration." The Brazilian people often feel that the United States is "allied only with the dominant domestic economic groups." For instance, agrarian reform "is only now beginning to come within sight because it has always been frustrated by the opposition of the dominant economic groups."

Kennedy: President Kennedy worries about the "the deterioration of the Brazilian economic situation." Inflation is rampant and private investment has declined from $169 million in 1961 to "almost nothing" in 1962.

Goulart: The real reasons for Brazil's economic troubles stem from the "drop in prices of the major export products."

Kennedy: "We have no quarrel with independence in Brazilian policy, but we [do] object" to systematic criticism of American policies and interests by Brazilian ministers and public officials.

Goulart: "It has been disappointing that the Alliance for Progress has not . . . yielded the hoped for results."

Kennedy: Brazil is free to seek loans from the Soviet Union. The United States is also prepared to extend such assistance. "But if all high officials in Brazil are either attacking the United States constantly or being silent in the face of such attacks, cooperation will not be possible."

Goulart: The cause of democracy has been losing much ground in Latin America in recent years "because the popular masses feel that their problems are not being solved through democratic means."[1]

The differences between Goulart's and Kennedy's views could not have been wider. President Goulart "reacted sharply" to the attorney general's demand that he dismiss several of his advisers. Kennedy insinuated that the responsibility for the poor relations between the two countries fell to President Goulart. Only he could take steps to reestablish trust and confidence. For his part, Brazil's president said that the United States should have confidence that he "will not play the Communist game." The Brazilian president added that, "in any showdown, there was no doubt that Brazil [stood] on the side of the United States." On the subject of agrarian reform, one of the major goals of the Alliance for Progress Charter, the US attorney general offered no verbal support. Kennedy said nothing positive about any of the social reforms that his host was advancing in Brazil. At one point in the lengthy conversations, Bobby Kennedy passed a note to Lincoln Gordon: "We seem to be getting no place."

The difficulties with Brazil typify the vexed relations the United States had with many constitutional governments in Latin America during the secret war. Since the 1930s, populists like Getúlio Vargas and Juan Domingo Perón had attempted to fashion urban-based alliances of the middle-class professionals and organized workers, leavened with generous amounts of nationalism and anti-oligarchy scapegoating. The populists in Brazil and Argentina had eclipsed the political power of the landowning elites, labeling them *vendepatrias* for selling out national resources to Standard Oil, Hanna Mining, and the British-owned railways and utilities.

Often, the armed forces of Latin America held the keys to a successful or a failed populist movement. Indeed, both Vargas and Perón succumbed to *golpes de estado,* one in 1954 and the other a year later. Populists could win elections. But the generals determined their job tenure. Rising national debt, inflation, political polarization, civil-military tension, and popular frustration—these conditions formed the backdrop of populism in 1959 when Fidel Castro introduced socialism to the Americas. How could Latin America's largest country become so unsettled by the Cuba issue that its armed forces, which had never before formed a military junta, came to rule continuously for twenty-one years?

Quite simply, the Cuban issue drove a wedge between democratic politicians in Washington and their counterparts in Brasília. In Latin America, the electorate seldom rewarded those politicians who appeared subservient to US policies. What better way to demonstrate independence than to befriend Fidel Castro! The dilemma was that elected officials needed to borrow from the United States in order to pay for social programs, which explains their acceptance of the Alliance for Progress. Yet officials back in Washington also depended on elections. To spend tax dollars on foreign governments that would not renounce Fidel Castro won no congressional approval for aid packages. Public spending without US financial backing led to inflation and social unrest. The specter of mass upheaval from below finally drove the propertied class to exercise the military option. Brazil in 1964 provided the first such case.

DIPLOMACY HIGH AND LOW

Frustrated by their inability to get rid of Fidel Castro, Presidents John F. Kennedy and Lyndon B. Johnson resolved to spare no effort in isolating the Cuban Revolution and preventing its spread. The White House would have preferred to defeat communism with democratic allies. However, the United States soon came to realize that most elected officials in Latin America did not measure up as anticommunists. Both Kennedy and Johnson spoke of communist subversion at every turn, as if Latin American leaders had no other problems to confront. Ironically, the very reformist politicians who shared Kennedy's commitments to the land reform and progressive taxes outlined in the Alliance for Progress refused to divorce revolutionary Cuba. Therefore, American diplomats had little choice but to identify with the very sectors of society that opposed social reforms in Brazil, just as President Goulart had pointed out to Bobby Kennedy. The military and the oligarchy, after all, professed anticommunism as their gospel.

Brazil's new constitutional president, João Goulart, continued with his predecessor's independence at the next important meeting of the Organization of American States. It took place at Punta del Este, Uruguay, at the end of January 1962. As if to reinforce his opposition to US influence in the OAS, President Goulart flew into the São Paulo airport, there to meet the plane taking President Osvaldo Dorticós, head of the Cuban delegation, to Uruguay.[2] They chatted for an hour while the plane was being refueled. Goulart told Dorticós that Brazil would not support the Peruvian and Colombian proposal that all OAS members must sever diplomatic relations with Cuba. Brazil's San Tiago Dantas voted no, along with the foreign ministers of Argentina, Chile, Uruguay, Bolivia, and Mexico. But Secretary of State Dean Rusk obtained victory by bribing Haiti's Papa Doc Duvalier. A gleeful member of the American delegation took to calling the Brazilian foreign minister "Santiago de Cuba."[3] Governments representing two-thirds of Latin America's population had lost the tally.

President Goulart himself paid a state visit to President Kennedy at the Oval Office two months later, in April 1962. Goulart began their chat with a long disquisition on Brazil's social problems and how he would like "to keep the confidence of the masses." Brazil was not threatened by the Communist Party, which was "weak and . . . divided on many issues." If social problems remained unsolved, Goulart told Kennedy, "democracy would be

President John F. Kennedy welcoming Brazilian president João Goulart to the White House in 1962. *Left to right:* Secretary of State Dean Rusk, Vice President Lyndon Johnson (behind Goulart), and a Brazilian military officer look on.

in great danger." Moreover, the financial stabilization measures of the International Monetary Fund (IMF) would "create serious social problems" such as unemployment. To combat Brazil's high inflation of 45 percent per annum, Goulart suggested an alternative solution based on growth and development, rather than one of stability and deflation.

The subject turned to loans. Kennedy told Goulart that financial assistance needed to demonstrate "results from the use of our money" in order to "keep Congress in the mood to support us." But the Brazilians must act to get those results. Cuba, the host said, posed the real "danger" to the "survival of democracy." Kennedy worried about "communist infiltration and subversion" of Latin American labor movements. Goulart studiously avoided agreeing with his host. The United States had "many misconceptions about Brazil," President Goulart concluded, such as the "accusations of communist sympathies leveled at [me]."[4]

Two other noteworthy incidents occurred during Goulart's state visit to Washington. The first was an expression of Brazilian concern about the activities of the CIA. At a dinner for some American officials at the Brazilian embassy, Foreign Minister Dantas said that the "fundamental purpose of [the] Central Intelligence Agency was to create a worldwide secret police force strong enough to influence the affairs of countries in which they operate." One invitee, CIA director John McCone, assured his host that he was mistaking his Agency with the KGB, for the intelligence services of the Soviet Union "definitely had such purposes in mind." McCone warned his hosts about communist "penetration in Brazil."[5] The second incident concerned the inevitable question that American reporters posed to President Goulart about communists serving in the government of Brazil. "There are no communists on my staff," Goulart responded curtly.[6] Goulart's state visit to Washington demonstrated more differences of opinion than policy agreements.

All during Goulart's presidency, the diplomatic, commercial, and cultural connections with the Socialist Bloc countries became tighter. Russians, Czechs, East Germans, Hungarians, Yugoslavians, and Chinese visited Rio de Janeiro. Brazilian delegations traveled to socialist countries. Brazilian writers, filmmakers, and artists collaborated with their Cuban counterparts. Trade unionists, students, and peasants joined groups supporting the Cuban Revolution against imperialist threats. Novelist Jorge Amado (*Gabriela: Clove and Cinnamon* and *Doña Flor and Her Two Husbands*) and the architect Oscar Niemeyer (who built Brasília's signature buildings) collaborated in several conferences with Cuban minister of education Armando Hart and the island's revolutionary poet Nicolás Guillén.[7] Outwardly, it appeared that the Goulart government could not or would not collaborate with North Americans on the same level.

If Goulart had wished to engineer a political rapprochement between Cuba and the United States, his opportunity came during the crisis of October 1962. Shortly after discovering missile bases in Cuba, the White House asked for Brazil's mediation. The Americans sought to negotiate a backdoor deal between Washington and Havana that cut out the Russians. Goulart accepted the offer. The Brazilian president told Ambassador Gordon that the Brazilians backed the United States, because he opposed the introduction of nuclear weapons into Latin America. Nonetheless, he also disavowed OAS sanctions against Cuba and deplored Kennedy's boycott against the Cuban people.[8] However, Castro had no intentions of giving up the missiles, and the Soviets really controlled them. Goulard also suggested that Washington accept Havana's five demands, one of which required the Americans to give up the Guantánamo Naval Base. US refusal doomed Brazil's mediation, and relations between Kennedy and Goulart sank appreciably thereafter.[9] Even Soviet missiles failed to unite the hemisphere's two biggest countries, the United States and Brazil. This was when Attorney General Robert Kennedy came to Brasília to confront Goulart.

Bobby Kennedy's visit preceded by one month the popular plebiscite that ended parliamentary rule. Five of every six voters cast ballots to restore the constitutional powers that the armed forces had removed from Goulart two years beforehand as a condition for allowing him as vice president to succeed constitutionally to the office vacated by the sudden resignation of Jânio Quadros. Goulart's triumph was so stunning that the opposition behaved as if there had been no plebiscite at all. His large margin of victory in the nationwide vote also passed unacknowledged by the Brazilian generals.[10] With this new power, the Brazilian president distanced himself even more from American policies. The CIA was reporting that pro-American army officers "have been gradually losing their good jobs" because of the "illegal or pro-Communist action" by Goulart. From January 1963, American analysts referred to all of Goulart's advisers as "pro-Communists."[11] They too almost never referred to Goulart's overwhelming victory in the plebiscite.

Moreover, the CIA informed White House advisers that Brazil's economic situation was deteriorating. "Inflation is rampant and accelerating." The cost of living rose by 50 percent in 1962, causing resentment among military personnel as well as workers. Consequently, financial aid from the International Monetary Fund slowed to a trickle. "The aid was to be contingent on Brazilian measures to set the economy in order, but these measures were not taken," the CIA reported. Brazil had fallen into arrears on its foreign debt payments.[12] Despite these dismal economic prospects, American officials insisted that President Goulart, who depended on support from labor and landless peasants, terminate all trade relations with Cuba and the Soviet Union.

Goulart's respected top minister San Tiago Dantas had moved from foreign affairs to finance and returned to Washington, DC, in March 1963 with a new IMF plan for financial stabilization. He met with Secretary of State Dean Rusk and Ambassador Lincoln Gordon at Foggy Bottom.[13] Did they talk seriously about Brazil's cost-of-living crisis that had sent desperate

workers and even noncommissioned military officers into the streets in protest? They did not. Instead, the American hosts wanted to talk about Cuba
and communism. What about the rumors of subversive activities in Bolivia
and Paraguay that the Cubans were launching from their embassy in Brazil?
asked Ambassador Gordon. The Brazilian delegation held its ground. Based
on information from our embassy in Havana, Minister Dantas said, we have
no Brazilians being trained in subversive techniques in Cuba. "In Brazil,"
Minister Dantas said, "the orthodox communists are now denouncing those
who have close ties with Cuba, such as [the leader of agrarian reform move-
ment] Francisco Julião."[14]

Questions about the rise of the communists, the peasant leagues, and the
labor unions took on new relevance with a strike by noncommissioned officers in air force and marine units stationed in the new capital of Brasília.[15]
Army sergeants did not participate in the strike. In September 1963, Brazil's Supreme Court ruled that noncommissioned soldiers could not vote or
stand for elections—though military officers could. The striking sergeants
occupied the telephone exchange building in Brasília, interrupting communications. They also invaded the Ministry of the Navy and killed a guard in
the scuffling. Driving military vehicles, the noncoms surrounded a section
of military housing and arrested some thirty officers. Others seized control
of the tower at Brasília's airport and shut down air traffic.

President Goulart was out of town and received news when the rebellion
was winding down. Politicians on the left explained the causes of rebellion:
inflation, falling real wages for enlisted personnel, and the right wing's
denial of political rights to subordinate members of the military services.
According to the Cuban embassy, one military commander called the rebels
"seditious and traitorous . . . to the democratic order."[16] He promised vigorous
military prosecutions.

In the meantime, investigators suspected that the sergeants' rebellion was
connected to labor organizers seeking to unionize the military's enlisted personnel. Court rulings that denied soldiers and sailors their political rights
also undermined their ability to organize a union. In some units, military
commanders arrested sergeants who were connected to the military union
movement. Noncommissioned officers had made connections to leftist
organizations such as the Communist Party of Brazil, the peasant leagues,
and the national labor confederation. They corresponded with land reformers

like Francisco Julião and with Governor Leonel Brizola, the president's brother-in-law. The issue of soldiers joining labor unions continued to fester between the right and left in Brazilian politics.

In January 1964, President Goulart rejected a call by Caracas for additional OAS sanctions against the Cuban Revolution. Venezuelan authorities had discovered a cache of arms that Havana had attempted to send to guerrillas in that country. The Cuban Ministry of Foreign Affairs admitted Havana's culpability in the incident in the way it phrased Brazil's opposition to the OAS sanctions. "The Brazilian government will maintain unaltered its position when the denunciation formulated for the OAS by President Rómulo Betancourt with respect to the finding of *arms coming from Cuba and destined for the Venezuelan patriots*." Following this declaration by Brasília, the Venezuelan government sent military officers bearing photos, serial numbers, and a copy of the Belgian manufacturer's letter that confirmed the sale of UZIs, FALs, and other weapons to Cuba.[17] President Goulart still intended to back Cuba at the OAS meeting scheduled for June 1964.

THE PEASANT LEAGUES

Clearly, Brazil's land reform movement did not begin with the Cuban Revolution. It only gained renewed traction because of Castro's momentous agrarian reform projects. The Brazilian attorney Francisco Julião came to be associated with peasant organization. Representing plantation tenants working in the cane fields of northeastern Brazil, Julião in 1959 convinced the state government of Pernambuco to confiscate an unproductive sugar *fazenda*. Its subdivision benefited the plantation's former workers. The Cuban Revolution had been their inspiration.[18] Julião made two trips to Cuba during the very next year, the first with president-elect Quadros and later with some one hundred of his own followers. On return to Brazil, he began demanding a radical version of agrarian reform in which owners would receive no compensation at all for land distributed to the peasants.[19] Fidel Castro impressed Julião greatly. "The Cuban Revolution is ours," he told a reporter. "Whoever dares to touch Cuba today . . . will be directly provoking the Brazilian people into an immediate and limitless struggle."[20] The noncommunist leftist Francisco Julião also impressed Fidel, much more than did members of the Brazilian Communist Party.

In the meantime, Julião continued his organizational efforts. One Cuban diplomat called him "a figure of great national prestige," which Francisco Julião utilized in organizing the first national conference of peasant leagues in November 1961. The conference convened 400 delegates representing 170 "different organizations. The newly formed National Confederation of Peasant Leagues claimed a membership of 70,000 workers and tenants nationwide." They adopted the motto "Land for Those Who Work It." Although the delegates spoke in terms of "radical agrarian reform," their project proposed confiscating land of the "latifundistas" in order to distribute it to peasants "in individual parcels, or cooperative and state farms." In other words, they allowed for some private ownership. Delegates spoke about unequal land distribution in the Brazilian countryside, in which less than 3.5 percent of the landowners possessed more than 62 percent of the arable land. The congress's final declaration referred to the underlying forces in Brazil's repressive system of tenancy. "The monopoly of land ownership," it stated, "is connected to foreign colonizing capital, principally from North Americans, which they use to dominate Brazil's political life, exploiting all its wealth."[21]

Although the Congress's organizer, Francisco Julião, had a right to be upbeat during the proceedings, his press conference betrayed some anxiety. He had competition. He mentioned the FLN (National Liberation Federation) of Governor Leonel Brizola, which had a strong presence in his home state of Rio Grande do Sul. Incidentally, Brizola's brother-in-law President Goulart owned one of the largest latifundias in the entire nation. Julião dismissed as insufficient the top-down property distribution projects of such politicians on the left. The church presented a more dangerous form of competition to the *ligas camponeses* because "the clergy makes many more compromises with the reactionaries than with the democratic forces," Julião told reporters. The authentic agrarian reform project represented by Julião's peasant leagues "will prosper with the bishops, without the bishops, or despite the bishops."[22] Our motto is "Agrarian Reform or Revolution," Francisco Julião said.

Julião and his confederates in the peasant leagues sought out Cuban patronage. In a meeting with Fidel Castro on that first trip with presidential candidate Jânio Quadros, Julião requested funding from Cuba in order to be able to finance the organization of the rural leagues. Apparently, Fidel went to Che Guevara, as president of the national bank, to discuss the request.

Before the Quadros party departed, Castro said he had to deny the financing until the peasant organizations could prove their viability. Julião took a trip to China in November 1960 with the same request. Then he flew back to Havana in December 1960. On return to Brazil, Julião appointed Clodomir Morais as the revolutionary director of the Northeast's peasant leagues. The Cubans had promised their support.

Clodomir Morais had also accompanied presidential candidate Jânio Quadros on that first Havana trip. Morais had been a member of the Communist Party of Brazil who broke with the party in order to join the peasant movement. When he returned from Cuba, he organized the Northeast Brazil Pro-Cuba Solidarity Committee. It distributed Cuban propaganda materials, held conferences and photo expositions, and wrote petitions in favor of pro-Cuba policies. Morais also wrote to the Cuban embassy in Rio de Janeiro requesting copies of journals such as *Revista INRA* and *Verde Olivo*. Moreover, Morais sought an invitation from Havana to revisit the island in the company of pro-Cuba legislators and other leaders of the *ligas camponeses*.[23] Morais received the invitation he sought.

In June 1961, at a euphoric time in Cuba due to Fidel's victory at the Bay of Pigs, a dozen Brazilians from the Northeast stepped off the plane at the airport in Havana. Clodomir Morais led the group. They arrived from Recife with a group of Argentineans and Paraguayans who had come on a Cubana flight ostensibly for guerrilla training. The government housed them all in the Hotel Riviera, the former gambling center along the Malecón coastal boulevard. Other delegations staying there included Czechs, Chinese, and Russians—though few of these groups could communicate with each other. The Brazilians met the Soviet cosmonaut Yuri Gagarin, the first man in space, and attended Fidel's speech on July 26.

Then a caravan of government "cadillacs" whisked the Brazilians off to the training camp at the Managua Army Base south of Havana together with a dozen Venezuelans, seventeen Argentineans, six Paraguayans, and five *panameños*. Separated by nationality, they took courses on ideology, marksmanship, guerrilla movement, Molotov cocktail making, and the assembly and disassembly of various weapons. The instruction featured common American weapons provided by US Military Assistance Programs that guerrillas could acquire back home. Only the Panamanians took demolition training, apparently to sabotage canal operations.[24]

Training for the Brazilians at least does not appear to have been the full six-month guerrilla curriculum, including forced marches and participation in the suppression of the *bandido* insurrection in Cuba's Escambray Mountains. Out of respect for the pro-Cuban government of Goulart, Fidel lent support to Brazilian peasant leagues. He invited their delegations to celebrate revolutionary events in Havana. But the Cubans refrained from training a guerrilla force as they did for other nationalities. The rule of thumb went that if the country's government voted for Cuba in the OAS and UN, then Castro entertained but did not train its citizens for military action. Because their governments supported Cuba in international forums, few Brazilians, Mexicans, Uruguayans, Bolivians, and Chileans received Cuban guerrilla instruction in the early 1960s.

Nonetheless, Clodomir Morais and his associates sought to militarize the Brazilian *ligas,* perhaps as a way of counteracting the suppression of the landowners' paramilitary thugs. Possibly with Cuban funding (which never came close to CIA expenditures), he purchased *fazendas* in the interior states of Brazil. He set up training camps such as the one he attended in Cuba. News articles in *O Globo* suggested that the *ligas* had established sites in several states of the interior. Clodomir Morais toured South America in order to meet with ultraleftist groups in Chile, Peru, Bolivia, Ecuador, and Venezuela. He wished to be a part of the international network of like-minded revolutionaries. The Chinese pledged support to the *ligas,* and Brazil's security forces suspected that Czechoslovakia smuggled arms to them from time to time.

Francisco Julião established offices for the *ligas* in Brasília and Rio de Janeiro. In the capital, as a national deputy Julião lobbied for government assistance. In Rio, he and Morais met frequently with personnel of the Cuban, Czech, Soviet, and Chinese embassies. Domestic and foreign intelligence services suspected that most diplomats in these posts were actually security agents rather than professional diplomats. Finally, in November 1962, army police moved on a rural property belonging to the *ligas* and detained Morais and others in possession of arms and propaganda.[25] Soon articles appeared in the conservative newspaper *O Globo,* raising the specter of an armed rebellion of the landless.

President Goulart distrusted Julião and had sought the assistance of Governor Miguel Arraes of Pernambuco to diminish the influence of Julião's leadership of impoverished Brazilian peasants of the Northeast. American reports described Arraes as "pro-Communist." To provide Julião with competition, the CIA gave money to priests who less militantly mobilized *campesinos.* The Catholic reform movement grew considerably nationwide.

"The worst problem was overcoming [the *campesinos'*] fear," said one priest. "They were afraid of their bosses and afraid of communism. But since I was a priest, it made it easier to overcome . . . objections."[26] But American diplomats failed—at least publicly—to acknowledge what President Goulart and Minister Dantas were telling them about the many divisions among Brazil's left wing. The White House could not sell such nuance to American voters or to Congress.

Yet CIA cables repeatedly informed Washington about the divisions in the Brazilian left. Two leaders of the Brazilian left, though from differing philosophies, visited Fidel in Havana: Luiz Carlos Prestes of the cautious Brazilian Communist Party and Francisco Julião of the militant peasant leagues. Prestes remained aligned to Moscow and disavowed Cuba's export of revolution to Venezuela and Peru. Castro criticized Prestes and other Latin American communist leaders for their timidity. Prestes replied that Julião had little prestige in Brazil and had "barely" won election as a federal deputy. "This proves my point," the Cuban prime minister told Prestes. "Communism cannot be achieved through elections."[27] Fidel found that he could not control Julião in every respect either. He cautioned Brazil's leading land reformer not to undermine the regime of President Goulart. In the January 1963 plebiscite, however, Francisco Julião actually declined to support Goulart.[28]

Despite Washington's apprehensions, the left in Brazil was unable to organize itself into a unity pact. There was no better demonstration of that discord than the Congress for Solidarity with Cuba, which the Brazilian Communist Party sponsored in March 1963. The conservative governor Carlos Lacerda used state troops to block the conference from being held in Rio de Janeiro, and organizers had to move the site across Guanabara Bay to Niterói, outside Lacerda's jurisdiction. President Goulart sent in federal troops to protect the conference center. Five hundred people attended the congress, including a few representatives from Europe, Asia, and Africa. The largest delegations came from Brazil, Argentina, and Uruguay. Nikita Khrushchev and Zhou Enlai sent greetings.

About the only issue the delegates agreed on was welcoming the Cuban delegation with "a wild salvo of applause." Brazilians chanted, "Down with the government of Rómulo Betancourt" and "Down with Yankee imperialism." Otherwise, the pro-Moscow delegates passed their resolutions and successfully stifled dissent. When one Brazilian Communist Party speaker rose to address the assembly, he acknowledged the presence of several dignitaries such as his party boss Luiz Carlos Prestes. But the speaker failed to mention the name of Francisco Julião, who was also present. A great cry of protest arose among dissidents, who stood for five minutes shouting Francisco Julião's name.[29]

Speakers at the Solidarity Conference could not even agree on Fidel. Prestes delivered a long speech praising the accomplishments of the Cuban Revolution without uttering—not even one time—the name of Fidel Castro. On the other hand, another speaker singled out the Cuban leader for special praise. "All the Indians, Blacks, Whites, and Mestizos exploited for centuries in Latin America see Fidel Castro and the heroic island of Cuba as the great champions of their historical causes."[30] But the Communist Party controlled the drafting of the Declaration of Niterói and maintained a very general formulation, without extolling the names of the revolutionary leaders. "We call, finally, for vigilance and action," it stated, "in order to assure the victorious defense of Cuban sovereignty. With this we will create the most favorable conditions for our own victory."[31] Because their leftist rivals held Fidel Castro in high regard, members of the Brazilian Communist Party could not mention his name.

Although it endorsed Brazil's diplomatic relations with Castro's Cuba, the Brazilian Communist Party (PCB) and its leader Luiz Carlos Prestes did not adopt the rural *foco* model of revolution. The Communists preferred the Moscow-anointed model of the "united front" between communists, socialists, and left-of-center parties of the bourgeoisie. The PCB made common cause with the nationalists. Its creed rejected the Alliance for Progress as "a US ploy to conciliate the bourgeoisie by isolating the most important sectors of the anti-imperialist front, particularly the communist parties." The Communists stated that the "policy of the Alliance for Progress, a form of neo-colonialism, runs counter to the fundamental interests of the people of Latin America." The PCB instead counted on the assistance of the socialist camp. "The Soviet Union and other socialist countries have come to contribute considerably to the acceleration of industrialization" in developing nations. Thus could the PCB leader, Luiz Carlos Prestes, collaborate with President Goulart.[32] The Brazilian Communists would not subscribe to Che Guevara's stratagem of rural guerrilla warfare.

Much to the chagrin of Washington, the formal relationship between Goulart and the Cuban revolutionary government remained close. The

Cubans considered Brazil to be a revolutionary partner on the left and dispatched one of the island's top diplomats to Brasília. Raúl Roa Kourí, son of Cuba's foreign minister, had accounted for himself very well in his previous posting to Prague. Fidel did not wish to sabotage Goulart's chances for a democratic revolutionary breakthrough in Brazil.[33] The Cuban ambassador met with Brazil's president in June 1963 and came away with Goulart's firm support for the principles of "non-intervention and self-determination." In fact, the Brazilian president praised the Cuban people for "fighting imperialism bravely and heroically" and promised that Brazil along with Mexico would continue resisting US overtures to break diplomatic relations with Cuba.[34] Goulart's foreign policies and the agitation of popular movements at home raised apprehensions not only among wealthy landowners but also among military officers.

CIVIL-MILITARY RELATIONS

The United States had maintained greater military cooperation with Brazil than with any other country of Latin America. The Joint Brazil-United States Military Commission, established in 1943 and lasting until 1977, grew out of Brazil's commitment to send an army division to fight alongside American soldiers in Italy during World War II. The Joint Military Commission, the only one of its kind in Latin America, coordinated the exchange of information, training, and arms purchases. When President Kennedy changed military policy from conventional warfare to counterinsurgency, the military commission facilitated quick communication of the new doctrine to the Brazilian Armed Forces. In 1962, the Defense Department issued a National Security Memorandum. It designated the Jungle Warfare School at Fort Gulick in the Canal Zone and the Special Forces School at Fort Bragg, North Carolina, as training sites for counterinsurgency. "The growth of doctrines of revolutionary warfare and, specifically, the rise of Castro," observed one political scientist, "engendered in [Brazil's] military officers a complex set of responses: fear of Communism (especially because of its threat to the regular army), growth of counterinsurgency doctrines, and a conviction that basic changes were necessary to avoid revolution."[35] About one-third of Brazil's line officers received training at US service schools, though only a minority in counterinsurgency.

Latin American armies embraced counterinsurgency doctrine with special enthusiasm. The Brazilians immediately instituted counter-guerrilla training at their general staff college and in one airborne division. US Special Forces conducted counterinsurgency training exercises for Brazilian officers and soldiers in the Xingu River valley. The course included twenty-four hours of instruction in civil disturbance operations and forty hours in counterinsurgency training. A three-day field exercise followed.[36] In the first three months of 1964, American diplomats had been cultivating a close relationship with the Brazilian military and the civilian opposition. In January, the US embassy authorized the sale of C-130 cargo planes to the Brazilian Air Force.[37]

Officers of the Brazilian Armed Forces in the early 1960s took every opportunity to demonstrate their solidarity with the American military. The arrival in São Paulo of Major General James G. Alger, chairman of the Joint Brazilian-United States Military Commission, provided one such occasion. General Amaury Kruel, commander of Brazil's 2nd Army, decided to host a banquet in General Alger's honor in February 1964. The guest list had to be enlarged several times over—so many high-ranking Brazilian officers insisted on attending. General Kruel offered a toast to General Alger by referring to the mission of the military in defending "the Christian regime" in Brazil.[38] There were no toasts to the constitutional commander-in-chief, President João Goulart. Brazilian officers held Goulart in low regard despite his popularity with the voters.

In mid-1963, President Kennedy apparently was changing his mind about supporting Latin American democracies at all costs. Colonel Vernon Walters, who received orders to report as military attaché to the American embassy in Brazil, had heard the rumor too: Kennedy would not be averse to seeing the overthrow of the Goulart government. In his initial interview with Ambassador Gordon, Colonel Walters asked for instructions. "From you I want three things," Gordon told him. "First I want to know what is going on in the Armed Forces; second, I want to be able in some measure to influence it through you; and third, most of all, I never want to be surprised."[39] The embassy's military attaché proved to be an invaluable asset in this regard. Colonel Walters, a brilliant linguist, had served in World War II as a liaison officer to the Brazilian division in the Italian Campaign. Young Walters had developed a friendship in Italy with Lieutenant Colonel Humberto de Alencar Castelo Branco. Two decades later, when the two men collaborated again, General Castelo Branco had become the chief of staff of the Brazilian army.

American diplomatic and intelligence personnel adopted the gloomy prognostications of these military officers to explain Brazilian current affairs to Washington. The embassy relied less on what the government officials said and more on the viewpoints of the opposition. Therefore, Ambassador Lincoln Gordon was sending home ominous reports about Goulart's preparations for a leftist coup at the top. "With near-daily crises of varying intensity here . . . and violence ready to become epidemic through rural land invasion, clashes of rival communist and democratic street meetings, or general strike efforts, and with programmed crescendo of Goulart actions with special commitment to having achieved basic reforms by August 24 (tenth anniversary of Vargas suicide)," Gordon wired, "real danger exists of irruption civil war at any time." The American ambassador urged Washington to support General Castelo Branco, who showed "prospects of wide support and competent leadership."[40]

The CIA kept Washington policymakers informed by circulating translated articles appearing in the most conservative newspapers. The headlines reveal the flavor of these articles: "Cacao Fazendas in Bahia Invaded," "Cuban Exhibits to Illustrate Progress of Revolution," "Anti-Communist Woman's League Organized by Governor Valadares," "Santos Municipal Chamber Split on Anti-Communist Tactics," "Communists Say Goulart Is a Revolutionary," "Peasants Invade Fragoso Mill in Pernambuco," and "Communist Agitator Reveals Plan for Armed Revolution." Such news articles abounded between January and March 1964. They portrayed a rise of violence between the propertied classes and landless peasants. The conservative press, such as *O Globo* of Rio de Janeiro, reported a true fact—that a limited number of peasant leaders received training in Cuba. Much else was exaggerated. *O Globo's* article on "Piaui on Verge of Large-Scale Invasion" mentioned how professional agitators had "incited" rural workers in the state of Minas Gerais to demand land from the large *fazendeiros*. "The workers used guerrilla tactics, distributed subversive literature and went around the area inciting the people to revolt," the article reported. Landowners were preparing to defend their properties. "They know well that the peasants are being armed," concluded *O Globo*, "but they do not fear them because [the *fazendeiros*] too are buying weapons."[41]

As the storm gathered, Lincoln Gordon invited Marshal Eurico Dutra to lunch at the ambassador's residence. The grand old marshal had turned eighty years old. He served as war minister during World War II, when the Estado Novo dictatorship of Getúlio Vargas sent the expeditionary force to Italy. For all this, Brazil received US technology for its iron and steel industry, lend-lease credits, and the most up-to-the-minute weaponry. When his troops returned home in 1945, the military forced Vargas to end the dictatorship, and General Dutra won the following presidential election. Dutra finished his presidential term, and Getúlio Vargas returned to win the 1950 election. Vargas's labor minister, João Goulart, had helped him garner the support of Brazil's working poor. Marshal Dutra played no part in the 1954 military coup that overturned Vargas for the second time and led to his suicide.

The US embassy wished to demonstrate its commitment to the legacy, not of Getúlio Vargas, but of Marshal Eurico Dutra. Brazilians understood the symbolism of Ambassador Gordon's gesture. "In sixty years of active observations of Brazil's public life," the ambassador wrote, "[Dutra has] never known political conditions as bad as they [are] at present. He regards President Goulart with the deepest suspicion, considering him both incompetent and wrongly oriented." Gordon also quoted Marshal Dutra speculating that "Goulart would like to perpetuate himself in office."[42]

The embassy did not portray Goulart as the president who restored his rightful constitutional powers through a popular plebiscite. No, he was the labor president who sought to subvert the constitution in order to perpetuate himself in office with the help of communists. Gordon suspected that Goulart intended "to assume dictatorial power as a populist in the mold of Vargas . . . or Juan Perón in Argentina." Gordon also likened him to "some communist Nasser."[43] The embassy of the United States and the CIA too had bought into the rhetoric of the Brazilian right wing.

ANATOMY OF A COUP

The idea of a *golpe de estado* against the Goulart presidency had germinated among a group of army generals. These plans coalesced following the plebiscite of January 1963. Immediately, the conspirators appeared to go out of their way to seek US approval. The CIA knew as early as May 1963 that General Olympio Mourão Filho, commander of the 1st Army, was meeting with fellow *golpistas* to plan the coup. Mourão Filho claimed to have the support of Governors Carlos Lacerda of Guanabara and Adhemar de Barros of São Paulo. The 1st Army commander was also telling his coconspirators that he had "tacit US support" and was counting on American recognition of the ruling junta he would set up.[44]

Brazilian businessmen and civil organizations also had formed clandestine associations that advocated a military strike against the Goulart government. CIA agents reported that these domestic opponents were "vitally interested in receiving assurance that leaders of the American Business Community and U.S. government officials [were] informed of what action was planned and for what reasons." American intelligence identified Dr. D. M. Lobo Rosa of São Paulo as the leader of the pro-coup civilian opposition. He reportedly said that it would be vital for the Americans to recognize the provisional government "if movement against federal government [was] successful."[45] Brazil's military *golpe de estado* did not come as a surprise to Washington.

In São Paulo, middle-class indignation was building in response to pro-Goulart political rallies. The land-expropriation decree of February 1964 met an enthusiastic response among urban and rural workers in the state, but the loudest reaction derived from the industrialists and the landowners. A leading Paulista industrial group forged links to dissident generals and raised a million dollars to advance the anti-Goulart cause within the army. "Democratic action" committees sprang up in order to plan defensive measures at the local level. Governor Adhemar de Barros attacked the president for having dictatorial pretensions, while local newspapers compared Goulart to Hitler. Even modest family farmers began to arm themselves in anticipation of land invasions. Adhemar reflected their alarm in a speech in the countryside. "I will not fire the first shot," he said, "but I will die fighting in defense of democracy." He ordered local police forces to prepare to defend private property in the state of São Paulo.[46]

When the conservative civilians organized the so-called pro-democracy rallies in São Paulo and Rio de Janeiro, the embassy provided financial assistance. It lent its resources to opposition congressmen, moderate labor and student groups, church prelates, and businessmen. "We may be requesting modest supplementary funds for other covert action programs," Gordon reported.[47] Then, on March 19, two hundred thousand people organized by "democratic-action" groups turned out in São Paulo to call for the fall of Goulart and his communist allies. Few rural workers participated. But middle-class women formed the vanguard of the movement and participated in great numbers in protest against the Goulart government, often appealing to family, religious, and patriotic values.[48] Indeed, some American observers felt that the militancy of the landowners seemed to be "out of proportion to the immediate threat." The state government of São Paulo and the police had the weapons to maintain order. As the landowners and farmers armed, the landless rural workers of São Paulo displayed "little active unrest or preparations for armed conflict."[49]

The issue of property redistribution provoked intense polarization in many other states as well. In Pernambuco, the peasant leagues invaded lands of two large sugar estates. Governor Arraes supported the landless workers and promised to expedite the transfer of property titles to them. In the meantime, middle-class women of Goulart's home state of Rio Grande do Sul formed the Democratic Crusade and sent a delegation of one hundred women to thank the commanding general of the 3rd Army for his criticism of labor and peasant strikes.[50] American consuls were reporting that the landowners of southern Brazil were acquiring arms "not usually found outside the military establishment."[51] In Curitiba, capital of the state of Paraná, eighteen thousand students and parents marched through the rain protesting the rumor that the government was preparing to expropriate private schools.[52]

In this frenzy of right-wing activity, the National Security Council at the White House prepared contingency plans for the expected showdown between pro- and anti-government forces in Brazil. Four months into his term, President Johnson had already decided that the United States would support the *golpistas,* the so-called Democratic Revolt against the excesses of the Goulart Regime. The plans proposed that, in the event of a Goulart offensive, "the United States might well be willing to provide covert or even overt support" to the opposition. Such aid would consist of petroleum, food, arms, and ammunition. It would intervene with American military forces "only if there were clear evidence of Soviet Bloc or Cuban intervention" to save Goulart. The White House drew up these contingency plans two and one-half months prior to the actual *golpe de estado.*[53]

The United States was ready to support the *golpistas.* Previous contacts with the plotters had indicated that the anti-Goulart military forces were anticipating a prolonged civil war. In such an event, they would need resupplies of ammunition and especially of fuel for their tanks, planes, and ships. President Goulart's control of the Brazilian national petroleum company, Petrobras, meant that the *golpistas* might quickly run out of fuel. The State

Department was ready to help. It utilized its friends in the oil industry to plan the diversion of several tankers from Venezuela to the ports of Rio de Janeiro or Santos. The Defense Department arranged to dispatch a naval task force of several destroyers and an aircraft carrier in support of the "democratic forces." Already, orders had gone to several US military installations to pack up 110 tons of ammunition for possible flights to rebel-held air bases in Brazil.[54]

Just two weeks before the Brazilian *golpe,* President Johnson moved to declare a new doctrine for Washington's policies toward Latin America. In truth, the policy shift had begun in the last days of Kennedy's presidency. Assistant Secretary of State Thomas Mann introduced the new policy during a conference at Foggy Bottom for ambassadors and Aid for International Development representatives in Latin America. Ambassador Gordon attended this State Department meeting. Mann stated that the United States "would no longer seek to punish military juntas for overthrowing democratic regimes." The assistant secretary of state promised no more sanctions against military regimes such as those that President Kennedy imposed on Argentinean and Peruvian generals in 1962.[55] Mann asked only that the military regime commit itself to four goals: economic growth, protection of foreign investments, nonintervention in the internal affairs of its neighbors, and opposition to communism. He did not once mention the Alliance for Progress.[56] Thereafter, the new Washington policy to combat communism in Latin America became known as the Mann Doctrine.

The only thing remaining was a pretext, which came in mid-March 1964. Many uniformed Brazilian enlisted men attended a labor union rally in support of President Goulart. They were planning to organize a union of Brazilian soldiers and sailors. The president himself addressed the crowd and announced a land confiscation decree in which the government would take over all lands within ten kilometers of rural highways. Following the rally, General Castelo Branco asked American military attaché Vernon Walters, his colleague from the days of the Italian Campaign, to stop by his home. "Did you see the rally on TV?" Castelo Branco asked, and Walters said that he had. "The only signs I saw were hammers and sickles," said the Brazilian general. "That man is not going to leave when his term is up."[57]

On March 20, General Castelo Branco circulated a memorandum to members of the high command. In it, he noted two threats to the nation: the constitutional assembly that was to meet on social reforms and "the illegal power of the CGT," the Brazilian labor confederation. He said that the armed forces would uphold the laws and not let themselves be manipulated by a labor union dictatorship. Colonel Walters brought a copy of the memo to Ambassador Gordon.[58] Just days before the coup, the conspirators consulted with Marshal Eurico Dutra, who told them that they should move quickly to oust Goulart.[59] General Castelo Branco's letter taking issue with Goulart's support for the unionization of the noncommissioned officers had finally galvanized enough unity among military officers to plot the end of the government.

The Brazilian coup d'état commenced while President Johnson was enjoying the springtime at his ranch at Johnson City, Texas. His secretary of state called him by phone and assured him that the expected *golpe* would probably proceed well. Nonetheless, after getting a lengthy briefing, Johnson turned to his staff. "Rusk expects something could happen tonight. So I rather expect we ought to go on back to Washington," he said. "I don't see anything to be gained to be in Johnson City with the Hemisphere going Communist."[60] It might seem a disquieting statement even though Rusk had assured him that the Brazilian military had things well in hand. But Johnson did have an election coming up in seven months, and "a second Cuba" in Latin America's biggest country would not please American voters. After all, the president too had been reading some of those alarming messages emanating from his embassy in Brazil.

The tanks and jeeps began to move on the last day of March. General Olimpio Mourão Filho of the 1st Army initiated the movement by advancing on Rio de Janeiro. Foreign Minister San Tiago Dantas called the president and told him that the US embassy approved of the coup. General Amaury Kruel of the 2nd Army in São Paulo dithered for twenty-four hours until he too decided to join the rebellion. President Goulart and General Kruel spoke by phone in the interim. Kruel asked him to denounce the Communists, even though the party remained illegal. "General," Goulart said, "I am a political being. I have compromises with the political parties and I cannot abandon them under pressure from the military. Nor can I leave aside the popular forces that support me." "Then, Mr. President," the army commander replied, "we can do nothing."[61]

Eight governors in key states called for the ouster of President Goulart. The 3rd Army in the southernmost state of Rio Grande do Sul remained loyal to Goulart and his brother-in-law, Governor Leonel Brizola. So did two

A light tank takes up a position in front of President João Goulart's apartment house in downtown Rio de Janeiro in the 1964 military coup d'état.

regiments of the 1st Army in Rio de Janeiro, which deployed to oppose the rest of the army's advance from Minas Gerais. But these troops very quickly switched allegiance to the *golpistas*. Support for the president collapsed in a matter of hours. The coup ended quickly on April 1 without bloodshed or any military engagements.[62] Nary a shot was fired.

The speed by which the coup succeeded prompted the US Defense Department to recall its naval task force before its arrival off Brazil, and the expedition's very existence remained a secret for three decades. On April 2, President Johnson's congratulatory telegram arrived at the office of Pascoal Ranieri Mazzilli, the leader of the Chamber of Deputies, who had just been sworn in as interim president according to the constitution. Mazzilli soon followed in the wake of Quadros and Goulart, as the generals decided that Brazil's constitution would be better served by one of them. The presidency then reverted to General Humberto de Alencar Castelo Branco. Pleased by what he believed to be the democratic actions of Brazil's armed forces, President Johnson promptly sent a telegram to Castelo Branco congratulating him on his "election."[63] The American president adhered to the new Mann Doctrine and was among the first heads of state to recognize the result of what the *golpistas* called the Brazilian revolution. The arrival of Johnson's telegram coincided with the new government's announcement of the closing of its embassy in Havana.

However, no one suspected that the nature of the intervention of the armed forces would differ from previous ones. In 1954, for example, Brazil's generals may have precipitated the resignation and suicide of Getúlio Vargas, but they did not establish military government. In that case, the officers forced out the sitting president and engineered the election of his successor. Indeed, Ambassador Gordon and the US embassy in Brazil believed that the Brazilian Armed Forces would intervene in 1964 only to remove the threat of a left-wing takeover of the government. The Americans expected the generals would move quickly to install a more moderate electoral regime.[64]

What the White House, the CIA, the State Department, and the American embassy did not anticipate was twenty-one years of military rule in Brazil. They had been relying on past history in which the generals "played a stabilizing role in the political life of Brazil" and intervened infrequently to provide for a new civilian regime to replace one that had performed badly. The State Department's experts in Brazil believed that the generals harbored no "penchant for politics or decreasing concern for constitutional processes." Moreover, American diplomats took comfort that many opposition members of Congress had wholeheartedly supported the military takeover. They quoted the anti-Goulart deputy Aliomar Baleiro of the National Democratic Union as saying, "Que belo golpe!"[65] What a beautiful coup!

How much did the American diplomats influence the coup? Both Lincoln Gordon and Vernon Walters subsequently denied US agency, citing domestic opposition as playing the decisive role.[66] However, the evidence indicates that no American officials, from the White House on down to the embassy, wanted João Goulart to succeed because he would not renounce Fidel Castro. Instead, American diplomats fraternized with the government's domestic enemies and even helped finance the opposition "pro-democracy" protests. Washington heavyweights from the Oval Office, the Defense Department, the State Department, and CIA headquarters—even Bobby Kennedy— openly disrespected Goulart.

Nevertheless, rather than Washington, it was the Brazilians themselves who set the agenda and the pace for the overthrow. As one Brazilian historian sums it up, "There was inflation rising daily, social anarchy, and great discontent in the middle class—sufficient ingredients for *um golpe de estado*."[67] The coup plotters, the business class, and the landowners wanted the Americans to adopt their view of the Goulart regime. Gordon, Rusk, and President Johnson himself accommodated them. This episode does not represent the State Department's finest hour, to be sure. But US diplomats resembled fans cheering for the team on the right, while players on the field actually determined the ultimate victors. In the end, it was not much of a contest. Their team won, but American decision makers found themselves with little leverage to moderate subsequent military rule. The generals governed, sometimes harshly, for the next two decades. Nor could American diplomats prevent the "Brazilian model" from spreading to other South American republics.

One thing is certain. Brazilian generals knew how to ingratiate themselves with Washington. They broke diplomatic relations with Cuba and backed the United States in the Organization of American States.[68] Latin America's largest country did demonstrate its newfound support for American foreign policies closer to home, in the Caribbean. The military government endorsed President Johnson's decision to send US troops into the Dominican Republic on the side of the militarists and against the Constitutionalists. President Castelo Branco instructed his diplomats to round up support in the OAS, pressing Peru, Ecuador, Chile, and Uruguay to vote for the American position.[69] He also ordered Brazilian military units to deploy in Santo Domingo as OAS peacekeepers. The United States agreed to pay the expenses and to provide modern weapons and equipment, which the Brazilian battalion could keep on its return home.[70]

But the hard-liners who increasingly took over Castelo Branco's agenda did not follow the State Department's script. Ambassador Gordon expected an interim military junta. Without consulting with the American embassy (as they had been accustomed to do before the coup), the generals issued the first *ato institucional,* or "institutional act." This took Brazilians as well as Americans by surprise. The dismissal of federal deputies and the deprivation of political rights shocked the people here, reported one US consul. Apparently, most *brasileiros* had believed that, once the revolt had succeeded, the military would "depart from the political scene in traditional Brazilian fashion" after arranging for a new election.[71] The military's decree stunned even Lincoln Gordon. He thought that the arrests of forty congressmen smacked of "an old-fashioned reactionary Latin American military coup." He sent Colonel Vernon Walters to reason with junta president Castelo Branco.

Walters learned that the real architect of the *linha dura* in the officer corps was the war minister, General Artur Costa e Silva. Described as pro-American, Costa e Silva had been one of several high-ranking officers who attended service schools in the United States, in his case the US Army Armor School at Fort Knox, Kentucky.[72]

The hard-liners were gathering strength, and they did not like the moderate Castelo Branco. As 1964 came to a close, they could say that "the revolution has not yet found its leader." The hard-liners identified themselves as the "authentic revolutionary conscience," to the exclusion of the fence-sitters and those who waited to support the coup only after it had succeeded. General Kruel lost his job as 2nd Army commander because he had hesitated too long during the coup. The hard-liners also deposed several governors who prevented "the revolution" from proceeding.[73] Moreover, officers identified as hard-liners received promotions, while politically moderate officers did not. The minister of war who determined these promotions: General Artur Costa e Silva.

On the first anniversary of the military "revolution," Minister Costa e Silva spoke to a group of army generals. He declared that the depths of the decay in the country necessitated a much longer period of military rule than had been reckoned in 1964. He believed that "at least ten years of revolutionary government would be necessary for the normalization of the Brazilian nation." Costa e Silva said that the army was "the strong party . . . the government [needed] in order that subversion and corruption never again return" to weaken the country.[74] What he told the generals annoyed President Castelo Branco. He reportedly reprimanded his war minister for advocating long-term military rule. In the end, the hard-liners prevailed. At this juncture, Robert F. Kennedy arrived on a whirlwind tour of Latin America. This was the same former attorney general who presided over Operation Mongoose and who encouraged the anti-Castro commandos in Miami. Now that Lyndon Johnson had made President Kennedy's policies his own, Bobby was free to reinvent himself. He had won election as senator from New York and launched his new "liberal" persona. In contrast to his first trip, to browbeat the Brazilian head of state, Bobby Kennedy returned in November 1965 saying he had "come to learn." He capitalized on the warm memory of Brazilians for his brother, the first Roman Catholic president of the United States. In Salvador da Bahia, on the second anniversary of John Kennedy's assassination, he and Ethel Kennedy attended mass at a small church in a slum. "President Kennedy was most fond of children. Can I ask you to do a favor for him?" he asked a group of poor boys and girls in the neighborhood. "Stay in school, study hard, study as long as you can, and then work for your city and Brazil."[75]

After touring the Brazilian Northeast with a retinue of twenty-five friends and reporters, Senator Kennedy flew to Rio de Janeiro. Four thousand students at the Catholic University greeted Bobby Kennedy with wild enthusiasm. He asked how many of them had worked in a *favela*. Only a few raised their hands. "If all we do is complain about the universities, criticize the government, carry signs, make speeches to one another and then leave to take a job," he told them, "we have not met our responsibility."[76]

Bobby Kennedy criticized neither President Johnson nor the Brazilian military. However, he did manage to shake the hand of soccer star Pelé.

CHAPTER ELEVEN

Soldiers and Revolution in Peru

AT 3:00 A.M. on a chilly July morning in 1962, thirty battle tanks rumbled into the Plaza de Armas in downtown Lima and took up positions at the front gate of Peru's Government Palace. Armed soldiers in trucks and jeeps stationed themselves in adjoining streets. Precisely at 3:35 A.M., an army colonel spoke over the loudspeaker mounted on the lead tank. He addressed the outgoing president, Manuel Prado Ugarteche, in the name of the joint command of the armed forces. Prado had two minutes to surrender the palace, the colonel announced. After several additional ultimatums went unanswered, a Sherman tank supplied to the Peruvian army by the US military aid program broke through the front gate. Troops and army vehicles poured into the palace's courtyard. At 4:00 A.M., President Prado and a group of civilians emerged from the Government Palace singing the Peruvian national anthem. Troops escorted the president into an army truck and took him to the navy arsenal for safekeeping. The president had only a few more weeks before he was to turn power over to his elected successor. This democratic transition is what irritated the generals.

Limeños awakened later that morning to radio and television broadcasts of the military communiqué. "Having exhausted all efforts to effect the annulling of the electoral process for the proven irregularities," the communiqué said, "the Armed Forces have seen themselves required to depose President Prado and assume the government of the nation." The generals were accusing the winning American Popular Revolutionary Alliance (APRA) party of widespread electoral fraud.[1] President-elect Víctor Raúl Haya de la Torre had won a plurality of 33 percent of the popular vote from a field of seven candidates. President Prado did not belong to the winning APRA party and had little reason to rig the election.[2]

American diplomats had tried hard to dissuade Peru's military from taking such action. President Prado's election in 1956, replacing the eight-year dictatorship of General Manuel Odría, had been part of democracy's rise in the 1950s. In conversation with the US ambassador during the campaign, the navy minister explained that the military distrusted Haya de la Torre. If elected, Haya would take over the military by promoting only officers affiliated with his party. Therefore, military officers "would use force if necessary to keep him out." Haya de la Torre did not admire the Cuban Revolution, and Peru's Communist Party did not support his candidacy. The ambassador pointed out that President John F. Kennedy had based his Latin American policy on elected leaders like Prado, who had even addressed the US Congress just the year before. He had been the first elected president in the Americas to break diplomatic relations with Cuba. The ambassador said that military action would be "disastrous" to Peru–United States relations, but the navy minister seemed unimpressed. "July 15 and 16 saw an almost frantic effort on our part to forestall a military coup," the US embassy reported.[3] By their action, the generals rebuffed the administration of President Kennedy.

THE *DICTABLANDA*

The junta consisted of anticommunist general officers, almost half of whom had had the benefit of US training in their careers. More than 150 Peruvian officers had attended the School of the Americas in the Canal Zone in the 1950s.[4] The eldest general officer on duty assumed the presidency of the junta; he had no American training but was considered staunchly anticommunist. Between them, the four other junta members had trained in US military stations such as Fort Leavenworth's US Army Command and General Staff College, at Forts Belvoir and Riley, as military attachés to Washington, and as staff members at the Inter-American Development Bank. Three of them had received the US Legion of Merit, the Pentagon's highest honor bestowed on foreign nationals.[5] These generals felt betrayed when the Kennedy administration refused to recognize the junta and suspended military and economic assistance.

The Peruvian *golpe de estado* disturbed President Kennedy and his advisers. They had invested their prestige in the Alliance for Progress and in the ability of elected governments in Latin America to carry out necessary social reforms in order to forestall both communism and military dictatorship. President Prado had formed an important piece of the pro-democratic puzzle. His administration collaborated with anti-Castro Cuban émigré organizations. Once financed by the CIA station in Miami, they ranged far and wide in their anti-Castro activities. One group connected to the Auténtico Party's Aureliano Sánchez Arango broke into the Cuban embassy in November 1960 in broad daylight. "At the point of a pistol," Cuban officials said, "five individuals threatened the chargé d'affaires and proceeded to ransack the files and destroy office furniture and equipment." According to Castro's diplomatic service, these five Cuban émigrés falsified documents to show Cuban interference in the internal affairs of Peru.[6] President Prado subsequently became the first in South America to break diplomatic relations with Cuba, in December 1961, much to the delight of the Kennedy administration.

President Prado also had been the first Latin American head of state to visit President Kennedy at the White House. He pledged solidarity in the struggle against "aggression from abroad, and against infiltration by foreign and disruptive ideologies." Prado addressed Congress, where he denounced the interventions of Fidel Castro in the internal affairs of other countries. He also expressed enthusiasm for the promises of the Alliance for Progress. Furthermore, American diplomats had always viewed the increasingly conservative political project of Haya de la Torre and his *apristas* (followers of the APRA party) as the perfect antidote for communism.[7] American policymakers had welcomed the 1962 election results in Peru.

One should take note that these generals did not object to the elections because of a communist threat. The military intervened because of a blood feud. The officer corps had nurtured a visceral hatred of Peru's APRA party that went back three decades. When the Depression-induced economic problems weakened an eleven-year dictatorship in 1930, two movements emerged that sought to bring electoral democracy to Peru. One was a group of junior army officers led by Colonel Luis Miguel Sánchez Cerro and the other, APRA. The latter had its center in the northern coastal city of Trujillo and proposed a reformist program that sought to integrate the indigenous peasantry of the Andean highlands into the modernized coastal regions of Peru. The APRA movement sought to break the political and economic control of the small group of *latifundistas* (large landowners), curb foreign interests, and modernize the economy.

Both movements presented their leaders as presidential candidates in the 1930 elections. Colonel Sánchez Cerro defeated the young APRA leader Haya de la Torre. The disappointed *apristas* responded by sacking the army garrison at Trujillo and killing many of its defenders. President Sánchez Cerro outlawed the APRA party, and the army destroyed the party's regional headquarters, killing or imprisoning resisters. Then, in 1933, an APRA party member shot and killed President Sánchez Cerro.[8]

These events poisoned civil-military relations for the next thirty years. Thereafter, whenever presidential elections projected a victory for the perennial candidacy of Haya de la Torre, the military stepped in to prevent his occupancy of the Government Palace. Haya himself spent many years in exile, allying with other Latin American democrats such as José "Pepe" Figueres of Costa Rica, Juan Bosch of the Dominican Republic, and Rómulo Betancourt of Venezuela.

Peru's civil-military breakdown prevented APRA leaders from taking over the government and carrying out their populist agenda. While other populists like Lázaro Cárdenas, Getúlio Vargas, and Juan Perón were wresting control of basic industries from foreign interests in Mexico, Brazil, and Argentina, Peruvian presidents proved powerless to reduce the domination of North American enterprises. The International Petroleum Corporation and the Cerro de Pasco mining company remained in control of Peru's two most important natural resources, oil and copper. That the populist project in Peru lagged meekly behind those of other countries encouraged the leftist uprisings of the 1960s. The Peruvian experience lent credence to Che's aphorism that only "bullets not ballots" would change the social structure. After 1959, the Cuban Revolution served as living proof.

In the early 1960s, therefore, the generals began to equate the reformist APRA party with the "Communists" in Cuba. The connection lacked substance. In reality, Haya de la Torre had moved to the right in recent years, attracting many supporters of the conservative president Prado. The *apristas* had even adopted the slogan *¡APRA, sí; comunismo, no!* It cost Haya de la Torre support among the masses and within his own party.[9] After the coup against Haya's election, the generals scoffed at US expressions of dismay. On one occasion, a general officer picked up the newspaper announcing the US loan of fifty million dollars to the military-backed government of Argentina and told the ambassador, "What the hell . . . the State Department had to support Peru." The United States had lost too much respect in Latin America by allowing the communists to take over Cuba, the general reasoned. He told the US embassy "to keep its nose out of purely Peruvian business." The junta wanted Ambassador James Loeb Jr. to know that Peru was in "danger of Communist penetration by Castro-Cuba."[10]

However, this military government soon came to be called the *dictablanda,* the "bland dictatorship," rather than the hard dictatorship, *dictadura.* Initially, the generals did not set out to oppress any political organization. President-elect Haya de la Torre had gone into hiding when the army tanks ousted President Prado's government, but reemerged as soon as he realized that the police were not searching for him.[11] In fact, the refusal of the military government to repress the Communist Party and union and university radical leaders alarmed American diplomats in Lima.

The US State Department in Peru soon gave up attempts to uphold President Kennedy's calls for democracy in Latin America. Secretary of State Dean Rusk showed American displeasure with the military junta for several months. Then he renewed diplomatic relations. Thereafter, the American envoy in Lima began encouraging the junta to take action against the domestic agitation that its coup had provoked. The State Department believed that radicals had taken over the Peruvian university student associations. "Communist organizers" were active in stirring up *campesino* unrest in the Southern Highlands, and "Communist dominated" unions were coordinating strikes against US companies. Even though he admitted that social inequities caused the unrest, Ambassador Loeb accused the military junta of "lacking the will" to take firm measures against those who were now exploiting these conditions.[12] American diplomats tended to see every protest by students, laborers, and peasants as communist inspired.

Eight months later, when the protests did not subside, the junta moved. They rounded up four hundred people throughout the country and sent nearly half of these to the infamous Sepa Prison in the eastern Peruvian rain forest. Interrogators there announced that they had uncovered the existence of a communist terrorist plan—though no arms to sustain it.[13] "We are encouraged that [the] Junta has at last identified the Communist menace and taken action against it," wrote Secretary Rusk. He particularly approved of the junta's "action against foci of Communist strength in [the] trade unions" and praised the generals' pronouncements about beginning agrarian reform according to Alliance for Progress recommendations.[14] In truth, pressure from below forced the junta to deal with the issue of land redistribution.

PEASANT UNIONS

Trotskyist labor organizers had been active among indigenous workers in the Peruvian highlands since 1960. The most successful of them operated in the valley of La Convención, north of Cuzco, where the cordillera descends into the Oriente, as the Peruvian Amazonia is called. The valley of La Convención is located close to the tourist site of Macchu Pichu. Fewer than one-third of the rural (mainly indigenous) workers in La Convención had been born there. Most had moved to the valley from rural districts higher up the cordillera to the west. Thus, land tenure favored the big hacienda owners, and the migrants served as *yanaconas,* "resident workers," or as renters and itinerants. The fact that the owners came from the white elite and the rural peons from indigenous background exacerbated what already were exploitative labor relationships. It also meant that the workers responded positively to labor recruiters. Some of the first unions of rural workers formed in 1960.[15] A growing population of indigenous rural workers, each year, increased the land hunger.

Hacendados and peasants in La Convención produced oranges, bananas, coffee, mangoes, and papayas, most of which grew year round. On the haciendas, a form of serfdom obtained in labor relations. The white owner permitted peasants and their families to cultivate a plot of land on the hacienda but required nearly all of them to provide unpaid labor in the fields and orchards, in the household, and in transport to market. The laborers had few alternatives but to accept the onerous conditions.[16] Indigenous and

Andean Rebellions of the 1960s

mestizo rural workers could never get ahead living on the hacendado's land, but eviction left them completely destitute.

Enter Hugo Blanco. He did not go to Cuba and did not profess guerrilla warfare. Blanco's ideological background consisted of a Trotskyist hostility toward the Stalinist Communist Party of Peru. He and other Trotskyists who attracted supporters among the indigenous highlanders in the Southern Andes resented the collaborationist attitudes of Peru's communists. The Cuban Revolution inspired Hugo Blanco's struggle. "It proved that the Latin American revolution is a socialist revolution, that [it] will not be made by peaceful means," he wrote, "and that it is indeed necessary to destroy—not reform—the capitalist system."[17] Blanco welcomed the Cuban example as an antidote to the Peruvian communists who refused to support his rural activism.

The Trotskyist Blanco intended to organize the peasants into labor unions in order to confront the exploitative landlords and their *gamonales*. In the Andes, *gamonales* referred to local officials who served as lackeys for the landlords. "We always spoke Quechua throughout the struggle," wrote Blanco, "and always exalted everything Indian."[18] But he recognized that the peasants would only achieve recognition of their rights not by legal but by violent means. The peasants were responding. In October 1962, Blanco could boast of some success. "We are reaching victory by means of stoppages, strikes, meetings, division of land contrary to bourgeois law."[19] Blanco had been encouraging the peasants to invade hacienda lands. After all, peasant leagues were then organizing in Brazil for the same purpose.

The union organizer Hugo Blanco had become head of the movement that counted on the support of lawyers, teachers, and technicians in Cuzco and other highland cities. Blanco enjoyed favorable publicity in the leftist newspapers. Labor and peasant groups responded to his example, once forming a mob of eight thousand rioters that prompted the resignation of a notorious prefect in the provincial capital of Cuzco. The military junta sent in three hundred police officers equipped with automatic weapons and riot shields to augment the local constabulary. They arrested one hundred demonstrators and flew them to Lima for trials before military tribunals. Seventeen people died in the melee, and fifty suffered injuries.[20]

Peasant unionizing in the Cuzco region often took on a tone of menace against the status quo. Youthful *campesinos* especially asserted themselves at the union meetings and exerted pressure to push for land reform. Many of these young men had served as army conscripts through the universal military draft, which scions of the middle class and elite families easily shirked. Thus one young union militant could announce to a reporter from the coast, "Here we all know how to handle weapons, machine guns, everything."[21] Most of the union leaders were sharecroppers, "given that the Cholo (mestizo) peasants constituted the vanguard of the struggle against the hacienda system." Women often made up one-third of the members in the assemblies and were sometimes more vocal and militant than the menfolk. An observer later described peasant women as "the real motor in the fight against the big landlords." In La Convención Valley alone, the union membership had grown rapidly to 12,500 rural proletarians. Like Che Guevara and the Cuban revolutionaries, Hugo Blanco did not believe in paying landlords for their confiscated lands.[22] He believed that the hacienda families had made fortunes over the years based on the labor of landless rural workers. The hacendados deserved no compensation.

Just before the 1963 elections, the military junta handed the highland radicals a hard setback. It proposed its own land reform project. Ideologists and politicians had talked about the need for agrarian reform since the 1920s. But the military's project in 1963 represented the first such effort by any Peruvian government. In a plan conforming to their US civic action training, army engineers had punched roads into the remote valley of La Convención. The military government announced a program of land appropriation with immediate compensation—an impossibly expensive project if carried out on a large scale. This pay-as-you-go type of agrarian reform would have been a tepid solution to a big problem, yet the junta's announcement had won the praise of Secretary of State Dean Rusk. Indeed, it met Alliance for Progress specifications: confiscation with compensation. It also weakened the allegiance of the peasantry toward Hugo Blanco and his labor organizers.

Army engineer battalions also added some civic action features to the reform package. The year 1963 had already been declared the "year of literacy" by the military government, which promised a modest educational project imitating Cuba's massive literacy project but without social revolution.[23] The generals were designing literacy campaigns and land reform as placebos—not the radical and far-reaching revolutionary restructuring of the Cuban Revolution.

The labor strike and land invasion became Hugo Blanco's main tactics of resistance. Where the hacendados resisted the union movement, often with violence, as at Hacienda Chaupimayo, the *yanaconas* achieved a rare combination of unity and courage in order to seize the property and expel the owner. This successful land invasion inspired other indigenous laborers to do the same. On these unusual occasions, the peasants designated themselves the owners of their plots of land and set aside collectivized fields for everyone to graze their livestock. They then formed an *ayllu,* a traditional community of peasant democracy, to govern the former hacienda estate.[24] The Ministry of War had a different opinion of the movement. "[The *campesinos*] became inebriated, stole the cattle, and acted like the owners and lords of the region." They took literacy courses "that had no other object than to fill the head with the subversive propaganda" of the Trotskyists.[25]

Blanco maintains that he was forced to turn to armed resistance without sufficient preparation, because the authorities had resolved to crush the rural labor movement. The peasants "had come to see that armed struggle was the only solution," Blanco wrote. Therefore, he recruited a band of peasants armed with pistols, rifles, and automatic weapons. They had acquired their weapons by disarming the rural police and buying additional arms with money from bank robberies. The peasants and the armed Trotskyists overwhelmed the Guardia Civil patrolmen assigned to La Convención. The military government sent hundreds of troops to La Convención to disarm the militias. Together, Blanco and his peasant followers attempted to form more local militias for self-defense.[26]

Soon Blanco went from labor leader to fugitive. He shot a local policeman who had committed violence on some of his followers and fled to the high mountains, "protected by the peasants."[27] Police patrols closed in by arresting one peasant, who gave up Blanco's location under interrogation and torture. Agents from the Civil Guard cornered Blanco, exhausted and hungry, in a small hut. A policeman spied the fugitive flattened out in a mud wallow. "I've found him," he shouted. "Shoot him," the commander ordered from afar. The policeman fired a shot to the side, purposefully missing the target. The commander vented his fury that his order had not been heeded, but with so many witnesses now gathering around, the prisoner gained a margin of safety.[28]

The policeman's disobedience saved Blanco's life. However, "it [was] not enough to destroy or paralyze the Marxist enemy," as one officer said. "It [was also] necessary to gain the support of the masses."[29] A Peruvian court sentenced Hugo Blanco to a long jail term. This victory greatly enhanced the junta's ability to bring off a presidential election in June 1963. It was at this moment that two hundred young Peruvians who had completed guerrilla training in Cuba attempted to return home.

GUERRILLAS EN ROUTE

The Peruvian fighters had split into two groups. The largest faction belonged to leftist radicals of the APRA youth movement. Party leader Haya de la Torre had expelled them from the party as he moved to the right. Che Guevara's first wife, Hilda Gadea, had joined the young *apristas,* many of whom spent time in exile in the 1950s. Gadea met the young Dr. Ernesto Guevara in Guatemala in 1954, and they later reunited in Mexico City. The APRA youth became even more radicalized upon arriving in Havana. "When Fidel declared that the Cuban Revolution was going socialist [in April 1961]," said one Peruvian, "we also had to accelerate our passage from the ideological standpoint."[30] Eventually, these APRA radicals formed the MIR, the Movement of the Revolutionary Left. MIR was becoming the name taken by noncommunist revolutionaries in several countries of South America, including Venezuela and later Chile.

By this time, Luis de la Puente Uceda had assumed the leadership of the MIR. De la Puente had joined the APRA in the 1950s and also spent time in exile in Mexico. Apparently, he did not meet Fidel Castro or Che Guevara. However, de la Puente did visit Havana in May 1959 and criticized the new land reform decree—he found it too moderate. He returned to Peru during the presidency of Manuel Prado and challenged his own APRA party with his radical ideas. During a political disturbance, de la Puente shot a militant of the mainline faction of the party and spent a year in jail.[31] He subsequently joined his MIR colleagues for military training in Havana.

The revolutionaries' principal problem concerned disunity on the left. In 1962, de la Puente journeyed to La Convención to interview Hugo Blanco, the labor organizer. But the two neither formed a friendship nor shared a philosophical kinship. Blanco learned to speak Quechua as a boy growing up in Cuzco and felt alienated from this white-skinned, Spanish-speaking son of a coastal landowner.[32] De la Puente of the MIR later voiced some animus toward Blanco and his flimsy self-defense militias.

Che Guevara disliked de la Puente's uncooperative attitude. Che had favored the faction of communist dissidents for their willingness to work with other rebel factions. These challengers to the Peruvian Communist Party doctrine of electoral participation chose the appellation of the Army of National Liberation, or ELN. Che encouraged unity on the left among guerrillas, and he much preferred the ELN, which pledged to join up with Blanco's peasant movement in the Southern Andes of Peru. Che and Fidel conspired to delay the MIR's return, sending them off to Cuba's Escambray Mountains to fight against the *bandido* counterrevolution.[33] That assignment had become something of a graduation exercise for guerrilla trainees in Cuba.

Personnel of the Peruvian ELN were the first Peruvian trainees to fly into Brazil protected by the pro-Cuba government of President Goulart. From Brazil, they entered Bolivia in small groups for the trek overland to the Peruvian border. The Cubans had already enlisted Bolivia's Communist Party to assist the movement of the Peruvians. Bolivian party militants provided safe houses and communications for the returning Peruvians but also threw up some obstacles. Neither the Bolivian nor the Peruvian Communist Parties believed in armed rebellion. The Bolivians felt obliged to inform their Peruvian fellow communists of the movement of the party dissidents who composed the Army of National Liberation.

Crossing the border even at remote locations presented problems as well. There the Peruvian police thought the young men were smugglers and pursued them, killing the ELN's Javier Heraúd, a celebrated poet. They captured several others.[34] This setback caused the ELN to lose the race to begin operations back in Peru before the military junta could hold the next election. In it, Fernando Belaúnde Terry defeated the generals' nemesis, Haya de la Torre of the APRA. The generals then turned over executive power to Belaúnde. Remaining members of the ELN met in La Paz, Bolivia, to discuss whether Belaúnde's electoral victory might disrupt their plans. They decided to go ahead anyway, according to Héctor Béjar, leader of the ELN. ELN fighters concluded that Belaúnde "would continue with the policies of repression against the peasants."[35] Nevertheless, it took two years for the ELN to regroup and prepare for the combat.

Now that its service in Cuba had concluded, the MIR also confronted a major obstacle to making the Peruvian revolution. They too wished to return before the elections but failed. To overcome the travel restrictions imposed by Washington and its allies in Latin America, the *miristas* split up into groups of five to ten individuals. Each group returned from Cuba on circuitous routes through Prague, Zurich, Paris, Rio de Janeiro, and then Bolivia or Ecuador. The MIR had a safe house in Paris and bank accounts in Switzerland with deposits from the People's Republic of China and other sources. Three women acted as couriers between the MIR offices in these major cities. Rank-and-file trainees were grumbling about how MIR leaders spent freely, while the foot soldiers received small salaries.[36] At least, this amounted to what some informers told agents of the CIA.

The Chinese proved their commitment to armed revolution in South America by lending assistance to Peru's Movement of the Revolutionary Left. One report indicated that the MIR leader Luis de la Puente told his supporters that he had received a letter from Mao Zedong, asking for unity of the left in Peru. The pro-China faction of Peru's Communist Party supported the MIR as requested, but pro-Soviet Peruvian Communists did not join in. In the meanwhile, eight *miristas* departed in 1964 for training in North Korea; twenty more were to go to China for guerrilla instruction. None of them were to travel through Moscow, which, de la Puente suspected, was working with the United States to identify Latin American radicals. The MIR claimed to have three million dollars with Beijing's compliments, with promises of forty million more. "The Chinese supported us economically more than anyone else," recalled one *mirista,* "and they demanded no political compromises to assume Maoist positions."[37]

The CIA succeeded in recruiting one of these Peruvian trainees who was apprehended in Ecuador on his journey home. "What he wants is financial assistance to get his wife and child out of Peru and to resettle in some other country," reported agent Philip Agee. "He says he became disillusioned during the training in Cuba, but my guess is that he's lost his nerve now that he's almost on the battlefield." The CIA's Lima station gathered information from this informant on MIR supporters, maps, names and addresses, and photographs. Eventually, the CIA turned all the information over to the Peruvian authorities. American agents subsequently arranged for the MIR informant's relocation to Mexico with a "generous retirement bonus."[38]

The elections came off before many of the *miristas* had even reached the border. Several groups of seven to ten returnees had arrived in Bolivia, but others were still passing from Prague through France, Brazil, and either Bolivia or Ecuador. All these groups were to cross the border separately and assemble in one of several points in the cordillera of Peru.[39] Seventy-two Cuban-trained *miristas* had returned. However, the MIR had yet to distribute weapons with which to begin the struggle. Those few activists who had returned home were busily attempting to assemble and stockpile arms at points along the border with Chile and Bolivia. Informants told American intelligence agents that the *miristas* had approached the Greek shipping magnate Aristotle Onassis to bring in arms via Cape Horn to northern Chile, there to be unloaded onto Peruvian fishing trawlers.[40] It did not matter. The newly elected president was about to take the oath of office, and Hugo Blanco was in prison.

BELAÚNDE IN POWER

The national elections held in 1963 came off without notable problems, satisfying the military junta but troubling US policymakers. APRA's longtime standard-bearer, Víctor Haya de la Torre, came in second to Fernando Belaúnde. Belaúnde garnered 39 percent of the popular vote among four candidates, but the *apristas* and two other parties had taken control of Congress. The president-elect promised to bring about land reform. He vowed to raise the incomes of the working classes without taxing the few wealthy families; Belaúnde said he would borrow funds for social improvements from foreign lending agencies.[41]

However, it gave Americans pause that the new president had promised that the first and foremost priority of his administration would be to make a tough new agreement with the International Petroleum Company, the IPC. This oil company was a wholly owned subsidiary of the Standard Oil Company of New Jersey. The president-elect's pledge did not resonate with the American embassy, defender of US investors in Peru, but the electorate loved this nationalistic appeal.[42] The popularity and sincerity of president-elect Belaúnde certainly created unfavorable conditions for fresh guerrilla activities. Public opinion accorded the new president a window of opportunity to achieve the reforms he was proposing. The MIR and ELN waited for a stumble from the Belaúnde government.

United States policymakers cooperated unwittingly with the guerrillas by doing what they could to trip up Belaúnde. They disliked his first priority, which was to reach a new agreement with International Petroleum. Economic nationalism may have helped elect Belaúnde, but it did not sit well with the designers of the Alliance for Progress. Private domestic and foreign investment remained the hallmark of the Alliance program. While Belaúnde requested loans for domestic social reforms, he insisted on increasing the taxes and royalties on Standard Oil's IPC. American policymakers feared that the new president might expropriate the foreign-owned petroleum assets as Mexico's president Lázaro Cárdenas had done in 1938. President Kennedy held up loans and aid for Belaúnde's government, and President Johnson continued this reactionary turn in foreign policy.[43]

In the meantime, Belaúnde inherited the rural unrest and had to deal with *campesino* seizures of lands owned by American mining companies and elite Peruvian families. The new president did not wish to alienate the indigenous majority of Peru's population. He personally visited some of the properties taken over by the peasant organizations and asked *campesinos* to await passage of the agrarian reform bill he had sent to Congress. Also, Belaúnde told them that such invasions would provoke "powerful [reactionary] forces" that wished to "obstruct the government in its plan of transformation."[44] He was referring to the powerful hacienda class and also to his political opponents in the APRA party. The opposition majority in Congress delayed action on President Belaúnde's agrarian and other reform legislation. Land for the peasants had been a cardinal project of the APRA since the 1930s. Yet they would not support a similar project of a political rival.

President Belaúnde pursued negotiations over a new petroleum contract that would please no one. Politicians from the right and left voiced criticism of a proposed 65–35 split in oil profits because the government would receive the lesser amount. It was well known that the Venezuelan government was receiving 50 percent of oil revenues at the time. Moreover, the cost of living in Peru increased to the point that it stretched the patience of impoverished workers and peasants. Inflation reached double digits in the first half of 1965. Poverty, population growth, and lack of land had augmented the flow of peasants out of the countryside and into Lima. Half a million migrants per year contributed to the spread of impoverished *barriadas,* slums on the outskirts of the capital.[45]

THE GUERRILLA UPRISING

Like other revolutionaries, Luis de la Puente Uceda sought to publicize the goals of his struggle at the outset. "We feel sure that American armed intervention in our country will come more quickly than in other nations," de la Puente wrote in the Marxist-oriented *Monthly Review*. "The Pentagon is perfectly aware of the importance of a triumphant or developing insurrection in the very heart of Latin America." He also said that "our national revolutionary struggle will become, sooner or later, a continental revolutionary struggle."[46] Despite his confident predictions, the United States did not intervene militarily in Peru. Even more ironic is the fact that the MIR leader was already dead when this *Monthly Review* article appeared.

Toward the end of May 1965, de la Puente summoned the high commanders of MIR to his headquarters in the Mesa Pelada. Héctor Béjar of the Army of National Liberation (ELN) did not attend and had not been invited. The *miristas* drew up their revolutionary "proclamation," by which they announced to the nation that the guerrilla struggle had begun. It amounted to a blueprint for social revolution of the type that attacked the bourgeois state, the landlord class, and foreign interests. They promised the "final destruction of the large estates, with ownership being given to the peasants."[47] The ELN also prepared for action—separately.

Héctor Béjar of the ELN said that the *miristas* refused to work with him because of a dispute about the role of "the revolutionary party." De la Puente and his confederates had formed the party, the MIR, before entering the armed struggle (as had the Bolsheviks in the Russian Revolution and Mao Zedong's Communist Party in the Chinese Revolution). On the relationship of the party to the army, Mao had said: "Our principle is that the Party commands the gun, and the gun must never be allowed to command the Party."[48] Meanwhile, the ELN followed the dictum of taking up arms first and later forming the revolutionary party out of the guerrilla movement itself (as in the case of Castro's 26th of July Revolutionary Movement).[49] Much of the disunity actually revolved around personal rivalries. De la Puente could not collaborate with either Hugo Blanco or Héctor Béjar, nor they with him.

By June 1965, nevertheless, the *miristas* had consolidated three principal areas of insurrection. In naming their encampments, rebel leaders invoked the ancient Inka kings. In the Northern Andes, they established the Manco Cápac front. In the center of the Peruvian cordillera, they placed the Túpac Amaru brigade. De la Puente himself commanded the rebels in the southern zone, named the Pachacútec. Curiously, none of these MIR leaders were even remotely indigenous. The guerrilla leaders from the coast did not know the Quechua language of the highland peasants.[50]

MIR leader Luis de la Puente Uceda gives a marksmanship lesson to his guerrilla fighters.

Luis de la Puente Uceda assumed overall command of the *miristas* with headquarters in the remote eastern peaks above La Convención, where the culturally savvy Hugo Blanco had once operated. The MIR issued a "call to arms" in a news release to the nation's major newspapers, appealing for unity on the left but putting the military on notice. Peruvian newspapers estimated that potential subversives now numbered some eight hundred men.[51] The number seems much exaggerated in view of subsequent events.

One leader of MIR, Guillermo Lobatón, would rise to mythic levels among the common folk of the Central Andes. He grew up in the Lima shantytowns as a young man of African origins, his name suggesting Haitian heritage. He found himself one of the few Afro-Peruvians attending the University of San Carlos, where he endured barbs because of his racially mixed and poor socioeconomic background. During the Odría dictatorship, he participated in student protests and spent time in prison. In 1954, he traveled as a political exile to Paris, attended classes at the Sorbonne, collected scrap paper for a living, and married a French woman of leftist political leanings. Lobatón started to travel a great deal beginning in 1961—Cuba, Argentina, Brazil, and Chile, eventually joining the Guevarist left. Above all, he had committed himself to revolution in Peru. When he went into the mountains with the MIR, he wrote to his mother. "Give me your blessing, mother, and let me go forward. Your son will never forget you."[52] Lobatón commanded the Túpac Amaru rebellion in the Central Andes.

Despite this final meeting of rebel chieftains at Mesa Pelada, the guerrilla campaign began almost too abruptly. Guillermo Lobatón's first armed onslaught in late June 1965 caught the other three guerrilla *foci* off guard. Neither Béjar nor de la Puente was prepared, and the northern guerrillas had only just started to establish their base. Lobatón and his Túpac Amaru rebels had recruited effectively beforehand, gaining about 120 volunteers, the greatest increment of peasant support of the three MIR contingents. Most indigenous highlanders distrusted white revolutionaries from the coast. The Afro-Peruvian Lobatón had secured the backing from the forest villagers, the Campa. One Túpac Amaru survivor testified about peasant support. He said the guerrillas numbered only thirteen with an auxiliary of indigenous peasants. "The peasantry helped us enthusiastically. They helped us carry provisions, arms, medicines, to take us from one site to another, to show us places and trails with great enthusiasm."[53]

Meanwhile, Lobatón and his guerrilla followers attacked a mining center, invaded two haciendas, and destroyed two bridges close to Huancayo. Arms of the Túpac Amaru consisted of a few light automatic rifles, but mostly pistols, shotguns, and carbines.[54] Newspapers in Lima described the attackers as "young men . . . about 18 years of age. They are armed with machine guns, bearded, [and] wearing long hair." The leaders, it was reported, had trained in Cuba, Czechoslovakia, China, North Korea, and North Vietnam.

No one died in this initial assault, although the leftists took two mine employees as hostages. The assault netted supplies and explosives from the mining company, and Lobatón claimed that "large numbers of campesinos are joining the guerrillas." They seemed to have proved the inadequacy of Belaúnde's land reform program, for Lobatón boasted that he had redistributed twice as much land to peasants in one guerrilla action as the government had in the previous two years. "You are our brothers," Lobatón was telling the peasants in his zone of combat. "What we have taken from your bosses belongs to you."[55] Later, this same group assaulted two Civil Guard posts and captured a sergeant and three guards. The Túpac Amaru guerrillas distributed fliers announcing that they would destroy police units sent against them. "We are well prepared to face police forces," the fliers announced. "We shall destroy those who attempt to attack our fortress."[56]

Less than two weeks following Lobatón's inaugural attack, his lieutenant, Máximo Velado, followed up with another guerrilla strike. Velado's column ambushed twenty-nine civil guardsmen in a narrow canyon, killing the commander and eight others. The guerrillas lectured the captives to "cease serving the rich." Then they released them and kept their weaponry.[57]

MIR propaganda maintained that members of the Ranger Battalions and Civil Guard were defecting and that the guerrillas were on the offensive. A communiqué of the MIR spun a very favorable image of the struggle. "Three months ago the heroic guerrilla groups of Pachacútec and Túpac Amaru began their victorious struggle against mercenary repressive forces, superior in numbers, but under the leadership of Yankee 'advisers.'" The rebels claimed to have inflicted heavy casualties on government forces. "The Peruvian revolution has begun," they said. "It is not a Communist Revolution (although the Communists may participate in it like all other Peruvians)."

MIR propagandists described the revolution as a multiclass coalition fighting against the "masters of Peru," the *latifundistas,* the bankers, and "the foreign master who directs them, Yankee imperialism." The guerrillas said this should not be a civil war between eleven million Peruvians and the army but between Peru and US imperialism. "Therefore, the army must unite with the people in order to liquidate the oligarchy, to make our sovereignty respected, and to liberate Peru, nationally and socially." Finally, the MIR rebels offered an immediate ceasefire with the army under a "pacification plan" that included "suffrage for all illiterate peasants," punishment of the reactionary elements, agrarian reform, and immediate nationalization of the petroleum industry.[58]

In the south, the MIR guerrillas had directed their propaganda to the soldiers in imitation of a successful campaign of Castro's rebels in the Sierra Maestra. "Think, brother soldier, whom are you defending in this struggle. Your families, your class or the exploiters, those responsible for all the shame of Peru?"[59]

CONFRONTING THE REBELS

The government of President Belaúnde responded to the attack by sending a thirty-three-man detachment of the highlands rural police called the Guardia Civil. It was they who fell into an ambush set up by Lobatón's guerrillas. The armed forces seized upon the police defeat as a call to arms. They especially worried that the guerrillas were gaining appreciable support of the peasantry. The generals gave their elected commander-in-chief an ultimatum: turn over the counterinsurgency to the armed forces, or they would overthrow his regime. President Belaúnde gave in to the pressure. He declared a state of siege and turned the guerrilla zones over to the military.[60] The rebels may have been ready for the rural police, but they were no match for the army.

In many ways, the army of Peru differed greatly from Batista's poorly disciplined troops. The Peruvian armed forces in the 1960s numbered some 5,000 officers and 50,000 conscripts, of which two-thirds were in the army. They had equipment and weapons of World War II and Korean War vintage. The officer corps ranked among the most professional in Latin America, each officer having been educated at the military academy. Most senior officers received foreign technical training, often in the Canal Zone or the United States. Promotion to general officer had favored those military students who had ranked in the top quarter of their classes.[61] Most had attended Peru's Center for Higher Military Studies. In this important educational institution, both military officers and civilian experts gathered together to talk more about national problems and economic planning than about military doctrine.[62] Consequently, they debated over foreign control of Peru's oil and mining industries and about the social and economic problems such as the oligarchy's control of landholding.

The Peruvian military already had two examples of the destruction of the military establishment, Bolivia right next door in 1952 and recently Batista's army in Cuba.[63] Therefore, early in the 1960s, the Peruvian army adopted counterinsurgency doctrines. They offered courses in the subject at their own service schools, and they sent potential instructors and practitioners of anti-guerrilla warfare to study in the US Canal Zone and at the military staff colleges in the United States.[64] Between 1947 and 1967, 324 Peruvians attended the US Army School of the Americas at Fort Gulick on the Atlantic side of the Panama Canal Zone. There the instructors taught courses in counterinsurgency, in jungle and airborne operations, and in military intelligence. Articles soon began to appear in the army's professional journals, such as the *Revista Militar del Perú,* on how the army's engineering corps might develop civic action capabilities of building roads and irrigation ditches in remote areas. Peruvian army generals established an intelligence school in 1959 and the first counterinsurgency unit in 1960. Peruvian Air Force enlisted personnel formed the largest group of students—562 airmen— attending the Inter-American Air Force Academy in the Canal Zone.[65] Ultimately, these military students adopted what suited them from the instruction and rejected US doctrines that did not apply to their national circumstances.

The high command of Peru's armed forces acted as if it already had a contingency plan for irregular warfare. The generals ordered the police to monitor university students in Cuzco for "terrorist" sympathies and shut down the University of Iquitos. The local police arrested leaders and members of peasant leagues and other people who had been known to have visited Cuba and Communist Bloc countries. Dentists, former town councillors, foreigners, students, and labor leaders fell into these categories. Also arrested was the president of the agricultural cooperative of Chaco Huayanay, whom President Belaúnde had recently decorated as a "responsible" leader of the government's agrarian reform.[66] The army concentrated its forces in Huancayo to suppress Lobatón's forces and in La Convención to deal with de la Puente's guerrillas.

The weight of the rebels and security forces in the highlands began to put pressure on supplies and foodstuffs. Army and police units also took scarce local supplies from towns and villages. One hundred and fifty soldiers in one highland town slaughtered a pig or sheep every three days and consumed about one hundred kilos of potatoes daily. Chickens, ducks, and geese disappeared from barnyards, and food prices rose. The security forces, manned by personnel from Lima and other coastal cities, assumed that the indigenous peasants supported the guerrillas and treated them with suspicion and contempt.[67] The generals did not permit US military advisers to accompany Peruvian units in the field, contrary to de la Puente's prediction. However, the Americans did speed up the delivery of helicopters and ammunition, even though they refused to supply more napalm than government forces already had.[68]

Units of the army formed a cordon around the MIR redoubt of Mesa Pelada in La Convención, bastion of de la Puente. They closed all roads leading up to the rebel camps. In the first clashes of the siege, the soldiers killed twenty rebels and began a bombardment of the guerrilla bases. Army casuality rates remained remarkably low. Two soldiers died in the early fighting. In the following weeks, a unit of rangers suffered only one casualty in capturing thirty-five guerrillas and killing three.[69]

The guerrilla forces began to disintegrate under army pressure. The rangers captured one rebel who had knowledge of the supply network. Under interrogation, he revealed the names of the principal urban suppliers, who were subsequently rounded up by the police. Other deserters fell into the hands of the rangers as well. These spoke of panic among the Pachacútec rebels in the Southern Andes. Army rangers reported a clash with guerrillas on a road heading into La Convención; two guerrillas were killed as well as two soldiers. A second encounter occurred as the army surprised a group of guerrillas attempting to fall back.[70]

The generals pressed their advantage over the rebels. Army intelligence set up roadblocks and debriefed refugees and suspected rebel couriers coming out of the valley of La Convención. Soldiers pinpointed the location of ten different rebel encampments. Obviously, de la Puente and the MIR were not observing Mao and Che's dictum that guerrilla fighters should maintain "constant vigilance, constant movement, and constant suspicion." Army units moved against these encampments one at a time, capturing guerrillas and weapons and confiscating communist propaganda materials.

De la Puente ensconced himself in the Mesa Pelada, scene of Hugo Blanco's land-or-death campaign of the early 1960s. But the rebels garnered very little popular support. Peruvian army intelligence surmised that the activities of the MIR had actually alienated the peasants of La Convención. Ninety percent of the peasants had favored Hugo Blanco over government forces in 1962. However, three years later, local support for the MIR had plummeted to just 15 percent. *Campesinos* turned against the rebels, said army spokesmen, because of de la Puente's white skin and his inability to speak Quechua. They called him "el gringo" and resented his brand of iron discipline.[71]

In fact, a local peasant leader, Albino Guzmán, denounced de la Puente for being out of touch with the local peasantry. Guzmán greatly assisted the troops in locating the various guerrilla encampments within La Convención Valley and particularly the secret paths leading up to Mesa Pelada. He had been an earlier collaborator of Hugo Blanco and, as an MIR committee member, knew of the locations of all hidden weapons and food supplies.[72]

Then, beginning on September 20, 1965, four thousand men in five separate army detachments began the siege of Mesa Pelada. Peruvian air force planes bombed and strafed the guerrilla fortress during the day, and artillery batteries kept the guerrillas awake with nightly barrages. Soldiers surrounded and captured individual guerrillas descending from the encampment to hunt for food or to escape. The army assaulted the ten encampments of the Pachacútec one by one. None of the guerrilla camps was able to help others under attack. The army merely pinpointed those bases and concentrated overwhelming firepower to reduce the redoubts.[73]

On October 10, infantry troops attacked Mesa Pelada, killing fifty-four guerrillas even though the MIR leader had escaped with a handful of associates. This small group made their way to a nearby hacienda. They demanded help and, according to the Defense Ministry account, shot several peasants who refused. The rifle shots alerted a combat squad nearby, which suppressed the renegades with rifle fire. Journalistic sources intimated that these three rebels had been executed on the spot. Soldiers captured de la Puente and a local indigenous chieftain at the end of October 1965, shackled their hands, and brought them to headquarters. Two ministers and an army general flew in to interrogate the prisoners. Afterward, the MIR leaders were taken into the countryside and executed.[74] The Pachacútec of de la Puente was defeated.

By August, fresh army units were arriving to Junín Province by plane for "Operation Clean-Up" of Comandante Guillermo Lobatón's guerrilla band. The generals mobilized the ranger and infantry battalions that already had undergone counterinsurgency training. They commandeered the airport at Ayacucho for their headquarters in the Andean region and declared a major portion of the surrounding area as a free-fire zone. The 43rd Infantry Battalion took Huancayo as its base of operations.[75]

The air force joined in the operation, and its light bombers forced the guerrillas to abandon their base camp at Pucutá. Helicopters ferried rangers' units to remote areas behind the guerrillas. The air force bombarded an area to which guerrillas retreated and announced that more than one hundred had been killed. It seems unlikely that all these had been guerrilla fighters. The napalm attacks at Pucutá proved to be devastating to the defenders. They consisted of napalm-filled gasoline drums with simple fuses that frightened crew members when they lit them as they pushed the drums out of the bay of a C-46 cargo plane.[76] Their explosions and destructive power on the ground terrified local residents.

In August, government forces went on the offensive against Lobatón in the Central Andes. Police units of the Republican Guard and Civil Defense engaged his Túpac Amaru guerrillas located at Pucutá. However, some men of these police units, most of whom came from the coastal lowlands, may not have been prepared for combat in the highlands. Rebels set up an ambush and killed nine policemen. Government forces responded by bombarding the rebels, killing twenty guerrillas.[77] However, the army's 2nd Light Infantry Division led the attack on Pucutá. By this time, army intelligence had hired informants from among the Campa people with gifts of radios, machetes, carbines, and flashlights. The assault on Pucutá killed eleven guerrillas and routed Lobatón's force. The survivors fled eastward toward the lowlands and suffered desertion among the highland recruits. Only a reduced number of Campa recruits remained.[78]

After the death of de la Puente, the MIR issued a statement that the struggle would continue. Guillermo Lobatón of the Túpac Amaru took command as the MIR's national leader. Yet Lobatón too was pulling back. Even in retreat, the guerrillas still had the ability to take over a hacienda here and there, occasionally executing the overseers. They still attacked towns in the search for supplies. The army caught several stragglers of Lobatón's command, who declared that their leaders were fleeing eastward, descending deeper into the Amazonian rain forests.[79]

Peruvian army units displayed great leadership and training. The Defense Ministry described how the León detachment carried out a surprise attack on the guerrilla base at Shuenti. Two Campa men guided the unit on a 130-kilometer march through rough terrain in five days on just two days' rations. The soldiers did not radio for a helicopter lift of new rations for fear of their position being discovered. They attacked Shuenti, killing eleven guerrillas and capturing seventeen others. They recovered weapons and equipment the rebels had previously taken from Civil Guard policemen.[80] Here one of the lieutenants of Lobatón committed suicide, army spokesmen averred, by repeatedly bashing his own head against the wall of his cell. Lobatón and a few supporters fled toward the Brazilian border pursued by airborne troops.[81]

As the Peruvian summertime passed into January 1966, MIR operatives in Lima attempted to divert government forces by exploding bombs and scattering leaflets proclaiming the Peruvian revolution. Yet the struggle in the countryside had long since turned against the rebels. Rangers took two brothers into custody as they were attempting to recruit peasants for the struggle. Next, the police captured two guerrillas linked to bank robberies. Meanwhile, the guerrillas in the center had abandoned their camp at Pucutá and regrouped to the east, where the rangers ambushed a rebel foray against coffee plantations and killed six of them. Then two thousand army parachutists dropped behind the remaining Túpac Amaru guerrillas of Comandante Guillermo Lobatón.[82] The rebel *comandante* succumbed in the last firefight, on the banks of the Sotziqui River, not far from the Brazilian border on January 7, 1966, ending all resistance of the Túpac Amaru guerrilla band. The army said that Lobatón died fighting, but more likely he was captured and executed.[83]

In the cordillera near the Ecuadorian border, the MIR commander Gonzalo Fernández Gasco and his guerrillas had rushed to establish a training camp in the remote mountains of Piura Province, close to the city of Ayabaca. Newspapers reported that they were training three hundred peasants there for guerrilla combat. However, the reports greatly exaggerated the preparations of the Manco Cápac guerrillas. The fighting farther south had caught them off guard. They had yet to set up their encampments and had no way of communicating with the other MIR groups. The MIR set up a radio station at its main camp in this mountainous region and was broadcasting calls for insurrection and the speeches of Fidel Castro. In mid-October, the Peruvian army reported that these fighters in the north had attacked an outpost of the Civil Guard, and the guards there had repelled the assault.[84] In reality, the Manco Cápac guerrillas never fought at all.

The army sent the 1st Cavalry Division against the Manco Cápac guerrillas. At the outset of the campaign in October, the troops captured six guerrillas over the course of two weeks. Intelligence indicated that Comandante Gonzalo placed his main encampments on the peaks of Cerro Negro. On December 11, 1965, three army detachments advanced on the mountain peak. They discovered four separate camps stocked with provisions, ammunition, and equipment—but the guerrillas had fled. Army spokespersons reported that thirty-five hard-core rebels in the area of Ayabaca had gone to Ecuador. Their commander crossed the border with them. Cleanup activities had concluded at the beginning of January 1966. "Peru's record in dealing with insurgency at the incipient stage is best of the hemisphere," a staff member of the National Security Council wrote to President Lyndon Johnson.[85] The White House, though distracted by the Vietnam War, had been keeping track of guerrilla problems in Latin America.

Official accounts of army operations emphasized guerrilla failings. Rebel leaders engaged in damaging infighting. They abused the peasantry just like "the exploiters and hacendados of the region." The guerrillas committed atrocities on two policemen, according to one account, and left their badly burned bodies unburied, pretending that they had been victims of an air force napalm attack.[86] It was guerrilla abuse, one general wrote, that motivated the indigenous highlanders voluntarily to come over to the side of the government. Many former guerrilla recruits among the Campa volunteered to become informers. When the Túpac Amaru rebels had finally dispersed at the end of September 1965, "the Campa villages were attended with special care and the families of those who had lost their lives were compensated [by the army]."[87] As usual, the victors claimed all the propaganda opportunities.

Héctor Béjar, commander of the Army of National Liberation, also led his men into action in 1965. Béjar chose Ayacucho in the Central Andes as his battleground. His ELN seized the Hacienda Chapi in September and shot the abusive owners, the Carrillo brothers, in the firefight. Hacienda workers showed their gratitude to the ELN guerrillas by raising their fists and hailing the *comunistas*. Some joined Béjar's rebels. Peasants throughout the department of Ayacucho responded positively to the presence of the guerrilla band, and many hacendados and overseers found it expedient to flee the countryside. "With the landowners removed and the army unable to locate us," Béjar wrote, "we became the only authority in the zone." However, the army would not ignore the ELN, for one of the slain Carrillo brothers had retired from the military at the rank of major.[88]

As soon as the soldiers defeated the MIR at La Convención, army commanders sent reinforcements into Ayacucho. Within days of the death of de la Puente, the air force transported five army detachments from Mesa Pelada to engage the ELN. These units began to tighten the noose. The soldiers "liberated" the Hacienda Chapi when the guerrillas retreated.[89] They terrorized and killed peasants suspected of collaborating with the guerrillas, or so claimed the rebels.

The ELN too had to escape down the eastern sierras among the forest people, the Campa. Footpaths led from one settlement to another. The Quechua-speaking highlanders deserted, leaving Béjar's group with only thirteen men. In a battle on December 17 near a village called Tincoj, the soldiers engaged the bedraggled guerrillas, killing three, dispersing the rest, and capturing Béjar.[90] "The troops were received with open arms by the inhabitants whose open collaboration, we have to admit, enabled us to rout the [ELN] guerrilla band in just 30 days," the Ministry of War reported. ELN commander Héctor Béjar was sentenced to prison, where he started writing his memoirs and giving interviews to journalists.[91]

In an interview published in Lima, Béjar reminded Peruvians that the conditions that had led to peasant unrest still existed. Although the army had killed many guerrilla leaders, the long-term revolution would not die, Béjar said. He denounced the "bloody system that rules our country in the name of democracy" and concluded that the "amount of abuse and the number of crimes committed in these regions are incredible."[92]

In the end, the army and the air force had prevailed. Fifty to seventy-five guerrilla leaders lost their lives and, as had been usual since the days of the Conquest, the indigenous *campesinos* suffered disproportionate losses—eight thousand killed. Thousands of other peasants fell victim to military repression. A French journalist recounted stories of military trucks loaded down with corpses.[93] An additional nineteen thousand refugees escaped napalm attacks that destroyed the vegetation over some fourteen thousand hectares of land. As many as fifty-six soldiers died too.[94] Two veterans of Héctor Béjar's ELN, Juan Pablo Chang Navarro (known by his code name, "Chino") and Lucio Edilberto Galván ("Eustaquio") later joined Che Guevara in the Bolivian guerrilla movement. A third Peruvian, Dr. Restituto José Cabrera Flores ("Negro") also joined the Bolivian guerrillas after several years practicing medicine in Cuba.[95]

No sooner had the Peruvian guerrillas met their doom than the theorists of revolution began arguing over the lessons learned. At the time of the Peruvian defeat, the French leftist intellectual Régis Debray was examining the Cuban revolutionary example as the path to be followed by Latin America. He had fallen under the spell of Che's reflections on the guerrilla war in the Sierra Maestra, though Debray could not interview Guevara himself, who was operating secretly in Africa. Debray talked to Fidel, Raúl, and other veteran comandantes in coming up with his *foco* theory of guerrilla revolution. In drawing conclusions about the failure of the Peruvians, Debray emphasized that the Asian models, formulated and practiced by Mao himself, did not apply to Latin America as much as did the Cuban model.

Debray charged the MIR fighters with following the incorrect strategies of guerrilla warfare that they had learned in their training in China— particularly by establishing "supportive bases" that army troops could then attack and destroy. The Peruvian rebels, he said, should have remained on the move, avoiding contact with superior government forces until they had built up support among the peasants. "To wage a short war, to destroy the *foco* in its embryonic stage, without giving it time to adapt itself to terrain or link itself closely with the local population or acquire a minimum of experience, is thus the golden rule of counter-insurgency," concluded Debray.[96] The Peruvian guerrilla war had come to an end in 1966 with a decisive victory for the army. However, the country's social problems endured.

SOLDIERS MAKING REVOLUTION

"Misión cumplida," announced the Ministry of Defense. All the guerrilla bands "have been broken and destroyed one after the other." The Peruvian Armed Forces prevented the communists from delivering the country "into the hands of foreign powers."[97] But the military did not declare victory, for it acknowledged that the "virus of subversion was still latent" in the country's social structure. Military officers cited the hacienda system, the poor distribution of wealth, the lack of transportation infrastructure, and foreign economic domination as enduring national problems. So long as social and economic problems remained unresolved, Peru still needed to complete "the social democratic revolution."[98]

In the process of crushing the guerrillas, the generals came face-to-face with the pressing need for basic social reforms in Peru. They had interrogated rebel prisoners and seized their philosophical texts. The generals were later to read these materials and tended to agree with some of the social criticism, particularly about the foreign control of the economy and hacendado abuse of peasants. One general wrote three chapters on Marxist-Leninist plans and programs in his book on the guerrilla campaign.[99] No doubt, officers at the Center for Higher Military Studies were discussing these subjects.

The armed forces had saved President Belaúnde from the menace of the guerrillas only to witness the further deterioration of the political and economic situation. Congress refused to consider tax reforms as a method of increasing revenues. Without United States financial bailouts, the government's budgetary deficit was growing by 96 percent per annum. The foreign debt rose from $120 million in 1963 to $670 million in 1967.[100] As inflation continued unabated, the armed forces had received no pay raises since the time of the military junta in 1962.

Moreover, political bickering continued as before over the petroleum contract with the IPC subsidiary of Standard Oil. The International Petroleum Company had purchased and operated the oil fields and refinery on the northern coast since 1917. The La Brea tract had been among the first oil fields in South America, dating from the 1880s, and had expanded under the IPC as a major exporter to California and the west coast of North America.[101] By the 1960s, however, most of the oil company's profits now came from sales within Peru, where the IPC had been the monopoly marketer of petroleum and lubricants. American corporations espousing the economics of free markets in the United States often enjoyed monopoly status in the smaller markets of Latin America.

Actually, the White House and State Department still rankled over the failure of President Belaúnde to reach a contract agreement satisfactory to the IPC. At the Punta del Este summit, Lincoln Gordon remembered the meeting between Presidents Johnson and Belaúnde as "the most interesting" presidential chat of the summit. Gordon described how Belaúnde spoke in English and sought to make the Texas connection to Johnson. The Peruvian head of state reminisced about his days as a student at the University of Texas and praised Lady Bird Johnson, who attended at the same time. President Johnson ignored these cues and appeared "as if he hadn't slept quite enough." Then Belaúnde spoke as a visionary about the physical integration of South America, by building roads through the Andes, damming up the Amazon River, and using atomic energy to dig irrigation canals.

Johnson finally interrupted him. "Well, have you thought about the financial side of it?" Belaúnde exclaimed that the "financial problems [are] secondary," a statement that provoked the American president to launch into a mini-lecture on budgetary problems in the United States. When the Peruvian president departed, Lyndon Johnson turned to his aides and said, "That man not only has his head in the clouds, he's got his feet in the clouds, too."[102]

Not long after the presidental summit, a frustrated President Belaúnde once again complained to American diplomats that the US Agency for International Development was not advancing as much funding to Peru as to Brazil, Chile, and Colombia. He reminded the envoys that he had received his master's degree in architecture from the University of Texas. Belaúnde told them "that he might as well have gone to the University of Oklahoma for all the good his relationship with Texas had done him."[103] But American advisers no longer had friends among Peruvian generals either. The Johnson administration refused to sell them advanced jet fighters and criticized the military when it turned to France for Mirage fighters.[104] American-Peruvian relations had reached low ebb when the IPC affair came to a climax.

In July 1968, President Belaúnde announced the successful conclusion of contract negotiations with the International Petroleum Corporation. It was written on plain onionskin paper without any official letterhead. The government agreed to give up its claims on the IPC's past evasion of taxes in exchange for the Standard Oil owners' turning over oil field production to the state. But the company's refinery would be able to continue its monopoly control of oil markets in the country. The document's table of contents stated that page 11 would indicate new taxes that the IPC refinery would pay the state for the right to process Peruvian-owned crude oil. Yet page 11 went missing!

The generals joined the political opposition in criticizing the deal. They believed that the foreign oilmen must have bribed officials of the Belaúnde government, for the contract absolved the IPC from having to pay back taxes. No one seemed satisfied with the terms of the contract—not even the chief negotiator. President Belaúnde offered to renegotiate. Presidential elections were approaching, and Haya de la Torre of the opposition APRA party appeared once again to be the leading candidate. The generals had had enough.

In October 1968, they seized control of the government. In one of their first acts as a governing junta, the military men nationalized the whole of the IPC—oil fields, refineries, tankers, railway cars, delivery trucks, and service stations. Furthermore, they said, Peru will not pay anything in compensation for its seizure of the company's assets in view of all the unpaid taxes Standard Oil's IPC had amassed over the years. In this one act, the new military government had scored the biggest victory ever for Peruvian national pride.[105] These actions represented a significant challenge to the United States, whose State Department had always insisted on prompt payment for nationalized properties of US investors in Latin America.

Remarkably, the Peruvian military did not adopt the conservative policies of Brazil's generals. Instead, the officer corps appeared to take the guerrilla program as its own. "We fought the guerrillas in the Andes, and we know," one general told former White House adviser Richard Goodwin. "We saw men so desperate that they faced certain death to fight us, and we asked ourselves what made them so brave. Then, look at Vietnam. You can't win against guerrillas unless you have the support of the people."[106] The generals of the "Peruvian revolution" eventually seized the highland haciendas of the country's most reactionary and aristocratic families and distributed the land to peasant communes.

The generals did not blame the left for these problems but lambasted electoral politics for not finding solutions. "Where are the profound reforms that [the politicians] promised so often at election time and then, once in power, whisked out of sight in order to serve the oligarchy?" asked General Juan Velasco Alvarado, head of the military junta. "We do not talk of revolution; we are making one."[107] In the countryside around Trujillo, they seized the coastal plantations and turned them over to the labor unions representing the sugar and agricultural workers. Then they made common cause with the mining workers by nationalizing the mines, smelters, and haciendas of the Cerro de Pasco group, owned by a US corporation.[108] The generals placed public funds into the construction of potable water facilities, sewage systems, parks, and schools in Lima's migrant shantytowns. They created a new bureaucracy called SINAMOS, "without owners." To run these social reform agencies, the generals hired a rich diversity of activists— some were progressive priests, and others former *apristas,* Christian Democrats, and leftist militants.[109]

The military government's amnesty of 1970 had set Hugo Blanco and Héctor Béjar free from imprisonment. Béjar took advantage of his freedom to publish his book on his ELN experiences and join the reformist government of General Velasco in SINAMOS. On the other hand, Hugo Blanco chose to support the teachers' strike of 1971, an act that led to his expulsion to Mexico, where he published a book on his rural labor organizing in La Convención.[110]

President Richard M. Nixon demonstrated great forbearance with the reformist generals of the Peruvian ruling junta. His administration provided Peru with face-saving loans to compensate the North American companies for their lost assets, and new credits to finance the social reforms. After all, what the generals accomplished measured up well with Washington's prescriptions in the now-defunct Alliance for Progress. The generals could be trusted more than the guerrillas, the communists, and the reformist politicians. The Nixon administration even overlooked the purchase of Soviet weapons systems by the Peruvian military.[111] The US government, which had been so parsimonious with the previous elected government, opened the financial spigot so that the Peruvian military authorities could finance expensive reforms and economic development projects. But Peru's international debt also rose precipitously. Peruvians owed less than $1 billion when the military seized power and were left with a debt larger than $6.5 billion when the generals relinquished power twelve years later.

The land and income redistribution of the military junta never measured up to revolutionary proportions. The Mexican revolution of 1910 and the Bolivian revolution of 1952 had more rigorous agrarian reform projects than Peru. Cuba under Castro had socialized most property—rural and urban— in the 1960s. Nevertheless, the Peruvian military junta had accomplished more reform in twelve years than ruling politicians had since independence. The military government between 1968 and 1980 distributed more than 9.5 million hectares of land to nearly 370,000 families.[112] As the government advertised on billboards everywhere, "La Revolución es tuya."[113] The Revolution is yours.

However, the most ironic event of all occurred when the very military government whose generals had defeated guerrillas trained in Cuba made an about-face and welcomed Fidel Castro to Lima in 1971. Castro had just completed his trip to Chile. On the way home from seeing President Salvador Allende, he accepted an invitation to meet General Velasco, head of the revolutionary military government. That visit culminated several months later in the formal reestablishment of diplomatic ties between Peru and Cuba. Immediately thereafter, Havana assigned none other than Antonio Núñez Jiménez as its first ambassador to Lima in more than a decade. He was the communist geography professor who fought at the battle of Santa Clara with Che Guevara and who then served as the top boss of Cuba's powerful Na-

Prime Minister Fidel Castro pays a visit to junta president Juan Velasco Alvarado in Lima, as the OAS isolation of the Cuban Revolution begins to disintegrate.

tional Institute of Agrarian Reform.[114] Kennedy's cherished isolation of Cuba was crumbling.

The Peruvian case of 1965 points out that an army well prepared and well disposed to confront the guerrilla *foco* can destroy the potential of the guerrillas to garner support among the *campesinos*. First, the state of the military institution matters greatly. A cohesive, unified, and committed armed force not sullied by corruption and political factionalism will defeat most challenges by irregular warriors. The key for the military revolves around taking the guerrilla threat seriously and recognizing the social conditions that make possible a popular explosion in the countryside. Where the military lacks these qualities, resistance fighters will have opportunities to rouse the masses. This was the case in four social revolutions of twentieth-century Latin America: Mexico in 1910, Bolivia in 1952, Cuba in 1959, and Nicaragua in 1979.

It is doubtful that Peruvian officers needed the Americans to tell them about the consequences of not acting decisively. They learned from seeing what happened to Batista's men, lined up at the *paredón* before the firing squads in January through March 1959. Once so motivated, the Peruvian high command sought out what the Americans were thinking about in terms of counterinsurgency. Fidel Castro himself had done the same. Confronted with *bandidos* in the Escambray Mountains, he sent some of his lieutenants off to Moscow to compare what the Bolsheviks had done in the 1920s. Not that he "learned" or "took orders" from Soviet advisers. He already had experienced the mistakes Batista's generals had made against his own M26 guerrillas.

This case of Peru warrants an additional conclusion about the hemisphere-wide differences between revolution and reaction. In many ways, this Andean instance stands apart from the classic 1960s struggle between the ultraleftist challenge and the ultrarightist response typified by the Brazilian counterrevolution of 1964. In contrast, the generals in Peru shared similar ideas with their adversaries about national development. Certainly, having an institution such as Peru's Center for Higher Military Studies encouraged diverse opinions and debate. Not just one tendency worked for all South American soldiers. The reformers would predominate in Panama and Bolivia, and the hard-liners prevailed in Brazil and Argentina and later in Chile.

This military junta, unlike that of 1962, remained in power for twelve years. Haya de la Torre died in the interim, and the election of 1980 brought victory to a non-*aprista* candidate. The new president was the very same Fernando Belaúnde who had suffered the *golpe de estado* of 1968. Latin American politics does have its ironies. And there was one more in the case of Belaúnde's second term. He oversaw the rise of a second and far more pernicious guerrilla war, that of the Shining Path (Sendero Luminoso). It prowled the ELN's old territory in Ayacucho and the surrounding departments. Shining Path had no foreign sponsors and lasted twelve years before the armed forces and police could control it. Shining Path's leaders, unlike those of the MIR, came not from the coast but from the highlands. They were men and women who had no foreign military training. They blended with the population of cities and countryside and established few base camps. The group's top leader, Abimael Guzmán, eluded police and soldiers for several years before he was captured.

General Velasco certainly exaggerated when he declared, "Civilians had been ruling Peru for 150 years, but it took the armed forces to make a revolution. . . . The oligarchy is now dead." Obviously, what reforms the generals accomplished after defeating the MIR and the ELN did not prevent the outbreak of the even greater guerrilla uprising of the Shining Path.

CHAPTER TWELVE

From Riots to *Golpe* in Panama

"SEÑOR PRESIDENTE," LYNDON Baines Johnson said via a long-distance telephone call from the Oval Office. "We are very sorry over the violence which you have had down there but gratified that you have appealed to the Panamanian people to remain calm."[1]

He was speaking to President Roberto F. Chiari of the Republic of Panama. This unusual phone conversation between two heads of state occurred on January 10, 1964, following the first full day of riots by Panamanian youths along the unfenced boundary between Panama City and the US-occupied Canal Zone. Johnson had not even completed his second month in office. The so-called flag riots posed the first foreign crisis of his presidency.

Remarkably, the Panamanian president more than held his own in this conversation between unequal powers. "Fine, Mr. President," responded Chiari, "the only way that we can remove the causes of friction is through a prompt and thorough revision of the treaties between our countries." Johnson answered that he understood Chiari's concern and said that the United States also had vital interests connected to this matter. But Chiari did not relent.

"This situation has been building up for a long time, Mr. President," said the Panamanian head of state, "and it can only be solved through a complete review and adjustment of all agreements. . . . I went to Washington in [1962] and discussed this with President Kennedy in the hope that we could resolve the issues," Chiari explained. "Two years have gone by and practically nothing has been accomplished. I am convinced that the intransigence and even indifference of the U.S. are responsible for what is happening here now."

Anti-American protests and violence occurred frequently in the decade of the 1960s. Why did President Johnson consider that this riot in Panama amounted to an international crisis that he had to handle personally? A number of factors explain the importance of Panama to American foreign policy. Johnson had just assumed office following the assassination of the popular John F. Kennedy, who successfully faced down the Russians in the 1962 Missile Crisis. The new president undoubtedly felt that he also needed to prove his toughness in foreign affairs. Moreover, the Cuban Revolution of 1959 and its challenge to American hegemony in the hemisphere raised the possibility that communism might take over another Latin American nation. No sitting president would win reelection if a "second Cuba" occurred during his watch. President Johnson already had his eye on the 1964 presidential election coming in just ten months. Moreover, intelligence reports from Panama were pouring into the White House warning of Castro's agents participating in the violence.

Finally, the continued existence of the American-controlled Canal Zone was becoming a prominent issue in inter-American relations. The Zone itself consisted of a ten-by-fifty-mile swath of land in which about forty-six thousand English-speaking administrators, operators, and military personnel lived. The Canal Zone divided the Spanish-speaking nations of Mexico and Central America from those of South America. To many, the Panama Canal symbolized US imperialist hegemony over the entire hemisphere. The Republic of Panama itself figures as a South rather than a Central American country because it once belonged to Colombia.

Panamanians had become indignant over the long-term refusal of the Americans to fly Panama's national flag in the Canal Zone, a sentiment that sparked the violence. In the original treaty between the two countries, Panama retained sovereignty over the Zone. It merely ceded operational control to the United States. Yet, few Panamanians felt sovereign in their own country. Therefore, when the violence broke out, Chiari immediately suspended diplomatic relations with the United States. Meanwhile, American politicians in Washington, DC, debated what they should do—if anything—to placate the little country that President Theodore Roosevelt had called into being in 1903. This debate was to continue through four American presidencies. Fidel Castro did not prevent resolution. Panamanian "unreasonableness" did not prevent resolution. Rather, the inability of politicians in Washington to fashion an intelligent policy led directly to the *golpe de estado* by a Panamanian military officer who would eventually convince the Americans to give up control of canal operations and the Canal Zone itself.

THE ZONIANS

The Panama Canal Zone divided this republic's capital of Panama City to the east from its secondary cities and its productive countryside to the west. Practically the only national territory to the southeast of the capital was the underpopulated vastness of tropical jungles known as the Darién. Here, dense tropical forests prevented the completion of the famous Pan-American Highway that connects Minneapolis, Minnesota, to the Tierra del Fuego, except through the Darién. Most of the Canal Zone had no fences. However, the Avenida Cuatro de Julio separated the Canal Zone from the commercial district of the capital. Hundreds of Panamanians drove to work on Fourth of July Avenue every day, turning into the unguarded Gorgas Road. There was nothing like Checkpoint Charlie. There was no equivalent of the Berlin Wall, although Canal Zone police officers did stop Panamanians who looked like they did not belong. Military police mounted tighter security at US bases.

Yet citizens of this South American nation experienced the interoceanic canal, reminding them of the presence of a mighty imperialist power in their midst. From Panama City on the Pacific coast to Colón on the Atlantic, they saw the ships sailing in to and out of the canal. On the streets of the capital, Panamanian pedestrians frequently walked past Zonians, the English-speaking employees of the Canal Zone, as well as US military personnel assigned to its defense. These Americans shopped at stores full of Japanese electronics and Indian linens. At night and on weekends, Panamanian national guardsmen patrolled the red-light districts of the capital.

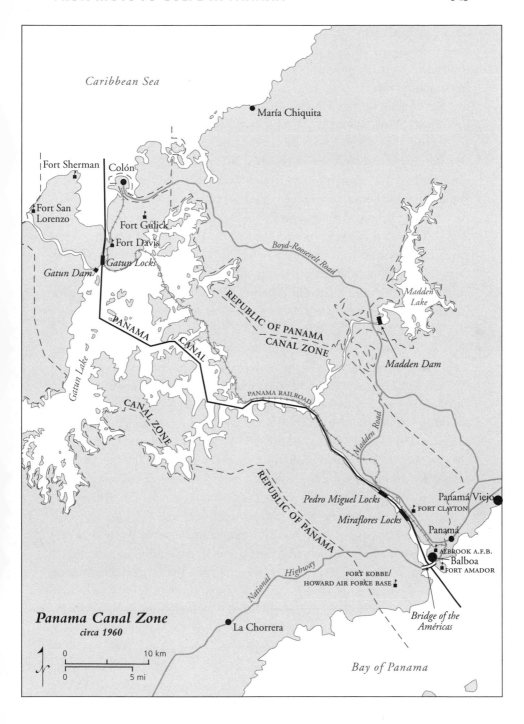

Caribbean Sea

María Chiquita

Fort Sherman
Colón
Fort San
Lorenzo
Fort Gulick
Fort Davis
Gatun Locks
Gatun Dam

Boyd-Roosevelt Road

*Madden
Lake*

REPUBLIC OF PANAMA
CANAL ZONE

PANAMA

CANAL

Madden Dam

Gatun Lake

CANAL ZONE

PANAMA RAILROAD

Madden Road

REPUBLIC OF PANAMA

Pedro Miguel Locks
FORT CLAYTON
Panamá Viejo

Miraflores Locks
Panamá
ALBROOK A.F.B.
Balboa
FORT AMADOR

FORT KOBBE/
HOWARD AIR FORCE BASE

National
Highway

*Bridge of the
Américas*

Panama Canal Zone
circa 1960

La Chorrera

0   10 km
0   5 mi

Bay of Panama

They provided some satisfaction to citizens when they broke up fights between strong-armed, drunken US servicemen. Occasionally, Americans toured the northern provinces and found weekend relief at the beaches or in the mountains.

Most of all, what rankled proud Panamanians was the method by which the United States had acquired the Canal Zone. Teddy Roosevelt stated it succinctly: "I took the Canal Zone and let Congress debate."[2] He meant that he precipitated a revolution there in 1903 after the Colombian government resisted US terms in negotiations over rights to build a ship canal through its northernmost province of Panama. The man most responsible for declaring Panamanian independence was Philippe Bunau-Varilla, a citizen of France. Bunau-Varilla had once worked for the De Lesseps Company. This French construction firm, which successfully had constructed the Suez Canal through the deserts of Egypt, had nonetheless failed miserably at building one through tropical Panama. When the government in Bogotá hesitated to transfer the De Lesseps concession to the Americans, Bunau-Varilla arranged for Dr. Manuel Amador to proclaim the independence of this Colombian province. President Roosevelt dispatched warships to Colón long before the news of the movement even reached Bogotá.

The United States recognized the newly sovereign nation of Panama and concluded a treaty by which it acquired the rights to construct the canal and to manage the newly created Canal Zone "as if it were sovereign." The treaty permitted the United States to lease the 150-square-mile property by paying the Panamanian government $10 million upfront and $250,000 per year "in perpetuity." Bunau-Varilla had acted as chief treaty negotiator, after which he stayed on in Washington as Panama's first ambassador.[3] The entire episode gave new meaning to the French term *fait accompli*.

The Americans came to dominate this new republic of the Western Hemisphere. They built the canal, truly a triumph of ingenuity and industrial technology. In the process, the Americans remade the Hispanic culture of this former province of Colombia by bringing in thousands of West Indian construction workers. They were overwhelmingly English speakers of African descent. By 1914, the canal opened in time for World War I traffic. Many West Indians stayed on as permanent employees—though not supervisors—and lived in segregated housing inside the Zone.[4] Every four years, Washington sent out a new governor, an army general of the Engineering Corps, to run the Canal Company and the Zone.

Anglo technicians moved into the Canal Zone to live in neat communities of tree-lined streets and homes with covered porches and screened windows and doors. Their West Indian gardeners kept the tropical vegetation at bay. Afro-Caribbean women tidied up their homes, cooked their meals, and cared for their children. Canal Zone police officers, recruited in the United States, maintained order. The Zonians had their own schools, clubs, hospitals, restaurants, and commissaries, many of which proudly unfurled the Stars and Stripes overhead. Neighborhoods outside the Zone in the capital of Panama, one visitor said, had "a kind of aimless shabbiness" to them.[5]

The US Armed Forces staffed a full complement of fourteen army forts, air bases, and naval posts around the canal. A four-star general presided over the Caribbean Command and the thousands of military personnel and civilian employees who staffed it. Yet military life, particularly following President Truman's order to racially integrate the armed services, began to differ strikingly from Zonian society. Officers and enlisted men inhabited housing according to rank rather than race, while segregation survived in the neighborhoods of company employees. For the Zonians, daily life developed a colonial atmosphere not unlike that of British India. They may have come from modest social backgrounds in the States, but in Panama they lived like a colonial elite. They stayed in the Zone for their social lives and recreation.[6] And Zonians zealously preserved their privileges.

Owning property did not count among their privileges. The Panama Canal Company owned and maintained the homes in which its employees lived and ran the businesses and shops in which they worked. The United States government had built the canal, and the canal company ran it like a welfare state. Zonians at the same rank received the same salaries. Schools and services were free. Free hospitalization and guaranteed pensions completed the cradle-to-grave benefits that only career military personnel also received.[7] What made the privileges all the dearer to the mainly white Zonians was that West Indians and Panamanians did not qualify for the same lavish benefits.

In 1959, when some eighty armed Cubans led by two Panamanians assaulted the small Atlantic port of Nombre de Dios, some 46,000 people lived in the Canal Zone. Military personnel and their families made up the largest group. Ten thousand active-duty servicemen and 20,000 dependents lived on eight different bases. The Panama Canal Company employed 3,500 American citizens, many for life, who had 6,500 dependents. There was little socialization between the military and the Zonians, the latter of whom felt that the officers looked down on them. Six thousand other employees, mainly West Indians, also lived in the Zone. An additional 9,000 mostly bilingual Panamanians entered the Canal Zone five days a week as nonresident workers.[8]

Panamanians resented the Americans for the wage differential and sought "equal pay for equal work." But they did not apply the same to the Afro-Caribbean workers. The West Indians held jobs requiring menial labor and found no sympathy among the Americans or the Panamanians. Panamanians referred to the West Indians as *chombos*. In the 1950s, the average "gold wage" of the Americans equaled $6,000 per year and the "local wage" averaged $1,300.[9] Some proud Panamanians came to resent the whole arrangement even though they made relatively good livings as canal employees. However, citizens of Panama could do nothing but complain. That is, until 1959.

Did Fidel Castro rile up the Panamanians in that fateful year of the so-called Caribbean War? Of course, he spoke disparagingly about the image of US imperialism that the Canal Zone represented. He did help organize the Cuban-Panamanian invasion at Nombre de Dios of April 1959, though he denied it publicly. However, Panamanians had another example of anti-imperialism besides that of Fidel. Colonel Gamal Abdel Nasser and his fellow army officers had made a coup d'état on the pro-Western king of Egypt, and in 1956 they seized the Suez Canal from its French and British owners. France and England sent troops, which President Dwight Eisenhower opposed. The United Nations intervened and eventually awarded Egypt possession of the Suez Canal with the guarantee of access by ships of all nations. Panamanians followed these far off events closely.

In November 1959, in any case, an anti-American riot broke out along the Avenida Cuatro de Julio. Canal Zone police officers sufficed to secure the main entrance and to post guards at the Tivoli Hotel, where Teddy Roosevelt had stayed on his trip in 1911, and at Gorgas Hospital.[10] It was at Gorgas that army doctors had introduced remedies against the debilitating tropical disease yellow fever, which were first used in the US Army's occupation of Cuba and which they derived from Dr. Carlos Finlay's research there on mosquito carriers. It was to this same hospital that the Americans in 1956 air-evacuated the Nicaraguan strongman Anastasio Somoza, mortally wounded by an assassin's bullet. His sons stayed on to run the country. President Eisenhower, who as an army captain had served in the Canal Zone in the 1920s, sympathized with Panamanian frustrations. Yet he did not entirely control Washington's reactions to the difficulties. He had to share that burden with Congress.

Representative Gordon H. Scherer, from Cincinnati, Ohio, spoke for many in Washington who blamed Panamanian frustrations on Panama's own failures. "If it were not for the Canal Zone and the millions of dollars which it pours into the economy . . . each year, the Panamanians would have some real problems." Scherer additionally iterated that "politicians and agitators, in order to divert the attention of the masses from their own short-comings and derelictions, use the United States . . . as a scapegoat for most of their troubles." Stand firm, the congressman advised President Eisenhower, so that "Panamanian agitators . . . [will] realize that we are not going to be blackmailed."[11] Sage advice to the former Allied supreme commander! Other members of Congress also urged a firm stance. "At no time was there any gratitude expressed for anything done for Panama by the United States," New York congressman Francis E. Dorn wrote to Eisenhower.[12]

RISING RESENTMENTS

Even before the Cuban invasion, Panamanian youth exhibited frustration over the national humiliation of a Yankee-owned strip of land running through the heart of their country. High school and college-aged youth identified sovereignty and national pride with the Panamanian national flag. The first flag incident occurred on May 2, 1958, at the moment that Vice President Nixon was touring South America. A group of students entered the Canal Zone and planted seventy Panamanian flags on the grounds. As the Canal Zone police were removing the display, anti-American protesters lined up along Fourth of July Avenue. Troops from the Guardia Nacional (GN), Panama's police force, confronted the rioters and violence broke out. Nine demonstrators lost their lives.[13] President Eisenhower subsequently sent his brother, Dr. Milton Eisenhower, president of Johns Hopkins University, on a trip to Latin America, including Panama. He was seeking solutions to US–Latin America problems with political leaders. Milton Eisenhower's advice on the flag issue motivated his brother, the president, to defy Congress.[14]

The second flag incident occurred in November 1959. On November 3, Panama's Independence Day, a group of students from the National Institute (a public secondary school) marched into the Zone and ran up a Panamanian flag on the closest flagpole. Canal Zone police responded with tear gas to disperse three hundred protesters. A mob attacked the US embassy downtown and tore down the American flag. However, on this occasion, President Ernesto de la Guardia declined to call out the Guardia Nacional.[15] In this second flag riot, no one died, though one hundred Panamanians sustained injuries.

Finally, President Eisenhower issued an executive order stipulating the flying of a Panamanian national banner alongside every Old Glory displayed in the Canal Zone. The president's directive went unheeded. The Zonians refused to run up the Panamanian flag over their schools, clubs, and shops.[16] For sure, the Canal Zone was not a democracy, and Zonians could not vote for the governor. But the Panama Canal Company did not rule by fiat. Zonians voted absentee in their states back home. Therefore, they could and did correspond with congressmen in Washington, DC, who voted to withhold funding for new flagpoles.[17] The only Panamanian banner fluttered at Shaler Triangle, near the front entrance to the Canal Zone on the Pacific side.

President John F. Kennedy too met resistance from the Zonians. He agreed to reduce the display of the Stars and Stripes to just eight locations in the Canal Zone. Panama's colors would also fly at these eight sites, according to Kennedy's directive. The agreement prevented the Zone's public schools from flying any flag, even the American one. One Zonian brought suit against the display of Panama's flag in the Zone, but American courts tossed it out.[18] Therefore, the flagpole in front of Balboa High stood alone without any flag whatsoever by order of the president of the United States. Patriotic students of military and Zonian families felt deprived of their national symbol. "Children become more American the longer they stay here," said one school administrator, "and perhaps less tolerant. They are prouder than ever of being American because of the contrasts."[19]

The sovereignty issue stood at an impasse when President Roberto F. Chiari, came to the White House in June 1962. Chiari wished to renegotiate the fifty-eight-year-old Canal Treaty. He suggested that the two countries "eliminate the [treaty] clauses that have caused misunderstandings between the two peoples for a great many years." Chiari told his American counterpart that he was convinced that Kennedy could persuade Congress to approve renegotiation of the treaty.

His host expressed little optimism. President Kennedy could not see "how he could demonstrate to two-thirds of the Senate that such a course [would advance] United States interests." On the issue of sovereignty, Kennedy added, the United States recognized Panama's ownership of the canal. We did this in Eisenhower's time, President Kennedy observed; "we are there [only] for operating, maintaining and defending it." Therefore, we should work to reduce the points of friction, such as the wage frustrations of Panamanian employees and the contraband of cheaper goods entering Panama from the Canal Zone.

President Chiari became emotional as he mentioned more serious problems with the treaty. He objected to the phrase "in perpetuity" appearing in the 1903 treaty. He expressed the bitterness of his citizens in not seeing the Panamanian flag flown in their own territory. The Panamanian head of state actually broke down sobbing in the Oval Office. Kennedy could only repeat his reluctance to renegotiate the treaty. He wanted to wait until a committee finished investigating the possibility of retiring the obsolete canal and replacing it with a sea-level canal. The committee had five separate locations under consideration in three countries: Nicaragua, Panama, and Colombia.[20] President Chiari returned home without convincing the one American president—a Catholic no less—most Latin Americans believed in.

Nevertheless, over the course of five months, a binational committee of Panamanians and Americans met to discuss several issues of contention between the two countries. They left aside the big issues, such as division of transit revenues. Moreover, one State Department staffer, Edwin Martin, had to admit "that Canal tolls had not been raised since the Canal opened in 1914."[21] As for the flags, these representatives agreed that the Panamanian national banner should be displayed with the Stars and Stripes at all public buildings in the Canal Zone. These talks dissatisfied President Chiari most of all. He said that the flag concessions did not go far enough. US stalling built up dangerous pressures in Panamanian public opinion, he warned, which "an extremist like Castro" might exploit.[22]

As leader of the aristocratic Liberal Party, Chiari supported the US diplomatic goal of isolating and embargoing Cuba. On taking office in 1960, he "maintained a frankly hostile policy towards Cuba," according to Cuban diplomats. Cuban exile "contrarrevolucionarios" shot at Castro's embassy on three occasions, once while a reception was going on inside. No one was injured. The National Guard also detained the embassy's driver, accusing him of selling marijuana, beating him, and burning his legs with cigarette butts. President Chiari broke relations with Cuba in December 1961.[23] He thought Kennedy would be grateful.

President Chiari suggested that payments to Panama be raised to ten million dollars per year. The Panamanians had some justification for the increase. A later study indicated that the US government was providing shipowners with subsidies of more than one-half billion dollars per year. Transit rates might well be doubled and tripled without loss of traffic, the study concluded.[24] Yet everyone in Washington acted like the Panamanians were ungrateful for such a gift.

In the meantime, Washington was becoming worried that the treaty controversy might incite anti-American agitation. The Panamanian communist party had an estimated 5,000 members out of a total national population of 1.2 million. American agents also knew that party members had visited Cuba, where Castro's intelligence operatives had asked them to spy on US military forces and on ship traffic in the canal. Panamanian communists were not fans of Fidel Castro, it turned out.[25] US agents reported that pro-Soviet communists posed no danger. The old-line communist party was "not directed against imperialism but against the national oligarchy" and specifically against the Chiari government, one CIA report concluded.[26] Among student groups, support for Castro and the Cuban Revolution rose much higher.

Before being kicked out of Panama in December 1961, Cuban diplomats had been in touch with local pro-Castro support groups. Young men and women periodically held rallies denouncing US retribution against Cuba. Members received propaganda tracts from the Cuban embassy. Members of radical student groups approached the embassy hoping to get free passage to Havana on learning and training trips.[27] The lists that the Cuban embassy and the ministry in Havana maintained for radical Panamanian supporters of the revolution conformed closely to those names that the CIA and US Army intelligence had assembled too.[28] Both the Cubans and the Americans identified those belonging to the group called the VAN.

Left-wing militants proved to be much more active against American imperialism than the communist party members. Pro-Castro activists of the clandestine Vanguard of National Action (VAN) had gained control of the university and declared a student strike in August 1962. Members of the Vanguard made Molotov cocktails and used firearms to prevent students from entering the campus for final exams. American observers were using the term "communists" to describe the student militants as well as the older party leaders, as if the same viewpoints motivated both groups.[29] In fact, the communists rejected revolutionary adventurism, and the militant youth embraced it.

President Chiari's invocation of the Castro threat to Panama did not fall on disbelieving ears. American agents were already collecting information on the Vanguard. Their informants provided details like the names of individual members and their travels and subversive training. Here was what the report said about Alvaro Menéndez Franco, the "official VAN representative in Cuba." Menéndez had traveled to Moscow in 1961 and to Cuba five different times since 1960. "His last trip was on 27 December 1962 to 9 April 1963, during which time he received guerrilla warfare training." An older member of the VAN, Pablo Cordero, notably received three years of training in Moscow from 1936 to 1939, the years of the Spanish Civil War. The intelligence listed five other younger members as receiving guerrilla training in Cuba.[30]

Suddenly, in October 1963, a flurry of CIA reports arrived in Washington that the Panamanian revolution would begin early in 1964. The Vanguard collected arms and initiated training activities for its recruits. VAN leaders traveled back and forth to Mexico, consulting with their handlers at the Cuban embassy there. Still others were going and coming from Cuba. Follow-up reports moved up the start of hostilities to coincide with the celebrations of National Independence Day, November 3, which had sparked the riots of 1959. Some activists lobbed Molotov cocktails at the US Information Service building as preliminary actions. US intelligence sources reported that Fidel Castro had been urging rebellion in Panama because it would destabilize the center of American imperialism in Latin America.[31] Yet Panamanian Independence Day came and went without an uprising.

American diplomats, in the meantime, believed that the United States had a good working relationship with the men of the Panamanian National Guard. This force combined police and national defense functions. The Guardia Nacional had its origin in the US policy of Dollar Diplomacy from 1903 to 1933. Two brutal dictators had come from US-trained National Guards—the elder Anastasio Somoza of Nicaragua and Rafael Trujillo of the Dominican Republic. In Panama, however, the Guardia generally refrained from direct interference in the electoral contests among conservative elite families. Only twice did the national police overturn elected presidents. On both occasions, in 1941 and 1951, the victim was the populist leader Arnulfo Arias, who still campaigned for the presidency in the 1960s.

The politics of the officers, all of whom came from the middle to lower-middle classes, contained no discernable ideology. They did not share the elite government's conservative social policies, but neither did they condone the leftism of the militant students. Guardia officers trained at US bases in the Canal Zone and generally supported American policies in Latin America. Because the National Guard was not technically an army, it did not participate in the Military Assistance Program of the United States. Yet by no means was it underequipped. The United States intended for the Panamanians to assist in the defense of the Canal Zone, which, of course, it did well in the April 1959 invasion by eighty Cubans. Also it had suppressed some of the earliest anti-American flag protests.

National guardsmen regularly attended the "internal security" courses given yearly at the Inter-American Police Academy at Fort Davis in the Canal Zone. The United States Agency for International Development (AID) conducted this training. The Guardia's elite Presidential Guard appeared in AID training films sent to police units throughout the Americas. In 1963, the Police Academy held its fourth training course for 127 students from eleven countries. Students received tours of the Canal Zone and Fort Lorenzo, the oldest Spanish fortress under American control. Two guest lecturers made presentations on the counterinsurgency campaigns being conducted currently by the Filipino and Colombian armies.[32] The Guardia Nacional also initiated civic action projects in the countryside and enjoyed popularity among the mixed-race working classes from which it recruited its soldiers. With justification, Washington expected the Panamanian National Guard to form the first line of defense of the canal. Yet, in the 1964 flag riots, the guardsmen never came out of the barracks.

THE 1964 FLAG RIOTS

The lack of progress to negotiate a new treaty aroused the students of the high school and university in the capital city. At 4:30 on Friday afternoon, January 9, two hundred male secondary school students from the National

Institute carried Panamanian flags as they passed on foot into the Canal Zone. They were heading to Balboa High School. A Canal Zone police patrol halted the column one block before it reached its destination. Negotiations ensued. Everyone agreed that five Panamanian youths could proceed with police escort to hoist a Panamanian flag—a banner stained with the blood of "martyrs" of previous protests—on the flagpole in front of the school. Five hundred Zonians gathered around the flagpole, and scuffling broke out between the two groups. An American girl fell to the pavement, and the jostling produced a tear in the Panamanian flag.

The police escort ordered the five Panamanians to retreat back to their colleagues. As the Panamanian students returned to the Fourth of July Avenue, a few stragglers started hurling stones at cars and buildings. By 7:00 P.M., the vice governor of the Canal Zone requested assistance from military police units to help expel the remaining marauders inside the Zone. "From that time on," reported Vice Governor David Parker, "the situation deteriorated." Parker was in charge, because the canal's governor was visiting in the United States at the time.[33]

Radio reports of the afternoon's events soon brought out a crowd of angry Panamanians onto the Fourth of July Avenue, where they rioted through the evening. They stopped cars and set them afire. Other rioters threw Molotov cocktails across the fence into the Zone. Vice Governor Parker went to survey the riot from the porch of the Tivoli Hotel. His car was stoned. By 8:00 P.M., the boisterous crowd had grown to number six thousand Panamanians, several of whom had entered the Zone and were causing property damage. Fifty Canal Zone policemen, practically the entire Pacific side force, had been shooting their weapons into the air with little effect. They could not hold the fenceless boundary between the Zone and Panama City.

In the meantime, the vice governor made several calls to the headquarters of the Guardia Nacional—even to the office of President Chiari—to request assistance in controlling the crowd. No guardsmen ever showed up. If we had arrived to quell the rioting, explained their commander Colonel Bolívar Vallarino, Panamanian citizens "would have accused us of being traitors and anti-patriots." The vice governor had to call on General Andrew P. O'Meara of the Caribbean Command. Armed American troops finally relieved the policemen, chased the Panamanian marauders out of the Zone, and secured the canal side of the Fourth of July Avenue. For the next week, General O'Meara retained command of the entire Canal Zone.[34]

A Canal Zone police captain attempts to halt a delegation of Panamanian students from raising their national flag in front of Balboa High School. This protest drew the world's attention to the American occupation of Panamanian sovereign territory.

Soon the rioters in Panama City turned their wrath on the buildings associated with US interests. Someone drove a car through the front door of the Pan American Building and dropped a match into the gas tank. The resulting fire consumed most of the structure. Arson attacks occurred at the library of the US Information Service and at the American embassy. US servicemen and families living in Panama prudently drove their cars into the Canal Zone for protection, as violence spread to the port city of Colón on the Atlantic side of the canal. Then, late at night and into the next day, snipers from streets and buildings on the Panama side of the Fourth of July fired random rounds of bullets into the Zone. Snipers climbed onto the roof of the Legislative Palace, seat of the Panamanian Congress, located across the street from the Zone's main entrance. The US Southern Command reported that the sniper fire over the succeeding two days amounted to some four hundred rounds and that American troops did not return fire.

This was the situation that prompted President Johnson's phone call to President Chiari. The foreign minister of Panama shared his president's views on these events. On Friday, he cabled Secretary of State Dean Rusk saying that US troops had inflicted "acts of ruthless aggression" on the Panamanians. Panama broke diplomatic relations with the United States and demanded indemnifications.[35] Twenty-four Panamanian citizens and five American servicemen died.[36] Hundreds, mainly Panamanians, were wounded.

President Johnson sent Thomas C. Mann, the assistant secretary of state for Latin America, and a team of foreign policy experts to Panama City. They were to determine the immediate causes of the riots. Mann's delegation made a point of turning over the names of five "known agitators" to the foreign minister and requested that the Guardia Nacional apprehend them.[37] When Mann visited President Chiari in his office in the Presidential Palace, he asked to speak alone with the president. When all their aides departed, Tom Mann told Chiari that US intelligence had determined that "the Castroites . . . have penetrated high positions in his Government and among them were advisors to the President himself." Then Mann added that "Castro would soon be trying to introduce arms into Panama."[38] As the Americans met with Chiari in his presidential office, a crowd of six hundred citizens outside were chanting, "Out with the gringos."[39] Still, none of the Panamanian officials would acknowledge communism or Castro as causes of the riots.

President Chiari demanded the immediate renegotiation of the Canal Treaty. Neither President Johnson nor his team of advisers were inclined to renegotiate the treaty. A *Washington Post* poll had just indicated that 85 percent of Americans agreed that the United States should *not* give in to Panama's demands. Johnson recounted in his memoirs about how he had told Chiari, "I will not negotiate under pressure of violence."[40]

The Southern Command's after-action report saw nothing but communist influence in the Panamanian riots. Military intelligence informed General O'Meara that "55 known Communist leftists, pro-Castroites, and VAN members have been identified as having been involved in the Panamanian violence." Pro-Cuban student leaders had urged on the violence both in Panama City and in Colón. Castroites "engaged in sniper activity." Consistent with "Communist patterns of agitation and violence," the Southern Command reported, Panamanian agitators engaged in "sniping, looting, burning, and hurling of Molotov cocktails." Moreover, many of these known activists had received training "in Cuba or Russia."[41]

Soon thereafter, air force intelligence prepared an additional report that described in detail the connections between Cuba and Panama. It mentioned the places where Panamanians obtained training and where they stayed in Cuba—jungle survival in Punta la Sierra, Pinar del Río Province; small-arms instruction in La Cabaña Fortress on the Bay of Havana; and guerrilla tactics at Minas del Frío in Oriente Province. Moreover, air force intelligence officers had constructed brief biographies of twenty-seven members of the Panamanian communist party and the Vanguard. The information included the precise dates in which each individual underwent travel and training in Cuba, the Soviet Union, and / or the People's Republic of China.

There was the communist Floyd Britton, a twenty-seven-year-old Panamanian of West Indian heritage. Curiously, the air force did not mention his being wounded in the Roberto Arias uprising of April 1959 during the Caribbean War. The document did list Britton's position as youth secretary of the communist party and his participation in the November 1959 student riots. In 1963, Britton joined forces with a terrorist group known as the United Popular Front. Other radicals included Vanguard member Gilberto Velásquez, who "underwent guerrilla training in Cuba 7 August 1962 [to] 26 February 1963. Andres Galvan Lorenzo traveled to the USSR and Communist China 25 September 1960 to 3 January 1961."[42] This intelligence report covered seventy-seven pages and contained specific information on dozens of "communists" and pro-Castro activists.

Back in Washington, members of Congress immediately thought of the Panama flag riots in terms of the Cuban threat. "If there's any one thing that is essential to the economic life as well as the defense of every nation in the hemisphere," Senator Richard Russell told President Johnson, "it is the Panama Canal, and we can't risk having it sabotaged or taken over by any Communist group. And there's no question in my mind . . . that's [Castro's] chief aim there."[43]

The Panamanians themselves attributed the causes of the riots neither to Castro nor to the Communists, as President Chiari forthrightly told President Johnson by phone. Chiari accused the US government of responsibility for the flag riots because it had refused to renegotiate the 1903 Canal Treaty.

VIEW FROM THE OVAL OFFICE

Following the riots, Panama continued to be a topic of concern in the White House. The CIA had sent over a report that the Communists and opposition politician Arnulfo Arias were planning a coup d'état on the Chiari government. A lengthy meeting occurred in the Oval Office in which President Johnson instructed General O'Meara to inform Arias as well as General Bolívar Vallarino of the Panamanian National Guard that the United States would not tolerate a communist takeover of Panama. For the time being, the Americans were placing Arias, because of his populist proclivities, on the side of the Castro Communists. Therefore, the White House instructed the Joint Chiefs of Staff to draw up contingency plans for a military intervention in Panama in the event that a "Communist / Castro oriented government has seized power in Panama."[44] In the minds of Washington politicians, Castro always popped up as the cause of the troubles over the Panama Canal. "I wish to hell . . . Castro'd seize it," Senator Russell told the president over the phone. "Then, maybe, dammit, those people in the State Department and these weepin' sob sisters all over the country would let us go in there and protect our rights."[45]

Johnson rejected the very suggestion that the United States negotiate a new treaty with the Panamanians. He briefed a group of senators at the White House about Chiari's demand for treaty renegotiation. The president regretted "the hell I caused by just mentioning it." Therefore, Johnson refrained from uttering the words "to negotiate" and "revise" the treaties in any discussions with the Panamanians.[46] He told the ambassador to the United Nations Adlai Stevenson that a treaty revision was out of the question. "I've talked to the leading people who would have to consider a treaty and I couldn't find one vote anywhere," said the president. "My honest judgment is I couldn't get 20 votes [in the United States Senate] for any treaty that substantially rewrote the present one."[47]

Later, the president told Secretary of State Dean Rusk that inaction on the part of the United States might bring the Panamanians around. "If you squeeze their nuts just a little bit," President Johnson explained in his downhome manner, "I think that maybe they're more willing to come along."[48] This stonewalling appeared to produce results. The Southern Command reported in March 1964 that "heavy pressures on Chiari are increasing daily from business men and publishers to restore [diplomatic] relations [with the United States] and arrest the economic decline." Laid-off workers were increasingly turning to opposition politician Arnulfo Arias. Though a Harvard-trained medical doctor married to a *rabiblanca*, Arnulfo Arias considered himself an outsider among the aristocracy.[49] His followers proudly called themselves *arnulfistas*, just as Juan Perón's supporters were *peronistas*.

At the time, the United States had its staunchest allies in the Panamanian oligarchy—that is, the very interrelated political families that had produced Presidents de la Guardia and Chiari. However, to continue to win elections, these aristocratic politicians of the Liberal Party needed to demonstrate some progress in treaty negotiations with the United States. American policymakers could do nothing to support their closest allies in Panama. Therefore, serious renegotiation of the 1903 Canal Treaty remained very difficult. It had to be conducted behind the scenes.

Panama's electoral season ended just as the US presidential election was also concluding. The Liberal Party of President Chiari had nominated his cousin, Marco Robles, and the election of December matched the *rabiblanco* Robles against the veteran populist Arnulfo Arias. Robles won the popular vote, and his opponent Arnulfo Arias claimed the election had been fraudulent. On the whole, the American diplomats were satisfied with the election of the new president. "We can communicate sensibly and candidly with [a] Robles government," the embassy reported. "Robles has pledged himself to stand firm against communist agitation, in welcome contrast to his predecessor [Chiari]."[50]

US elections too played a role. As soon as the November 1964 polling results confirmed a Johnson landslide victory, President Johnson instructed the State Department to begin talks on a new agreement if it was possible not to use the word "negotiate." He proposed to reaffirm the country's sovereignty over the Canal Zone and raise payments to the government of Panama. Although events in Vietnam prevented the president from submitting the treaty revisions for a vote in the US Senate, the unsigned agreement would lead eventually to the 1977 treaty concluded between President Jimmy Carter and General Omar Torrijos.[51] Unfortunately for the aristocrats, the eventual treaty came too late to save them. The Liberal Party oligarchs did not realize that Marco Robles would be their last hurrah if he did not secure an acceptable new treaty by the end of his tenure in 1968.

Meanwhile, the US intelligence community kept an eye out for the old master of Panamanian politics, Arnulfo Arias. His political star seemed to rise as the treaty negotiations lagged. The CIA reported that Arias was planning a coup d'état for March 1965. The CIA picked up rumors that he was cooperating with members of the Panamanian communist party like Thelma King and, through her, with Fidel Castro. Arias also had his nephew Roberto Arias conspiring on his behalf in Czechoslovakia.[52] Roberto was the Arias scion who had married the prima ballerina Margot Fonteyn and who had invited the 1959 Cuban invasion. The CIA continued to link Arias, the defeated presidential candidate of 1964, to left-wing forces, suggesting that the veteran populist encouraged student disturbances. Communist leaders in the universities "have repeatedly intimidated politicians, demanded and received audiences with Panamanian ministers and presidents, and occasionally had a direct impact on government policy," reported the CIA.[53]

American intelligence agents did not actually believe that Arias had become a communist agent but only that he might strike a deal with the devil in order finally to get into power. Twice elected and twice prevented by the Guardia Nacional from completing his term of office, Arias felt that he had been cheated by Robles's fraud in the 1964 elections.[54] As leader of the political party the Panameñistas, Arias was determined to take power with the help of student leftists if necessary. Arias's deputies in Congress, moreover, would never accept a treaty that Robles might negotiate with obstinate American officials.

The leftist threat to President Robles actually receded—or so it seemed—as his government made feeble progress on the new Canal Zone treaty. Yet the leftists still agitated. American intelligence analysts speculated that Arias might be able to depend on five hundred members of the Panamanian communist party and an additional thousand sympathizers. "Between 1959 and the present," the Department of Defense reported in 1965, "about 190 Panamanians have traveled to Cuba, behind the Iron Curtain and Red China to train in revolutionary tactics, guerrilla warfare, or . . . communist indoctrination."[55] The CIA also acknowledged that the Vanguard of National Action had split into rival leftist groupings.[56] However, intelligence operatives in Panama did uncover a new pro-Chinese movement among university students that was planning anti-American protests over the US occupation of Santo Domingo in April 1965.[57]

American intelligence analysts explained the political activity of Panamanian students at public schools like the National Institute and the University of Panama with the lack of jobs befitting their education. With a sluggish economy, only the students whose families could afford private education tended to snare the few opportunities. Modest families sent their children to public schools, which, over the years, became overcrowded. The classrooms at the University of Panama accommodated three thousand students comfortably, yet seventy-five hundred students were enrolled there in

1966. More than two thousand additional students took university exten-sion courses. For these reasons, the CIA concluded, the "students are easily manipulated by dedicated and well-organized Communists at the Univer-sity of Panama." Arias and the radicalized students, said a CIA report, might produce a potent threat against both President Robles and US inter-ests in Panama.[58]

The American negotiators, constrained back home by a Congress wedded to the idea of a US-controlled canal, could not give Robles the kind of treaty that Panamanian nationalists demanded. As the 1968 election ap-proached, the ruling aristocracy appeared unlikely to retain control of the presidency—unless the Guardia Nacional once again denied Arnulfo Arias and his supporters. To that end, the United States poured money into ex-panding the National Guard.

In 1966, Panama's National Guard numbered forty-three hundred men. Washington picked up the bill for the first year's expenses of an additional five hundred new recruits. President Robles requested that the American gov-ernment continue to pay the expenses for the new trainees into the second year and also pay the bill for one thousand more recruits in 1967. American taxpayers assumed the cost of the civic action programs of the Guardia in the countryside of Panama.[59]

With United States encouragement and AID funding, the Panamanian National Guard expanded in size. By 1968, the Guardia had grown to number 5,400 men and an officer corps of 235 men drawn primarily from the middling sectors of society. The United States provided most of the pro-fessional schooling and arms for this police force. Approximately half of its enlisted personnel and all of its officers had taken training courses at the AID Police Academy and at the School of the Americas at Fort Gulick on the Atlantic side of the Canal Zone. Panama's future leader serves as a case in point.

Omar Torrijos obtained his commission on a scholarship at the Cadet Academy of El Salvador. Panama had no officer training facility at the time. Thereafter in 1959, Torrijos attended the Jungle Warfare Center at Fort Sherman, Canal Zone, which would subsequently become a major training site for Vietnam-bound American soldiers. Torrijos took preventive mainte-nance and command and general staff courses, all offered at the School of the Americas. He called his course on counterinsurgency "Guerra de Guerrillas," the title of Che Guevara's 1960 book on the subject. Another junior officer who would come to prominence in the military government of the 1970s, Manuel Noriega, also took courses at the School of the Americas. Noriega specialized in military intelligence. Expansion cost money, and the National Guard budget rose from $6.2 million in 1966 to $9.2 million in 1968.[60] American taxpayers footed the bill.

PRELUDE TO A COUP

Lyndon Johnson met his Panamanian counterpart for the first time at the 1967 presidential summit conference of the Organization of American States. Unlike John Kennedy, Johnson had not hosted many heads of state from Latin America at the White House. Instead, the president had been preoccupied with the likes of President Nguyen Van Thieu and Vice President Nguyen Cao Ky of South Vietnam.[61] Johnson needed a break from pursuing his war policies in Southeast Asia and from taking criticism from student protesters and Senator Robert F. Kennedy. "I don't know how to get out and I don't know what to do," he once said about Vietnam to Lady Bird Johnson. In April 1967, the president took off for South America in Air Force One. He had with him his foreign policy team, Secretary of State Rusk, Special Adviser Walt Rostow, and Assistant Secretary of State for Latin America Lincoln Gordon. They were going to the Uruguayan resort city of Punta del Este on the South Atlantic coast. They were to attend the Organization of American States meeting of all the heads of state in the hemisphere but Fidel Castro, who was expelled from the OAS in 1962. These advisers also attended Johnson's private meetings with several Latin American presidents.

President Marco Robles of Panama dropped by Johnson's villa for a chat. The Panamanian president tried to put his American counterpart at ease, speaking to him like "one farmer to another." Three years of treaty discussions had preceded the meeting, and President Robles said Panamanians were not pleased with the result. He wanted to demonstrate sovereignty over the Canal Zone by placing it under the Panamanian justice system. Another issue pertained to Robles's intent to increase his country's share of revenues. He told President Johnson that the national debt was leading the Panamanian economy to a state of "asphyxiation." Therefore, Panama needed a much fairer return on the canal's operations. Finally, Robles wanted to sign a satisfactory new treaty with the United States before his term ended. Failing that, he might not be able "to eliminate the nationalist passions and emotional effects" that might lead to domestic unrest. Presidential electioneering had already begun in Panama for the next presidential race.

"We share Panama's sense of urgency," Johnson replied, and he would talk to his negotiators when he returned to Washington. On revenue sharing, President Johnson said that he assumed it would be based on "traffic volume" through the canal and on "earnings derived from that volume." He expressed his happiness to "review the question of civil justice." Johnson too did not want the Panama Canal negotiations to "drag on" fruitlessly.[62] No doubt, the president had been reading the CIA briefings. They predicted the last remaining conservative democracy of South America would be "hard pressed" in the coming elections. If no new canal treaty was signed, the plutocratic families might not be able to retain control of the government, wrote the analysts.[63]

The differences between the Panamanian and American negotiators were not trivial, especially over revenue sharing. The Panamanians wanted eighty million dollars per year and the Americans were offering only twenty million.[64] The US leader at the treaty talks actually told Rostow that "the atmosphere has got increasingly emotional as the climax" drew near. His counterpart on the Panamanian side told everyone that he would probably have to resign if the Americans did not accept the Panamanian proposals.[65] Nevertheless, three months later, Presidents Johnson and Robles announced that the negotiators had an agreement. Each would present it to their legislators for ratification. But since the Panamanians would receive three-quarters less in revenues than the eighty million they demanded, President Robles hesitated to present it to the National Assembly. Robles's own advisers had found seventy items in the treaty that they wanted to renegotiate.[66] President Robles was backing out.

The treaty impact loomed large in the coming elections. It had not helped that Robles's Liberal Party had chosen his *rabiblanco* brother-in-law, David Samudio, as its candidate in the elections. The opposition *arnulfistas* suspected that the two would commit electoral fraud to keep the presidency within the oligarchy. Everyone knew that a free and fair election would result in a victory for Arias. Robles counterattacked. He placed pressure on General Vallarino, commander of the National Guard, to close down the assembly and relied on the Supreme Court to invalidate the impeachment vote by the legislators. At this point, Rostow told President Johnson that only Vallarino and his National Guard had "the power to enforce a settlement on both sides."[67] Failure might mean bloodshed and a possible military coup.

How would the Guardia Nacional respond to the political standoff? Without expressing a preference toward Robles, General Vallarino ordered troops to surround the assembly building. They prepared themselves to use tear gas, if necessary, to prevent mobs of *arnulfistas* from entering along with a replacement president. Rostow worried that the US-equipped Guardia would drag the Americans into the dispute, yet he saw hope in the fact that the students and "the communists and their allies" had not taken sides.[68] In the end, the intervention of the Guardia proved decisive. Robles managed to complete his term as president, and the party of Arnulfo Arias returned to electioneering as a way to gain power. National Guard officers preferred the aristocrat over the populist. Even American diplomats believed that the president-controlled electoral system would deliver a Samudio victory—by fraud, if necessary.

Robles turned the tables on everyone. He presided over a fair election despite his brother-in-law's vote "irregularities." Out of a total of 309,000 ballots, Arias won by a decisive, landslide victory of 41,000 votes. The next challenge appeared to be whether Arias would be allowed to take office on October 1, 1968. General Bolívar Vallarino promised no interference from the Guardia Nacional. "I will enforce the decision of the constitutionally created National Elections Board," Vallarino said, "and I will not tolerate any act that would void the will of the people."[69] Democracy in Panama hung in the balance.

President-elect Arias did not act magnanimously in victory. Several days prior to his inauguration, he notified General Vallarino that he and five other senior officers would be dismissed from the Guardia.[70] Nonetheless, the inaugural ceremony proceeded without a hitch, and American officials and businessmen sued for peace. They treated President Arias to an elaborate reception on a yacht. Among his first official acts, Arias fired General Bolívar Vallarino. Other senior officers of the Guardia Nacional immediately sounded out the US embassy. We are not fools, one lieutenant colonel told the American military attaché, "and [can] see the handwriting on the wall." American diplomats suspected that Colonels Omar Torrijos and Boris

The National Guard mounted armed troops around the National Assembly to save
Marco Aurelio Robles from losing his presidency to impeachment in March 1968.
His failure to obtain a satisfactory Canal Zone treaty from the United States nearly
ended his tenure in office.

Martínez, both being "strong-minded" and "vulnerable," were directing
the Guardia's opposition to Arias's presidency.[71]

The Americans did not want another *golpe de estado* in Latin America.
The secretary of state immediately wired a message to the ambassador in
Panama City. "A coup in Panama in [the] wake of [the] Peruvian Coup would
be very disturbing." Rusk advised Ambassador Charles W. Adair Jr. to make
it clear that "any coup attempt by GN officers would be very badly received
by the [United States government]." Military assistance to the Guardia Nacional might depend on the outcome.[72] The embassy so informed military
officers on October 10.

Nevertheless, the coup against the newly inaugurated president Arnulfo
Arias got under way on the evening of the very next day. Martínez and his
troops west of the capital rebelled first, provoking Torrijos to do the same.
As troops formed up in Panama City, Torrijos was told by the US Army li-
aison officer that the officer needed to call his superiors in the Canal Zone.
"Like hell you will," replied Torrijos. The colonel ordered his men to lock up

the American for the night, together with a bottle of whisky.[73] Guardsmen surrounded the Presidential Guard at the Arias home. Gunfire broke out but no one died. By 9:00 P.M., National Guard troops controlled the city, the airport, and most radio and television stations. Pro-Arias supporters did not take to the streets, despite the president's plea for his *arnulfistas* to "support the constitutional majority."[74] Arnulfo Arias took refuge in the nearby Canal Zone. He had not even served two weeks as president.

Despite Arias's landslide electoral victory, Panamanians greeted news of his ouster with relative calm. "The coup appears to be headed by Lt Col Omar Torrijos and supported by Major Boris Martinez and Major Federico Boyd," the US Southern Command reported. "Lt Col Urrutia, the newly appointed commandant of the GN, is under arrest." SouthCom further mentioned that General Vallarino had been taken unawares by the coup, which occurred while the former commander of the Guardia was fishing off Las Perlas Islands. The first statements by Secretary Rusk showed alarm and expressions of deep distress. "We have a close relationship with Panama and a stake in the stability of the isthmus in view of our presence there as stewards of the vital Panama Canal," he said. "This coup d'etat must be equally disturbing to our sister republics in the hemisphere."[75]

The Americans soon realized who wielded the real power behind the coup. "Torrijos is the spark plug, most determined, perhaps least civilian oriented, most power-minded" officer involved in the *golpe de estado*, the US embassy reported.[76] The US Army commander at Fort Amador knew Torrijos well and decided to invite him to his quarters for a drink. Their chat turned ugly when Major General Chester L. Johnson suggested that Torrijos return power to President Arias. Torrijos became enraged. He later told his aides that he would "burn the Canal Zone" if the Americans continued to support Arias.[77] Secretary of State Dean Rusk finally intervened. "We should not facilitate any attempts by Arias [to] overturn the junta by violence," he advised President Johnson. "He cannot now be successful and any effort would lead to bloodshed without satisfactory solution."[78]

Not that Torrijos worried about fighting the United States. If the Americans invaded Panama, Torrijos vowed to defend the nation to his last breath. "We could hold Panama City for forty-eight hours," he later told his friend, the novelist Graham Greene. "As for the Canal, it is easy to sabotage. Blow a hole in the Gatún Dam and the Canal will drain into the Atlantic. It would take only a few days to mend the dam, but it would take three years of rain to fill the Canal. During that time it would be guerrilla war."[79] The statement sounded as if it had been uttered by Fidel Castro.

In the immediate aftermath of the 1968 coup, Arias remained a burden for the Americans. He refused to leave the Canal Zone, and his presence nearby gave courage to his supporters in the capital city. They declared a general strike and threatened violence, but nothing happened. The United States government wanted him out nonetheless. So did Colonel Torrijos. He called for Arias's expulsion from the Canal Zone because he was a "threat to political stability in Panama." We can live without US recognition, the junta said, but "Arias' presence in the Zone continually threatened bloodshed."[80] On October 22, eleven days following the *golpe de estado,* ex-president Arias finally boarded a US Air Force flight out of the Canal Zone.[81] His departure marked the end of more than sixty years of civilian political domination of the Republic of Panama.

While Washington still withheld recognition of the new junta, Commander Seddon of the Military Group invited Colonels Omar Torrijos and Boris Martínez to lunch at his home in Panama City. They stayed talking for three hours, and the most powerful Guardia officers in the new junta never once complained about the lack of US recognition. They also responded to American concerns by saying that the junta planned to reinstate civil liberties in due time. The two colonels made the point to remind the Americans that the coup d'état had come off without civilian casualties.[82]

Back in Washington, Special Adviser Walt Rostow suggested to the president that the time had arrived to recognize the government of the junta. Thirteen other Latin American governments representing the largest countries (many now ruled by military governments, Rostow neglected to mention) had already renewed diplomatic relations. The junta had dismissed the only two suspected leftists in the government and restored most civil liberties. Moreover, said Rostow, Arias was using the withholding of recognition by the United States as an excuse to promote "guerrilla warfare" from neighboring Costa Rica.[83] Recognition came on November 13, two months following the *golpe.* The State Department had waited less than one month to recognize the other coup of 1968, that of Peru.

Meanwhile, the CIA estimated (wrongly as it turned out) that the junta would retain power "for some time, perhaps a year," before it would permit elections for a civilian government. Analysts said that "Torrijos himself . . .

has shown no sympathy for the [Communist] Party in the past." Their pre-diction that the junta would "impose rightist authoritarian solutions" also missed the mark.[84]

MILITARY REFORMISM

Colonel Torrijos ultimately promoted himself to general and opted for pop-ulist military reformism on the Peruvian model rather than the reactionary type of Brazil. He and his confederates had just displaced the oligarchy. Therefore, to consolidate power, Torrijos needed to outflank his own military colleagues who coveted the top job. Also he needed to mobilize international support to confront the United States over the canal. To achieve unity at home, Torrijos moved to the left to appeal to workers, peasants, stu-dents, and Afro-Panamanians.

Omar Torrijos consolidated his regime much as Fidel Castro had done. Following the October 1968 coup, the first to go was Colonel Boris Mar-tínez, the doctrinaire anticommunist who also had a puritanical bent. He had actually alienated many pragmatic and corruptible National Guard of-ficers who desired to use their positions for personal gain. These men gravi-tated to Colonel Torrijos as the better alternative. Majors Amado Sanjur and Ramiro Silvera joined Torrijos in disarming and arresting Martínez one eve-ning in February 1969 at GN headquarters. Captain Manuel Noriega later claimed that Torrijos and Martínez had never really gotten along. Martínez could only count on the support of Major Boyd, who subsequently accom-panied him on his military flight to Miami and exile.[85]

Martínez was not the only challenger from within the Guardia Nacional. Following the ouster of Boris Martínez, Colonel Amado Sanjur became chief of staff in recognition for his assistance in arresting his predecessor in that job. But he represented the right wing of the Guardia officer corps. He had attended the Colegio Militar in Caracas, Venezuela, during the time of Pérez Jiménez and continued to admire the Venezuelan military dictator there-after. American intelligence agents recognized Sanjur as pro-American. His wife worked in the offices of the US Information Service. He also took the usual military courses at the School of the Americas—none of which con-cerned counterinsurgency doctrine. They instead instructed him and other

Panamanian officers in staff officers' duties, preventive maintenance, and medical orientation. In the 1968 election, he opposed the candidacy of Arnulfo Arias because he shared a fear of Arias's planned interventions into the leadership of the Guardia. Following the coup, Colonel Sanjur styled himself as an expert on communism and wrote occasionally in the newspapers about his objections to this leftist ideology.[86]

Colonel Ramiro Silvera also received a promotion after he supported Martínez's dismissal. He had attended cadet schooling in Guatemala during the presidency of Arévalo and gained a reputation for opposing the promotion of nonmilitary school graduates. Silvera's officer training did include counterinsurgency and jungle warfare courses, as well as police training in Italy and "traffic control" courses at Northwestern University and the University of Indiana. US intelligence agencies considered him a pro-American as well as a man who "drinks heavily" and "engages in extra-marital affairs." In the latter two proclivities, Silvera differed little from most of his fellow officers—including Torrijos.[87] It bears repeating that the Panamanian military officers had other cultural and training influences than those introduced at the School of the Americas.

Torrijos's coconspirators Sanjur and Silvera perceived an opportunity to maximize their business holdings in December 1969. General Torrijos had flown to Mexico City in order to cheer on the Panamanian horse entered in the Carrera de las Américas, at the Mexico City racetrack. He received a phone call in his hotel room. Two other junta members, Colonels Bolívar Urrutia and José María Pinilla, were calling to advise Torrijos not to return to Panama. "We have decided that you should not come back home again." Urrutia and Pinilla indicated that they represented some Panamanian businessmen who worried about "communists" in the government. "I can't leave this poor country in your hands," Torrijos shouted into the phone. "I'm coming back."[88]

At the time, Major Manuel Noriega commanded the GN base in Chiriquí Province on the western border with Costa Rica. He arranged to guide the secret night landing of the small plane that brought Torrijos in from San Salvador. "The plane flew out over the Pacific Ocean undetected," Noriega testified. "I had ordered jeeps and trucks to be brought down to the landing strip after dark, awaiting the arrival. When we made radio contact, I ordered the vehicles to turn on their lights. The plane landed and I saluted Torrijos as he alighted. There was a cheer from our men: 'Viva Torrijos!'"

Before General Torrijos arrived in Panama City, junior officers moved to detain Colonels Urrutia and Pinilla. Only Torrijos's personal intercession prevented the conspirators from being hanged. All of these December *revoltosos* had been intimate coconspirators of Torrijos since the 1968 military coup d'état against the civilian regime.[89]

However, when he arrived back at GN headquarters, General Torrijos could not contain his fury. While he understood that the American diplomats were not happy with him, the leader of the Guardia Nacional had grown to trust the army men from the 407th Army Intelligence Group, located at the headquarters of the US Army's Southern Command at Fort Amador. Especially Sergeant Efraín Angueira. This intelligence noncommissioned officer had been assigned to Torrijos for many months. Torrijos had told him of the Guardia's unhappiness with President-elect Arias, and Angueira reported to his superiors about the possible coup attempt of October 1968. It was Angueira who was locked up with a bottle of whisky when the coup came off. But, more importantly, Torrijos entrusted the American NCO to house his wife and children at his quarters at Fort Amador during the tense days of the crisis. But now, six months later, Torrijos blamed Sergeant Angueira for not warning him of Sanjur's conspiracy. "He said I was involved in the coup," Angueira said later.[90] The Guardia Nacional began to shut out the officers and men of the 407th.

However, the US agency that had actually put Colonel Sanjur up to the coup attempt was the Central Intelligence Agency. The CIA also had an operations center at Fort Amador, an unmarked, unassuming building a block away from the 407th. Most officers and men at Fort Amador had no knowledge of who or what was inside the windowless air-conditioned building. Yet agents of the CIA developed a jealousy of the 407th now that their clients, the officers of the Guardia Nacional, were running the country. They developed a plan to get rid of Torrijos and offered Colonel Amado Sanjur one hundred thousand dollars to remove him. Not even the new ambassador representing the Nixon White House knew of the CIA's coup plot. "This blew up in my face," Ambassador Robert M. Sayer said later. "Torrijos was furious."[91]

Eventually, the 407th Intelligence Group declined in influence, and the CIA took over. They paid their informants more money, including Torrijos and Noriega, though they failed to save the Panama Canal for the United States. "We had close relations with the CIA for years," Noriega claims, "and both Torrijos and I felt comfortable with the succession of CIA station chiefs posted in Panama City."[92] Each showdown increased Torrijos's hold on power and resulted in quick promotions for his loyal troop commander Manuel Noriega. He had moved up four complete ranks from lieutenant to lieutenant colonel in a little over two years. After his triumph of December 1969, Omar Torrijos and his military government began to lean to the left, purposely cultivating popular support.

Panamanian officers started to travel to South America for courses offered by the military schools in Peru, for example. "It started with Fidel Castro," Omar Torrijos said later. "Suddenly, there was a new orientation. We had more contact with the people. In all the military schools, the orientation changed immediately. After Cuba, there was a preoccupation with social forces in the courses. We studied the case of Cuba . . . social justice. We came to the conclusion that there was a direct relationship between social justice and social violence."[93]

Perhaps the new chief of the Southern Command, General William O. Porter, had these national guardsmen in mind when he lamented the cultural distance between Latin American and US military officers. Moreover, just as military juntas were establishing long-term rule over their nations' governments, American budget cuts for embassies were reducing the number of military attachés by 50 percent. The reductions formed part of Washington's relocation of foreign assets to Vietnam. As General Porter observed, these American officers would be needed "to help the Ambassadors maintain good communications with the Latin American military."[94] Porter did not think that the 1964 Mann Doctrine, whereby the United States recognized military coups without prejudice, sufficed to mitigate the hostility between Latin American and US militaries. "There exists among the military in each country mistrust of the US State Department and the Department of Defense," General Porter said in 1970. "This is almost instinctive."[95]

To officers of the 407th Military Intelligence Group, neither Sanjur nor Silvera seemed much of a threat to Torrijos. "[Silvera] is an ostentatious swaggerer who lacks the capacity to support his presumptuousness," Army intelligence officers concluded, "and Colonel [Sanjur] is only a sincere plodder who lacks the cunning wit necessary to succeed as leader of the GN."[96] Most of the civilian cabinet members resigned when Torrijos returned triumphantly in December 1969. He reappointed four of them, but, as the CIA reported, they no longer enjoyed the confidence that Torrijos had accorded to them before the attempted coup.[97]

The conspirators in the December revolt languished in the fetid prison of the Guardia Nacional in Panama City. In June 1970, however, Colonels Silvera, Sanjur, and another prisoner managed to escape after bribing a sergeant in charge of the cellblock. The Panamanian government communiqué said that the escapees had paid bribes amounting to "large sums of money." They fled with the sergeant directly into the Canal Zone and turned themselves over to American security personnel.[98] The Canal Zone proved to be an ideal escape route for politicians and officers in the political turbulence of the late 1960s.

The CIA took note of the reformist tinge of the Torrijos regime at the end of its first year. Analysts mentioned the moderate land reforms and the expansion of military civic actions in the countryside. But the CIA also corroborated that the regime had moved to incarcerate known agitators and dismiss left-wing professors from university classrooms. The return of strong economic growth had helped Torrijos blame the country's problems on the corruption of aristocratic former politicians. The middle class responded well to his anti-oligarchic political rhetoric. General Torrijos also canceled the American leasehold on the Río Hato training ground in Western Panama. He thus struck a blow for national pride.[99] This became the first round in the eight-year struggle that resulted in the treaty revisions of 1977.

Nineteen sixty-nine turned out to be a busy year for Torrijos. Nelson Rockefeller visited Panama in May 1969 on his Latin American tour for President Nixon. He departed very much impressed with the new military government. Governor Rockefeller invited General Torrijos to visit New York City, which he did just days after the December coup attempt. There, the Panamanian strongman addressed a meeting of American businessmen at the Goldman Sachs financial firm. He did not talk about the coup he had just avoided. But he did invoke the refrains that American investors liked to hear from Latin American leaders. "In short, gentlemen, with a political economy well defined, private enterprise will develop the economy . . . with agile capital markets," General Torrijos told the American financiers. "We know that you frequently listen to these appeals and presentations and, with good reason, many times you are skeptical about what you hear. . . . For this I invite you to come and see for yourselves."[100]

Since independence in 1903, Panama had maintained an enviable record with regard to human rights, on a par with that of Costa Rica, for example. But the coup marked a departure. Officers of the Guardia Nacional dealt harshly with pro-*arnulfista* activists as well as student protesters. Repression, beatings, and imprisonment became quite common against those who spoke out or protested the coup d'état. Communists of the pro-Moscow Party of the People were rounded up and jailed or sent into exile. The guardsmen treated the Maoists even more rigorously. Seven of them were sent to the prison camp on Coiba Island. There Floyd Britton, the Afro-Panamanian student rebel who had participated in the 1959 uprising, which young Captain Torrijos had helped put down, was beaten and starved. He died. Likewise, an activist priest, Father Héctor Gallego, fell afoul of powerful landowners in Veraguas Province. Gallego had organized landless peasants; he was last seen alive in the custody of guardsmen.[101] Noriega became chief of military intelligence in the Guardia in 1971 and guarded the regime from dissenters and conspirators. Human rights reports placed the number of political murders by the regime at thirty-four, a low figure by the standards of the day for Latin American military regimes.[102] The Torrijos government gradually mellowed and preferred social alliances over outright repression.

However, as Omar Torrijos moved to the left, he sought to incorporate members of the communist party into the regime by placing them in charge of popular reform programs. Torrijos even made amends to the students, whom, over the decades, the Guardia Nacional had repressed time and again. He once referred to his own wounds suffered while putting down the 1959 rural revolt at Cerro Tuti. "The bodies of these young, dead guerrillas were not the end of the discontent," he said. "If it were not for the uniform, I would have been with them."[103] Torrijos expressed identical sentiments to the British novelist Graham Greene. "If the students break into the Zone again I have only the alternative of crushing them or leading them," he told Greene. "I will not crush them."[104]

The 1972 Labor Code solidified Torrijos's ties to laborers. Membership in unions proliferated as private sector and government jobs multiplied in the economic boom of the 1970s. The pronouncements about meaningful land reform won many adherents in the countryside, even though commercial landholdings and agricultural exports burgeoned as well as subsistence farming.[105] The Torrijos government also reached out to the previously excluded West Indian descendants, calling them Afro-Panamanians. Torrijos, himself a mestizo, suggested that they formed part of the nation just as much as he did. Several black professionals received appointments to high government positions. Juan Materno Vásquez became minister of the presidency and spoke forcefully for the Hispanicization of black Panamanians through education and assimilation.[106]

However, it took more than economic prosperity and social reforms to bring the Americans back to the negotiating table. General Torrijos used his close proximity to US hegemony just as Castro had been doing. He appealed to the sympathy of the nonaligned world as well as to anti-imperialist sentiments throughout Latin America. Moreover, General Torrijos's tough criticism of United States intransigence toward renegotiation of the Canal Zone Treaty was burnishing the Panamanian leader's reputation as a nationalist.

Relations with Argentina warmed when Juan Perón returned to the presidency in 1973. As it turned out, Perón and Torrijos knew each other. A young Lieutenant Torrijos in 1955 commanded a small force charged with the security of ex-president Perón during his brief exile in Colón, Panama. In fact, during his stay, Perón met María Estella (Isabel) Martínez, a member of an Argentinean traveling dance company who was destined to be his third wife and (on his death in 1974) the first female president in the Western Hemisphere. The affable, relaxed Perón made a great impression on the young Panamanian lieutenant. Torrijos thereafter considered him "America's great leader."[107]

He accepted President Perón's invitation to make a state visit to Buenos Aires in January 1974. Argentinean citizens greeted him enthusiastically, cheering and applauding at the theater newsreels that covered his activities. The leftist youth known as the Montoneros turned out at his public appearances beating their bass drums, jumping up and down, and chanting anti-US slogans. It was becoming clear to bystanders at the time that, despite the enthusiasm, Perón and his motorcycle police escorts were losing patience with the Montonero militants.[108] Despite their mounting political polarization, Argentineans broadly supported Panama's struggle with the Goliath of the North.

Later that same year, Torrijos invited a visiting delegation of Peronist youth to his home for an informal talk. Being anti-America, the visiting youngsters brought up the subject of the School of the Americas. Someone asked about American "indoctrination" of Latin American armed forces "in order to inculcate a mentality of dependence." Torrijos responded by alluding to two officers who resisted such indoctrination: Colonel Francisco Caamaño, leader of the Constitutionalist rebellion in the Dominican Republic, and General Juan Velasco Alvarado, chief of the reformist military junta of Peru. "Well, we send officers there to the military schools of the United States. I am a product of [the School of the Americas] also," he said. "Cáamaño came from there. Velasco Alvarado also. It is not easy to indoctrinate a man—especially us, because we have [the schools] here within our own fatherland."[109] Here Torrijos alluded once again to the ability of Latin American military officers to chart their own way despite what appeared to be overwhelming subservience to US tutelage.

Most telling of all, the reformist government of General Omar Torrijos reached out to Fidel Castro. By the early 1970s, Fidel had become the link to African and Asian votes in the United Nations. Since December 1961, the Cuban Revolution had no diplomatic relations with Panama. But Panamanians had traveled to the island, and some even trained there. In the 1960s, the Guardia Nacional had little tolerance for the communist party or for student radicals. Yet frustration at the slow progress of canal negotiations motivated Torrijos to enlist assistance from the Non-Aligned Movement now led by Fidel Castro. Panama began a secretive trade with Cuba in US spare parts and commodities that violated the American embargo. Torrijos sponsored students and labor leaders to exchange visits with their Cuban counterparts. Foreign ministers did so as well.[110] Fidel spoke to Panamanian students in Havana, and Cuban *universitarios* came to Panama to attend a conference held at the University of Panama commemorating the twentieth anniversary of Castro's attack on Moncada Barracks.

Torrijos hosted a breakfast for the latter delegation of Cubans at his Río Hato military headquarters. Torrijos talked principally about Cuba's assistance to Panamanian peasants. He thanked his guests for sending a team of agronomists to Panama. Torrijos told them, "I had some ideas about agricultural reforms, but I had doubts about putting them into action." After talking with the Cuban technicians, he was able to confirm those ideas. It gave Torrijos the confidence to put his plans into action. He also spoke about dealing with Nixon's treaty negotiators, who "treated the [Panamanians] like the Viet Cong." However, he took solace in Panama's successes at the United Nations, where the Yankees had just lost a major vote.[111]

The diplomatic breakthrough came in 1974, when Panama and Cuba once again exchanged ambassadors. General Torrijos made his first trip to Havana in 1975. After signing the Canal Treaty of 1977, Torrijos returned to Cuba for the Non-Aligned Nations Conference. Unlike many reformers in Latin America, Torrijos balanced alliances with Castro and with Wall Street. The former linked his regime to other emerging countries of Africa and Asia—and votes in the United Nations.

America's investment banks, meanwhile, provided the economic growth he needed to secure the backing of peasants and workers without alienating the middle class. Torrijos did not confiscate or cancel contracts with foreign companies like other reformers in the region. Instead, his government wrote up brochures in English inviting foreign businesses. Three selling points could not but appeal to capitalists and to "modernization" economists in the US government. Panama touted its open economy with bank reforms in 1971 that accepted unlimited infusions of foreign capital. The one-to-one convertibility of the dollar to the Panamanian balboa assured investors that Brazil's style of inflation would not wreak havoc there. The City Bank of New York (Citibank), Bank of America, Chase Manhattan, and some eighty other US, Asian, and European financial institutions conducted operations in Panama.[112] Skyscrapers dramatically changed the cityscape of the nation's capital.

Given this expansive community of supporters, Omar Torrijos proved himself a much tougher negotiator than the Americans had previously encountered. Attending one of his first meetings with the American envoys, led by the diplomat Robert B. Anderson, General Torrijos seemed bored by the small talk. He interrupted and said bluntly, "Let's get to our problem." Thereupon, chief negotiator Anderson launched into a long preamble emphasizing the opposition of Congress to a new Canal Zone treaty. We need flexibility and half measures, Anderson said. We cannot go from full US control of the Canal Zone "to zero" in one treaty agreement. Above all, Anderson added, we must avoid "mob violence" that "would be extremely damaging to Panama's interests."

General Torrijos replied that some of Panama's youth were talking of fighting the Americans. "Ho Chi Minh had fought the colonialists twice and achieved great successes." Torrijos said that he thought "good will" could solve problems, but it was not easy to persuade Panamanians. Many people say that "good will had not achieved anything since 1964 and patience [is] wearing thin."[113]

Torrijos found supporters in the United States. Besides Wall Street, Hollywood offered another in none other than John Wayne. The movie star spent an afternoon with the Panamanian strongman in March 1973, after which he promptly fired off a letter to another friend, Richard Nixon at the White House. "I found [Torrijos's] attitude most congenial toward us, willing to be helpful if we wanted to invest in their country—quite a contrast to our other neighbors. Signed, Duke."[114] Still, Richard Nixon stalled on canal negotiations. So did Gerald Ford after him.

President Jimmy Carter took the Canal Zone situation seriously. He sent his secretary of state, Cyrus Vance, to handle the final rounds of negotiation with Torrijos. No stranger to Panama, the veteran diplomat Vance had actually visited President Chiari with Tom Mann's delegation during the flag riots of 1964. Vance's new role pleased Torrijos. The general had remembered when Cyrus Vance and the other Americans entered the Presidential Palace through a phalanx of angry hecklers. "It is a good thing that Vance is Carter's Secretary of State," Torrijos said. "He was in Panama City when the rioting began and we had to smuggle him out of his hotel into the Zone, so he knows what a Panamanian riot can be like. He was a very frightened man."[115] The treaty that Torrijos and Carter signed at the White House in 1977 provided that Panama would come into full possession of the canal on the first day of the third millennium in 2000. And so it did.

Panama represents a case in which the military establishment had depended on the United States for arms, equipment, and training. The Guardia Nacional could not match the power of the American armed forces stationed at military bases located but a few kilometers from its headquarters. Nevertheless, GN officers defied the Americans by not protecting them from Panamanian rioters in 1964. Four years later, they ignored the warnings of American diplomats and US military attachés. They defied the US embassy in bringing about the downfall of a conservative oligarchic regime dependent on US backing. Once in power, a junta president who had trained at the School of the Americas renewed diplomatic relations with the communist government of Cuba and sold proscribed US goods to Fidel Castro. Torrijos actually visited Havana in 1975 at the same moment that Castro had Cuban troops fighting in Angola against CIA-backed forces.[116] Finally, General Torrijos proceeded to mobilize international pressures to force Washington to renegotiate a treaty against the wishes of the White House, the US Congress, and American public opinion. Panama—the poster child of dependency or of the limitations of hegemony?

"I'm not interested in going down in history," General Omar Torrijos was fond of saying. "I just want to go into the Canal Zone."[117]

CHAPTER THIRTEEN

Origins of Argentina's Armed Struggle

NEWS REPORTERS NAMED them "Uturuncos" after the nom de guerre of the guerrilla leader who, in 1959, began the insurrection in Argentina's western provinces of Tucumán and Salta. "I read about the triumphs of Fidel Castro, the mountains, the oppressed people there," exclaimed one guerrilla, "and I said: 'We can do this.'"[1] Indeed, the parallels to Cuba are striking. A group of young men in their teens and twenties hiking up to encampments in the foothills, a surprise attack on a rural police station to secure arms, supplies and sympathy coming from the local families, and foot marches in the rain—all these resemble tactics utilized by Castro's guerrillas in the Sierra Maestra. The fighters of Tucumán and Salta also reflected a national Peronist resistance movement germinating fitfully since 1956.

In October 1959, this faction of the Peronist opposition decided to act. Members of the Peronist Youth in Tucumán who called themselves the Comando 17 de Octubre chose to raise the resistance to the level of armed conflict. Leaders of the Uturuncos came from provincial families whose fathers worked on the Mitre Railway connecting Tucumán to far-off Buenos Aires. Their national unions became powerful well before the rise of

Colonel Juan Perón as labor minister in 1943. The railroad workers received the best pay in the country and enjoyed travel privileges and dining halls along the rail lines that other workers could not equal.[2] They prominently supported Colonel Perón. Tucumán's workers took pride in participating in the nationwide general strike of October 17, 1945, that sprang Colonel Perón from military detention and vaulted him to the presidency in the 1946 and 1952 elections. The children of these workers subsequently grew up on a steady diet of loyalty to Perón. Whether their families had *gringo* (European immigrant) or *criollo* (mestizo) origins, they constituted what passed for the middle class in northwestern Argentina. Sons and daughters of railway workers were able to study at the University of Tucumán.

The youth of Tucumán shared this history of union militancy. The eastern plains of Tucumán formed the cradle of the sugar industry, and many locals there depended on cutting cane and working in the sugar mills. Workers also came from Bolivia and Paraguay to cut cane. Fathers and older brothers of the youthful guerrillas belonged to the pro-Perón sugar workers union, which did not match the railway unions in national importance but mattered locally. Both the railway and the sugar workers unions had participated in strikes against President Arturo Frondizi's policies that froze wages and fired excess workers.

Moreover, *tucumanos* identified with the lore of the interior plains and Andean foothills. One leader, Juan Carlos Díaz, took the name Uturunco, which in the indigenous Quechua language means *tigre,* "mountain lion." Another leader who hailed from Salta Province, Félix Serravalle, assumed the nom de guerre of another feline hunter of the Andes, Puma. Just as guerrillas of Cuba's Sierra Maestra protected their identities with battle names, so did the Tiger-men. They called each other Rulo, Iván, El Tano, Búfalo, Polo, Azúcar, León, El Mexicano, Toto, Pocho, and Negro. They demanded Perón's return to Argentina, as well as the cadaver of "the protectress of the humble," Eva Duarte de Perón.[3] The military's 1955 coup d'état had exiled Juan Perón and "disappeared" the body of his deceased wife.

The Tiger-men pulled off only one successful operation. They executed a well-planned attack on a police station in Farías, a city of twenty-five thousand people in Salta Province. The operation replicated on a small scale Fidel Castro's 1953 attack on Moncada Barracks—except that no one died. The Uturuncos collected a few guns and dressed in military uniforms. As did Castro, they chose a day of local celebration, in this case Christmas morning of 1959. Arriving at the Farías *comisaría* (police station) at 4:10 A.M., they advanced into the building through the front and rear entrances. The Tiger-men used a Castro-like subterfuge that referenced current rumors of a military coup against President Frondizi. "The revolution has triumphed!" they shouted. "We come to take charge." The few sleepy guards and desk cops on duty that morning quickly surrendered and were escorted to a holding cell. The attackers took uniforms and small arms from the *comisaría,* shouting "Comandante Uturunco, mission completed! Viva Perón!" and driving off in a car and a stolen truck.[4] Arriving back in Tucumán Province, they pushed the getaway vehicles into a ravine and began to climb up toward El Callao Peak. Meanwhile, the summer rainy season had arrived.

But the Tiger-men, hungry and wet, had already begun to descend from the mountain and return to their family homes. Their parents beseeched the provincial police to treat their teenagers with leniency.[5] The authorities rounded up many of them without firing a shot, and the local magistrates eventually released most of the apprehended rebels as a gesture of magnanimity.

Their adventure ended in a whimper by June 1960, when the remaining Tiger-men fled to Bolivia. Puma, Uturunco, and a few other captured leaders spent time in jail. The next elected president, Arturo Illia, freed them in the amnesty of 1965.[6] Nevertheless, like Castro in 1953, the Tiger-men had announced the arrival of armed rebellion on the national scene. Politicians were starting to take note. The administration of Arturo Frondizi had alienated the expectations of the democratic left in Argentina. His anti-union economic policies and subservience to military pressures accomplished much in convincing the new generation of youth that the popular vote could not bring about needed reforms.[7] Within a decade, armed insurrection would absolutely define Argentina's political crisis.

Why did some Argentinean youth increasingly resort to armed insurrection in the 1960s? The decision of young men of the Uturunco to become revolutionary fighters probably typified the attitudes of many Latin Americans of this generation. They longed for change yet were not certain that they personally wanted to engage in armed struggle to accomplish it. It took more than Cuba's revolutionary example and training to mobilize young people. That many eventually did take up arms testifies to the human toll produced by Argentina's fifteen years of political unrest following the 1955 coup that sent Perón into exile. Economic stagnation, middle-class frustration, working-class unrest, military intransigence, and the country's ideological heritage all played roles in the evolving political crisis of the 1960s.[8] This analysis only suggests that the historian cannot discount the larger cycle of revolution and reaction that Castro's triumph of 1959 had set in motion within Latin America.

While some university students engaged in armed resistance, one should not conclude that disaffected middle-class youth carried the heaviest load in the Peronist movement. Actually, the working class had borne that burden. Resistance from below originated in the factories and industrial suburbs in Buenos Aires and Córdoba as well as in the ports of Bahía Blanca and Rosario and in the sugar mills of Tucumán. Towns up and down the lines with railway workers seethed with animus toward a military that kept their hero Juan Perón in exile. Rank-and-file laborers felt no respect for Radical politicians, who would have lost to Peronist candidates in open elections. In the early 1960s, workers more frequently clashed with police than did university students. The rank and file chose younger militants to replace union bosses who collaborated with Perón's political enemies in power. Laborers formed commando groups that engaged in sabotage and bombings. In September 1959, working-class militants committed some 106 acts of terrorism in Buenos Aires.[9] If anything, student radicals took more inspiration from the Argentinean working class than from the Cuban Revolution.

PERÓN'S MAN IN HAVANA

John William Cooke attended the University of La Plata, graduating with a law degree in 1943. The rise of Colonel Perón with that year's military *golpe* gradually caught the fancy of John William, now in his mid-twenties. He appreciated Perón's politics of appealing to the masses and his stand against US meddling in the 1946 presidential election. He won congressional elections as a Peronist. Cooke made himself useful to Perón with his forceful oral and written defenses of government policies. He helped write the 1949 Constitution that allowed for President Perón's reelection to a second term in 1952.

Once the 1955 military coup forced Perón to flee from Argentina, Cooke became even more important. He was one of the ex-president's designated *dirigentes,* "directors." John William directed the opposition to the military's exclusion of the Peronists from public life. Meanwhile, the Conductor, as his followers called Perón, remained in exile. Cooke played an important role in negotiating the secret accord between Perón and Frondizi. Keeping the military in the dark, the Conductor ordered his loyalists to vote for the Radical candidate. As president, Frondizi was to permit Peronist participation in national politics.[10] Cooke would later turn against Frondizi, especially for his pro-US policies.

Always a nationalist, John William Cooke adopted anti-imperialist doctrine as early as November 1959. He was already linking Peronism to Cuba's developing ideology. "The struggle for liberation is revolutionary as well as national and social," he said. "Peronism constituted an authentic political, economic, and social revolution."[11] Cuba's leaders did entertain some doubts about the revolutionary credentials of Perón. After all, the former president of Argentina spent nearly all of his exile in countries ruled by right-wing dictators—Stroessner of Paraguay, Pérez Jiménez of Venezuela, Trujillo of the Dominican Republic, and Franco of Spain. Perón's itinerary hardly pointed to revolutionary proclivities.

However, Cooke worked to pull Perón further to the left. The Conductor grudgingly accepted the developing Argentinean left wing as possibly useful for his own return to the country. Therefore, the CIA had good reason to keep up surveillance of Cooke. He and his wife, the poet and leftist activist Alicia Eguren, made their first trip to Havana in 1960. They found themselves detained by Cuban security on advance reports about Cooke's "fascist" background. As he awaited his fate in the airport security office, Cooke decided to sit down at a table with his portable typewriter. Someone from behind touched him on the shoulder and said, "What's going on, Cooke? Are you in the clink?" It was El Che.[12]

Cooke and Eguren's presence in Havana accomplished much to change Perón's image among Cuban revolutionaries. They circulated among the revolutionary leadership, voicing approval of armed resistance and anti-imperialism. Cooke attended the youth conference that celebrated the 26th of July holiday of 1960 along with fifteen hundred *jóvenes* from all over the world. He wrote to Perón that he took the opportunity to correct many of the misconceptions in Cuba that Peronism had fascist leanings.[13] Cooke also mentioned that Fidel's speech to the conference had announced that "the Cordillera de los Andes will be the Sierra Maestra of the American continent."[14] In other words, social revolution was coming to South America. Eventually, Cooke and Eguren joined the Cuban militia, took some training, and deployed with their unit during the Bay of Pigs invasion. They did not see action, but the Argentinean visitors partook of the revolutionary victory with their fellow *milicianos*. Cooke subsequently obtained a university teaching position.

John William's correspondence from Cuba helped bring Perón around to accepting support from the Latin American left. Cooke emphasized that Peronismo and the Cuban Revolution had anti-imperialist antecedents, shared the same friends, and drew opposition from the same enemies. Fidel Castro began to speak well of Perón, and the latter responded in kind. "They called us fascists in 1943, Nazis in 1946, and communists in 1955, even though we were not anything else but good Argentineans wanting to liberate our land," the Conductor wrote in 1962. "It is logical that now Fidel Castro and the patriots that accompany him are also called 'communists' ever since they dared to speak the truth, to liberate their people, and to hold the firm decision to defeat their true enemies."[15]

For Cooke, Havana represented "the revolutionary Mecca." As Cooke wrote to Perón, "Cuba is the obligatory passage of hundreds of men of all continents who come to learn, whether as triumphant revolutionaries, as representatives of peoples in the struggle, as members of parties or movements that seek to throw themselves into the fight."[16] Both Cooke and Alicia Eguren acted as magnets to draw visitors into the revolutionary orbit of Che Guevara. "Alicia was a kind of front-line explorer fishing for Argentineans, who were then sucked up into the sorcerer's cave," Ciro Bustos observed years later. "¡El Che es mío!" she told him.[17] Che is mine.

Cooke transmitted the 1962 invitation of Fidel Castro for the exiled Perón, as the "authentic leader" of the Argentine nation, to take up residence in Cuba.[18] However, the Peronist *dirigente* Cooke may have overplayed his hand. Perón refused to meet him on Cooke's next trip to the ex-president's home in Madrid. Then the missile crisis intervened, giving pause to some Peronists who worried about the unsavory impact of Cuba's close alliance to the Soviet Union. Perón neither accepted nor refused Fidel's invitation. John William Cooke lost his status as a Peronist *dirigente,* and his correspondence with the Conductor tapered off. Nonetheless, his writings and his work in Havana continued to nurture the Argentinean left.

FROM HAVANA TO MONTEVIDEO

Cooke's leftist Peronists set up headquarters in Havana and Montevideo, attracting Argentineans to both cities. In 1962 alone, approximately five hundred Argentineans had traveled to Havana to experience the revolution firsthand. Cooke also maintained an apartment in Uruguay with his wife, whom the CIA identified as a "terrorist" and "guerrilla recruiter."[19] Fidel told Cooke that Argentina ranked second after Venezuela in Cuba's plans for revolution. CIA informants in Madrid were reporting that Juan Perón had received the equivalent of US$750,000 via Cuba in support of the revolutionary struggle in the Southern Cone. Peronist operatives moved back and forth between Uruguay and Argentina. The left wing in Montevideo was engaging in pro-Castro propaganda, which its members had smuggled into Argentina.[20] At the time, American security agents equated Peronism with Castro-communism.

The CIA station in Montevideo kept a close eye on the "Left-Wing Peronists and Argentine Terrorists." Its agents discovered a high level of cooperation between these and security agents in the Cuban embassy. Philip Agee admitted that the CIA in Uruguay actually found itself outnumbered. The Soviet embassy had sixteen intelligence officers, and Agee suspected that most Cuban diplomats and the journalists of Prensa Latina were also enemy agents. "Czechoslovakia, Poland, Bulgaria, Hungary, Romania and Yugoslavia also have diplomatic missions in Montevideo," he wrote. Moreover, the immigration police at the international airport refused to share passenger lists with the CIA, because they had contraband operations to protect. On top of it all, the CIA's workload increased in 1964. Two *golpes de estado* in Brazil and Bolivia in 1964 contributed additional political refugees to the hundreds of Argentineans and Paraguayans already living in Montevideo.[21] The city festered with coffeehouse conspiracies.

United States diplomacy achieved a small victory in Uruguay—when the government broke relations with the Castro regime in September 1964. The domestic left wing predictably reacted with violence. Students rioted at the University of the Republic, taking over several buildings on campus; leftists planted bombs at the business offices of the First National City Bank, General Electric, and Coca-Cola. A crowd of several thousand demonstrators turned out to bid farewell to the Cuban diplomats at the airport and ended up in a pitched battle with police.[22]

The anti-Yankee outbursts in Montevideo reappeared in the very next year. The US military invasion of the Dominican Republic provoked street demonstrations and attacks on American businesses and on the embassy. "Opposition to the [Dominican] invasion is a popular issue," CIA agent Agee wrote.[23] Secretary of State Dean Rusk personally fell victim to Uruguayan outrage. On an official visit in November 1965, Rusk was laying a wreath at the statue of José Gervasio Artigas, father of Uruguayan independence. Three hundred police officers were protecting him at the site. "Suddenly a young man slipped through the cordon and ran all the way up to Rusk, expelling an enormous wad of spittle in the Secretary's face," according to Philip Agee's eyewitness account. The police beat up the young man, putting him in a coma.[24]

Taking refuge in Montevideo in the early sixties proved every bit as stimulating to anti-imperialism as being in Havana. Uruguay lacked the Peronist tradition, it was true. But populist reforms of the early twentieth century had already established Uruguay as Latin America's most advanced welfare state. A large percentage of the population depended on government employment. Yet the executive branch wielded considerably less power than all other presidents of Latin America. The army and police force rivaled those of Costa Rica in their small numbers and reluctance to intervene in politics. (The generals finally did take over, but not until 1973.) Uruguayans also tolerated outside dissidents and honored human rights. At the same time, Uruguay was experiencing many of the same pains of populist maturation as Brazil and Argentina. The state had grown large and inefficient. Economic dynamism declined as politicians rejected the liberal export-oriented policies that had made Uruguay progressive before World War I. Uruguay also held the dubious distinction of reaching triple-digit inflation before most other South American countries.

These national conditions led Uruguay to develop one of the more successful urban guerrilla movements in Latin America—the Tupamaros. Their legendary leader, Raúl Sendic, a young socialist law student, found much inspiration in the Cuban Revolution. He left university in order to organize the long-oppressed sugar workers in the north and the west. Sendic organized unions among these rural proletarians, who then went on strike for higher wages and for rights to the fields. Much of his activity mirrored that pursued by Brazil's reformer Francisco Julião and Peru's Hugo Blanco in the early 1960s. "Raúl [Sendic] was a person of very few words who listened a lot but when he spoke, you listened because he did not speak nonsense," said one labor supporter. "I always say that thanks to Raúl I knew my rights."[25] But often his followers gained little more than dismissal from their jobs. When Raúl Sendic and his closest followers abandoned rural labor organization for armed resistance, they moved to the city. Uruguay contains no mountainous terrain where they could follow the Cuban example.

Sendic and his acolytes had adopted the name of "Tupamaros" after the indigenous leader Túpac Amaru, whose uprising of 1789 paralyzed the Spanish colonial order in highland Peru and Bolivia for several years. Not many Uruguayans went to Cuba for training. "By far the most significant Cuban efforts in Montevideo have been put into the recruitment of Argentines for guerrilla training," a British diplomat reported.[26] Nonetheless, the Uruguay youth did take inspiration from Che Guevara's speech at the University of the Republic in 1961. The twenty-year-olds who joined the Tupamaros in 1970 referred to Che's visit by the date of his talk—"the 17th of August 1961," or simply "17-8-61."

The CIA suspected that this group of militants had begun a series of bombings intended not to cause casualties but to demonstrate opposition to US involvement in the Vietnam War.[27] The police responded with torture. Plainly, the halcyon days of Uruguayan tolerance for domestic dissent and political refugees were waning as the Tupamaros became a nuisance to the weak government. The police even started to harass members of labor unions and the Communist Party, which might have sympathized with yet did not join the urban guerrillas. Foreign leftists came under suspicion.[28] The Tupamaros were becoming a force in Uruguay at a time when Peronist exiles were losing Montevideo as a sanctuary in their battle for Argentina.

COMANDANTE SEGUNDO

On a crisp winter day in June 1963, a band of five armed men crossed the Bolivian border into a sparsely settled zone of Salta Province. Four were Argentinean and the fifth was a Cuban, the Sierra Maestra veteran Hermes Peña. These were the men whom Che Guevara had trained in Cuba to commence his revolution in Argentina. They identified themselves as members of the Ejército Guerrillero del Pueblo (Guerrilla Army of the People, or EGP). Its commander was Comandante Segundo, the journalist Jorge Ricardo

Masetti. The EGP's war chest consisted of some fifty thousand US dollars, and each officer carried on his person some two thousand US dollars and also local currency for emergencies.[29] The money facilitated the acquisition of supplies without alienating the local population. The expedition aimed to plant one in a series of guerrilla uprisings in many countries that would present Yankee imperialism with a coordinated Latin American revolution.

One of the group, Ciro Bustos, went on to Buenos Aires and Córdoba to coordinate the recruitment of an additional thirty guerrillas from a number of radical groups in Argentina. Almost none of these had undergone training in Cuba. One such group consisted of the Gramscian intellectuals who founded the journal *Pasado y Presente* in Córdoba, the home province of Che Guevara.[30] These *cordobeses* agreed to form an urban support group to provide recruits and supplies to EGP guerrillas. A few members of the Communist Party volunteered, but no one from the Peronist left. Che had not informed its leaders, John William Cooke or Alicia Eguren, of his plans and did not favor having Peronists in his guerrilla group. "They are very infiltrated [by police informants]," he said.[31] Only a few of the hundreds of Argentineans who had traveled to and/or trained in Cuba participated in the Guerrilla Army of the People.[32]

Only the Cuban peasant Hermes Peña was familiar with living in the countryside. Later, a recruit asked Peña why he was risking his life to fight in Argentina. "If El Che is in Cuba," replied the Cuban, "why shouldn't I be here? Why not give back to El Che that which he did for us?"[33] Che had instructed them to establish a camp at a remote farm purchased for guerrilla training. They were to stockpile locally secured arms and equipment. The recruitment of the local peasantry would begin upon Che's arrival to take command. "The comrades who came did not once walk through the countryside or the Hills of Córdoba," one survivor testified. "Therefore, I say that there was a poor selection process in the sense that no one knew the physical and athletic capacities of the recruits."[34] Two of the recruits were secret agents of the federal police. They had previously infiltrated leftist groups in Buenos Aires, just as Che had feared.

This guerrilla *foco* had poor timing. A mild-mannered country doctor from Córdoba had just assumed the presidency. Arturo Illia of the Radical Party had received only 25 percent of the vote; the Peronist blank votes totaled 19 percent. Illia's government performed ineptly, but it was not rule by the hard-line generals. It was not repressive. Even so, Comandante

Segundo proceeded to announce the presence of the EGP. He wrote a communiqué that his *guerrilleros* intended to liberate Argentina from international imperialism and its Argentine allies—the armed forces, the landed oligarchy, and an Illia government. Masetti sent his message to a leftist publication in Buenos Aires, but the public reacted with scant excitement. Not even the nation's army responded.

Within a few months, Comandante Segundo decided to toughen up his thirty new guerrilla fighters by undertaking forced marches into the thickets of the wilderness area. In separate incidents, two of the youngest recruits exhibited some "deviant" behavior—homosexuality in one case and homesickness in the other. Once, while near a reconnaissance target on patrol, the recruit known as El Pupi "began to play the fool," the Cuban Hermes Peña wrote in his diary, "and we had to disarm him." Comandante Segundo ordered his trial and execution soon thereafter in November 1963.

Another new recruit subsequently angered Masetti because he lagged behind on patrol and isolated himself in a profound depression. "Nardo had been tried and condemned to death," Hermes noted in his diary. "I was chairman of the tribunal."[35] Both were Jews and sons of bourgeois intellectual parents, dedicated Trotskyists from Córdoba. The hint of anti-Semitism in Masetti's behavior reflected his youthful affiliation with the Argentinean right wing.[36] The executions outraged some of Comandante Segundo's men who were out on maneuvers at the time. "You don't execute a man for masturbating in his hammock," one *cordobés* survivor, Héctor Jouvé, said later.[37] Shortly after this second execution, the guerrilla band began to unravel.

In February 1964, authorities in Salta Province sent an eight-man patrol of the rural police into the remote area where locals had reported the presence of suspicious outsiders, possibly smugglers. Young men with beards dressed in military uniforms reportedly were using cash to purchase supplies. Comandante Segundo had divided up his guerrilla force into several smaller units for work details. The two police infiltrators created dissension and fled from the group, only to fall into the hands of the eight rural policemen. Four of the rural police advanced to the site where a few guerrillas were setting up camp. Policemen captured two combatants, while others fled only to end up in the arms of the remaining members of the Salta police. Two other guerrillas decided to run away back home; one succeeded, and the other was apprehended by police. Finally, the small patrol, now reinforced by another handful of rural policemen, stumbled on the main camp and se-

questered all the arms, ammunition, and food supplies stored there. Comandante Segundo and about twenty others were left stranded, virtually incommunicado, in separate areas of the wilderness.

Over the course of the next month, the guerrillas wandered through the
selva seeking food and refuge and finding little of either. Three of these died
of hunger. All told, a total of thirteen fell into the hands of police with little
or no resistance and spent several years in jail. Three others died in firefights
with the police, one of whom was the Cuban Hermes Peña. What happened
to Jorge Ricardo Masetti, Comandante Segundo, remains a mystery to this
day. He and one unfortunate recruit had taken flight through the *selva* in
possession of the group's cash funds, amounting to twenty thousand dollars. Neither their bodies nor the money was ever recovered. As Héctor Jouvé
said, "I think that [Masetti] had many talents for diplomacy and politics,
but I could not see him as a military chief."[38]

Guerrilla recruiter Ciro Bustos was visiting Córdoba at the time. He
picked up the local newspaper to read that the border police had raided the
camp of a group of *guerrilleros* in Salta. His heart sank. When Bustos got
back to Havana for the postmortem, Che told him to begin all over again.
"Put your plan into action."[39] Indeed, other schemes for armed resistance
were already under way in Argentina.

LA TACUARA

As a teenager, José "Joe" Baxter adhered to the dogma of Catholic nationalism and hostility to the "dictatorship" of Juan Perón. He became an important leader of the Argentinean right wing, composed of Acción Católica
activists, wealthy elites, and military officers. The ultraconservatives (as well
as the leftists and Radical opponents) did not view Juan Perón's rule from
1946 to 1955 as authentic democracy. Instead they equated Peronism with
demagoguery, whipping up the fickle masses with denunciations of the
landed oligarchy and the Catholic Church. The right in the 1950s called
Perón a dictator, despite his electoral majorities approaching 60 percent of
the vote. Baxter and his coreligionists celebrated the military's *golpe de
estado* of September 1955, the so-called Revolución Libertadora, as a return
to democracy. Like John William Cooke, Joe Baxter was also the son of Irish
immigrant forebears.

Baxter was twenty-one years old when he and Alberto Ezcurra Uriburu founded the right-wing action group called the Tacuara. In the Mapuche language, *tacuara* refers to the battle lance that mounted Indian warriors used to terrorize Spanish-speaking settlers on the Pampas. Ezcurra had family ties to General José F. Uriburu who, in 1930, led Argentina's first military *golpe* of the twentieth century. Police officers tolerated even the unlawful activities of the Tacuara because they shared its ideas and honored the Uriburu family.[40] In the turbulent years following Perón's 1955 ouster, Tacuara militants at the University of Buenos Aires fought pitched battles against leftist students with fists, clubs, and pistols. When Celia de la Serna, the mother of Che Guevara, gave a talk in 1961 at the university, a melee broke out between the right-wing and left-wing students, and she escaped unharmed when a few were able to enforce a brief truce. Later, Alberto Ezcurra and an associate went to her apartment house and shot up the outside wall with some twenty bullet holes.[41]

The Tacuara particularly sought to prevent the return of Juan Perón to Argentina, which placed them at odds with the majority of the working class. Right-wing youth did not oppose making a revolution in Argentina, but it would align itself neither with the United States nor with the Sino-Soviet Bloc. "We have sympathized with the Cuban Revolution as far as possible," said Alberto Ezcurra. "At present we consider that Cuba has changed only to another Imperialism." Members of the Tacuara wanted a Catholic revolution because they believed that religion formed the "historical essence" of the Argentinean nation.[42] A Catholic Argentina would not be subservient either to the Kremlin or to Wall Street.

These right-wing university students disliked the pro-US foreign policies of President Arturo Frondizi. They even took the side of union workers employed by foreign-owned enterprises. In January 1959, thousands of laborers seized one of the largest state-owned meat processing factories, or *frigoríficos,* in protest against Frondizi's proposed sale of the plant to foreign capital. Tacuara militants mobilized to support labor's nationalistic defiance. They even went into the streets to join Peronist workers in a forty-eight-hour general strike. Fifteen hundred police officers forced their way into the *frigorífico* and jailed hundreds of the striking workers. President Dwight D. Eisenhower's subsequent visit to Argentina, in which he intended to demonstrate overdue US support for democratically elected presidents such as Frondizi, also drew public opposition from Tacuara militants.[43]

Above all, the *tacuaristas* stood for nationalism. One of his followers once asked Alberto Ezcurra, "The Troskyites say I'm a reactionary and the reactionaries call me a Troskyite. What the hell am I?" The Tacuara leader replied, "You are a nationalist."[44] When Prime Minister Fidel Castro came to Buenos Aires in May 1959, the Tacuara took little note. Although still suspicious of socialism, Joe Baxter was one who gave the Cuban Revolution the benefit of the doubt. Then, in 1960, Castro's government seized all properties belonging to the foreign interests. Shortly afterward, Baxter and his Tacuara associates attended the university talk given by the visiting president of Cuba, Osvaldo Dorticós. "This is the nationalism that I want for Argentina," he told a friend.[45] The Cubans took note that the revolution had greater support among students than any other group in Argentina.

The young men of the Tacuara particularly despised Argentina's Jewish population and blamed them for socialism and communism. Joe Baxter and his friends took solace in breaking windows of Jewish grocers and haberdashers in the Buenos Aires neighborhood of Plaza Once. Israel's Mossad agents scandalized the young men of the Tacuara. In the aftermath of the Mossad's capture in Argentina of the fugitive Nazi war criminal Adolf Eichmann in May 1960, militants sought revenge. They shot and wounded a Jewish student. "¡Viva Eichmann!" they shouted. "¡Judíos a Israel!" These anti-Semitic antics attracted some seven thousand adherents to the Tacuara in the early 1960s.[46] Rightist youths extolled the virtues of Mussolini, Hitler, and General Francisco Franco as well as the supremacy of the Catholic religion. Some critics referred to the *tacuaristas* as "half monks, half soldiers."[47] Still splintered and factionalized, many youth organizers on the left became envious of Ezcurra and Baxter for their capacity to gain public attention.

Joe Baxter began to exercise more intellectual curiosity than his coleader, Alberto Ezcurra. In coffeehouse conversations with priests who worked in the poor shantytowns, Baxter began to soften his attitude toward the exiled Juan Perón. After all, Perón had taken control of the railways and meatpacking plants from British owners. Perón too had admired Mussolini, welcomed former Nazis to Argentina after the war, and defied North American imperialism. Thus began the long journey of many—but certainly not all— *tacuaristas* from opposing Peronism to supporting it. Baxter's faction of the Tacuara drew closer to the nationalistic anti-imperialism they saw in Castro and Perón, while the supporters of Ezcurra Uriburu remained closer to Catholic nationalism.

The Baxter faction within Tacuara began slowly to move toward the center when Joe's followers acquired money to finance their travel and political activities. In August 1963, they robbed a bank of fourteen million pesos and gunned down two guards. The robbery also drove them into the clandestine lifestyle of militants. Alberto Ezcurra broke publicly with the Grupo Baxter. He denounced them as the idiots of Marxism. "You, little reptile," wrote Ezcurra, "are on a road that will end your low-life crime-ridden career with an affiliation in the Communist Party."[48] In trouble with the police, Baxter and his close associates took sanctuary in Montevideo, that haven of political refugees. Joe Baxter also came into contact with Raúl Sendic and the Tupamaros at the moment that the Uruguayan leader was making the transition from a rural labor organizer to urban guerrilla leader. The slide leftward accelerated when El Grupo Baxter joined in opposition to the US military interventions in the Dominican Republic and Vietnam. The exiles started listening to the protest music of Joan Baez and Bob Dylan.

In Uruguay, Joe Baxter fell in with the Peronist financier Héctor Villalón. The latter reputedly held the Cuban concession for selling Cohiba cigars in Europe. According to his police dossier, Villalón dedicated himself to financing trips to Cuba for "Trotskyist militants." Baxter eventually traveled to Spain, where Villalón introduced him to Juan Perón himself. "A fantastic man," Perón said following his chat with Baxter. "He seems capable of making the revolution all by himself."[49]

Baxter and some of his colleagues traveled to Beijing for training in rural guerrilla warfare. One colleague later reminisced about the China trip. It began with travel around the country and finished with two weeks of military training. "The routine was: get up early, military formation, running, this kind of thing, but at 10 in the morning you put your ass in the chair studying Marxism."[50] Baxter did not have an audience with Chairman Mao, but he had heard an anecdote from a friend. In it, Mao says that if he had been born in Argentina, he would be a *peronista*.[51] The Baxter *tacuaristas* formed a new association of militants that they called the Tacuara Revolutionary Nationalist Movement. Its members adopted an internationalist perspective and sent members to visit Havana and Beijing.[52] They avoided going to Moscow.

Finally, Baxter made his way to Cuba for military training. He took a course in combat leadership, called the *curso de comandantes*. Baxter took additional combat training and qualified as a shooting instructor for other

Latin Americans. He never did meet his countryman Che Guevara, because the revolutionary was then serving in Africa (as only a few Cuban leaders knew). But Baxter did meet a Guevara collaborator, the Bolivian-born journalist named Ruth Arrieta. She had reported on Guevara during the latter's visit to Punta del Este for the 1961 Economic Ministers Conference. She followed him back to Cuba, where she found work at the international radio station. Ruth Arrieta and Joe Baxter eventually married and lived together in Havana. Marriage did not end the radical career of Joe Baxter, for he would help organize the last rural *foco* of Argentina.

ARMED PERONISTS

The failure to return Juan Perón to Argentina spawned several small armed resistance groups made up of middle-class students. These supplemented the shop-floor unions having the same purpose. Roberto Quieto ultimately became the most important leader among the armed Peronists. As a law student at the Universidad de Buenos Aires, he received a US embassy travel grant to study comparative legal systems in Miami and New York. The group of ten students on the trip with Quieto included the future president Carlos Menem. Quieto took advantage of his travel to the United States in 1960 to take a side trip to Cuba. This was the year in which Soviet vice premier Anastas Mikoyan visited the island and Castro nationalized first the foreign oil companies and then the sugar mills. "[Quieto] returned dazzled," his widow later told a journalist, "more than dazzled, fascinated."[53] While completing his studies, Quieto became active in leftist politics, becoming a member of Argentina's Communist Party. Quieto attended that 1961 talk of Che's mother, Celia de la Serna, which ended in violence between leftists and the *tacuaristas*. Fellow students gave Quieto credit for escorting de la Serna to safety.[54]

Quieto received an invitation to participate in the delegation that traveled to Cuba in 1966 for the Tricontinental Conference. Some took military training courses and, as they remembered later, received vague instructions to be ready to join a future insurrection. Back in Argentina, they stockpiled arms, but the summons to action never came. Quieto's former colleagues, informed by subsequent events, believe that Che was planning to call them to Bolivia in 1967.[55]

Eventually student leftists came to support Perón as the only answer. At first, Argentinean youths may have regarded the Cuban Revolution with indifference. News dispatches from Havana written by Jorge Ricardo Masetti and Rodolfo Walsh helped to change the attitudes of many Peronists. Che's denunciations of the Alliance for Progress at Punta del Este also inspired. Then a man of impeccable links to Peronism, the *dirigente* John William Cooke, also challenged his countrymen to contemplate the example of the Cuban Revolution. Cooke and his wife, Alicia Eguren, founded the Peronist Revolutionary Action, whose acolytes received Cuban guerrilla training in 1962.[56] Among these were two men who would be instrumental in fashioning the most important Peronist action group of the 1960s, the Peronist Armed Forces, or FAP. They were Gustavo Rearte and Raimundo "El Negro" Villaflor. Both had been among the three hundred Argentineans who attended Che's Gran Asado.

Rearte and Villaflor became involved in throwing bombs and creating disturbances. Rearte paid for his activism with numerous jailings and beatings by police. In 1964, he helped organize the FAP.[57] Subsequently, Rearte joined the Argentine delegation for the 1967 OLAS conference in Havana. Later that year, ten men of the FAP finished a six-month course in guerrilla warfare. Néstor Verdinelli trained with them.[58]

In the meantime, Argentinean police uncovered an arms smuggling operation in Tucumán that was preparing for another, separate rural *foco* to be set up in that province. Vasco Bengoechea may have agreed to open up yet a third uprising among union militants in the southern industrial neighborhoods of Buenos Aires. Their separate operation came to naught in July 1964 when Bengoechea (who had debated El Che at the Gran Asado) and nine others blew themselves up while making bombs at a safe house.[59]

There developed a number of militant groups increasingly mobilized by the repression of the military dictatorship of General Juan Carlos Onganía beginning in 1966. The armed forces returned to power during an economic crisis. Onganía was creating that which the military sought to repress—leftist insurrection and labor resurgence. The junta wasted public support on a campaign against immorality. Kissing on the street became suspect, and the news kiosks could no longer sell pornography. Police officers harassed young women who wore miniskirts and young men with long hair. Onganía's son-in-law assumed leadership of the morality campaign. "Many inhabitants of the country," Colonel Enrique Green announced, "are ill with a contagious disease, immorality." He intimated ominously that "undesirable people" might have to be eliminated.[60]

Onganía especially directed his morality campaign at the universities. "It is the intellectuals who are the protagonists of subversion, not the masses," one Catholic theologian informed the military. "The national universities are today the central headquarters of the communist ruling class within our country."[61] The generals brought in right-wing rectors to shake up the faculty and administrators. They fired leftist professors and summoned the police to crush student protests. Onganía was alienating the youth of middle-class origin. For the first time, university students began to identify with the political champion of the poor, Juan Domingo Perón. They perceived that those who opposed Perón also were repressing the universities. Moreover, sons and daughters of working-class families were enrolling in secondary schools and universities in unprecedented numbers, so any government repression of students affected more than just middle-class families. The radicalization of Argentina's youth quickened in the late 1960s.

The Onganía junta did not make headlines so much for its innovative economic policy as for its repression of students and professors. The general admired Brazil's hard-line military regime and sought to emulate it. Soon after he seized power, the police surrounded several faculties of the University of Buenos Aires and ordered students to vacate the classrooms. This intervention violated the law of university autonomy. Therefore, many students and their professors barricaded themselves in the classrooms as dusk approached. A visiting professor from the Massachusetts Institute of Technology remained inside when the police fired tear gas and charged into the classrooms with gas masks and batons. "As we stood blinded by the tear gas against the walls of the classrooms, the police . . . began hitting us," Professor Warren Ambrose told a reporter. "Then one by one we were taken out and forced to run between rows of police spaced about 10 feet apart. That was when I got seven or eight wallops and a broken finger."[62] The police detained more than two hundred students and faculty. The *New York Times* ran a story about the incident, which became known as the Night of the Long Sticks, a euphemism for police batons. The dictatorship's repression made it easier for militants to recruit for the armed resistance.

In 1968, one group of *fapistas* finally entered into combat with a Che-like rural uprising at Taco Ralo, a rugged area "of low vegetation and spiny shrubs" in Tucumán Province. Fourteen members composed the *guerrilla,* among them Verdinelli and others who had just returned from Cuba. Their adopted motto, besides those demanding the return of Perón, gave away the Cuban influence of the Taco Ralo group: *¡Patria o muerte! ¡Venceremos!* But they also demonstrated their determination to succeed: *Caiga quien caiga, cueste lo que cueste.* (Whoever falls, whatever the cost.) The guerrillas had just established an encampment and went on an unarmed reconnaissance march into the wilderness. Before their return, a neighboring peasant noti-fied the local police about the *muchachos extraños* camped nearby. The rural police, always on the lookout for smugglers, sent out a patrol of one hun-dred men that captured the unarmed guerrillas without firing a shot. On that very day, September 19, 1968, the intellectual author of the armed re-sistance, John William Cooke, died of cancer in a Buenos Aires hospital.[63]

After one year in prison, the remaining ten jailed members of the FAP's Taco Ralo *foco,* including Néstor Verdinelli, explained their philosophy. They declared that the Peronist Youth favored "socialist forms of production" and the "creation of the new man." The FAP obviously had adopted Che Gue-vara's vision of a continent-wide solution to Latin America's problems. Just as the United States dominates all the other republics of the Western Hemi-sphere, so the struggle for liberation must be pursued simultaneously in many countries, the Taco Ralo communiqué said. "Total liberation can only be a product of the defeat of imperialism on a continental level."[64]

The Argentinean left was adopting the program of Che Guevara, who had just died in Bolivia while expecting his *paisanos* to join him there. Other *fapistas* back in Buenos Aires regrouped. They commenced their urban guer-rilla movement late in 1969 with two assaults on the police stations in suburban Greater Buenos Aires. The second attack garnered a cache of weapons, which the group utilized for additional armed actions.[65]

From his Spanish exile, Perón considered these leftist followers committed to armed insurrection with some trepidation. He encouraged them because their violent acts might hasten his return to power. His youth movement had developed Cuban linkages, and they did not demonstrate the same def-erence as did his labor leaders. As long as the military repressed Peronism, the Conductor nurtured the left within his movement.[66] "As you know very well," Perón wrote to the Fuerzas Armadas Peronistas, "the moment is now for the fight, not for political dialectics, because the dictatorship that afflicts the Fatherland has not given up its violence but commits ever greater vio-lence."[67] Perón encouraged the FAP but did not trust it.

Younger workers, in the meantime, had also begun to embrace the Juan Perón of their parents. A new generation of workers in the 1960s came around to Peronism because they saw themselves as disenfranchised. The reactionary junta made labor bear the brunt of economic stabilization. In the auto factories of Córdoba, managers reduced wages and fired Peronist activists. The junta's modernization schemes provoked a backlash among factory workers. The jobs were good, but even those who kept them could not prevent inflation from reducing purchasing power.

The events of May 1969 in Córdoba marked the beginning of the end for General Onganía's "Argentinean Revolution." When their employers extended the workweek by four hours with no additional pay, a group of metal workers held a rally. They marched into the downtown area in defiance of police barricades. Students at the Universidad Nacional de Córdoba joined the march. The protesters seized control of the city center, setting fire to the offices of multinational corporations like Xerox and Citroën. Army forces descended on the city and drove the protesters back into the university and working-class barrios. The uprising's toll included fourteen deaths, hundreds of wounded, and the arrests of at least one thousand protesters.[68] The Cordobazo weakened public confidence in the junta. "This man who had been chosen by his peers because of his great capacity for leadership, for command, for decisiveness, turned into another man," observed a fellow military officer. "The impact of the Cordobazo on [Juan Carlos] Onganía was not ordinary, it was greater than the ordinary; he was visibly impaired inside."[69]

The FAP began to cooperate with other armed groups as the rebellion against military rule gained momentum. Roberto Quieto's armed group launched a spectacularly coordinated operation in 1970. Governor Nelson Rockefeller arrived in Buenos Aires on a goodwill tour for the Nixon administration. His family owned a chain of modern grocery stores in Argentina called Minimax. The Peronist combatants firebombed thirteen Minimax supermarkets in a matter of hours while Rockefeller was meeting with the new junta chief, General Alejandro Lanusse. After the attacks, the Rockefeller family sold the Minimax chain to an Argentinean financial group.[70] In time, these militants of the Peronist Youth became fused to Latin America's largest urban guerrilla group. Yet, the Guevara-style rebellion in the countryside still attracted militants.

Rioting by workers and students known as the Cordobazo challenged the military rule of General Juan Carlos Onganía and inspired subsequent resistance from the armed left in Argentina.

SANTUCHO, THE LAST RURAL FIGHTER

The *foco* theory meshed well with the revolutionary tradition of the Andean province of Tucumán. Rebellion in the countryside came naturally to Argentina's Northwest, where cities were not large, and the majority of residents made a living from agricultural exports and subsistence farming. Roberto Mario Santucho, known as Robi to his friends, remained true to his *noroeste* roots. He belonged to the generation mobilized politically by the 1955 Revolución Libertadora and the Cuban Revolution. In his late teens, Santucho took obligatory military training as a conscript airman in 1957. He became a paratrooper and an expert marksman who competed in national shooting tournaments. As an accounting student at the University of Tucumán, Santucho subscribed to a Trotskyist philosophy of union militancy. He helped organize sugar workers.

Santucho also won a traveling fellowship for study at Princeton and Harvard, an experience that accomplished nothing to change his ideological predilections. He wrote home to his family about "the inexorable decadence of the empire, the farce that capitalist development contributes to the welfare of the majority." On the return trip from the United States, Santucho took a detour to Cuba. He arrived just days before the Bay of Pigs invasion in April 1961. The subsequent six months he spent in Cuba confirmed Robi's political convictions. "On seeing the miserable life of our Latin American brothers and the beautiful future that Cuba shows," he said, "my desire to work for the revolution has multiplied."[71] Another student fellowship to study in the United States backfired on its donors.

For Robi Santucho, his struggle began with the foundation of a political party, the Revolutionary Party of the Workers. Together with other Argentinean visitors to Cuba, the party devoted itself to providing legal assistance to workers. General Onganía's *golpe* made peaceful protest more difficult and armed resistance more logical. The failure of the sugar workers' strike in 1967 proved that political organization alone would achieve nothing. The economic modernization of the 1960s in rural Tucumán resulted in the closure of several sugar mills and the destitution of hundreds of families. Men, women, and children marched on the town of Bella Vista to protest the firing of excess workers at the local mill. When someone in the crowd tossed a homemade bomb, the provincial police responded with gunfire, killing one woman. The protesters regrouped and pushed their way into the police station and took control of Bella Vista. On the following day, police reinforcements arrived to break the strike. Thereafter, Roberto Mario Santucho began to advocate armed resistance, a decision that cost him some defections from Peronist moderates.

Robi's selection to participate in the Latin American Solidarity Organization (OLAS) came at a propitious moment in his transition from political to armed struggle. This 1967 conference in Havana served Fidel's purpose of unifying the left and stimulating multiple revolutionary outbreaks while Che was engaged in his Bolivian venture. John William Cooke again chaired the Argentine delegation, as he had for the Tricontinental conference of the previous year. For OLAS, Cooke selected leftists such as Juan Carlos Coral of the Socialist Party and Alcira de la Peña of the Communist Party. His delegation also consisted of a who's who of Argentina's guerrilla movement. Future Montoneros Norma Arrostita, Fernando Abal Medina, and Emilio

Maza attended. Juan García Elorrio, who dropped out of the Catholic seminary to edit the influential journal *Critianismo y Revolución,* represented Argentina's movement of the Third World priests, or *tercermundistas.*[72]

While in Cuba, many Argentineans undertook guerrilla training at the time of the OLAS conference. For security reasons, names were not used in the training camps; trainees answered to code names. A rare Chilean trainee—rare because Fidel respected the peaceful (electoral) road to revolution of his friend Salvador Allende—took the same guerrilla courses. He counted upward of thirty trainees from Argentina. The Chilean came from a socialist party background and did not get along with the Argentineans. The latter had strong Peronist, nationalist, or Catholic backgrounds. One ordained priest (perhaps the ex-seminarian García Elorrio) trained alongside his *paisanos* from Argentina. These men and a few women, too, took classes in "marksmanship, explosives, homemade artillery, urban fighting, mapreading and other arts of irregular war."[73] One might suppose that the Cuban trainers wanted these Argentineans to join Guevara in Bolivia.

During the OLAS sessions, Santucho met the ex-fascist Joe Baxter, and he also chatted briefly with two of the tallest men in attendance, Fidel Castro and the Brazilian guerrilla theorist Carlos Marighella. Not only did the attendees have an opportunity to meet each other, but also they conferred at length with Manuel Piñeiro, alias Redbeard, and other members of the Americas section of the Cuban Interior Ministry. Che Guevara was conspicuous for his absence at both the Tricontinental Conference of 1966 and the OLAS conference in 1967. However, it was common knowledge among the 350 delegates at OLAS that Che was making the revolution.[74] The highlight of the conference came on the last night when an announcer read again Che's letter of April 1967 to the Tricontinental. "Hay de crear dos, tres . . . Vietnam." The Argentinean attendees especially were moved.

Many received news of Che's death in Bolivia as they were completing their final field maneuvers in October 1967. Che Guevara's demise permitted Juan Perón finally to say something positive about this Argentinean-born revolutionary. The Conductor called Guevara "a hero, the most extraordinary youth that the Latin American revolution has produced" and "one of ours, perhaps the best."[75]

After the conference, Carlos Marighella remained in Cuba until June 1968. While he was undertaking guerrilla training, the Brazilian Communist Party rescinded Marighella's longtime membership. The Brazilian radical responded that he had no wish to be associated with "that faculty of fine arts," indicating that Marighella would not renounce armed struggle.[76] A squadron of São Paulo policemen ambushed and killed the fifty-seven-year-old guerrilla leader Carlos Marighella in November 1969. He left behind his booklet *A Mini-Manual for Guerrillas* as a primer on urban warfare for the armed insurrectionaries of the 1970s.

Most importantly, the Revolutionary Tacuara's Joe Baxter, the former "half monk, half soldier," established a warm friendship with the anticlerical Santucho. Together they formed the most radical of all Argentine guerrilla groups, the Revolutionary Army of the People (ERP). The ERP would take up guerrilla warfare in the countryside, ironically at a time when Che's death and also the defeat of the Venezuelan rebels had tarnished the theory of the rural *foco*. Marighella's Brazilian followers, the Tupamaros of Uruguay, the Chilean MIR, and—largest of them all—the Montoneros in Argentina came to dominate the urban wave that typified the 1970s.

Comandante Che's death in October 1967 came as a shock to leftists all over Latin America. It may have dampened the spirit of the Venezuelan fighters, but it increased the resolve of Santucho. "He was our Comandante," said Robi. "Now he inspires us to follow his example, take up the rifle until conquering or dying for the socialist revolution in Argentina."[77] In 1968, Santucho traveled back to Cuba with three colleagues and took additional training in combat arms. Thereafter, he and Joe Baxter journeyed together to seek additional ideological training in Trotskyism at the Fourth International Conference in Paris, there to bear witness to the seizure of the Sorbonne by Daniel Cohn-Bendit's student radicals.

Back in Argentina, Robi planned and carried out the successful robbery of a provincial bank, yielding more than two hundred thousand dollars for weapons and equipment. Baxter went on to spent time with his Bolivian-born wife and daughter in Santiago de Chile during the presidency of Salvador Allende. He collaborated with the armed youths of the MIR and prepared a Chilean sanctuary for Robi's guerrillas from neighboring Tucumán.[78] In this manner, Baxter made himself the foreign minister of Argentina's guerrilla movements, having nurtured relations with leftists in Cuba, France, Brazil, Uruguay, and Chile.

In 1970, Santucho, Baxter, and other militants considered linking forces with the nascent group known as the Montoneros, whose younger leaders

they met at the OLAS meeting. Ultimately, they rejected such an association for ideological reasons. The Montoneros had Catholic, nationalist,
Peronist, and right-wing origins. The *erpistas* subscribed strictly to Marxism-
Leninism and Trotskyism with an internationalist outlook. Although neither
Baxter nor Santucho had attended the Gran Asado of 1962, Manuel Gaggero of the ERP remembered well Che's speech at that national day celebration in Havana. The People's Revolutionary Army remained committed
to Guevara's ideals. "General San Martín and Comandante Che Guevara
are our maximum examples," said the ERP's charter.[79] With these origins,
the *erpistas* sallied forth into the foothills of Tucumán to meet the fate of
most rural uprisings. In the meantime, the urban fighters that Santucho and
Baxter refused to join succeeded in mounting the most serious revolutionary
threat in all Latin America since the Sierra Maestra.

LOS MONTONEROS

The terroristic turn that Argentinean youth took in the late 1960s had as
much to do with their nation's economic downturn and military repression
as with the Cuban Revolution. A whole new generation of militants came
forth who did not share an *asado* with Che Guevara. Only a few of them
had even traveled to Havana. Yet the Cuban example lingered in their minds.
The eclectic origin of the urban guerrilla group the Montoneros serves as an
example.[80] The generation that defined the early 1970s spent their formative days in secondary school in a national atmosphere of military rule,
Peronist labor strikes, and growing armed resistance. Their curriculum
had espoused democratic principles, but school administrators often supported dictators.[81] Social and political unrest approached crisis levels under
the military rule of General Juan Carlos Onganía from 1966 to 1970.

This alienated generation would coalesce around a small nucleus of urban
activists in both Buenos Aires and Córdoba. Some came from right-wing
terrorist groups that abhorred Peronism. Their participation in Catholic
youth organizations connected to priests of the Third World ministries
converted them to a national populism that differed little from Peronist
models—a kind of Peronism with or without Perón. Fernando Abal Medina
and Mario Firmenich attended the Colegio Nacional de Buenos Aires. This
prestigious secondary school had launched the careers of many public fig-

ures. With the growing inflation and industrial stagnation of the late 1960s, however, the future looked very bleak. It appeared the very antithesis of early twentieth-century growth that had placed Argentina among the most progressive nations of the Western world.

Many Catholic youths found purpose in collaborating with Father Carlos Mugica and other Third World priests. They went into the poorest *villas miserias,* or shantytowns, to work on sanitation and health projects. They ministered to disadvantaged children. In summertime, they camped in isolated rural communities both for public service to poor rural workers and for religious retreat. Their political activism stemmed from Onganía's harsh reactions to labor strikes and from protests among students. The elder Montoneros leader, Abal Medina, had participated in the Tacuara movement. His younger colleague Mario Firmenich's first act of political activism consisted of throwing stones at police during the Buenos Aires port workers' strike of 1966.[82] Eventually, these relatively conservative young people came around to sympathizing with Peronist workers suffering the blows of military dictatorship. Padre Mugica embraced the Peronist left wing while rejecting communist revolutions such as the Russian and Chinese. These upheavals only produced a new "parasitic bureaucracy that dominated others," he wrote. "For us Christians, the authentic proletariat cultural revolution would mean the forming of men who live for the function of serving others."[83]

Future Montonero leaders devoured issues of the new magazine *Cristianismo y Revolución,* edited by the prominent Catholic thinker Juan García Elorrio. Influenced by the example of the Cuban Revolution, García Elorrio had left the seminary in the early 1960s. He traveled to Havana as if on a pilgrimage. He attended the OLAS conference and may have trained as a guerrilla. García established a friendship and intellectual exchange with John William Cooke. He became affiliated with the powerful movement of Third World priests, the *tercermundistas,* which had four hundred members in Argentina alone and more than two thousand in the rest of Latin America. García Elorrio engaged in a debate over the social role of the church as protector of the poor in a time of great structural inequalities. The *tercermundista* movement of priests recruited Catholic acolytes to work in the *villas miserias.*[84] Che's texts inspired the proto-Montoneros somewhat, but so did those of the Colombian guerrilla priest Camilo Torres. When Torres was martyred in 1966, Abal Medina adopted the rebel priest's name for his first action group.

The Comando Camilo Torres made headlines in Argentina shortly after the coup by General Onganía. The new military junta had come to participate in a celebratory mass at the National Cathedral. During the service, four young activists passed out handbills to the congregation. "Lord Jesus," the flyers read, "in this painful day for our Fatherland, in which workers cannot freely express the anguish of their families, and labor unions, in the face of the devastating action of an economic plan at the service of capitalism, imperialism, and the oligarchy, and against the people, we beseech You, Lord: that the union liberties destroyed by the government be recuperated through and for the working class."[85] These middle-class youths declared their solidarity with Peronist workers against the military government.

Adherents to both Catholic and Marxist doctrines joined Abal Medina's group and found common purpose in supporting Peronism. It seemed the only movement that could unify the working class and the bourgeoisie in overturning military rule. For tactics and strategies, such as "decentralization and security," the young urban-based activists looked to the Tupamaros of Uruguay. Decentralization meant operating in small groups whose members do not know other militants so as not to compromise their identities under torture.

They attracted urban adherents who did not come from families claiming wealth and status. The twenty-year-old Norma Arrostita, whose father was an artisan and an anarchist, joined the nascent group with her communist husband. When the latter went to Cuba for a year of military and ideological instruction, the couple separated. Norma and Abal Medina eventually became lovers. They themselves made the pilgrimage to Cuba in August 1967 for the OLAS conference. Attendance at the OLAS conference motivated the leaders to transform the fledgling organization. Abal Medina and his colleague Emilio Maza decided to detach themselves from the Christian left, changing the group's name to the Peronist Liberation Command, the direct forerunner of the Montoneros.[86]

The Abal Medina gang, still numbering only some dozen members in their early twenties, came to national prominence following another national awakening, the Cordobazo. It inspired Abal Medina to plan a spectacular and meticulous operation—the kidnapping of General Pedro Aramburu. The latter held particular symbolism for supporters of the exiled Juan Perón, because Aramburu took a leading role in the Revolución Libertadora that overturned the Perón presidency in 1955. As interim president from 1956 to

1958, he engineered the heavy-handed proscription of Peronist politicians, army officers, and labor leaders. President Aramburu presided over the execution of twenty-seven Peronist supporters.[87] Aramburu also had arranged for the disappearance of the corpse of Evita Perón, patron saint of the urban resistance movement.

Norma Arrostita and Mario Firmenich, both of whom participated in the general's kidnapping, later revealed details of the operation.[88] Months of observations of Aramburu's apartment house and his personal movements went into the planning. They chose Army Day, August 29, 1970. Wearing a wig as a disguise, Arrostita acted as a lookout on the street, and Firmenich, in police uniform, guarded the entrance to the apartment house. Dressed as junior army officers, Abal Medina and Maza arranged to escort General Aramburu to a military ceremony. The general's wife admitted them to the apartment and even served them coffee as her husband put on his dress uniform. After a few pleasantries, Abal Medina pulled a pistol and shuffled the general down the elevator and into an awaiting car.

The kidnappers and victim switched from car to van on the outskirts of Buenos Aires and drove some four hundred kilometers to a small estancia. There they subjected the general to a "people's court" and had Aramburu answer for "crimes" against the Patria and the Peronist movement. Abal Medina and his associates sentenced him to death and prepared to execute him in the cellar of the farmhouse. Standing at attention, unbound and unblindfolded, the former chief executive of the Argentine Republic gave the order for his own death. "Proceed," Aramburu said.[89] They shot him with pistols at point-blank range.

The execution of General Pedro Aramburu jolted the nation. The junta of General Onganía immediately reinstated the death penalty for crimes of terrorism, but it was not enough. Onganía's fellow officers came together to cut short his reign and continued military rule without him for another three years. Investigators identified some of the kidnappers, and photos of Abal Medina, Arrostita, Maza, and Firmenich appeared on the front pages of newspapers across the nation. The audacity of this new armed group inspired and mobilized university youth throughout the country.

These upstart rebels embraced the urban guerrilla model practiced in Montevideo. Like the Tupamaros, they assumed the name of heroic fighters of the patriotic past. In this case, they chose the nineteenth-century gaucho horsemen who, despite heroic resistance, had lost control of the nation to the landholding oligarchy.[90] The youngsters of the late 1960s converted the landowners' pejorative expression for the gaucho horsemen, *los montoneros* (the mounted rabble), into a call to arms. Few of these early Montonero leaders had actually come from the Peronist movement. But by 1970 they had embraced Perón. Be they *tacuaristas,* Peronists, socialists, communists, or proponents of Catholic Action, the Montoneros appeared to represent a remedy for the repressive stagnation gripping the Republic of Argentina. They had decided to stop arguing over ideological semantics, just as Che had urged eight years beforehand at the Gran Asado. "Actions unite us," said one Montonero, "words separate us."[91]

By way of a postscript to the development of urban armed resistance, one should note that the divide between anti-Peronists and Peronists widened in 1970 rather than narrowed. Funerals showed evidence. Police eventually discovered the body of President Aramburu and returned it to his family. Subsequently, a large number of supporters accorded him a hero's funeral in Buenos Aires. In December 1970, barely four months after the kidnapping, Fernando Abal Medina and several associates died in a firefight with police. The funeral of these rebels drew a crowd of mostly secondary school and university-aged youth. Father Carlos Mugica conducted the funeral mass. The young mourners dispersed chanting, "¡Ni yanquis, ni fascistas, peronistas!"[92] Many of them had come round from the right and center to become the "soldiers of Perón." The final battle for Argentina had commenced.

Together, these Cuban-inspired campaigns contributed to political polarization, undermined elected governments, emboldened the right wing, justified military intervention, and ultimately led to the torture and death of thousands of Argentinean citizens. Most of these victims never threw a bomb or shot at police.[93] Yet, many guerrillas whose exploits are recounted in these pages did suffer for their militancy.

The right-wing *tacuarista* Alberto Ezcurra was not one of them. He later took vows as a Catholic priest and from the pulpit celebrated the 1976 coup d'état that installed Argentina's last military dictatorship.[94] He thus fell in with the reactionaries who persecuted those former associates of the Grupo Baxter who had made the move from the right to the left. Joe Baxter made the leap from the Tacuara to the Revolutionary Army of the People (ERP). He died in a mysterious air crash at Paris Orly Airport in 1973. French authorities recovered forty thousand dollars in cash that Baxter was carrying,

The widow of General Pedro Eugenio Aramburu standing before the casket of her husband, surrounded by high-ranking military officers. Interim president Aramburu was the most prominent victim of the Montoneros.

apparently intended for the *sandinista* rebels in Nicaragua. He had met Carlos Fonseca and other *sandinistas* at the OLAS conference in Havana in 1967.

And so, what became of the leftist guerrillas when Juan Perón himself returned in 1973 to denounce them and when the military resumed power in 1976 in order to liquidate the leftist resistance forces? Argentina's state terrorism crushed them underfoot like *cucarachas*. The Peronist government itself turned on the Montoneros, whose armed rebellion had forced the military generals to call Perón back from exile. Perón had never trusted the revolutionary left. He therefore unleashed his own right-wing Peronists on his own *guerrilleros*. The Argentine Anticommunist Alliance, the notorious Triple A (whose leaders shared the right-wing ideology of the old Tacuara), was made up of a core of police and other right-wing hitmen. Nine thousand guerrillas, leftists, and many innocents died at the hands of this paramilitary group. Father Carlos Mugica became one of the first victims of the Triple A in 1974. He died in a hail of bullets. As one of the leaders of the *tercermundista* priests' movement, Father Mugica had brought some conservative Catholic youths around to supporting social revolution for the poor.[95]

Many others died less suddenly and more gruesomely. Roberto Quieto, founder of the Fuezas Armadas Revolucionarias implicated in the Minimax bombings, was captured in 1971. He went to Rawson Prison, from which he escaped along with Roberto Mario Santucho and others, eventually ending up for a third time in Cuba. Back in Buenos Aires in 1973, Quieto merged his group, the FAP, with the Montonero movement and became the latter's second-in-command. In 1975, while he was returning from a family swimming party at a park on the Río de la Plata, a large force of the federal police apprehended him. Apparently, the police turned him over to the army at Campo de Mayo. President María Estela Martínez de Perón had succeeded her husband, Juan Perón, who died in July 1974. She gave special immunities to the armed forces to combat terrorism, and the soldiers subjected Quieto to torture. Shortly after his capture, the security forces raided several safe houses and arrested many of Quieto's militant associates. The Montonero high command responded by condemning its erstwhile second-highest leader to death for revealing secrets while under torture.[96] Quieto "disappeared," according to the lexicon of the security services. To this day, no one has recovered his body.

The army captured Robi Santucho and also Enrique Gorrián Merlo of the ERP in 1971. Both managed to escape the infamous Rawson Prison in 1972 (together with Roberto Quieto, mentioned above) and commandeered a plane for a freedom flight to Salvador Allende's Chile, whence they left for Cuba. Santucho's wife and several other prisoners did not succeed in escaping and were shot in cold blood by prison guards. Santucho soon returned to lead remnants of the ERP in resistance to the military until he died in a Buenos Aires shoot-out in 1976. His associate Gorrián Merlo survived the dictatorship, remained active in radical politics, and participated in the 1980 assassination in Paraguay of the Nicaraguan ex-dictator Anastasio Somoza.

Norma Arrostita and Mario Firmenich survived to see the return of Juan Perón in 1973, by which time the Montoneros had grown to number some three thousand combatants and several thousand supporters. Most lived to witness Argentina's last military *golpe* in 1976.[97] The coup d'état returned the generals to power for one last time, and they vowed to finish the job begun by the Triple A. Ten to thirty thousand more citizens were to "disappear" in action or in custody of the military.[98] In the year of the coup, surviving activist Gerardo Bavio remembers meeting by chance Alicia Eguren de Cooke on Buenos Aires's Corrientes Street strolling with Héctor Jouvé. The latter served with Comandante Segundo and spent years in prison until pardoned when the Peronists returned to power in 1973. Jouvé escaped death during the last military dictatorship, but Eguren did not. Members of a *patota* (action squad) from the Naval Mechanics School captured the widow of John William Cooke and "disappeared" her body over the ocean on one of many "death flights."[99] In 1978, the *montonera* Norma Arrostita died in custody after spending more than four hundred days incarcerated at the infamous ESMA, the Naval Mechanics School, that became a center of torture and death.[100]

Only Firmenich and several other leaders of the Tupamaros survived the last military dictatorship, which ended in 1983. Firmenich spent some of this time as a refugee in Mexico, Cuba, and Nicaragua. Captured in Brazil, the former military commander of the Montoneros was extradited to Argentina to stand trial for murder. Having no death penalty, the court gave him a prison sentence of thirty years. Firmenich walked out of jail with a pardon from President Carlos Menem in 1990 and eventually obtained a doctorate in economics from the University of Barcelona.

Journalist Rodolfo Walsh, who had once worked in Havana for Jorge Ricardo Masetti's Prensa Latina, joined the Montoneros. Then he quit, believing that Firmenich erred in assassinating armed forces personnel. He also criticized the military government and had to go into hiding after the *golpe* of 1976. The death squads found him nonetheless. Moments before his capture in 1977, he posted an open letter to the leaders of the military regime. In it, Walsh accused the generals of "the most profound terror that Argentinean society has known." Already in the second year of state repression, Walsh counted fifteen thousand *desaparecidos,* ten thousand prisoners, four thousand deaths, and several thousand exiles. Moreover, he said that "the refusal of this Junta to publish the names of prisoners is the same as the covering over of a systematic execution of captives in the open and at early hours of the morning under the pretext of contrived combat and imaginary attempts at flight."[101] The investigative journalist Rodolfo Walsh died in the torture chambers of the Naval Mechanics School.

As for the Tupamaros, they too succumbed in the early 1970s, after the Uruguayan military entered the battle against them. In 1973, the army captured five hundred suspected leftists, virtually crippling the Tupamaro organization. More than sixteen hundred Uruguayan leftists took refuge in Cuba and Chile.[102] The generals themselves took power from the elected civilian government and ruled until 1984. The Tupamaros' legendary leader Raúl Sendic died in exile suffering from head and face wounds he developed when soldiers tortured him.

Mao Zedong expressed it succinctly when he said, "Revolution is not a dinner party!" Fidel Castro added a corollary: "But reactionaries and counter-revolutionaries are always more cruel than revolutionaries."[103]

CHAPTER FOURTEEN

The Last Campaign of Che Guevara

ERNESTO "CHE" GUEVARA and the Bolivian Communist Party (PCB) leader Mario Monje greeted each other with friendly jibes. "Coño, Che, how skinny you are!" said Monje. "Coño, Mario, what a potbelly you have!" replied the Argentinean.[1]

It was the last day of 1966, just eight years since Che's victory at Santa Clara ended Cuba's revolutionary war. The mood at the Río Ñancahuazú camp was festive despite the spartan surroundings. The woman known by the code name of Tania, who had brought Monje to camp, passed around the camera, taking pictures and having her picture taken too. The introductions all around confirmed the party boss's worst fears. Monje counted fifteen Cubans at the base. Of nearly an equal number of Bolivians already in camp, he recognized fewer than a handful from the PCB. The rest came from splinter groups on the left.

According to Monje's recollection, Che began the conversation. "I have to apologize; we have misled you," he said. "We could not explain our plans. I know that you could not understand the Cuban comrade (Pombo) . . . that this region is the ideal territory."[2] We have selected Bolivia "because [the

Cubans] have done an evaluation of certain characteristics," Guevara explained. "First: a weak army, a reactionary government of [René] Barrientos [and] a weak bourgeoisie that can be defeated."

Mario Monje did not agree. No objective conditions for revolution existed in Bolivia, said the party boss. Monje did not believe in Che's well-known adage that the guerrillas could create those conditions. The success of Cuba's revolution had been a complete aberration. "But nonetheless I think that I understand the Bolivian problem better than you," Monje told El Che.[3] Mario Monje demanded that he, as Bolivia's communist leader, take command of the guerrilla expedition.

Che Guevara refused to yield on this very point. "I will be the military chief and I will not accept any ambiguities about it," the Argentinean said.[4] Subsequent discussion between El Che and Monje led nowhere, and they adjourned in disagreement. "In effect," Monje recalled, "we could not understand each other; we were talking about two different things."[5]

Later that afternoon, Monje met separately with four members of the PCB who had joined the guerrillas. All of them had previously trained in Cuba. He asked them to abandon Che's venture; none did. According to the Bolivian Inti Peredo, the party boss warned them of the futility of the uprising. "When Bolivians discover that this guerrilla group is directed by a foreigner, they will turn their backs. They will deny you their support," Monje said. "You will die very heroically, but you do not have the slightest chance of triumphing."[6] Nevertheless, at midnight, everyone raised a cup to toast the coming year.

Bolivia's pro-Moscow communist leader prepared to depart early on New Year's Day. Mario Monje announced that he was going to La Paz to inform his *compañeros* on the Central Committee about the guerrillas' intentions. Then Monje would offer to resign his leadership of the Communist Party. This would free him up to return in a couple of weeks to join the group as a foot soldier. "Good, we will wait for you," said Che.[7]

Tania was told never to return to the camp again. She could escort invited visitors to the nearby town of Camiri. No closer. Guevara did not want her to blow her cover as a Cuban spy. If she did, Che stood to lose his connections through her to the urban infrastructure in La Paz and beyond.

The quest for security underlay Cuba's original strategy to export the revolution. This meant having friendly neighbors that would oppose US efforts to overturn socialism. Also, one has to acknowledge the missionary aspect. Revolutionaries believe they have the secret of salvation—that capitalism is the work of the devil, and socialism, of paradise. This rationale also works in reverse. Such was the motivation for Cuba's military training camps for foreign fighters. But to train Cubans whose sole purpose was to make the revolution in another country—that was unusual. Moreover, by this time, 1966, the danger of direct United States military intervention in Cuba had receded greatly.

Che Guevara created this new strategy of guerrilla warfare in Bolivia and chose himself as its commander. After the failures of the rural *focos* in Argentina and Peru, why did El Che attempt another uprising in the heart of South America?

Che Guevara the prophet believed that only he could ignite the Latin American revolution. Only he had the experience and the leadership skills. Eventually, Che would assemble some fifty fighters in the Bolivian wilderness. Twenty of them had been born outside the country, and thirty were Bolivians who were to learn irregular warfare from the Cubans. Bolivia served to prove that the guerrilla struggle, properly carried out by a master revolutionary, could create the conditions for the anti-imperialist revolution on a continental scale. Guevara was willing to be a martyr for this belief. Once Che set his mind to it, Fidel Castro also threw his support behind the Andean venture. The anti-imperialist revolution, after all, would not succeed if the best guerrilla fighters stayed at home.

THE BOLIVIAN NATIONAL REVOLUTION

Bolivia remains a curious choice for Che's guerrilla *foco*. It already had its social upheaval in the 1950s. The bourgeois electoral party of the MNR (National Revolutionary Movement) gained control of the government, yet the armed workers and peasants pushed its politicians to the left. Shortly after the mine workers defeated and destroyed the army, they distributed weapons to peasants who formed their own *sindicatos* to press for agrarian reform. In the Bolivian highlands, armed peasants seized the rural properties of wealthy hacendado families. They then began cultivation on their own accounts. Later, political leaders of the middle-class MNR party could only acquiesce to the fait accompli by conferring formal titles to the peasants.[8]

Dr. Ernesto Guevara himself traveled through the country in July and August 1953 as the Bolivian national revolution had entered its second year.

He and a friend, Carlos "Calica" Ferrer, stayed in La Paz for most of the time. But they also toured Lake Titicaca and visited the archeological sites at Copacabana. They traveled to a mine in the Yungas, stopping along the road so that Ernesto could snap a photograph of armed miners. He knew that the agrarian reforms had just begun, and he wrote and spoke about the "unique" process occurring in that Andean republic.

Ernesto penned a letter to a friend from medical school, Tita Infante, a member of Argentina's communist youth movement. In it, Guevara mentioned the revolutionary violence in Bolivia, the explosions of the "cartridges of dynamite" carried by workers on their belts, and the two or three thousand deaths in the countryside ("nobody knows exactly how many"). "In the end," he wrote, "they have fought without fear." He also observed that the government of the MNR did not incline toward radical social reforms but that its labor and peasant allies pushed the revolution leftward. He informed Infante about the revolutionary program of the union movement led by Juan Lechín. "Power probably remains definitely in the hands of the Lechín Group, which counts on the powerful help of the armed miners, but the resistance of his colleagues in the government could be serious above all now that the army is being reorganized."[9]

Bolivia remained on Ernesto's mind as he passed on to Central America on his way to Guatemala and Mexico City. The interview Dr. Guevara gave months later to a Costa Rican newspaper provides additional proof that he perceived that social change in "the Bolivian experiment" merited serious consideration. The news reporter asked him about his impressions of the nations he had just passed through. "The country that most impressed us is, without any doubt, Bolivia," *Diario de Costa Rica* quoted Guevara as saying. "With minimum capacity, they were bringing about extraordinary enterprises that are producing a profound transformation in multiple aspects of the political, social and economic life of Bolivia," Dr. Guevara said. "And certain it is that all the countries of the hemisphere have eyes placed on that powerful and revolutionary Republic."[10]

The young Dr. Guevara also recognized that the armed workers had been responsible for destroying the Bolivian army in 1952.[11] The full implication of that fact might not have occurred to him until he had lived through the CIA-instigated military revolt that toppled the Guatemalan revolution in 1954. To succeed in the real revolution, rebels had to destroy the standing army. Only then could the redistribution of property proceed. When he

Che Guevara snapped this photograph of a truckload of armed miners in Bolivia in 1953. His traveling companion, Carlos "Calica" Ferrer, stands at the left.

reached Mexico City in 1955 and met with Raúl and Fidel Castro, Guevara told them as much.

Che Guevara in 1966 could have raised a Cuban expedition to reinforce ongoing rebellions then raging in Guatemala or Venezuela. Yet he chose Bolivia. He opted to open a new front. Moreover, to justify his choice, Che could utilize the ideology that he himself had constructed for the export of revolution. The MNR governments had never adopted Marxist-Leninist doctrine, and, worst of all, Bolivia accepted military and economic aid from the United States, the enemy. "You cannot be a revolutionary without being anti-imperialist," Che used to say.[12] It was also true that a coup in 1964 had installed a military government and that an air force general, René Barrientos, won the subsequent presidential election. Che himself had preached for years that the guerrilla conflict would expose elected officials as tools of the nation's military and of imperialism. But no homegrown leftist *foco* had sprouted in Bolivia. The ideological hairsplitting could not cover up that Bolivia's attraction to Che Guevara consisted in the fact that he would be close to his real revolutionary goal, *la patria argentina*.

THE TRAINING MARCH

The group eventually chose to call itself the National Liberation Army, known by its Spanish acronym ELN. Che intended to utilize Ñancahuazú's remote site in Bolivia in order to train one or more guerrilla bands that would spawn a continent-wide, anti-imperialist, and socialist revolution. In turn, Che planned that this guerrilla campaign would eventually spill over into Argentina and Brazil. It was to reignite the Peruvian insurrection that had ended in defeat just months beforehand. Che Guevara posed as the chief planner and instigator of this long-term project. He intended to present imperialist powers in the Americas with many rural rebellions that would spread thin the repressive forces of international imperialism until the ELN and its progeny guerrilla groups liberated all Latin America from United States domination.

Loyola Guzmán arrived at camp shortly after Tania and Monje left. She was the daughter of a communist militant in the schoolteachers union. Her dedication and aptitude gained Loyola a scholarship to attend the Communist Party's cadre school in Moscow. She returned to attend law school at the University of La Paz. On Che's behalf, she was to coordinate the raising of money and to lead the urban support network for the guerrillas. Importantly, Loyola as treasurer of the group took charge of eighty thousand pesos, one quarter of which was set aside to buy a truck. She departed Ñancahuazú after two weeks of instruction from Che.

Meanwhile, Che Guevara prepared for the campaign. His group began stockpiling weapons, provisions, and medicines (particularly inhalants, pills, and morphine to control Che's asthma) and explored the *finca* and the surrounding wilderness. The region of the Ñancahuazú River is located in the rugged, tropical southeastern foothills of the Andean Cordillera. It is shot through with deep arroyos, raging streams in the rainy season, and dense jungle growth. This was not like the Sierra Maestra, a tropical forest set in steeply undulating typography. Southeast Bolivia was a tropical jungle, where Cuban veterans of the Sierra Maestra had learned to hack passages through the thick undergrowth with machetes. Travel would be slow and laborious—not quite conducive to Che's guerrilla tactics of "bite and flee; wait; move close; return to bite and flee." But the jungle canopy would offer cover.

Activity in the guerrilla camp picked up pace as Comandante Che prepared the men for the tasks ahead. Before Monje's visit, they had already begun construction of two encampments several kilometers from the tin-roofed house close to the only road in. The men received more instruction in the Quechua language, the better to speak to the peasants. The group acquired two mules for carrying equipment on the trek. Hunters caught armadillos in the traps for dinner. The Bolivian code-named Loro took off in the jeep on an unassigned errand. Confronted by Che, he admitted that he went to see a woman. Che assembled the men to publicly rebuke Loro for compromising the revolutionary mission. Che again reminded the men about the need for discipline "and threatened [Loro] with death if he became a traitor."[13]

In the Cuban revolutionary war, Che Guevara had fully participated in several such executions for betrayal of Castro's guerrilla band. Revolutionary justice had been codified in the Sierra Maestra and utilized several times. Comandante Segundo convened tribunals twice in Argentina. Yet, in the nine and one-half months of the Bolivian campaign, Che never once formed up the firing squad for any breach of discipline. The few Bolivian recruits who defected got clean away. Loro went on to die in battle. Nor did Che kill Bolivian army captives accused of stealing from locals. He reasoned that "it should be the enemy, not us, that starts the repression."[14]

The surrounding territory in which he was to operate for the next eleven months lay between 700 and 2,500 meters above sea level. By January 1967, when Che's patrols began exploring the wilderness for trails and river crossings in the deep canyons, Che started jotting down the altitude of the areas in which he was operating—to find his locations on the sometimes-inaccurate maps he was using. Che indulged himself with his old pastime of photography. He and others took photos of the training and of each other, processing the films and hiding away the collection with other documents (such as their false passports) in caves back at the base camp. As in the Sierra Maestra and the Congo, Che kept a diary for future instruction. He missed not one day's entry from November 7, 1966, to October 7, 1967.

In February 1966, he fielded about thirty-five combatants when he set out on a training march that was supposed to end up back in the base camp at Ñancahuazú within two weeks. In the challenging wilderness, the exercise lasted six weeks. Guerrilla patrols set out in all directions to gather intelligence on people and terrain.

Inti Peredo, one of the Bolivians trained in Cuba's School of National Liberation, made first contact with the *campesinos* but succeeded in nothing. "This peasant is typical: capable of helping us, but incapable of foreseeing the dangers involved and therefore potentially dangerous," Che noted in the diary.[15] In fact, the guerrillas were not operating among the highland peasants who, in 1953, were seizing land from the elite and tilling the soil on their own accounts. In contrast, the country people of Santa Cruz Province were hearty frontiersmen and -women who had descended to the semitropical lowlands to become squatters. They ran a few cows and horses. One of them had borrowed money to buy and fatten pigs. "He has capitalist ambitions," Che observed.[16] His diary also mentions "rich peasants," which accurately describes the smallholder aspirations the rebels confronted in Santa Cruz.

On the long training march, Che divided his column of thirty-five men into three groups: a scouting vanguard commanded by Miguel, a main group led by Che that carried provisions and equipment and herded the livestock, and a rear guard commanded by Joaquín. Miguel and Joaquín were Cubans with experience in the island's revolutionary war. With heavy supplies to carry, the main group always had trouble fording the dangerous streams and rivers during the rainy season. The three columns marched forward at some distance from each other, staying in touch via walkie-talkies or runners. When in retreat, the first two groups would pass through the rear guard, which set up an ambush to cover the withdrawal from enemy pursuit.

The column's first casualty came in this training exercise. As he crossed a rain-swollen river with a heavy knapsack, the Bolivian schoolteacher Benjamín fell into the water and disappeared. He did not know how to swim. "Now we have our baptism of death," Che wrote.[17] He observed that the march was meant to toughen up the men. Yet the Bolivians lagged behind as the trek entered its fifth week, and the infrequent meals weakened their enthusiasm. The men bickered, and Che began to suffer bouts of asthma.

While Che continued the training march, additional recruits showed up back at Ñancahuazú. Conspicuously absent from recruitment were members sent by the PCB. On returning to La Paz, Mario Monje convened a meeting of the party's Central Committee. He resigned his position as general secretary of the party and his successor, who also believed in "peaceful coexistence," refused to send any party militants to join Che's uprising.[18] One Maoist splinter group led by Moisés Guevara, on the other hand, decided to recruit for the guerrillas. Moisés himself came to Ñancahuazú with several other pro-Beijing activists and waited for Che's return from the training march. "I do not come here to impose conditions," he told his new companions, "but to apply for acceptance as one more soldier. For me it is an honor to fight alongside of El Che, the revolutionary I most admire."[19]

Peruvians too arrived at camp. They included three men who had escaped the defeat of the ELN of Héctor Béjar. They were El Negro, Eustaquio, and El Chino. All three had received their Cuba military training in 1962. Che Guevara also had plans to meet with representatives of the Tupamaros of Uruguay as well as Brazilian rebels from the hills of Espíritu Santo. But the Brazilian army obliterated the latter before contact was made.[20]

Tania, whose real name was Tamara Bunke Bider, was charged to perform liaison functions between the isolated guerrillas of the ELN and the outside world. As the daughter of refugee communists from Hitler's Germany, she grew up in Argentina speaking both Spanish and German. Bider returned to East Germany after World War II, and her parents became minor officials in the communist state apparatus. At twenty-two, she worked as a translator for East German state security. In December 1960, she accompanied Che Guevara on his first tour of East Germany. Records of the Stasi secret police reveal that Bider subsequently traveled to Havana, where she began training as a spy under the tutelage of Guevara and Manuel "Barba Roja" Piñeiro of Cuban state security.[21] There she became the undercover agent Tania.

In 1964, with an assumed name, Tania received orders to infiltrate to La Paz as a German-Argentine society lady interested in Bolivian folklore and antiquities. She even married a Bolivian engineering student in order to apply for a Bolivian passport in the name of Laura Gutiérrez Bauer. The Cubans arranged to award her husband a scholarship to study engineering in Moscow, and the couple divorced. Soon Laura was circulating in the high society of La Paz and sharing cocktails with President René Barrientos and his ministers. Thus, she had achieved an impeccable cover story to be able to coordinate the infiltration of fifteen Cuban fighters and Comandante Che Guevara in October 1966.[22] Che expected the spy Tania to accomplish a great deal more while he directed the guerrilla uprising in eastern Bolivia.

Tania was to bring two foreigners to Ñancahuazú whom Che Guevara very much wished to see when he returned from the training march. He devised ambitious plans for the French journalist Régis Debray and for the Argentinean radical Ciro Bustos. It was to be the first time that Debray would meet El Che, whose works had inspired the Frenchman's *foco* theory. "[Debray's task] was to meet with Che . . . then go out with a plan for publicizing and obtaining European solidarity for the revolutionary struggle in Bolivia and in other South American countries," according to Cuba's spy chief, Barba Roja Piñeiro.[23]

Tania had gone to Argentina as instructed. El Che had assigned her to make contact with potential recruits in Argentina, who were to come to Bolivia for field training and combat experience. To accomplish this, Tania went to Buenos Aires in early February to find Bustos, whom she had never met before. She used her spy training to locate him and pass him a cryptic message to meet her on a downtown street in his hometown of Córdoba. Perplexed, Bustos stood gazing through a storefront window at the appointed time. Finally, a woman approached dressed in a broad brimmed hat covering her face. "El Che quiere verte," she said mysteriously. "Che wants to see you."[24] Subsequently, she informed him that she would escort him to the Bolivian base camp and that he would be back in Argentina by the ides of March. Che had asked Tania to bring Bustos and Debray to the camp on March 1, a meeting that was timed for the return of the training march.

However, Tania behaved with disregard for security procedures. She arranged to accompany Bustos and Debray on the same public bus leaving La Paz. They each boarded separately and sat in different seats, but they were the only whites on a bus full of indigenous peasants. At the bus stop, all three jumped into Tania's jeep, which she had stored nearby. She drove too fast, and, at a roadside restaurant, she spoke too loudly using Cuban slang. They met Moisés Guevara and his Maoist recruits at the tin-roofed house. She pulled out the photos she had taken at the New Year's gathering, pointing out Che Guevara and naming all the other Cubans. Finally, the Cuban in charge of the camp stepped in to gather up the photos. No one in camp was aware that Tania's presence violated orders Che had given her.

Before Che Guevara returned to the base camp, the Bolivian recruits from the Maoist splinter group had seen the photos and learned of Che Guevara's presence. As it turned out, the Maoist collaborators in La Paz had recruited several young volunteers with the promise of a free education in Cuba. But the Cubans left to care for the base camp welcomed them as new guerrilla fighters and thrust weapons and knapsacks into their arms. Uninterested in the prospect of combat, two recruits defected, taking a rifle to the nearby town, where they sold it for cash. The local policemen apprehended the two Bolivians on suspicion of being drug traffickers. They interrogated the men and could scarcely believe the story. But they dutifully sent a report to La

Paz that a guerrilla force was operating in Santa Cruz Province. The police recounted that Che Guevara might be leading it.[25]

Within the week, the 4th Army Division sent out two separate patrols to investigate the camp at Ñancahuazú. Soldiers commanded by Captain Silva arrived by truck at the tin-roofed house at 4:00 one afternoon. At the sound of the truck's engine, the inhabitants of the house ran into the woods, leaving dinner cooking on the stove. They also abandoned Tania's jeep, containing incriminating documents, which Captain Silva impounded. Silva's soldiers heard shots coming from the interior of the property. The second patrol had captured another Bolivian recruit while exchanging gunfire with still others. One Bolivian soldier died.[26] Among those fleeing to safety in the *monte* were Tania, the Frenchman, and the Argentinean. Before nightfall, the two army patrols withdrew from the area and returned to their base at Camiri.

The 4th Army Division traced the ownership of the commandeered jeep to a certain Laura Gutiérrez of La Paz. Soon police investigators in the capital entered her apartment. There they discovered a shortwave radio, transmission codes, and some weapons hidden deep in a closet. With her radio equipment, Tania had been able to communicate with Che's column and also with the state security agency in Havana.[27] The raid blew her cover. She had defied Che's orders never to return, and now she could not leave. Two years of spying came undone overnight. Tamara Bunke Bider thus became La Guerrillera Tania.

Che and his men on the training march still had two weeks of treacherous terrain to cover. During a rainstorm the column became separated. Joaquín and the rear guard remained behind, while Che and his larger group followed the vanguard across a raging torrent at the bottom of an arroyo. The guerrillas purposely chose not to use radios whose messages might be intercepted by the enemy. They had to rely on couriers' running back and forth between Che in the middle and his vanguard and rearguard commanders. Thus, the runners sent out by Joaquín and Che could not locate each other for two weeks. This miscommunication presaged a problem that would prove fatal later on.

By the middle of March, Joaquín and the rear guard found and rejoined the main group. The men celebrated Joaquín's return by feasting on horsemeat. Then the guerrilla column set out for the main camp at Ñancahuazú. On the return, another man died in a dangerous flash flood, and knapsacks, ammunition, and rifles were lost too. When the horsemeat ran out, the hunters brought down "four birds that became our meal, not as bad as one might anticipate." Then Che jotted down in his diary about the first flyover of a military airplane. His men ducked and covered immediately. "That did not presage anything good," he wrote.[28] He soon learned the reason for the flyover.

Guevara's training column was making its way slowly back to the base camp. A scout from the vanguard brought the report that two men had deserted and the army had raided the tin-roofed house. He also learned that the army patrols did not discover the arms, ammunition, and medicine that the guerrillas had hidden away in five caves on the property. Guevara reacted with fury toward those he had left behind. "Whoever heard of retreating before ever making contact with the enemy," he wrote.[29]

When the column returned to base camp, the guerrillas appeared dehydrated, skinny, and haggard. Their uniforms had been torn to shreds by thorny bushes. Their appearance cannot have impressed the new recruits. Che immediately ordered double rations and rest for the marchers. Then he had to deal with the situation that Tania had created. She had abandoned her mission in the city to remain in camp with the Frenchman and Argentinean. Comandante Che was in no mood to see Tania in camp wearing a combat uniform. The guerrilla band was now isolated, with no communication to Loyola and other students in La Paz and no way to get messages to Fidel in Havana. "What the fuck do I tell you things for!" Che yelled at her for all to hear.[30]

He banished her to the rear guard and assigned her to a lot of cooking duty. "She was not prepared for the guerrilla life," the Cuban fighter Pombo wrote in his own diary. "El Che was furious when he found her in the camp, because on leaving the city, she was leaving us completely without communication with the outside world."[31] Tania's presence also disrupted the macho milieu of the guerrilla *foco*.

FIRST ENCOUNTERS

After a short time of rest, Comandante Che ordered everyone to prepare for the defense of the encampment. He expected the army to return. His fighters posted guards and set up an ambush along the main trail. On March 23, an unsuspecting army patrol walked into an ambush. The guerrillas killed seven soldiers, took eighteen prisoners, and attended to the wounds of four of them. They also relieved the enemy of three mortars, sixteen rifles, and two radios. The two captured officers, a major and a captain, talked like "parrots," and Che eventually released all the captives in their underwear. Three days later, President Barrientos himself flew into the Camiri military base. He visited the tin-roofed house at Ñancahuazú and declared an all-out offensive against "Castro-communism."[32]

At the time of the guerrilla outbreak, Bolivia had an army of fifteen thousand ill-trained conscript soldiers. Most of the conscripts were illiterate indigenous peasants who could not easily avoid the draft and who barely spoke Spanish. Each of them owed one year of mandatory military service. Only three thousand of these soldiers were "combat ready." Even these combat troops could not operate for long in the field, because the army lacked combat food kits and field mess facilities. The entire army force was divided into eight army divisions throughout the country. Two of these, the 4th Division at Camiri and the 8th Division at the provincial capital, had bases in the province of Santa Cruz. The troops of these army divisions served in small outposts spread throughout the province. Soldiers had access to outdated Mauser bolt action rifles, of which only three out of ten functioned properly. Conscripts spent a lot of time in civic action programs, laboring on construction and road building.[33] The armed forces had prepared poorly for counterinsurgency. A secret report to President Johnson described the weaknesses of the Bolivian military in stark terms:

> The Army is handicapped by the fact that most officers have been training in traditional warfare and have no comprehension of guerrilla tactics. The majority of the men are raw recruits with little or no training. All are unfamiliar with the terrain. Officers are arbitrarily assigned to squads, and frequently issue orders to soldiers not even under their command, causing endless confusion. Soldiers are demoralized by the lack of food, medical facilities, faulty weapons, and the terrifying ferocity of guerrilla attacks from the dense jungle.[34]

By March 27, President Barrientos alerted the nation in a nationwide radio broadcast to the presence of the guerrillas, quite possibly led by the notorious foreign subversive Ernesto "Che" Guevara.

Their discovery by the enemy now forced Che to commit his fighters to battle before they were prepared. Moreover, he was stuck with Tania, the Argentinean Bustos, and the French intellectual Debray until he could find a way to expel the latter two from the band without being apprehended. They were supposed to be at the base camp only for a few days in order to receive instructions, then return to La Paz. From there, Bustos had orders to return to Buenos Aires and Córdoba in order to dispatch some twenty Argentinean young men to the National Liberation Army. The Frenchman Debray was to communicate with Havana and Paris, enlisting the assistance of Jean-Paul Sartre and Bertrand Russell. The Frenchman presented the comandante with a copy of his book *Revolution in the Revolution?*, which had formalized the theory of the rural *foco,* also known as *foquismo.* Che read it in one sitting and took extensive notes and scribbled amply in the margins of the pages.

His diary of the Bolivian guerrilla campaign often referred to President Barrientos as a military dictator. He never acknowledged that the army general who led the 1964 military coup d'état actually won the next year's presidential election with 60 percent of the vote against two other presidential candidates. He never acknowledged Barrientos's ability to speak Quechua and his popularity with peasant organizations. He ignored the fact that the military junta he led briefly in 1964 had not reversed any of the revolutionary reforms of the previous decade. Communiqué number one of the ELN, circulated at the end of March 1967, demonstrated how Che viewed the government of President René Barrientos. "The military thugs . . . have usurped power, murdered workers, and laid the groundwork for surrendering our resources to U.S. imperialism."[35]

When Che issued his first communiqué from the guerrilla fighters, he had the document signed by his guerrillas of the Maoist faction, well known in the mines of Oruro. Moisés Guevara, Simón Cuba, and two other Bolivians had been active in workers' circles. "Only through socialism would we get a more just, a more human world, without hunger, without misery, without malnutrition, without injustice, without lay-offs by the company," they promised.[36] The *maoistas* and Che had credibility in the mines, while President Barrientos appealed more to the indigenous peasants.

Communication failure posed a serious drawback for the guerrilla band. The number of men in the ELN's guerrilla force now amounted to forty-seven, including the two visitors and Tania. While miners in Oruro wished to send recruits and supplies to the ELN, the guerrillas had no way to coordinate such aid. They even voted in union meetings to donate one day's wage to the rebels.[37]

The transistor radio receivers of the guerrillas began to crackle with newscasts from La Paz concerning guerrilla ambushes and troop movements in Santa Cruz. Larger numbers of army conscripts ("almost children," Che called them) were arriving in the province, and the guerrilla band had to stay on the move nearly every day. The army's second and third encounters with the guerrillas demonstrated the lack of preparedness on the part of the conscripts.

On April 10, Che's fighters successively pulled off two ambushes. In the first, a small patrol walked into a trap laid by the rear guard. Three soldiers died, seven were captured, and four escaped back up the road. Later that day, a company of 120 men came back down the trail to retrieve the wounded. But Che's rear guard had advanced farther up the road and ambushed this relief column. Six more soldiers fell, and the company commander and a dozen others were captured along with their weapons. "We came to look for our dead and to investigate what happened," the Bolivian commander told his captors. "Because we were taught [in military classes] that the guerrillas strike and then retreat, we didn't imagine that you were here again waiting for us."[38] The ELN just had its best day of the military campaign.

Suddenly, a third foreigner showed up unexpectedly. George Andrew Roth, a stringer for *Life* magazine, had hired a peasant guide to take him to Che's column for an interview with the famous comandante. Bustos describes Roth as a "maverick, intrepid and enthusiastic." He was an Anglo-Chilean freelance photographer.[39] Che now had four unwanted civilians in his column, counting Tania. He managed to expel Roth, Debray, and Bustos near the village of Muyupampa. These three quickly walked into an army patrol tipped off by townspeople.

Once captured, Roth, Debray, and Bustos were held incommunicado in the Camiri jail until July. Foreign reporters descended on Camiri in search of Che Guevara. "We were never tortured," Bustos writes. The prisoners' guardian angel turned out to be none other than the president of France, Charles de Gaulle. The French aristocratic mother of Régis Debray arrived in La Paz, and de Gaulle sent a personal plea for clemency to President Barrientos. The Bolivian head of state reminded de Gaulle that the guerrillas had already killed twenty-seven soldiers defending the patria from foreign invasion. "I ask you to admit that if for Your Excellency the first priority is

France and the French People," Barrientos wrote, "my prime duty is Bolivia and the Bolivians."[40]

The three captives subsequently cooperated with interrogators and told the Bolivians everything they knew about guerrilla operations. Interrogations of Debray and Bustos provided proof to the world that Che Guevara was alive and fighting again as a guerrilla comandante.[41] The Argentinean artist Ciro Bustos drew sketches of the guerrillas, including a portrait of Che Guevara. Régis Debray gave interviews to foreign journalists. Finally, the Bolivian court at Camiri convicted Debray and Bustos to lengthy prison sentences. The Anglo-Chilean photographer received a short sentence.

In the meantime, the great foreign newspapers such as the *New York Times,* the *Times* of London, and *Le Figaro* of Paris were running unflattering articles about Bolivia. President Barrientos and his advisers grew weary of the foreign press characterizing their country as "backward, illiterate, and impoverished." Barrientos resolved then and there not to have another trial for foreign rebels. Che Guevara would have to die in battle.

At Muyupampa, the vanguard and Che's center became separated from Joaquín's rear guard when the first two elements retreated after dropping off the three foreigners. Army patrols pursued them, and the Bolivian Air Force dropped bombs aimlessly around them. The rearguard fighters stationed themselves, as ordered, on the other side of the river. The main column did not have any radio contact with the rear guard. Subsequently, they lost each other. Eleven men and Tania remained with Joaquín. Explorers sent by Che to find the rear guard returned without discovering their trail and without making contact with Joaquín's own runners.[42] From then on, Joaquín and Che learned of each other's whereabouts by monitoring Bolivian newscasts on their radio receivers. They never reunited during the remainder of the campaign. Tania remained with the rear guard until the end.

Patrols of the 4th Army Division now flooded the areas where peasants indicated they had spotted the guerrillas. The sheer numbers of conscript soldiers took their toll on the ELN. On April 25, a "black day," as Che noted in his diary, the guerrilla Rolando received a mortal wound in a botched ambush. His fellow fighters carried him back to the main group for medical treatment, and he died as Che and the Peruvian doctor El Negro attempted to deliver blood plasma. "We have lost the best man of the guerrilla band," Che wrote of the Cuban who had served as Che's messenger during the decisive battle of Santa Clara.[43]

THE YANKS ARE COMING

The White House received the first credible news that Che Guevara was still alive on March 16, the day a top-secret message arrived from President René Barrientos that two guerrillas (Debray and Bustos) had been apprehended. The message claimed that Che had forty guerrillas operating there "independent of any Bolivian party."[44] President Johnson decided to take action. As he and his advisers mulled over the options, he requested and received a CIA assessment. Intelligence analysts in Washington remained unconvinced of any great danger. They discounted Che's effectiveness as a guerrilla leader, stating that the man was nothing but legend. "With his myth he is ten feet tall, without it, he is a mortal of normal stature."[45]

President Johnson resolved to send military aid and advisers to bolster the capacity of the Bolivian Armed Forces—something low-key. The Southern Command in the Panama Canal Zone already had had experience training guerrilla-hunting rangers in Venezuela and Colombia. In fact, American military advisers had assisted their Bolivian counterparts in creating the 1st Ranger Battalion in 1963, but the army wanted to keep these rangers in reserve for possible deployment against another strike by the mine workers. La Paz now requested just such a unit to find and destroy Che's guerrilla force. The Bolivian Armed Forces began recruiting immediately for a new ranger battalion, the 2nd, while the US Southern Command in the Panama Canal Zone prepared to deliver the training.[46]

Early in April, the commander of the 8th Special Forces Group at Fort Gulick received the order. He was to prepare a mobile training team (MTT) for a "classified, very sensitive" mission in Bolivia. The commander appointed Major Ralph W. "Pappy" Shelton, the only ranger-qualified officer available. "It was simply 'luck of the draw,'" Pappy recalled.[47] Guerrillas had just badly mauled a Bolivian army patrol. No other details were available about the nature of the guerrillas, except that Cubans accompanied the force.

Pappy Shelton chose sixteen men, five of them officers and the rest noncommissioned officers. Together they had expertise in intelligence, demolitions, infantry weapons, communications, and medical services. All of the men had prior assignments to Vietnam, and some had even served in World War II and Korea. Several were native Spanish speakers, having Hispanic family roots in the southwestern United States and Puerto Rico.[48]

The Special Forces team and its equipment flew in to the Santa Cruz air-port in mid-April on two C-130 cargo planes. They brought stocks of Korean War weapons from storage in the Panama Canal Zone. "As we taxied to the small terminal, I spotted [Master Sergeant] Milliard and [Sergeant First Class] Rivera Colon waiting for us. They were wearing their green berets," Pappy Shelton recalled. "So much for a low profile."[49] Several trucks carried men and equipment to an abandoned sugar mill outside of La Esperanza. The American military attaché in La Paz had orders not to enter the zone of combat. He and Bolivian army officers settled on the training site at La Esperanza, at least sixty kilometers from any sighting of guerrilla activity.[50] Food supplies arrived at the Santa Cruz airport continuously via C-130 transport planes in the next three months. Trainers realized the need to get some "extra calories" into the Bolivian trainees. The mobile training team communicated to headquarters at Fort Gulick via shortwave radio.

The MTT divided up instruction into four phases. The first six weeks were devoted to individual basic training. Three weeks of advanced individual training followed. In the third phase, Special Forces personnel provided unit exercises. The final phase consisted of advanced unit and counterinsurgency schooling, followed by a two-week field exercise. At one point, President Barrientos came to address the trainees. "His address was a great morale booster to the Battalion," Pappy recalled. "It came at an opportune time and carried them through some of the more arduous training in Phase IV."[51]

Five hundred sixty soldiers successfully completed the course to make up the 2nd Ranger Battalion of the Bolivian 8th Army. Their commander was Major Manuel Ayoroa. The advanced unit training imbued the men with a sense of combat superiority. "Also they stood their ground with patriotic sentiments," said Major Ayoroa, "and put us on guard that Bolivia had been invaded by a foreign army that wanted to dominate us."[52] The 2nd Bolivian Ranger Battalion held its graduation parade on September 17. The White House took credit for its wisdom in sending in the Special Forces. As it turned out, however, the MTT training mission was *not* decisive in Che's defeat.

At the White House, special assistant Walt W. Rostow reported to President Johnson on the rumor that Che might be alive. "We need more evidence before concluding that Guevara is operational—and not dead, as the intelligence community, with the passage of time, has been more and more inclined to believe," Rostow wrote.[53]

Che seemed to welcome the arrival of the American advisers, about whom he had heard in the news broadcasts on the radio. "Perhaps we are witnessing the first episode of a new Vietnam," Che speculated.[54] He was referring to the message he had written for the Tricontinental Conference before he left Cuba. Che entitled the message, "To create two, three . . . many Vietnams is the watchword." He began by quoting the famous sugar mill metaphor of José Martí: "It is the time of the furnaces and no one can see anything but the blazing light." His message to the Tricontinental noted that the world had had twenty-three years of peace since World War II but that the results for the world's poor were disastrous—more misery, degradation, and exploitation. "How close and bright would the future appear if two, three, many Vietnams flowered on the face of the globe, with their quota of death and their immense tragedies, with their daily heroism, with their repeated blows against imperialism, forcing it to disperse its forces under the lash of the growing hatred of the peoples of the world!"[55]

Che envisioned the revolutionary redemption. He took heart in the prominent role played by socialists in the decolonization of Africa and Asia, particularly the war of liberation in Vietnam that provoked US military intervention. Once again he reiterated that the dangers and sacrifices of one man did not matter when the destiny of humanity entered into play. "Our every action is a battle cry against imperialism and a call for the unity of peoples against the great enemy of the human race, the United States of North America."[56] So it was that Che seemed to be expecting and welcoming US intervention in another hot spot he hoped would become the second Vietnam.

In the eastern province of Santa Cruz, Che's guerrilla group had become completely isolated. Rural residents in the vicinity of the rebel movement tended to cooperate more with the army than with the rebels—though they probably would have preferred being left absolutely alone by both. Bolivian army troops were moving about in great numbers wherever the guerrillas had been sighted. Not surprisingly, the poor Bolivian peasants sold victuals to the armed, Cuban-led rebels. But they remained "very frightened by our presence here," as Che admitted.[57]

In this rural *foco,* the theoretically expected peasant support never materialized. Even if Che had gained the support of the smallholders and squatters of Santa Cruz Province, it might not have mattered that much. Beginning in April 1967, Bolivian troops seemed to be everywhere, which encouraged the peasants to treat the rebels with even more wariness. While inefficient, the Bolivian army was not corrupt or unpopular enough to teeter on the point of collapse. The military chief of staff General Alfredo Ovando dispatched several thousand extra troops to the province of Santa Cruz to patrol the villages and towns. The reinforced 4th Division hemmed in the rebel guerrillas, in the south, and the 8th Army Division, in the north.

THE WINTER OF DISCONTENT

In the winter months of 1967, Che Guevara proved himself to be a great military tactician—contrary to the CIA assessment that he was "all myth." His tragedy lay in the simple fact that his tactical talents of keeping his men alive and fighting could never make up for the strategic blunders. He had no exit plan whatsoever.

Nevertheless, Che the master tactician survived despite having lost contact with the outside world and even his own rear guard. His vanguard and center groups now consisted of twenty-five men. Increasingly, the guerrillas avoided the roads, except at night, and kept to the *monte*. They acquired food along the way. They still paid peasants for corn, pigs, horses, and cows when the opportunity presented itself—sometimes it did not. The main group herded livestock through rushing waters and up and down steep arroyos. They cut trails with machetes. The slaughter of a horse resulted in a feast and leftover meat for up to four days.

But there were days and nights of intense hunger too. And thirst. And rain. In the dry season, the rivulets dried up. Che had to dispatch guerrilla patrols to isolated farms and villages to procure water. Such contacts with the population endangered the guerrillas because peasants tended to report them to the army. Che began to fill up his diary not so much with news of skirmishes won or lost but of desperate searches for food and water and the satisfaction of the occasional meat roast. "Ricardo killed a rodent-like creature [*hochi*]," wrote Che, "and with that and a corn stew we passed the day."[58]

The men thought often about food—especially the lack of it. On his twenty-seventh birthday, Pombo wrote in his diary: "I've been hungry for the last two days. The only thing I have eaten is lard soup, which is all we have left." Months later, hunger remained his preoccupation. "The mules were able to get down [the canyon], but the horse fell into a ditch," Pombo noted. "In point of fact, as hungry as we were, we wished the horse had died, forgetting that Che needed to ride it."[59] Pombo had been with Che in the Sierra Maestra and the Congo.

While crisscrossing the steep valleys of the Grande and Ñancahuazú Rivers searching for Joaquín's rear guard, climbing from 800 to 2,000 meters above sea level and back down again, the group heard bad news on the radio. They learned of the capture of a Cuban landing party in Venezuela and the parading of two Cuban guerrilla advisers before President Raúl Leoni's news conference. Che did not recognize the names of the prisoners. Then came the inevitable breakdown of guerrilla discipline. Aníceto and Luis were found asleep at their guard posts. Che sentenced them to seven days as "kitchen helpers" and one day without roasted or fried pork.[60] His asthma was occurring frequently and condemned him to two or three sleepless nights in a row. By now, El Che had run out of medicines, and Bolivian soldiers were removing asthma remedies from all pharmacies in the zone.

On June 14, the group rested beside a mountain stream huddling around the fire. Che celebrated his thirty-ninth birthday "thinking about my future as a guerrilla; for now I am 'whole.'"[61] General Ovando, the Bolivian chief of staff, confirmed on the radio that Ernesto "Che" Guevara was leading the guerrilla forces in Santa Cruz Province. The comandante took satisfaction.[62]

Yet, the broadcasts also brought him annoyance. Not only did Che denounce every utterance of President Barrientos and General Ovando, but he also reacted to criticism from the socialist camp as well. The radio news broadcast had reported that Premier Brezhnev disparaged Che for his guerrilla activities and that the Hungarian press had called him "a pathetic figure." "How I would like to come into power, for nothing more but to unmask the cowards and lackeys of every sort and rub their snouts in pig shit," he fumed in the diary.[63]

Militarily, the guerrillas continued to be a force to be reckoned with, and their morale remained remarkably high. On June 26, they successfully ambushed a patrol of Bolivian rural policemen, killing four, taking eleven prisoners, and acquiring nine horses. But one guerrilla died, and another suffered injuries in the ambush. Death came to the Cuban code-named Tuma. Che inscribed in his diary that Tuma was "an inseparable comrade of all the last years, of a loyalty passing every test and whose absence from now on would be like that of a son."[64] The troop was down to twenty-four men. Che had to plan on making contact with the city in order to acquire equipment, medicine, and fifty to one hundred more recruits.

The guerrillas captured ten more rural policemen at the beginning of July and released them without clothing, as was the custom, about one kilometer from the nearest village. Even the Bolivian guerrillas were earning their laurels with Che. "There are only two or three slackers," he wrote.[65] Luckily, in this winter campaign, the army was not performing effectively despite its overwhelming numbers, except in intimidating the peasants to run away at the sight of the armed rebels. "The legend of the guerrilla force expands like foam," he boasted in his diary. "We are now invincible super-humans."[66] But Che was reading too much into the news he was hearing. Every small announcement of a splinter group's disaffection with the Barrientos regime and every miners' strike he took as a sign of the government's disintegration. "What a pity that I do not have 100 more men at this moment," he lamented.[67]

The presence of an active guerrilla movement may have caused the military to crack down on the workers even more decisively than usual. Miners very much supported the guerrillas. They collected contributions and took target practice with old rifles in hopes of joining up. In June and July, Barrientos responded to miners' support for the ELN guerrillas by sending army units by train to the mining camps. Soldiers advanced shooting at miners, women, and children; over one hundred people died during these winter months.[68] Since the 1952 revolution, the army had refrained from attacking workers until this moment of the guerrilla threat in the Andean winter of 1967.

Slowly, the military balance of power shifted away from the guerrillas, even before the rangers got into the action. At the end of July, while the main group lagged behind, attempting to coerce recalcitrant horses to move up a steep arroyo, the vanguard on the road above walked into an ambush by 150 soldiers. The Bolivian code-named Raúl died on the spot. The Cuban veteran Ricardo suffered gunshot wounds, and his comrades had to carry him back in a hammock. Another Cuban, Pacho, limped back with a bullet to the buttock.

This battle turned out to be costly. The men lost taped messages from Havana, Debray's book with Che's annotations in the margins, and seven backpacks with medicines and plasma. Without medical supplies, Che and the Peruvian doctor El Negro could not revive Ricardo. He bled to death before midnight, and they buried his body. "Ricardo was the most undisciplined member of the group . . . but he was an extraordinary fighter," Che noted in his diary.[69] Ricardo had been with Che in the Cuban revolutionary war and in the Congo too. Now the guerrilla group of Che was reduced to twenty-two men, who still lacked contact with Joaquín, Tania, and nine others in the rear guard.

Bolivia entered international discussions like never before. In July 1967, President Johnson himself brought up the issue to Alexei Kosygin at their meeting in Glassboro, New Jersey. Cuba's interventions into the internal affairs of other Latin American nations posed unnecessary dangers, Johnson said. It might force the Americans to retaliate militarily. Kosygin subsequently headed to Cuba. There he restated Soviet objections toward Cuba's policy of spreading revolution. His conversation turned testy when Kosygin called Cuba's export of revolution "adventurist." "So was the Cuban revolution adventurist?" Castro replied. "Most of the communist parties in Latin America are not parties . . . but Marxist clubs." Kosygin had his own retort. "I have not heard that [Che] had been invited by the Bolivians."[70] Fidel would not give up on armed revolution. In fact, many Latin American radicals were then preparing to travel to Havana for Fidel's first conference of the Latin American Solidarity Organization (OLAS), which would be dedicated to the encouragement of even more guerrilla movements in the hemisphere.[71]

By that time, other Americans had arrived to assist as well. On the last day of July, two Spanish-speaking agents from the CIA deplaned in La Paz. Both were Bay of Pigs veterans. One of them, Special Agent Félix I. Rodríguez, had infiltrated into Cuba before the landing in order to assist the anti-Castro underground in its rebellion. None occurred, and Castro defeated the invasion. Subsequently, Félix Rodríguez escaped from the island by taking refuge in the Venezuelan embassy. Later, he joined the CIA-supported anti-Castro commando group of Manuel Artime. In 1965, Rodríguez returned to civilian life when Johnson shut down Artime's operations.

Special Agent Gustavo Villoldo had also joined Brigade 2506, the CIA's invasion force of 1961. A pilot, Villoldo flew a B-26 on strafing runs twice over the Bay of Pigs. Later, Villoldo received additional military training with the United States Armed Forces and got on the CIA payroll as an agent trainee in 1964.[72] He served among the fighter pilots in the Congo when Che Guevara (unbeknownst to the CIA) advised the rebel forces there.

Now, in 1967, the CIA gave Félix Rodríguez and Gustavo Villoldo orders to work with Bolivian military intelligence services. They had instructions to persuade the Bolivians to capture Guevara alive and turn him over to the United States for interrogation in the Panama Canal Zone. The CIA men paid courtesy calls on President Barrientos and on the commander-in-chief of the Bolivian Armed Forces, General Alfredo Ovando.[73] The new arrivals coordinated their activities with John Tilton, the CIA station chief at the American embassy.

By August, the accumulation of flight, fatigue, hunger, and asthma had finally got on Che's nerves. He had to ride a horse or mule more often now because he was physically incapable of keeping up the pace on foot. One of the mares he rode because of his asthma had been slowing down in the previous few days. Finally she stopped altogether. Che lost his temper and stabbed the horse in the neck with a knife. That evening he assembled the men for a lesson in discipline, confessing his own failure of self-control and stressing that "we need to be more revolutionary." Guevara saw the necessity of bolstering morale. He rose to the occasion as only El Che was capable of doing:

> We are in a difficult situation. Pacho is recovering but I am a mess and the incident of the mare indicates that there are moments in which I lose control of myself; that will change, but we must all share alike the burden of the situation and whoever feels he cannot stand it should say so. This is one of those moments in which great decisions must be made, because a struggle of this type gives us the opportunity to become revolutionaries, the highest step in the human ladder and also allows us to test ourselves as men. Those who cannot measure up to these two requirements should say so and abandon the struggle.[74]

The radios still picked up news stories from Havana. Che and his men were amazed to learn that they had sent a message of greetings to the delegates attending the inaugural meeting of the OLAS in Havana. What? Did we do that by mental telepathy? they asked.[75] Once again, Fidel Castro had wished to strike a note of optimism about the insurrections still proceeding in Venezuela and Bolivia. After all, he had convened the Latin American Solidarity Organization to inspire even more.

Joaquín, Tania, and the other members of the rear guard still wandered through the *monte* searching for Che's main group. Two Bolivians, among the youngest of the band, found an opportunity to desert from the rear guard early in August. The deserters saved their lives by informing their army interrogators about the caves of supplies that the earlier military occupation of the base camp had not found. The army reentered Ñancahuazú and discovered the caves, confiscating the radio equipment, provisions, and Che's anti-asthma medicine. They found photos, several of which appeared in newspapers around the country. The front page of *El Diario* in La Paz featured Che's passport photos and shots of his activities at the training camp.[76]

Several of the photos found in the caves revealed the collaboration of the university student Loyola Guzmán. She had the equivalent of US$28,000 in her possession when authorities arrested her in La Paz shortly thereafter. Loyola never broke faith with her revolutionary ideals. Under interrogation at the Ministry of the Interior, she broke free and leapt out the window of the fourth floor. A tree broke her fall, and she survived. Imprisoned thereafter, Loyola gave interviews to news reporters. "I hold to my ideas," she told them. "Although this is a blow to us, the struggle will go on, even if many more people must die."[77]

More bad news soon reached the dwindling group of fighters. Joaquín's lost rear guard of nine men and Tania were heading north, still searching for Che's main element. They stopped in for a meal and supplies at a merchant's home near the Río Grande. The owner, Honorato Rojas, had sold them provisions before, so the guerrillas believed him to be trustworthy. Rojas overheard their plan to cross the Río Grande, and he notified Captain Mario Vargas of the Bolivian army, who was patrolling nearby. His troops set up an ambush on both banks of the Río Grande on the last day of August.

Captain Vargas watched as the line of guerrillas approached the riverbank slowly, then entered one by one to ford the river. "With the majority of them in the water and when they were coming directly towards us, we opened fire," reported Vargas. "Immediately they threw off their backpacks, which the current started to carry downstream, and they tried to take shelter in the water. They fled in all directions, obliging us to abandon our positions and go down to the riverbank. From both sides of the river we went shooting and eliminated them one by one. The whole thing lasted less than twenty minutes. Tania was one of the first to fall."[78] The guerrilla Tania did not even have the time to throw off her backpack and fire her weapon.

As the South American winter turned to springtime, radio broadcasts began reporting the results of the ambush, though not one of them mentioned the recovery of the body of a female. Tania's corpse had washed downstream and became snagged under a rock. The broadcasters mentioned the fact that one Bolivian in Joaquín's rear guard had managed to surrender to the soldiers. On hearing the news, Che expected that the captive would be tortured and executed. The radio also brought the news that the government had placed a bounty of 50,000 pesos (US$4,200) on the capture of Che Guevara, dead or alive.

In the meanwhile, the guerrilla defeat on the banks of the Río Grande provided a unique opportunity for CIA agent Félix Rodríguez. One man, a Bolivian who had the code name Paco, survived the initial firefight and was captured. The Bolivian commanders did torture him. They obtained some information and prepared to execute him. Rodríguez and his companion, a Bolivian army intelligence officer, obtained the prisoner along with a diary kept by the Cuban Braulio, one of Joaquín's men. Paco told his captors that Tania had been in Joaquín's rear guard and had gone underwater after the first salvo. But the Bolivians had not recovered the body of a woman. They returned and found her corpse still underwater, weighed down by the knapsack. Rodríguez used Braulio's diary to learn details of the internal organization of the guerrillas as well as the relationship between Che and his followers. Then he corroborated the evidence with Paco's recollections.

Paco, a Bolivian, had never intended to be a guerrilla and freely admitted as much to Agent Rodríguez. He and an uncle had gone to several meetings of the Maoist faction in La Paz. He met Moisés Guevara. In January 1967, Moisés Guevara promised Paco a scholarship to study in Cuba and Russia and delivered him to the farm at Ñancahuazú. There he received a backpack, a hammock, and a Mauser. Together with a number of other Bolivian "recruits," Paco was told he was now a guerrilla fighter. Many of his Bolivian colleagues had likewise been tricked into joining the guerrillas. The Maoist leader Moisés Guevara also had been a member of the rear guard. He too died in the ambush at the Río Grande.

Moreover, Paco the reluctant guerrilla fighter began to regale his interrogators with gossip, especially on Tania. She was Guevara's lover, he testified, and tried to hang on Che's arm whenever Che entered camp. Tania also had the habit of writing down all the slights and insults she suffered in order to report them to El Che. She often argued in tears with Joaquín, who called her a "high-class lady" from a wealthy family. But after Joaquín's rear guard became separated from the main column, Tania could no longer confide in Che.[79] Paco and the other men in the rear guard speculated that Tania was sick with cancer.

As the new Bolivian rangers completed the last month of their training, the regular army conscripts were closing in on the guerrillas of the ELN. By September 9, one month before the end, the twenty-two remaining Cuban and Bolivian guerrillas were surrounded on nearly all roads and hamlets by soldiers and harassed daily by flyovers of planes and helicopters. They remained day and night in the *monte,* hacking pathways for torturous movement through the thick underbrush. One day in mid-September, Che Guevara wrote matter-of-factly in the diary, "After something like 6 months, I bathed. That constitutes a record that already others are approaching."[80]

On the evening of September 22, the guerrillas entered Alto Seco, a village of fifty houses left unguarded by the army. Che assembled "15 terrified and silent peasants" in a small schoolhouse.[81] The Bolivian Inti Peredo addressed the townspeople as the ostensible commander of the guerrillas. "I explained our objectives," Inti wrote later. "I emphasized their hard condition of life, the significance of our struggle and its importance for the people, because their future improvement depended on our triumph."[82]

Che also spoke, asking for volunteers to join the struggle against imperialism. The townspeople listened respectfully. Only the schoolteacher asked questions, especially about the finer points of socialism. This amounted to the first and only occasion in which the insurgents could explain their program before a group of townspeople. Soon thereafter the guerrillas abandoned Alto Seco. At the last minute, a young man approached one of the Bolivian fighters and asked in Quechua if he could join up. "Don't be a fool," Pablo whispered. "We're all washed up and we don't know how to get out of here."[83]

The conscript soldiers of the Bolivian army were becoming more effective in their combat skills. Their superior numbers emboldened them, and they had placed the guerrillas in a defensive posture. On September 26, a company of the 8th Division ambushed Che's vanguard at the village of La Higuera. Three of the guerrillas went down—Coco, Miguel, and Julio, the latter two Cuban revolutionary veterans. Miguel had commanded Che's vanguard. Three others suffered wounds, and Camba removed his knapsack and fled. In an instant, Che's column suffered its heaviest casualties of any previous engagement. Che and others retreated chaotically to the canyons below La Higuera. The men heard shots in the distance and presumed that Camba and another missing guerrilla, León, had also met their deaths. Che had never liked Camba and reported in the journal that his loss was "a net gain" for the guerrilla band.[84]

Second Lieutenant Eduardo Galindo Marchant of the 8th Division later described the ambush to an Argentinean journalist. "When we saw the enemy coming toward us, we opened fire bringing down three of them." Galindo described how the rest of the guerrilla column was coming out of the town of La Higuera. "I gave the order to my men to leave their positions and go on to assault directly at them," the lieutenant recalled. "The insurgents took flight deep into the bushes."[85] Che's diary confirms these recollections.

The conscript soldiers did not in fact kill Camba and León but captured them both alive. Lieutenant Galindo then brought the men of his entire company to view the "mythic" enemy against whom they were fighting. "Camba, exhausted, weak, ragged, inspired more pity than fear," one officer recalled.[86] Three days of retreat followed for the rebel force. The guerrillas listened as Bolivian broadcasters announced the guerrilla casualties and that Che Guevara himself was "corralled" in the canyons below La Higuera. Che noted in his journal that the army was demonstrating "more effectiveness in its action."[87] This notation amounts to Che's first praise for the fighting capacity of the Bolivian army.

At this moment, the government ordered the 2nd Ranger Battalion, which had been in training with the Green Berets, into action against the guerrillas.

LAST DAYS

The first six days of October consisted of more life-on-the-run for the fighters of the National Liberation Army. Che recounted one notable occurrence in glowing terms: one of his final guerrilla "feasts." "Towards nightfall we came down and prepared coffee which tasted wonderful despite the bitter water and the grease in the pot in which it was prepared. We then prepared porridge to eat there and rice with tapir meat to take with us."[88] After the meal, the group undertook a night march to get down to a canyon at 1,360 meters above sea level, but they were unable to find water.[89] The men listened to the radio about how the two Bolivian prisoners fared after their capture. "To our surprise," Pombo wrote in his diary, "Camba conducted himself more firmly than León."[90]

As the guerrilla column climbed back up to an altitude of 2,000 meters searching for water, the radio crackled with the news that the army had dispatched eighteen hundred troops to La Higuera in the hunt for Che Guevara. Among them was the 2nd Ranger Battalion. The guerrillas now numbered eighteen men. They passed the morning of October 7 "bucolically" marking their eleventh month of the campaign.

Then just after noon, an old woman herding goats wandered into the canyon where the guerrillas were camped. She professed to know nothing of the soldiers' whereabouts but placed the guerrillas several kilometers below La Higuera. They gave the women fifty pesos not to say a word to anyone about their location. Che entertained "few hopes that she would comply notwithstanding her promises."[91] Therefore, the rebels moved down the canyon in a march that ended after midnight.

On the morning of the next day, the fatigued and battered guerrilla force found itself encircled in its canyon campsite. The third platoon of the newly deployed ranger company of Captain Gary Prado had moved on to the heights above the canyons east of the town of La Higuera. Several of the ELN fighters hiding below had received wounds in previous fights and were in poor condition to fight. Still others suffered from illness, particularly dysentery.

The guerrillas now found themselves at 2,000 meters, no longer under trees but among clumps of thorn bushes offering scant camouflage. Che crawled over to Benigno and ordered him to scout out the weakest point in the Bolivian rangers' positions. The guerrillas might have to fight their way through the encirclement. "Prepare yourself," Benigno remembered Che saying, "because I think this will be the last combat." At the time, Benigno, who was injured in the previous firefight, had wanted this to be the last battle. We all wanted to die, recalled Benigno. "We couldn't do anything more, but neither did we want to become prisoners."[92]

Che reasoned that they might be able to break through if the rangers made no advance until dusk. He ordered his fighters to lie low and counterattack at nightfall. Instead, shortly after noon, one flank of the Bolivian rangers spotted a guerrilla crossing a clearing. They shot the Bolivian fighter Aníceto. "Cayó uno, cayó uno," the soldiers shouted. "One's down, one's down."[93] The entire platoon of rangers commenced the fusillade, which lasted for some twenty minutes. The guerrillas fired back selectively to save ammunition but still dropped three attackers.

Che immediately reacted to save the sick and injured, numbering half of his men. He ordered Pablito to lead this group in retreat down the canyon, while the others returned fire and covered the retreat. A bullet struck the chamber of Che's rifle, disabling it. Che pulled out his pistol but discovered it had no bullets in the chamber. At that moment, Che felt a sharp pain in the calf of his right leg. He had been shot. The Bolivian rebel Willy Cuba helped Che regain his footing. They attempted to climb out of the canyon. But they were met by several rangers with rifles at the ready. "Stop! Don't shoot!" yelled the Argentinean guerrilla leader. "I'm El Che, and I'm worth more to you alive than dead."[94] The rangers seized the Argentinean and his Bolivian comrade.

The ranger commander, Captain Prado, arrived to take charge of the prisoners. He called for an immediate ceasefire. Prado organized guards to march Comandante Che, Willy, and another injured rebel, Pacho, back to La Higuera. Pacho collapsed and died on the march. Arriving at his command post, Captain Prado radioed a message to battalion headquarters. "Tenemos el Papá," he reported in code. "We have Daddy."[95] Major Pappy Shelton later took note of Che's bad luck. He "was trapped by and tried to break through the best platoon of the best company in the Ranger [Battalion]," he wrote, "Gary Prado's 'C' Co. and the 3rd [Platoon] commanded by Sgt. Huaca."[96]

The rangers placed Che in one small room of a dilapidated schoolhouse, and Willy in the other. They threw in the corpses of three dead guerrillas too. A Bolivian medic entered to bind Che's wound in the right calf and discovered that the bullet had torn through the flesh but missed the bone. The battalion commander, Major Ayoroa, arrived and removed Che's personal possessions. "Why did you choose to come to Bolivia?" Ayoroa asked.[97] Che replied, "Can't you see the state in which the peasants live? They are almost like savages, living in a state of poverty that depresses the heart, having only one room in which to sleep and cook and no clothing to wear, abandoned like animals."[98] The guerrilla comandante asked about his own fighters. "They are good people," he said. "At this time they could be living comfortably with their families."[99] He displayed not a trace of defeatism and looked everyone in the eye when he spoke. The two prisoners received a meal.

Subsequently, the officers divided up the contents of Che's money belt, some 2,500 US dollars and 20,000 Bolivian pesos. Others took his smoking pipes, German 9-millimeter pistol, maps, altimeter, and personal documents. Major Ayoroa took possession of the diaries. Three of their own rangers had also fallen in battle, but Ayoroa and Captain Prado treated the prisoners with dignity. Other officers and some soldiers who were celebrating with rounds of beer had begun to taunt them. In the meanwhile, the fate of Che himself was being discussed.

That evening in La Paz, President Barrientos convoked a meeting of his military staff. General Ovando attended, as did five other general officers. Barrientos had suffered intense international scrutiny regarding the court case pending against Régis Debray. Apparently, the president had no desire to endure the even greater pressure if he placed Che Guevara on trial. Bolivia did not have the death penalty.[100] Therefore, Barrientos decided on summary execution. He would not be able to control the university students, the MNR left wing, and the mine workers if Che Guevara was brought to La Paz for a trial.[101] General Ovando transmitted the order to the 8th Division and the 2nd Ranger Battalion. Next morning, General Ovando left for the airport with several other field grade officers and reporters for a trip to Vallegrande, a garrison town northwest of the hamlet of La Higuera. Government spokesmen informed the press that Che Guevara had died in battle at noon on the previous day, October 8.

That morning Che was very much alive. CIA agent Félix Rodríguez arrived early at La Higuera via helicopter and went straight to talk to the prisoner. Most of the other Bolivian officers were leaving to meet General Ovando in Vallegrande. They left Agent Rodríguez, who wore captain's bars on his Bolivian army fatigues, as the highest-ranking officer at La Higuera. Rodríguez wanted to debrief the guerrilla commander for his report to CIA headquarters at Langley. "Nobody interrogates me!" said Che, although he did consent to have a conversation with the CIA officer. Rodríguez untied the wounded prisoner and invited him outside into the bright sunlight for a photo, snapped by the helicopter pilot with the CIA agent's camera.[102] The two returned inside for the "conversation."

From that talk with the famous comandante, Rodríguez was able to file a "top secret" report. Che refused to denounce Fidel, stated that Castro was not a communist until after he came to power, and cleared Raúl and Fidel Castro of responsibility in the death of Camilo Cienfuegos. He advised his wife to marry again. Guevara also wanted Fidel to know that the revolution in Latin America would ultimately succeed. The prisoner knew he was going to die, reported Rodríguez, but "Che never lost his composure." (For Rodríguez's interview of Che Guevara, see the Appendix.)

Numerous members of the international press corps were gathering in Vallegrande. Colonel Zenteno, commander of the 8th Army, expected the arrival of General Ovando at any moment. The body of Che Guevara, supposedly killed in battle on the previous day, had not yet been delivered. Zenteno put in a call to La Higuera, and CIA agent Rodríguez answered. Zenteno ordered him to have Guevara shot immediately and to fly the body via helicopter to Vallegrande. Rodríguez, as a captain, passed on the execution order to 2nd Lieutenant Pérez, who assigned it to Sergeants Huanca and Mario Terán. The two Bolivian NCOs drew straws. The lieutenant asked Che if he had any last wishes. Yes, food. "I want to die on a full stomach." Pérez accused him of being a materialist, interested only in food. "Quizás," replied Che. "Maybe."[103]

The CIA agent advised the soldiers not to shoot Che in the face, for reasons of identification. At 1:00 P.M., Sergeant Huanca walked into the schoolroom where the Bolivian Willy was held prisoner. They exchanged loud insults, and Huanca shot him. Sergeant Terán entered Che's room, and Guevara said, "So you have come to kill me?" And then Che told him to change the name "El Ché" printed on the blackboard. "Che is not spelled with an accent over the e. Tell your commander to remove the accent," said the Argentinean. Terán departed as instructed. Sergeant Terán's fellow soldiers teased him for his lack of nerve, and he reentered the room.[104] Che got himself to his feet and spoke to Terán in a firm voice.

"Now you will see how a man dies! Shoot now, dammit!"[105] Terán obeyed, getting off several shots to the upper torso, one piercing the heart.

The corpse was still warm when it arrived in Vallegrande on the skids of a helicopter. The soldiers removed the shirt, cleaned up the blood, and cut Che's hair. They placed the body on a stretcher in the washroom, eyes open and lips slightly parted. Rigor mortis had not yet set in. When the soldiers moved the corpse, the arms flopped about. Reporters waiting outside did not see this. When they entered, army officers instructed them not to touch the body. It had already been announced that Che had been dead for twenty-four hours, and the officers did not want the international press to know that President Barrientos had lied.

CIA agent Rodríguez had accompanied the body during the flight from La Higuera and ducked out of sight immediately after landing. He did not want to implicate the United States in Che's death. On the other hand, CIA agent Villoldo rushed to see the body being prepared. He grabbed a few locks of hair cut from Che's head (which he would sell forty-five years later on eBay). He remained at the site in his Bolivian captain's battle dress for the rest of the afternoon. Journalists identified him later in their photos, arousing suspicion that the CIA had orchestrated Che's execution.

According to Agent Villoldo's memoir, the armed forces chief of staff, General Ovando, ordered him to bury Che and two others of his men. Villoldo requisitioned a driver, a security guard, and a pickup truck from the 8th Army. He buried the three guerrillas at a cemetery near the new tarmac at a military airport.[106] The actual burial site remained a secret for the next thirty years.

THE CURSE OF CHE GUEVARA

Che had told his fighters that he had come to Bolivia to succeed or die. Yet, he actually surrendered during the final battle on October 8. The experienced guerrilla commander might have planned ahead that his surrender would save the lives of his men. Indeed, Captain Prado's troops held their positions for the rest of the afternoon, permitting the sick and injured guerrillas to escape down the canyon. Still, units of the 2nd Ranger Battalion caught up to them several days later and killed all but six of them.

Benigno and five others managed to escape the rangers for a second time. These survivors of the National Liberation Army included the Bolivians Inti, Darío, and Ñato and the Cubans Pombo, Urbano, and Benigno. Ñato died of his gunshot wounds after escaping the army dragnet. Miraculously, the remaining five men hid from Bolivian patrols while fleeing westward across the Altiplano and through the Andes Mountains into Chile. There the three Cubans contacted Senator Salvador Allende. After convalescing, they boarded planes flying across the Pacific and the Middle East to Prague. Castro greeted them as heroes when they returned to Cuba. Pombo and Urbano stayed in the revolution. Benigno broke publicly with Fidel, accusing him of treason in the death of Che Guevara. Today he lives in exile in Paris.[107]

The Bolivian guerrilla survivors, Inti and Darío, later died at the hands of police assassins. They had been instrumental in the unsuccessful resurrection of the ELN in 1969. They attempted to begin a second guerrilla war with additional Bolivians who trained at the School of National Liberation on the Isle of Pines, Cuba. The second ELN failed much more rapidly than the first. But it had been able to execute the merchant Honorato Rojas for his responsibility in the army's lethal ambush of Joaquín's rear guard.

President Johnson rewarded Bolivian president René Barrientos with a rare invitation (for a Latin American head of state) to visit the Johnson ranch in Stonewall, Texas. The afternoon's entertainment featured an outdoor Texas barbeque and a frontier pageant along the Pedernales River with covered wagons, cowboys, and faux Indians. Johnson the cattleman presented Barrientos the aviator with a western saddle. Not two weeks later, his government in La Paz had to confront a new crisis.[108] The Bolivian left erupted in protest rallies as the official version of Che's death was leaking out.

While El Che led the guerrilla rebellion, the nation rallied around President Barrientos. The trouble began after Guevara was executed. Barrientos's popularity declined when his version of Che's death proved to be a lie. The president ridiculed Captain Prado and a few other officers who had exposed the falsehood. They were dismissed from the armed forces. Antonio Arguedas, interior minister in the cabinet of President Barrientos, had to flee the country for releasing to the press the real story behind the execution of Comandante Che Guevara. His report implicated American officials in Che's death. Arguedas's version of events placed CIA agent John S. Tilton and the embassy's military attaché at the meeting in which the Bolivian president and generals had decided on Che's execution.[109]

Finally, photocopies of Che's diary came to light in 1968, when Fidel Castro had them published in Havana. Bolivian president Barrientos denounced the publication as a fabrication, and Castro challenged him to compare the Cuban publication to the actual diary still in the hands of the Bolivian government. Barrientos's spokesmen had to concede the truth of the matter. A British reporter, Richard Gott, revealed that he had paid a Bolivian general US$5,000 for copies of the diary, which eventually ended up in the hands of Fidel Castro.

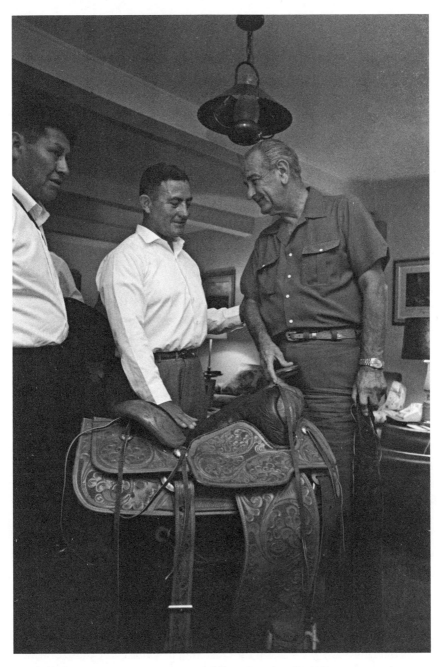

Lyndon Johnson presenting a western saddle to President René Barrientos at the former's ranch on the Pedernales River, Texas. The Bolivian leader had little time to enjoy the gift; he died in a helicopter accident a few months later.

Then there occurred the denials concerning Che's corpse. Three requests arrived at the Presidential Palace in La Paz for Che's remains. One came from his brother Roberto Guevara, another from Castro, and the third from the president of the Chilean Senate, Salvador Allende. Barrientos announced falsely that Che's body had been cremated.[110] Even so, before "disappearing" the body, Bolivian officials wanted to make sure they had the real Che Guevara. They sawed off both hands before disposing of his body. A Bolivian military officer flew with the severed hands to Buenos Aires, where Argentinean forensic experts confirmed that the fingerprints were those of Ernesto Guevara de la Serna. Minister Arguedas subsequently delivered Che's hands, sealed in a jar of formaldehyde, to Fidel Castro. The severed hands showed up in Havana in 1970 and were stored at the Palacio de la Revolución.[111]

Che's remains arrived much later. In 1997, the Bolivian government revealed the secret burial site of Guevara and other Cubans who had died with him. Castro had the remains repatriated to Santa Clara, Cuba. There Che and his followers lie within a mausoleum that commemorates his greatest military victory in the Cuban revolutionary war. Tania's remains rest there too.

Communist party leader Mario Monje returned from Chile after the government had defeated Che's uprising. But Inti Peredo had begun the brief rebellion of the second National Liberation Army in 1970. One morning, Monje emerged from his residence to find a death threat nailed to his front door, signed by the ELN. He left Bolivia and retired to Moscow, where Che Guevara's biographers traveled to interview him.

Sergeant Terán, Che's executioner, admitted later to be wracked with doubt about his role. President Barrientos promoted him to sergeant major and gave him some money. At times he considered himself a national hero, and at others, a common killer who did not deserve to live. Ultimately the Cubans forgave him. He traveled later in life to Havana for cataract surgery to save his eyesight—completely free.[112] By then, the president of Bolivia was Evo Morales, a firm ally of the Cuban revolutionary government.

Soon enough, the Bolivian triumph turned into a curse in which many of the top leaders involved in the death of Che met violent ends. President René Barrientos died in 1969 in the crash of a helicopter, the cause of which was never determined. General Juan José Torres, the army commander who attended the meeting that generated the order of execution, governed the country briefly as president over a left-wing government in 1971. He released Régis Debray and Ciro Bustos from prison. Torres was assassinated in Buenos Aires in 1976 by the right-wing terrorist group known as the Argentine Anticommunist Alliance (AAA, or Triple A). General Alfredo Ovando succeeded Barrientos in office for a brief period and later fell into a well and died in 1982.

The commander of the 8th Bolivian Army, Colonel Joaquín Zenteno (who passed on the order to execute the prisoner), died on a Paris street in 1976 at the hands of assassins belonging to a group called the Che Guevara Command. In another assassination attempt in 1972, Che's captor, Captain Gary Prado, suffered a gunshot wound to the spine. Prado has used a wheelchair ever since.

Author and former CIA agent Brian Latell, who interviewed defectors from the Cuba state security agencies, claims that Castro's hit squads were responsible for some of these killings. Those involved in the execution of Che Guevara, including President Barrientos, succumbed to Fidel's wrath, Latell says. For good measure, Cuban security agents arranged the assassination in Paraguay of former Nicaraguan dictator Anastasio Somoza Jr.[113]

Che's life defies easy analysis. He was a man who overcame chronic asthma in order to pursue a full and active life. He was a revolutionary, a disciplinarian, an executioner, and a rigid ideologue. But Guevara advocated ceaselessly for social justice and for the rights of the poor and diseased, believing that they had a right to education and health care. Most of all, he detested the exploitation of the powerless by the powerful.

Ernesto Guevara—El Che—believed he was destined to reshape the world. As minister of industry, he thought he could industrialize a tropical island via sheer willpower and a strict reading of Karl Marx. His errors in economic planning deeply hurt his pride, and he returned with a vengeance to his first love: revolutionary activism. Indeed, he had never abandoned it, even as president of the Cuban National Bank and minister of industry. Che had a hand in the Caribbean War in 1959. Subsequently, he designed the guerrilla training curriculum for foreign fighters, and he propagandized in favor of revolutionary warfare on an international scale. He aged restlessly, afraid he would soon be too old to fight. Therefore, he forced the mission in the Congo as well as the guerrilla uprising in Bolivia. It did not matter that neither country had conditions conducive to revolution. Che convinced him-self that he could create them. Communist naysayers merely stoked his un-quenchable yearning to show up his critics.

What happened to Ernesto "Che" Guevara in Bolivia illustrates the re-sult of personalities imposing themselves on process. This fact makes the his-tory of the secret war in South America so interesting and paradoxical. Che Guevara himself misrepresented the revolutionary formula in order to jus-tify the power that Fidel Castro's 26th of July Movement had gained in the aftermath of Batista's flight. His writings discounted the role played by the urban middle class in the Cuban revolutionary war. Why? Because it was from the middle class that the counterrevolution arose in resistance to the communist turn that Castro was taking afterward, during the consolidation. Moreover, when Cuban radicals wanted socialist neighbors, Che Guevara exported the revolution not as it had been but as what it had become— Marxist rather than nationalist. Ironically, the communist parties in the target countries opposed this export of the armed revolution. Bolivia was no exception.

Che suffered the consequences of his mistaken revolutionary strategies. His own death was hardly tragic. But the demise of one hundred men (guer-rillas and soldiers) and one woman (Tania) constitutes the real Bolivian tragedy of 1967. Add that number to the hundreds of thousands of people who would be tortured, raped, and killed in Latin America in the years following the Cuban Revolution, and one gains perspective of the real calamity.[114] No one can blame all this mayhem solely on El Che. Kennedy, Johnson, Khrushchev, Brezhnev, Mao, and Castro also share that burden. So do countless right- and left-wingers who entered the fray throughout the hemisphere.

El Che could have been the character in one of Mariano Azuela's novels who said, "I love the volcano because it's a volcano, the revolution because it's the revolution! What do I care about the stones left above or below after the cataclysm? What are they to me?"[115]

Conclusion

PRIOR TO 1962, Latin America had been undergoing a surge of democratization. One dictatorship after another ended in the late 1950s, to be replaced by elected governments. Manuel Prado's election in 1956 had even followed a dictatorship in Peru. Argentina and Venezuela made the electoral transition in 1958. When strongman Fulgencio Batista fled from Cuba on New Year's Day, 1959, it appeared that the "twilight of the dictators" had arrived. Subsequently, President John F. Kennedy staked the Alliance for Progress on these democratic movements. He made it a policy to invite only elected presidents to the White House while purposely ignoring the four remaining dictators.[1] Shortly after his inauguration, Kennedy honored Peru's President Prado as one of his first foreign guests.

Then the tide turned. Of the fifteen Latin American heads of state with whom Kennedy personally conferred, eight suffered military overthrows before the end of Kennedy's thousand days in the presidency.[2] Brazilian generals in 1964 contributed a new element to the interventions. There they established long-term, institutional military rule that became the standard into the 1970s. Subsequent coups in Bolivia, Argentina, Peru, and Panama replicated the Brazilian pattern. The cycle of long-term rule by juntas gained additional strength in the 1970s with military takeovers in Chile, in Uruguay, and in Argentina once again in 1976.[3] Only Colombia and Venezuela in South America did not revert back to military control.

The military coups d'état of the 1960s occurred in a unique confluence of national and international currents. Rising foreign debts, inflation, political polarization, civil-military tension, and popular frustration—these formed the backdrop in 1959, when Fidel Castro introduced a new development model to the Americas. First the Cuban revolutionaries destroyed the old military establishment that certainly would have resisted wholesale economic and social change. Then Fidel utilized members of the domestic communist party and formed alliances with the Socialist Bloc countries. He socialized rural and urban properties and confiscated virtually all foreign and domestic businesses. The revolutionary regime provided universal and free programs in public education and health care. In 1961, Castro and his worker and peasant militias defeated a counterrevolutionary invasion engineered by the Central Intelligence Agency.

Consequently, the Cuban Revolution caught the imagination of Latin America's youth. Many who flocked to Havana to celebrate Cuba's victories gained the support of Fidel Castro and Che Guevara in order to return home to start guerrilla rebellions. Cold War currents interpenetrating with the hot waters of unresolved national problems created a volatile mixture.

In their textbooks on US–Latin America relations, students commonly read about the havoc caused by American policies aimed at preventing the spread of communism and the Cuban revolutionary example. There is no point in attempting to whitewash US foreign policy. American diplomatic conduct in the cases of Guatemala in 1954 or in Chile in 1973 does conform to this blanket indictment. US actions prior to the Brazilian military coup in 1964 also appear highly suspect. Historians agree that President Lyndon Baines Johnson's decision in 1965 to send American troops into the Dominican Republic vastly overreacted to the danger of a communist takeover.[4]

However, in other cases, American diplomats sought to prevent the fall of elected governments. The generals often defied the embassies of the United States. In fact, an earlier generation of scholars—mostly political scientists—who studied the "breakdown of democracy" dismissed international relations as a factor. "Those who assume that the source of Latin America's political turmoil and democratic failures is primarily external—U.S. intervention and manipulation; economic dependence—may be disappointed with the historical analyses in this volume," began one anthology of case studies. "Without exception, each of our authors attributes the course of political development and regime change primarily to internal structures and actions."[5] In a more recent study, a scholar warns of the limits of Washington's power to shape events. "The United States was the strongest imperial power in Latin America in the twentieth century, and it got what it wanted often enough, frequently with tragic results," Patrick Iber states. "Still it was not omnipotent."[6]

Yet, there is no denying that a tsunami of military interventions washed over Latin America in the 1960s. The Cuban Revolution provided the shock that set off the wave. Moreover, the method by which the Cuban Revolution exported both its counterrevolution and its brand of guerrilla warfare tended to multiply the energy of the island's revolutionary example. America's support of the Cuban counterrevolution also contributed to the strength of the reactionary wave. The evidence in this book suggests that the secret war waged between the Cuban revolutionaries and Washington's policymakers profoundly affected the political balance in every republic of Latin America. Sometimes it led to overdue social reforms, as in the cases of Venezuela, Peru, and Panama. In others, it hastened the repression of popular demands.

To this point, few scholars have researched the Cuban Revolution as a motivating factor in the surge of military *golpes* in the 1960s and 1970s. The reason is understandable. Cuban officials simply do not permit access to the documentation of the General Directorate of Intelligence or of Fidel Castro's papers in the Council of State. These two institutions really determined and carried out Havana's foreign policies. But when both Cubans and non-Cubans write about inter-American affairs in the 1960s, they rely on US documents—and Fidel's speeches—on such subjects as the Bay of Pigs, the Cuban Missile Crisis, Operation Mongoose, and the CIA. Most of Washington's smoking guns are exposed. Havana's weapons are hidden. No wonder there have been few in-depth studies of Cuba's export of revolution.[7] Admittedly, this book cannot be the last word on the Cuban Revolution and the secret war in Latin America. Until historians gain access to Castro's papers and the archives of the Cuban Interior Ministry, we will never know what American intelligence analysts got wrong.

The revolution in Cuba created a dilemma for democracy in the Western Hemisphere. To wit, American elected officials had difficulty talking to their South American counterparts. President Kennedy could not find agreement with Presidents Frondizi and Goulart on questions of Cuba and communism. Johnson did not see eye to eye with Belaúnde on American oil operations in Peru or with Robles on negotiations over the Panama Canal. Congress disapproved of financing civilian presidents who criticized US policy and who spoke the language of nationalism. Yet those were the very leaders South American voters in the 1960s tended to support. Washington's blessing did not always guarantee success for Latin American politicians either. In 1962, the Americans would have been happy with Haya de la Torre as president of Peru. Washington wanted Frondizi to finish his term of office in Argentina. Even though US officials in Panama celebrated the inauguration of President Arias with an elaborate party, he had to flee a coup d'état just two weeks later.

On the other hand, the generals offered the policy pronouncements that pleased the Americans, even if they seldom delivered. The juntas welcomed capital investment, and their ministers at the OAS voted to punish the Cubans. True, the military rulers of the 1960s did not privatize the state industries as the Americans suggested, but neither did they denounce the foreign corporations. Finally, military men were anticommunist, a product of their own survival in revolutionary times. In contrast to the civilian politicians, few generals sought the popular vote.

The Kennedy administration had wanted every military junta of Latin America to provide a transition of power via elections to a "responsible" civilian leader. In the end, the American diplomats had to settle for long-term military rule. The generals could be counted on to be anticommunists, fiscal conservatives, proponents of the OAS boycott of Cuba, protectors of private foreign capital, and advocates for economic integration through the Alliance for Progress.

Brazil in 1964 proved to be the only domestic military intervention approved beforehand by United States diplomats, because the constitutional heads of state, Quadros and Goulart, unabashedly supported Fidel Castro and forcefully criticized American foreign policies and capital investments. Therefore, US policymakers bought into the anticommunist rhetoric of the Brazilian right wing. Ambassador Gordon, Secretary Rusk, and President Johnson too believed the opposition's improbable contention that President Goulart was planning a left-wing coup d'état of his own government. In South America, no president has made a coup of his own government (the so-called *autogolpe*) without backing from the military.[8]

However, when the militaries defied US expectations, Washington could do naught but acquiesce. Its opposition to Cuba trumped all other policies for Latin America. As a result, the generals ruled Brazil for twenty-one years and Argentina for most of the thirty years after the fall of Perón in 1955. Peru's junta controlled the government for twelve years, while only a full-blown invasion of US troops in 1985 could dislodge the Panamanian military after seventeen years in power. Moreover, the United States did not achieve all its policy objectives with junta rulers. The Peruvian military expropriated US-owned petroleum and mining companies, and Peru and Panama renewed diplomatic relations with Fidel Castro. At least the military governments restored enough stability to permit the United States to shift its Cold War crusade to Southeast Asia. Instances of right-wing savagery—Argentina, Chile, and Guatemala—derived from local causes rather than US engagement.[9]

Most military governments pursued reactionary policies. How then does one account for the more reformist tendencies adopted by the Peruvian and Panamanian *golpistas?* Generals Velasco and Torrijos befriended Fidel Castro and called themselves "revolutionaries" without having to invert the lexicon, as did the Brazilian generals. The difference lies in the country's previous experience with populism. Peru and Panama had never had leaders powerful enough to achieve the populist agenda: nationalizing basic industries and bringing urban workers into the body politic. The military had suppressed the elections, respectively, of Haya de la Torre and Arnulfo Arias. Therefore, the officers in power assumed the responsibility to tackle problems of land tenure, foreign domination of the economy, and lack of incorporation of the popular classes into national politics. Argentina and Brazil had had powerful experiences with populism; not so Peru and Panama.

Finally, how did Venezuela, which had no tradition of democracy, manage to keep the generals at bay despite battling the most serious pro-Castro guerrilla insurrection of the 1960s? The civilian politicians played the pro–United States card. President Betancourt broke diplomatic relations with Cuba while carrying out the measured land reforms (though no progressive taxation) suggested by Kennedy's Alliance for Progress. He and his successors also professionalized the military with US equipment and training, though they were careful not to embarrass the officer corps by publicizing this dependence. Cuba rather than the United States posed the greatest foreign danger to Venezuela. Moreover, as President Leoni told Lyndon Johnson at Punta del Este, both of their governments shared an overriding interest in keeping up the northward flow of Venezuelan petroleum. Consequently, the Venezuelans seldom had to beg for US development funds.

In general, Che Guevara's oft-repeated prediction did not materialize. He said that guerrilla struggle in the countryside would ultimately sweep all Latin America toward the revolutionary anti-imperialist triumph. The *sandinistas* who overthrew the Somoza regime came close in the 1970s to establishing Cuban-style socialism, but neither the Soviets nor the Chinese had sufficient economic dynamism to support a second Cuba. True, the administration of Ronald Reagan sold weapons to the Iranian revolution in order to fund the Nicaraguan counterrevolution. However, peace and elections resulted from the efforts of all Central American heads of state to prevent the Americans from crushing the *sandinistas*, making it possible for the Nicaraguans themselves to vote *sandinista* leader Daniel Ortega out of power for more than two decades.[10] All other guerrilla uprisings—whether rural or urban—met defeat by the domestic armed forces. Che's legacy reinforced the reactionary trend that won out in many Spanish- and Portuguese-speaking nations of the Western Hemisphere.

"If given the choice between social justice and order," Henry Kissinger once said, "I would always choose order." Many Latin Americans agreed with him—but at what a cost!

APPENDIX

NOTES

ACKNOWLEDGMENTS

ILLUSTRATION CREDITS

INDEX

Statements by Ernesto "Che" Guevara prior to His Execution in Bolivia

Washington, October 13, 1967

MEMORANDUM FOR
    The Secretary of State
    The Secretary of Defense
    Mr. Walt W. Rostow
    Assistant Secretary of State for Inter-American Affairs

SUBJECT
    Statements by Ernesto "Che" Guevara Prior to His Execution in Bolivia

1. Further details have now been obtained from [*less than 1 line of source text not declassified*] who was on the scene in the small village of Higueras [*sic*] where Ernesto "Che" Guevara was taken after his capture on 8 October 1967 by the Bolivian army's 2nd Ranger Battalion.
2. [*less than 1 line of source text not declassified*] attempted to interrogate Guevara on 9 October 1967 as soon as he got access to him at around 7 A.M. At that time "Che" Guevara was sitting on the floor in the corner of a small, dark

schoolroom in Higueras. He had his hands over his face. His wrists and feet were tied. In front of him on the floor lay the corpses of two Cuban guerrillas. Guevara had a flesh wound in his leg, which was bandaged.

3. Guevara refused to be interrogated but permitted himself to be drawn into a conversation with [*less than 1 line of source text not declassified*] during which he made the following comments:

   a. *Cuban economic situation:* Hunger in Cuba is the result of pressure by United States imperialism. Now Cuba has become self-sufficient in meat production and has almost reached the point where it will begin to export meat. Cuba is the only economically self-sufficient country in the Socialist world.

   b. *Camilo Cienfuegos:* For many years the story has circulated that Fidel Castro Ruz had Cienfuegos, one of his foremost deputies, killed because his personal popularity presented a danger to Castro. Actually the death of Cienfuegos was an accident. Cienfuegos has been in Oriente Province when he received a call to attend a general staff meeting in Havana. He left by plane and the theory was that the plane became lost in low-ceiling flying conditions, consumed all of its fuel, and crashed in the ocean, and no trace of him was ever found. Castro had loved Cienfuegos more than any of his lieutenants.

   c. *Fidel Castro Ruz:* Castro had not been a Communist prior to the success of the Cuban Revolution. Castro's own statements on the subject are correct.

   d. *The Congo:* American imperialism had not been the reason for his failure there but, rather, the Belgian mercenaries. He denied ever having several thousand troops in the Congo, as sometimes reported, but admitted having had "quite a few".

   e. *Treatment of Guerrilla Prisoners in Cuba:* During the course of the Cuban Revolution and its aftermath, there had been only about 1,500 individuals killed, exclusive of armed encounters such as the Bay of Pigs. The Cuban Government, of course, executed all guerrilla leaders who invaded its territory. . . . (He stopped then with a quizzical look on his face and smiled as he recognized his own position on Bolivian soil.)

   f. *Future of the Guerrilla Movement in Bolivia:* With his capture, the guerrilla movement had suffered an overwhelming setback in Bolivia, but he predicted a resurgence in the future. He insisted that his ideals would win in the end even though he was disappointed at the lack of response from the Bolivian campesinos. The guerrilla movement had failed partially because of Bolivian Government propaganda which claimed that the guerrillas represented a foreign invasion of Bolivian soil. In spite of the lack of popular response from the Bolivian campesinos, he had not planned an exfiltration route from Bolivia in case of failure. He had definitely decided to either fall or win in this effort.

4. According to [*less than 1 line of source text not declassified*] when Guevara, Simon Cuba, and Aniceto Reynaga Gordillo were captured on 8 October, the Bolivian Armed Forces Headquarters ordered that they be kept alive for a time. A telegraphic code was arranged between La Paz and Higueras with the numbers 500 representing Guevara, 600 meaning the phrase "keep alive" and 700 representing "execute". During the course of the discussion with Guevara, Simon Cuba and Aniceto Reynaga were detained in the next room of the school house. At one stage, a burst of shots was heard and [*less than 1 line of source text not declassified*] learned later that Simon Cuba had been executed. A little later a single shot was heard and it was learned afterward that Aniceto Reynaga had been killed. When the order came at 11:50 A.M. from La Paz to kill Guevara, the execution was delayed as long as possible. However, when the local commander was advised that a helicopter would arrive to recover the bodies at approximately 1:30 P.M., Guevara was executed with a burst of shots at 1:15 P.M. Guevara's last words were, "Tell my wife to remarry and tell Fidel Castro that the Revolution will again rise in the Americas." To his executioner he said, "Remember, you are killing a man."

5. At no time during the period he was under [*less than 1 line of source text not declassified*] observation did Guevara lose his composure.

Dick

Source: Lyndon Baines Johnson Presidential Library, National Security File, Country File, Bolivia, vol. 4, Memoranda, Jan 1966–Dec 1968. Secret.

Notes

INTRODUCTION

1. Rafael Fermoselle, *The Evolution of the Cuban Military: 1492–1986* (Miami: Editiones Universal, 1987), 267; R. Hart Phillips, *Cuba: Island of Paradox* (New York: McDowell, Obolensky, 1959), 394; Ramón L. Bonachea and Marta San Martín, *The Cuban Insurrection, 1952–1959* (New Brunswick, NJ: Transaction Books, 1974), 311–13; C. Fred Judson, *Cuba and the Revolutionary Myth: The Political Education of the Cuban Rebel Army, 1953–1963* (Boulder, CO: Westview Press, 1984), 158–59.

2. As quoted in Robert E. Quirk, *Fidel Castro* (New York: W. W. Norton, 1993), 211.

3. Carlos Franqui, *Diary of the Cuban Revolution,* trans. Georgette Felix et al. (New York: Viking Press, 1980), 483, 487, 1026–27. The general strike of early January 1959 succeeded because laborers—both noncommunists and some communists—had already forged an alliance with Castro's M26. See Stephen Cushion, "Organized Labour and the Cuban Revolution, 1952–1959" (doctoral thesis, University of London, 2012), chap. 7.

4. Fidel Castro, *Revolutionary Struggle, 1947–1958,* ed. Rolando E. Bonachea and Nelson P. Valdés (Cambridge, MA: MIT Press, 1972), 447.

5. Hart Phillips, *Cuba: Island of Paradox,* 397–98.

6. Castro, *Revolutionary Struggle,* 449.

7. Franqui, *Diary of the Cuban Revolution,* 484; Hart Phillips, *Cuba: Island of Paradox,* 397–98; T. J. English, *Havana Nocturne: How the Mob Owned Cuba . . . and Then Lost It to the Revolution* (New York: Harper, 2007), 302.

8. Howard Hunt, *Give Us This Day* (New Rochelle, NY: Arlington House, 1973), 28. The head of the Bacardí rum distillery, Orlando Bosch, donated several thousand dollars to Castro's rebel group. See Tom Gjelten, *Bacardi and the Long Fight for Cuba* (New York: Penguin Books, 2008), 195. Earl E. T. Smith, *The Fourth Floor: An Account of the Castro Communist Revolution* (New York: Random House, 1962), 18–26.

9. Franqui, *Diary of the Cuban Revolution,* 489; Bonachea and San Martín, *The Cuban Insurrection,* 318–21.

10. "Fidel Castro Speaks to Citizens of Santiago," 3 Jan 1959, Castro Speech Database: Latin American Network Information Center (hereafter cited as Castro Speech Database, LANIC), http://lanic.utexas.edu/project/castro/db/1959/19590103 .html, accessed 27 Aug 2013.

11. E. J. Hobsbawm, *The Age of Revolution, 1789–1848* (Cleveland: World, 1962). The wave of revolution still reverberates in academic literature. See Kurt Weyland, "The Diffusion of Revolution: '1848' in Europe and Latin America," *International Organization* 63, no. 3 (2009): 391–423; Weyland, *Making Waves: Democratic Contention in Europe and Latin America since the Revolutions of 1848* (New York: Cambridge University Press, 2013).

12. See especially Henry Kissinger, *A World Restored: Metternich, Castlereagh, and the Problems of Peace, 1812–22* (Boston: Houghton Mifflin, 1973). On Fidel Castro as a student of the French Revolution, see Fidel Castro, *Fidel en la memoria del jovén que es* (Melbourne: Ocean Press, 2005), 155, 157.

13. See Theda Skocpol, *States and Social Revolutions: A Comparative Analysis of France, Russia, and China* (Cambridge: Cambridge University Press, 1979), 4–5, 288. For Latin America, see Alan Knight, "Social Revolution: A Latin American Perspective," *Bulletin of Latin American Research* 9 (1990): 175–202.

14. See Jorge I. Domínguez, *To Make a World Safe for Revolution: Cuba's Foreign Policy* (Cambridge, MA: Harvard University Press, 1989), 114–15; Tad Szulc, "Exporting the Cuban Revolution," in *Cuba and the United States: Long-Range Perspectives,* ed. John Plank (Washington, DC: Brookings Institution Press, 1967), 69–97; Ernesto F. Betancourt, "Exporting the Revolution to Latin America," in *Revolutionary Change in Cuba,* ed. Carmelo Mesa-Lago (Pittsburgh: University of Pittsburgh Press, 1971), 105–26; Piero Gleijeses, *Conflicting Missions: Havana, Washington, and Africa, 1959–1976* (Chapel Hill: University of North Carolina Press, 2002).

15. Senator Frank Church provided the numbers in "United States Military Policies and Programs in Latin America," *Hearings before the Subcommittee on Western Hemisphere Affairs of the Committee on Foreign Relations,* United States Senate,

91st Cong., 1st sess., 24 Jun and 8 Jul 1969 (Washington, DC: U.S. Government Printing Office, 1969), 69.

16. Jorge I. Domínguez, *Cuba: Order and Revolution* (Cambridge, MA: Belknap Press of Harvard University Press, 1978), 137.

17. Christopher Andrew and Vasili Mitrokhin, *The World Was Going Our Way: The KGB and the Battle for the Third World* (New York: Basic Books, 2005), 3–6.

18. The following analysis owes much to Odd Arne Westad's *The Global Cold War: Third World Interventions and the Making of Our Times* (Cambridge: Cambridge University Press, 2007), 396, which states that "the most important aspects of the Cold War were neither military nor strategic, nor Europe-centered but connected to the political and social development in the Third World."

1. HOW TO CONSOLIDATE A REVOLUTION

1. T. J. English, *Havana Nocturne: How the Mob Owned Cuba . . . and Then Lost It to the Revolution* (New York: Harper, 2007), 101–2.

2. On the failure of the so-called summer offensive of 1958, see Fidel Castro, *Fidel and Religion: Talks with Frei Betto* (Havana: Publications Office of the Council of State, 1988), 218. Paul J. Dosal, *Comandante Che: Guerrilla Soldier, Commander, and Strategist, 1956–1967* (University Park: Penn State University Press, 2003), 131–46.

3. Michelle Chase, "The Trials: Violence and Justice in the Aftermath of the Cuban Revolution," in *A Century of Revolution: Insurgent and Counterinsurgent Violence during Latin America's Long Cold War,* ed. Greg Grandin and Gilbert M. Joseph (Durham, NC: Duke University Press, 2010), 167, 184.

4. R. Hart Phillips, *Cuba: Island of Paradox* (New York: McDowell, Obolensky, 1959), 397–98; Chase, "The Trials," 177.

5. Carlos Franqui, *Camilo Cienfuegos* (Barcelona: Editorial Seix Barral, 2001), 105.

6. Hart Phillips, *Cuba: Island of Paradox,* 391.

7. Jules Dubois, *Fidel Castro: Rebel, Liberator or Dictator?* (Indianapolis, IN: Bobbs-Merrill, 1959), 353–55. Also see Nancy Stout, *One Day in December: Celia Sánchez and the Cuban Revolution* (New York: Monthly Review Press, 2013), 316–20; Luis Báez, *Secretos de generales* (Havana: Editorial Si-Mar, 1996), 255.

8. Julia E. Sweig, *Inside the Cuban Revolution* (Cambridge, MA: Harvard University Press, 2002), 181.

9. Aran Shetterly, *The Americano: Fighting with Castro for Cuba's Freedom* (Chapel Hill, NC: Algonquin Books, 2007), 138, 146–47.

10. "Fidel Castro Interview on Ed Sullivan—1959," video, from an *Ed Sullivan Show* episode televised by CBS on 11 Jan 1959, posted on 10 Jan 2011, accessed 13 Oct 2014, http://wn.com/fidel_castro_1959.

11. Robert E. Quirk, *Fidel Castro* (New York: W. W. Norton, 1993), 217; Neill Macaulay, *A Rebel in Cuba: An American's Memoir* (Chicago: Quadrangle Books, 1970), 156.

12. Macaulay, *A Rebel in Cuba,* 153–54. Returning to the United States, Macaulay pursued graduate studies at the University of Texas and eventually taught history at the University of Florida.

13. Dubois, *Fidel Castro,* 362. On Fidel's entrance into the city, see Dick Cluster and Rafael Hernández, *The History of Havana* (New York: Palgrave Macmillan, 2006), 210–11.

14. "Castro Speech Delivered in Ciudad Libertad," 9 Jan 1959, Castro Speech Database, LANIC, accessed 14 Aug 2013, http://lanic.utexas.edu/project/castro/db /1959/19590109-1.html.

15. Ramón L. Bonachea and Marta San Martín, *The Cuban Insurrection, 1952– 1959* (New Brunswick, NJ: Transaction Books, 1974), 322–31.

16. As quoted in William Gálvez, *Camilo: Señor de la vanguardia* (Havana: Editorial de Ciencias Sociales, 1979), 458.

17. Mario Mencía, *The Fertile Prison: Fidel Castro in Batista's Jails* (Melbourne: Ocean Press, 1993), 39, 41, 47. Mencía, a Cuban author, suggests that he also read extensively on Marxist and Leninist doctrine including four volumes of *Das Kapital.* If so, Castro actually never uttered any socialist jargon until 1961. Also see Wendy Gimbel, *Havana Dreams: A Story of Cuba* (New York: Alfred A. Knopf, 1998), 118, 121, 136–37. My thanks to Carolin Brown for this book. See also Quirk, *Fidel Castro,* 63–65, 68.

18. Gimbel, *Havana Dreams,* 132–33; Hugh Thomas, *Cuba, or the Pursuit of Freedom,* rev. ed. (New York: Da Capo Press, 1998), 854.

19. Castro's letter condemning the Pact of Miami is reproduced in Ernesto Che Guevara, *Reminiscences of the Cuban Revolutionary War* (Melbourne: Ocean Press, 2006), 205–20. On the Pact of Caracas, see Thomas, *Cuba,* 103–4; Louis A. Pérez Jr., *Cuba between Reform and Revolution,* 4th ed. (New York: Oxford University Press, 2011), 234; Bonachea and San Martín, *The Cuban Insurrection,* 238; Patrick Iber, *Neither Peace nor Freedom: The Cultural Cold War in Latin America* (Cambridge, MA: Harvard University Press), 126.

20. Bonachea and San Martín, *The Cuban Insurrection,* 244–45; Thomas, *Cuba,* 985; Lars Schoultz, *That Infernal Little Cuban Republic: The United States and the Cuban Revolution* (Chapel Hill: University of North Carolina Press, 2009), 55–57, 74–76.

21. Hart Phillips, *Cuba: Island of Paradox,* 346.

22. Weeka Report, 6 Jun 1959, 737.00(W)/6-659, Confidential US State Department Central Files, Cuba: Internal Affairs, 1955–1959, reel 8; Weeka Reports, 31 May 1960, 737.00(W)/5.3160; 10 Oct 1960, 737.00(W)/10-360; 25 Nov 1960, 737.00(W)/11-2560, Confidential US State Department Central Files, Cuba:

Internal Affairs, 1960–1963, reel 23. On Prío Socarrás and labor, see Charles D. Ameringer, *The Cuban Democratic Experience: The Auténtico Years, 1944–1952* (Gainesville: University Press of Florida, 2000), 48–49; Serafino Romualdi, *Presidents and Peons: Recollections of a Labor Ambassador in Latin America* (New York: Funk & Wagnalls, 1967), 65, 200–201; Efrén Córdova, *Castro and the Cuban Labor Movement: Statecraft and Society in a Revolutionary Period* (Lanham, MD: University Press of America, 1987), 294–95.

23. Jorge I. Domínguez, *Cuba: Order and Revolution* (Cambridge, MA: Belknap Press of Harvard University Press, 1978), 145.

24. Louis A. Pérez, *Army Politics in Cuba, 1898–1958* (Pittsburgh: University of Pittsburgh Press, 1976), 148–49.

25. As quoted in Thomas, *Cuba,* 1075. Also see Chase, "The Trials," 164.

26. Quirk, *Fidel Castro,* 227.

27. Thomas, *Cuba,* 1065–90, 1197.

28. Weeka Reports, 10 Mar 1959, 737.00(W)/3-1059; 14 Apr 1959, 737.00(W)/4-1459, Confidential US State Department Central Files, Cuba: Internal Affairs, 1955–1959, reel 8.

29. Carlos Franqui, *Diary of the Cuban Revolution,* trans. Georgette Felix et al. (New York: Viking Press, 1980), 327; Sweig, *Inside the Cuban Revolution,* 116–17, 162–63; Guevara, *Reminiscences,* 248.

30. Thomas, *Cuba,* 1229–30, 1232.L

31. Rufo López-Fresquet, *My Fourteen Months with Castro* (Cleveland: World Publishing, 1966), 170; Quirk, *Fidel Castro,* 248–49; Weeka Report, 16 Jun 1959, 737.00(W)/6-1659; 23 Jun 1959, 737.00(W)/6-2359, Confidential US State Department Central Files, Cuba: Internal Affairs, 1955–1959, reel 8; *Foreign Relations of the United States, 1958–1960,* vol. 6, *Cuba* (Washington, DC: US Government Printing Office, 1991) (hereafter *FRUS, 1958–1960, Cuba),* 58–60, 544–45.

32. Sweig, *Inside the Cuban Revolution,* 12–14; Thomas, *Cuba,* 970; Antonio Rafael de la Cova, *The Moncada Attack: Birth of the Cuban Revolution* (Columbia: University of South Carolina Press, 2007), 158–59, 205; Quirk, *Fidel Castro,* 156.

33. Manuel Urrutia Lleó, *Fidel Castro & Company, Inc.: Communist Tyranny in Cuba* (New York: Frederick A. Praeger, 1964), 49.

34. Ibid., 57.

35. Rodolfo Walsh, "Fidel renuncia, Fidel se queda," in *El violento oficio de escribir: Obra periodística, 1953–1977* (Buenos Aires: Planeta, 1995), 114.

36. Ibid., 119–20; Weeka Report, 14 Jul 1959, 737.00(W)/7-1459, Confidential US State Department Central Files, Cuba: Internal Affairs and Foreign Affairs, 1955–1959, reel 8. Also see Samuel Farber, *Cuba since the Revolution of 1959: A Critical Assessment* (Chicago: Haymarket Books, 2011), 40–41.

37. Herbert L. Matthews, *Fidel Castro* (New York: Simon & Schuster, 1969), 106; Hart Phillips, *Cuba: Island of Paradox,* 299. "Since the dawn of the Cold War," writes

author Vann Gosse, "few Third World figures of any sort have received such sustained, sympathetic coverage from the journalistic establishment in the US as did Fidel Castro in the two years before Batista fell." Van Gosse, *Where the Boys Are: Cuba, Cold War America and the Making of a New Left* (London: Verso, 1993), 67.

38. "Sierra Maestra Manifesto," 12 Jul 1957, LatinAmericanStudies.org, accessed 24 Sep 2014, http://www.latinamericanstudies.org/cuban-rebels/manifesto.htm.

39. Weeka Report, 4 Apr 1959, 737.00(W) / 4-459, Confidential US State Department Central Files, Cuba: Internal Affairs and Foreign Affairs, 1955–1959, reel 8; Leycester Coltman, *The Real Fidel Castro* (New Haven, CT: Yale University Press, 2003), 156–57.

40. Weeka Reports, 4 Apr 1959, 737.00(W) / 4-459; 1 Dec 1959, 737.00(W) / 12-159, Confidential US State Department Central Files, Cuba: Internal Affairs and Foreign Affairs, 1955–1959, reel 8; Weeka Report, 8 Aug 1960, 737.00(W) / 8-1860; Confidential US State Department Central Files, Cuba: Internal Affairs, 1960–1963, Reel 23. On the breakup of the first revolutionary cabinet, see Jorge I. Domínguez, "Cuba since 1959," in *Cuba: A Short History,* ed. Leslie Bethell (Cambridge: Cambridge University Press, 1993), 105.

41. R. Hart Phillips, *The Cuban Dilemma* (New York: Ivan Obolensky, 1963), 33.

42. Dubois, *Fidel Castro,* 215; Gerald E. Poyo, *Cuban Catholics in the United States, 1960–1980: Exile and Integration* (Notre Dame, IN: University of Notre Dame Press, 2007), 46–47; Alberto Müller, interview with author, 20 Jun 2013; Thomas, *Cuba,* 1215.

43. Fabián Escalante, *The Cuba Project: CIA Covert Operations, 1959–62* (Melbourne: Ocean Press, 2004), 37–38, 70–71, 78–79.

44. Franqui, *Diary of the Cuban Revolution,* 439.

45. Eduardo García, " 'No éramos aliados de los Estados Unidos': Entrevista a Manuel Ray Rivero," *Temas: Cultura, Ideología, Sociedad,* no. 55 (2008): 48–50; Bonachea and San Martín, *The Cuban Insurrection,* 207, 213.

46. Huber Matos, *Cómo llegó la noche: Memorias* (Barcelona: Tusquets Editores, 2002), 337–52.

47. Weeka Report, 1 Dec 1959, 737.00(W) / 12-159, NADS, Cuba, 1955–1959. Ambassador Bonsal reported on the retreat of Ray, Felipe Pazos, and López-Fresquet: "Reports are that some [moderates] may be on [the] way out, others would like to resign but fear treatment similar to that accorded Urrutia and Matos." *FRUS, 1958–1960, Cuba,* 649, 1138.

48. *FRUS, 1958–1960, Cuba,* 1158; García, " 'No éramos aliados de los Estados Unidos,' " 50–51; Howard Hunt, *Give Us This Day* (New Rochelle, NY: Arlington House, 1973), 92.

49. Arthur M. Schlesinger Jr. *A Thousand Days: John F. Kennedy in the White House* (Boston: Houghton Mifflin, 1965), 230–31, 283.

50. Matos, *Cómo llegó la noche*, 66.

51. Benigno [Dariel Alarcón Ramírez], *Memorias de un soldado cubano: Vida y muerte de la Revolución* (Barcelona: Tusquets Editores, 1997), 74–75.

52. Quirk, *Fidel Castro*, 265.

53. Matos, *Cómo llegó la noche*, 344.

54. Gálvez, *Camilo*, 455–65; Franqui, *Camilo Cienfuegos*, 152–59. Valdés was not a member of Camilo's entourage but was close to Raúl and Che. He served as Che's executive officer in the battle of Santa Clara.

55. Ray claims to have helped spring a dozen of Matos's staff officers from jail and spirited them all into exile, undoubtedly with the assistance of the US embassy and the CIA. García, " 'No éramos aliados de Estados Unidos,' " 50–51.

56. López-Fresquet, *My Fourteen Months with Castro*, 57.

57. Matos, *Cómo llegó la noche*, 331. Some say Raúl Castro had ordered a Sea Fury to shoot down Camilo's plane. Robert Quirk suggests that a Cuban fighter plane mistook Camilo's Cessna for a counterrevolutionary flyover and shot him down by accident. Quirk, *Fidel Castro*, 27.

58. Weeka Reports, 10 Nov 1959, 737.00(W) / 11-1059; 17 Nov 1959, 737.00(W) / 11-1759, Confidential US State Department Central Files, Cuba: Internal Affairs and Foreign Affairs, 1955–1959, reel 8.

59. See his speeches in the annex of Gálvez, *Camilo*, 501–62.

60. Franqui, *Camilo Cienfuegos*, 141–42. Camila had a closer relationship with Che. When Guevara first gained command of a column in the Sierra Maestra, Camila Cienfuegos served in his vanguard. According to one of Che's men, "Realmente se querían como hermanos." (They loved each other like brothers.) Yet the serious Che did have to temper the jokester in Camilo. "Camilo, recuerda que están mis hombres presentes." (Camilo, remember that my men are present.) Luis Báez, *Secretos de generales* (Havana: Editorial Si-Mar, 1996), 189.

61. Gerónimo Besánguiz Legarreta and Osiris Quintero Fernández, *Camilo en la batalla de Yaguajay* (Havana: Editora Política, 2004), 46, 92–93, 120–21; Jorge G. Castañeda, *Compañero: The Life and Death of Che Guevara* (New York: Alfred A. Knopf, 1997), 133; Benigno, *Memorias de un soldado cubano*, 53–54; Dosal, *Comandante Che*, 255. Guevara mentions later that the siege of Yaguajay went on for eleven days. Guevara, *Reminiscences*, 266.

62. Thomas, *Cuba*, 1032.

63. Weeka Report, 30 Sep 1959, 737.00(W) / 9-3059, Confidential US State Department Central Files, Cuba: Internal Affairs, 1955–1959, reel 8.

64. Weeka Report, 5 May 1959, 737.00(W) / 5-559, Confidential US State Department Central Files, Cuba: Internal Affairs, 1955–1959, reel 8; "Raúl Chibás," tape 5, 21 Oct 1984, Tad Szulc Collection, box 2, Cuban Heritage Center, University of Miami Libraries, Coral Gables, FL (hereafter CHC). Chibás was one dissident who did not believe that Fidel had had Camilo killed.

65. Franqui, *Camilo Cienfuegos*, 41; López-Fresquet, *My Fourteen Months with Castro*, 58.

66. Weeka Report, 19 May 1959, 737.00(W) / 5-1959, Confidential US State Department Central Files, Cuba: Internal Affairs, 1955–1959, reel 8.

67. As quoted in Victor Franco, *The Morning After*, trans. Ivan Kats and Philip Pendered (New York: Frederick A. Praeger, 1963), 115. Artime subsequently published a detailed version of the INRA meeting in Manuel F. Artime, *Traición! Gritan 20,000 tumbas cubanas* (Mexico City: Editorial Jus, 1960), 53–72.

68. Hans Tanner, *Counterrevolutionary Agent* (London: G. T. Foulis), 64–65.

69. Hunt, *Give Us This Day*, 47; Haynes Johnson with Manuel Artime, *The Bay of Pigs: The Leaders' Story* (New York: W. W. Norton, 1964), 23–26, 33; Félix I. Rodríguez and John Weisman, *Shadow Warrior* (New York: Simon & Schuster, 1989), 117. Manuel Artime has never mentioned the accusation of embezzlement except in the public trial of captured *brigadistas*. "For each check that was delivered it was necessary to present proof that the last one had been spent," he testified. "So it would have been difficult for me to have taken two of those checks." He also stated that the five hundred dollars he used to escape from Cuba had come from a Manzanillo rice grower. *History of an Aggression: Testimony and Documents from the Trial of the Mercenary Brigade Organized by the U.S. Imperialists That Invaded Cuba on April 17, 1961* (Havana: Ediciones Venceremos, 1964), 75, 239.

70. Shetterly, *The Americano*, 55–58; Bonachea and San Martín, *The Cuban Insurrection*, 134–38; Hart Phillips, *Cuba: Island of Paradox*, 342–43; Rafael Hernández, "'Siempre me he considerado un socialista': Max Lesnik habla sobre la Revolución cubana," *Temas: Cultura, Ideología, Sociedad*, no. 55 (2008): 36–37.

71. Castañeda, *Compañero*, 134–45; John Lee Anderson, *Che Guevara: A Revolutionary Life* (New York: Grove Press, 1997), 354; Dosal, *Comandante Che*, 152–53; *The Miami News*, 13 Aug 1961, Jay Mallin Papers, box 4, CHC.

72. Weeka Reports, 11 Aug 1959, 737.00(W) / 8-1159; 19 Aug 1959, 737.00(W) / 8-1959, Confidential US State Department Files, Cuba, 1955–1959. Gutiérrez Menoyo performed this service for the revolution despite having previously been denounced in the communist newspaper *Hoy* for being "a tool of Yankee imperialism" for a goodwill trip he took to the United States. See Weeka Report, 24 Mar 1959, 737.00(W) / 3-2459, Confidential US State Department Files, Cuba: Internal Affairs, 1955–1959, reel 8; López-Fresquet, *My Fourteen Months with Castro*, 133–38.

73. Weeka Report, 16 Feb 1960, 737.00(W) / 2-1660, Confidential US State Department Central Files, Cuba: Internal Affairs, 1960–1963, reel 23.

74. Weeka Report, 16 Mar 1960, 737.00(W) / 3-1660, Confidential US State Department Central Files, Cuba: Internal Affairs, 1960–1963, reel 23. Also see Eloy Gutiérrez Menoyo, *El Radarista* (Madrid: Editorial Playor, 1985).

75. "Max Lesnick," 8 Oct 1984, Tad Szulc Collection, box 2, CHC.

76. Press clipping, El Mundo, Miami, 22 Oct 1960; "Morgan Executed in Cuba," n.d., Jay Mallin Papers, box 4, CHC.

77. Hunt, *Give Us This Day,* 105.

78. Philip W. Bonsal, *Cuba, Castro, and the United States* (Pittsburgh: University of Pittsburgh Press, 1971), 145. Also see Daniel F. Solomon, *Breaking Up with Cuba: The Dissolution of Friendly Relations between Washington and Havana, 1956–1961* (Jefferson, NC: McFarland, 2011), 127–38.

79. Says Samuel Farber, "Fidel Castro had political designs that he shared with no one. They were pragmatic in the sense that although Castro wanted to make a radical revolution, he left it to historical circumstances, the existing relations of forces and tactical possibilities, to determine specifically what kind of revolution it would be, all along making sure that he would remain in control." Samuel Farber, *The Origins of the Cuban Revolution Reconsidered* (Chapel Hill: University of North Carolina Press, 2006), 63.

2. THE CARIBBEAN WAR OF 1959

1. Testimony of C. P. Cabell, "Communist Threat to the United States through the Caribbean," *Hearings before the Subcommittee to Investigate the Administration of the Internal Security Act of the Committee on the Judiciary, United States Senate,* pt. 8 (Washington, DC: US Government Printing Office, 1960), 163. Also see Carlos Franqui, *Camilo Cienfuegos* (Barcelona: Editorial Seix Barral, 2001), 122–23; Teresa Casuso, *Cuba and Castro,* trans. Elmer Grossberg (New York: Random House, 1961), 216. At the time, Cuban communist labor leader Lázaro Peña was visiting Moscow as an emissary of Raúl Castro. See Alan McPherson, "The Limits of Populist Diplomacy: Fidel Castro's April 1959 Trip to North America," *Diplomacy and Statecraft* 18 (2007): 242, 244; Robert O. Kirkland, *Observing Our Hermanos de Armas: U.S. Military Attachés in Guatemala, Cuba, and Bolivia, 1950–1964* (New York: Routledge, 2003), 33.

2. Christian Herter to J. William Fulbright, 19 Mar 1959; Herter, "Memorandum for Roy R. Rubottom, Jr.," Dulles-Herter Collection, box 11, Dwight D. Eisenhower Presidential Library, Abilene, KS. On Fidel's trip, see Hugh Thomas, *Cuba, or the Pursuit of Freedom,* rev. ed. (New York: Da Capo Press, 1998), 1208–13; McPherson, "The Limits of Populist Diplomacy," 237–68; Rufo López-Fresquet, *My Fourteen Months with Castro* (Cleveland: World Publishing, 1966), 106–12.

3. Jeffrey J. Safford, "The Nixon-Castro Meeting of 19 April 1959," *Diplomatic History* 4 (1980): 425; Lee Lockwood, *Castro's Cuba: Cuba's Fidel* (New York: Macmillan, 1967), 186.

4. "Síntesis cronológica de los principales momentos de las relaciones bilaterales Cuba-Panamá después de 1959," n.d., Fondo Panamá, Archivo del Ministerio de Relaciones Exteriores, Havana, Cuba (hereafter cited as MINREX).

5. Anon., "Unofficial Visit of Prime Minister Castro of Cuba to Washington," Whitman File, International Series, box 8, Eisenhower Library.

6. Weeka Reports, 30 Jun 1959, 737.00(W) / 6-3059; 7 Jul 1959, 737.00(W) / 7-759, State Department Central Files, Cuba, 1955–1959.

7. "Síntesis cronológica," n.d., Fondo Panamá, MINREX; Weeka Reports, 5 May 1959, 737.00(W) / 5-559; 12 May 1959, 737.00(W) / 5-1259; 6 Jun 1959, 737.00(W) / 6-659, Confidential US State Department Central Files, Cuba: Internal Affairs, 1956–1959, reel 6. Also see R. Hart Phillips, *The Cuban Dilemma* (New York: Ivan Obolensky, 1963), 93.

8. *Foreign Relations of the United States, 1958–1960,* vol. 5, *American Republics* (hereafter *FRUS, 1958–1960, American Republics*) (Washington, DC: US Government Printing Office, 1991), 324–25, 453, 493.

9. Thanks to Jorge I. Domínguez for this insight.

10. Bureau of Intelligence and Research, "Castro's Revolution and Subversive Plotting in the Western Hemisphere (February–April 1959)," 18 May 1959, *O.S.S. / State Department Intelligence and Research Reports,* vol. 14, *Latin America: 1941–1961,* ed. Paul Kesaris (Washington, DC: University Publications of America, 2001), microfilm.

11. CIA, "Current Intelligence Weekly Summary," 5, 17, 18, 19, 20 Mar, 8 Jun 1959, Central Intelligence Agency Records Search Tool, National Archives and Records Administration, College Park, MD (hereafter cited as CREST).

12. Embassy Havana, Weeka Report, 24 Mar 1959, 737.00(W) / 3-2459, Confidential State Department Central Files, Cuba: Internal Affairs and Foreign Affairs, 1956–1959, reel 6. Also see Stephen G. Rabe, "The Caribbean Triangle: Betancourt, Castro, and Trujillo and U.S. Foreign Policy, 1958–1963," *Diplomatic History* 10, no. 1 (Winter 1996): 55–78.

13. César Vega, interview, *Alcance* (Miami), 2 Dec 1960.

14. Alan Cowell, "For Prima Ballerina, 1950s Coup Attempt Was All But Graceful," *New York Times,* 30 May 2010.

15. The following story of the MAR comes from Carlos H. Cuestas G., *Hijos de la rebeldía* (Panama City: L & J Publicaciones, 2008).

16. Ibid., 208–9.

17. Ibid., 290.

18. Ibid., 254–67; Cowell, "For Prima Ballerina, 1950s Coup Attempt Was All But Graceful." The resourceful Roberto Arias later attempted to revise his image as a Castroite by meeting Attorney General Robert F. Kennedy and hobnobbing in Washington, DC, social circles. The Panamanian government again appointed him as ambassador to the Court of St. James, then fired him from that job in 1962. See C. K., "Memorandum for Mr. Ralph Dungan," 21 Jan 1963, National Security File (hereafter NSF), box 150, John F. Kennedy Presidential Library, Boston.

19. Vega, interview, *Alcance,* 2 Dec 1960.

20. Cablegram from Cuban embassy in Panama, 26 Apr 1959, Fondo Panamá, MINREX; John C. Shillock Jr., "Comments on Recent Invasion Crisis," 6 May 1959, 719.00/5-659; Henry C. Reed, "Meeting of the COAS," 11 May 1959, 719.00/5-1159; R. Austin Acly, "Review of Selected Political Developments," 13 May 1959, 719.00/5-1359, Records of the Department of State Relating to the Internal Affairs of Panama, 1955–1959, decimal files 719, 819, and 919, microfilm. Enrique Morales Brid's father served as president of Panama's Supreme Court of Justice, additionally solidifying the aristocratic leadership of the invasion forces.

21. CIA, "Central Intelligence Bulletin," 27 Apr 1959, CREST.

22. Bureau of Intelligence and Research, "Castro's Revolution."

23. Manuel Piñeiro, *Che Guevara and the Latin American Revolutionary Movements,* ed. Luis Suárez Sálazar, trans. Mary Todd (Melbourne: Ocean Press, 2001), 43.

24. The CIA named the following as Nicaraguan graduates of Cuba's training camps: Carlos Adan Perez Bermudez, Eligio Alvarez Montalvan, Reinaldo Viquez Ruiz, and Francisco Rolando Alvarado Lopez, Juan Jose Lorio Garcia, Adrian Sanchez Sancho, and Abdul Sirker Urroz of the PSN [exact title unknown]; Ricardo Francisco Osojo Zeledon, Orlando Quinones Torres, and Guillermo Andres Baltodano Serrano, all student leaders; Marco Antonio Melendez Delgado, Socrates Noel Flores Vivas, Ivan Sanchez Arguello, Orlando Quintana, and German Pomares Ordonez of the FLN [exact title unknown]; and Agapito Fernandez Garcia of the Conservative Party. See CIA, "Cuban Training of Latin American Subversives," 27 Mar 1963, in *C.I.A. Research Reports: Latin America, 1946–1976* (Frederick, MD: University Publications of America, 1982), microfilm. Matilde Zimmermann of Sarah Lawrence College wrote in a personal email to the author on January 13, 2007: "At least some of them were early members of the FSLN (which was called the FLN c. 1961–63, until Carlos Fonseca convinced the others to add 'Sandinista' to the name) who participated in the FLN / FSLN guerrilla operation known as Rios Coco y Bocay in 1963. Most of the sixty or so young participants in that action (all male) trained in Cuba between 1960 and 1963. Ivan Sanchez was a founder of the FLN / FSLN, who was killed at Rios Coco y Bocay in 1963. The most famous of the names you list was German Pomares, who fought in RCyB and was killed by the National Guard just weeks before the 1979 victory. Efrain (not Adrian) Sanchez Sancho was a leader of the FSLN who was kicked out for indiscipline and womanizing around 1970. Most of the other names I don't recognize. Some of the ones listed as PSN could have been FSLN—the situation was still pretty fluid and it's hard to see how the CIA could have been sure which of these individuals still had some kind of affiliation with the PSN, since sometimes the individuals weren't all that sure themselves. Some of the central leaders who aren't listed—Carlos Fonseca, Tomas Borge, Silvio Rodriguez, Rodolfo Romero—trained in Cuba earlier, beginning in 1959."

25. Hart Phillips, *The Cuban Dilemma,* 93.

26. Conservative youth leaders included Pedro Joaquín Chamorro and Luis Cardenal, who were to figure prominently in the revolution against the Somozas of the late 1970s. Luis G. Cardenal, *Mi rebelión: La dictadura de los Somoza* (Mexico: Ediciones Patria y Libertad, 1961), 314; Weeka Reports, 12 May 1959, 737.00(W) / 5-1259; 6 Jun 1959, 737.00(W) / 6-659, Confidential State Department Central Files, Cuba: Internal Affairs and Foreign Affairs, 1955–1959, reel 6; Bureau of Intelligence and Research, "Castro's Revolution."

27. "General Anastasio Somoza Debayle," National Security Council, Internal Meetings and Travel File, box 18, Lyndon Baines Johnson Presidential Library, Austin, TX. Anastasio Somoza Jr. received the Legion of Merit medal from the US government in 1957.

28. Bernard Diederich, *Somoza and the Legacy of U.S. Involvement in Central America* (Maplewood, NJ: Waterfront Press, 1989), 252–53, 259.

29. As quoted in ibid., 58–59.

30. Cardenal, *Mi rebelión,* 262, 279–80.

31. Then a smaller, rival group of twenty armed men under Chester Lacayo debarked at the mouth of Río Patuca in Honduras. Lacayo's group had apparently set sail from Cuba in defiance of Che Guevara. *FRUS, 1958–1960, American Republics,* 328, 330.

32. Matilde Zimmermann, *Sandinista: Carlos Fonseca and the Nicaraguan Revolution* (Durham, NC: Duke University Press, 2000), 54–55.

33. Weeka Reports, 6 Jun 1959, 717.00(W) / 6-659; 12 Jun 1959, 717.00(W) / 6-1259; 19 Jun 1959, 717.00(W) / 6-1959; 1 Jul 1959, 717.00(W) / 7-159, Confidential State Department Central Files: Nicaragua, Internal Affairs and Foreign Affairs, 1955–1959, reel 6. See Claudia Patricia Rueda, "Students of Revolution: Youth and Protest in Somoza-era Nicaragua, 1937–1979" (PhD diss., University of Texas at Austin, 2014), 230–40; Zimmermann, *Sandinista,* 57–58; Tomás Borge, *The Patient Impatience: From Boyhood to Guerilla* (Willimatic, CT: Curbstone Press, 1992), 110; Francisco J. Barbosa, "July 23, 1959: Student Protest and State Violence as Myth and Memory in León, Nicaragua," *Hispanic American Historical Review* 85, no. 2 (May 2005): 187–94.

34. CIA, "Cuban Training of Latin American Subversives, 27 Mar 1963."

35. *FRUS, 1958–1960, American Republics,* 453, 906–7.

36. See Thomas, *Cuba,* 754–55, 811–12; Tad Szulc, *Fidel: A Critical Portrait* (New York: First Road Press, 2000), 154–56.

37. Bureau of Intelligence and Research, "Castro's Revolution." Jiménez Moya had joined up with M26 in Caracas in 1958, where several exile groups had congregated after the fall of the dictator, General Andrés Pérez Jiménez. Jiménez Moya had flown into Oriente Province on board one of several Venezuelan planes delivering arms to Castro. Matilde Zimmermann, "Exporting Revolution: Cuba and the Caribbean Revolutionary Expeditions of 1959" (unpublished paper presented at the 2007 meeting

of the Latin American Studies Association). Dr. Felipe Maduro Sanabria, known to American diplomats as a communist, headed the UPD in Havana.

38. See Delio Gómez Ochoa, *Constanza, Maimón y Estero Hondo: La victoria de los caídos* (Santo Domingo: Editora Alfa & Omega, 1998).

39. A. J. Goodpastor, "Memorandum of Conversation with the President," 26 Apr 1960, Whitman File, International Series, box 6, Eisenhower Library. Also see Herter, "Possible Actions to Prevent Castroist Takeover of Dominican Republic," 14 Apr 1960, White House, Office of the Staff Secretary, 1952–1961, Alphabetical Subseries, box 15, Eisenhower Library.

40. Bureau of Intelligence and Research, "Castro's Revolution"; *FRUS, 1958–1960, American Republics,* 387–88.

41. Cabell, "Communist Threat," 497.

42. Ibid., 516–17; Miguel Guerrero, *Trujillo y los héroes de junio* (Santa Domingo: Editora Corripio, 1996), 82. The Dominican pilot who did not fly on that day was Juan de Díos Ventura Simó. He appeared to have been a spy for the dictator Rafael Trujillo. After troops loyal to Trujillo had snuffed out the invasion forces, Ventura Simó returned home as a hero of the regime. After his propaganda usefulness ended, Ventura Simó faced execution like most of the men he had betrayed.

43. In January 1960, Captain Del Río testified at a hearing of a Senate subcommittee. Cabell, "Communist Threat," 518.

44. As quoted in Zimmermann, "Exporting Revolution," 11; Guerrero, *Trujillo y los héroes de junio,* 39–40.

45. Ministerio de Estado, "Visita del exilado dominicano Tomás Reyes Cerdo," 13 Nov 1959, Fondo República Dominicana, MINREX. My thanks to Aaron Moulton for sending me a copy of this manuscript.

46. Guerrero, *Trujillo y los héroes de junio,* 38.

47. Bernard Diederich, *1959: The Year That Inflamed the Caribbean* (Princeton, NJ: Markus Wiener, 2009), 129–34; Jules Dubois, *Operation America: The Communist Conspiracy in Latin America* (New York: Walker, 1963), 9, 74; Juan J. Cruz Segura, *Bajo la barbarie: La Juventud Democrática Clandestina (1947–1959)* (Santo Domingo: Biblioteca Taller, 1997), 89.

48. Raúl Roa to Gonzalo Escudero, 26 Jun 1959, Fondo República Dominicana, MINREX; CIA, "Central Intelligence Bulletins," 18, 20, 22, 27 Jun 1959, CREST; *FRUS, 1958–1960, American Republics,* 325–26.

49. Weeka Reports, 18 Aug 1959, 737.00(W) / 8-1959; 1 Sep 1959, 737.00(W) / 9-159, Confidential US State Department Central Files, Cuba: Internal Affairs, 1956–1959, reel 6; Diederich, *1959,* 32, 145–47; Alex von Tunzelmann, *Red Heat: Conspiracy, Murder, and the Cold War in the Caribbean* (New York: Henry Holt, 2011), 153–54.

50. Weeka Report, 11 Aug 1959, 737.00(W) / 8-1159, Confidential US State Department Central Files, Cuba: Internal Affairs, 1956–1959, reel 6. Trujillo may have

extorted four million dollars from his guest Fulgencio Batista to help finance this conspiracy. See Robert D. Crassweller, *Trujillo: The Life and Times of a Caribbean Dictator* (New York: Macmillan, 1966), 345, 350–52; Fabián Escalante, *The Cuba Project: CIA Covert Operations, 1959–62* (Melbourne: Ocean Press, 2004), 20–32; Clara Nieto, *Masters of War: Latin America and United States Aggression from the Cuban Revolution through the Clinton Years,* trans. Chris Brandt (New York: Seven Stories Press), 38–39; Luis Báez, *Secretos de generales* (Havana: Editorial Si-Mar, 1996), 256. Also see Jonathan C. Brown, "Contrarrevolución en el Caribe: La CIA y los paramilitares cubanos en los 60," *Temas: Cultura, Ideología, Sociedad,* no. 55 (2008), 60.

51. Hart Phillips, *The Cuban Dilemma,* 81.

52. Weeka Reports, 19 May 1959, 737.00(W) / 5-1959; 16 Jun 1959, 737.00(W) / 6-1659; 30 Jun 1959, 737.00(W) / 6-3059, Confidential US State Department Central Files, Cuba: Internal Affairs, 1956–1959, reel 6; CIA, "NSC Briefing," 30 Jun 1959, CREST. Also see Alan McPherson, *Yankee No! Anti-Americanism in U.S.-Latin American Relations* (Cambridge, MA: Harvard University Press, 2003), 53–59; Jorge I. Domínguez, "Cuba since 1959," in *Cuba: A Short History,* ed. Leslie Bethell (Cambridge: Cambridge University Press, 1993), 98–99.

53. As Jorge Domínguez says, "The Castro government's support for revolution [abroad] began before the [US] government's attacks on Cuba." Jorge I. Domínguez, *To Make a World Safe for Revolution: Cuba's Foreign Policy* (Cambridge, MA: Harvard University Press, 1989), 114–15.

54. *Foreign Relations of the United States, 1958–1960,* vol. 6, *Cuba* (Washington, DC: US Government Printing Office, 1991), 419.

55. As quoted in Norman Hampson, *A Social History of the French Revolution* (Toronto: University of Toronto Press, 1974), 132.

3. CUBA AND THE SINO-SOVIET DISPUTE

1. Sergo Mikoyan, *The Soviet Cuban Missile Crisis: Castro, Mikoyan, Kennedy, Khrushchev, and the Missiles of November,* ed. Svetlana Savranskaya (Washington, DC: Woodrow Wilson Center Press; Stanford, CA: Stanford University Press, 2012), 173. The author accompanied his father, Anastas Mikoyan, on both the 1960 and 1962 trips.

2. "Memorandum of Conversation between Castro and Mikoyan," Havana, 5 Nov 1962, Russian Foreign Ministry archives, Cold War International History Project (hereafter CWIHP), accessed 20 Apr 2015, http://digitalarchive.wilsoncenter.org /document/110980. On the public view of Mikoyan's visit, see issues of *Revolución* (Havana) from 3, 4, 9, 26, 27 Nov 1962.

3. *Revolución* (Havana), 13 Nov 1962. Editors identified the "CIA agent" as Miguel Angel Orozco Crespo.

4. "Notes of Conversation between A. I. Mikoyan and Fidel Castro," Havana, 3 Nov 1962, CWIHP, http://digitalarchive.wilsoncenter.org/document/110955, accessed 20 Apr 2015. Also see "Reunión del secretariado de la O.R.I. con Mikoyan," Havana, 4 Nov 1962, CWIHP, http://digitalarchive.wilsoncenter.org/document /110879, accessed 14 Nov 2016. Also see Leycester Coltman, *The Real Fidel Castro* (New Haven, CT: Yale University Press, 2003), 201–2; Lars Schoultz, *That Infernal Little Cuban Republic: The United States and the Cuban Revolution* (Chapel Hill: University of North Carolina Press, 2009), 208–9.

5. "Record of Conversation between A. I. Mikoyan and F. Castro," 13 Nov 1962, CWIHP, http://digitalarchive.wilsoncenter.org/document/115099, accessed 20 Apr 2015.

6. Carlos Rafael Rodríguez, "Informe de la conversación sostenida por el compañero Carlos R. Rodríguez con el compañero Nikita Jruschov," Moscow, 11 Dec 1962, CWIHP, http://digitalarchive.wilsoncenter.org/document/115171, accessed 20 Apr 2015.

7. CIA, "Soviet Bloc Efforts at Penetration of Latin America," 14 Mar 1958; "Observation of Latin American CP Delegations to the 21st CPSU Congress and Their Experiences with CP China in Beijing," [date blocked out], White House, Office of the Staff Secretary, Alphabetical Side Series, box 7, both in Dwight D. Eisenhower Presidential Library, Abilene, KS.

8. C. P. Cabell to A. J. Goodpaster, 11 Apr 1959, WH, box 7, Eisenhower Library.

9. CIA, " 'Big Leap' Falters because of Mismanagement," Feb 1959, Central Intelligence Agency Records Search Tool, National Archives and Records Administration, College Park, MD. Historians estimate that between thirty and fifty-five million Chinese perished as a result of the failures of the Great Leap Forward. Maurice J. Meissner, *Mao's China and After: A History of the People's Republic,* 3rd ed. (New York: Free Press, 1999), 237. Chris Bramall calls it the "worst famine in human history." See Bramall, *Chinese Economic Development* (London: Routledge, 2009), 126; Frank Dikötter, *Mao's Great Famine: The History of China's Most Devastating Catastrophe, 1958–1962* (New York: Walker, 2010), 114–33, 325.

10. Sergey Radchenko, *Two Suns in the Heavens: The Sino-Soviet Struggle for Supremacy, 1962–67* (Washington, DC: Woodrow Wilson Center, 2009), 47; Lorenz Luthi, *The Sino-Soviet Split: Cold War in the Communist World* (Princeton, NJ: Princeton University Press, 2008), 194–200; Lowell Dittmer, *Sino-Soviet Normalization and Its International Implications, 1945–1990* (Seattle: University of Washington Press, 1992), 29–34.

11. Alexandr Fursenko and Timothy Naftali, *One Hell of a Gamble: Khrushchev, Castro, and Kennedy, 1958–1964* (New York: W. W. Norton, 1997), 11, 33; Brian Latell, *After Fidel: The Inside Story of Castro's Regime and Cuba's Next Leader* (New York: Palgrave Macmillan, 2005), 135.

12. Fursenko and Naftali, *One Hell of a Gamble*, 27, 29. The authors base this valuable study on Soviet documentation.

13. "Discussion at the 411th Meeting of the NSC," 25 Jun 1959, Ann Whitman Files, National Security Council [NSC] Series, box 11, Eisenhower Library.

14. Aleksandr Alekseyev had previous assignments in Buenos Aires and in Mexico City, where Ramiro Valdés, Fidel's first intelligence chief, consulted with him in July 1959. Christopher Andrew and Vasili Mitrokhin, *The World Was Going Our Way: The KGB and the Battle for the Third World* (New York: Basic Books, 2005), 3–6, 35–37.

15. CIA, "Current Intelligence Weekly Summary," 19 May 1960, WH, Eisenhower Library. In August, Cuban diplomat Miguel Ángel Campos visited China and made the point that Fidel Castro's policies were not procommunist. Campos claimed that Castro aimed to raise the people's standard of living and wipe out the poverty that bred communism. Anon., "Memo from the Far East Department," 24 Aug 1959, Foreign Office Files for Cuba 1959–1963, microfilm, 26, 411.

16. Weeka Reports, 9 Sep 1959, 737.00(W)/9-959; 17 Nov 1959, 737.00(W)/ 11-1759, Confidential US State Department Central Files, Cuba: Internal Affairs, 1955–1959, microfilm, reel 8.

17. "Soviet Bloc Efforts at Penetration of Latin America," 14 Mar 1958, White House, box 7, Eisenhower Library; Rufo López-Fresquet, *My Fourteen Months with Castro* (Cleveland: World Publishing, 1966), 174. "While American hostility was later to reinforce Castro's alliance with the Soviet Union, it did not cause it," write Christopher Andrew and Vasili Mitrokhin. "The initiative for the alliance came from Havana." Andrew and Mitrokhin, *The World Was Going Our Way*, 35.

18. "Partial Chronology of Events Leading Up to the Present Situation in Cuba," 15 Mar 1960, Whitman Files, NSC Briefing Notes Subseries, box 6, Eisenhower Library.

19. R. Hart Phillips, *The Cuban Dilemma* (New York: Ivan Obolensky, 1963), 173.

20. CIA, "Special National Intelligence Estimate: Communist Influence in Cuba," 22 Mar 1960, White House Office of Special Assistant for National Security Affairs, box 6, Eisenhower Library.

21. Hugh Thomas, *Cuba, or the Pursuit of Freedom,* rev. ed. (New York: Da Capo Press, 1998), 1290.

22. Aleksandr Fursenko and Timothy Naftali, *Khrushchev's Cold War: The Inside Story of an American Adversary* (New York: W. W. Norton, 2006), 296–97, 302, 306; Fursenko and Naftali, *One Hell of a Gamble,* 54; Andrés Suárez, *Cuba: Catrosim and Communism, 1959–1967,* trans. Joel Carmichael and Ernst Halperin (Cambridge, MA: MIT Press, 1967), 80.

23. Sergei N. Khrushchev, *Nikita Khrushchev and the Creation of a Superpower,* trans. Shirley Benson (University Park: Penn State University Press, 2002), 411.

24. Jung Chang and Jon Halliday, *Mao: The Unknown Story* (New York: Alfred A. Knopf, 2005), 461, 572; Yinghong Cheng, "Sino Cuban Relations during the Early Years of the Castro Regime, 1959–1966," *Journal of Cold War Studies* 9, no. 3 (Summer 2007): 92.

25. Chargé d'Affaires to Chancery, Beijing, 3 May 1960; Michael Stewart to H. A. A. Hankey, Beijing, 30 Jul 1960, Foreign Office: General Correspondence, 1906–1966, Political Correspondence, National Archives, London, 371/148202; "Minutes, 447th National Security Council meeting," 8 Jun 1960, Eisenhower: Papers, 1953–1961, Ann Whitman Files, NSC Series, Eisenhower Library.

26. "Notes on a Consultation in the Chinese Foreign Ministry," 17 Jun 1960, Ministerium für Auswärtige Angelegenheiten, Politisches Archiv des Auswärtiges Amt, Berlin, Germany (hereafter MfAA, Politisches Archiv).

27. "Discussion at the 447th Meeting of the NSC," 8 Jun 1960, Ann Whitman Files, NSC Series, box 12; "Discussion at the 455th Meeting of the NSC," 12 Aug 1960, Ann Whitman Files, NSC Series, box 13, Eisenhower Library.

28. "Discussion at the 461th Meeting of the NSC," 26 Sep 1960, Ann Whitman Files, NSC Series, box 13, Eisenhower Library.

29. CIA, "Current Intelligence Weekly Summary," 3 Nov 1960, White House; "Minutes, 472 NSC Meeting," 29 Dec 1960, Ann Whitman File, Eisenhower Library. Jorge G. Castañeda asserts that Che was the principal architect of Cuba's alliance with the Soviets and Chinese. Castañeda, *Compañero: The Life and Death of Che Guevara,* trans. by Marina Castañeda (New York: Alfred A. Knopf, 1997), 174–75, 183. Also see Paul J. Dosal, *Comandante Che: Guerrilla Soldier, Commander, and Strategist, 1956–1967* (University Park: Penn State University Press, 2003), 60–61.

30. *Foreign Relations of the United States, 1958–1960,* vol. 19, *China* (Washington, DC: US Government Printing Office, 1996), 742. A member of the communist old guard, Aníbal Escalante, attended the Moscow conference as Cuba's representative. Vladislav Zubok and Constantine Pleshakov, *Inside the Kremlin's Cold War: From Stalin to Khrushchev* (Cambridge, MA: Harvard University Press, 1996), 206–7. On military training, see Luis Báez, *Secretos de generales* (Havana: Editorial Si-Mar, 1996).

31. Michael Ratner and Michael Steven Smith, eds., *Che Guevara and the FBI: The US Political Police Dossier on the Latin American Revolutionary* (Melbourne: Ocean Press, 1997), 59.

32. "Memorandum of Conversation between Mao Zedong and Ernesto 'Che' Guevara," 19 Nov 1960, in *Cold War International Project Bulletin,* nos. 17 / 18 (Fall 2012): 50–57; Cheng, "Sino Cuban Relations," 95; Paco Ignacio Taibo II, *Guevara, Also Known as Che,* trans. Martin Michael Roberts (New York: St. Martin's Press, 1997), 314–15; Luiz Bernardo Pericás, *Che Guevara e o debate econômico em Cuba* (São Paulo: Xamã Editora, 2004), 64–66. Raúl Castro once confided to his Bulgarian hosts that the Chinese had donated antiaircraft weapons at no cost to the Cubans. See Radchenko, *Two Suns in the Heavens,* 41. For the Chinese leaders' early favoritism of the

Cuban revolutionaries, see Cecil Johnson, *Communist China & Latin America, 1959–1967* (New York: Columbia University Press, 1970), 134–36, 143–45.

33. CIA, "Current Intelligence Weekly Summary," 26 Jan 1961, *C.I.A. Research Reports: Latin America, 1946–1976* (Frederick, MD: University Publications of America, 1982), microfilm; Weeka Reports, 8 Dec 1960, 737.00(W)/12-860; 15 Dec 1960, 737.00(W)/12-1560, Confidential US State Department Central Files, Cuba: Internal Affairs, 1960–1963, microfilm, reel 23.

34. Other sympathetic visitors such as the future French president, François Mitterrand, also missed the signs of famine in 1961. Dikötter, *Mao's Great Famine*, 114. Subsequently, Cuban president Osvaldo Dórticos made a state visit to Beijing complete with a meeting with Chairman Mao. See *Revolución* (Havana), 6 Oct 1961.

35. Bureau of Intelligence and Research, "Cuban Economic Mission to the Sino-Soviet Bloc," 23 Mar 1961, in *O.S.S./State Department Intelligence and Research Reports*, vol. 14, *Latin America: 1941–1961*, ed. Paul Kesaris (Frederick, MD: University Publications of America, 1979), microfilm.

36. K. S. Karol, *Guerrillas in Power: The Course of the Cuban Revolution*, trans. Arnold Pomerans (New York: Hill & Wang, 1970), 52.

37. Orlando Borrego, *Che: El camino del fuego* (Havana: Imagen Contemporánea, 2001), 103.

38. CIA, "Current Intelligence Weekly Summary," 12 Jan 1961, in *C.I.A. Research Reports*.

39. Carlos Franqui, *Family Portrait with Fidel: A Memoir*, trans. Alfred MacAdam (New York: Vintage Books, 1985), 260. On the economic debate within socialism between Che, Charles Bettelheim, and Carlos Rafael Rodríguez, see Borrego, *Che*, 201–42. Also see Ernesto Che Guevara, *El Gran Debate sobre la economía en Cuba, 1963–1964* (Havana: Editorial de Ciencias Sociales, 2004); Pericás, *Che Guevara e o debate econômico em Cuba;* Carmelo Mesa-Lago and Luc Zephirin, "Central Planning," in *Revolutionary Change in Cuba*, ed. Carmelo Mesa-Lago (Pittsburgh: University of Pittsburgh Press, 1971), 145–84; Andrew Zimbalist, "Cuban Economic Planning," in *Cuba: Twenty-Five Years of Revolution, 1959–1984*, ed. Sandor Halebsky and John M. Kirk (New York: Praeger, 1985), 213–30. On Khrushchev's economic reforms, see Martin McCauley, *The Khrushchev Era, 1953–1964* (London: Longman, 1995), 53; Karol, *Guerrillas in Power*, 193.

40. Richard Goodwin, *Remembering America: A Voice from the Sixties* (Boston: Little, Brown, 1988), 172.

41. Dobrynin was the Soviet ambassador in Washington, DC. CIA, International Intelligence Communication, 18 Dec 1963, National Security Files (hereafter NSF), Country File (hereafter CF), box 32, Lyndon Baines Johnson Presidential Library, Austin, TX. Also see Karol, *Guerrillas in Power*, 225; Carmelo Mesa-Lago, *The Economy of Socialist Cuba: A Two Decade Appraisal* (Albuquerque: University of New Mexico Press, 1981), 157–62.

42. Ernesto Che Guevara, *Guerrilla Warfare,* ed. Brian Loveman and Thomas M. Davies Jr. (Lincoln: University of Nebraska Press, 1985), 7, 11.

43. CIA, "Situation and Prospects in Cuba," 14 Jun 1963, NSF, CF, box 9, LBJ Library.

44. CIA, "The New State of the Sino-Soviet Dispute," ca. Dec 1961, NSF, Department of Agencies, box 271, John F. Kennedy Presidential Library, Boston.

45. Thomas, *Cuba,* 1379–81, 1468–69. On Castro and the communists, see D. Bruce Jackson, *Castro, the Kremlin, and Communism in Latin America* (Baltimore, MD: Johns Hopkins University Press, 1969); Jacques Lévesque, *The USSR and the Cuban Revolution: Soviet Ideological and Strategical Perspective, 1959-1977;* Suárez, *Cuba, Castroism and Communism;* Jorge I. Domínguez, *Cuba: Order and Revolution* (Cambridge, MA: Belknap Press of Harvard University Press, 1978).

46. Hart Phillips, *The Cuban Dilemma,* 208, 275; Robert Taber, *M-26: Biography of a Revolution* (New York: Lyle Stuart, 1961), 334–35.

47. *Foreign Relations of the United States,* vol. 5, *Cuba, 1958–1960* (Washington, DC: US Government Printing Office, 1991), 863, 1128.

48. "Notes on a Discussion with Cuban Ambassador to China, Mr. Pinos-Santo," 7 Jan 1961, MfAA, Politisches Archiv.

49. *The Kennedy Presidential Press Conferences* (New York: Earl M. Coleman, 1978), 76. Allen Dulles, CIA director at the time, denies that the "massive uprising" had been promised. Yet that idea had spread among the Cuban expatriates who trained for this mission. Allen Dulles, *The Craft of Intelligence* (New York: Harper & Row, 1963), 169.

50. More than twelve hundred militiamen died to only one hundred fourteen men of Brigade 2506. Howard Jones, *The Bay of Pigs* (Oxford: Oxford University Press, 2008), 122.

51. What could the CIA have done better? "There was no really detached body of experts giving a critical evaluation as to the chances of success or failure," writes Lyman Kirkpatrick. "There should be a clear separation between those who evaluate intelligence and those who mount operations based on that intelligence." Lyman B. Kirkpatrick Jr., *The Real CIA* (New York: Macmillan, 1968), 204. On the Bay of Pigs debacle, see chapter 10 of Arthur M. Schlesinger Jr.'s *A Thousand Days: John F. Kennedy in the White House* (Boston: Houghton Mifflin, 1965); James Blight and Peter Kornbluh, eds., *Bay of Pigs Declassified: The Secret CIA Report on the Invasion of Cuba* (New York: New Press, 1998); Jones, *The Bay of Pigs;* Juan Carlos Rodríguez Cruz, *La batalla inevitable: La más colosal operación de la CIA contra Fidel Castro* (Havana: Editorial Capitán San Luis, 1996); Piero Gleijeses, "Ships in the Night: The CIA, the White House and the Bay of Pigs," *Journal of Latin American Studies* 27, no. 1 (1995): 1–42; Don Bohning, *The Castro Obsession: U.S. Covert Operations against Cuba, 1959–1965* (Washington, DC: Potomac Books, 2005), 34, 61.

52. "Documents on Raul Castro's Visit to Eastern Europe," Mar–May 1965, in *Cold War International Project Bulletin,* nos. 17 / 18 (Fall 2012): 781.

53. DDR [German Democratic Republic] Embassy, Warsaw, "Notes on Discussion with Amado Palenque, Cultural Attaché to Cuban Embassy," 25 Apr 1961; DDR Embassy, Beijing, "Notes on a Visit by Mrs. Ana Galbis, Cuban Embassy," 25 May 1961, MfAA, Politisches Archiv. Translation by David Brown.

54. *Foreign Relations of the United States, 1961–1963, the Soviet Union* (Washington, DC: US Government Printing Office, 1998), 184–86 (hereafter *FRUS, 1961– 1963,* vol. 5, *The Soviet Union).* On the Kennedy-Khrushchev meetings, see Michael R. Beschloss, *The Crisis Years: Kennedy and Khrushchev, 1960–1963* (New York: Harper Collins, 1991), chaps. 8–9.

55. As quoted in John Lewis Gaddis, *The Cold War: A New History* (New York: Penguin, 2005), 115.

56. Anatoly Dobrynin, *In Confidence: Moscow's Ambassador to America's Six Cold War Presidents (1962–1986)* (New York: Random House, 1995), 70, 72; Zubok and Pleshakov, *Inside the Kremlin's Cold War,* 219–20, 231, 260–62.

57. Dobrynin, *In Confidence,* 73.

58. Fursenko and Naftali, *Khrushchev's Cold War,* 438–39, 444–45. In deciding to place missiles in Cuba, Khrushchev did not seek the KGB's advice on how it thought the United States might react. Andrew and Mitrokhin write, referring to Khrushchev, "Few world leaders have been guilty of greater foreign policy misjudgments." Andrew and Mitrokhin, *The World Was Going Our Way,* 45. Says historian Piero Gleijeses: "Kennedy's reckless policy of aggression against Cuba precipitated the decision to install missiles in the island and brought the world to the brink of nuclear war." Gleijeses, "Cuba and the Cold War, 1959–1980," in *The Cambridge History of the Cold War,* 3 vols., ed. Melvyn P. Leffler and Odd Arne Westad (Cambridge: Cambridge University Press, 2010), 2: 346.

59. CIA, "Chinese Use Soviet Position on Cuba and India to Press Attack on Khrushchev," 1 Nov 1962, NSF, box 51, Kennedy Library.

60. See Tomás Diez Acosta, *Octubre de 62: Un paso del holocausto; Una mirada cubana a la crisis de los misiles* (Havana: Editora Política, 1999); Daniela Spenser, "The Caribbean Crisis: Catalyst for Soviet Projection in Latin America," in *In from the Cold: Latin America's New Encounter with the Cold War,* ed. Gilbert M. Joseph and Daniela Spenser (Durham, NC: Duke University Press, 2008), 77–112; James G. Hershberg, "The United States, Brazil, and the Cuban Missile Crisis, 1962," pt. 2, *Journal of Cold War History* 6, no. 3 (Summer 2004): 40. Interestingly, US military intelligence had no idea that some of the Soviet missiles were already armed with nuclear warheads at the time of the US naval blockade. That fact emerged from the conferences of former Soviet, American, and Cuban officials in 1992 and 2002. See James G. Blight, Bruce J. Allyn, and David A. Welch, *Cuba on the Brink: Castro, the Missile Crisis, and the Soviet Collapse* (New York: Pantheon Books, 1993); Michael Dobbs,

One Minute to Midnight: Kennedy, Khrushchev, and Castro on the Brink of Nuclear War (New York: Alfred A. Knopf, 2008). For more on hostilities between the PRC and the USSR during the missile crisis, see Radchenko, *Two Suns in the Heavens,* 33–41.

61. CIA, "Soviet Personnel Intelligence Activities," 4 Dec 1962, NSF, box 51, Kennedy Library; CIA, "Cuba 1962: Khrushchev's Miscalculated Risk," 13 Feb 1964, NSF, CF, box 35, LBJ Library. See Zubok and Pleshakov, *Inside the Kremlin's Cold War,* 260, 269. The Soviets did leave behind some military personnel and the surface-to-air missiles (SAMs) that they trained the Cubans in operating. See *FRUS, 1961–1963,* vol. 5, *The Soviet Union,* 694. One Cuban communist, Juan Marinello, lost his job as rector of the University of Havana for defending the Soviet decision in the missile crisis. See CIA, "Cuban Government Official's Views on the Cuban Internal Political Situation," 23 Mar 1963, NSF, box 52A, Kennedy Library.

62. Robert E. Quirk, *Fidel Castro* (New York: W. W. Norton, 1993), 449.

63. The Venezuelan insurrection lasted through the 1960s but eventually failed; the Argentine insurrection ended within five months. See Aragorn Storm Miller, "Precarious Paths to Freedom: The United States and International Communism in the Contest for Venezuela, 1961–1968" (MA thesis, University of Texas, 2008); Daniel Avalos, *La guerrilla del Che y Masetti en Salta, 1964* (Córdoba, Argentina: La Intemperie, 2005).

64. "Propaganda Report," 18 Jan 1963, NSF, Cuba, box 59, Kennedy Library. On Soviet opposition to Cuba's early interventions in Latin America and Africa, see Gleijeses, "Cuba and the Cold War, 1959–1980"; Sergey Radchenko, "Cuba and the Cold War, 1959–1980," in *The Cambridge History of the Cold War,* 3 vols., ed. Melvyn P. Leffler and Odd Arne Westad (Cambridge: Cambridge University Press, 2010), 2: 349–72.

65. "Opinions of Cuban Government Officials on Internal Situation, Relations with the Soviet Union," 15 Feb 1963; "Cuban Attitude toward the Sino-Soviet Struggle," 30 Jan 1963, NSF, box 52A; "Radio Propaganda Report," 18 Jan 1963, NSF, box 59, Kennedy Library.

66. Foy D. Kohler to Secretary of State, Moscow, 31 May 1963, NSF, box 44, Kennedy Library; Tad Szulc, *Fidel: A Critical Portrait* (New York: Avon Books, 1986), 654–57; Coltman, *The Real Fidel Castro,* 205–6.

67. James G. Blight and Philip Brenner, *Sad and Luminous Days: Cuba's Struggle with the Superpowers after the Missile Crisis* (Lanham, MD: Rowman and Littlefield,, 2002), 64. Also see Carlos Lechuga, *In the Eye of the Storm: Castro, Khrushchev, Kennedy and the Missile Crisis* (Melbourne: Ocean Press, 1995), 65–66.

68. Quirk, *Fidel Castro,* 459–69; Khrushchev, *Nikita Khrushchev,* 658–62.

69. Andrew and Mitrokhin, *The World Was Going Our Way,* 46–47.

70. Fursenko and Naftali, *One Hell of a Gamble,* 332–34; Lévesque, *The USSR and the Cuban Revolution,* 92, 96. Fidel's first trip to the Soviet Union lasted from April 27 to June 5, 1963.

71. Johnson, *Communist China & Latin America,* 155.

72. The East Germans, at least, took the joint US-Latin American strike force seriously. "Moscow, Comments on Discussion between DDR Ambassador Rittner with . . . Raul Castro," 15 Nov 1963, MfAA, Politisches Archiv.

73. CIA "International Intelligence Communication," 17 Mar 1964, NSF, CF, box 32, LBJ Library.

74. Secretary of State to All American Diplomatic Posts, 28 Jan 1964, NSF, CF, box 16, LBJ Library. Cuban diplomats in Eastern Europe began expressing Havana's acknowledgment of Moscow's leadership of the international socialist movement. See "Letter to Comrade Stibi from Comrade Grünstein regarding the Visit of Comrade Galeano, Representative of the Ministry of the Interior of Cuba," 15 Aug 1963, MfAA, Politisches Archiv.

75. Thomas L. Hughes to Secretary of State, 28 Jul 1964, NSF, CF, box 20, LBJ Library. However, Castro was annoyed at the Czechs, Poles, and East Germans because they were not willing to pay the high prices for Cuban sugar that the Chinese and Soviets paid. CIA, "International Intelligence Communication," 19 Feb 1964, NSF, CF, box 32, LBJ Library.

76. Fursenko and Naftali, *One Hell of a Gamble,* 354; Luthi, *The Sino-Soviet Split,* 285–95.

77. CIA, "International Intelligence Communication," 26 Jan 1965, NSF, CF, box 32, LBJ Library.

78. Ciro Bustos, *El Che quiere verte: La historia jamás contada en Bolivia* (Buenos Aires: Javier Vergara, 2007), 244.

79. CIA, "Chinese Communist Activities in Latin America," 30 Apr 1965, NSF, CF, box 2, LBJ Library. On Sino-Cuban trade, see He Li, *Sino-Latin American Economic Relations* (New York: Praeger, 1991), 20–33; Frank Dikötter, *Mao's Great Famine,* 114.

80. CIA, "Visit to Beijing of Latin American Leaders following the November Conference in Havana," 24 Mar 1965, NSF, CF, box 31, LBJ Library. The CIA had a good source for this story as Raúl Castro corroborated this exchange, though without Mao's attack on Fidel. See "Documents on Raul Castro's Visit to Eastern Europe," 769, 781. See Johnson, *Communist China & Latin America,* 163–64. On the number of Uruguayan militants, see "Communist Threat to the United States through the Caribbean," *Hearings before the Subcommittee to Investigate the Administration of the Internal Security Act of the Committee on the Judiciary,* United States Senate, pt. 3 (Washington, DC: US Government Printing Office, 1960), 161. The Uruguayan Communist Party membership amounted to six thousand in 1964, and its electoral strength to 3.5 percent of the popular vote in 1962. See Philip Agee, *Inside the Company: CIA Diary* (New York: Stonehill, 1975), 331.

81. Directorate of Intelligence, "Weekly Cuban Summary," 3 Feb 1965; CIA, "Weekly Cuban Summary," 17 Feb 1965, NSF, CF, box 36; CIA, "International In-

telligence Communication," 31 Mar 1965, NSF, CF, box 32, LBJ Library; Jon Lee Anderson, *Che Guevara: A Revolutionary Life* (New York: Grove Press, 1997), 610–11, 620–21; Castañeda, *Compañero*, 288–89.

82. I. J. M. Sutherland to William G. Bowdler, 20 Apr 1965, NSF, CF, box 18, LBJ Library; Cheng, "Sino Cuban Relations," 104. On the breakdown of relations, see Canadian Embassy, Havana, to Undersecretary for External Affairs, 2 Jun 1965; A. E. Donald to E. Youde, Beijing, 17 Feb 1965; A. P. McLaine, "Sino-Cuban Relations and the Chinese Students in Havana," 16 Jun 1966; Foreign Office: General Correspondence, 1906-1966, Political Correspondence, National Archives, London, 371/179444, / 179521, / 1848555.

83. Latell, *After Fidel*, 136; Suárez, *Cuba*, 94, 159.

84. Franqui, *Family Portrait with Fidel*, 219.

85. "At the Asian-African Conference in Algeria (February 24, 1965)," in *Che Guevara Reader*, ed. David Deutschmann, 2nd ed. (Melbourne: Ocean Press, 2003), 342. Also see Jorge I. Domínguez, *To Make a World Safe for Revolution: Cuba's Foreign Policy* (Cambridge, MA: Harvard University Press, 1989), 66–67.

86. Different versions of these encounters are found in Luiz Alberto Moniz Bandeira, *De Martí a Fidel: A Revolução Cubano e a América Latina* (Rio de Janeiro: Civilização Brasileira), 550–55; Pacho O'Donnell, *Che: La vida por un mundo mejor* (Buenos Aires: Debolsillo, 2004), 235–37. Another of Che's biographers, Jon Lee Anderson, attests to the seriousness of the meetings; he says that Fidel accepted Che's views on the USSR but suggested that Che depart for the training mission to the Congo as soon as possible so as not to antagonize Cuba's principal benefactor. Anderson, *Che Guevara*, 626–27.

87. "Statement of Raul Castro pertaining to Ernesto 'Che' Guevara," 1 Mar 1985, CWIHP, http://digitalarchive.wilsoncenter.org/document/116563, accessed 20 Aug 2015; "Documents on Raul Castro's Visit to Eastern Europe," 777. Che's and Fidel's biographers note March 1965 as the decisive moment of Guevara's departure from the revolution. See Hugo Gambini, *El Che Guevara: La biografía* (Buenos Aires: Planeta, 2004), 287–89; Castañeda, *Compañero*, 296–300; Domínguez, *To Make a World Safe for Revolution*, 68–69; Quirk, *Fidel Castro*, 522–23; Szulc, *Fidel: A Critical Portrait*, 670. According to Fidel, "[Che] had no conflicts with the Soviets, but it's obvious that he was closer . . . to China, or more sympathetic to that country." Fidel Castro and Ignacio Ramonet, *Fidel Castro: My Life, a Spoken Autobiography*, trans. by Andrew Hurley (New York: Scribner, 2006), 292.

88. Ratner and Smith, *Che Guevara and the FBI*, 131; Agee, *Inside the Company*, 437–38. One of Che's closest associates in the export of revolution, Manuel Piñeiro of the Interior Ministry, claimed that Guevara did not break with the Soviets or with the Chinese. But the story spread that Fidel had shot Che and had him buried secretly. "That's how one of the most incredible tall tales of all time was created," he

wrote. Piñeiro, *Che Guevara and the Latin American Revolutionary Movements,* ed. Luis Suárez Salazar, trans. Mary Todd (Melbourne: Ocean Press, 2001), 44.

89. Mao's associates viewed African independence movements as duplicating the beginning of the Chinese Revolution in the days of the Boxer Rebellion. See Philip Snow, "China and Africa: Consensus and Camouflage," in *Chinese Foreign Policy: Theory and Practice,* ed. Thomas W. Robinson and David Shambaugh (Oxford: Clarendon Press, 1998), 284.

90. Ernesto 'Che' Guevara, *The African Dream: The Diaries of the Revolutionary War in the Congo,* trans. Patrick Camiller (New York: Grove Press, 1999), 1, 29. Under Castro's leadership, Cuba returned to Africa in the 1970s, despite Guevara's defeat in 1966. It did so not in support of subversion of pro-Western regimes but as a military ally of national liberation governments. The difference between the two kinds of interventions underwrote Cuba's success in Africa in the 1970s and 1980s.

91. "Havana: A Meeting with Comrade Torres to Get a Cuban Analysis of the U.S. and Cuban Policies in Latin America," 15 Dec 1965, MfAA, Politisches Archiv. This message also mentioned that "Cuba is expecting Chinese attempts to disrupt the Tricontinental and is prepared for such attempts." Translation by David Brown.

92. The Cubans did not disseminate the list of attendees at this conference so as not to expose the world's foremost revolutionaries to undue scrutiny by foreign security forces. The noncommunist West only knew of the identity of the speakers. See *First Solidarity Conference of the Peoples of Africa, Asia and Latin America* (Havana: General Secretariate of the OSMFAAL, 1966); Comisión Especial de Consulta sobre Seguridad, *La "Primera Conferencia Tricontinental": Otra amenaza a la seguridad del sistema interamericano* (Washington, DC: Pan American Union, 1966). Also see Renata Keller, *Mexico's Cold War: Cuba, the United States, and the Legacy of the Mexican Revolution* (New York: Cambridge University Press, 2015), 182-90.

93. Thomas L. Hughes, "The Tri-continent Conference at Havana: A Preliminary Assessment," n.d., NSF, CF, box 18, LBJ Library. Also see Jackson, *Castro, the Kremlin, and Communism,* chap. 6.

94. Fidel Castro, *Betrayal by Chinese Government of Cuban People's Good Faith, February 6, 1966* (n.p., n.d.), 17; Domínguez, *To Make a World Safe for Revolution,* 68–69; Lévesque, *The USSR and the Cuban Revolution,* 188; Suárez, *Cuba,* 234; Johnson, *Communist China & Latin America,* 164–69. See also "[Telegram from Havana to London]," 5 Jan 1966; Canadian Embassy, Havana, "The Tricontinental Conference and Osmany Cienfuegos," 23 Feb 1966, Foreign Office: General Correspondence, 1906–1966, Political Correspondence, National Archives, London, 371/184847.

95. CIA, "The Chinese Culture Revolution," 25 May 1967; "The Short-Term Outlook in Communist China," 23 May 1968, NSF, National Intelligence Estimates, box 5, LBJ Library. Also see Cheng, "Sino Cuban Relations," 108–11; Roderick

MacFarquhar and Michael Schoenhals, *Mao's Last Revolution* (Cambridge, MA: Belknap Press of Harvard University Press, 2006), 52.

96. Guevara, *Guerrilla Warfare,* 153. Historians point out that Bolivia had already had its "National Revolution" in 1952. Ironically, young Ernesto Guevara had been there briefly as a witness. Ernesto Che Guevara, *Otra vez: El diario inédito del segundo viaje por América Latina (1953–1956)* (Buenos Aires: Editorial Sudamericana, 2000); José M. Gordillo, *Campesinos revolucionarios en Bolivia: Identidad, territorio y sexualidad en el Valle Alto de Cochabamba, 1952–1964* (La Paz: Promec, 2000); James Dunkerley, *Rebellion in the Veins: Political Struggle in Bolivia, 1952–82* (London: Verso, 1984); James W. Wilkie, *The Bolivian Revolution and the U.S. since 1952* (Los Angeles: Latin American Center, University of California, 1969).

97. Blight and Brenner, *Sad and Luminous Days,* 122.

98. *Foreign Relations of the United States, 1964–1968,* Vol. 14, *The Soviet Union* (Washington DC: US Government Printing Office, 2001), 553, 559.

99. Blight and Brenner, *Sad and Luminous Days,* 125. Also see "A Report from the Mexican Embassy in Havana," 4 Jul 1967, CWIHP, http://digitalarchive.wilsoncenter .org/document/115799, accessed 17 Oct 2015.

100. Carmelo-Mesa Lago and Fernando Gill, "Soviet Economic Relations with Cuba," in *The USSR and Latin America: A Developing Relationship,* ed. Eusebio Mujal-León (Boston: Union Hyman, 1989), 183–84; Yuri Pavlov, *Soviet-Cuban Alliance, 1959–1991* (New Brunswick, NJ: Transaction Publishers, 1994), 88–89; W. Raymond Duncan, *The Soviet Union and Cuba: Interests and Influence* (New York: Praeger, 1985), 70–75; Andrew and Mitrokhin, *The World Was Going Our Way,* 54.

101. On Guevara in Bolivia, see Henry Butterfield Ryan, *The Fall of Che Guevara: A Story of Soldiers, Spies, and Diplomats* (New York: Oxford University Press, 1998); Benigno [Dariel Alarcón Ramírez], *Memorias de un soldado cubano: Vida y muerte de la Revolución* (Barcelona: Tusquets Editores, 1997); Luiz Bernardo Pericás, *Che Guevara e a luta revolucionária na Bolívia,* 2nd ed. (São Paulo: Xamã, 2008).

102. Says Daniela Spenser, "The tensions between the two countries [Cuba and the USSR] were reduced as a result of the elimination of [Che's] guerrillas." Spenser, "The Caribbean Crisis," 105.

103. Blight and Brenner, *Sad and Luminous Days,* 219. Also see Quirk, *Fidel Castro,* 598–99; Duncan, *The Soviet Union,* 76–79; Pavlov, *Soviet-Cuban Alliance,* 90–94. Cuba's commitment to the USSR is reflected in meetings of Cuban diplomats with DDR officials. "[We had] a relationship with the USSR since 1959," one Cuban official told the East Germans. "From the beginning, Cuba never accepted [the Yugoslavians]." "Meeting between Minister Mielke and Minister del Valle," 19 Sep 1969; "Suggestions for Discussions with Representatives of Cuba's Interior Ministry," 7 Oct 1969, Archiv der Zentralstelle, Mfs Zaig, NR 6409, NR 5485, BStU [acronym for Stasi Archive in Berlin]. Translation by David Brown.

104. "Comments of Soviet Diplomat on Soviet Relations with Cuba and China," London, 4 Jun 1963, NSF, box 53, Kennedy Library.

4. THE *GUSANO* COUNTERREVOLUTION

1. José Martí used the term to denigrate Cubans who opposed the independence movement of the late nineteenth century against Spanish colonial rule. See Lillian Guerra, *Visions of Power in Cuba: Revolution, Redemption, and Resistance, 1959–1971* (Chapel Hill: University of North Carolina Press, 2012), 100.

2. Antonio R. Zamora, *What I Learned about Cuba by Going to Cuba* (Miami: Cuba Libre Publications, 2013), 35.

3. Antonio R. Zamora, interview with author, Miami, 17 Jun 2013.

4. Ibid.

5. Ibid.; Alberto Müller, interview with author, Miami, 20 Jun 2013. Also see Gerald Poyo, *Cuban Catholics in the United States, 1960–1980* (Notre Dame, IN: University of Notre Dame Press, 2007), 37–38; Oscar Cerrallo, interview, *Avance* (Miami), 2 Dec 1960.

6. Weeka Report, 21 Apr 1959, 737.00(W)/4-2159, Confidential US State Department Central Files, Cuba: Internal Affairs, 1955–1959, microfilm, reel 8.

7. Victor Franco, *The Morning After,* trans. Ivan Kats and Philip Pendered (New York: Frederick A. Praeger, 1963), 165.

8. John M. Kirk, *Between God and the Party: Religion and Politics in Revolutionary Cuba* (Tampa: University of South Florida Press, 1989), 67.

9. Ibid., 69.

10. "Carta abierta del episcopado al Sr. Primer Ministro Dr. Fidel Castro," Havana, 4 Dec 1960, Jay Mallin Papers, box 2, Cuban Heritage Center, University of Miami (hereafter CHC).

11. See Weeka Reports, 10 Mar 1959, 737.00(W)/3-1059; 21 Apr 1959, 737.00(W)/4-2159; 6 Jun 1959, 737.00(W)/6-659, Confidential US State Department Central Files, Cuba: Internal Affairs, 1955–1959, reel 8.

12. The FEU had been the institutional foundation of the Directorio Revolucionario in 1954, when its president José Antonio Echeverría took his armed rebellion off campus.

13. Weeka Report, 23 May 1952, 737.00(W)/5-2352, Confidential US State Department Central Files, Cuba, Internal Affairs, 1955–1959, reel 8. Also see Jamie Suchlicki, *University Students and Revolution in Cuba, 1920–1968* (Coral Gables, FL: University of Miami Press, 1969).

14. Weeka Reports, 17 Nov 1959, 737.00(W)/11-1759; 5 Jan 1960, 737.00(W)/1-560, Confidential US State Department Central Files, Cuba, Internal Affairs, 1955–1959, reel 8. Also see *Revolución* (Havana), 2, 7 Jan 1960.

15. Weeka Reports, 5 Apr 1960, 737.00(W) / 4-560; 3 May 1960, 737.00(W) / 5-360; 10 May 1960, 737.00(W) / 5-1060, Confidential US State Department Central Files, Cuba, Internal Affairs, 1955–1959, reel 8. Also see Franco, *The Morning After,* 169–70.

16. Weeka Reports, 6 July 1960, 737.00(W) / 7-660; 1 Dec 1960, 737.00(W) / 12-160, Confidential US State Department Central Files, Cuba: Internal Affairs, 1960–1963, microfilm, reel 23. My thanks to Iliyana Hadjistoyanova for her research notes on this topic. For more on Cubela, see Guerra, *Visions of Power in Cuba,* 128–32.

17. Poyo, *Cuban Catholics,* 65–66.

18. Müller, interview, 20 Jun 2013.

19. I met one of these foreign advisers, Liu Wen Long, at a luncheon at Fudan University in Shanghai in March 2009. We chatted in Spanish, but we did not have time to talk in detail about his experiences. After his assignment in Cuba, he returned to China and became one of the pioneers of Latin American studies in Chinese academia.

20. Kirk, *Between God and the Party,* 73–74.

21. *Avance* (Miami), 2 Mar 1962; *Miami Herald,* 6 Mar 1962, box 27, Directorio Revolucionario Estudiantil (DRE) Records, CHC; Kirk, *Between God and the Party,* 77; Guerra, *Visions of Power in Cuba,* 122–25. The elder Müller was released in 1970. Juan Manuel Salvat to US Consul, n.d., Mexico, D.F., box 37, DRE Records, CHC. The author's conversations with Alberto Müller, Jun 2013.

22. Richard R. Fagen, *The Transformation of Political Culture in Cuba* (Stanford, CA: Stanford University Press, 1969), 69–71.

23. Jose Yglesias, *In the First of the Revolution: Life in a Cuban Country Town* (New York: Vintage Books, 1969), 283; Samuel Farber, *Cuba since the Revolution of 1959: A Critical Assessment* (Chicago: Haymarket Books, 2011), 16–17.

24. *Foreign Relations of the United States, 1958–1960,* vol. 6, *Cuba* (Washington, DC: US Government Printing Office, 1991), 1149, 1152; Philip W. Bonsal, *Cuba, Castro, and the United States* (Pittsburgh: University of Pittsburgh Press, 1971), 141. The chargé d'affairs was Daniel Braddock.

25. Pedro Etcheverry Vázquez and Santiago Gutiérrez Oceguera, *Bandidismo: Derrota de la CIA en Cuba* (Havana: Editorial Capitán San Luis, 2008), 82–83.

26. Ibid., 42, 44–45.

27. "Castro's Invasion Scare and Other Steps Causing Ridicule," 31 Jan 61, in *C.I.A. Research Reports: Latin America, 1946–1976* (Frederick, MD: University Publications of America, 1982), microfilm.

28. CIA, "Early Castro Meetings with Communists," 20 Jan 1961; "Current Intelligence Weekly Summary," 26 Jan 1961, in *C.I.A. Research Reports.*

29. CIA, "Increasing Opposition to Castro," Jan 1961, in *C.I.A Research Reports.*

30. CIA, "Indications in Camaguey of Increasing Dissatisfaction with CASTRO Government," 10 Mar 1961; "Decreasing Popular Support of the CASTRO Government," 16 Mar 1961, in *C.I.A. Research Reports*.

31. CIA, "Current Intelligence Weekly Summary," 13 Apr 1961, in *C.I.A Research Reports*.

32. Isidro "Chilo" Borja, interview with author, Miami, 18 Jun 2013.

33. Alberto Müller to John F. Kennedy, 24 Jan 1961, in Alberto Müller's personal collection.

34. CIA, "Supplement to the Current Intelligence Digest," 19 Apr 1961; "Current Intelligence Weekly Summary," 20 Apr 1961, in *C.I.A Research Reports;* Pedro Etcheverry Vázquez and Santiago Gutiérrez Oceguera, "El Bandidismo en La Habana" (unpublished manuscript, n.d.), 11–12, Museo de la Lucha Contra los Bandidos, Trinidad, Cuba; Félix I. Rodríguez and John Weisman, *Shadow Warrior* (New York: Simon & Schuster, 1989), 75–76; Alberto Müller, personal email to author, 28 Sep 2013.

35. Rodríguez and Weisman, *Shadow Warrior,* 87–88.

36. "Reaction within Cuba to Attempt to Overthrow CASTRO Regime," 19 May 1961, in *C.I.A Research Reports;* Jorge I. Domínguez, *Cuba: Order and Revolution* (Cambridge, MA: Belknap Press of Harvard University Press, 1978), 253; Daniel F. Solomon, *Breaking Up with Cuba: The Dissolution of Friendly Relations between Washington and Havana, 1956–1961* (Jefferson, NC: McFarland, 2011), 205; Louis A. Pérez Jr., *Cuba: Between Reform and Revolution,* 4th ed. (New York: Oxford University Press, 2011), 252.

37. *Diario de las Américas,* 19 Sep 1961, DRE Records, box 40, CHC.

38. Rodríguez and Weisman, *Shadow Warrior,* 95.

39. "Datos Biográficos, Miguel García Armengol" [ca. 1962], DRE Records, box 37, CHC; Hans Tanner, *Counterrevolutionary Agent* (London: G. T. Foulis, 1962), 38; Etcheverry Vázquez and Gutiérrez Oceguera, *Bandidismo,* 152–54.

40. Zamora, interview, 17 Jun 2013.

41. Lyman Kirkpatrick, "Paramilitary Case Study—The Bay of Pigs," n.d., Lyman Kirkpatrick Papers, National Archives and Records Administration, College Park,, MD (hereafter NARA). The CIA calculated that the Cuban forces had suffered ten casualties for every one *brigadista* killed or wounded.

42. Kirk, *Between God and the Party,* 95–96; Poyo, *Cuban Catholics,* 34.

43. Kirk, *Between God and the Party,* 97.

44. Poyo, *Cuban Catholics,* 76–80; Kirk, *Between God and the Party,* 102–3; Rafael Hernández, "'Siempre me he considerado un socialista': Max Lesnik habla sobre la Revolución cubana," *Temas: Cultura, Ideología, Sociedad,* no. 55 (2008): 43–44.

45. Fidel Castro, *Fidel and Religion: Talks with Frei Betto* (Havana: Publications Office of the Council of State, 1988), 212.

46. CIA, "Experiences before, during and after the Attempted Invasion," 5 Jun 61, in *C.I.A Research Reports*.

47. CIA, "Living Conditions / Anti-Castroist Reaction to Regime's Activities," 11 May 61, in *C.I.A Research Reports;* Dick Cluster and Rafael Hernández, *The History of Havana* (New York: Palgrave Macmillan, 2006), 228–29.

48. Samuel Farber, *The Origins of the Cuban Revolution Reconsidered* (Chapel Hill: University of North Carolina Press, 2006), 135.

49. "Minutes: 473rd Meeting of the NSC," 5 Jan 1961, box 12, Ann Whitman Files, National Security Council (NSC) Series, Dwight D. Eisenhower Presidential Library.

50. "Staff Notes No 854," 20 Oct 1960, box 54, Ann Whitman Files, Dwight David Eisenhower (DDE) Diary Series, Eisenhower Library.

51. Lloyd A. Free, "The Cuban Situation," 13 Apr 1960, box 8, Ann Whitman Files, International Series, Eisenhower Library.

52. "Cuban Refugees in Florida," 8 Nov 1960, Ann Whitman Files, Diary Series, box 54, Eisenhower Library.

53. Tanner, *Counterrevolutionary Agent,* 13.

54. Kathryn D. Goodwin to Jarold A. Keiffer, 9 Nov 1960, Robert E. Merriam Records, Eisenhower Library.

55. Christian A. Herter, "The Problem of Cuban Refugees," 23 Dec 1960; Bonsal, "Statement by the US Interim Representative to the OAS," n.d., Ann Whitman Files, Dulles-Herter Series, box 13; Monsignor John J. Fitzpatrick, "Cardinal Spellman's Check for Cuban Refugee Relief," 11 Jan 1961, Merriam Records, Eisenhower Library.

56. Guy E. Coriden, "Report on Hungarian Refugees," approved for release 1994, posted 2 Jul 1996, CIA Historical Review Program, https://www.cia.gov/library/center-for-the-study-of-intelligence/kent-csi/vol2no1/html/v02i1a07p_0001.htm, accessed 27 Aug 2015. The total number of refugees settled throughout Western Europe and North America amounted to two hundred thousand Hungarians. "Fall of the 1956 Revolution" (unpublished manuscript, n.d.), Museum of Communism, Budapest, Hungary.

57. Tracy S. Voorhees, "Interim Report to the President on the Cuban Refugee Problem," 19 Dec 1960, Merriam Records, Eisenhower Library.

58. C. V. Clifton, "Cuban Focal Point in the Miami Area," 19 Dec 1962; Department of Health, Education, and Welfare, "Resources of Cuban Prisoner Returnees," 7 Jan 1963, National Security Files (hereafter NSF), box 48, John F. Kennedy Presidential Library; Jorge I. Domínguez, personal communication, 9 Sep 2015. Also see *Foreign Relations of the United States, 1961–1963,* vol. 11, *Cuban Missile Crisis and Aftermath* (Washington, DC: US Government Printing Office, 1996) (hereafter *FRUS, 1961–1963,* vol. 11, *Missile Crisis*), 647.

59. As quoted in María Cristina García, *Havana USA: Cuban Exiles and Cuban Americans in South Florida, 1959–1994* (Berkeley: University of California Press, 1996), 17.

60. Enrique G. Encinosa, *Cuba: The Unfinished Revolution* (Austin, TX: Eakin Press, 1988), 150.

61. Yglesias, *In the First of the Revolution,* 158. Also see Anita Casavantes Bradford, *The Revolution Is for the Children: The Politics of Childhood in Havana and Miami, 1959–1962* (Chapel Hill: University of North Carolina Press, 2014), 129.

62. Carlos Eire, *Waiting for Snow in Havana: Confessions of a Cuban Boy* (New York: Free Press, 2003), 300.

63. Ibid., 377, 390; Tanner, *Counterrevolutionary Agent,* 53; Cluster and Hernández, *The History of Havana,* 220–21.

64. "Operation Pedro Pan: The Journey of the Cuban Children to America, 1960–1962," n.d., Pedro Pan Collection, box 2, CHC; "Family Reunion of Cuban Refugees in the United States," 3 Jun 1965, NSF, Country File (hereafter CF), box 30, Lyndon Baines Johnson Presidential Library, Austin [hereafter LBJ]. Also see Felix Roberto Masud-Piloto, *From Welcomed Exiles to Illegal Immigrants: Cuban Migration to the U.S., 1959–1995* (Lanham, MD: Rowman & Littlefield, 1996), 39–41; Monsignor Bryan O. Walsh, "Cuban Refugee Children," in *The Cuban Reader: History, Culture, Politics,* ed. Aviva Chomsky, Barry Carr, and Pamela Maria Smorkaloff (Durham, NC: Duke University Press, 2003), 557–60.

65. Donald Wheeler Jones to Robert King High, 13 Oct 1965, NSF, CF, box 30, LBJ Library.

66. Haydon Burns to Lyndon B. Johnson, 5 Oct 1965, NSF, CF, box 30, LBJ Library.

67. John W. Gardner to Haydon Burns, 11 Oct 1965; Gardner to the President, 4 Nov 1965, NSF, CF, box 30, LBJ Library.

68. Chase to Bundy, 27 Nov 1963; Woodward to State, 24 Apr 1964, NSF, CF, box 30, LBJ Library.

69. "Press Release from the White House," 5 Apr 1965, NSF, CF, box 30, LBJ Library.

70. Gordon Chase, "Cuban Refugee Flow—Miami Problem," 28 Feb 1963, NSF, box 56A, Kennedy Library.

71. Chase, "Relocation of Cuban Refugees," 9 Apr 1963, NSF, box 56A, Kennedy Library.

72. Quoted in "As Forces Grow, Cuban Refugees Find New Hope," *National Observer* (Washington, DC), 19 Aug 1963.

73. John A. McCone, "Payments to Dependents of Cuban Brigade Members," 20 Jul 1962, NSF, box 48, Kennedy Library.

74. CIA, "Opposition Situation in Cuba as of 18 May 1961," 5 Jun 1961, in *C.I.A Research Reports.*

75. CIA, "Conditions and Life for the Brigade Prisoners in Cuban Prisons," 9 Oct 1962, in *C.I.A Research Reports.*

76. Judith Edgette, "Domestic Collection on Cuba," n.d.; Andrew Wixson, "Portrait of a Cuban Refugee," n.d., Kirkpatrick Papers, NARA. For example, see CIA, "Recent Soviet Military Aid to Cuba," 22 Aug 1962, in *C.I.A. Research Reports;* Don Bohning, *The Castro Obsession: U.S. Covert Operations against Cuba, 1959–1965* (Washington, DC: Potomac Books, 2005), 146.

77. *FRUS, 1961–1963,* vol. 11, *Missile Crisis,* 685–86, 695–96.

78. Robert Hurwitch, "Subject: Possible Resignation of Dr. Miro Cardona," 6 Apr 1963, NSF, box 56A, Kennedy Library. Also see García, *Havana USA,* 130.

79. Department of State, "US Military Training for Cubans," ca. Jul 1963, NSF, box 48, Kennedy Library.

80. Hal Hendrix, "Backstage with Bobbie," *Miami News,* 14 Jul 1963, NSF, box 48, Kennedy Library.

81. Borja knew the hotel by the name of the Rosita Hornedo Hotel. Borja, interview, 18 Jun 2013; "Complete Information on the Raid of Castro's Cuba," 31 Aug 1962, DRE Records, box 23, CHC; *Miami News,* 26 Aug 1962; *Time,* 7 Sep 1962; *Albany (NY) Times Union,* 30 Aug 1962, as collected in DRE Records, boxes 27, 35, CHC. Also see Bohning, *The Castro Obsession,* 120; García, *Havana USA,* 128; Jefferson Morley, *Our Man in Mexico: Winston Scott and the Hidden History of the CIA* (Lawrence: University Press of Kansas, 2008), 130–32, 163. Morley writes that the CIA was giving the DRE $51,000 per month, or about $300,000 in 2008 dollars.

82. Luis Fernández Rocha to J. F. Kennedy, 13 Dec 1962; *Palm Beach (FL) Post-Times,* 22 Apr 1962, boxes 26, 27, DRE Records, CHC.

83. Philip Agee, *Inside the Company: CIA Diary* (London: Allen Lane, 1975), 231, 369.

84. "Text of Castro Communique on Shelling," 25 Aug 1962, Castro Speech Database, Latin American Network Information Center (LANIC), http://www.lanic .utexas.edu/project/castro/db/1962/19620825.html; "Castro Condemns Recent Havana Raid by Counter-revolutionaries," 28 Aug 1962, Castro Speech Database, LANIC, http://www.lanic.utexas.edu/project/castro/db/1962/19620828.html, accessed 21 Oct 2015. Also see *Revolución,* 28 Aug 1962.

85. Editorial, *Revolución,* 23 Feb 1959, as quoted in Richard R. Fagen, "Mass Mobilization in Cuba: The Symbolism of Struggle," in *Cuba in Revolution,* ed. Rolando E. Bonachea and Nelson P. Valdés (Garden City, NY: Anchor Books, 1972), 201.

86. A recurrent theme in Ambassador Bonsal's book is that Castro's enemies relied on Washington to rid them of "the dictator" rather than uniting to do the job themselves. They could not believe that the Americans would allow the communists to maintain control of the island. Bonsal, *Cuba, Castro, and the United States,* 145. Also see Jesús Arboleya, *The Cuban Counterrevolution,* trans. Rafael Betancourt

(Athens: Ohio University Press, 2000), 79, 109. Also see "Memorandum of Conversation between Mao Zedong and Cuban President Osvaldo Dorticos," 28 Sep 1961, in *Cold War International Project Bulletin,* nos. 17 / 18 (Fall 2012), 75.

87. British Embassy, Havana, "Miscellany," 17 Aug 1963, NSF, box 39, Kennedy Library.

5. THE *BANDIDO* COUNTERREVOLUTION

1. See Louis A. Pérez Jr., *Lords of the Mountain: Social Banditry and Peasant Protest in Cuba, 1878–1918* (Pittsburgh: University of Pittsburgh Press, 1989); Rosalie Schwartz, *Lawless Liberators: Political Banditry and Cuban Independence* (Durham, NC: Duke University Press, 1989).

2. Víctor Dreke, *From the Escambray to the Congo: In the Whirlwind of the Cuban Revolution* (New York: Pathfinder Press, 2002), 170; Enrique G. Encinosa, *Escambray: La guerra olvidada* (Miami: Editorial CIBI, 1989), 26, 32; José R. Herrera Medina, *Operación Jaula: Contragolpe en el Escambray* (Havana: Casa Editorial Verde Olivo, 2006), 72–73.

3. Enrique G. Encinosa, *Cuba: The Unfinished Revolution* (Austin, TX: Eakin Press, 1988), 81.

4. *Revista Moncada* 12 (Jun 1978): 12–13, as quoted in Pedro Etcheverry Vázquez and Santiago Gutiérrez Oceguera, *Bandidismo: Derrota de la CIA en Cuba* (Havana: Editorial Capitán San Luis, 2008), 119–20.

5. Richard R. Fagen, *The Transformation of Political Culture in Cuba* (Stanford, CA: Stanford University Press, 1969), 42. Also see Jesús Arboleya, *The Cuban Counter-Revolution,* trans. Rafael Betancourt (Athens: Ohio University Press, 2000), 113–19.

6. Encinosa, *Cuba: The Unfinished Revolution,* 83.

7. Julio Crespo Francisco, *Bandidismo en el Escambray, 1960–1965* (Havana: Editorial de Ciencias Sociales, 1986), 75.

8. Etcheverry Vázquez and Gutiérrez Oceguera, *Bandidismo,* 228, 243.

9. "Analisis de algunos aspectos de la actividad bandesca," n.d., doc. 555-(4.1), Museo de la Lucha Contra los Bandidos, Trinidad, Cuba (hereafter MLCB).

10. Laura Bergquist, "Epitaph for a Big Loser," *Look Magazine,* 25 Apr 1961; R. Hart Phillips, *The Cuban Dilemma* (New York: Ivan Obolensky, 1963), 259, 311.

11. Etcheverry Vázquez and Gutiérrez Oceguera, *Bandidismo,* 92. A French journalist reported that the INRA nationwide ran 800 cooperatives, 604 cane *copos,* 268 people's farms, 150 sugar mills and food factories, and 2,000 *tiendas del pueblo.* See Victor Franco, *The Morning After,* trans. Ivan Kats and Philip Pendered (New York: Frederick A. Praeger, 1963), 115.

12. Herrera Medina, *Operación Jaula,* 126–27.

13. William Gálvez, *Camilo: Señor de la Vanguardia* (Havana: Editorial de Ciencias Sociales, 1979), 341, 395; Ernesto Che Guevara, *Reminiscences of the Cuban*

Revolutionary War (Melbourne: Ocean Press, 2006),, 265. Chapters of Guevara's book first appeared as short articles in *Verde Olivo*. For more on Félix Torres, see Encinosa, *Cuba,* 49, 57–59; Rafael Hernández, " 'Siempre me he considerado un socialista': Max Lesnik habla sobre la Revolución cubana," *Temas: Cultura, Ideología, Sociedad,* no. 55 (2008): 37; Jon Lee Anderson, *Che Guevara: A Revolutionary Life* (New York: Grove Press, 1997), 338–39; 400.

14. Ejército Rebelde, "Orden del día de la conferencia del Escambray," 24 Sep 1961, doc. 503-(4.1), MLCB.

15. "All Cuban mass organizations were founded at times when the revolutionary government was threatened," writes Jorge I. Domínguez. "ANAP was no exception." Domínguez, *Cuba: Order and Revolution* (Cambridge, MA: Belknap Press of Harvard University Press, 1978), 445, 447–48. Also see Aviva Chomsky, Barry Carr, and Pamela Maria Smorkaloff, eds., *The Cuba Reader: History, Culture, Politics* (Durham, NC: Duke University Press, 2003), 380–81.

16. "El Departamento de Seguridad del Estado en la Lucha Contra Bandidos," n.d. [ca. 1962], doc. 215-(0), MLCB.

17. Rafael Rojas, *Essays in Cuban Intellectual History* (New York: Palgrave Macmillan), 128.

18. "Operación de cerco," n.d.; "Operación de cerco y peine," n.d., 19/3-3/5-6/1-37, Colección Fuerzas Armadas Revolucionarias, Fondo Lucha Contra los Bandidos, Instituto de Historia de Cuba (hereafter Fondo LCB).

19. DSE, "Expediente EI 138," n.d. [ca. 1963], doc. 401-(4.1), MLCB. According to Jorge I. Domínguez, the farmers "revolted against what they perceived as an intrusion of arbitrary outside power that threatened the security of the land and of their way of life." Domínguez, *Cuba: Order and Revolution,* 443.

20. Crespo Francisco, *Bandidismo en el Escambray,* 296–97.

21. "Fichas biográficas del A.B.S.," 19/6.1/2.1/1-301, Fondo LCB; Crespo Francisco, *Bandidismo en el Escambray,* 103–4.

22. Crespo Francisco, *Bandidismo en el Escambray,* 119.

23. Joanna Beth Swanger, "Lands of Rebellion: Oriente and Escambray Encountering Cuban State Formation, 1934–1974" (PhD diss., University of Texas at Austin, 1999), 287–88, 304.

24. Carlos Moore, *Castro, the Black, and Africa* (Los Angeles: Center for Afro-American Studies, University of California Press, 1988), 21; Lillian Guerra, *Visions of Power in Cuba: Revolution, Redemptions, and Resistance, 1959–1971* (Chapel Hill: University of North Carolina Press, 2012), 182–83.

25. Crespo Francisco, *Bandidismo en el Escambray,* 98; Encinosa, *Escambray,* 47; Gerald E. Poyo, *Cuban Catholics in the United States, 1960–1980* (Notre Dame, IN: University of Notre Dame Press, 2007), 76–77.

26. "Hechos cometidos en zonas donde operan bandas," Jun 1962, 19/1-2/8-10/39-61, Fondo LCB.

27. See Ada Ferrer, *Insurgent Cuba: Race, Nation, and Revolution, 1868–1898* (Chapel Hill: University of North Carolina Press, 1999), 99–100, 144; Gillian Mc-Gillivray, *Blazing Cane: Sugar-Communities, Class, and State Formation in Cuba, 1868–1959* (Durham, NC: Duke University Press, 2009), 4.

28. "Distintos hechos ocurridos en zona de Rodas y Cartagena desde el 9 de noviembre," 28 Jan 1962, 19/3-4/3:4.2/1-2, Fondo LCB.

29. Evelio Duque Miyar, *Mis memorias: Importantes revelaciones del proceso revolucionario de Cuba* (Miami: Evelio Duque Miyar, 1995), 107, as quoted in Swanger, "Lands of Rebellion," 301.

30. Crespo Francisco, *Bandidismo en el Escambray,* 28, 105–6; Herrera Medina, *Operación Jaula,* 76–77. Women too signed up for militia duty. See Michelle Chase, *Revolution within the Revolution: Women and Gender Politics in Cuba, 1952–1962* (Chapel Hill: University of North Carolina Press, 2015), 129–31.

31. Crespo Francisco, *Bandidismo en el Escambray,* 40; Hart Phillips, *The Cuban Dilemma,* 300.

32. Crespo Francisco, *Bandidismo en el Escambray,* 99–100; Hart Phillips, *The Cuban Dilemma,* 146.

33. Etcheverry Vázquez and Gutiérrez Oceguera, *Bandidismo,* 26–27.

34. Orlando Lorenzo Castro, "Desarrollo de la entrevista," 17 Apr 1984, doc. 392-(4.1); Augusto Sandino to Sinesio Walsh Rice, 18 Sep 1960, doc. 368-(4.1), MLCB.

35. Encinosa, *Cuba: The Unfinished Revolution,* 77; Hans Tanner, *Counterrevolutionary Agent* (London: G. T. Foulis, 1962), 47. For more on Sinesio Walsh, see Dreke, *From the Escambray,* 173; Hart Phillips, *The Cuban Dilemma,* 255.

36. "Muerte de Piti," n.d. [ca. 1962], doc. 452-(4.1), MLCB.

37. Norberto Fuentes, *Cazabandidos* (Montevideo: Libros de la Pupila, 1970), 133.

38. Tanner, *Counterrevolutionary Agent,* 15; Herrera Medina, *Operación Jaula,* 106; Etcheverry Vázquez and Gutiérrez Oceguera, *Bandidismo,* 70, 74–75; Fuentes, *Cazabandidos,* 146.

39. "Operación de Cerco," n.d., 19/3.3/5.6/1-37, Fondo LCB.

40. Armando Torre to Raúl Castro Ruz, 1 Oct 1962, 19/1-2/8-9/1-14, Fondo LCB.

41. Crespo Francisco, *Bandidismo en el Escambray,* 121.

42. Domínguez, *Cuba: Order and Revolution,* 208.

43. Raúl Menéndez Tomassevich, "(Decirlo)," n.d. [ca. 1965], doc. 328-(0), MLCB.

44. "Análisis de algunos aspectos de la actividad bandesca," n.d., doc. 555-(4.1); Comandante Sandino to Osvaldo Ramírez, 8 Nov 1961, doc. 522-(4.1), MLBC.

45. Crespo Francisco, *Bandidismo en el Escambray,* 70–72; David Atlee Phillips, *The Night Watch* (New York: Atheneum, 1977), 123.

46. Etcheverry Vázquez and Gutiérrez Oceguera, *Bandidismo,* 127–28, 138–39.

47. Encinosa, *Cuba: The Unfinished Revolution,* 75; Crespo Francisco, *Bandidismo en el Escambray;* Herrera Medina, *Operación Jaula,* 36, 140.

48. "Minutes, 461st NSC Meet," 26 Sep 1960; "Minutes, 464th NSC Meeting, 20 Sep 1960, Ann Whitman Files, NSC series, box 12, Dwight D. Eisenhower Presidential Library, Abilene, Kansas; [Deleted] to Allen W. Dulles, 12 Sep 1960, Central Intelligence Agency Records Search Tool, National Archives and Records Administration, College Park, MD.

49. Cuban government officials counted thirty-five infiltrations of arms, money, and trained men in the six years of the rebellion. The CIA supposedly provided the mother ship, the freighter *Rex,* and the fast boats used in these operations. An unreported number of these attempts were intercepted by State Security troops. Etcheverry Vázquez and Gutiérrez Oceguera, *Bandidismo,* 336.

50. "Análisis de algunos aspectos de la actividad bandesca," n.d., doc. 555-(4.1), MLBC; Félix I. Rodríguez and John Weisman, *Shadow Warrior* (New York: Simon & Schuster, 1989), 87–88.

51. Jorge I. Domínguez, personal message to author, 9 Sep 2015.

52. Ted Shackley with Richard A. Finney, *Spymaster: My Life in the CIA* (Dulles, VA: Potomac Books, 2005), 65. Another CIA agent, Warren Frank, said, "It wasn't hard to get agents in Cuba, but a lot of them weren't effective. . . . At the time of the [missile] crisis, we had about forty agents reporting from Cuba." Bayard Stockton, *Flawed Patriot: The Rise and Fall of CIA Legend Bill Harvey* (Washington, DC: Potomac Books, 2006), 130.

53. John Meples Spíritto served a term in prison. When released in 1970, he worked for a decade in the Ministry of Construction. Then he departed for the United States. Etcheverry Vázquez and Gutiérrez Oceguera, *Bandidismo,* 97, 221–41; Herrera Medina, *Operación Jaula,* 66–67.

54. "Bandas existentes en fecha junio 3/62," 19/3.3/6:1–4/3-67, Fondo LCB.

55. Ibid.; Roberto Roca, "Relaciones de bandidos capturados," 19/1-3/2-2/1-54, Fondo LCB.

56. Herrera Medina, *Operación Jaula,* 100–101; Etcheverry Vázquez and Gutiérrez Oceguera, *Bandidismo,* 59, 90–91.

57. Dreke, *From the Escambray,* 94–95, 102; Etcheverry Vázquez and Gutiérrez Oceguera, *Bandidismo,* 110–11; Herrera Medina, *Operación Jaula,* 81–82; Crespo Francisco, *Bandidismo en el Escambray,* 54–55; Encinosa, *Escambray,* 68.

58. Tanner, *Counterrevolutionary Agent,* 146.

59. Ibid., 20, 40, 74; Etcheverry Vázquez and Gutiérrez Oceguera, *Bandidismo,* 162.

60. Vázquez and Oceguera, 194–95.

61. "Frente Nacional Democrático, Comandancia General de Operationes Escambray," n.d. [ca. 1962], doc. 348-(4.1), Fondo LCB.

62. Historian Encinosa claims that the revolutionary government's crimes outweighed those of Osvaldo Ramírez. Encinosa, *Escambray,* 50–51.

63. Etcheverry Vázquez and Gutiérrez Oceguera, *Bandidismo,* 203.

64. Ibid., 199, 206–7.

65. Crespo Francisco, *Bandidismo en el Escambray,* 87–89, 149–51.

66. Ibid., 141–43, 146–49.

67. The government deployed two battalions to eliminate the group of Tomás San Gil in March 1963. Luis Báez, *Secretos de generales* (Havana: Editorial Si-Mar, 1996), 199; Encinosa, *Cuba: The Unfinished Revolution,* 85; Encinosa, *Escambray,* 55–56; Crespo Francisco, *Bandidismo en el Escambray,* 149–51. Also see Fuentes, *Cazabandidos,* 30.

68. Báez, *Secretos de generales,* 387, quoting Ernio Hernández Rodríguez.

69. Pedro Etcheverry Vázquez and Santiago Gutiérrez Oceguera, "El bandidismo en Matanzas" (unpublished manuscript, MLCB), 21.

70. Menéndez Tomassevich, "(Decirlo)"; Encinosa, *Cuba: The Unfinished Revolution,* 75.

71. Dreke, *From the Escambray,* 111. Víctor Dreke later served with Che Guevara in the Congo.

72. Crespo Francisco, *Bandidismo en el Escambray,* 162, 176.

73. *Mártires del Minint: Semblanzas biográficas,* 2 vols. (Havana: Editora Política, 1990), 1: 25, 29–30, 61, 172, 235.

74. Ibid., 9–13, 40; Etcheverry Vázquez and Gutiérrez Oceguera, *Bandidismo,* 314–15; Dreke, *From the Escambray,* 114–15.

75. Crespo Francisco, *Bandidismo en el Escambray,* 321. For an outlaw's view of imprisonment, see Lorrin Philipson and Rafael Llerena, *Freedom Flights: Cuban Refugees Talk about Life under Castro and How They Fled His Regime* (New York: Random House, 1980), 6–7, 13–14, 41–43, 61.

76. CIA Intelligence Information Cable, 6 May 1964; Directorate of Intelligence, "Weekly Cuban Summary," 21 Apr 1965, National Security Files, Country File, boxes 22 and 36, Lyndon Baines Johnson Presidential Library, Austin, Texas. In 1966, a Stanford University professor visited one resettlement camp of Escambray peasants in Pinar del Río Province. Fagen, *The Transformation of Political Culture,* 170. Also see Guerra, *Visions of Power,* 181–86.

77. Fagen, *The Transformation of Political Culture,* 170, 173–75. Also see Crespo Francisco, *Bandidismo en el Escambray,* 164, 294.

78. "Fidel Castro Speech on 26 of July Anniversary," Santa Clara, 26 Jul 1965, Castro Speech Database, LANIC, http://www.lanic.utexas.edu/project/castro/db/1965/19650726.html, accessed 28 Jan 2015.

79. Pedro Etcheverry Vázquez and Santiago Gutiérrez Oceguera, "El Bandidismo en La Habana" (unpublished manuscript, MLCB), 15.

80. Etcheverry Vázquez and Gutiérrez Oceguera, *Bandidismo,* 214, 327–28, 330. On the US naval base and the counterrevolution, see Jana K. Lipman, *Guantánamo: A Working Class History between Empire and Revolution* (Berkeley: University of California Press, 2009), 168–69.

81. Domínguez, *Cuba: Order and Revolution,* 345–46; Encinosa, *Cuba: The Unfinished Revolution,* xii; Etcheverry Vázquez and Gutiérrez Oceguera, *Bandidismo,* 336; Guerra, *Visions of Power,* 185–86.

82. Weeka Report, 14 Sep 1960, 737.00(W)/9-1460, Confidential US State Department Central Files, Cuba: Internal Affairs, 1960–1963, microfilm, reel 23.

83. "Bandidos capturados por año," n.d., doc. 334-(4.1), Fondo LCB. President Johnson shut down the CIA's Miami office in 1965. Shackley, *Spymaster,* 62; David Corn, *Blond Ghost* (New York: Simon & Schuster, 1994), 116; Stockton, *Flawed Patriot,* 74–75.

84. "Fidel Castro Speech on 26 of July Anniversary."

6. COMMANDOS OF THE CARIBBEAN

1. Department of Defense, National Military Command Center, cable, 15 Sep 1964, National Security Files (hereafter NSF), Country File (hereafter CF), box 15; Department of State, incoming telegram, 15 Sep 1964, NSF, CF, box 22, both in Lyndon Baines Johnson Presidential Library, Austin, TX.

2. Associated Press release, 15 Sep 1964, NSF, CF, box 22, LBJ Library. Also see Félix I. Rodríguez and John Weisman, *Shadow Warrior* (New York: Simon & Schuster, 1989), 122–23.

3. News release, 16 Sep 1964, NSF, CF, box 22; AmEmbassy Santo Domingo to State, 9 Nov 1964; Department of Defense, National Military Command Center, to White House, 6 Nov 1964, NSF, CF, box 22, LBJ Library. AmEmbassy Santo Domingo to Sec. of State, 9 Nov 1964, NSF, CF, box 20, LBJ Library.

4. "Future of CIA's Cuban Paramilitary Program; Proposed UDT Sabotage Operations," 18 Jan 1965, NSF, CF, box 22, LBJ Library. For President John F. Kennedy's policy directive establishing the covert program, see *Foreign Relations of the United States, 1964–1968,* vol. 32, *Dominican Republic, Cuba, Haiti, Guyana* (Washington, DC: US Government Printing Office, 2005) (hereafter *FRUS 1964–1968,* vol. 32, *Dominican Republic*), 720–21.

5. On the themes of nationalism, exile, and the betrayed revolution, see Rafael Rojas, *Essays in Cuban Intellectual History* (New York: Palgrave Macmillan, 2008), 120.

6. Rafael L. Díaz-Balart to President Eisenhower, 9 Jul 1960, Cuba, Country File (hereafter CF), box 805, Dwight D. Eisenhower Presidential Library, Abilene, KS. The White Rose refers to a poem by José Martí: "I cultivate a white rose / In June

as in January, / for the true friend / who offers me his hand of loyalty." Rafael Díaz-Balart, *Cuba: Intra-history; An Unremitting Struggle* (Mexico: private printing, 2006), 97, 104, http://www.larosablanca.org/LAROSABLANCA/RDB_files/libro%20Cuba%20spread.pdf, accessed 1 Nov 2014.

7. Ann Louise Bardach, *Cuba Confidential: Love and Vengeance in Miami and Havana* (New York: Random House, 2002), 42–50.

8. Don Bohning, *The Castro Obsession: U.S. Covert Operations against Cuba, 1959–1965* (Washington, DC: Potomac Books, 2005), 130.

9. CIA, "Cuban Covert Program Report," 13 Oct 1961, NSF, box 319, John F. Kennedy Presidential Library; Bohning, *The Castro Obsession*, 158.

10. CIA Intelligence Information Cable, 14 Jun 1964, NSF, CF, box 22, LBJ Library; James Blight and Peter Kornbluh, eds., *Bay of Pigs Declassified: The Secret CIA Report on the Invasion of Cuba* (New York: New Press, 1998), 96; *Bohemia* (Havana), 11 May 1974.

11. Ernesto "Che" Guevara, "Address to the General Assembly," 11 Dec 1964, https://www.marxists.org/archive/guevara/1964/12/11.htm, accessed 16 Nov 2016.

12. *Foreign Relations of the United States, 1964–1968,* vol. 31, *South and Central America: Mexico* (Washington, DC: US Government Printing Office, 2004) (hereafter *FRUS, 1964–1968,* vol. 31, *South and Central America*), 11.

13. Gordon Chase to MacGeorge Bundy, 14 May 1964; 16 Jun 1964; Peter Jessup, "Memorandum for the Record," 9 Apr 1964, NSF, CF, box 22, LBJ Library. Also see *Cien horas con Fidel: Conversaciones con Ignacio Ramonet,* 3rd ed. (Havana: Publicaciones del Consejo del Estado, 2006), 284.

14. Bohning, *The Castro Obsession*, 79–80; Lars Schoultz, *That Infernal Little Cuban Republic: The United States and the Cuban Revolution* (Chapel Hill: University of North Carolina Press, 2009), 175–82; Jacinto Valdés-Dapena Vivanco, *Operación Mangosta: Preludio de la invasión directa a Cuba* (Havana: Editorial Capitán San Luis, 2002); Fabián Escalante, *The Cuba Project: CIA Covert Operations, 1959–62,* trans. Maxine Shaw (Melbourne: Ocean Press, 2004).

15. *FRUS, 1964–1968,* vol. 32, *Dominican Republic,* 611.

16. John F. Kennedy, "Remarks of the President to Inter-American Press Association," Miami Beach, FL, 18 Nov 1963, https://www.jfklibrary.org/Asset-Viewer/Archives/JFKPOF-048-014.aspx, accessed 16 Nov 2016.

17. W. W. Rostow, "Handling of the Cuban Revolutionary Council (Frente)," n.d., NSF, box 48, Kennedy Library; Arthur M. Schlesinger Jr. *A Thousand Days: John F. Kennedy in the White House* (Boston: Houghton Mifflin, 1965), 283.

18. CIA, "Current Intelligence Weekly Summary," 19 Apr 1963, Central Intelligence Agency Records Search Tool, National Archives and Records Administration, College Park, MD (hereafter CREST); *Foreign Relations of the United States, 1961–1963,* vol. 10, *Cuba, 1961–1962* (Washington, DC: US Government Printing Office, 1997), 116, 430, 630; *Foreign Relations of the United States,* vol. 11, *Cuban Mis-*

sile Crisis and Aftermath (Washington, DC: US Government Printing Office, 1996), 25, 843 (hereafter *FRUS, 1961–1963,* vol. 11, *Missile Crisis*). Other leaders of the Revolutionary Council distrusted Ray's leftist politics, and, to a certain extent, so did the CIA. One young diplomat in the US embassy in Havana suggested in 1960 that the CIA help Ray escape from the country. "Absolutely not," replied the agent. "Ray is anti-Castro, but he's something of a socialist himself." Wayne S. Smith, *The Closest of Enemies: A Personal and Diplomatic Account of U.S.-Cuban Relations since 1957* (New York: W. W. Norton, 1987), 72. Also see Jesús Arboleya, *The Cuban Counter-Revolution,* trans. Rafael Betancourt (Athens: Ohio University Press, 2000), 73.

19. CIA Information Report, 22 Jan 1964, Country File, NSF, CF, box 22, LBJ Library.

20. The analyst was referring to the death of Martí in 1895 and the battle of Alegría del Pío in December 1956 that nearly wiped out Castro's landing party from the *Granma*. Cuban Coordinator, Miami to Sec. of State, 7 Jun 1963, NSF, box 44, Kennedy Library; Department of State, "JURE Plans to Stimulate Cuban Liberation Efforts," 20 Mar 1964, NSF, CF, box 22, LBJ Library. Philip W. Bonsal, *Cuba, Castro, and the United States* (Pittsburgh: University of Pittsburgh Press, 1971), 68.

21. *CIA Objective: To Destroy the Cuban and Latin American Revolutions* (New Delhi: New Age Printing Press, ca. 1968), 12.

22. CIA Intelligence Information Cable, 20 Mar 1964, NSF, CF, box 22, LBJ Library.

23. Richard Helms to Director, 20 May 1964; CIA Intelligence Information Cables, 27 Mar 1964; 4 Oct 1964, NSF, CF, box 22, LBJ Library.

24. John H. Crimmins, Memorandum of Conversation, 27 May 1964, NSF, CF, box 22, LBJ Library.

25. Tad Szulc, "Exiles Proclaim Anti-Castro War," *New York Times,* 21 May 1964; "Silence Shrouds Anti-Castro War," *New York Times,* 22 May 1964; CIA Intelligence Information Cable, 23 May 1964, NSF, CF, box 22, LBJ Library.

26. CIA Intelligence Information Cable, 26 May 1964, NSF, CF, box 22, LBJ Library.

27. CIA Intelligence Information Cables, 28 May 1964; 1 Jun 1964, NSF, CF, Box 22, LBJ Library.

28. *Bohemia* (Havana), 29 May 1964.

29. Chase to Bundy, 3 Jun 1964, NSF, CF, box 22, LBJ Library. Other collaborators of Ray included Orlando Acosta Suárez, former councilman of Marianao Municipality in Havana, and Carlos Zárraga Martínez, formerly associated with the paramilitary group Cuba Libre. CIA Intelligence Information Cable, 3 Jun 64, NSF, CF, box 22, LBJ Library; *FRUS, 1964–1968,* vol. 32, *Dominican Republic,* 656, 663–64. Also see Richard Eder, "Cuba Uses Humor as Political Tool," *New York Times,* 4 Jun 1964. Ray's passengers included the freelance writer John Thomas Duncan and photographer Andrew St. George of *Life* magazine. St. George had

gained notice in 1958 for having photographed Fidel and his M26 guerrillas in the Sierra Maestra.

30. CIA Intelligence Information Cables, 27 Jun 1964; 2 Jul 1964; 13 Jul 1964, NSF, CF, box 22, LBJ Library. Like many former payees of the CIA in Miami, Manuel Ray denies having been an "ally" of the US government. Ray claims to have helped spring a dozen of Comandante Huber Matos's staff officers from jail and spirited them all into exile, undoubtedly with the assistance of the US embassy and the CIA. Eduardo García, "'No éramos aliados de Estados Unidos': Entrevista a Manuel Ray Rivero," *Temas: Cultura, Ideología, Sociedad,* no. 55 (2008): 54–55.

31. CIA Intelligence Information Cable, 24 Dec 1964, NSF, CF, box 22; Directorate of Intelligence, "Weekly Cuban Summary," 30 Dec 1964, NSF, CF, box 36, LBJ Library.

32. CIA Intelligence Information Cables, 26 Jan 1965; 27 Jan 1965; 16 Feb 1965, NSF, CF, box 22, LBJ Library.

33. *CIA Objective,* 45–47. The testimony of numerous prisoners in Cuba indicates that these ex-commandos were rootless young men motivated more by a monthly salary than by ideological differences with the revolution.

34. Ted Shackley with Richard A. Finney, *Spymaster: My Life in the CIA* (Dulles, VA: Potomac Books, 2005), 70.

35. Enrique G. Encinosa, *Cuba: The Unfinished Revolution* (Austin, TX: Eakin Press, 1988), 195. Despite Menoyo's role in Alpha 66's formation, the collection of this group housed at the Cuban Heritage Center of the University of Miami does not contain any mention whatsoever of his name or his participation in its founding. His associates claim that Menoyo's role in exposing the Trujillo assault against Castro in August 1959 created much opposition to him later in Miami. See Rafael Hernández, "'Siempre me he considerado un socialista': Max Lesnik habla sobre la Revolución cubana," *Temas: Cultura, Ideología, Sociedad,* no. 55 (2008): 38, 41.

36. CIA, "Alpha 66," n.d., NSF, CF, box 48; CIA, "American Support in Collection of Funds for MRP-A," 24 Mar 1963, NSF, box 52, Kennedy Library.

37. Department of State, "Alpha 66 / II Frente del Escambray Press Conference," 19 Mar 1963, NSF, box 48, Kennedy Library. The CIA suspected too that "a number of Soviets were killed." CIA, "Anti-Castro Raid of 17 March in Isabela de Sagua Area," 20 Mar 1963, NSF, box 48, Kennedy Library. The CIA determined that the offshore base was Riding Rocks Cay in the Bahamas. CIA, "Location of SFNE Operations Base," n.d., NSF, box 48, Kennedy Library.

38. Kohler to Sec. of State, 27 Mar 1963; CIA, "Further Information of the L-66 Raid on Caibarien on 27 March," n.d.; CIA, "Attacks of Soviet Freighters L'GOV and BAKU," 8 Apr 1963, NSF, box 48, Kennedy Library.

39. "Anti-Castro Exile Raids: Press Conference," 3 Apr 1963, NSF, box 61, Kennedy Library.

40. *FRUS, 1961–1963,* vol. 11, *Missile Crisis,* 739–42.

41. Richard Helms, "The Effects of the President's Miami Visit on the Cuban Exile Community," 21 Nov 1963, NSF, box 52, Kennedy Library. Also see, Department of State, "For the Press, no. 169," 30 Mar 1963, NSF, box 48, Kennedy Library.

42. *FRUS, 1961–1963,* vol. 11, *Missile Crisis,* 906. Also see Bradley Earl Ayers, *The War That Never Was: An Insider's Account of CIA Covert Operations against Cuba* (Indianapolis, IN: Bobbs Merrill, 1976).

43. "Planned Activation of Plan Omega," 28 Nov 1963, NSF, CF, box 22, LBJ Library. Among his collaborators were Ociel González, former chief of the Havana fire department, and Amaury Fraginals Alonso, ex-leader of the Havana electrical workers. Also see Aran Shetterly, *The Americano: Fighting with Castro for Cuba's Freedom* (Chapel Hill, NC: Algonquin Books, 2007).

44. Department of State Telegram, 17 Dec 1963, NSF, CF, box 22, LBJ Library.

45. Department of State Airgram, 27 Feb 1964, NSF, CF, box 22, LBJ Library.

46. Richard Dudman, "Cuban Exiles Recruiting Drive Is Reported," *St. Louis Post-Dispatch,* n.d., CREST.

47. Department of State Airgram, 20 May 1964, NSF, CF, box 22, LBJ Library.

48. CIA Intelligence Information Cables, 13 May 1964; 15 May 1964; 22 May 1964, NSF, CF, box 22, LBJ Library. Both Eloy and his late older brother Carlos had been born in Spain, where Carlos had fought for the leftists in the Spanish Civil War.

49. CIA Intelligence Information Cable, 19 May 1964, NSF, CF, box 22, LBJ Library.

50. "Report on Capture of 4 Agents in Oriente," Prensa Latina, Havana, 27 Jan 1965, CREST; Directorate of Intelligence, "Weekly Cuban Summary," 19 Jan 1965; 27 Jan 1965, NSF, CF, box 36, CIA Intelligence Information Cable, 20 Jan 1965, NSF, CF, box 22, LBJ Library.

51. "Translation of Havana Prensa Latina Report," 27 Jan 1965, NSF, CF, box 22, LBJ Library. The prisoners were identified as Menoyo, Ramón Quesada Gómez, Domingo Ortega Acosta, and Noel Salas.

52. Navy Department Report, 30 Jan 1965, NSF, CF, box 22, LBJ Library; "Weekly Cuban Summary," 10 Feb 1965, NSF, CF, box 36, LBJ Library.

53. The translated transcript of the televised interview was furnished to the Johnson White House by US security agents. "Gutierrez Menoyo Questioned by State Security," 3 Feb 1965, NSF, CF, box 22, LBJ Library. For Cuban accounts of Menoyo's capture, see *Bohemia* (Havana), 5 Feb 1965; *Verde Olivo* (Havana), 28 Feb 1965. Also see Norberto Fuentes, *Cazabandidos* (Montevideo: Libros de la Pupila, 1970), 57–60.

54. Chase to Bundy, 26 Jan 1965, NSF, CF, box 20, LBJ Library.

55. "Cuba Airs 'Confession' by Menoyo," *Washington Post,* 2 Feb 1965; Directorate of Intelligence, "Weekly Cuban Summary," 3 Feb 1965, NSF, CF, box 36, LBJ Library.

56. CIA, "Weekly Cuban Summary," 7 Apr 1965, NSF, CF, box 36, LBJ Library; *Cien horas con Fidel,* 550. Ransoming counterrevolutionaries was not novel. In December 1962, Cuba received fifty-three million dollars' worth of medicine and baby foods in exchange for the Bay of Pigs prisoners. Haynes Johnson with Manuel Artime et al., *The Bay of Pigs: The Leaders' Story of Brigade 2506* (New York: W. W. Norton, 1964), 329.

57. Directorate of Intelligence, "Weekly Cuban Summary," 10 Feb 1965; CIA, "Weekly Cuban Summary," 24 Feb 1965, NSF, CF, box 36, LBJ Library.

58. Johnson et al., *The Bay of Pigs,* 23–26, 33; Félix I. Rodríguez and John Weisman, *Shadow Warrior* (New York: Simon & Schuster, 1989), 117; Pedro Etcheverry Vázquez and Santiago Gutiérrez Oceguera, *Bandidismo: Derrota de la CIA en Cuba* (Havana: Editorial Capitán San Luis, 2008), 50–52.

59. "Manifesto to the World-Wide Public Opinion," Costa Rica, 8 Jun 1960, Jay Mallin Papers, box 1, Cuban Heritage Collection, University of Miami, Miami, FL.

60. Schlesinger, *A Thousand Days,* 236–37.

61. Johnson et al., *The Bay of Pigs,* 281.

62. "Remarks of the President and Mrs. John F. Kennedy," 29 Dec 1962, NSF, Files of Gordon Chase, box 5, LBJ Library. Jefferson Morley, *Our Man in Mexico: Winston Scott and the Hidden History of the CIA* (Lawrence: University Press of Kansas, 2008), 160–61; Shackley and Finney, *Spymaster,* 50, 54, 56.

63. Bohning, *The Castro Obsession,* 150, 187–88. Ted Shackley is the source of the quote.

64. *Chicago Tribune,* 29 Dec 1962, CREST.

65. *Tampa (FL) Times,* 19 Aug 1963, CREST.

66. CIA, "Cuban Exile Endeavors to Form a New Cuban Exile Unity Group," 1 May 1963, NSF, box 52A, Kennedy Library.

67. CIA, "Activities of Enrique Jose Ruiz-Williams in Regard to Cuban Exile Unity," 18 May 1963, NSF, box 52A, Kennedy Library; Bohning, *The Castro Obsession,* 192–93.

68. CIA, "Report of U.S.-Sponsored Anti-Castro Exile Activities," 11 Jul 1963, NSF, box 48A, Kennedy Library.

69. CIA, "Plans of Former Nicaraguan President Luis Somoza for an Actions Program against Cuba," 7 Aug 1963, NSF, box 53, Kennedy Library.

70. Richard Helms, "Report of Manuel Artime's Visit with President Luis Somoza of Nicaragua," 3 Apr 1963, NSC, CF, box 48, Kennedy Library; Richard Helms, "Information Obtained by Hal Hendrix of the Miami News," 13 Jul 1963, NSF, box 51A, Kennedy Library.

71. CIA Information Reports, 3 Dec 1963; 6 Dec 1963, NSF, CF, box 22, LBJ Library. The MRR maintained a naval refueling station in the Dominican Republic. Rodríguez and Weisman, *Shadow Warrior,* 122; Ayers, *The War That Never Was,* 211.

72. Rodríguez and Weisman, *Shadow Warrior,* 116, 119. The CIA funneled the money through a dummy corporation called Marítima BAM. Also see "As Forces Grow, Cuban Refugees Find New Hope," *National Observer,* 19 Aug 1963.

73. Summer to Sec. of State, 15 Aug 1963, NSF, box 48A, Kennedy Library.

74. Encinosa, *Cuba: The Unfinished Revolution,* 164.

75. AmEmbassy San Jose to State, 27 Dec 1963, NSF, CF, box 16, LBJ Library,

76. CIA Intelligence Information Cable, 19 Mar 1964, NSF, CF, box 22; AmEmbassy San Jose to Sec. of State, 24 Mar 1964, NSF, CF, box 16, LBJ Library; José Gómez Abad, *Cómo el Che burló la CIA* (Sevilla: RD Editores, 2007), 158.

77. AmEmbassy San Jose to Sec. of State, May 22, 1964, NSF, CF, box 16; CIA Intelligence Information Cable, 10 Jul 1964, NSF, CF, box 22, LBJ Library.

78. *FRUS, 1964–1968,* vol. 31, *South and Central America,* 179.

79. CIA Intelligence Information Cable, 15 Apr 1964, NSF, CF, box 22, LBJ Library.

80. CIA Intelligence Information Cable, 16 Apr 1964, NSF, CF, box 22, LBJ Library. In point of fact, two Nicaraguan revolutionary groups aided by the Cubans had challenged his regime, in 1959 and again in 1963. See "Security Threat in Isthmian Area," Panama City, 12 Jul 1965, NSF, CF, box 31, LBJ Library. Also see Matilde Zimmermann, *Sandinista: Carlos Fonseca and the Nicaraguan Revolution* (Durham, NC: Duke University Press, 2000).

81. CIA Intelligence Information Cable, 2 Jul 1964, NSF, CF, box 22, LBJ Library.

82. CIA Intelligence Information Cable, 10 Jul 1964, NSF, CF, box 22, LBJ Library; R. P. Pinsent, "Cuban Subversion," Managua, 13 Jan 1965, Foreign Office: General Correspondence, 1906–1966, Political Correspondence, National Archives, London, 371/179476. Félix I. Rodríguez, who served as communications officer with the MRR in Nicaragua, writes of catching one spy and saboteur in Nicaragua. He claims that the suspect, Gabriel Albuerne, later escaped from Nicaraguan custody during the 1972 Managua earthquake. Rodríguez and Weisman, *Shadow Warrior,* 121.

83. Department of State Airgram, 22 Apr 1964, NSF, CF, box 22, LBJ Library.

84. Ibid.; CIA Intelligence Information Cable, 14 May 1964, NSF, CF, box 22, LBJ Library.

85. Manuel Artime, "First War Communique 15 C," n.d., Jay Mallin Papers, box 1, CHC; "Attack on Sugar Mill at Puerto Pilon," 5 Jun 1964, NSF, CF, box 22, LBJ Library.

86. Dean Rusk to AmEmbassy Rio de Janeiro, 25 May 1964, NSF, CF, box 30; CIA Intelligence Information Cable, 1 Jun 1964, NSF, CF, box 32, LBJ Library. Félix I. Rodríguez supports the MRR claim of extensive damage and quotes Artime as saying, "It is . . . the hardest blow Cuban communism has received since the Bay of Pigs." Rodríguez and Weisman, *Shadow Warrior,* 122–23.

87. Chase to Bundy, 8 Jun 1964; 15 Jun 1964, NSF, CF, box 20, LBJ Library.

88. "Raid," 31 Aug 1964, NSF, CF, box 22, LBJ Library.

89. Robert F. Woodward to W. W. Rostow, 3 Oct 1964, NSF, CF, box 22, LBJ Library.

90. Chase to Bundy, 10 Nov 1964, NSF, CF, box 20, LBJ Library. Secretary of State Dean Rusk told subordinates to make the findings "as indeterminate as is possible." *FRUS, 1964–1968,* vol. 32, *Dominican Republic,* 688.

91. "For the Noon Briefing," 18 Jan 1965, NSF, CF, box 30, LBJ Library. The CIA did fund Artime and Manolo Ray but not Menoyo. Mac Bundy noted that "we cannot expect too much effect from their raids." *FRUS, 1961–1963,* vol. 11, *Missile Crisis,* 907.

92. J. C. King, "Meeting with General Anastasio Somoza," 17 Sep 1964, NSF, CF, box 22, LBJ Library.

93. "Future of the Autonomous Group Headed by Manuel Artime," 6 Nov 1964, Country File, NSF, CF, box 22, LBJ Library.

94. Chase to Bundy, 5 Jan 1965; "Activities of Manuel Artime Buesa during December and Early January," 6 Jan 1965, NSF, CF, box 22, LBJ Library. Don Bohning suggests the CIA may not have delivered the weapon to Cubela. Bohning, *The Castro Obsession,* 225.

95. At the subsequent trial, Cubela confessed his personal failings due to "a disorderly life of parties, cabarets, vices, and all the things involved, including drugs." Because of Cubela's past contributions to the revolution, Fidel commuted his death sentence to twenty-five years in prison. Four accomplices were convicted as well. CIA, "Bi-weekly Propaganda Guidance," 28 Mar 1966, CREST.

96. Directorate of Intelligence, "Weekly Cuban Summary," 10 Feb 1965; CIA, "Weekly Cuban Summary," 10 Feb 1965, NSF, CF, box 36, LBJ Library; *Bohemia* (Havana), 12 Feb 1965. Ameijeiras was demoted and censored for corruption, although it is unclear if the censure had anything to do with the above conspiracy. Almeida continued to serve in his army position. Jorge I. Domínguez, *Cuba: Order and Revolution* (Cambridge, MA: Belknap Press of Harvard University Press, 1978), 231. On the new CIA strategy, see *FRUS, 1964–1968,* vol. 32, *Dominican Republic,* 747. The CIA's connection to Artime began in 1961, and Cuban intelligence subsequently learned nearly all the details. See *FRUS, 1964–1968,* vol. 32, *Dominican Republic,* 742–43; Jacinto Valdés-Dapena Vivanco, *La CIA contra Cuba: La actividad de la CIA y la contrarrevolución (1961–1968)* (Havana: Editorial Capitán San Luis, 2002), 226–37.

97. Chase to Bundy, 9 Feb 1965, NSF, CF, box 22, LBJ Library.

98. "Withdrawal of Support from Artime Group," 23 Feb 1965, NSF, CF, box 22, LBJ Library. The White House urged all US officials to treat the severing of ties with Artime with the greatest delicacy. "We do not want to precipitate any messy situ-

ation with him in the next few weeks." See "Proposed Script for Conversation with Somoza on Artime," n.d., NSF, CF, box 22, LBJ Library. Author and former CIA employee Brian Latell believes that Cubela was a double agent working for the General Directorate of Intelligence (DGI) and that Castro personally directed Cubela's activities. Brian Latell, *Castro's Secrets: The CIA and Cuba's Intelligence Machine* (New York: Palgrave Macmillan, 2015), 150–51, 173, 189.

99. Schoultz, *That Infernal Little Cuban Republic,* 216.

100. *FRUS, 1964–1968,* vol. 32, *Dominican Republic,* 555.

101. Some analysts hoped that disgruntled officers in the Cuban revolutionary armed forces, stimulated by offshore raids, would stage a coup d'état. *FRUS, 1964–1968,* vol. 32, *Dominican Republic,* 550, 554.

102. CIA, "Weekly Cuban Summary," 17 Mar 1965, NSF, CF, box 36, LBJ Library. As Jorge I. Domínguez writes, "All Cuban mass organizations were founded at times when the revolutionary government was threatened." Domínguez, *Cuba: Order and Revolution,* 445.

103. Richard Helms, "Analysis of the Reaction of the Cuban Government and Cuban Exiles to Recent Anti-Castro Activity," 21 May 1964, NSF, CF, box 22, LBJ Library.

104. *FRUS, 1964–1968,* vol. 32, *Dominican Republic,* 659–60.

7. THE EXPORT OF REVOLUTION

1. CIA, "The Training of Latin Americans in Cuba," Jan 1963, National Security Files (hereafter NSF), box 51, John F. Kennedy Presidential Library, Boston. The document does not name the student. Therefore, the author has given him the fictitious name of Julio García.

2. "26 July Ceremonies," 26 Jul 1962, Castro Speech Database, LANIC, http://lanic.utexas.edu/project/castro/db/1962/19620726.html, accessed 24 Nov 2014.

3. Sergio M. Nicanoff and Axel Castellano, *Las primeras experiencias guerrilleras en la Argentina: La historia del "Vasco" Bengochea y las Fuerzas Armadas de la Revolución Nacional* (Buenos Aires: Ediciones del Centro Cultural Floreal Gorini, 2006), 73.

4. Historian Piero Gleijeses has had access to state security documents for Cuba's African policies. See his two books, *Conflicting Missions: Havana, Washington, and Africa, 1959–1976* (Chapel Hill: University of North Carolina Press, 2002) and *Visions of Freedom: Havana, Washington, Pretoria, and the Struggle for Southern Africa, 1976–1991* (Chapel Hill: University of North Carolina Press, 2013).

5. See Andrés Suárez, "Leadership, Ideology, and Political Party," in *Revolutionary Change in Cuba,* ed. Carmelo Mesa-Lago (Pittsburgh: University of Pittsburgh Press, 1971), 4.

6. CIA Intelligence Information Cable, 10 Jul 1964, NSF, Country Files (hereafter CF), box 22, Lyndon Baines Johnson Presidential Library, Austin, TX. The DGI was known as the Department of State Security (DSE) until 1962.

7. Christopher Andrew and Vasili Mitrokhin, *The World Was Going Our Way: The KGB and the Battle for the Third World* (New York: Basic Books, 2005), 46–47.

8. CIA, "Cuban Subversion in Latin America since June 1964," 15 Nov 1965, NSF, CF, box 31, LBJ Library.

9. [Mexican Intelligence], "Dirección General de Inteligencia, el servicio exterior de inteligencia cubano," 10 Sep 1968, iv, 5–6, Fondo Dirección General de Inteligencia Políticas y Sociales, Archivo General de la Nación, Mexico City. The author thanks Renata Keller for sharing a copy of this report.

10. "Havana, Notes on the Content of Cuban Press," 4 Sep 1963, Ministerium für Auswärtige Angelegenheiten, Politisches Archiv des Auswärtiges Amt, Berlin, Germany (hereafter MfAA, Politisches Archiv).

11. Under the orders of the Auténtico leader, Dr. Manuel Antonio de Varona, members of one of Miami's anti-Castro groups committed this caper. Jules Dubois, *Operation America: The Communist Conspiracy in Latin America* (New York: Walker, 1963), 58; Philip Agee, *Inside the Company: CIA Diary* (London: Allen Lane, 1975), 146.

12. Orlando Castro Hidalgo, *Spy for Fidel* (Miami: E. A. Seemann, 1971), 35. Also see CIA, "Decision of Raul Roa Garcia to Abolish Assignment of Intelligence Personnel within the Foreign Ministry," 1 Jun 1963, NSF, box 53, Kennedy Library.

13. [Mexican Intelligence], "Dirección General de Inteligencia, el servicio exterior de inteligencia cubano," 10 Sep 1968, iv, 18–19, 22, Fondo Dirección General de Inteligencia Políticas y Sociales, Archivo General de la Nación, Mexico City. My thanks to Renata Keller for sending me a copy of this valuable report.

14. Castro Hidalgo, *Spy for Fidel,* 20.

15. Stéphane Lefebvre, "Cuban Intelligence Activities Directed at the United States, 1959–2007," *International Journal of Intelligence and CounterIntelligence* 22, no. 3 (Jun 2009): 453–54.

16. Rafael Hernández, "'Siempre me he considerado un socialista': Max Lesnik habla sobre la Revolución cubana," *Temas: Cultura, Ideología, Sociedad,* no. 55 (2008): 43; Francisco Wong-Diaz, *Castro's Cuba: Quo Vadis?* (Carlisle, PA: US Army War College, 2006), 4; Castro Hidalgo, *Spy for Fidel,* 107. One such double agent was Manuel Hevia, recruited by the CIA in 1963 and assigned as a translator in the CIA station in Montevideo. See Manuel Hevia Cosculluela, *Pasaporte 11333: Ocho años con la CIA* (Havana: Editorial de Ciencias Sociales, 1978).

17. Brian Latell, *Castro's Secrets: The CIA and Cuba's Intelligence Machine* (New York: Palgrave Macmillan, 2012), 98, 113.

18. CIA, "Decision of Raul Roa Garcia," 1 Jun 1963.

19. CIA, "Training in Cuba for Subversion in Latin America," 19 Jul 1963, NSF, box 53, Kennedy Library.

20. David Atlee Phillips, *The Night Watch* (New York: Atheneum, 1977), 95–96.

21. Agee, *Inside the Company*, 498; Thomas C. Field Jr., *From Development to Dictatorship: Bolivia and the Alliance for Progress in the Kennedy Era* (Ithaca, NY: Cornell University Press, 2014), 67.

22. CIA, "Cuban Contact with Latin America for Purpose of Subversion," 15 Mar 1963, NSF, box 52A, Kennedy Library; CIA, "Expected Activities of Latin Americans Trained in Guerrilla Warfare in Cuba," 2 Oct 1963, NSF, box 53, Kennedy Library; Agee, *Inside the Company*, 263.

23. CIA, "Briefing Notes: Conclusion," 18 Feb 1963, NSF, box 53, Kennedy Library. On US efforts to curtail air and sea travel to Cuba, see Edwin McCammon Martin, *Kennedy and Latin America* (Lanham, MD: University Press of America, 1994), 205–7.

24. Martin, *Kennedy and Latin America*, 208.

25. Agee, *Inside the Company*, 198.

26. Che Guevara, *Guerrilla Warfare* (Lincoln: University of Nebraska Press, 1998), 7.

27. Ibid., 8.

28. "10 Anniversary of the 26th of July," 26 Jul 1963, Castro Speech Database, LANIC, http://lanic.utexas.edu/project/castro/db/1963/19630726.html, accessed 1 Dec 2014.

29. CIA, "Cuban Subversion in Latin America," 9 Aug 1963, Central Intelligence Agency Records Search Tool, National Archives and Records Administration, College Park, MD.

30. For a complete analysis of the *foco* theory, see Matt D. Childs, "An Historical Critique of the Emergence and Evolution of Ernesto Che Guevara's *Foco* Theory," *Journal of Latin American Studies*, 27, no. 3 (Oct 1995): 593–624.

31. Ernesto Che Guevara, "Guerra de guerrilla: Un método," *Cuba Socialista* 3, no. 25 (September 1963), 6, 9. Also see CIA, "Castro's Plans for Subversion in Latin America," 15 Oct 1963, NSF, box 52, Kennedy Library. Writes Wickham-Crowley about Che's abandonment of his dictum on the inadvisability of rising up against a democratic regime, "The desire for active 'praxis' apparently overcame the desire for accurate theory." Timothy P. Wickham-Crowley, *Guerrillas and Revolution in Latin America: A Comparative Study of Insurgents and Regimes since 1956* (Princeton, NJ: Princeton University Press, 1992), 170.

32. "This Information Was Received from the Canadian JIC Representative in Washington," 13 Sep 1963, NSF, box 39, Kennedy Library.

33. These articles today form the basis for Che's *Reminiscences of the Cuban Revolutionary War* (Melbourne: Ocean Press, 2008). Also see Paul J. Dosal, *Comandante Che: Guerrilla Soldier, Commander, and Strategist, 1956–1967* (University Park: Penn

State University Press, 2003), 189–90. Dosal says that Guevara was a strategist, not a theorist.

34. Guevara, "Guerra de guerrilla: Un método," 13.

35. Régis Debray, *Revolution in the Revolution? Armed Struggle and Political Struggle in Latin America,* trans. Bobbye Ortiz (New York: MR Press, 1967), 22, 63. Batista's most capable battle commander, Colonel Sánchez Mosquera, commanded the assault on Hombrito.

36. Ibid., 69, 75, 77, 80. Commenting on the Cuban combatants fighting in the cities against the Batista regime, Fidel said that "many more people died in the [urban] underground that in the guerrilla struggle." Fidel Castro, *Fidel and Religion: Talks with Frei Betto* (Havana: Publications Office of the Council of State, 1988), 220.

37. General Robert W. Porter, "Look South to Latin America," *Military Review* 48 (Jun 1968): 86–87.

38. CIA, "Castro's Plans for Subversion in Latin America," 15 Oct 1963.

39. Andrew and Mitrokhin, *The World Was Going Our Way,* 47–51.

40. Cecil Johnson, *Communist China & Latin America, 1959–1967* (New York: Columbia University Press, 1979), 160–62.

41. "Record of Conversation between Mikoyan and Ernesto 'Che' Guevara," Havana, 16 Nov 1962, from the personal papers of Dr. Sergo A. Mikoyan, donated to the National Security Archive, Cold War International History Project, http://digitalarchive .wilsoncenter.org/document/115100, accessed 20 Apr 2015. Also see Sergo Mikoyan, *The Soviet Cuban Missile Crisis: Castro, Mikoyan, Kennedy, Khrushchev, and the Missiles of November,* ed. Svetlana Savranskaya (Washington, DC: Woodrow Wilson Center Press; Stanford, CA: Stanford University Press, 2012), 85.

42. W. W. Rostow, *The Diffusion of Power: An Essay in Recent History* (New York: Macmillan, 1972), 265.

43. See Guevara, "Guerra de guerrilla: Un método"; Anon., "Cuban Relations with Latin America," n.d. [ca. Mar 1964], NSF, CF, box 33, LBJ Library.

44. See Bureau of Intelligence and Research, "The 26th of July Movement since the Abortive General Strike of April 9, 1958," 15 Aug 1958, in *O.S.S./State Department Intelligence and Research Reports,* vol. 14, *Latin America: 1941–1961,* ed. Paul Kesaris (Washington, DC: University Publications of America, 2001), microfilm. Most historians do not believe that Fidel Castro professed communist ideals, either secretly or openly, as a guerrilla leader. See C. Fred Judson, *Cuba and the Revolutionary Myth: The Political Education of the Cuban Rebel Army, 1953–1963* (Boulder, CO: Westview Press, 1984), 37; Luiz Alberto Moniz Bandeira, *De Martí a Fidel: A Revolução Cubano e a América Latina* (Rio de Janeiro: Civilização Brasileira), 172–78.

45. Jorge Ricardo Masetti, *Los que luchan y los que lloran: El Fidel Castro que yo vi* (Buenos Aires: Freeland, 1958), 48.

46. Castro's quip about "hiding under the bed" was widely quoted, even by the CIA. See National Intelligence Estimate (NIE), "Potential for Revolution in

Latin America," 28 Mar 1968, NSF, NIE, box 8, LBJ Library. For reasons of state, Castro later promoted the idea that the communists contributed to the fight against Batista. It is an idea prominently displayed today in the revolutionary museums throughout the country, all of which are operated by the Cuban communist party. The ideology of the Second Front and the Directorio Revolucionario also had few Marxist elements. See Hernández, "'Siempre me he considerado un socialista,'" 37.

47. *Fidel en la memoria del jovén que es* (Melbourne: Ocean Press, 2002), 106, 120; Castro, *Fidel and Religion.*

48. José Gómez Abad, *Cómo el Che burló la CIA* (Sevilla: RD Editores, 2007), 287–89.

49. Navy Department, "Travel of Salvadorans from Cuba to Costa Rica via Grand Cayman," 2 Jun 1963; Clinton E. Smith, "Memorandum to Sub-committee on Cuban Subversion," 10 Sep 1963, NSF, box 60, Kennedy Library.

50. Gómez Abad, *Cómo el Che burló la CIA,* 342, 348. On the 1960s guerrilla uprising in Guatemala, see Virginia Garrard-Burnett, *Terror in the Land of the Holy Spirit: Guatemala under General Efraín Río Montt, 1982–1983* (New York: Oxford University Press, 2013), 26–31; Giovanni Batz, "Military Factionalism and the Consolidation of Power in 1960s Guatemala," in *Beyond the Eagle's Shadow: New Histories of Latin America's Cold War,* ed. Virginia Garrard-Burnett, Mark Atwood Lawrence, and Julio E. Moreno (Albuquerque: University of New Mexico Press, 2013), 51–75.

51. On Mexico's assistance identifying travelers coming to and from Cuba, see Agee, *Inside the Company,* 266; Renata Keller, *Mexico's Cold War: Cuba, the United States, and the Legacy of the Mexican Revolution* (New York: Cambridge University Press, 2015), 6, 165.

52. CIA, "Travel of Latin American Students to Cuba for Subversive Training," n.d. [ca. 1963], NSF, box B39, Kennedy Library.

53. CIA, "Communist Plans for Central America in the Event of an Invasion of Cuba," 26 Sep 1962, NSF, box 52, Kennedy Library. The Honduran rebel was identified as Lorenzo Zelaya Romero.

54. CIA, "Cuba: The Movement of Subversives and Subversive Trainees," n.d. [ca. March 1963], NSF, box 59, Kennedy Library. To continue surveillance on the Mexico City–Havana flights explains why Secretary of State Dean Rusk thought it advantageous that Mexico maintain diplomatic relations with Cuba.

55. CIA, "Security Conditions in Mexico," 7 Apr 1966, in *C.I.A. Research Reports: Latin America, 1946–1976* (Frederick, MD: University Publications of America, 1982), microfilm. See Keller, *Mexico's Cold War,* 42–48; Cindy Forster, "Not in All of America Can There Be Found a Country as Democratic as This One: Che and Revolution in Guatemala," in *Che's Travels: The Making of a Revolutionary in 1950s Latin America,* ed. Paulo Drinot (Durham, NC: Duke University Press, 2010), 213;

Eric Zolov, "Between Bohemianism and a Revolutionary Rebirth: Che Guevara in Mexico," in *Che's Travels,* 267–68, 270.

56. CIA, "Briefing Notes: The Communist Threat in Latin America," 16 Feb 1963, NSF, box 53, Kennedy Library.

57. CIA, "Briefing Notes: Conclusion," 18 Feb 1963, NSF, box 53, Kennedy Library; Benigno [Dariel Alarcón Ramírez], *Memorias de un soldado cubano: Vida y muerte de la Revolución* (Barcelona: Tusquets Editores, 1997), 97–98.

58. Office of Special Investigations, US Air Force, "Panama: An Analysis of Castro/Communist Subversive Activity," Feb 1964, NSF, box 65, LBJ Library.

59. Ibid.

60. CIA, "Draft Briefing Notes: The Plan," 18 Feb 1963, NSF, box 53, Kennedy Library. Also see R. Hart Phillips, *The Cuban Dilemma* (New York: Ivan Obolensky, 1963), 56; Judson, *Cuba and the Revolutionary Myth,* 237.

61. "Che is the best fighter I know," Alberto Bayo told a French reporter. Victor Franco, *The Morning After,* trans. Ivan Kats and Philip Pendered (New York: Frederick A. Praeger, 1963), 99–101; "Communist Threat to the United States through the Caribbean," *Hearings before the Subcommittee to Investigate the Administration of the Internal Security Act of the Committee on the Judiciary, United States Senate,* pt. 8 (Washington, DC: US Government Printing Office, 1960), 499.

62. CIA, "Castro's Plans for Subversion in Latin America," 15 Oct 1963.

63. Miguel Aguirre Bayley, *Che: Ernesto Guevara en Uruguay* (Montevideo: Cauce Editorial, 2002), 75.

64. CIA, "Briefing Notes: The Communist Threat in Latin America," 16 Feb 1963, NSF, box 53, Kennedy Library.

65. CIA, "Draft Briefing Notes: Weapons," 18 Feb 1963, NSF, box 53, Kennedy Library.

66. Ciro Bustos, *El Che quiere verte: La historia jamás contada del Che en Bolivia* (Buenos Aires: Javier Vergara Editores), 143, 237.

67. Department of State, "Possible Clandestine Arms Shipments in Latin America," 20 Mar 1963, NSF, box 44, Kennedy Library; CIA, "Castro's Subversive Capabilities in Latin America," 9 Nov 1963, NSF, box 37, LBJ Library.

68. Fifth Meeting of Ministers of Central America, "Arms Control in the United States," 12–15 Jul 1965, NSC, box 51, LBJ Library.

69. Héctor Béjar, former leader of Peru's ELN, as quoted in Michael F. Brown and Eduardo Fernández, *War of Shadows: The Struggle for Utopia in the Peruvian Amazon* (Berkeley: University of California Press, 1991), 85, from Héctor Béjar, "Aquellos años sesenta," *30 Días* 1, no. 8 (Jul 1984): 10. Also see Ernesto F. Betancourt, "Exporting the Revolution to Latin America," in *Revolutionary Change in Cuba,* Carmelo Mesa-Lago, ed. (Pittsburgh: University of Pittsburgh Press, 1971): 105–26.

70. Anon., "Havana's International Broadcasting," 31 Jan 1963, NSF Cuba, box 59, Kennedy Library.

71. Ernesto Che Guevara, *Otra vez: El diario inédito del segundo viaje por América Latina (1953–1956)* (Buenos Aires: Editorial Sudamericana, 2000), 68, 162.

72. Gabriel Rot, *Los orígenes perdidos de la guerrilla en la Argentina* (Buenos Aires: Waldhuter, 2010), 74.

73. Ibid., 93, 106.

74. "Reporte sumario sobre Prensa Latina," 25 Nov 1968, Expediente 65–92–68, Fondo Dirección Federal de Seguridad, Archivo General de la Nación, Mexico City. The author thanks Renata Keller for forwarding a copy of this report. As Gabriel Rot writes, "La lucha por la hegemonía política en Prensa Latina se convertirá en el primer gran campo de batalla entre los antiguos comunistas y los *guevaristas*." Rot, *Los orígenes perdidos,* 119. Also see Keller, *Mexico's Cold War,* 79–85.

75. Department of State, "Havana Meeting of Latin American Communist Parties," 4 Mar 1965; CIA, "Cuban Subversion in Latin America," 23 Apr 1965, NSF, CF, box 31, LBJ Library.

76. CIA, "Cuban Subversion in Latin America," 23 Apr 1965. The Cubans overestimated the Guatemalan movement. The guerrilla fighters led by Yon Sosa, reported the British embassy there, "have so far confined their activities to attacks against individuals, mainly military [and] ex-military . . . and their openly announced intention is the eventual overthrow of the Government." See Léon Mayrand, "A Cuban View on the Guerrilla Movement in Latin America," 1 Jun 1965; J. D. Atkinson to G. E. Hall, 2 Jan 1966, Foreign Office: General Correspondence, 1906–1966, Political Correspondence, National Archives, London, 371/179478, 371/179476.

77. McCarthy and Che met on December 16, 1964, in the apartment of Lisa Howard of NBC News who earlier had had a ten-hour interview with Fidel. Che was in New York to address a meeting of the United Nations. *Foreign Relations of the United States, 1964–1968,* vol. 32, *Dominican Republic, Cuba, Haiti, Guyana* (Washington, DC: US Government Printing Office, 2005), 699.

78. NIE, "Potential for Revolution in Latin America," 28 Mar 1968. Also see Piero Gleijeses, *The Dominican Crisis: The 1965 Constitutionalist Revolt and American Intervention,* trans. Lawrence Lipson (Baltimore: Johns Hopkins University Press, 1978); Tad Szulc, *Dominican Diary* (New York: Delacorte Press, 1965).

79. Moniz Bandeira, *De Martí a Fidel,* 562–63. On the Tricontinental, see Keller, *Mexico's Cold War,* 235–44; Enrique Ros, *Castro y las guerrillas en Latinoamérica* (Miami: Ediciones Universal, 2001), 188–89.

80. Carlos Moore, *Castro, the Blacks, and Africa* (Los Angeles: Center for African-American Studies, 1988), 256–57. Also see Peniel E. Joseph, *Stokely: A Life* (New York: Basic Civitas, 2014).

81. Castro Hidalgo, *Spy for Castro,* 97.

82. Robert Moss, *Urban Guerrillas: The New Face of Political Violence* (London: Temple Smith, 1972), 236.

83. Gabriela Saidon, *La Montonera: Biografía de Norma Arrostito* (Buenos Aires: Editorial Sudamérica, 2005), 44–45.

84. "Report Based on Information Coming Out of the Havana Embassy related to OLAS and Tricontinental," Oct 1966; "On OLAS and Speeches of Castro," 10 Aug 1967, MfAA, Politisches Archiv. Translations by David Brown. Also see Moore, *Castro, the Blacks, and Africa,* 266–67.

85. CIA, "Propaganda Report," 18 Jan 1963, NSF, box 59, Kennedy Library.

86. Ibid.; CIA, "Ernesto Guevara's Talk on Fomenting Revolution in Latin America," 25 Jan 1963, NSF, box 52, Kennedy Library.

87. NIE, "Potential for Revolution in Latin America," 28 Mar 1968.

88. Martin C. Needler, *Anatomy of a Coup d'État: Ecuador, 1963* (Washington, DC: Institute for the Comparative Study of Political Systems, 1963), 41.

8. REVOLUTIONARY DIPLOMACY AND DEMOCRACY

1. Manuel Urrutia Lleó, *Fidel Castro & Company, Inc.: Communist Tyranny in Cuba* (New York: Frederick A. Praeger, 1964), 25.

2. *New York Times,* 24 Jan 1959; 25 Jan 1959.

3. Francisco Pividal to Carlos Olivares, 6 Apr 1961, Fondo Venezuela, Archivo del Ministerio de Relaciones Exteriores, Havana, Cuba (hereafter MINREX); Robert J. Alexander, *Rómulo Betancourt and the Transformation of Venezuela* (New Brunswick, NJ: Transaction Books, 1982), 542. For other versions, see Tad Szulc, "Exporting the Cuban Revolution," in *Cuba and the United States: Long-Range Perspectives,* ed. John Plank (Washington, DC: Brookings Institution Press, 1967), 78; Hugh Thomas, *Cuba, or the Pursuit of Freedom,* rev. ed. (New York: Da Capo Press, 1998), 1090. William John Green, "Revolution for Export? Cuba and the Insurgent Left of Venezuela" (MA thesis, University of Texas at Austin, 1989), 34.

4. *New York Times,* 28 Jan 1959.

5. John William Cooke, *Obras completas,* ed. Eduardo L. Duhalde, vol. 2, *Correspondencia Perón-Cooke* (Buenos Aires: Colihue, 2007), 470; Pablo Bavini, "Cuba en la caída de Frondizi," *Todo Es Historia,* 25, no. 297 (Mar 1992): 31.

6. Manuel Mora y Araujo, "Fidel Castro y la Argentina de Frondizi," *Todo Es Historia,* 25, no. 297 (Mar 1992): 11.

7. *The Review of the River Plate* (Buenos Aires), 9 May 1959.

8. Leycester Coltman, *The Real Fidel Castro* (New Haven, CT: Yale University Press, 2003), 156–57.

9. *The Review of the River Plate* (Buenos Aires), 9 May 1959. Also see Daniel F. Solomon, *Breaking Up with Cuba: The Dissolution of Friendly Relations between Washington and Havana, 1956–1961* (Jefferson, NC: McFarland, 2011), 119–20.

10. Walter LaFeber, "Thomas C. Mann and the Devolution of Latin American Policy: From the Good Neighbor to Military Intervention," in *Behind the Throne: Ser-*

vants of Power to Imperial Presidents, 1898–1968, ed. Thomas J. McCormick and Walter LaFeber (Madison: University of Wisconsin Press, 1993), 181.

11. Luiz Alberto Moniz Bandeira, *De Martí a Fidel: A Revolução Cubano e a América Latina* (Rio de Janeiro: Civilização Brasileira), 316.

12. "Relación de personas y organizaciones a favor y en contra de la Revolución Cubana en Uruguay," n.d.; Mario García Incáustegui to Ramón Aja Castro, 23 Feb 1961, Fondo Uruguay, MINREX.

13. Embassy Montevideo to Raúl Roa, 15 Jun 1961; "Informe sobre las actividades del clero en Uruguay contra Cuba," 17 Jul 1961; "Informe sobre posible golpe militar en Uruguay," 24 Jun 1964, Fondo Uruguay, MINREX.

14. Asdrúbal Pereira Cabrera, ed., *1961 / Ernesto Che Guevara en Uruguay* (Montevideo: Rumbo Editorial, 2011), 153.

15. Ibid., 313.

16. Ibid., 399.

17. Haedo was a conservative politician not well disposed to the Cuban Revolution, but he and other critics of Fidel Castro made few public announcements of these views because of the overwhelming public opinion favoring Castro. Haedo and others did not criticize the United States for the Bay of Pigs invasion for the same reason. "Posiciones negativas ante la agresión a Cuba," 24 Apr 1961, Fondo Uruguay, MINREX.

18. Miguel Aguirre Bayley, *Che: Ernesto Guevara en Uruguay* (Montevideo: Cauce Editorial, 2002), 34.

19. Ibid., 54.

20. In 1962, Che had denigrated the contribution of Pazos to the revolution against Batista. He dismissed Pazos and others who spent time in Miami during Batista's dictatorship as men of "stone age minds immune to the call of the people's struggle." Ernesto Che Guevara, *Reminiscences of the Cuban Revolutionary War* (Melbourne: Ocean Press, 2006), 120.

21. Pereira Cabrera, *1961 / Ernesto Che Guevara en Uruguay,* 747.

22. Aguirre Bayley, *Che: Ernesto Guevara en Uruguay,* 51, 58, 64.

23. Pereira Cabrera, *1961 / Ernesto Che Guevara en Uruguay,* 308.

24. Aguirre Bayley, *Che: Ernesto Guevara en Uruguay,* 53.

25. Ibid., 77; Pereira Cabrera, *1961 / Ernesto Che Guevara en Uruguay,* 112, 327–29, 463; Aguirre Bayley, *Che: Ernesto Guevara en Uruguay,* 77; Jon Lee Anderson, *Che Guevara: A Revolutionary Life* (New York: Grove Press, 1997), 511–18. The other anticommunist Cubans were José Ignacio Rasco, Manuel Antonio (Tony) Varona, and Luis Conte Agüero.

26. Aguirre Bayley, *Che: Ernesto Guevara en Uruguay,* 133. Some American officials did not agree with Che's prediction. Years later, at a time when military governments were on the rise in Latin America, the consummate modernization economist Walt Rostow wrote that he believed that the Alliance for Progress had "dimmed

longer-run prospects for communist expansion in Latin America." W. W. Rostow, *The Diffusion of Power: An Essay in Recent History* (New York: Macmillan, 1972), 252.

27. "Relación de personas y organizaciones a favor y en contra de la Revolución Cubana en Uruguay," n.d.

28. Pereira Cabrera, *1961 / Ernesto Che Guevara en Uruguay,* 604.

29. Aguirre Bayley, *Che: Ernesto Guevara en Uruguay,* 165–74; José Carrillo to Carlos Olivares, 6 Sep 1961, Fondo Uruguay, MINREX.

30. Richard N. Goodwin, *Remembering America: A Voice from the Sixties* (Boston: Little, Brown, 1988), 199–203; Pereira Cabrera, *1961 / Ernesto Che Guevara en Uruguay,* 675–81. Apparently, Fidel Castro only learned after the fact that Che Guevara was meeting with the White House aide Richard Goodwin. See Don Bohning, *The Castro Obsession: U.S. Covert Operations against Cuba, 1959–1965* (Washington, DC: Potomac Books, 2002), 167; James G. Hershberg, "The United States, Brazil, and the Cuban Missile Crisis, 1962," pt. 1, *Journal of Cold War Studies* 6, no. 2 (Spring 2004): 7–8.

31. Pereira Cabrera, *1961 / Ernesto Che Guevara en Uruguay,* 743, 761.

32. As quoted in Bavini, "Cuba en la caída de Frondizi," 26. Also see Ricardo Rojo, *Mi amigo, el Che* (Buenos Aires: Merayo Editor, 1974), 151–54.

33. McKintock to Sec. of State, 14 Apr 1962, National Security Files (hereafter NSF), box 6, John F. Kennedy Presidential Library, Boston.

34. Arturo Frondizi, *La política exterior argentina* (Buenos Aires: Transición, 1962), 164; Félix Luna, *Diálogos con Frondizi* (Buenos Aires: Editorial Desarrollo, 1963), 89–90.

35. *Washington Daily News,* 25 Sep 1961, Jay Mallin Papers, box 2, Cuban Heritage Collection, University of Miami.

36. Memorandum of Conversation, "Alliance for Progress; Argentine Economic Problems," 26 Dec 1961; Dean Rusk, "Argentine Aid Request," n.d., NSF, box 6, Kennedy Library; Luna, *Diálogos con Frondizi,* 90. Also see David M. K. Sheinin, *Argentina and the United States: An Alliance Contained* (Athens: University of Georgia Press, 2006).

37. Kennedy could be just as blunt to other heads of state when discussing communism. On a visit to Mexico City, he asked his host, President Adolfo López Mateos, what Mexico had done to fight communism. See Renata Keller, *Mexico's Cold War: Cuba, the United States, and the Legacy of the Mexican Revolution* (New York: Cambridge University Press, 2015), 136.

38. "Summary of Conversation between President Kennedy and President Frondizi," 24 Dec 1961; R. F. Woodward to AmEmbassy Buenos Aires, 26 Dec 1961, NSF, box 6, Kennedy Library. Edwin McCammon Martin, *Kennedy and Latin America* (Lanham, MD: University Press of America, 1997), 270–72.

39. *Foreign Relations of the United States, 1961–1963,* vol. 12, *American Republics* (Washington, DC: US Government Printing Office, 1996) (hereafter *FRUS 1961–*

1963, vol. 12, *American Republics)*, 295–96; Stephen G. Rabe, *The Most Dangerous Area in the World: John F. Kennedy Confronts Communist Revolution in Latin America* (Chapel Hill: University of North Carolina Press, 2002), 60; Martin, *Kennedy and Latin America*, 245; Hershberg, "The United States, Brazil," pt. 1, 10; Alex von Tunzelmann, *Red Heat: Conspiracy, Murder, and the Cold War in the Caribbean* (New York: Henry Holt, 2011), 262.

40. Robert F. Kennedy, *Thirteen Days: A Memoir of the Cuban Missile Crisis* (New York: W. W. Norton, 1969), 92.

41. Robert McClintock to Sec. of State, 20 Feb 1962, NSF, box 6, Kennedy Library.

42. McClintock to Sec. of State, 14 Mar 1962, NSF, box 6, Kennedy Library; M. A. Cárcano, "El presidente de la nación argentina decreta," 8 Feb 1962, Fondo Argentina, MINREX.

43. Robert A. Potash, *The Army and Politics in Argentina, 1945–1962: Perón to Frondizi* (Stanford, CA: Stanford University Press, 1980), 345–50; Marvin Goldwert, *Democracy, Militarism and Nationalism in Argentina, 1930–1966* (Austin: University of Texas Press, 1972), 185.

44. Potash, *Army and Politics in Argentina*, 368. The CIA had predicted the military coup. CIA, "The Argentine Elections," 23 Mar 1962; Steward to Sec. of State, 29 Mar 1963; H. R. Wellman to AmEmbassy, Buenos Aires, 28 Mar 1962, NSF, box 6, Kennedy Library. At least two historians surmise that Kennedy had already grown weary of supporting democrats like Frondizi. See David F. Schmitz, *Thank God They're on Our Side: The United States and Right-Wing Dictatorships, 1921–1965* (Chapel Hill: University of North Carolina Press, 1999), 258; Rabe, *The Most Dangerous Area*. This author agrees with them.

45. As quoted by Cuban embassy in Brazil (hereafter CEB), "Declaraciones de Janio Quadros favorable a la Revolución Cubana," 11 Apr 1960, Fondo Brasil, MINREX. For additional praise from Quadros for Cuba, see CEB, "Janio Quadros apoya gobierno revolucionario," 29 Jun 1960, Fondo Brasil, MINREX.

46. This was the question posed by the president's leading critic, Governor Carlos Lacerda of Guanabara State. See Vera Lúcia Michalany Chaia, *A liderança política de Jânio Quadros, 1947–1990* (Ibitinga, São Paulo: Humanidades, 1992), 218.

47. CEB, "Informe sobre el Brasil," 10 Sep 1960, Fondo Brasil, MINREX; Chaia, *A liderança política de Jânio Quadros*, 182.

48. "Brazilian Finance Minister's Call on President Kennedy," 16 May 1961, NSF, box 12, Kennedy Library.

49. Thomas E. Skidmore, *Politics in Brazil, 1930–1964: An Experiment in Democracy* (London: Oxford University Press, 1967), 194–200.

50. *FRUS, 1961–1963*, vol. 12, *American Republics*, 439–40. Not all Brazilians escaped the Oval Office without a lecture on communism. Kennedy told the Brazilian ambassador in Washington that "Brazil underestimates the dangers of Cuban

ideological expansionism." As quoted in Hershberg, "The United States, Brazil," pt. 1, 9.

51. As quoted in Túlio Velho Barreto and Laurindo Ferreira, eds., *Na trilha do golpe: 1964 revisitado* (Rio de Janeiro: Fundação Joaquim Nabuco, 2004), 150. Also see Patrick Iber, *Neither Peace nor Freedom: The Cultural Cold War in Latin America* (Cambridge, MA: Harvard University Press, 2015), 181–82.

52. Cooke, *Correspondencia Perón-Cooke*, 483.

53. CEB, "Estudiantes del Brasil pelean contra el ejército," 11 Jun 1961, Fondo Brasil, MINREX.

54. Ney Eduardo Possapp d'Avila, *Um olhar sobre a legalidade, 1961* (Passo Fundo, Brazil: Berthier, 2011), 43–45.

55. Gustavo Henrique Marques Bezerra, *Da revolucão ao reatamento: A política externa brasileiro e a questão cubana (1959–1986)* (Brasília: Fundação Alexander de Busmõ, 2012), 108–19.

56. Ibid., 120–22. Conditions for asylum seekers at the Brazilian embassy in Havana continued to be a vexing issue in Brazil-Cuba relations through 1963. See B. Hitch to J. M. Brown, Havana, 15 Feb 1963, 371/168152, Foreign Office: General Correspondence, 1906–1966, Political Correspondence, National Archives, London.

57. Moniz Bandeira, *De Martí a Fidel,* 328–32; Pereira Cabrera, *1961/Ernesto Che Guevara en Uruguay,* 770–99. Moniz saw the 1961 military pressure on President Quadros to resign as a military *golpe.* See especially Luiz Alberto Moniz Bandeira, *O 24 de agôsto de Jânio Quadros* (Rio de Janeiro: Editora Melso, 1961); Cliff Welch, *The Seed Was Planted: The São Paulo Roots of Brazil's Rural Labor Movement, 1924–1964* (University Park: Penn State University Press, 1999), 244. Lacerda was a staunch conservative who, from 1961 to 1965, used anticommunism to destroy two dozen favelas, displacing thousands of residents whose poverty might make them susceptible to political radicalization. See Brodwyn Fischer, "The Red Menace Reconsidered: A Forgotten History of Communist Mobilization in Rio de Janeiro's Favelas, 1945–1962," *Hispanic American Historical Review* 94, no. 1 (2014): 2.

58. CEB, "Sobre la crisis política," Aug 1961, Fondo Brasil, MINREX.

59. Jorge Ferreira, *João Goulart: Uma biografia,* 2nd ed. (Rio de Janeiro: Editora Civilização Brasileira, 2011), 224–27.

60. John W. F. Dulles, *Vargas of Brazil: A Political Biography* (Austin: University of Texas Press, 1967), 319–33.

61. Possapp d'Avila, *Um olhar sobre a legalidade, 1961,* 112–19, 141–42; Cecil Johnson, *Communist China & Latin America, 1959–1967* (New York: Columbia University Press, 1970), 27–28; Lincoln Gordon, *Brazil's Second Chance: En Route toward the First World* (Washington, DC: Brookings Institution Press, 2001), 51.

62. CIA, "Communist Inroads in the Brazilian Government," 27 Sep 1961, in *C.I.A. Research Reports: Latin America, 1946–1976* (Frederick, MD: University Publications of America, 1982), microfilm.

63. Claudia Korol, "Cooke y el Che: En el cruce de caminos," in *Cooke, de vuelta: El gran descartado de la historia Argentina,* ed. Miguel Mazzeo (Buenos Aires: Ediciones la Rosa Blindada, 1999), 93. For more on the Gran Asado, see Gabriel Rot, *Los orígenes perdidos de la guerrilla en la Argentina* (Buenos Aires: Waldhuter, 2010), 144–48.

64. As quoted in Korol, "Cooke y el Che," 94–95. Also see Michael Ratner and Michael Steven Smith, eds., *Che Guevara and the FBI: The U.S. Political Police Dossier on the Latin American Revolutionary* (Brooklyn, NY: Ocean Press, 1997), 88.

65. As quoted in Claudia Korol, *Che y los argentinos* (Buenos Aires: Ediciones, 1987), 87.

66. Sergio M. Nicanoff and Axel Castellano, *Las primeras experienceas guerrilleras en la Argentina: La historia del "Vasco" Bengochea y las Fuerzas Armadas de la Revolución Nacional* (Buenos Aires: Ediciones del Centro Cultural de la Coop. Floreal Gorini, 2006), 68–70.

67. As recollected by Manuel Gaggero in Korol, "Cooke y el Che," 97–98.

68. As remembered by Gerardo Bavio, "Cooke y el Che: Recuerdos, realidad y ficción," in *Cooke, de vuelta,* 106–7. Influential Argentinean leftist leaders in Cuba at the time included Ángel Bengoechea, also known as "El Vasco," Gustavo Rearte, Juan García Elorrio, Nahuel Moreno, Carlos Olmedo, Fernando Abal Medina, Norma Arrostita, Marcos Osatinsky, Roberto Quieto, Elías Seman, José "Joe" Baxter, Raimundo Villaflor, Francisco "Paco" Urondo, Emilio Jáuregui, Roberto Mario Santucho, Domingo Menna, Benito Urteaga, Rodolfo Walsh, and Haroldo Conti. Cooke informed Juan Perón about the Gran Asado without many details (perhaps not wanting to arouse jealousy) except that Che spoke in favor of a revolution of national liberation in Argentina. Cooke, *Correspondencia Perón-Cooke,* 532.

69. Rojo, *Mi amigo, el Che,* 188. Also see Jorge Ricardo Masetti, *Los que luchan y los que lloran: El Fidel Castro que yo vi* (Buenos Aires: Freeland, 1958).

70. Rojo, *Mi amigo, el Che,* 35–36; "Reporte sumario sobre Prensa Latina," 25 Nov 1968, Expediente 65–92–68, Fondo Dirección Federal de Seguridad, Archivo General de la Nación, Mexico City. The author thanks Renata Keller for forwarding a copy of this report.

71. Piero Gleijeses, *Conflicting Missions: Havana, Washington, and Africa, 1959–1976* (Chapel Hill: University of North Carolina Press, 2002), 31, 52.

72. Ciro Bustos, *El Che quiere verte: La historia jamás contada del Che en Bolivia* (Buenos Aires: Javier Vergara Editores), 106.

73. Ibid., 96–97, 108–9.

74. Ibid., 92, 99–100.

75. Ibid., 121.

76. Rot, *Los orígenes perdidos,* 159–60.

77. Ibid., 165–67; Bustos, *El Che quiere verte,* 281.

78. Rot, *Los orígenes perdidos,* 170–71.

79. Thomas C. Field Jr., *From Development to Dictatorship: Bolivia and the Alliance for Progress in the Kennedy Era* (Ithaca, NY: Cornell University Press, 2014), 73; Rot, *Los orígenes perdidos,* 140–41.

80. Bustos, *El Che quiere verte,* 170–71. Inti and Coco Peredo also served in Che's Bolivia venture in 1967.

81. Field, *From Development to Dictatorship,* 73; Rot, *Los orígenes perdidos,* 140–41.

9. VENEZUELA'S GUERRILLA WAR

1. Richard Gott, *Guerrilla Movements in Latin America* (Garden City, NY: Doubleday, 1971), 93–98.

2. Gabriel García Márquez, *Obra periodística,* vol. 3, *De Europa y América (1955–1960)* (Buenos Aires: Editorial Sudamericana, 1997), 619.

3. As quoted in Alan McPherson, *Yankee No! Anti-Americanism in U.S.–Latin American Relations* (Cambridge, MA: Harvard University Press, 2003), 11; H. W. Brands Jr., *Cold Warriors: Eisenhower's Generation and American Foreign Policy* (New York: Columbia University Press, 1988), 41–42, 44. Also see Lars Schoultz, *That Infernal Little Cuban Republic: The United States and the Cuban Revolution* (Chapel Hill: University of North Carolina Press, 2009), 68–70; Vernon A. Walters, *Silent Missions* (Garden City, NY: Doubleday, 1978). Colonel Walters translated for the Nixons on the goodwill tour. The justification for awarding Pérez Jímenez the Legion of Merit in 1954 had to do with the "protection of our vast economic interests in Venezuela." "Vice President's South American Tour," 22 Apr 1958, Pre-presidential Papers of Richard Nixon, Robert E. Cushman Jr. Files, pps. 325, box 10, Richard M. Nixon Presidential Library.

4. See Philip B. Taylor Jr., *The Venezuelan Golpe de Estado of 1958: The Fall of Marcos Pérez Jiménez* (Washington, DC: Institute for the Comparative Study of Political Systems, 1968), 48, 50–51, 55, 61.

5. Daniel H. Levine, "Venezuela since 1958: The Consolidation of Democratic Politics," in *The Breakdown of Democratic Regimes: Latin America,* ed. Juan J. Linz and Alfred Stepan (Baltimore: Johns Hopkins University Press, 1978), 93, 97; John D. Martz, *Acción Democrática: Evolution of a Modern Political Party in Venezuela* (Princeton, NJ: Princeton University Press, 1966), 103–5.

6. "Soviet Bloc Efforts at Penetration of Latin America," 14 Mar 1958, White House, Office of the Staff Secretary Series, Alpha Side Series, box 7, Dwight D. Eisenhower Presidential Library, Abilene, KS.

7. CIA, "National Intelligence Estimate: Venezuela," 16 Dec 1965, National Security Files (hereafter NSF), National Intelligence Estimates (hereafter NIE), box 9, Lyndon Baines Johnson Presidential Library, Austin, TX.

8. John Duncan Powell, *Political Mobilization of the Venezuelan Peasant* (Cambridge, MA: Harvard University Press, 1971), 107, 110, 180.

9. Robert J. Alexander, *The Communist Party of Venezuela* (Stanford, CA: Hoover Institution Press, 1969), 73.

10. Martz, *Acción Democrática,* 22–23.

11. Jonathan C. Brown and Peter S. Linder, "Trabajadores en petróleo extranjero: México y Venezuela, 1920–1948," in *Las inversiones extranjeras en América Latina, 1850–1930: Nuevos debates y problemas en historia económica comparada,* ed. Carlos Marichal (Mexico City: Fondo de Cultura Económica, 1995), 244–71.

12. Ernesto Che Guevara, *Otra vez: El diario inédito del segundo viaje por América Latina (1953–1956)* (Buenos Aires: Editorial Sudamericana, 2000), 34.

13. Robert J. Alexander, *Rómulo Betancourt and the Transformation of Venezuela* (New Brunswick, NJ: Transaction Books, 1982), 456; Aragorn Storm Miller, "Season of Storms: The United States and the Caribbean Contest for a New Political Order, 1958–1961," in *Beyond the Eagle's Shadow: New Histories of Latin America's Cold War,* ed. Virginia Garrard-Burnett, Mark Atwood Lawrence, and Julio E. Moreno (Albuquerque: University of New Mexico Press, 2013), 89.

14. Rómulo Betancourt, *Venezuela: Política y petróleo* (Mexico City: Fondo de Cultura Económica, 1956).

15. Jonathan C. Brown, "Jersey Standard and the Politics of Latin American Oil Production, 1911–1930," in *Latin American Oil Companies and the Politics of Energy,* ed. John D. Wirth (Lincoln: University of Nebraska Press, 1985), 1–50; "Why Foreign Oil Companies Shifted Their Production from Mexico to Venezuela in the 1920s," *American Historical Review,* 90, no. 2 (1985): 362–85.

16. Talton F. Ray, *The Politics of the Barrios of Venezuela* (Berkeley: University of California Press, 1969), 35; Alexander, *The Communist Party of Venezuela,* 67. In the decade following 1959, more than 166,000 peasant heads of household benefited from land reform. James W. Wilkie, *Measuring Land Reform* (Los Angeles: UCLA Latin American Center Publications, 1974), 63.

17. James W. Wilkie and Peter Reich, eds., *Statistical Abstract of Latin America,* vol. 18 (Los Angeles: UCLA Latin American Center Publications, 1977), 273.

18. Ibid., 427.

19. CIA, "National Intelligence Estimate: Venezuela," 19 Feb 1964, NSF, NIE, box 9; "The Venezuelan Communist Split and Present Insurgency," 7 Jun 1967, NSF, Country Files (hereafter CF), box 75, Lyndon Baines Johnson Presidential Library, Austin, TX.

20. "It was a costly mistake and a heavy blow to the forces of the people," he admitted. Augusto Velardo, "Entrevista con el dirigente máximo del MIR Moisés Moleiro," *¿Por Qué?* (Mexico City), 8 May 1968, as quoted in Gott, *Guerrilla Movements in Latin America,* 102.

21. CIA, "Daily Brief," 31 Jan 1962; "Counter-Insurgency Critical List," 25 Jul 1962, Central Intelligence Agent Records Search Tool, National Archives Records Administration, College Park, MD (hereafter CREST); Jean Lartéguy, *The Guerrillas,* trans. Stanley Hochman (New York: World Publishing Company, 1970), 191–92.

22. "La Republic Comments on Establishment of FALN Office in Havana," 20 Nov 1964, CIA Press Information, box 3, National Archives and Records Administration, College Park, MD (hereafter NARA).

23. Fidel Castro, "4th Anniversary of the Cuban Revolution," 2 Jan 1963, Castro Speech Database, LANIC, http://lanic.utexas.edu/project/castro/db/1963/19630102 .html, accessed 1 Mar 2015; "Propaganda Report," 18 Jan 1963, NSF, box 59, John F. Kennedy Presidential Library, Boston. Raúl Castro reiterated this commitment later, telling Bulgaria's communist leaders, "We think that the only way to seize power is via armed struggle, the massive struggle of the people, the way things are now in Venezuela." "Documents on Raul Castro's Visit to Eastern Europe," Mar–May 1965, in *Cold War International Project Bulletin,* no. 17 / 18 (Fall 2012): 780.

24. One revolutionary claims that Venezuela's guerrilla uprising cost the Cubans "millions of dollars." Ciro Bustos, *Che Wants to See You: The Untold Story of Che in Bolivia,* trans. Ann Wright (London: Verso, 2013), 277.

25. Moscoso to State, 1 Sep 1961; ANAF Attaché, Caracas, 14 Dec 1961, NSF, box 192, Kennedy Library.

26. Moscoso to State, 17 Oct 1961, NSF, box 192; Leo J. Moser, "Joint Weeka No. 31," 3 Aug 1963, NSF, box 192, Kennedy Library.

27. Stewart to State, 6 May, 1 Jun 1962, NSF, box 192, Kennedy Library.

28. The leader was Captain Jesús Teodoro Molina. Gott, *Guerrilla Movements in Latin America,* 116–17.

29. Ibid., 119.

30. "Cuban Subversive Activities," 5 Oct 1962, NSF, box 52; CIA, "Disturbances in Caracas," 5 Jun 1962; CIA, Stewart to State, 14 Feb, 14 Aug 1963, NSF, box 192, Kennedy Library.

31. CIA, "National Intelligence Estimate: Venezuela," 19 Feb 1964.

32. CIA, "Demands on President Romulo Betancourt," 5 Jun 1962, NSF, box 192, Kennedy Library. The State Department concluded that the "high command and great bulk [of the] officers remain[ed] loyal to [the] government and [were] prepared to defend it." Hill to State, 29 Apr 1963, NSF, box 192, Kennedy Library.

33. *Foreign Relations of the United States, 1961–1963,* vol. 12, *American Republics* (Washington, DC: US Government Printing Office, 1996), 273.

34. "Second and Final Conversation between President Kennedy and President Betancourt," memo, 20 Feb 1963, NSF, box 192, Kennedy Library.

35. As quoted in Robert Moss, *Urban Guerrillas: The New Face of Political Violence* (London: Temple Smith, 1972), 164, 170; CIA, "The Venezuelan Communist Split and Present Insurgency," 7 Jun 1967, NSF, CF, box 75, LBJ Library.

36. As quoted in Moss, *Urban Guerrillas,* 136.

37. Stewart to State, 1 Oct 1963; Department of State, "Cuban Propaganda and Subversive Activities Venezuela," 18 Mar 1963; Stewart to State, 5 Jun, 1 Jul, 1 Oct 1963, NSF, box 192, Kennedy Library. Five of the nine hijackers of the oil ship that put in at Belém, Brazil, flew to Cuba to find refuge. Brazil already had granted asylum to all nine of the hijackers. Edwin McCammon Martin, *Kennedy and Latin America* (Lanham, MD: University Press of America, 1997), 364.

38. Hughes, "Venezuela: Government Acts Forcefully to Quell Terrorists," 14 Jun 1963; CIA, "The Political Crisis in Venezuela and Prospects for Democracy," 11 Oct 1963; Stewart to State, 1 Oct, 11 Oct 1963; Leo J. Moser, "Possible Clandestine Arms Shipments in Latin America: Venezuela," 3 Jul 1963, NSF, box 192, Kennedy Library.

39. Stewart to State, 18 Nov 1963; CIA, "Terrorism in Venezuela," 16 Sep 1963, NSF, box 192, Kennedy Library.

40. *Foreign Relations of the United States, 1964–1968,* vol. 32, *South and Central America, Mexico* (hereafter *FRUS, 1964–1968,* vol. 32, *South and Central America*) (Washington, DC: US Government Printing Office, 2004), 8; Raúl Roa, "Respuesta al presidente de la comisión investigadora de la O.E.A.," 3 Feb 1964, Fondo Venezuela, Archivo del Ministerio de Relaciones Exteriores, Havana (hereafter MINREX).

41. *New York Times,* 23 Feb 1964; CIA, "International Intelligence Communiqué," 18 Dec 1963, NSF, CF, box 32, LBJ Library. Kennedy and Johnson staffer Edwin Martin certified the authenticity of the Cuban arms, saying it had been "confirmed by an OAS investigating committee in a Report of December 3, 1963." Martin, *Kennedy and Latin America,* 203, 209, 370. At least two former CIA operatives suspect the arms cache to have been a CIA plant rather than a Cuban drop. Neither have any direct evidence. See Philip Agee, *Inside the Company: CIA Diary* (London: Allen Lane, 1975), 322; Joseph Burkholder Smith, *Portrait of a Cold Warrior* (New York: G. P. Putnam's Sons, 1976), 383. Journalist Don Bohning does not even suggest that the CIA planted those weapons. He based his information on extensive interviews with former agents of the CIA's Miami station. Don Bohning, *The Castro Obsession: U.S. Covert Operations against Cuba, 1959–1965* (Washington, DC: Potomac Books, 2002), 198. Also see Schoultz, *That Infernal Little Cuban Republic,* 227; Walter LaFeber, "Thomas C. Mann and the Devolution of Latin American Policy: From the Good Neighbor to Military Intervention," in *Behind the Throne: Servants of Power to Imperial Presidents, 1898–1968,* ed. Thomas J. McCormick and Walter LaFeber (Madison: University of Wisconsin Press, 1993), 193. Additional evidence comes from transcripts of Raúl Castro's meetings with East European leaders. See "Documents on Raul Castro's Visit to Eastern Europe," Mar–May 1965, in *Cold War International Project Bulletin,* no. 17 / 18 (Fall 2012): 776, 780.

42. "Discurso pronunciado por el Comandante Fidel Castro Ruz . . . en la Ciudad Deportiva, el 6 de diciembre de 1963," speech, http://cuba.cu/gobierno/discursos /1963/esp/f061263e.html, accessed June 18, 2015.

43. CIA, "Conclusions of the Fifth Plenum of the Central Committee of the Communist Party of Venezuela," 19 May 1964, NSF, CF, box 16, LBJ Library.

44. As quoted in Lartéguy, *The Guerrillas,* 194.

45. Gott, *Guerrilla Movements in Latin America,* 131; Tad Szulc, "Exporting the Cuban Revolution," in *Cuba and the United States: Long-Range Perspectives,* ed. John Plank (Washington, DC: Brookings Institution Press, 1967), 77.

46. Gott, *Guerrilla Movements in Latin America,* 108, 110–11.

47. Ibid., 113, 154.

48. "FALN Member Interviewed in Uruguay," 6 Oct 1964, CIA Press Information, box 3, Kennedy Library.

49. "Venezuela, Insurgency and Counterinsurgency," 31 Dec 64, CIA Press Information, box 4, NARA.

50. The Joint Chiefs of Staff, "Memorandum for the President," 30 Nov 1961, NSF, Departments, box 276, Kennedy Library.

51. US Commander in Chief, South to Joint Chiefs, 28 Feb 1964, NSF, CF, box 16, LBJ Library.

52. David Marcus Lauderbeck, "The U.S. Army School of the Americas: Mission and Policymaking in the Cold War" (PhD diss., University of Texas at Austin, 2004), 213, 255, 266–67, 275.

53. Robert G. Foote, 8th Special Forces Group (Airborne), Ft. Gulick, Canal Zone, "MTT to Venezuela," 8 July 1963; Record Group 548, "US Army Forces in the Caribbean," stack 631, row 50, compartment 32, shelf 1–2, "Office of Military Assistance Program Files 1963–66," box 1, NARA. My thanks go to Ian Lyles for bringing these documents to my attention.

54. *FRUS, 1964–1968,* vol. 32, *South and Central America,* 1120–28.

55. "Defense Minister Discussed Anti-guerrilla Action," 18 Nov 1964, CIA Press Information, box 3, NARA.

56. "The Protection of U.S. Personnel and Installations against Acts of Terrorism in Latin America," 12 May 1965, NSF, CF, box 2, LBJ Library. On Raúl Castro's good treatment of American hostages in 1958, see Jana K. Lipman, *Guantánamo: A Working Class History between Empire and Revolution* (Berkeley: University of California Press, 2009), 140–41; Julia E. Sweig, *Inside the Cuban Revolution: Fidel Castro and the Urban Underground* (Cambridge, MA: Harvard University Press, 2002), 171.

57. "The Protection of U.S. Personnel and Installations against Acts of Terrorism in Latin America," 12 May 1965.

58. "Venezuela," 22 Jul 1965, CIA Press Information, box 6, NARA.

59. "Venezuela," 1 Nov 1965, CIA Press Information, box 7, NARA.

60. CIA, "Plans of Cuba to Increase Support of the Communist Revolution in Venezuela," cable, 15 Jan 1965, NSF, CF, box 31, LBJ Library.

61. Miguel Acoca, "Downfall of 'The Man with the Dog,'" *Special Report Venezuela,* 30 Apr 1965, CREST.

62. State Department, "Latin American Communist Party Meeting in Havana," 1 Mar 65, NSF, CF, box 31, LBJ Library.

63. "Che Guevara at the United Nations," speech, 11 Dec 1964, Marxists Internet Archive, https://www.marxists.org/archive/guevara/1964/12/11.htm, accessed 2 Mar 2015.

64. CIA "Possibility of Cuban Arms for the Army of National Liberation," 14 Oct 67, NSF, CF, box 19, LBJ Library.

65. "FALN Document Pledges Long War," 6 Feb 65, CIA Press Information, box 4, NARA.

66. "Troops Continue Anti-guerrilla Activities," 15 Mar 1965, CIA Press Information, box 4, NARA.

67. "Venezuela," 21 Jun 1965, CIA Press Information, box 6, NARA.

68. "Defense Minister Reports Death of Guerrillas," 9 Jun 1965, CIA Press Information, box 5, NARA.

69. The defector was José Díaz. "Venezuela," 17 Sep 1965, CIA Press Information, box 6, NARA.

70. "Captured Guerrilla Chief Reveals Guerrilla Weaknesses," 2 Sep 1965, CIA Press Information, box 6, NARA.

71. "Venezuela," 8 Oct 1965, CIA Press Information, box 7, NARA.

72. "Venezuela," 30 Apr 1965, CIA Press Information, box 7, NARA.

73. "Venezuela," 8 Jul 1965, CIA Press Information, box 6, NARA.

74. "Venezuela," 30 Apr 1965, CIA Press Information, box 7, NARA.

75. "Venezuela," 8 Jul 1965, CIA Press Information, box 6, NARA.

76. "Venezuelan Communists Losing," 6 Dec 1965, CREST.

77. "Venezuela," 13 Jun 1965, CIA Press Information, box 7, NARA; Martz, *Acción Democrática,* 256.

78. "Venezuelan Communists Losing," 6 Dec 1965, CREST.

79. Ibid.; "Venezuela," 22 Jul 1965, CIA Press Information, box 6, NARA.

80. "Venezuela," 8 Jul 1965, CIA Press Information, box 6, NARA.

81. "Venezuela," 22 Jul 1965.

82. "Venezuela," 8 Jul 1965; 1 Nov 1965, CIA Press Information, box 7, NARA.

83. "Venezuela," 8 Oct 1965, CIA Press Information, box 7, NARA.

84. "Venezuelan Communists Losing," 6 Dec 1965.

85. Gott, *Guerrilla Movements in Latin America,* 153; Benigno [Dariel Alarcón Ramírez], *Memorias de un soldado cubano: Vida y muerte de la Revolución* (Barcelona: Tusquets Editores, 1997), 219–20.

86. CIA, "Revolt of Hard-Line Dissidents in the FALN against Established Leadership," 30 Dec 1965, NSF, CF, box 75, LBJ Library. Also see Aragorn Storm Miller, *Precarious Paths to Freedom: The United States, Venezuela, and the Latin American Cold War* (Albuquerque: University of New Mexico Press, 2016), chap. 5.

87. The author derived this analysis from the following extensive report: CIA, "The Venezuelan Communist Split and Present Insurgency," 7 Jun 1967, NSF, CF, box 75, LBJ Library.

88. As quoted in Alexander, *The Communist Party of Venezuela,* 105. Also see William John Green, "Revolution for Export? Cuba and the Insurgent Left of Venezuela" (MA thesis, University of Texas at Austin, 1989),54; Committee on the Judiciary, US Senate, *The First Conference of the Latin American Solidarity Organization* (Washington, DC: US Government Printing Office, 1967), ix, 102; Levine, "Venezuela since 1958," 100; Maurice Halperin, *The Taming of Fidel Castro* (Berkeley: University of California Press, 1981), 233–34.

89. Tomás Almodóvar to Raúl Roa García, Prague, 22 Jun 1966; "Las guerrillas venezolanas," Nov 1967, Fondo Venezuela, MINREX.

90. Fidel Castro read aloud Ojeda's letter during his speech at the University of Havana on March 13, 1967, cited in Gott, *Guerrilla Movements in Latin America,* 149. Castro denounced the PCV again in his closing address to the Latin American Organization of Solidarity conference. Fidel Castro, speech to the OLAS Conference, 10 Aug 1967, Marxists Internet Archive, https://www.marxists.org/history/cuba/archive/castro/1967/08/10.htm, accessed 3 Mar 2015. Also see A. D. Brighty to P. Hartahome, Havana, 30 Jun 1966, 371/184863, Foreign Office: General Correspondence, 1906–1966, Political Correspondence, National Archives, London.

91. CIA, "Evidence of Cuban Violations of Venezuelan Sovereignty," n.d.; "Speech of 13 March 1967," NSF, Intelligence File, box 2, LBJ Library.

92. Castro, speech to the OLAS Conference, 10 Aug 1967.

93. AmEmbassy Caracas to State, 23 Jun 1967, NSF, Intelligence Files, box 2, LBJ Library.

94. Orlando Castro Hidalgo, *Spy for Fidel* (Miami: E. A. Seemann, 1971), 49; *FRUS, 1964–1968,* vol. 32, *South and Central America,* 144, 1091; Gott, *Guerrilla Movements in Latin America,* 162; CIA, "Fidel Castro and Prospects for Revolution in Latin America," 28 Dec 1967, NSF, CF, box 19, LBJ Library.

95. Quoted in Gott, *Guerrilla Movements in Latin America,* 162. On the demise of the Venezuelan guerrillas, see Miller, *Precarious Paths to Freedom,* chap. 6.

96. "Si me descubrían me mataban." Luis Báez, *Secretos de generales* (Havana: Editorial Si-Mar, 1996), 107–9; José A. Gárciga Blanco, *General Tomassevich: Un héroe de la Revolución cubana* (Havana: Editorial Política, 2009), 170–73.

97. CIA, "Venezuela Legalizes the Communist Party," *Weekly Summary,* 4 Apr 1969, CREST; Donald L. Herman, *Christian Democracy in Venezuela* (Chapel Hill: University of North Carolina Press, 1980), 66.

98. Herman, *Christian Democracy in Venezuela,* 132–35; Robert J. Alexander, *International Maoism in the Developing World* (Westport, CT: Praeger, 1999), 188–89.

99. See Ian Bradley Lyles, "Demystifying Counterinsurgency: U.S. Army Internal Security Training and South American Responses in the 1960s" (PhD diss., University of Texas at Austin, 2016), 165, 196–98, 468.

100. Judith Ewell, "Che Guevara and Venezuela: Tourist, Guerrilla Mentor, and Revolutionary Spirit," in *Che's Travels: The Making of a Revolutionary in 1950s Latin America,* ed. Paulo Drinot (Durham, NC: Duke University Press, 2010), 170.

10. MILITARY COUNTERREVOLUTION IN BRAZIL

1. "Minutes of Conversation between President João Goulart and Attorney General Robert Kennedy," 19 Dec 1962; Lincoln Gordon to State Department, 18 Dec 1962, National Security Files (hereafter NSF), box 13A, John F. Kennedy Presidential Library, Boston. I thank Renata Keller for forwarding copies of these documents. Another version of the meeting is provided by Jorge Ferreira, *João Goulart, uma biografia,* 2nd ed. (Rio de Janeiro: Editora Civilização, 2011), 318–20. Yet another account, totally unsympathetic to Goulart, is by Arthur M. Schlesinger Jr., *Robert Kennedy and His Times* (Boston: Houghton Mifflin, 1978), 581–83. Schlesinger quotes Robert Kennedy later saying, "I didn't like [Goulart]. He looks and acts a good deal . . . like a Brazilian Jimmy Hoffa. I didn't think he could be trusted."

2. "Cronología de las relaciones bilaterales Cuba-Brasil, 1959–2000," Fondo Brasil, Archivo del Ministerio de Relaciones Exteriores (hereafter MINREX).

3. The member was Senator Burt Hickenlooper of the Senate Foreign Relations Committee. See Gustavo Henrique Marques Bezerra, *Da revolução ao reatamento: A política externa brasileiro e a questão cubana (1959–1986)* (Brasília: Fundação Alexander de Busmô, 2012), 161–68; Quintañeiro, *Cuba e Brasil: Da revolução ao golpe, 1959-1964* (Belo Horizonte: Editora UFMG, 1988), 71–75.

4. *Foreign Relations of the United States, 1961–1963,* vol. 12, *American Republics* (Washington, DC: US Government Printing Office, 1996), 461–63, 466.

5. Ibid., 468.

6. Stanley J. Grogan to the Director of the CIA, 5 Apr 1962, Central Intelligence Agent Records Search Tool, National Archives Records Administration, College Park, MD (hereafter CREST). For more on Goulart's trip to the United States, see James G. Hershberg, "The United States, Brazil, and the Cuban Missile Crisis, 1962," pt. 1, *Journal of Cold War Studies* 6, no. 2 (Spring 2004): 11–12.

7. The correspondence of these exchanges abounds in the archives of the Cuban Foreign Ministry. A quick guide to the subject can be found in "Cronología de las relaciones bilaterales Cuba-Brasil, 1959–2000," Fondo Brasil, MINREX. I extend my thanks to Joel Wolfe for his comments on Niemeyer's contributions to the building of Brasília.

8. James G. Hershberg, "The United States, Brazil, and the Cuban Missile Crisis, 1962," pt. 2, *Journal of Cold War Studies* 6, no. 3 (Summer 2004): 13, 19.

9. Ibid., 2, 35, 43, 46, 48, 58, 63. Without US acquiescence to Cuba's five conditions, Brazil's mediation met resistance in Cuba.

10. Ferreira, *João Goulart*, 323. By comparison, Goulart became vice president in 1961 by taking 36 percent of the vote in a field of two other candidates. Quadros, the presidential victory in that election, represented a different political party than did Goulart. See Vera Lúcia Michalany Chaia, *A liderança política de Jânio Quadros, 1947–1990* (Ibitinga, São Paulo: Humanidades, 1992), 183; "Situación política actual," 11 Apr 1963, Fondo Brasil, MINREX; Edwin McCammon Martin, *Kennedy and Latin America* (Lanham, MD: University Press of America, 1997), 305.

11. CIA, *Daily Brief,* 26 Feb, 21 Jun 1963, CREST.

12. CIA, "Current Intelligence Memorandum: Brazil," 1 Oct 1963, NSF, box 14A, Kennedy Library; Werner Baer, *The Brazilian Economy,* 6th ed. (Westport, CT: Praeger, 2008), 410. The causes of rising inflation, says Gordon, were the "unwise policies" going back to Vargas and Kubitschek: loose fiscal practices, wage increases for labor and the military, and bureaucratic overstaffing in government and state industries. Lincoln Gordon, *Brazil's Second Chance: En Route toward the First World* (Washington, DC: Brookings Institution Press, 2001), 36, 49–50.

13. "Views of San Thiago Dantas, Brazilian Finance Minister," 11 Feb 1963, NSF, box 13A, Kennedy Library.

14. "Cuba and Communist Activities in Latin America," 12 Mar 1963, NSF, box 13A, Kennedy Library.

15. The following comes from a twenty-page study on the incident by Cuban diplomats in Rio de Janeiro. They based their report on Brazilian newspaper accounts. CEB, "El levantamiento de los sargentos en Brasilia," Sep 1963, Fondo Brasil, MINREX.

16. Ibid.

17. "Cronología de las relaciones bilaterales Cuba-Brasil, 1959–2000"; Raúl Roa to Osvaldo Dorticós, 4 Mar 1964, Fondo Brasil, MINREX. Brazil's position on the Venezuelan charges changed after the April military coup. In the June 1964 OAS meeting, it voted additional sanctions against Cuba for sending arms to Venezuelan guerrillas, leaving Mexico, Bolivia, Uruguay, and Chile in the pro-Cuba camp. By 1966, only Mexico remained. See Marques Bezerra, *Da revolucão ao reatamento,* 241.

18. Cliff Welch, *The Seed Was Planted: The São Paulo Roots of Brazil's Rural Labor Movement, 1924–1964* (University Park: Penn State University Press, 1999), 230.

19. Ibid., 245–56; Seth Garfield, "From Ploughshares to Politics: Transformations in Rural Brazil during the Cold War and Its Aftermath," in *Beyond the Eagle's Shadow: New Histories of Latin America's Cold War,* ed. Virginia Garrard-Burnett, Mark Atwood Lawrence, and Julio E. Moreno (Albuquerque: University of New Mexico Press, 2013), 154.

20. As quoted in Joseph A. Page, *The Revolution That Never Was: Northeast Brazil, 1955–1964* (New York: Grossman, 1972), 92, 94.

21. Helio Armenteras, "Informe sobre las Ligas Campesinas," 28 Nov 61; "Declaración del primer Congreso Nacional de Labradores y Trabajadores Agrícolas de Brasil," 17 Nov 1961, Fondo Brasil, MINREX.

22. José Leandro Bezerra da Costa, "Mensagem ao povo cubano e ao seu goberno revolucionario de Fidel Castro," 29 Apr 1961, Fondo Brasil, MINREX.

23. Clodomir Morais to Departamento Latinoamericano de Divulgación (Latin American Department of Publication), 28 Apr 1960, Fondo Brasil, MINREX. Other pro-Cuba organizations sprang up in Brazil, many of which sought communication with the Cuban government. For example, see Maria Barboza Dias et al. to Ambassador of Cuba, 6 May 1960, Fondo Brasil, MINREX; Bezerra da Costa, "Mensagem ao povo cubano."

24. A series of articles in *O Globo* divulged the 1961 itinerary of Clodomir Morais and his colleagues. The articles appeared in January 1963, at a time when Morais languished in prison on charges of violating national security laws. *O Globo* cited no sources, leaving the researcher only to speculate. Yet the accounts seemed accurate enough that both the Cuban Ministry of Foreign Relations and the CIA reproduced them. "Traducción de artículos aparecidos en el periódico 'O Jornal' las días 27–29–30 de enero de 1963," Fondo Brasil, MINREX; CIA, "Cuban Training of Latin American Subversives," 27 Mar 1963, in *C.I.A. Research Reports: Latin America, 1946–1976* (Frederick, MD: University Publications of America, 1982), microfilm. The CIA and Cuba reports listed the same names of the Brazilians who allegedly received guerrilla training in Cuba: Clodomir dos Santos Morais, Joaquím Ferreira, Pedro Motta Barros, Rivadiva Braz de Oliveira, Amaro Luíz de Carvalho, Florentino Alcantara de Moraes, Carlos Danielli, Angel Arroyo, Mauricio Gravois, and João Amazonas. Mostly, the Cubans refrained from imparting military training to Brazilians until after the 1964 military coup and the formation of an urban resistance movement in 1967. See Denise Rollemberg, *O apoio de Cuba à luta armada no Brasil: O treinamento guerrilheiro* (Rio de Janeiro: Mauad, 2001), 11, 24, 25, 40.

25. "Traducción de artículos aparecidos en el periódico 'O Jornal.'"

26. As quoted in Welch, *The Seed Was Planted,* 281. Also see Ibid., 257, 261; CIA, *Daily Brief,* 11 Apr, 10 Oct 1963, CREST; Page, *The Revolution That Never Was,* 88, 108, 115, 154–55, 159.

27. CIA, "Continued Support of Leader of Brazilian Peasant League by Cuban Government," 26 Mar 1963, NSF, box 25A, Kennedy Library; CIA, "Desire of Fidel Castro to Ensure That Activity of Francisco Julião's Pleasant Leagues Does Not Topple Government of President Goulart," 19 Mar 1963, NSF, box 52, Kennedy Library.

28. CIA, "Continued Support of Leader of Brazilian Peasant League by Cuban Government," 26 Mar 1963; CIA, "Desire of Fidel Castro," 19 Mar 1963.

29. AmEmbassy Rio de Janeiro, "Continental Congress for Solidarity with Cuba (CCSC)," 6 May 1963, NSF, box 44, Kennedy Library.

30. Luis Carlos Prestes, "Movilizar a las masas para la defensa de Cuba y eligir respeto a la autodeterminación," 31 Mar 1963; "El Congreso de Solidaridad con Cuba celebrado en Brasil," 30 Mar 1963, Fondo Brasil, MINREX.

31. "La Declaración de Niteroi," 30 Mar 1963, Fondo Brasil, MINREX.

32. Edward J. Bash, "Economic Program of Brazilian Communist Party," 7 May 1964; John Keppel, "Luís Carlos Prestes' Views on the Goulart Regime," 8 Jun 1964, Central Foreign Policy Files, box 1935, NARA. Also see S. Hitch to J. M. Brown, Havana, 28 Mar 1963; H. S. Burroughs to I. J. M. Sutherland, Rio de Janeiro, 27 Jun 1963, 371/168152, Foreign Office: General Correspondence, 1906–1966, Political Correspondence, National Archives, London.

33. CIA, "A Review of Reporting on Cuba," 15 Jul 1963, NSF, box 52, Kennedy Library.

34. CIA, "Cuban Ambassador Raul Roa Observations about Political Relations between Brazil and Cuba," 2 Jul 63, in *C.I.A. Research Reports.*

35. Alfred Stepan, *The Military in Politics: Changing Patterns in Brazil* (Princeton, NJ: Princeton University Press, 1971), 173. Also see Sonny B. Davis, *A Brotherhood of Arms: Brazil-United States Military Relations, 1945–1977* (Niwot: University Press of Colorado, 1996), x, 175, 181, 224.

36. Joint Chiefs of Staff, "Status of Military Counterinsurgency Programs," n.d., NSF, Departments, box 280, Kennedy Library.

37. *Foreign Relations of the United States, 1964–1968,* vol. 31, *South and Central America; Mexico* (Washington, DC: US Government Printing Office, 2004) (hereafter *FRUS, 1964–1968,* vol. 31, *South and Central America*), 399; George Ball to AmEmbassy, Rio de Janeiro, 20 Feb 1964; Ralph J. Burton to Thomas Mann, 18 Feb 1964, Department of State, Political and Defense, box 1611, NARA. Also see Ian Bradley Lyles, "Demystifying Counterinsurgency: U.S. Army Internal Security Training and South American Responses in the 1960s" (PhD diss., University of Texas at Austin, 2016), Chapter 8.

38. Niles W. Bond, "Current Brazilian Politics," 20 Feb 1964, Central Foreign Policy Files, box 1932, NARA.

39. Vernon A. Walters, *Silent Missions* (Garden City, NY: Doubleday, 1978), 374–75; Phyllis R. Parker, *Brazil and the Quiet Intervention, 1964* (Austin: University of Texas Press, 1979), 28, 65.

40. Lincoln Gordon to Secretary of State, 27 Mar 1964, NSF, Country Files (hereafter CF), box 9, Lyndon Baines Johnson Presidential Library, Austin, TX. Many documents concerning the White House and the 1964 Brazilian coup are translated and collected in Marcos Sá Correa, *1964: Visto e comentado pela Casa Branca* (Porto Alegre, Brazil: L&PM Editores, 1977).

41. Translation, *O Globo* (Rio de Janeiro), 19 Feb 1964, Record Group 263, Records of the Central Intelligence Agency, Press Information relating to Insurgency and Counterinsurgency: Latin America, Entry (A) 64, box 1, NARA.

42. Gordon, "Memorandum of Conversation," 9 Jan 1964, Central Foreign Policy Files, box 1932.

43. Gordon, *Brazil's Second Chance*, 52, 63. The idea of a Goulart dictatorship arose in the minds of the right-wing opposition. In a meeting with a group that included journalists in January 1963, the chief of staff of the armed forces, Castelo Branco, was quoted as saying, "I believe that Communist infiltration is facilitated by the placement of disseminators of Communism in posts of the administration, of teaching, and of government-controlled corporations." Castelo Branco also declared in February 1964 that the armed forces would not support any movement giving dictatorial power to Goulart. See John W. F. Dulles, *Castelo Branco: The Making of a Brazilian President* (College Station: Texas A & M University Press, 1978), 270, 328.

44. CIA, "Plans to Overthrow the Administration of President Goulart," 4 May 1963, in *C.I.A. Research Reports.*

45. CIA, "Plans of Sao Paulo Civilian Sector of Movement to Overthrow Goulart Administration," 24 May 1963, in *C.I.A. Research Reports.*

46. Barbara Weinstein, *For Social Peace in Brazil: Industrialists and the Remaking of the Working Class in São Paulo, 1920–1964* (Chapel Hill: University of North Carolina Press, 1996), 321–22; AmConGen, São Paulo, "Weekly Summary no. 12," 19 Mar 1964; American Consul, Salvador, "Weekly Summary," 20 Mar 1964, Central Foreign Policy Files, box 1930, NARA. Also see Alzina Alves de Abreu, "A participação da imprensa na queda do Governo Goulart," in *1964–2004, 40 anos do golpe: Ditadura militar e resistência no Brasil* (Rio de Janeiro: 7Letras, 2004), 23.

47. *FRUS, 1964–1968,* vol. 31, *South and Central America,* 417. Also see Davis, *A Brotherhood of Arms,* 178–79; Gordon, *Brazil's Second Chance,* 61–62.

48. AmConGen, São Paulo, "Political Panorama Vastly Changed," 30 Apr 1964, Central Foreign Policy Files, box 1930; AmConGen, São Paulo, "Weekly Summary no. 5," 30 Jan 1964; Niles W. Bond, "Sao Paulo Not as Calm as It Sounds," 7 Feb 1964, Central Foreign Policy Files, box 1932. On women in the anti-Goulart movement, see Janaina Martins Cordeiro, *Diretas em movimento: Campanha da Mulher pela Democracia e a ditadura no Brasil* (Rio de Janeiro: Editora FGV, 2009); Margaret Power, "Who But a Woman? The Transnational Diffusion of Anti-communism among and between Conservative Women in Brazil, Chile, and the United States from the 1960s to the 1980s," unp. ms. presented at the American Historical Association meeting, New York, 2015.

49. AmConGen, São Paulo, "Weekly Summary," 28 Feb 1964, Central Foreign Policy Files, box 1932.

50. AmConGen, Recife, "Weekly Summary no. 35," 26 Mar 1964, Central Foreign Policy Files, box 1930.

51. AmConsul, Porto Alegre, "Weekly Summary no. 102," 31 Mar 1964, Central Foreign Policy Files, box 1930.

52. AmConsul, "Political Report of March 28–April 3," 16 Apr 1964, Central Foreign Policy Files, box 1930.

53. Benjamin H. Read, "Proposed Contingency Plan for Brazil," 8 Jan 1964, Central Foreign Policy Files, box 1943.

54. *FRUS, 1964–1968,* vol. 31, *South and Central America,* 427–28, 430, 435, 443. Also see "Advance Materials," 1 Apr 1964, NSF, NSC Meetings, box 1, LBJ Library.

55. Parker, *Brazil and the Quiet Intervention, 1964,* 61–62.

56. Walter LaFeber, "Thomas C. Mann and the Devolution of Latin American Policy: From the Good Neighbor to Military Intervention," in *Behind the Throne: Servants of Power to Imperial Presidents, 1898–1968,* ed. Thomas J. McCormick and Walter LaFeber (Madison: University of Wisconsin Press, 1993), 187; David F. Schmitz, *Thank God They're on Our Side: The United States and Right-Wing Dictatorships, 1921–1965* (Chapel Hill: University of North Carolina Press, 1999), 264–68.

57. Walters, *Silent Missions,* 383, 386; Dulles, *Castelo Branco,* 334. Also see Garfield, "From Ploughshares to Politics," 155.

58. Dulles, *Castelo Branco,* 340; Parker, *Brazil and the Quiet Intervention, 1964,* 65.

59. Dulles, *Castelo Branco,* 351.

60. *FRUS, 1964–1968,* vol. 31, *South and Central America,* 429.

61. As quoted in Ferreira, *João Goulart,* 484; Ibid., 471–72. Colonel Walters had a midnight meeting with Kruel, one of the last pro-Goulart generals, and reported that the commander had finally decided to support the opposition. See *FRUS, 1964–1968,* vol. 31, *South and Central America,* 425–26.

62. Department of State, "Circular to All ARA Diplomatic Posts," 2 Apr 1964, NSF, CF, box 10, LBJ Library; AmEmbassy Rio de Janeiro, 3 Apr 1964, Central Foreign Policy Files, box 1932; *FRUS, 1964–1968,* vol. 31, *South and Central America,* 450. For additional documents detailing last-minute US monitoring of the coup, see "Brazil Marks 40th Anniversary of Military Coup: Declassified Documents Shed Light on U.S. Role," National Security Archive, George Washington University, http://nsarchive.gwu.edu/NSAEBB/NSAEBB118/index.htm, accessed 17 Apr 2015.

63. Davis, *A Brotherhood of Arms,* 181.

64. George Philip, *The Military in South American Politics* (London: Croom Helm, 1985), 213.

65. AmEmbassy Brasília, "Goulart's Ouster and the Military Tradition in Brazil," 4 Apr 1964, Central Foreign Policy Files, box 1943, NARA.

66. "The United States did not participate in any way in this change," Vernon Walters wrote later. Former ambassador Gordon too denies "that the United States government took an active part in engendering or executing the coup d'etat." Walters, *Silent Missions,* 388; Gordon, *Brazil's Second Chance,* 60. Many historians disagree

with Gordon and Walters. See W. Michael Weis, *Cold Warriors & Coups d'État: Brazilian American Relations, 1945–1964* (Albuquerque: University of New Mexico Press, 1993), 5, 162; Stephen G. Rabe, *The Most Dangerous Area in the World: John F. Kennedy Confronts Communist Revolution in Latin America* (Chapel Hill: University of North Carolina Press, 2002), 63–71. "Never did one foreign ambassador determine so much in Brazil as this active and able Mr. Lincoln Gordon." Edmar Morel, *O golpe começou em Washington* (Rio de Janeiro: Editôra Civilização Brasileira, 1965), 208. Brazilian journalist Morel interpreted the coup as a conspiracy of the US embassy and foreign capital.

67. Plauto Mesquinta de Andrade, "1964: Jogo de cena e Guerra Fria," in *O jogo da verdade: Revolucão de 64, 30 anos depois,* ed. Nonato Guedes (João Pessoa, Brazil: A União, 1994), 57. As one Brazilian biographer wrote: "The possibility of resistance was nil, given the adhesion of the major contingents of the armed forces with the principal state governors, the national congress and the press." See Ferreira, *João Goulart,* 526. A more recent study agrees but adds the following caveat: "Nevertheless, the Washington policymakers still chose to intervene behind the scenes, pushing the outcome in their desired direction through a myriad of means." James N. Green, *We Cannot Remain Silent: Opposition to the Brazilian Military Dictatorship in the United States* (Durham, NC: Duke University Press, 2010), 46–47.

68. AmEmbassy, Weeka Report, 14 May 1964, Central Foreign Policy Files, box 1932, NARA.

69. *FRUS, 1964–1968,* vol. 31, *South and Central America,* 481.

70. AmEmbassy Rio de Janeiro to Sec. of State, 15 Jan 1966, Political and Defense, box 1611, NARA.

71. Herbert S. Okun, "Weekly Summaries no. 12–14," 2 May 1964, Central Foreign Policy Files, box 1930.

72. *FRUS, 1964–1968,* vol. 31, *South and Central America,* 460, 464; Defense Intelligence Agency to White House Situation Room, 2 Apr 1964, NSF, CF, box 10, LBJ Library.

73. "Organization of a Hard Line Group in the Army," 10 Dec 1964, Department of State, Political and Defense, box 1611, NARA.

74. "War Minister Sounds Strange Notes," 8 Apr 1965, Political and Defense, box 1611, NARA.

75. *New York Times,* 22 Nov 1965.

76. *New York Times,* 25 Nov 1965; AmConGen, Recife, "Weekly Summary," 29 Nov 1965, Central Foreign Policy Files, box 1927, NARA.

11. SOLDIERS AND REVOLUTION IN PERU

1. Lima to State, 28 Jun, 18 July 1962, 3:40 p.m., National Security Files (hereafter NSF), box 151, John F. Kennedy Presidential Library, Boston.

2. George Ball to AmEmbassy, 21 Jul 1962, NSF, box 151, Kennedy Library; Arnold Payne, *The Peruvian Coup d'État of 1962* (Washington, DC: Institute for the Comparative Study of Political Systems, 1968), 21, 23, 27.

3. Edwin M. Martin, *Kennedy and Latin America* (Lanham, MD: University Press of America, 1997), 348–50; Luis Ricardo Alonso F. to Miguel Angel Duque de Estrada, Lima, 24 May 1960, Fondo Argentina, Archivo del Ministerio de Relaciones Exteriores, Havana, Cuba (hereafter MINREX).

4. Luigi R. Einaudi, "Peruvian Military Relations with the United States," Rand Corporation, Jun 1970, in *Latin America: Special Studies, 1962–1980,* Paul Kesaris, ed. (Frederick, MD: University Publications of America, 1982), microfilm, 37–38.

5. Lima to State, 18 July 1962, 10:22 P.M., NSF, box 151, Kennedy Library.

6. Raúl Roa to Miguel Angel Cárcano, 7 Oct 1961, Fondo Perú, MINREX. On the embassy break-in by Frank Díaz Silveira of the Democratic Revolutionary Front (FRD) and four accomplices, see "Editorial—Communist Intervention," 18 Mar 1961, Jay Mallin Papers, box 2, Cuban Heritage Center, University of Miami.

7. Richard J. Walter, *Peru and the United States, 1960–1975* (University Park: Penn State University Press, 2010), 14, 24; Cynthia McClintock and Fabián Vallas, *The United States and Peru* (New York: Routledge, 2003), 21. On Prado's visit to the White House, see "Welcome to President Prado of Peru," 19 Sep 1961, Papers of John F. Kennedy, Presidential Papers, President's Office Files, Speech Files, Kennedy Library, http://www.jfklibrary.org/Asset-Viewer/Archives/JFKPOF-035-043.aspx, accessed 1 Dec 2011.

8. On the early civil-military relations, see Steve Stein, *Populism in Peru: The Emergence of the Masses and the Politics of Social Control* (Madison: University of Wisconsin Press, 1980); Peter F. Klaren, *Mobilization, Dislocation, and Aprismo: Origins of the Peruvian Aprista Party* (Austin: University of Texas Press, 1973).

9. AmEmbassy Lima, "Political Situation in Peru," 19 Apr 1962, NSF, box 151, Kennedy Library.

10. AmEmbassy Lima to State, 9 Jun 1962; Henderson to State, 19 Sep 1962, NSF, box 151A, Kennedy Library.

11. François Bourricaud, *Power and Society in Contemporary Peru,* trans. Paul Stevenson (New York: Praeger, 1970), 308; Daniel M. Masterson, *Militarism and Politics in Latin America: Peru from Sanchez Cerro to Sendero Luminoso* (New York: Greenwood Press, 1991), chap. 8.

12. Henderson to State, 2 Jan, 6 Jan, 28 Feb 1963, NSF, box 151, Kennedy Library.

13. Henderson to State, 8 Jan 1963, NSF, box 151, Kennedy Library.

14. Rusk to All ARA Diplomatic Posts, 10 Jan 1963; David W. Traub, "Mobile Training Team on Comptrollership for Peru," 9 Jul 1962, NSF box 151, Kennedy Library.

15. Héctor Béjar, *Peru 1965: Notes on a Guerrilla Experience,* trans. William Rose (New York: Monthly Review Press, 1970), 36–37.

16. Hugo Blanco, *Land or Death: The Peasant Struggle in Peru* (New York: Pathfinder Press, 1972), 29.

17. Ibid., 74.

18. Ibid., 30.

19. Richard Gott, *Guerrilla Movements in Latin America* (Garden City, NY: Doubleday, 1971), 239. Enrique Mayer also has a fine analysis of this stage of Blanco's movement. Mayer, *Ugly Stories of the Peruvian Agrarian Reform* (Durham, NC: Duke University Press, 2009), 47–50.

20. USCINCSO to Joint Chiefs, 28 Feb 1964, NSF, Country File (hereafter CF), box 16, Lyndon Baines Johnson Presidential Library, Austin, TX.

21. Hugo Neira, *Cuzco: Tierra y muerte* (Lima: Populibros Peruanos, 1964), 78.

22. Eduardo Fioravanti, *Latifundio y sindicalismo agrario en el Perú: El caso de los valles de la Convención y Laras* (Lima: Instituto de Estudios Peruanos, 1974), 18, 178–79, 201–3, 212, 214. Also see George D. E. Philip, *The Rise and Fall of the Peruvian Military Radicals, 1968–1976* (London: Athlone Press, 1978).

23. Masterson, *Militarism and Politics in Latin America,* 187–88; Luigi Einaudi, "U.S. Relations with the Peruvian Military," in *U.S. Foreign Policy and Peru,* ed. Daniel A. Sharp (Austin: University of Texas Press, 1972), 23.

24. Blanco, *Land or Death,* 34, 47.

25. Anon., *Las guerrillas en el Perú y su represión* (Lima: Ministerio de Guerra, 1966), 21.

26. Blanco, *Land or Death,* 57, 62, 66; Leon G. Campbell, "The Historiography of the Peruvian Guerrilla Movement, 1960–1965," *Latin American Historical Review* 8, no. 1 (Spring 1973): 45, 49.

27. Blanco, *Land or Death,* 69–70, 72.

28. Ibid., 11, 90; Anon., *Las guerrillas en el Perú y su represión;* Einaudi, "Peruvian Military Relations with the United States," 10.

29. As quoted in Masterson, *Militarism and Politics in Latin America,* 211.

30. Hilda Gadea, *Mi vida con el Che* (Lima: Arteidea Editores, 2005), 25–26; Jan Lust, *Lucha revolucionaria: Perú, 1958–1967* (Barcelona: RBA, 2013), 249, 277.

31. Gadea, *Mi vida con el Che,* 127–29; Michael F. Brown and Eduardo Fernández, *War of Shadows: The Struggle for Utopia in the Peruvian Amazon* (Berkeley: University of California Press, 1991), 89–91.

32. Lust, *Lucha revolucionaria,* 275–77; Gott, *Guerrilla Movements in Latin America,* 253, 256; Campbell, "The Historiography of the Peruvian Guerrilla Movement," 52; José Luis Rénique, "Del APRA rebelde a la lucha armada: Perú (1965)," in *Por el camino del Che: Las guerrillas latinoamericanas, 1959–1990,* ed. Pablo A. Pozzi and Claudio Pérez (Buenos Aires: Imago Mundi, 2011), 139.

33. Jon Lee Anderson, *Che Guevara, a Revolutionary Life* (New York: Grove Press, 1997), 560.

34. Roger Mercado, *Las guerrillas del Perú y la revolución de Trujillo* (Lima: Fondo de Cultura Popular, 1982), 55–60; Thomas C. Field Jr., *From Development to Dictatorship: Bolivia and the Alliance for Progress in the Kennedy Era* (Ithaca, NY: Cornell University Press, 2014), 73.

35. Lust, *Lucha revolucionaria*, 189–92, 301–2.

36. Richard Helms, "Activities of Cuban-Trained Peruvian Guerrillas," 11 Apr, 14 May 1963, NSF, box 51, Kennedy Library.

37. CIA, "Decision by the MIR to Begin Preparations for Revolution," 11 Feb 1964; "Plans of the MIR for Revolutionary Action," 12 Feb 1964, in *C.I.A. Research Reports: Latin America, 1946–1976* (Frederick, MD: University Publications of America, 1982), microfilm; Lust, *Lucha revolucionaria*, 281. Also see Rénique, "Del APRA rebelde," 142.

38. Philip Agee, *Inside the Company: CIA Diary* (New York: Stonehill, 1975), 268, 313, 440.

39. Richard Helms, "Activities of Cuban-Trained Peruvian Guerrillas," 11 Apr 1963, NSF, box 51, Kennedy Library.

40. Helms, "Activities of Cuban-Trained Peruvian Guerrillas," 14 May 1963, NSF, box 51; Thomas L. Hughes, "Cuban-Trained Peruvians Captured," 10 Jun 1963, NSF, box 50; AmEmbassy Lima to State, 1 Jun 1963, NSF, box 151, Kennedy Library; Lust, *Lucha revolucionaria*, 277.

41. Hughes, "Peru's New Administration and Reform Prospects," 11 Jul 1963, NSF, box 151, Kennedy Library.

42. On the IPC in Peru, see Jonathan C. Brown, "Jersey Standard and the Politics of Latin American Oil Production, 1911–1930," in *Latin American Oil Companies and the Politics of Energy*, ed. John D. Wirth (Lincoln: University of Nebraska Press, 1985), 1–50; A. J. Pinelo, *The Multinational Corporation as a Force in Latin American Politics: A Case Study of the International Petroleum Company in Peru* (New York: Praeger, 1968); George Philip, *Oil and Politics in Latin America: Nationalist Movements and State Oil Companies* (Cambridge: Cambridge University Press, 1982).

43. Walter, *Peru and the United States*, 34, 36, 65; McClintock and Vallas, *The United States and Peru*, 22–23.

44. Jones to State, 12 Sep 1963, NSF, box 151, Kennedy Library.

45. Sherman Kent, "Prospects in Peru," 29 Jul 1965, NSF, CF, box 72, LBJ Library.

46. As quoted from the November 1965 issue of the *Monthly Review* in Gott, *Guerrilla Movements in Latin America*, 261.

47. Ibid., 263–64.

48. As quoted in Cecil Johnson, *Communist China & Latin America, 1959–1967* (New York: Columbia University Press, 1970), 123; Lust, *Lucha revolucionaria,* 267–68.

49. Héctar Béjar, *Perú: Apuntes sobre una experiencia guerrillera* (Havana: Casa de las Américas, 1979), 69.

50. Ibid., 96.

51. "More Than 800 Peruvians Trained in Bloc Countries," 6 Dec 1964, NSC, CF, box 4, LBJ Library; Mercado, *Las guerrillas del Perú,* 136–37.

52. Brown and Fernández, *War of Shadows,* 100–103.

53. See Steve J. Stern, "The Age of Andean Insurrections, 1742–1782: A Reappraisal," in *Resistance, Rebellion, and Consciousness in the Andean Peasant World, 18th to 20th Centuries,* ed. Steve J. Stern (Madison: University of Wisconsin Press, 1987), 34–92; Brown and Fernández, *War of Shadows,* 99.

54. Brown and Fernández, *War of Shadows,* 97.

55. Jean Lartéguy, *The Guerrillas* (New York: New American Library, 1972), 209.

56. Allan Evans to State Department, n.d., NSF, CF, box 72, LBJ Library; "Peru: Guerrilla Activities," 28 Jun, 30 Jun, 1 Jul 1965, box 6; 19 Nov 1965, box 7, Record Group 263, Records of the Central Intelligence Agency, Press Information relating to Insurgency and Counterinsurgency: Latin America, Entry (A) 64, National Archives and Records Administration, College Park, MD (hereafter CIA Press Information).

57. Brown and Fernández, *War of Shadows,* 105.

58. "El Guerrillero Reviews Three Months of Struggle," 8 Nov 1965, box 7, CIA Press Information.

59. Artola Azcárate, *¡Subversión!* (Lima: Editorial Jurídica, 1976), 93, 96.

60. Lartéguy, *The Guerrillas,* 210–11; Masterson, *Militarism and Politics in Latin America,* 215.

61. Einaudi, "Peruvian Military Relations with the United States," 5.

62. Bourricaud, *Power and Society in Contemporary Peru,* 314. Even within the military one could find reception for the anti-oligarchic thought nurtured by Peruvian intellectuals. See Stephan M. Gorman, "The Intellectual Foundations of Revolution in Peru: The Anti-Oligarchic Tradition," in *Post-Revolutionary Peru: The Politics of Transformation,* ed. Stephan M. Gorman (Boulder, CO: Westview Press, 1982), 214–16; Philip, *Peruvian Military Radicals,* 42–43; Julio Cotler, "A Structural-Historical Approach to the Breakdown of Democratic Institutions: Peru," in *The Breakdown of Democratic Regimes: Latin America,* ed. Juan J. Linz and Alfred Stepan (Baltimore: Johns Hopkins University Press, 1978), 193.

63. Timothy P. Wickham-Crowley, *Guerrillas and Revolution in Latin America: A Comparative Study of Insurgents and Regimes since 1956* (Princeton, NJ: Princeton University Press, 1992), 67–68.

64. Sonny B. Davis, *A Brotherhood of Arms: Brazil-United States Military Relations, 1945–1977* (Niwot: University Press of Colorado, 1996), 170–71.

65. Joint Chiefs of Staff, "Status of Military Counterinsurgency Programs," NSF, Departments, box 280, Kennedy Library; Masterson, *Militarism and Politics in Latin America,* 159, 163, 204, 212–13, 217, 234; Einaudi, "U.S. Relations with the Peruvian Military," 45.

66. "Peru: Insurgency and Counterinsurgency," 28 Jul, 3 Aug, 17 Aug 1965, box 6, CIA Press Information.

67. "Peru: Insurgency and Counterinsurgency," 25 Jul 1965, box 6, CIA Press Information.

68. Walter, *Peru and the United States,* 75, 77.

69. "Insurgency and Counterinsurgency," 8, 18, 21 Oct 1965, box 7, CIA Press Information.

70. "Insurgency and Counterinsurgency," 27 Oct, 5 Nov 1965, box 7, CIA Press Information.

71. "Insurgency and Counterinsurgency," 24 Nov 1965, 7 Feb 1966, box 7, CIA Press Information; Campbell, "The Historiography of the Peruvian Guerrilla Movement," 54; Wickham-Crowley, *Guerrillas and Revolution in Latin America,* 8. In Peru, 70 percent of the MIR leadership had urban and middle-class backgrounds. See Lust, *Lucha revolucionaria,* 252.

72. Béjar, *Perú 1965,* 80; Artola Azcárate, *¡Subversión!,* 84; *Las guerrillas en el Perú y su represión,* 17; Wickham-Crowley, *Guerrillas and Revolution in Latin America,* 116, 137; Mercado, *Las guerrillas del Perú,* 167; Masterson, *Militarism and Politics in Latin America,* 215–16.

73. Béjar, *Perú 1965,* 82–85.

74. Anon., *Las guerrillas en el Perú y su represión,* 66–67; Lartéguy, *The Guerrillas,* 212. The local chief was identified as Rubén Tupayachi.

75. "Peru: Insurgency and Counterinsurgency," 26 Aug, 27 Aug 1965, box 6, CIA Press Information.

76. Brown and Fernández, *War of Shadows,* 114, 127; "Insurgency and Counterinsurgency," 23 Jul 1965, box 6, CIA Press Information; Artola Azcárate, *¡Subversión!,* 66.

77. "Insurgency and Counterinsurgency," 18 Oct 1965, box 7, CIA Press Information.

78. Artola Azcárate, *¡Subversión!,* 67–71.

79. "Insurgency and Counterinsurgency," 24 Nov 1965, box 7, CIA Press Information.

80. Anon., *La guerra de guerrilleros y su repression,* 62.

81. Artola Azcárate, *¡Subversión!,* 72–79.

82. "Insurgency and Counterinsurgency," 4, 6, 25 Jan, 7 Feb 1966, box 7, CIA Press Information.

83. Anon., *La guerra de guerrilleros y su repression,* 64; Lust, *Lucha revolucionaria,* 351; Gott, *Guerrilla Movements in Latin America,* 272.

84. "Insurgency and Counterinsurgency," 11 Oct, 27 Oct 1965, box 7, CIA Press Information.

85. "Insurgency and Counterinsurgency," 17 Feb 1966, box 7, CIA Press Information; W. G. Bowdler, "Guerrilla Problems in Latin America," 5 Jul 1967, NSF, Intelligence File, box 2, LBJ Library.

86. Artola Azcárate, *¡Subversión!,* 51, 64–65.

87. Ibid., 70, 71, 76, 49; Anon., *La guerra de guerrilleros y su repression,* 63.

88. Béjar, *Peru 1965,* 100; Just, *Lucha revolucionaria,* 224; Anon., *Las guerrillas en el Perú y su represión,* 68.

89. Anon., *Las guerrillas en el Perú y su represión,* 69.

90. Béjar, *Peru 1965,* 107–9.

91. Anon., *Las guerrillas en el Perú y su represión,* 70; Gott, *Guerrilla Movements in Latin America,* 283.

92. "Insurgency and Counterinsurgency," 17 Feb 1966; Campbell, "The Historiography of the Peruvian Guerrilla Movement," 57.

93. Lartéguy, *The Guerrillas,* 211.

94. Walter, *Peru and the United States,* 71–72; Gott, *Guerrilla Movements in Latin America,* 271.

95. Paulo Drino, "Awaiting the Blood of a Truly Emancipating Revolution: Che Guevara in 1950s Peru," in *Che's Travels: The Making of a Revolutionary in 1950s Latin America,* ed. Paulo Drinot (Durham, NC: Duke University Press, 2010), 116.

96. Régis Debray, *Revolution in the Revolution? Armed Struggle and Political Struggle in Latin America,* trans. Bobbye Ortiz (New York: Grove Press, 1967), 59, 62.

97. Anon., *Las guerrillas en el Perú y su represión,* 70.

98. Ibid., 80–81.

99. Ibid., 106–92.

100. Cotler, "A Structural-Historical Approach," 200.

101. See Brown, "Jersey Standard," 1–50; Jonathan C. Brown, "British Petroleum Pioneers in Mexico and South America," Texas Papers on Latin America, no. 89-17 (1989), Netti Lee Benson Library, University of Texas at Austin.

102. "Lincoln Gordon Transcript," Baltimore (10 July 1969), 88–89, Oral History Collection, LBJ Library.

103. J. Wesley Jones to President, 13 Nov 1967, NSF, CF, box 73, LBJ Library.

104. Walter, *Peru and the United States,* 92, 102, 104, 140; McClintock and Vallas, *The United States and Peru,* 25.

105. CIA, "Economic Implications of Peru's Expropriation of U.S. Oil Properties," Oct 1968; CIA, "Peru's Expropriation of U.S. Oil Properties: Background

and Possible Consequences," 2 Nov 1968, NSF, CF, box 73, LBJ Library. Besides the unpopular agreement with the IPC, two other reasons for the coup suggest themselves. One had to do with predictions of a victory in the 1969 presidential elections for Víctor Raúl Haya de la Torre of the APRA. The second concerned an impending congressional investigation of a smuggling operation conducted by the top commanders of the armed forces. However, neither of these explains the leftist tendencies of the first military junta under General Velasco. See Richard Lee Clinton, "The Modernizing Military: The Case of Peru," *Inter-American Economic Affairs* 24 (Spring 1971): 45–46; Philip, *Peruvian Military Radicals,* 69–71.

106. Richard Goodwin, "Letter from Peru," *New Yorker,* 17 May 1969, 99–100. Also see Einaudi, "U.S. Relations with the Peruvian Military," 22.

107. "Speech by Juan Velasco Alvarado, 1968," in *The Politics of Antipolitics: The Military in Latin America,* 2nd ed., ed. Brian Loveman and Thomas M. Davies Jr. (Lincoln: University of Nebraska Press, 1989), 254; Campbell, "The Historiography of the Peruvian Guerrilla Movement," 46.

108. Josh DeWind, "Continuing to Be Peasants: Union Militancy among Peruvian Miners," in *Workers' Control in Latin America, 1930–1979,* ed. Jonathan C. Brown (Chapel Hill: University of North Carolina Press, 1997), 244–69; McClintock and Vallas, *The United States and Peru,* 27.

109. Einaudi, "U.S. Relations with the Peruvian Military"; Campbell, "The Historiography of the Peruvian Guerrilla Movement," 63.

110. Peter Camejo, introduction to Blanco, *Land or Death,* 15–18; Campbell, "The Historiography of the Peruvian Guerrilla Movement," 59.

111. McClintock and Vallas, *The United States and Peru,* 28.

112. Masterson, *Militarism and Politics in Latin America,* 250, 252. Also see Philip, *Peruvian Military Radicals.* On SINAMOS, see Henry A. Dietz, *Poverty and Problem-Solving under Military Rule: The Urban Poor in Lima, Peru* (Austin: University of Texas Press, 1980), chap. 8. On the military coup of 1968, see Masterson, *Militarism and Politics in Latin America,* 219–34. Said one army colonel, "The central, profound, permanent and substantive goal of the [military] government was raising mass living standards" (231).

113. Dietz, *Poverty and Problem-Solving under Military Rule,* 23, 28.

114. "Acta declarativa de la reanudación de relaciones diplomáticas entre la república de Cuba y el Perú," Lima, 8 Jul 1972, Fondo Perú, MINREX.

12. FROM RIOTS TO *GOLPE* IN PANAMA

1. "Interpreter's Notes of a Conversation Which Took Place by Telephone between President Johnson and President Chiari on January 10, 1964," National Security Files (hereafter NSF), Country Files (hereafter CF), box 67, Lyndon Baines Johnson Presidential Library, Austin, TX.

2. David Howarth, *Panama: Four Hundred Years of Dreams and Cruelty* (New York: McGraw-Hill, 1966), 215.

3. Ibid., chap. 9; Noel Maurer and Carlos Yu, *The Big Ditch: How America Took, Built, Ran, and Ultimately Gave Away the Panama Canal* (Princeton, NJ: Princeton University Press, 2011), chap. 3.

4. John Weeks and Phil Gunson, *Panama: Made in the United States* (London: Latin America Bureau, 1991), 34–35.

5. Ibid., 26.

6. The following came from my own experience working and living at Fort Amador as an army lieutenant from 1968 to 1970. Also see John and Mavis Biesanz, *The People of Panama* (New York: Columbia University Press, 1955), 231, 234, 376. An international commission of jurists investigating the 1964 flag riots noted the intense "resentment" built up over the decades between Panamanians and Zonians, living divergent ways of life in such close proximity. See Alan McPherson, "Courts of World Opinion: Trying the Panama Flag Riots of 1964," *Diplomatic History* 28, no. 1 (Jan 2004): 108.

7. Michael E. Donoghue, *Borderland on the Isthmus: Race, Culture, and the Struggle for the Canal Zone* (Durham, NC: Duke University Press, 2014), 69–73.

8. Herbert and Mary Knapp, *Red, White, and Blue Paradise: The American Canal Zone in Panama* (New York: Harcourt Brace Jovanovich, 1984), 47, 207; Alan McPherson, *Yankee No! Anti-Americanism in U.S.-Latin American Relations* (Cambridge, MA: Harvard University Press, 2003), 89.

9. Biesanz and Biesanz, *The People of Panama*, 68, 81, 92; Michael L. Conniff, *Black Labor on a White Canal: Panama, 1904–1981* (Pittsburgh: University of Pittsburgh Press, 1985), 110, 118, 122.

10. Donoghue, *Borderland on the Isthmus*, 17–18.

11. Gordon H. Scherer to the President, 16 Nov 1959, Whiteman Files, Panama, Government and Embassy, box 884, Dwight D. Eisenhower Presidential Library, Abilene, KS. Also see McPherson, *Yankee No!*, 91; McPherson, "Courts of World Opinion," 90.

12. Francis E. Dorn to the President, 13 Jan 1960, Whitman Files, Panama, Government and Embassy, box 884, Eisenhower Library.

13. Paul B. Ryan, *The Panama Canal Controversy: U.S. Diplomacy and Defense Interests* (Stanford, CA: Hoover Institution Press, 1977), 42.

14. Milton Eisenhower, *The Wine Is Bitter* (Garden City, NY: Doubleday, 1963), 222.

15. Ryan, *The Panama Canal Controversy*, 43; Robert C. Harding II, *Military Foundations of Panamanian Politics* (New Brunswick, NJ: Transaction, 2001), 44; McPherson, "Courts of World Opinion," 90–91.

16. *Foreign Relations of the United States, 1958–1960*, vol. 5, *American Republics* (Washington, DC: US Government Printing Office, 1991), 910.

17. Knapp and Knapp, *Red, White, and Blue Paradise,* 258.

18. "Chronology of Events relating to Flag Controversy," n.d.; "Panamanian Situation Report for the President of the United States," 10 Jan 1964, in *Crisis in Panama and the Dominican Republic: National Security Files and NSC Histories,* ed. Paul Kesaris (Frederick, MD: University Publications of America, 1982), microfilm. Also see Maurer and Yu, *The Big Ditch,* 236–38.

19. Biesanz and Biesanz, *The People of Panama,* 340.

20. "United States–Panamanian Relations," 12 Jun 1962, NFS, box 149A, John F. Kennedy Presidential Library, Boston; Edwin McCammon Martin, *Kennedy and Latin America* (Lanham, MD: University Press of America, 1994), 141–48, 150. Martin was a White House staffer and specialist on Latin America. He mentioned that his colleagues in the Kennedy administration "felt strongly that any concession on treaty revision ought to be given to a President whose qualities as a leader were superior to those of Chiari."

21. Martin, *Kennedy and Latin America,* 141, 144.

22. Dept. of State, "US-Panamanian Conversations in Panama," 8 Nov 1962, NSF box 150, Kennedy Library. The sea-level study that American negotiators thereafter used to pressure the Panamanians ultimately ended in 1978 with a conclusion that the dangers of nuclear excavations far outweighed any cost savings. John Lindsay-Poland, *Emperors in the Jungle: The Hidden History of the U.S. in Panama* (Durham, NC: Duke University Press, 2003), 87, 96.

23. "Panamá, informe especial sobre el rompimiento de relaciones con Cuba," n.d., Fondo Panamá, Archivo Histórico del Ministerio de Relaciones Exteriores, Havana (hereafter MINREX).

24. Roberto F. Chiari to John F. Kennedy, 22 Feb 1963; William H. Brubeck to McGeorge Bundy, 2 Mar 1963, NSF, box 150, Kennedy Library; Ryan, *The Panama Canal Controversy,* 80–81; Harding, *Military Foundations of Panamanian Politics,* 111; Walter LaFeber, "Latin American Policy," in *The Johnson Years: Foreign Policy, the Great Society, and the White House,* ed. Robert A. Divine (Lawrence: University Press of Kansas, 1987), 69.

25. CIA, "Cuban Proposal to the Partido del Pueblo," 17 Dec 1962, NSF, box 52, Kennedy Library.

26. CIA, "Communist Estimate of the Political Situation in Panama," 10 May 1962, NFS, box 149A, Kennedy Library.

27. "Comite de la Defensa de la Revolución Cubana," 14 Dec 1959, Fondo Panamá, MINREX.

28. "Esta agrupación de nueva creación," 28 Jun 1961, Fondo Panamá, MINREX.

29. Farland, "Panama Uprising," 26 Aug 1962, NSF, box 149A, Kennedy Library.

30. CIA, "Vanguardia de Acción Nacional," 24 Jun 1963, NSF, box 44, Kennedy Library.

31. CIA, "Statements of Panamanian Revolutionary," 3 Oct 1963, NSF, box 53; "Attempt to Export Molotov Cocktails," 26 Oct 1963, NSF, box 150A, Kennedy Library.

32. Stuart, "IAPA Monthly Report for August 1963," 13 Sep 1963, NSF, box 150A, Kennedy Library; Charles W. Adair Jr., "Annual Politico-Economic Assessment," 4 Jun 1965, NSF, CF, box 67, LBJ Library; Philip Agee, *Inside the Company: CIA Diary* (New York: Stonehill, 1975), 262.

33. Major General Robert Fleming Jr. was the governor at the time. For descriptions of these events, see "Panamanian Situation Report for the President of the United Sates," 10 Jan 1964; Calileo Solís to Dean Rusk, 10 Jan 1964; "Background and Chronology of the Events in Panama and the Canal Zone on the Ninth, Tenth, and Subsequent Days in January 1964," in Kesaris, *Crisis in Panama and the Dominican Republic;* William J. Jorden, *Panama Odyssey* (Austin: University of Texas Press, 1984), chap. 3. Also see McPherson, "Courts of World Opinion," 86–88; McPherson, *Yankee No!,* 88; Harding, *Military Foundations of Panamanian Politics,* 48–49.

34. *Foreign Relations of the United States, 1964–1968,* vol. 31, *South and Central America; Mexico* (Washington, DC: US Government Printing Office, 2004) (hereafter *FRUS, 1964–1968,* vol. 31, *South and Central America*), 771. McPherson, *Yankee No!,* 97–98; Jorden, *Panama Odyssey,* 63.

35. Calileo Solís to Dean Rusk, 10 Jan 1964, in Kesaris, *Crisis in Panama and the Dominican Republic.*

36. H. W. Brands, *The Wages of Globalism: Lyndon Johnson and the Limits of American Power* (New York: Oxford University Press, 1995), 33; McPherson, *Yankee No!,* 97.

37. *FRUS, 1964–1968,* vol. 31, *South and Central America,* 788.

38. Ibid., 794.

39. Ibid., 784.

40. Lyndon Baines Johnson, *The Vantage Point: Perspectives of the Presidency, 1963–1969* (New York: Holt, Rinehart and Winston, 1971), 180–82; Brands, *The Wages of Globalism,* 39.

41. "U.S. Southern Command After-Action Report of Panama Disorders," 9–16 Jan 1964, NSF, CF, box 63, LBJ Library.

42. Office of Special Investigations, US Air Force, "Special Report: Panama—an Analysis of Castro / Communist Subversive Activity," Feb 1964, NSF, box 65, LBJ Library.

43. *FRUS, 1964–1968,* vol. 31, *South and Central America,* 776–77.

44. Ibid., 796, 798, 808; McPherson, *Yankee, No!,* 84.

45. *FRUS, 1964–1968,* vol. 31, *South and Central America,* 810.

46. Ibid., 827.

47. Ibid., 833.

48. Ibid., 836.

49. *Rabiblanco* refers to the "white-tailed" songbird of Panama and also to the oligarchic families that proudly traced their racial heritage to European ancestry. Ibid., 839; R. M. Koster and Guillermo Sánchez Borbón, *In the Time of the Tyrants, Panama: 1968–1990* (New York: W. W. Norton, 1990), 59.

50. AmEmbassy Panama to Sec. of State, 8 Dec 1964, NSF, CF, box 67, LBJ Library. On Robles, see McPherson, *Yankee No!,* 111.

51. LaFeber, "Latin American Policy," 70–71.

52. CIA, "Revolutionary Plotting of Arnulfo Arias Madrid," 23 Jan 1965, NSF, CF, box 67, LBJ Library.

53. CIA, "Communist Control of Panamanian Student Groups," 18 Jul 1966, NSF, CF, box 67, LBJ Library.

54. Koster and Sánchez Borbón, *In the Time of the Tyrants,* 60–63.

55. US Southern Command to US Embassy Panama, 23 Sep 1965, NSF, CF, box 67, LBJ Library.

56. CIA, "Revolutionary Plotting of the Panamanian Nationalist Union," 22 Sep 1965, NSF, CF, box 67, LBJ Library.

57. Ibid.; CIA, "MUR's Plans to Picket the Foreign Ministry and the American Embassy," 7 May 1965, NSF, CF, box 67, LBJ Library.

58. CIA, "Communist Control of Panamanian Student Groups," 18 Jul 1966, NSF, CF, box 67, LBJ Library.

59. W. W. Rostow, "Where We Stand on Panama," 1 Jul 1966, NSF, CF, box 67, LBJ Library.

60. The latter expenditure amounted to only 7.1 percent of Panama's national budget, a low figure by Latin American standards. By comparison, Argentina's military budget comprised 15 percent of its national budget. "Country Analysis, Panama," pp. 70–391, in Organization of the Joint Chiefs of Staff, The Military Establishment in Latin America, Aug 1969, NSC Institutional ("H") Files, Policy Papers (1969–1974), National Security Decision Memorandums, box H-159, Richard Millhouse Nixon Presidential Library, Yorba Linda, CA; *Nuestra revolución: Discursos fundamentales del Omar Torrijos Herrera* (Panama City: Ministerio de Relaciones Exteriores, 1974), 24.

61. Mark Atwood Lawrence, *The Vietnam War* (Oxford: Oxford University Press, 2010), 109–10, 121–22.

62. *FRUS, 1964–1968,* vol. 31, *South and Central America,* 925–28.

63. Ibid., 929–31.

64. Ibid. Also see John Major, *Prize Possession: The United States and the Panama Canal, 1903–1979* (Cambridge: Cambridge University Press, 1993), 339–40.

65. *FRUS, 1964–1968,* vol. 31, *South and Central America,* 933.

66. Ibid., 934–35, 937–39; Jorden, *Panama Odyssey,* 118–19.

67. *FRUS, 1964–1968,* vol. 31, *South and Central America,* 941–42.

68. Ibid., 943–44.

69. Adair, "Minotto-Vallarino Conversation," 20 May 1968; AmEmbassy Panama to Secstate, 18 Jul 1968, NSF, CF, box 69, LBJ Library.

70. Adair to Sec. of State, 30 Sep 1968, NSF, CF, box 69, LBJ Library.

71. Adair to Sec. of State, 9 Oct 1968, NSF, CF, box 6, LBJ Library.

72. Rusk to AmEmbassy Panama, 10 Oct 1968, NSF, CF, box 6, LBJ Library.

73. Jorden, *Panama Odyssey,* 134.

74. AmEmbassy Panama to Sec. of State, 12 Oct 1968, NSF, CF, box 69, LBJ Library; Juan Materno Vázquez, *Omar Torrijos* (Panama City: Ediciones Olga Elena, 1987), 56–57; Frederick Kempe, *Divorcing the Dictator: America's Bungled Affair with Noriega* (New York: G. P. Putnam's Sons, 1990), 62–64; Steven C. Ropp, *Panamanian Politics: From Guarded Nation to National Guard* (Stanford, CA: Hoover Institution Press, 1982), 36–37.

75. "Actions and Decisions of the Department of State in the Panama Crisis of October–November 1968," White House Central Files, Subject Files, box 69, Nixon Library.

76. Adair to Sec. of State, 13, 14, 15 Oct 1968, NSF, CF, box 6, LBJ Library.

77. Jorden, *Panama Odyssey,* 138.

78. *FRUS, 1964–1968,* vol. 31, *South and Central America,* 953.

79. Graham Greene, *Getting to Know the General: A Story of an Involvement* (New York: Simon & Schuster, 1984), 71.

80. "Actions and Decisions of the Department of State in the Panama Crisis of October–November 1968."

81. *FRUS, 1964–1968,* vol. 31, *South and Central America,* 956–57.

82. Adair to Sec. of State, 8 Nov 1968, NSF, CF, box 69, LBJ Library.

83. *FRUS, 1964–1968,* vol. 31, *South and Central America,* 960; Rusk to AmEmbassy Panama, 5 Nov 1968, NSF, CF, box 69, LBJ Library; "Actions and Decisions of the Department of State in the Panama Crisis of October–November 1968."

84. *FRUS, 1964–1968,* vol. 31, *South and Central America,* 958–59.

85. Manuel Noriega and Peter Eisner, *The Memoirs of Manuel Noriega: America's Prisoner* (New York: Random House, 1997), 36–37; Carlos Guevara Mann, *Panamanian Militarism: A Historical Interpretation* (Athens: Ohio University Center for International Studies, 1996), 108; Ropp, *Panamanian Politics,* 48–49.

86. "Biographical Data: Col Amado Silvio SANJUR Atencio," Jul 1969, White House Special Files, White House Central Files (hereafter WHCF), Subject Files, TS Files, 1969–1974, Nixon Library.

87. "Biographical Data: Col Ramiro SILVERA," Jul 1969, White House Special Files, WHCF, Subject Files, TS Files, 1969–1974, Nixon Library.

88. Kempe, *Divorcing the Dictator,* 66–70.

89. See Michael L. Conniff, *Panama and the United States: The End of the Alliance,* 3rd ed. (Athens: University of Georgia Press, 2012), 126–27; Harding, *Military Foundations of Panamanian Politics,* 86–87.

90. Seymour M. Hersh, "Our Man in Panama," *Life* magazine, Mar 1990, 83, 85.

91. Ibid., 85; Noriega and Eisner, *The Memoirs of Manuel Noriega*, 37, 43; Guevara Mann, *Panamanian Militarism*, 109.

92. Noriega and Eisner, *The Memoirs of Manuel Noriega*, 52.

93. Georgie Anne Geyer, *The New Latins* (Garden City, NY: Doubleday, 1970), 266, as quoted in Ropp, *Panamanian Politics*, 49.

94. Robert W. Porter to Nelson Rockefeller, 16 Feb 1970, NSC Institutional ("H") Files, Policy Papers (1969–1974), National Security Decision Memorandums, box H-158, Nixon Library.

95. Ibid.

96. "Comments on Possible 1970 Elections," 2 Oct 1969, White House Special Files, SHCF, Subject Files, TS Files, 1969–1974, Nixon Library.

97. CIA, "Ambassador-Designate to the United States: José DE LA OSSA," 7 Jul 1970, NSC Files, Country Files—Latin America, boxes 768–799, Nixon Library.

98. "Colonels in Canal Zone"; "Panama City Radio MIA Network," 8 Jun 1970, NSC Files, Country Files—Latin America, boxes 768–799, Nixon Library.

99. CIA, "Panama One Year after the Coup," 10 Oct 1969; CIA, Central Intelligence Bulletin, Aug 15, 1970, NSC Files, Country Files—Latin America, boxes 768–799, Nixon Library. Also see Jeanne W. Davis, "Panama Canal: NSSM 86," 27 Jan 1970, NSC Institutional ("H") Files, Policy Papers (1969–1974), National Security Decision Memorandums, box H-169, Nixon Library.

100. *Nuestra revolución*, 35. Also see Guevara Mann, *Panamanian Militarism*, 111, 122.

101. Guevara Mann, *Panamanian Militarism*, 145–48; Koster and Sánchez Borbón, *In the Time of the Tyrants*, 127; Ropp, *Panamanian Politics*, 46.

102. Harding, *Military Foundations of Panamanian Politics*, 89.

103. Ibid., 93; Guevara Mann, *Panamanian Militarism*, 118–19.

104. Greene, *Getting to Know the General*, 37.

105. Sharon Phillipps Collazos, *Labor and Politics in Panama: The Torrijos Years* (Boulder, CO: Westview Press, 1991); Harding, *Military Foundations of Panamanian Politics*, 96–97, 104; Conniff, *Panama and the United States*, 129.

106. Conniff, *Black Labor on a White Canal*, 150, 165–66.

107. Guevara Mann, *Panamanian Militarism*, 103.

108. While a Fulbright-Hayes student in Buenos Aires, the author witnessed the Torrijos visit firsthand.

109. *Nuestra revolución*, 169.

110. "Síntesis cronológica de los principales momentos de las relaciones bilaterales Cuba-Panamá después de 1959," Fondo Panamá, MINREX; Guevara Mann, *Panamanian Militarism*, 118–19.

111. "Informe de la delegación a los actos conmemorativos del XX anniversario del asalto al cuartel Moncada en Panamá," 18–27 Jul 1973, Fondo Panamá, MINREX.

112. Banco Nacional de Panamá, *Invest in Panama* (Panama City: n.p., 1979), 44. Also see Banco Nacional de Panamá, *Investment Opportunities in Panama* (Panama City: n.p., 1973); Ropp, *Panamanian Politics,* 111.

113. "Panama Treaty Negotiations," 29 Mar 1971, NSC Institutional ("H") Files, Policy Papers (1969–1974), National Security Decision Memorandums, box H-216, Nixon Library.

114. Richard Nixon Presidential Library.

115. Greene, *Getting to Know the General,* 37.

116. Ryan, *The Panama Canal Controversy,* 74–75.

117. José de Jesús Martínez, *Mi general Torrijos* (Managua: Editorial Nueva Nicaragua, 1987), 225.

13. ORIGINS OF ARGENTINA'S ARMED STRUGGLE

1. As quoted by Ernesto Salas, *Uturuncos: El orígen de la guerrilla peronista* (Buenos Aires: Editorial Biblos, 2003), 69.

2. Joel Horowitz, "Occupational Community and the Creation of a Self-Styled Elite: Railroad Workers in Argentina," *The Americas,* July 1985, 55–81.

3. Roberto Baschetti, ed., *Documentos de la resistencia peronista, 1955–1970* (Buenos Aires: Editorial De la Campana, 1997), 172.

4. Salas, *Uturuncos,* 76–79.

5. Ibid., 42, 44.

6. Ibid., 45; Paul H. Lewis, *Guerrillas and Generals: The "Dirty War" in Argentina* (Westport, CT: Praeger, 2002), 12. Also see Rosendo Fraga, *El ejército y Frondizi, 1958–1962* (Buenos Aires: Editorial Emecé, 1992), 138–41.

7. "Posición de Argentina frente al Imperialismo," n.d. [ca. 1961], Fondo Argentina, Archivo del Ministerio de Relaciones Exteriores, Havana, Cuba (hereafter MINREX); Mariano Ben Plotkin, *Freud en las pampas: Orígenes y desarrollo de una cultura psicoanalítica en la Argentina (1910–1983)* (Buenos Aires: Editorial Sudamericana, 2003), 261, 293.

8. See especially Federico Finchelstein, *The Ideological Origins of the Dirty War: Fascism, Populism, and Dictatorship in Twentieth Century Argentina* (New York: Oxford University Press, 2014).

9. "While the growing attraction of the guerrilla strategy was significant," writes Daniel James, "it had only a minor impact on most of the militants of the Peronist Resistance at this time." See Daniel James, *Resistance and Accommodation: Peronism and the Argentine Working Class, 1946–1976* (Cambridge: Cambridge University Press,

1988), 147–50; Valeria Manzano, *The Age of Youth in Argentina: Culture, Politics, and Sexuality from Perón to Videla* (Chapel Hill: University of North Carolina Press, 2014), 159.

10. Norberto Galasso, *Cooke: De Perón al Che; Una biografía política* (Rosario, Argentina: Homo Sapiens Ediciones, 1997), 7–18, 89–93; Silvia Sigal and Eliseo Verón, *Perón o muerte: Los fundamentos discursivos del fenómeno peronista* (Buenos Aires: Editorial Legasa, 1980), 101; Alain Rouquié, *Radicales y Desarrollistas en Argentina* (Buenos Aires: Schapire Editor, 1975), 96.

11. John William Cooke, *Obras completas,* ed. Eduardo L. Duhalde, vol. 2, *Correspondencia Perón-Cooke* (Buenos Aires: Colihue, 2007), 122, 126, 131.

12. Galasso, *Cooke: De Perón al Che,* 121.

13. Cooke, *Correspondencia Perón-Cooke,* 460–61.

14. Ibid., 462.

15. Ibid., 125.

16. Ibid., 456, 483.

17. Ciro Bustos, *El Che quiere verte: La historia jamás contada del Che en Bolivia* (Buenos Aires: Javier Vergara Editores), 53.

18. Cooke, *Correspondencia Perón-Cooke,* 532, 621. But see *Cooke, de vuelta: El gran descartado de la historia argentina,* comp. Miguel Masseo (Buenos Aires: Ediciones de la Rosa Blindada, 1999), 570. Perón's definitive refusal came in 1965.

19. Other Argentines identified as receiving training in Cuba include María Josefa de Mastroberti, Osaías León Schujman, and Jorge Francisco Timossi of Prensa Latina in Buenos Aires. CIA, "Cuban Training of Latin American Subversives," 27 Mar 1963, in *C.I.A. Research Reports: Latin America, 1946–1976* (Frederick, MD: University Publications of America, 1982), microfilm.

20. "A Summary of Information concerning Cuban Subversive Activities in Latin America," 31 Jul 1963, National Security Files (hereafter NSF), box 60, John F. Kennedy Presidential Library, Boston; CIA, "Castro's Subversive Activities before the Missile Base Crisis," 9 Nov 1962, NSF, National Intelligence Estimates, box 9, Lyndon Baines Johnson Presidential Library; CIA, "A Review of Reporting on Cuba," 15 Jul 1963, NSF, box 52, Kennedy Library; CIA, "Cuban Subversion in Latin America," 9 Aug 1963, CIA Records Station, National Archives and Records Administration, College Park, MD (hereafter CREST).

21. Philip Agee, *Inside the Company: CIA Diary* (New York: Stonehill, 1975), 334–35, 385.

22. Ibid., 390–92.

23. Ibid., 420–21.

24. Ibid., 447–48.

25. Gustavo Guerrero Palermo, *Los orígenes del MLN en el Interior* (Montevideo: Fin del Siglo, 2014), 92.

26. A. K. Milne to G. E. Hall, Montevideo, 16 Feb 1965, 371/179476, Foreign Office: General Correspondence, 1906–1966, Political Correspondence, National Archives, London.

27. Agee, *Inside the Company,* 385; Arturo C. Porzecanski, *Uruguay's Tupamaros: The Urban Guerrilla* (New York: Praeger, 1973), 15–16; José Harari, *Contribución a la historia del ideario del MLN Tupamaros* (Montevideo: Editorial Plural, 1987), 85. On the original Túpac Amaru rebellion in Peru, see Jonathan C. Brown, *Latin America: A Social History of the Colonial Period,* 2nd ed. (Belmont, CA: Wadsworth, Cengage Learning, 2005), chap. 11; Charles F. Walker, *The Tupac Amaru Rebellion* (Cambridge, MA: Belknap Press of Harvard University Press, 2014).

28. See Robert Moss, *Urban Guerrillas: The New Face of Political Violence* (London: Temple Smith, 1972), chap. 10; Alain Labrousse, *Una historia de los Tupamaros: De Sendic a Mujica* (Montevideo: Fin de Siglo, 2009); Julio María Sanguinetti, *La agonía de una democracia: Proceso de la caída de las instituciones en el Uruguay (1963–1973)* (Montevideo: Tauras, 2008); Clara Aldrighi, "El Movimiento de Liberación Nacional Tupamaros (1965–1975)," in *Por el camino del Che: Las guerrillas latinoamericanas, 1959–1990,* ed. Pablo A. Pozzi and Claudio Pérez (Buenos Aires: Imago Mundi, 2011), 243–82.

29. Bustos, *El Che quiere verte,* 176.

30. Raúl Burgos, *Los gramscianos argentinos: Cultura y política en la experiencia de Pasado y Presente* (Buenos Aires: Siglo XXI, 2004), 85, 89–90; Manzano, *The Age of Youth in Argentina,* 45. José Aricó, *La cola del diablo: Itinerario de Gramsci en América Latina* (Buenos Aires: Puntosur, 1988), 75.

31. Gabriel Rot, *Los orígenes perdidos de la guerrilla en la Argentina* (Buenos Aires: Waldhuter, 2010), 189, 194, 198.

32. CIA, "Planned Trip to Havana by Hector Villalon," 12 Dec 1964, NSF, CF, box 32, LBJ Library.

33. As quoted in "Los sueñeros del Che, Oran, 1964," *Sudestada: Cultura, Arte y Actualidad,* Jun 2007, 7.

34. This story comes from a variety of secondary and primary sources. Daniel Avalos, *La guerrilla del Che y Masetti en Salta, 1964,* 2nd ed. (Córdoba, Argentina: La Intemperie, 2005), 189. The quoted vignette comes from the Avalos book, which contains interviews with survivors. *Misión cumplida: Una historia olvidada* (Buenos Aires, 2005) by Eduardo W. Garay, a former member of the Salta rural police, presents the story of Salta's rural police force. Two other secondary works relate the episode: Jorge G. Castañeda, *Compañero: The Life and Death of Che Guevara* (New York: Knopf, 1997), 244–51; and Jon Lee Anderson, *Che Guevara: A Revolutionary Life* (New York: Grove Press, 1997), 537–60, 573–94.

35. On these two incidents, see Captain Hermes, "War Diary of the EGP," in Louis Mercier Vegas, *Guerrillas in Latin America: The Technique of the Counter-State*

(London: Pall Mall Press, 1969), 163–64, 169–70. Also see Rot, *Los orígenes perdidos,* 231–35.

36. Rot, *Los orígenes perdidos,* 14–15, 34–35.

37. Avalos, *La guerrilla del Che y Masetti,* 204.

38. "Los sueñeros del Che," 15. Gabriel Rot's book is an exception to the historical neglect.

39. Bustos, *El Che quiere verte,* 215–16, 228–30.

40. Richard Gillespie, *Soldiers of Perón: Argentina's Montoneros* (Oxford: Clarendon Press, 1982), 49. Federico Finchelstein analyzes the homegrown fascist ideology of the Tacuara. See Finchelstein, *The Ideological Origins of the Dirty War,* chap. 5.

41. Alejandra Dandan, *Joe Baxter: Del nazismo a la extrema izquierda; La historia secreta de un guerrillero* (Buenos Aires: Grupo Norma Editorial, 2006), 119–21; Marcelo Larraquy and Roberto Caballero, *Galimberti: Crónica negra de la historia reciente de Argentina* (Buenos Aires: Aguilar, 2002), 100–101.

42. Juan Esteban Orlandini, *Tacuara, hasta que la muerte nos separe de la lucha: Historia del Movimiento Nacionalista Tacuara, 1957–1972* (Buenos Aires: Centro Editor Argentino, 2008), 189, 215.

43. Dandan, *Joe Baxter,* 98–101; Daniel Gutman, *Tacuara: Historia de la primera guerrilla urbana argentina* (Buenos Aires: Ediciones B Argentina, 2003), 82; Larraquy and Caballero, *Galimberti,* 83.

44. Gutman, *Tacuara,* 114.

45. Dandan, *Joe Baxter,* 105–6; "Informe sobre el estudiantado argentino," 5 Apr 1961; "Provocaciones de autoridades argentinas contra Cuba," n.d. [ca. 1961], Fondo Argentina, MINREX.

46. Finchelstein, *The Ideological Origins of the Dirty War,* 99; Dandan, *Joe Baxter,* 79, 106–8; Lewis, *Guerrillas and Generals,* 12, 23, 34; Gutman, *Tacuara,* 91.

47. Dandan, *Joe Baxter,* 61.

48. Ibid., 198; On the bank robbery, see Gutman, *Tacuara,* 173–83.

49. Dandan, *Joe Baxter,* 176–77, 181.

50. Ibid., 231–32; Eduardo L. Duhalde and Eduardo Pérez, *De Taco Ralo a la alternativa independiente: Historia documental de las "Fuerzas Armadas Peronistas" y del peronismo de base,* vol. 1, *Las FAP* (La Plata, Argentina: De la Campana, 2002), 48, 50.

51. Dandan, *Joe Baxter,* 233.

52. Alejandro Guerrero, *El peronismo armado: De la resistencia a Montoneros* (Buenos Aires: Grupo Editorial Norma, 2009), 165.

53. Alejandra Vignollés, *Doble condena: La verdadera historia de Roberto Quieto* (Buenos Aires: Sudamericana, 2011), 59.

54. Ibid., 66.

55. Ibid., 72; Ciro Bustos, *Che Wants to See You: The Untold Story of Che in Bolivia,* trans. Ann Wright (London: Verso, 2013), 276–77.

56. Anderson, *Che Guevara,* 539–40.

57. Duhalde and Pérez, *De Taco Ralo a la alternativa independiente,* 19, 37–38, 47; Sergio M. Nicanoff and Axel Castellano, *Las primeras experiencias guerrilleras en la Argentina: La historia del "Vasco" Bengochea y las Fuerzas Armadas de la Revolución Nacional* (Buenos Aires: Ediciones del Centro Cultural de la Coop. Floreal Gorini, 2006), 74–75, 78, 99, 107, 115, 124–27. Gustavo Rearte died of leukemia in 1973.

58. Nicanoff and Castellano, *Las primeras experiencias guerrilleras en la Argentina,* 53; Marcelo Raimundo, "Izquierda peronista, violencia armada y clase obrera," in Pozzi and Pérez, *Por el camino del Che,* 156–57.

59. Nicanoff and Castellano, *Las primeras experiencias guerrilleras en la Argentina,* 202.

60. Cyrus Steven Cousins, "General Onganía and the Argentine [Military] Revolution of the Right: Anti-communism, Morality, Economic Growth, and Student Militancy, 1966–1970" (MA thesis, University of Texas at Austin, 2008), 25.

61. Ibid., 41.

62. *New York Times,* 1 Aug 1965; Guerrero, *El peronismo armado,* 160; Manzano, *The Age of Youth in Argentina,* 65–66.

63. Baschetti, *Documentos de la resistencia peronista,* 548; Duhalde and Pérez, *De Taco Ralo a la alternativa independiente,* 58–59, 135; Larraquy and Caballero, *Galimberti,* 76–77.

64. Duhalde and Pérez, *De Taco Ralo a la alternativa independiente,* 149, 152, 157.

65. Ibid., 60–62.

66. James P. Brennan, *The Labor Wars in Córdoba, 1955–1976* (Cambridge, MA: Harvard University Press, 1994), 218–19; Donald C. Hodges, *Argentina's "Dirty War:" An Intellectual Biography* (Austin: University of Texas Press, 1991), 98–99.

67. Baschetti, *Documentos de la resistencia peronista,* 731.

68. Luna, *Argentina, de Perón a Lanusse, 1943/1973,* 202–4; Manzano, *The Age of Youth in Argentina,* 163–67; Luis Alberto Romero, *A History of Argentina in the Twentieth Century,* trans. James P. Brennan (Mexico City: Fonda de Cultura Económica, 2006), 180–84.

69. Robert A. Potash, *The Army and Politics in Argentina, 1962–1973* (Stanford, CA: Stanford University Press, 1996), 253–55.

70. Ibid., 65; Larraquy and Caballero, *Galimberti,* 91.

71. As quoted in María Seoane, *Todo o nada* (Buenos Aires: Planeta Bolsillo, 1977), 57, 59.

72. See Gustavo Morello, *Cristianismo y revolución: Orígenes intelectuales de la guerrilla argentina* (Córdoba, Argentina: Editorial de la Universidad Católica de Córdoba, 2003).

73. Max Marambio, *Las armas de ayer* (Santiago de Chile: Random House Mondadori, 2007), 50. Three years after his military training in Cuba, Marambio recognized one of the Argentineans who had been with him. From a news photo of a

Montonero killed by police in 1970, he learned his name, Fernando Abal Medina, leader of the Montoneros.

74. Lewis, *Guerrillas and Generals,* 37–39; Galasso, *Cooke: De Perón al Che,* 205–7. Also see Gabriela Saidon, *La montonera: Biografía de Norma Arrostito* (Buenos Aires: Editorial Sudamérica, 2005), 44–45. One source mentions that, in 1968, a functionary at the Cuban embassy defected with the travel lists of many Latin American leftists who traveled back and forth to Havana under Cuba's diplomatic auspices. That Cuban diplomat turned the list over to American security agents.

75. Baschetti, *Documentos de la resistencia peronista,* 510.

76. See Mário Magalhães, *Marighella: O guerrilheiro que incendiou o mundo* (São Paulo: Companhia das Letras, 2012), chap. 26. My thanks to Professor Nila Burns for a copy of this important biography. Also see Moss, *Urban Guerrillas,* 194.

77. Seoane, *Todo o nada,* 94.

78. See Tanya Harmer, *Allende's Chile and the Inter-American Cold War* (Chapel Hill: University of North Carolina Press, 2011), 185.

79. Seoane, *Todo o nada,* 126.

80. See Jonathan C. Brown, *A Brief History of Argentina,* 2nd ed. (New York: Checkmark Books, 2011), 92, 94, 119.

81. Isabella Cosse, "*Mafalda:* Middle Class, Everyday Life and Politics in Argentina, 1964–1973," *Hispanic American Historical Review* 94, no. 1 (Feb 2014): 56–57.

82. Felipe Celesia and Pablo Waisberg, *Firmenich: La historia jamás contada del jefe montonero* (Buenos Aires: Aguilar, Altea, Taurus, Alfaguara, 2010), 21–23. On student protests to the Onganía coup, see Manzano, *The Age of Youth in Argentina,* 65.

83. P. Carlos Mugica, "Los valores cristianos del peronismo," in *La batalla de las ideas (1943–1973),* by Beatriz Sarlo (Buenos Aires: Ariel, 2001), 239.

84. Guerrero, *El peronismo armado,* 162. Also see Lewis, *Guerrillas and Generals,* 28.

85. Lewis, *Guerrillas and Generals,* 29; Celesia and Waisberg, *Firmenich,* 74.

86. Celesia and Waisberg, *Firmenich,* 81–82; Marambio, *Las armas de ayer,* 50.

87. Guerrero, *El peronismo armado,* 76.

88. "Mario Firmenich and Norma Arrostita cuentan cómo murió Aramburu," *La Causa Peronista,* no. 9, 3 Sep 1974.

89. Saidon, *La montonera,* 22.

90. Celesia and Waisberg, *Firmenich,* 86, 88.

91. Saidon, *La montonera,* 42.

92. Celesia and Waisberg, *Firmenich,* 105. For more on the church, see Gustavo Morello, *The Catholic Church and Argentina's Dirty War* (Oxford: Oxford University Press, 2015).

93. See Manzano, *The Age of Youth in Argentina,* chap. 8; Gillespie, *Soldiers of Perón;* John Simpson and Jana Bennett, *The Disappeared and the Mothers of the Plaza:*

The Story of the 11,000 Argentineans Who Vanished (New York: St. Martin's Press, 1985); Martin E. Anderson, *Dossier Secreto: Argentina's Desaparecidos and the Myth of the "Dirty War"* (Boulder, CO: Westview Press, 1993); Alison Brysk, *The Politics of Human Rights in Argentina: Protest, Change, and Democratization* (Stanford, CA: Stanford University Press, 1994); Lisa Cox, "Repression and Rank-and-File Pressure during the Argentine Process of National Reorganization, 1976–1983" (MA thesis, University of Texas at Austin, 1995); Wayne Magnusson, "Institutionalizing State-Sponsored Terrorism: A Decade of Violence in Argentine Terrorism, 1970–1979" (MA thesis, University of Texas at Austin, 1998).

94. Gutman, *Tacuara,* 267.

95. Finchelstein, *The Ideological Origins of the Dirty War,* 117, 120.

96. Vignollés, *Doble condena,* 11–12; Gillespie, *Soldiers of Perón,* 218–23.

97. Some observers at the time actually believed that the Argentinean radical left had corrected the mistaken notions of the rural *foco* originated by Che Guevara and embellished by Régis Debray. Writing euphorically in 1976, Donald Hodges predicted the ultimate victory of the Peronist Youth, the "largest youth formation on the continent to constitute a Marxist-Leninist tendency," in its looming internal war with the Argentinean armed forces. "The left has much to learn from the experience of the convergence of guerrilla nuclei with mass organizations," he said. Donald C. Hodges, *Argentina, 1943–1976: The National Revolution and Resistance* (Albuquerque: University of New Mexico Press, 1976), 143. However, the hoped-for revolutionary unity of urban guerrillas of bourgeois origin and organized labor turned out to be a chimera. Among the best English-language treatments of the terror of the 1970s are Gillespie's *Soldiers of Perón* and Lewis's *Guerrillas and Generals.*

98. Finchelstein, *The Ideological Origins of the Dirty War,* chap. 6.

99. Bavio, "Cooke y el Che: Recuerdos, realidad y ficción," in *Cooke, de vuelta,* 126.

100. Saidon, *La montonera,* 125.

101. Rodolfo Walsh, *El violento oficio de escribir: Obra periodística (1953–1977)* (Buenos Aires: Planeta, 1998), 415, 417.

102. Porzecanski, *Uruguay's Tupamaros,* 62; Labrousse, *Una historia de los Tupamaros,* 155.

103. Arthur M. Schlesinger Jr., *Journals, 1952–2000,* ed. Andrew and Stephen Schlesinger (New York: Penguin Press, 2007), 604. An interesting variation of Mao's aphorism is when he wrote that "una revolución no es un paseo por un jardín," literally translated as "a revolution is not a walk in the park." As quoted in Claudia Gilman, *Entre la pluma y el fusil: Debates y dilemas del escritor revolucionario en América Latina* (Buenos Aires: Siglo XXI, 2003), 189.

14. THE LAST CAMPAIGN OF CHE GUEVARA

1. As quoted in Pacho O'Donnell, *Che: La vida por un mundo mejor* (Buenos Aires: Editorial Sudamericana, 2003), 295.

2. Humberto Vázquez Viaña, *"Mi campaña junto al Che," atribuido a "Inti" Peredo, es una falsificación* (Santa Cruz, Bolivia: Editorial El País), 160.

3. Ibid., 161. Monje made these comments to an Italian TV journalist in 1971.

4. Ernesto Che Guevara, *El diario del Che en Bolivia* (Barcelona: Ediciones Metropolitanas, 1984), 48–49.

5. Vázquez Viaña, *"Mi campaña junto al Che,"* 161.

6. Inti Peredo, *Mi campaña con El Ché* (Buenos Aires: Schapire Editor, 1973), 40.

7. Benigno [Dariel Alarcón Ramírez], *Memorias de un soldado cubano: Vida y muerte de la Revolución* (Barcelona: Tusquets Editores, 1997), 133–35.

8. Robert L. Smale, "Above and Below: Peasants and Miners in Oruro and Northern Potosí, Bolivia (1899–1929)" (PhD diss., University of Texas at Austin, 2005), 3–4; Andrew Boeger, "Struggling for Emancipation: Tungsten Miners and the Bolivian Revolution," in *Workers' Control in Latin America, 1930–1979,* ed. Jonathan C. Brown (Chapel Hill: University of North Carolina Press, 1997), 217–43; Laura Gotkowitz, *A Revolution for Our Rights: Indigenous Struggles for Land and Justice in Bolivia, 1880–1952* (Durham, NC: Duke University Press, 2007), 268–80; Dwight B. Heath, *Land Reform and Social Revolution in Bolivia* (New York: Praeger, 1969); Paul Alfonso García, *Diez años de reforma agraria en Bolivia* (La Paz: Dirección Nacional de Informaciones, 1963).

9. Adys Cupull and Froilán González, *Cálida presencia: La amistad del Che y Tita Infante a través de sus cartas* (Rosario, Argentina: Ameghino Editora, 1997), 44, 120.

10. Ernesto Che Guevara, *Otra vez: El diario inédito del segundo viaje por América Latina (1953–1956)* (Buenos Aires: Editorial Sudamericana, 2000), 125.

11. Ernesto Guevara Lynch, *Aquí va un soldado de la América* (Buenos Aires: Sudamericana-Planeta, 1987), 14.

12. As quoted by Ulises Estrada, *Tania: Undercover with Che Guevara in Bolivia* (Melbourne: Ocean Press, 2005), 29.

13. Guevara, *El diario del Che en Bolivia,* 58.

14. Harry Villegas, *Pombo, A Man of Che's Guerrilla* (New York: Pathfinder, 1997), 196.

15. Ibid., 68. English translation in Daniel James, *The Complete Bolivian Diaries of Ché Guevara and Other Captured Documents* (New York: Stein and Day, 1968), 111.

16. James, *The Complete Bolivian Diaries,* 71. "Peasants [in Santa Cruz] generally had sufficient land and no history of autonomous organization or connections

with radical politics," one historian writes. Ann Zulawski, "The National Revolution and Bolivia in the 1950s: What Did Che See?," in *Che's Travels: The Making of a Revolutionary in 1950s Latin America,* ed. Paulo Drinot (Durham, NC: Duke University Press, 2010), 203.

17. Guevara, *El diario del Che en Bolivia,* 75; Paul J. Dosal, *Commandante Che: Guerrilla Soldier, Commander, and Strategist, 1956–1967* (College Park: Penn State University Press, 2003), 268.

18. Vázquez Viaña, *"Mi campaña junto al Che,"* 153–54.

19. Ibid., 81; Jorge G. Castañeda, *Compañero: The Life and Death of Che Guevara* (New York: Knopf, 1997), 347.

20. Régis Debray, *Che's Guerrilla War,* trans. Rosemary Sheed (Harmondsworth, England: Penguin Books, 1975), 80–81.

21. José Gómez Abad, *Cómo el Che burló la CIA* (Sevilla: RD Editores, 2007), 52; Estrada, *Tania,* 105; José A. Friedl Zapata, *Tania: Die Frau, die Che Guevara Liebte* (Berlin: Aufbau Verlag, 1997), 25–30; Jon Lee Anderson, *Che Guevara: A Revolutionary Life* (New York: Grove Press, 1997), 491–92.

22. Mariano Rodríguez Herrera, *Tania: La guerrillera del Che* (Mexico City: De Bolsillo, 2005), 76–78; Estrada, *Tania,* 86, 106; Anderson, *Che Guevara,* 688–89.

23. Manuel Piñeiro, *Che Guevara and the Latin American Revolutionary Movements,* ed. Luis Suárez Sálazar, trans. Mary Todd (Melbourne: Ocean Press, 2001), 61.

24. Ciro Bustos, *El Che quiere verte: La historia jamás contada del Che en Bolivia* (Buenos Aires: Javier Vergara Editores), 242.

25. Ciro Bustos, *Che Wants to See You: The Untold Story of Che in Bolivia,* trans. Ann Wright (London: Verso, 2013), 257–60; Richard Gott, *Guerrilla Movements in Latin America* (London: Thomas Nelson & Sons, 1970), 328–31.

26. Ibid., 58–59, 70–71; Gary Prado Salmón, *The Defeat of Che Guevara: Military Response to Guerrilla Challenge in Bolivia,* trans. John Deredita (Westport, CT: Praeger, 1987), 58–59; Luiz Bernardo Pericás, *Che Guevara e a luta revolucionária na Bolívia,* 2nd ed. (São Paulo: Xama VM Editora, 2008), 87; Henry Butterfield Ryan, *The Fall of Che Guevara: A Story of Soldiers, Spies, and Diplomats* (New York: Oxford University Press, 1998), 68–70.

27. Anderson, *Che Guevara,* 491–92, 549–52, 688–89.

28. Guevara, *Diario del Che en Bolivia,* 84, 86.

29. Ibid., 87; Peredo, *Mi campaña con El Ché,* 73–75.

30. "Account by Ciro Roberto Bustos of His Stay with Guevara's Guerrillas in Bolivia," in *"Che" Guevara on Revolution: A Documentary Overview,* ed. Jay Mallin (Coral Gables, FL: University of Miami Press, 1969), 186–224; Anderson, *Che Guevara,* 705, 708–9.

31. Villegas, *Pombo,* 157; Castañeda, *Compañero,* 362. Benigno, *Memorias de un soldado cubano,* 147.

32. Dosal, *Commandante Che*, 271.

33. CIA, "Assessing Military Expeditures in Latin America," Jul 1968, National Security Files (hereafter NSF), Country Files (hereafter CF), box 4, Lyndon Baines Johnson Presidential Library, Austin, TX; "Special Forces in Bolivia," *Veritas: Journal of Army Special Operations History* 4, no. 4 (2008): 43, 45.

34. CIA, "Cuban-Inspired Guerrilla Activity in Bolivia," 14 Jun 1967, NSF, Intelligence File, Latin America, box 2, LBJ Library.

35. Villegas, *Pombo,* 159.

36. Domitila Barrios de Chungara, *Let Me Speak: Testimony of Domitila, a Woman of the Bolivian Mines* (New York: Monthly Review Press, 1978), 113.

37. Debray, *Che's Guerrilla War,* 120; Rodolfo Saldaña, *Fertile Ground: Che Guevara and Bolivia* (New York: Pathfinder Press, 1997), 60.

38. Peredo, *Mi campaña con El Ché,* 78–79. Also see Hugo Gambini, *El Che Guevara*, 3rd ed. (Buenos Aires: Paidos, 1973), 315; Guevara, *El diario del Che en Bolivia,* 102–3.

39. Bustos, *Che Wants to See You,* 312–13; Villegas, *Pombo,* 171; Prado Salmón, *The Defeat of Che Guevara,* 88; Jean Lartéguy, *The Guerrillas,* trans. Stanley Hochman (New York: World Publishing, 1970), 248.

40. Prado Salmón, *The Defeat of Che Guevara,* 99–100; Ryan, *The Fall of Che Guevara,* 75.

41. Anderson, *Che Guevara,* 717; Dosal, *Commandante Che,* 284.

42. Prado Salmón, *The Defeat of Che Guevara,* 100–102.

43. Guevara, *El diario del Che en Bolivia,* 114. "Hemos perdido el mejor hombre de la guerrilla."

44. *Foreign Relations of the United States, 1964–1968,* vol. 31, *South and Central America; Mexico* (Washington, DC: US Government Printing Office, 2004) (hereafter *FRUS, 1964–1968,* vol. 31, *South and Central America),* 369.

45. Ibid., 370.

46. Gott, *Guerrilla Movements in Latin America,* 334.

47. "Special Forces in Bolivia," 3.

48. Ibid., 5, 27.

49. Ibid., 47, 66.

50. Dosal, *Commandante Che,* 282.

51. "Special Forces in Bolivia," 65, 77.

52. O'Donnell, *Che,* 337. Also see Donn [*sic*] W. Yoder, "Bolivia," 20 Jul 1967, Central Intelligence Agency Records Station, National Archives and Records Administration, College Park, MD (hereafter CREST). Yoder was the defense attaché at the American embassy in La Paz.

53. *FRUS, 1964–1968,* vol. 31, *South and Central America,* 371.

54. Guevara, *El diario del Che en Bolivia,* 105.

55. As quoted in Villegas, *Pombo,* 55. "Quizás estamos asistiendo al primer episodio de un nuevo Viet Nam."

56. As quoted in Gambini, *El Che Guevara,* 311.

57. Guevara, *El diario del Che en Bolivia,* 106.

58. Ibid., 141.

59. Villegas, *Pombo,* 178, 233.

60. Guevara, *El diario del Che en Bolivia,* 142.

61. Ibid., 140.

62. Ibid., 140, 161.

63. Ibid., 189–190.

64. Ibid., 145; Prado Salmón, *The Defeat of Che Guevara,* 124.

65. Guevara, *El diario del Che en Bolivia,* 148.

66. Ibid.

67. Ibid., 157.

68. Debray, *Che's Guerrilla War,* 19; June Nash, *We Eat the Mines and the Mines Eat Us: Dependence and Exploitation in Bolivian Tin Mines* (New York: Columbia University Press, 1979), 278–79, 282; Ryan, *The Fall of Che Guevara,* 98; Gott, *Guerrilla Movements in Latin America,* 354. In 1969, anthropologist June Nash found it ironic that university students plastered the walls with Che posters even though none had joined him two years earlier.

69. Guevara, *El diario del Che en Bolivia,* 165; Villegas, *Pombo,* 222; Prado Salmón, *The Defeat of Che Guevara,* 143; CIA, "The Bolivian Guerrilla Movement: An Interim Assessment," 10 Aug 1967, CREST.

70. Philip Brenner, "New Evidence on Soviet Premier Alexei Kosygin's Trip to Cuba, June 1967," in *Cold War International Project Bulletin,* no. 17 / 18 (Fall 2012): 793.

71. Castañeda, *Compañero,* 382, 383–84; Carlos Moore, *Castro, the Blacks, and Africa* (Los Angeles: Center for African-American Studies, 1988), 273.

72. Gustavo Villoldo, *Che Guevara: The End of a Myth* (Miami: Rodes Press, 1999), 13; Moore, *Castro, the Blacks, and Africa,* 167, 183.

73. *FRUS, 1964–1968,* vol. 31, *South and Central America,* 376; Villoldo, *Che Guevara,* 69, 77.

74. Guevara, *El diario del Che en Bolivia,* 169–70; James, *The Complete Bolivian Diaries,* 193.

75. Anderson, *Che Guevara,* 729.

76. *El Diario* (La Paz), 23 Sep 1967. The *New York Times* had been reporting the rumors in Bolivia of Che's guerrilla leadership since July 1967. *New York Times,* 9 Jul 1967.

77. Bowdler to Rostow, 6 Sep 1967, NSF, Intelligence File, box 2, LBJ Library; Carlos Hurtado Gomez, "Notes on the Experience of the Bolivian Army in Their

Struggle against the Castro-Communist Guerrillas," 7 Feb 1968, CREST; Prado Salmón, *The Defeat of Che Guevara*, 165.

78. Gambini, *El Che Guevara*, 321; Prado Salmón, *The Defeat of Che Guevara*, 151–53;, *FRUS, 1964–1968*, vol. 31, *South and Central America*, 377.

79. Félix I. Rodríguez and John Weisman, *Shadow Warrior* (New York: Simon & Schuster, 1989), 143–53.

80. Guevara, *El diario del Che en Bolivia*, 191.

81. Ibid., 198.

82. Peredo, *Mi campaña con El Ché*, 108.

83. Prado Salmón, *The Defeat of Che Guevara*, 169–70.

84. Guevara, *El diario del Che en Bolivia*, 203; Villegas, *Pombo*, 229; Prado Salmón, *The Defeat of Che Guevara*, 172.

85. O'Donnell, *Che*, 336.

86. As quoted in Ibid., 336–38.

87. Guevara, *El diario del Che en Bolivia*, 203.

88. Ibid., 206, as translated by James, *The Complete Bolivian Diaries*, 221.

89. O'Donnell, *Che*, 336–38.

90. Villegas, *Pombo*, 263.

91. Guevara, *El diario del Che en Bolivia*, 209.

92. As quoted in O'Donnell, *Che*, 350.

93. Peredo, *Mi campaña con El Ché*, 118.

94. Prado Salmón, *The Defeat of Che Guevara*, 247. Also see E. T. Nance, "Death of Ernesto (Che) Guevara," 9 Nov 1967, Depart of Defense Intelligence Information Report, USAF Defense Attaché, La Paz, CREST.

95. For Captain Prado's account, see Prado Salmón, *The Defeat of Che Guevara*, 186–90.

96. Nance, "Death of Ernesto (Che) Guevara."

97. As quoted in Rodríguez and Weisman, *Shadow Warrior*, 162.

98. Prado Salmón, *The Defeat of Che Guevara*, 249.

99. Anderson, *Che Guevara*, 735; O'Donnell, *Che*, 359. The following is a summary of the versions of Che's death covered in O'Donnell, *Che*, chap. 61; Gambini, *El Che Guevara*, 17–21, 324–332; Castañeda, *Compañero*; Anderson, *Che Guevara*; Rodríguez and Weisman, *Shadow Warrior*; Prado Salmón, *The Defeat of Che Guevara*, 252.

100. Castañeda, *Compañero*, 400.

101. Pericás, *Che Guevara e a luta revolucionária*, 172–73.

102. Rodríguez and Weisman, *Shadow Warrior*, 12–16. Also see O'Donnell, *Che*, 363.

103. John David Waghelstein, "A Theory of Revolutionary Warfare and Its Application to the Bolivian Adventure of Che Guevara" (MA thesis, Army Command and General Staff College, Fort Leavenworth, KS, 1973), in "Latin America: Special

Studies, 1962–1980," a microfilm project of University Publications of America, Frederick, MD. Waghelstein had access to a Special Forces after-action report.

104. Pericás, *Che Guevara e a luta revolucionária,* 113.

105. Nance, "Death of Ernesto (Che) Guevara"; Pericás, *Che Guevara e a luta revolucionária,* 113.

106. Villoldo, *Che Guevara,* 150, 166; Bjorn Kumm, "The Death of Ché Guevara," *New Republic,* 11 Nov 1967, 13–15.

107. On the escape, see Villegas, *Pombo,* 288–307; Benigno, *Memorias de un soldado cubano,* 163–65; Peredo, *Mi campaña con El Ché,* 127–33. The men were Inti (Inti Peredo), Darío (David Adriazola Veizaga), Ñato (Julio Luis Méndez), and the Cubans Pombo (Harry Villegas Tamayo), Urbano (Leonardo Tamayo Núñez), and Benigno (Dariel Alarcón Ramírez).

108. *FRUS, 1965–1968,* vol. 31, *South and Central America,* 395.

109. *Washington Star* (Washington, DC), 16 Nov 1967; Gambini, *El Che Guevara,* 18.

110. *FRUS, 1964–1968,* vol. 31, *South and Central America), America,* 386.

111. Villoldo, *Che Guevara,* 170; Castañeda, *Compañero,* 405.

112. Pericás, *Che Guevara e a luta revolucionária,* 113.

113. Brian Latell, *Castro's Secrets: The CIA and Cuba's Intelligence Machine* (New York: Palgrave MacMillan, 2012), 120–21, 124.

114. Upward of 200,000 mostly Mayans met violent deaths from 1954 to 1990, for example. Virginia Garrard-Burnett, *Terror in the Land of the Holy Spirit: Guatemala under General Efraín Ríos Montt, 1982–1983* (New York: Oxford University Press, 2011), 7.

115. Mariano Azuela, *The Underdogs,* trans. E. Munguía (New York: Signet, 1963), 136.

CONCLUSION

1. They were Alfredo Stroessner of Paraguay, François "Papa Doc" Duvalier of Haiti, Rafael Trujillo of the Dominican Republic, and Luis Somoza of Nicaragua.

2. In addition to Prado, the coup victims were Presidents Arturo Frondizi of Argentina, Juan Bosch of the Dominican Republic, Miguel Ydígoras Fuentes of Guatemala, Ramón Villeda Morales of Honduras, Carlos Julio Arosemena Monroy of Ecuador, João Goulart of Brazil, and Víctor Paz Estenssoro of Bolivia. Presidents Alberto Lleras Camargo of Colombia, Rómulo Betancourt of Venezuela, Francisco Orlich Bolmarcich of Costa Rica, Jorge Alessandri Rodríguez of Chile, and Roberto Chiari of Panama visited Kennedy and successfully finished their terms. The constitutional presidents of Uruguay did not visit Washington, DC.

3. For a list of the coups, see Peter H. Smith, *Democracy in Latin America: Political Change in Comparative Perspective* (New York: Oxford University Press, 2005),

355. Also see Alan McPherson, *Intimate Ties, Bitter Struggles: The United States and Latin America since 1945* (Washington, DC: Potomac Books, 2006), 59.

4. Michael Grow, *U.S. Presidents and Latin American Interventions: Pursuing Regime Change in the Cold War* (Lawrence: University Press of Kansas, 2008).

5. Larry Diamond and Juan J. Linz, "Introduction: Politics, Society, and Democracy in Latin America," in *Democracy in Developing Countries: Latin America,* ed. Larry Diamond, Juan J. Linz, and Seymour Martin Lipset (Boulder, CO: Lynne Rienner, 1989), 47. Hal Brands also makes a case for local agency. See Brands, *Latin America's Cold War* (Cambridge, MA: Harvard University Press, 2010), 256–59.

6. Patrick Iber, *Neither Peace nor Freedom: The Cultural Cold War in Latin America* (Cambridge, MA: Harvard University Press, 2015), 242.

7. See Jorge I. Domínguez, *To Make a World Safe for Revolution: Cuba's Foreign Policy* (Cambridge, MA: Harvard University Press, 1989), 114–15; Tad Szulc, "Exporting the Cuban Revolution," in *Cuba and the United States: Long-Range Perspectives,* ed. John Plank (Washington, DC: Brookings Institution Press, 1967), 69–97; Ernesto F. Betancourt, "Exporting the Revolution to Latin America," in *Revolutionary Change in Cuba,* ed. Carmelo Mesa-Lago (Pittsburgh: University of Pittsburgh Press, 1971), 105–26. The exception to the lack of books on Cuba's export of revolution is the work of Piero Gleijeses on Cuba's military interventions in Africa. The present government in Havana counts Africa as such a glorious success in Cuba's foreign policies that it allowed Gleijeses access to state documents. See Gleijeses, *Conflicting Missions: Havana, Washington, and Africa, 1959–1976* (Chapel Hill: University of North Carolina Press, 2002); *Visions of Freedom: Havana, Washington, and Pretoria and the Struggle for Southern Africa, 1976–1991* (Chapel Hill: University of North Carolina Press, 2013).

8. The examples are Getúlio Vargas in Brazil in 1937, Juan María Bordaberry in Uruguay in 1974, and Alberto Fujimori of Peru in 1992.

9. Federico Finchelstein, *The Ideological Origins of the Dirty War: Fascism, Populism, and Dictatorship in Twentieth Century Argentina* (Oxford: Oxford University Press, 2014); Tanya Harmer, *Allende's Chile and the Inter-American Cold War* (Chapel Hill: University of North Carolina Press, 2011); Virginia Garrard-Burnett, *Terror in the Land of the Holy Spirit: Guatemala under General Efraín Ríos Montt, 1982–1983* (Oxford: Oxford University Press, 2011).

10. See the fine summary of this episode in Brands, *Latin America's Cold War,* chap. 7.

Acknowledgments

My generation grew up profoundly influenced by the Cold War. In grade school, we held duck-and-cover exercises under the desks. I recall overhearing my Little League coaches talking about Senator Joe McCarthy. As college students, we experienced the March on Washington, the Cuban Missile Crisis, the Beatles, and antiwar protests. My instructors in the Reserve Officer Training Corps had fought in Korea. The deaths of John Kennedy, Martin Luther King Jr., and Bobby Kennedy unfolded before us on television. So did the Vietnam War. I fulfilled my military obligation in the Panama Canal Zone and Thailand. In graduate school, Walt W. Rostow taught me economic history; Nixon resigned and Perón died while I was doing doctoral research in Argentina. Now I am writing the history I have lived.

I started researching this project in microfilmed State Department records at the Benson Latin American Collection and in National Security Council documents at the Lyndon Baines Johnson Presidential Library. I had no idea what aspect of the revolution required more investigation, for Cuba already had a vast historiography. Then I stumbled onto a cache of CIA memos on the activities of anti-Castro commandos in Miami. The Cuban counterrevolution fascinates me. It was not manufactured by the CIA but had deep roots in Cuban politics and in divisions within the armed rebellion against Fulgencio Batista.

Jorge Domínguez chaired the panel at the Latin American Studies Association meeting in Montréal in which I presented this initial research. In Montréal, I became reacquainted with Jorge Mario Sánchez Egozcue and met Rafael Hernández for the first time. Subsequently, I found a lot of materials in US archives on the export of revolution, another neglected topic. I followed this line of inquiry across the waters of the Caribbean into Panama, Venezuela, Peru, Brazil, Argentina, and Bolivia.

Then I began to delve into how Cuba's revolution fit into the rift between the Soviet Union and China. I wrote up a preliminary paper for a conference that I organized with Professor Dong Jingsheng at Peking University. He had my essay translated into Chinese and published in that university's journal of Asian Pacific studies.

I took my first trip to Cuba in 2006: Havana, Santa Clara, Bayamo, Santiago de Cuba, and Fidel's old headquarters in the Sierra Maestra. On August 1, I was standing before the beds in which Fidel and Raúl had slept during their incarceration at Modelo Prison on the Isle of Pines (today the Isle of Youth). The museum guide said, "Haven't you heard? Fidel just took sick leave and appointed Raúl as interim president." A meaningful moment for a historian.

In the next two visits, I became acquainted with John Parke Wright. He introduced me to Ramón Castro, the older brother of Fidel and Raúl. Parke's own Florida family had lost a cattle ranch in Oriente Province to Castro's land reform program of 1959. Having participated in opening China in the 1980s, Parke sought to reintroduce United States–Cuban trade in the twenty-first century. Our highlights together included sitting in with a street band after mass at Cathedral Plaza, Parke on harmonica and I on bongos, and riding horses with Captain Miguel Jinartes, a former member of Camilo Cienfuegos's guerrilla column. This equine adventure made page 3 of the *New York Times*. Majel Reyes had arranged all the details in Cuba.

Research is a collaborative process. While it remains an individual effort to choose the documentation and to assess which evidence seems the most relevant, the scholar still relies on a community of searchers of truth. Several people stand out as among the most indispensable in my work.

First and foremost, Lynore Brown helped me through more than ten years of Cuban research. She accompanied me to all the research sites, foreign and domestic. Moreover, Lynore read and commented on every last word of this book manuscript. She is researcher, editor, and muse. My nephew David Brown, who grew up in Munich, acted as my research assistant for work in the East German materials in Berlin. He also translated into English key parts of the documentation, some of it on the guerrilla Tania.

Several professional colleagues contributed immensely to this volume. They composed letters and offered encouragement. The veteran *cubanólogo* Jorge Domínguez wrote two foundational texts on the revolution, *Cuba: Order and Revolution* and *To Make a World Safe for Revolution*. I had the benefit of conferring at length with Jorge five years ago when he accepted my invitation to speak about the October Missile Crisis to cadets of the United States Air Force Academy. He had attended the retrospective conferences of the late 1990s on the Bay of Pigs and the Cuban Missile Crisis that brought together surviving Cuban, American, and Russian participants. Jorge wrote countless letters on my behalf for research funding. Finally, he lent me many insights as he read the Cuban chapters in this volume.

Rafael Hernández gave me another tutorial on the revolution when he accepted the University of Texas at Austin's offer of a visiting professorship in 2009. Rafael edits Cuba's premier intellectual journal, *Temas*. He stayed at my home for about two weeks while looking for an apartment in Austin. Rafael told me about his upbringing at the base of the Escambray Mountains and about his memory of Che Guevara's guerrilla column passing through town on the way to the decisive battle of Santa Clara. Rafael also served as a young teacher in the Escambray during the literacy campaign of 1961.

A letter of agreement between the University of Texas and the Universidad de La Habana that I negotiated with Vice Rector for International Relations Cristina Díaz López proved critical to my work. LLILLAS Director Bryan Roberts and Paloma Díaz provided logistical support on the UT Austin side. Vice President for International Affairs Terri Givens signed the letter of agreement with Dr. Díaz López and toasted the event with the finest Havana Club *añejo* rum. This *convenio* gave me entrée to the Instituto de Historia de Cuba as well as to the Centro de Estudios sobre Estados Unidos, where Jorge Mario Sánchez and Rosa López Oceguera hosted me. At the Instituto, I benefited from the historical expertise of Tomás Díez and the administrative skill of Belquis Quesada Guerra. Personnel at the Museo de la Lucha contra los Bandidos in Trinidad, Cuba, cast new light on the so-called outlaw counterrevolution. On this last trip to Cuba in 2013, Daybel Panellas graciously hosted us for dinners at her home and at that of her parents.

Besides sharing documentation with me, Renata Keller and Aaron Moulton put me in touch with the newly opened archives of the Cuban Ministry of Foreign Relations, MINREX. There, Director Eduardo Valido helped with the search for Cuba's activities in Central and South America. While the Cuban diplomats wrote many informative reports of their activities, the real foreign policy of Havana originated in the Council of State of Fidel Castro. Yet MINREX documentation does reveal how Cuba affected domestic politics abroad.

Additional colleagues who have supported grant applications over the years include John Womack Jr., Carlos Marichal, Emilio Kourí, Joel Wolfe, John Tutino, and the late Friedrich Katz. Their letters helped me obtain a semester off from teaching and travel grants from the Lozano Long Institute of Latin American

Studies, the Dean of Graduate Studies, and the History Department. Martin Melosi, John Tutino, and Jorge Garcés have been among my closest friends and intellectual collaborators since graduate school.

In Miami, Attorney Antonio Zamora and several of his friends granted me lengthy interviews. They are Alberto Müller, Max Lesnik, and Isidro "Chilo" Borja. Zamora also advised Lynore Brown and me to stop by the Brigade 2506 Museum. I am glad we did, for we spoke to Emilio Martínez Venegas, Pablo Pérez Cisneros, Aurelio Pérez Lugones, and Vicente Blanco Capote.

I have benefited from the cooperation of a handful of colleagues pursuing similar interests in the study of Cold War Latin America. I exchanged leads and sources with Renata Keller. I also exchanged research information with the following: Aaron Moulton and Aragon Storm Miller, who work on Caribbean relations in the 1950s and 1960s; Mila Burns, who researches Brazilian political refugees during the 1970s; Thomas Field, who studies Bolivian foreign relations in the 1960s and 1970s; Ian Lyles, who researches the US Army in Latin America; James Hershberg, who investigates Cuban-Brazilian relations; and Luiz Bernardo Pericás, an expert on Che Guevara and the Brazilian left. Teresa Meade, Tanya Harmer, Aviva Chomsky, Michael Gonzales, Michelle Chase, and Jana Lipman commented on various preliminary findings. Francisco Zapata of the Colegio de México helped me with research in Córdoba, Argentina, after our chance meeting there in 2007. A native of Chile, he informed me that he played basketball with Fidel Castro on the latter's visit to Antofagasta in 1971.

Finally, I owe a debt of gratitude to the selflessness of country experts who made sure I committed no egregious errors. Gerald Poyo gave me feedback on Cuba's counterrevolution. Mathew Rothwell commented on the Sino-Soviet dispute. Doug Yarrington offered suggestions on Venezuela. Michael Conniff and John Mallett examined my interpretations of Panamanian history. Joel Wolfe, James Hershberg, and Luiz Bernardo Pericás gave me advice on the Brazilian chapter. Joel Horowitz, Martín Unzué, and Ricardo Salvatore critiqued two chapters on Argentina, while Thomas Field read two others on Bolivia. Peru proved tricky. I needed the wise counsel of Michael Gonzales, Henry Deitz, Richard Walter, and Peter Cleaves. Peter also made sure that my tennis game did not deteriorate during the writing of the book—though he allowed me very few match points. Jan Lust provided invaluable corrections based on his interviews with former Peruvian guerrilla fighters.

As for the illustrations of the Cuban Revolution, I am grateful for the assistance of the staff of the Sterling Memorial Library of Yale University and the Cuban Heritage Center of the University of Miami. Tomás Díez and the staff of Belquis Quesada Guerra assisted with photo acquisition at the Instituto de Historia de Cuba. Additional photographic consultation came from Claudia Freidenraij and

Ricardo Salvatore for Argentina, Natalia Jaira del Águila and Valeria Rey de Castro for Peru, John Mallett for Panama, and Mila Burns of New York City College and Marcelo Campos of Agência O Globo for Brazil. I am also indebted to Susan Flaherty for Rodrigo Moya's brilliant photographs of Cuba, Venezuela, and Guatemala.

While these and many others offered cogent suggestions, they cannot be blamed for my occasional stubbornness in not adopting them.

Illustration Credits

123   Two young girls wait at the Cuban Refugee Center in Miami. Cuban Heritage Center, University of Miami Libraries, Coral Gables, Florida.

145   Militiamen in training. Courtesy of Instituto de Historia de Cuba, Havana.

158   A unit of militiamen captures two rebels. Courtesy of Instituto de Historia de Cuba, Havana.

182   President John F. Kennedy and First Lady Jacqueline Kennedy. Cecil Stoughton. White House Photographs. John F. Kennedy Presidential Library and Museum, Boston. ST-19-3-62.

193   Eleventh anniversary of the Moncada Attack. Courtesy of Archivo Fotográfico Rodrigo Moya.

218   A guerrilla band in the Sierra de Minas of Guatemala, 1966. Courtesy of Archivo Fotográfico Rodrigo Moya.

232   Che Guevara and President Eduardo Haedo of Uruguay. Courtesy of Archivo General de la Nación, Departamento de Documentos Fotográficos, Buenos Aires, Argentina.

258   An FALN guerrilla unit. Courtesy of Archivo Fotográfico Rodrigo Moya.

284   President John F. Kennedy welcoming Brazilian president João Goulart. Abbie Rowe. White House Photographs. John F. Kennedy Presidential Library and Museum, Boston. AR 7144-E.

302   A light tank takes up a position in downtown Rio de Janeiro in 1964. Courtesy of Agência O Globo. Neg. 32849/Golp1037.

323   MIR leader Luis de la Puente Uceda gives a marksmanship lesson. Courtesy of *Caretas*.

339   Fidel Castro and junta president Juan Velasco Alvarado in Lima. Courtesy of *Caretas*.

356   A Canal Zone police captain attempts to halt a delegation of Panamanian students. Lyndon Baines Johnson Presidential Library.

366   The National Guard saving Robles from impeachment by the National Assembly, Panama. Private Collection.

400   Rioting by workers and students in the Cordobazo. Courtesy of Archivo General de la Nación, Departamento de Documentos Fotográficos, Buenos Aires, Argentina.

409   The widow of General Aramburu standing before the casket of her husband. Courtesy of Archivo General de la Nación, Departamento de Documentos Fotográficos, Buenos Aires, Argentina.

417   Photograph of a truckload of armed miners in Bolivia in 1953 by Che Guevara. Reproduced from Carlos Ferrer, *De Ernesto al Che: El Segundo y Último Viaje de Guevara por Latinoamérica* (Buenos Aires: Editorial Marea, 2000). Courtesy of Casa Editorial Marea, Buenos Aires, Argentina.

447   Lyndon Johnson presenting a western saddle to President René Barrientos. Lyndon Baines Johnson Presidential Library.

Index